Social Psychology as Social Process

Donald E. Allen
Oklahoma State University

Rebecca F. Guy
Memphis State University

Charles K. Edgley
Oklahoma State University

Wadsworth Publishing Company
Belmont, California
A Division of Wadsworth, Inc.

Acquisition Editors: *Bonnie Fitzwater*
                     Todd Lueders
Manuscript Editor: *Bill Waller*
Production Editor: *John Bergez*
Designer: *Katherine Minerva*
Cover: *Janet Wood*

Printed in the United States of America

1 2 3 4 5 6 7 8 9 10—83 82 81 80

Credits
Pages 27 and 311: Ziggy, copyright 1975 Universal Press Syndicate. Reprinted by permission. *Page 59:* Polston cartoon reproduced by special permission of *Playboy* Magazine. Copyright © 1974 by Playboy. *Page 197:* Orehek cartoon reproduced by special permission of *Playboy* Magazine. Copyright © 1975 by Playboy. *Pages 200 and 228:* "Dennis the Menace" cartoons by Hank Ketchum copyright © 1976 Field Newspaper Syndicate. Reproduced by permission. *Page 201:* "Dennis the Menace" cartoon by Hank Ketchum copyright © 1975 Field Newspaper Syndicate. Reproduced by permission. *Page 205:* "The Family Circus" by Bil Keane, 1975. Reprinted courtesy of The Register and Tribune Syndicate, Inc. *Page 274:* Cartoon copyright © by Bob Schochet. Reprinted by permission. *Pages 283–284:* Quotation from "That Powerful Drop," by Langston Hughes. In *Simple Takes a Wife.* Copyright 1953 by Langston Hughes. Reprinted by permission of Harold Ober Associates Incorporated. *Page 329:* "Peanuts" cartoon © 1976 United Feature Syndicate, Inc. Reproduced by permission. *Page 345:* Sidney Harris cartoon reproduced by special permission of *Playboy* Magazine. Copyright © 1974 by Playboy. *Cover:* Drawing from *Smile in a Mad Dog's i,* by Richard Stine. Copyright © 1980 Richard Stine.

Library of Congress Cataloging in Publication Data

Allen, Donald E
    Social psychology as social process.

    Bibliography: p. 417
    Includes index.
    1. Social psychology I. Guy, Rebecca F.,
joint author. II. Edgley, Charles K., joint
author. III. Title.
HM251.A529   301.1   79–14815
ISBN 0–534–00809–7

Preface

Social psychology, bridging as it does the gap between two social sciences, requires a careful balance of the two primary viewpoints: that of the individual as a psychological construct and that of social relationships as sociological constructs. Psychologists have dominated social psychology for many years, and the individualistic approach has prevailed. This text is especially prepared to restore the needed balance by emphasizing interpersonal relationships, social development, group phenomena, and other fundamental social factors. It was begun with the conviction that materials dealing with the social aspects of social psychology could be incorporated from sociological sources. We hope that it will be one of an expanding series of social-psychology textbooks that present new materials emerging from research on social processes and from the application of social theories.

The book is designed primarily for a one-semester undergraduate course in social psychology. Its organization into 15 chapters offers a reasonable compromise between the requirements of the semester system of 17 weeks and the quarter system of 12 weeks. The chapters are integrated units and can stand more or less by themselves. There is a logical progression in the text from the symbolic interaction implicit in language (Section One) to the socialization process in childhood, adolescence, and adulthood (Section Two). Socialization, which in a sense incorporates all of the processes and problems of human interaction, becomes the foundation for an examination of the self. In Section Three, the self is described, in a discussion of motives, as an interactional phenomenon. Social roles become the focus for treating interpersonal relationships in defined settings. The development of social roles permits the emergence of social groups, and the text deals next with   v group processes. The complex demands on teams of persons to sustain collective operation leads to the dramaturgical approach and to the social psychology implicit in Goffman's analysis of the individual's relation to societal institutions. This process is influenced by personal attitudes and by the conditions of attractiveness that develop among individuals.

Section Four incorporates the ideas of morality, deviance, and collective behavior. At this level the treatment becomes almost exclusively sociological. Social morality, although often excluded from social psychology texts because it is "value laden" and thought to be unsuitable for scientific investigation, is actually a primary requirement for the simplest kind of relationship. Thus, it is an essential part of any adequate treatment of the social factors in social psychology. The discussions of deviance, social control, and collective behavior proceed logically from social morality.

The text concludes with an overview assessment of the field of social psychology: its problems, prospects, and promises. Such an effort is filled with pitfalls, but we felt the book would be incomplete without an honest assessment of the shortcomings as well as the great promise offered by theory and research in social psychology.

To sum up, we have tried to attune this work to the needs of teachers interested in bringing the social side of the subject more vigorously to the student. We solicit and welcome criticisms and suggestions from those who use this text.

Many collegial and personal debts are accumulated in the years of struggle it takes to see a book like this to conclusion. The people at Brooks/ Cole have had faith in this project, and we have come to appreciate them very much. Bonnie Fitzwater gave of her time, intelligence, and good humor beyond the usual requirements of her role. Todd Lueders took over this project late in its development and brought just the right touch in pulling together loose ends.

We are deeply grateful to the following reviewers, who read part or all of the manuscript in earlier versions and strengthened the book immeasurably by their comments: Herbert Blumer, University of California, Berkeley; William Corsaro, Indiana University; Carl Couch, University of Iowa; David Graeven, California State University, Hayward; Mark Hutter, Glassboro State College; Suzanne Kurth, University of Tennessee; David Lundgren, University of Cincinnati; Robert Suchner, Northern Illinois University; Ronny Turner, Colorado State University; and Lyle Warner, University of Nevada, Reno.

Our colleagues at Oklahoma State and Memphis State were extremely helpful, and one of the authors owes a special debt to some people at Morehead State University who kept him going through one cold and lonely winter. Jan Fitzgerald and Jean Ryan contributed more than they will ever know. And Gene Acuff deserves special recognition for being the rare department chairman who believes in his faculty even when they are taking an unconscionably long time to complete a piece of work. He has somehow emerged from his long years in sociology with the belief that people count more than structures. For that we are grateful.

Finally, Dennis Brissett of the University of Minnesota, Duluth, has never seen this manuscript but needs to be thanked anyway for intellectual debts that could not possibly be enumerated here.

Donald Allen
Rebecca Guy
Charles Edgley

Contents

Section One

Foundations and Origins

If you is goin' anywhere in particular
Up here, yu'd better figger fust
How ta git thar
Cuz by jest goin'
Afore ya know where yere goin'
Ya can get to a powerful lotta places
Ya might not wanta be.

Anonymous

Social Psychology: Puzzles and Solutions   1

A. INTRODUCTION

Social psychology is a vibrant, exciting inquiry into what must stand as the most interesting of all subjects: ourselves. This subject is obviously familiar to all of us. And yet the most familiar things are frequently the most elusive. Social psychology studies the individual in a social context, in his or her continuing relationships with others. But observing the process of these relationships is more difficult than people often realize. Marshall McLuhan once observed that the last thing a fish would ever notice is water. Studying human beings in their social environment presents a similar problem. We are so immersed in social relationships that to see just how they influence us and how we influence them is no easy task.

In this sense social psychology serves as a platform on which to stand as we try to gain a perspective on our lives with other people. In this book we will look at how social psychologists have increased our understanding of the individual as a social being.

Part of the difficulty of studying a field as large as social psychology is its multiplicity of concerns. Just what constitutes *social psychology* is unclear, for psychologists and sociologists have both competed for the term. Furthermore, social psychologists have studied virtually everything. Rats, pigeons, ants, bees, chickens, apes, fish, and even human beings have been the subjects. Within this bewildering array, some distinctions need to be drawn.

1. Social Psychology as the Study of Human Interaction

For us social psychology is the study of human interaction. What happens when human beings come into contact with one another? How can we explain how people are held together in something loosely called a *society* but at the same time are set apart as unique creatures with their own identities? This concern with people means that we will not be worried about studies using animal subjects. We take this position not because we believe that animal studies do not tell us a great deal—about animals. But we think such studies tell us precious little about human beings as people. Because it is not

Social psychology is the study of human interaction. What happens when human beings come into contact with one another? (Photo by © Eric Kroll, Taurus Photos)

possible to study everything simultaneously, we will restrict our inquiry to those varieties of social psychology that tell us the most about human beings as human beings.

Furthermore, the study of human *interaction* is for us a key concern. We are not interested in varieties of "social" psychology that tend toward an individual psychological treatment of human beings. Personal psychology is an important matter, perhaps, but we feel that it is based too often on a misunderstanding of the relationship between the individual and others. In talking about the individual, people frequently fall into the trap that philosophers call *dualism*. That is, they inappropriately dichotomize the individual and society, minds and bodies, appearance and reality, the self and others. In our view these terms are really part of a single process and cannot be understood apart from that process. As we will show later in the sections on socialization, an *individual* simply does not exist without the presence of others. Gregory Stone (Stone and Farberman, 1970) has called attention to Carl Sandburg's poem asking "What did the last man on earth say?" The answer: "Where *is* everybody?" It should not be difficult for the reader to identify with this response, for what we are, what we think, and what we do are all tied up with others. For socialized creatures, at least, other people always exist. They are taken into account in some fashion even in the most seemingly isolated situations. The hermit who departs for a desert retreat is nonetheless engaging in a social act. His knowledge of other people and his interactions with them have led him to the conclusion that he wants to be apart from them.

Throughout a day, we act in ways that anticipate the actions of others. "What will she think if I do this?" "How will that affect Harold?" "I wonder how impressed they were when I said that?" Everyday life consists of these and similar questions and actions multiplied a thousand times. Even the implied presence of others, reflected in our awareness that we are part of something else—a group, a family, a job, or a church—may have something to do with the way we construct our behavior (Allport, 1968).

Such observations as these leave us with the feeling that what is called *individual psychology* must really be regarded as a social psychology, because it is inextricably tied up with the responses and actions of other people. There is no act that does not (at least potentially) have communicative value, and these communications between self and others form the subject matter for a fully developed social psychology.

2. Social Psychology as Social Process

The title of this book represents another important way of thinking about human interaction. When we speak of process we simply mean that social reality is a continuous *flow*. Much of social psychology, in its attempts to find answers to the question of what causes people to act the way they do, has ignored time and change. If we are making love, we may want the moment to last forever. But the flow of time is an inescapable fact of human existence. Nothing lasts forever. Take, for example, the meaning of a historical event. Russell Baker (1965) has shown the shifting sands of time in a poignant fable:

Observer: V-E Day Plus 7,305

After the last gun was silenced in World War II, a man in a six-button suit and Beatle haircut appeared from a time machine one night and wandered among a barracks full of servicemen who were awaiting discharges.

"Do you understand what this war was all about?" he asked a G.I. "Sure," the G.I. said. "We fought to save the Brooklyn Dodgers, the two-pants suit and mom's apple pie."

"Then you have lost," said the man from the time machine. "Within twenty years, the Dodgers will be sold out to Los Angeles. The two-pants suit is even now gone from the haberdashery rack. And by the time all of you are dads, mom's apple pie, like almost everything else mom used to whip up in the kitchen before Pearl Harbor, will be delivered by teamsters, frozen or ready-mixed."

The men in the barracks hooted and said that if they were not so tired of fighting they would bloody the visitor's nose on account of his feminine haircut. A cynic interrupted, however. "That mom's apple pie is just a crude way of saying we fought for democracy," he said. "Pure applesauce. Actually, we fought to save the British Empire."

"Then you have lost," said the visitor. "The British Empire will be dissolved, at American insistence, within the decade."

"You talk like a Nazi propagandist," said a sailor. "You're trying to drive a wedge between us and the British. Next you'll be trying to divide us and our great Soviet allies."

"Within five years," the visitor said, "any of you who calls them 'our great Soviet allies' will be accused of treason."

"Throw the bum out," shouted a corporal of infantry.

"What did you fight for, corporal?" the visitor asked.

"Easy," the corporal said. "Germany had to be destroyed."

"Then you have lost," the visitor said, "for within five years you will be paying to rebuild Germany out of your salary. For fifteen years after that, America will risk new wars to help put Germany back together again."

The men laughed and laughed. "Tell us about Asia!" shouted a Marine. "Yeah," said an Air Corps private, "tell us how we're all going to wind up loving the Japs and fighting the Chinese." And the barracks rocked with laughter.

"Don't tell me you fought to destroy Japan, too," the visitor said. "What else?" a sergeant asked.

"Then you have lost," said the visitor. "Within twenty years you will rebuild Japan. It will be your warmest friend in the Pacific. When your children are born, you will teach them not to say 'Japs.' You will train them to say 'our Japanese friends.' "

"That'll be the day," said a waist gunner. "The Jap bombing of Pearl Harbor will live in infamy. We've fought to guarantee that."

"Then you have lost," said the visitor. "Within twenty years you will have large, unhappy children who will not remember Pearl Harbor. They will say, however, that your own bombing of Hiroshima and Nagasaki were acts of infamy."

"If any of my kids ever say that," a staff sergeant said, "they'll get a punch in the nose. What I fought for was none of that fancy stuff—just the good old American right to beat some sense into your own kids."

"Then you have lost," said the visitor, "for within twenty years children who don't remember a thing about your war will outnumber you in the population, and though you may punch a few it will make no difference because your legs will be shot and your wind will be gone and your stomachs will be flabby with steak and beer."

A supply clerk who had listened solemnly spoke up. "I fought to keep America the way it is," he said. "That's right," said a Navy gunner. "I heard Jimmy Stewart say that in the movies. I fought because I didn't want anybody changing things around in America."

"Then you have lost," said the visitor, "for within twenty years everything will change. Farmers will live in the cities. City people will live in the suburbs. The country will be covered with asphalt. The cities you have known will be torn down. Money will be replaced by the credit card. Major Bowes, Charlie McCarthy and the Singing Lady will disappear."

"Your children"—here he paused to display his six-button jacket, his stove-pipe pants, leprechaun boots and seaweed hair—"will look like me."

"All right, men," roared the top sergeant, "grab the Fascist rat!" The visitor disappeared under a mass of uniformed bodies. "We'd better take him up to Intelligence for interrogation," the sergeant said. "He's probably part of a die-hard Axis scheme to destroy American morale."

When the men had untangled, of course, the visitor had spun off through the time-space continuum into 1965 and was dancing the Jerk at the GoGo. "Tell me, bird," he asked his partner between twitches, "did you ever hear of a two-pants suit?"*

So the reality of any event is constantly changing, so much so that you may at this very moment be wondering what a "Jerk" or a "GoGo" is. As the Greek philosopher Heraclitus said more than 2000 years ago, "No man can step into the same river twice, for the second time it's not the same river, and he's not the same man." Change is a basic assumption to be made about social life, and all phenomena must be understood in terms of their development. The subject matter of social psychology must be seen in "creative, emergent terms: it is neither fixed nor finite, nor independent of human conception and subsequent redefinition" (Strauss and Schatzman, 1973, 7). This is the idea of process in social psychology.

3. The Historical Background of Modern Social Psychology

Like all other systems of ideas, social psychology has a past. We will not try to be comprehensive about that past, but making some links to it should prove helpful. Philosophers have long thought about the relationship be-

---

* © Copyright CBS, Inc. 1969. All rights reserved. Originally broadcast May 20, May 27, and June 3, 1969 over the CBS Television Network as part of the CBS NEWS: GENERATIONS APART program.

tween the individual and society. Plato and Aristotle, for example, directed a considerable amount of attention to this question. However, rooted as they were in philosophical questions of first cause, ultimate ends, and the like, they simply never constructed a fully developed social psychology.

As a modern social science, social psychology has the same point of origin as other social sciences: the 17th-century revolution in our knowledge of the universe (Fernandez, 1977). Scientists and the scientific method undermined previous ways of thinking, especially those that were religious or spiritual. Before the scientific revolution God was the pivot on which the universe revolved. After the scientific revolution and the revelation that the sun, not the earth, was the center of the universe, religious explanations were increasingly shunted aside in favor of ones rooted in the natural and physical world. It was not long afterward that an external, scientific view was also applied to human behavior.

The first theories in social psychology were terribly simplistic, at least in the light of present understanding. They tended either toward simple propositions—such as Bentham's notion that all social behavior could be explained in terms of the desire to obtain pleasure and avoid pain—or grandiose schemes—such as Comte's superscience human behavior that would make obsolete all other forms of explanation. Comte (1798–1857) reasoned that during the early years of the 20th century biology and sociology would be combined in a new science he termed *la morale*. This true, final science would deal with the "individual unity" of man (Martineau, 1853).

The French reaction to Comte took two major directions. One was exhibited in the work of Gabriel Tarde (1903), who made individual psychology the basis of his sociology. Tarde's main work, *The Laws of Imitation*, was an attempt to explain social phenomena in terms of the interactions of individuals who imitate one another. This reduction of all behavior to imitation proved to be too simplistic to survive as an adequate theory for social psychology, but it did serve to indicate that patterns of interaction should be studied in their own right—a point that was to have profound influence on the later development of social psychology.

The other major French reaction to Comte can be seen in the work of Emile Durkheim (Pollock, 1953), who reduced all psychological processes to social ones. Durkheim's system of social determinism left little or no place for the person. At least in his early work (Stone and Farberman, 1967) Durkheim took the position that the individual is subordinate to the group in every way, virtually a piece of plastic stamped out of a societal mold. This perspective also proved to be too narrow for a complete social psychology.

The discipline of social psychology was christened formally in 1908 when its first two textbooks were published. E. A. Ross (1908) and William McDougall (1908) both adopted the title *Social Psychology*, but here the similarities ended. Adopting Tarde's position that imitation is a law of social life, Ross believed that the socialization process is largely a matter of learning what social behavior is acceptable in certain situations. To use a contemporary example, one would not attend church with a transistor radio and listen to it during the worship service. One might, though, go to a football game with a transistor radio. For Ross this tendency to imitate others' behavior in various social situations provided the basis for an understanding of human conduct. With all of its shortcomings, Ross's social psychology at least stressed the role of social processes in accounting for behavior.

McDougall's understanding of social psychology, in contrast, was heavily influenced by the Darwinian conception of instinct. The work of Charles Darwin had pointed toward human beings' animal origins. McDougall believed there were a small number of instincts (the parental instinct, curiosity, fear, repulsion) that led people to perceive their environment and to act accordingly. These native instincts, which were inborn and immutable, dictated people's behavior, which in turn shaped society. Society, then, was a mere outcome of native elements in human beings. Rather than people's being a reflection of their society, their society was a reflection of them.

McDougall's assertions about instincts received mixed reviews from his colleagues. In a landmark article entitled "Are There Any Instincts?" Dunlap (1919) denounced the idea as absurd. The criticism became so intense that McDougall himself recanted slightly, substituting in his later works the term *propensity* for *instinct* (Baron, Byrne, and Griffitt, 1974, 7).

Following these early efforts, social psychology began finally to take a shape and direction as competing frameworks asserted themselves. After sketching the basic tack taken by each of these theoretical perspectives, we will discuss the nature and methods of social-psychological research.

B. THE INDIVIDUALISTIC PERSPECTIVE

Some varieties of social psychology have begun with the person and proceeded to show how the individual is the locus of all action. Such individualistic psychologies have been, for example, a characteristic of English scholarship since the writings of John Locke (1632–1704). Locke was really a political philosopher, but involved in his writings were major statements about the relationship between individual and society. In Locke's view individuals precede society but form social contracts with each other in order to assure their common survival. Society, then, is a contractual arrangement between self-serving individuals who band together out of necessity. People must give up some of their rights in order to preserve their lives, but society is no more than the contractual agreements of the sum of its individual parts (Locke, 1928).

Another social-contract theorist, who took a slightly different position but nonetheless rooted his social psychology in the person, was Jean Jacques Rousseau (1712–1778). Rousseau (1910) advanced the thesis that human beings are born in a state of perfection and then promptly corrupted by society. "Men are born free, yet everywhere we find them in chains." The state of original nature is just, free, and peaceful, but our social institutions, especially private property, force people to act in negative and tragic ways. The relationship of the individual to society, then, is not a contractual agreement but a corrupting form of extortion. Not an eternal pessimist, however, Rousseau admitted the possibility of a just world in which inequality could be lessened through the construction of more humane social institutions.

1. Psychoanalytic Theory

The social-psychological perspective that placed perhaps the most singular emphasis on the person is that advanced by Sigmund Freud (1856–1939). Like the social-contract theorists Freud wrestled with the problem of basic human nature. He was a doctor, and his background in medicine proved to be an important influence on his work. It was this influence that was probably responsible for his emphasis on the individual and his relative neglect of society.

Freud believed that humans are basically egoistic. However, self-centered human beings fear what others might do to them and so reluctantly allow themselves to become social. The personality is composed of three primary elements: the id, the ego, and the superego. The id arises first. It is basically asocial and seeks self-gratification. The id in all its biological passion seeks fulfillment of its needs with no regard for how this will affect others. In response, society provides the superego, an internalized system of rules and constraints, to hold self-centered humans in check. The ego mediates inevitable conflicts that arise between the id and the superego. As a result the ego frequently exhibits pathologies arising out of the conflict between the asocial id and social constraints.

Freud's personal perspective can be seen most clearly in his concept of the unconscious. Using his own method of psychoanalysis, Freud probed the depths of the psyche and uncovered the irrational side of human nature (Collins and Makowsky, 1972, 120). The Enlightenment dream of a rationally ordered world may have died forever in the work of Freud, who argued so persuasively that human beings are collections of irrational forces, driven by sexual strivings and repressed wishes. With the individual in conflict with society, the resultant turmoil takes its toll in psychological destruction.

2. Cognitive Theories

The term *cognitive theory* is used in social psychology to refer to a constellation of ideas that emphasize the mind of the actor as the basic source of all external behavior. Historically, the cognitive viewpoint is most closely identified with the theoretical position known as *Gestalt psychology*, at least insofar as it focuses on the processes of perception and thinking (Ausubel, 1965, 5). In other words, the present mental state of the person is responsible for his or her behavior and must be understood if we are to understand that behavior. The mind is seen as a kind of information-processing computer centrally located between external stimuli and behavioral response. Neisser

(1967) says the term *cognitive* refers to "the processes by which any sensory input is transformed, reduced, elaborated, stored, recovered, and used." Cognition, then, is the act of knowing. It also includes the knowledge thereby acquired (Shaw and Costanzo, 1970).

The major influence on the development of various cognitive theories in social psychology has come from the Gestalt school of psychology. Experimentally oriented in their research, Gestalt psychologists have conducted literally hundreds of studies trying to understand the nature of human perception. The Gestaltists assert that their studies show that people do not respond to discrete stimuli but to their configurations of the world—in other words to the whole picture, or Gestalt. If we take five lines and arrange them on a page, as in Figure 1-1, we get one picture and see them in one way. If we arrange these same five lines in a different Gestalt (Figure 1-2), we get a different perception. And if we arrange them as we have done in Figure 1-3, we get still a different perception. The question "How long is line 'e'?" can be answered in terms of which Gestalt we are talking about. Line "e" looks very different in Gestalt 2 than it does in Gestalt 3 (Stone and Farberman, 1970, 15–16).

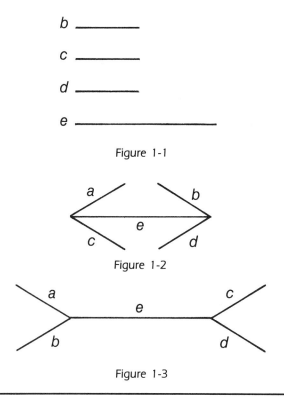

Figure 1-1

Figure 1-2

Figure 1-3

In each case, it is the mental Gestalt that determines the perception of the same five lines.

The approach of the Gestaltists has been more influential among psychologically oriented social psychologists than it has among sociologically based ones. The list of influential social psychologists who have been Gestaltists is impressive indeed. It includes such scholars as Kurt Lewin, Fritz Heider, Solomon Asch, Leon Festinger, and Theodore Newcomb, all of whom have contributed to our understanding of how human beings perceive the world they live in, all from the standpoint of a set of cognitive assumptions.

C. THE BEHAVIORAL PERSPECTIVE

1. Stimulus/Response and Reinforcement Theories

At the opposite extreme from cognitive theories, which stress internal processes as the explanation for external behavior, is the radical behaviorism offered by stimulus/response theories. These theories focus on the external conditions that are said to stimulate behavior as a response to prior learning. In this view present behavior is a product of past episodes of learning, and the task of social psychology is to discover what forms of environmental reinforcement are most likely to be associated with that behavior.

The ideas of *conditioning theory*, as this branch of social psychology is sometimes known, go back hundreds of years, but they are usually derived from the work of the Russian physiologist Pavlov (1849–1936) and his studies of dogs. These studies showed that various stimuli become associated with reward and that organisms can be taught to do a variety of things through the use of rewards and punishments designed to stamp in wanted responses and stamp out unwanted ones.

The most famous stimulus/response theorist of recent vintage is B. F. Skinner, whose work has become extremely controversial. There are three major assumptions on which the work of Skinner and other reinforcement theorists rests: 1) behaviorism, 2) associationism, and 3) hedonism (Deutsch and Krauss, 1965). Behaviorism stresses that behavior is the basic subject matter of social psychology and that the researcher should deal only with phenomena that are observable. So-called "internal" states and processes (such as those stressed by cognitive theories) are excluded in favor of direct observation of the concrete properties of human behavior. Behaviorism arose as a revolt against the subjectivism of the late 19th century, in which psychologists used terms like *instinct, will, sensation,* and so on as basic explanations for complex social behavior as well as simple behavioral acts. Primarily through the work of John Watson (1878–1958), behaviorism stressed that psychology should deal only with observable phenomena that are open to inspection by everyone. One can see the stimuli and one can see the response. Everything else is pure speculation and magic.

Associationism is a very old idea which holds that the primary units of the mind are paralleled (or "associated") with outer behavior. In other words, what we see as outward conduct is matched precisely by some inner version of the same thing. The behaviorists rejected the notion of mental units but retained the principle of association, substituting for mental states the conditioned response as the basic unit of analysis (Deutsch and Krauss, 1965, 78–79). Because inside and outside were now regarded as basically one unit, the entire analysis could focus on external, observable behavior and the person's "inner" life could effectively be ignored.

Reinforcement theories are further supported by the assumption that the human being is an economic creature driven to seek pleasure and avoid pain. This idea, which is the basis for what has come to be known as *exchange theory*, sees people's behavior as a simple response to their conditioning about costs and rewards. Behavior can be understood as attempts to maximize rewards and minimize costs (Homans, 1961, 13).

In recent years Skinner has increasingly left laboratory work to others and has become something of an advocate of the use of behaviorism to solve social problems and reorganize society. He advocates the use of behavioral principles to develop what he calls a "technology of behavior, which would use behavior modification to discourage anti-social conduct and reward through reinforcement desired conduct" (Schellenberg, 1978, 106). Skinner's work remains controversial, but it has been influential. The work of social psychologists Daryl Bem on attitudes and self-perceptions and George Homans on exchange theory bears the Skinnerian stamp, as do Ronald Akers's studies of deviant behavior.

D. THE INTERACTIONIST PERSPECTIVE

The personal perspective in both experimental and clinical versions has held sway among psychologically oriented social psychologists for some time, and behavioral perspectives have had a long and rich tradition within the dialogue of the discipline. As such, both perspectives and their associated theories continue to reflect psychological assumptions about human nature. Sociologists, however, have also recognized the necessity of including people and their behavior in their analyses of human society and have made important contributions to social psychology. It is worth noting that one of the founders of modern social psychology, Auguste Comte, is also known as the father of sociology.

Probably the most important sociologically based perspective is called *symbolic interactionism*. The interactionist perspective, which will be especially in evidence in this book, has steadfastly refused to separate the individual and society, insisting instead on the reciprocal relationship between the two.

Originating in the early 1900s in the United States, symbolic interactionism rapidly became one of the dominant perspectives in sociology and social psychology. Two of its earliest advocates were Charles Horton Cooley and George Herbert Mead, and two leading contemporary interactionists are Herbert Blumer, a student of Mead's at the University of Chicago in the 1930s, and Erving Goffman, a student of Blumer's. The essentials of interactionist thought are well illustrated in the work of these four men.

1. Charles Horton Cooley

The controversy over the primacy of the individual versus that of society is by no means new. The fallacy of this conceptualization was apparent to many early thinkers, including Charles Horton Cooley (1864–1929). Rejecting any attempt to separate the individual and society, Cooley insisted that they were linked organically. Cooley (1902) likened the self and society to an object and its looking-glass reflection. The self arises reflectively in its own reaction to three principal elements: (1) the imagination of our appearance to another person, (2) our imagination of the other's judgment of that appearance, and (3) some sort of resultant self-feeling, such as being proud or being mortified.

Perhaps the ultimate expression of the interrelatedness of the individual and society is to be found in the formation of what Cooley called the *primary group*. Primary groups, found everywhere human beings congregate, are those characterized by (1) face-to-face associations, (2) no specified or formal goals, (3) relative permanence, (4) smallness of size, and (5) relative intimacy of participants. Within such groups, self-consciousness develops easily as persons interact closely with one another.

For Cooley the self is always a feeling and an imagination that we have of what we have seen in the looking glass comprising other people. Cooley's attempt to use an interactionist framework slips a bit when he observes that the self is not necessarily the actual outcome of how we appear to others but exists only in the subject's own imagination of that appearance. Objects are reduced to subjects in his analysis, which goes against a consistently interactionist perspective. Despite this problem, Cooley's emphasis on the intensely personal way in which reflections of others are held and his insistence on looking at the individual and society within the same framework are notable advances in bridging the gap between psychology and sociology.

2. George Herbert Mead

George Herbert Mead (1863–1931), a contemporary and close friend of Cooley's, is generally considered the father of the interactionist perspective. A major difference between Mead and Cooley has been expressed by Angell (1968, 14): "Whereas Cooley saw communication as arising within mind, Mead saw mind arising in communication; he held that communication begins in gestures and preverbal sounds to which words are gradually added to create mind." It is difficult in a short sketch to appreciate the importance of Mead's work. He taught the first course anywhere entitled "Social Psychology" and gave the new discipline some impressive tools with which to start.

Mead taught in the Department of Philosophy at the University of Chicago at the turn of the century. His philosophy was known as *pragmatism*, and it is necessary to know something of this school of thought to grasp Mead's social psychology. Pragmatism was a radical departure from traditional modes of philosophical thinking. Arising in the context of the impressive achievements of science, pragmatism held that the majority of philosophical problems should be recast in the light of scientific knowledge, especially evolutionary theory. Charles Darwin's work, which we mentioned earlier, led Mead to take seriously the idea of process. This idea had been considerably neglected prior to Darwin. Nature was regarded as being fixed, consisting of unalterable substances that existed independently of one another (Desmonde, 1970). The substances of which nature was supposedly composed were regarded as eternal. The task of philosophy was to determine just what these eternal forms were and to show how human life was affected by them.

Darwin's work demolished this fixed conception of the universe and led to the acceptance of the idea of process and change. The developing social sciences were heavily influenced by this idea, as the work of Mead quickly showed. Organisms and their environment were not to be construed as separate entities, but the mutually dependent relationship between them was to be stressed. In addition, the reciprocal influence of organism and environment included an analysis of the shifting reconstruction that each was accomplishing on the other. Our current problems of pollution are a good example of this conception of the universe. People are reshaping the very environment in which they live through the products of industrial technology. As the environment changes, corresponding changes in human beings occur, and our heightened awareness of this process leads to efforts to restructure the environment in ways that are more livable and less destructive.

Mead did not refer to his own system of social psychology as *symbolic interactionism*. That term was coined later by Herbert Blumer in reference to what he believed were the essentials of Mead's position. Instead, Mead called his social psychology *social behaviorism*, and an understanding of why he chose that term will help us comprehend the strands of thought with which he was dealing.

By destroying the dualism between a person's mind and body, Darwin's theory gave support to those schools of thought that regarded human beings as part of a natural, evolutionary process. One of these was behaviorism, which we have already encountered. Mead agreed with the behaviorists that behavior is the basic datum of social psychology. From that point, however, Mead's thinking departed from theirs in some highly critical ways. First, Mead contended that the behaviorists' description of individual conduct stripped the organism away from the context in which its behavior occurred. The total behavior of an acting human organism includes not only those external, directly observable aspects but also covert, internal ones *that are accessible*, albeit indirectly. The behaviorists, according to Mead, tended to reduce human behavior to the model of billiard balls, acting and reacting against one another with no regard to the meaning their actions have for them (Desmonde, 1970, 57). The behaviorist model of stimulus/response, action, and reaction could be regarded as meaningful in the case of human beings only when weighed against a total social situation.

Mead also rejected the behaviorists' image of human organisms as passive. While a dog, rat, or pigeon may await an activating stimulus and then respond, human beings from the beginning of their lives are continually active (Dewey, 1922). People dynamically select the stimuli they are going to respond to and do not simply react to perceptions. In this sense human beings in many ways determine their own environment. Objects in the social world may be put there in an effort to elicit a certain type of behavioral response, but in the final analysis what they are depends on how they are acted on by people. A table or a chair is created in order to be used as something to eat from or sit on. In a pinch, however, a human being might well decide to forgo the conventional responses toward those objects and chop them up for firewood.

All of this means that the program of the behaviorists, as empirically sound as many of its tenets are, needs to be revised somewhat in the light of the special abilities of human organisms. Mead proposes, then, in contrast to psychological behaviorism a kind of social behaviorism in which human acts are taken to be social responses and not mere organic movements. Human movements, for example, usually begin with an idea. The idea, even though it is relatively covert, is an essential phase of the act. If we regard ideas and other mental processes as behavioral in their own right, then a behavioristic introspection is possible, because people—unlike rocks, trees, or pigeons—can be asked about their ideas and the role these play in their behavior. An empirically based social psychology is therefore possible, even though some aspects of social acts are not directly observable.

Human consciousness, rooted in the ability to communicate symbolically, means that human beings can learn new responses and new meanings without having gone through the trial/error, stimulus/response operant conditioning that the behaviorists offered as an adequate account of human functioning. Watching another person burn his or her fingers by putting them into a fire can mean that we might want to avoid such an exercise ourselves, even though we have never actually experienced the pain. The meaning of any event, then, is not necessarily in the direct experience of it but rather in the response we make toward it. This is why the "same" stimuli can mean radically different things to different people, because they respond to the stimuli from different social perspectives. During the Vietnam War, for example, peace symbols came to elicit radically different responses from people. Any other symbol is subject to the same kind of differing response, a point we will make again in our chapter on language.

Human social life, then, consists of a series of symbolic interactions with the world people experience themselves as being in. And it is important to recognize, as Mead did, that the process by which these interactions go on is collective, plural, and social—not individual. Meaning arises as a joint activity, even though the entire process may take place within the person's own "skin." Thinking, for example, is a social process—a kind of internal conversation—that takes place within people but involves considerably more than themselves. Mind, as Mead pointed out, emerges in communicative interaction with others and continues to have a life only with regard to these others. In this sense those who are defined as "mentally ill" are not so much out of *their* minds as they are out of the minds of others whose response they are no longer able to mobilize with their actions. Because mind is a social process that occurs in interaction, the components of interaction are essential to an understanding of even the most mental of all human activities. This understanding squares with Mead's definition of mind:

> Mind arises in the social process only when that process as a whole enters into or is present in the experience of any one of the given individuals involved in that process. . . . It is by means of reflexiveness—the turning-back of the experience of the individual upon himself—that the whole social process is thus brought into the experience of the individuals involved in it; it is by such means, which enable the individual to take the attitude of the other toward himself, that the individual is able consciously to adjust himself to that process, and to modify the results of that process in any given social act in terms of his adjustment to it. Reflexiveness, then, is the essential condition, within the social process, for the development of mind [1934, 134].*

For Mead, then, mind is simply the ability of one organism to take another into account as its action develops. Human beings, in fact, do that all of the time, and this ability considerably changes the way the social psychologist studies them, a point we will make later in our discussion of methodology. Many of Mead's riches are contained in his discussions of the self, and we will take up these insights in Chapter 9. But Mead's account of the mind, his discussion of the social nature of human acts, and his disagreement with the behaviorists over how far the concept of behavior should be extended all provide us with a rich foundation for a sociologically based social psychology.

3. Herbert Blumer

The major advocate of the Meadian tradition in social psychology has been Herbert Blumer, a student of Mead's at the University of Chicago at the time of Mead's death in 1931. Primarily through Blumer's work (especially his teaching) Mead's ideas have stayed at the forefront of modern social psychology. Much of Blumer's work has been critical of the remainder of

---

*This and all other quotations from this source are from *Mind, Self, and Society*, by G. H. Mead. Copyright 1934 by The University of Chicago Press. Reprinted by permission.

social psychology for not taking into account Mead's trenchant observations on social life. Like Mead, Blumer believes that human society consists of an interpretive process through which meanings are used to give events their particular character. Blumer has summarized five of Mead's key concepts that social psychology must take into account: the self, the act, social interaction, objects, and joint action. We will discuss each of these five points briefly.

a. The self.   Mead saw the human being as an organism having a self, and "the possession of a self converts the human being into a special kind of actor, transforms his relation to the world, and gives his action a unique character. In asserting that the human being has a self, Mead simply meant that the human being is an object to himself" (Blumer, 1969, 62). This self transforms human action into something quite different from animal behavior. People can act back on themselves in the same or similar terms as they act toward others and others act toward them. They can judge, analyze, evaluate, define, and guide their own conduct. Furthermore, the self is viewed as a *process* and not a structure. This idea separates interactionist thought from the personal approach, which stresses cognitive structures as the source of human action.

Much of psychology has identified the self with a structure, or organization. Freud's notion of the ego qualifies as such a structured view. But Mead insisted that a self is a social process characterized by the prospect of reflexivity. To be an object to one's own behavior changes the individual from one who merely responds to internal or external demands to one who acts toward the world, interpreting and organizing action on the basis of that interpretation:

> To illustrate: a pain one identifies and interprets is very different from a mere organic feeling and lays the basis for doing something about it instead of merely responding organically to it; to note and interpret the activity of another person is very different from having a response released by that activity; to be aware that one is hungry is very different from merely being hungry; to perceive one's "ego" puts one in the position of doing something with regard to it instead of merely giving expression to the ego. As these illustrations show, the process of self-interaction puts the human being over against his world instead of merely in it, requires him to meet and handle his world through a defining process instead of merely responding to it, and forces him to construct his action instead of merely releasing it. This is the kind of acting organism that Mead sees man to be as a result of having a self [Blumer, 1969, 63–64].

b. The act.   Because human beings have selves, human action is built up in the process of coping with the world rather than being released out of preexisting structures. Despite all the material available socially and culturally to persons (or perhaps because of the wide variety of such material), acts must be put together by the self-reflective organism each time they are done. This means that human behavior is a continual accomplishment, not a mere routine carried out under the influence of some direct stimulus. Among the things that human beings indicate to themselves are their needs, wants, goals, and feelings; the expectations of others; the rules of the group; the nature of the situation they are in; conceptions of themselves; recollections; and images of possible lines of action to be taken toward others. This means that the person is not the mere recipient of these things but must handle them as behavior unfolds.

Blumer notes that viewing behavior in this way is directly opposite to those perspectives that tend to be used in the psychological and social sciences. Traditionally, human behavior is seen as the result of factors that play on the organism, as though the resulting conduct were a mere response to activating mechanisms. Human beings are rarely seen as having selves but rather are viewed as mere vehicles through which other forces express themselves.

c. Social interaction. Human beings respond to one another in two ways: symbolically and nonsymbolically. In nonsymbolic interaction people respond directly to one another's gestures. In symbolic interaction, however, they respond to their interpretations of one another's acts. Most human interaction is of the symbolic variety. It consists of defining and interpreting the acts of ourselves and others and acting on the basis of such definitions. The definitions may well be wrong, but people are, nevertheless, condemned to a world of meanings in which their actions must be constructed out of their definitions of what is going on.

Social interaction is, therefore, a process to be understood in its own right, not simply another variable to be plugged into schemes that lodge determinants of behavior in attitudes, values, feelings, or the organization of personality. Human interaction is a positive shaping in its own right, and cannot, according to Blumer, be simply inserted beneath other factors that are deemed more important. Anyone who has had the opportunity to observe a wide variety of social situations is aware that the nature of the unfolding interaction is a highly significant process that in large measure accounts for the differences that occur in these situations.

A recognition of how social life involves the dual process of definition and interpretation enables social psychologists to deal with both permanence and change in the same analytic framework. Established patterns such as the family, religion, and economic systems exist and are sustained only through the continued use of some framework of interpretation. The defining acts of members of society regularly confirm various social arrangements, and change occurs when the definitions change. Relationships as varied as cooperation, conflict, domination, exploitation, consensus, and disagreement all hold this definitional basis in common. According to Blumer, an emphasis on social interaction overcomes the narrow tendency in social psychology to construct a general model of human interaction on the basis of one particular type of relationship. Conflict, exchange, and mutual expectations represent only a few of the many types of social interactions possible, and none of these by itself will serve as an adequate model of all human relationships.

d. Objects.   It is easy to observe that social life revolves around various kinds of objects that exist in the world. Blumer reminds us, however, that for Mead the concept of object had a very different meaning from that currently in use. Objects, for Mead, are *human constructs*, not self-existing entities with intrinsic properties. The nature of an object depends on how people act toward it. An object is anything that can be designated or referred to, including various physical classes of things such as buildings and cars but also—and importantly—social events such as a race riot or the activities of the middle class. The meaning of any of these classes of objects is not intrinsic to the object but flows from the nature of the social interaction that human beings have with the object. The object world, then, is created as human beings act toward it. We usually think of objects as *physical things*, but in social terms life consists primarily of the manipulation of *social objects*, which are the objects of *social acts*. A good example of a social object has been described by McCall and Simmons:

> A rather young man, in a park in the Bronx, is standing quietly but very alertly in the afternoon sun. Suddenly he tenses and scurries a few tentative steps to his right, still rather frozen, his gaze locked on a man only a few feet away. This other man makes a sudden movement with his right arm, and the first fellow breaks into sudden flight. Twenty or thirty yards away, still another fellow starts to run to cut him off, and the first man falls flat on his face, skidding and bouncing roughly along the ground for several feet as a result of his great momentum [McCall and Simmons, 1966, 51–52].

The acts being described here have created a social object—the stolen base in a game of baseball. It has no physical structure but is purely a social object, a kind of symbol created by the cooperative action of 18 men laboring under a common rule. "A stolen base cannot be touched, smelled, or tasted, but it does exist, through the joint efforts of human actors" (52).

Social objects such as the stolen base are all around us. In fact, most of the things we strive for—marriage, grades, academic degrees, positions in society, and so on—exist not in nature but only as social objects created jointly by the persons involved.

e. Joint action.   A final concept in Blumer's framework for social psychology is the idea of *joint action*. Social objects and social acts are accomplished not by individuals acting alone but by people acting together. Individual lines of action must join. Marriage, sex, intimacy, and love all involve other people. None of the social realities that compose our lives can be understood as an outcome of individual acts, but only as a result of joint acts, undertaken in common with others. A fully developed social psychology, according to Blumer, must take this fundamental principle into account.

4. Erving Goffman

A contemporary advocate of the interactionist perspective is Erving Goffman. In a classic work entitled *The Presentation of Self in Everyday Life* (1959), Goffman suggests that the image of self we present to others is strongly influenced by the presence of those others. Using a dramaturgical metaphor stressing the relationship between actor and audience, Goffman contends that, when we enter the presence of another person, we are primarily concerned with presenting and preserving face. He characterizes social interaction as a "face ritual." To Goffman, we arrange our performances so as to reveal some things and conceal others. In the presence of certain audiences, for example, there are topics that one would simply not discuss. To do so would be to threaten the face the person was trying to present to the others. Persons traffic in "impressions" and seek to manage them so that the immediate audience will accept the face that is being presented.

Goffman's most interesting—and by far most controversial—contribution to social psychology has been his theoretical attempt to relocate the self in the person's performances rather than in his or her mind, brain, body, or consciousness. People do not have substantive selves located inside of them but rather create the self as a dramatic effect arising diffusely in social experience and built purely out of social material. The details of Goffman's intriguing argument about the self will be presented in Chapter 10.

In addition to his important contributions to the social-psychological problems of the self, Goffman has undertaken studies of face-to-face interaction, the interactional structure of personal experience, behavior in public and semipublic places, and the interpersonal dynamics of mental hospitals and other institutions of total control (Goffman, 1967, 1971, 1963, 1961a). The work and theories of this important scholar will be much in evidence in our attempt in this book to treat social psychology sociologically.

E. ETHNOMETHODOLOGY

As the interactionist perspective grew, inevitable offshoots and derivatives emerged. Drawing on different philosophical traditions, various schools developed. One of the most important of these is called by its adherents *ethnomethodology* (Garfinkel, 1967). Based on the phenomenology of such European thinkers as Alfred Schutz and Edmund Husserl, ethnomethodology is based on several assumptions. First, human behavior is to be understood subjectively from the standpoint of the experience of the acting individual. Second, there are as many different social worlds of reality as there are individuals. Third, social order and social action are seen as problematic constructions, despite the fact that they are taken for granted by the individual. Fourth, in the process of interacting with other people the individuals involved suspend many of their own common-sense assumptions and act as if they know and understand what the others are saying. Finally, these common-sense assumptions make up what we call human society (Lindesmith, Strauss, and Denzin, 1975, 20).

Studying the commonplace, however, is not an easy task. We are so buried in our common-sense understandings and take them so much for granted that the social psychologist must devise a strategy with which to make these scenes visible. Harold Garfinkel, who coined the term *ethnomethodology*, has done this ably with a series of small experiments designed to disrupt the usual routines of everyday life and, by so doing, make their features visible. The major feature of everyday life is the existence of a series of *background expectancies*. These consist of those taken-for-granted social understandings that are "seen but unnoticed" and are usually perceived only when they are violated (Garfinkel, 1967).

The term *ethnomethodology* is a compound phrase taken from two words—*ethno*, meaning people, and *methodology*, meaning procedure. As a theory and strategy in social psychology, then, ethnomethodology focuses on the procedures people use to make sense out of everyday life.

Garfinkel reports that his standard procedure is to find a common routine in which people are engaged and then "see what can be done to make trouble." By observing how people respond he can presumably uncover all the features and characteristics of these scenes. For example:

Case 1

The subject was telling the experimenter, a member of the subject's car pool, about having had a flat tire while going to work the previous day.
(S) I had a flat tire.
(E) What do you mean, you had a flat tire?
She appeared momentarily stunned. Then she answered in a hostile way: "What do you mean, 'What do you mean?' A flat tire is a flat tire. That is what I meant. Nothing special. What a crazy question!" [Garfinkel, 1967, 42].

Case 6

(S) How are you?
(E) How am I in regard to what? My health, my finances, my school work, my peace of mind, my . . . ?
(S) (Red in the face and suddenly out of control.) Look! I was just trying to be polite. Frankly, I don't give a damn how you are! [44].

Case 7

My friend and I were talking about a man whose overbearing attitude annoyed us. My friend expressed his feeling.
(S) I'm sick of him.
(E) Would you explain what is wrong with you that you are sick?
(S) Are you kidding me? You know what I mean.

(E) Please explain your ailment.
(S) (He listened to me with a puzzled look.) What came over you? We never talk this way, do we? [44].

The reactions of people to these violations of common-sense expectations demonstrate how much of social life is routine and based on a series of background expectations that ethnomethodologists are trying to specify. When these small rules of interaction are violated, the results are startling, immediate, and devastating.

In another procedure, Garfinkel had students spend time in their own homes with their families acting as if they were merely boarders. They were told to conduct themselves in a polite and formal way, speak only when spoken to, and the like. Interestingly, some students found that they could not do this simple experiment because of the problems that arose. One student said her mother had a heart condition and she was afraid the shock might kill her.

For students who did try, the results were spectacular. Family members were stupefied. They sought to make the strange actions intelligible by providing accounts of the student's behavior, by acting angry or anxious, and by charging the student with being mean, inconsiderate, selfish, nasty, or impolite. One student embarrassed his mother in front of her friends by asking if she minded if he had a snack from the refrigerator before turning in for the night. The mother exploded: "Mind if you have a little snack? You've been eating snacks around here for years without asking me. What's gotten into you?" Family members responded routinely to these violations with the most savage attacks on the student (Garfinkel, 1967, 47–49).

To the ethnomethodologist these experiments show how important common-sense social structures are. We act routinely in terms of shared assumptions about what reality is, and, when these assumptions are challenged through behavior that does not validate them, the results are striking indeed.

Ethnomethodology is young and has few adherents at this time, although its influence among sociologically based social psychologists seems to be growing. Thus far, much of its theoretical work has been an effort to define itself and to distinguish it from other points of view, especially general symbolic interactionism. This attempt to carve out theoretical distinctions seems to be a common first stage in the development of competing points of view within social psychology. Some social psychologists see ethnomethodology and symbolic interactionism as parallel theories (Denzin, 1970). Others contend that it is a radically different theory having profound implications for all of social psychology (Zimmerman and Wieder, 1970).

It appears to us that the differences between symbolic interactionism and ethnomethodology *are* profound and stem from their different points of philosophical departure. Symbolic interactionism, as we have already suggested, is rooted in pragmatic philosophy and George Herbert Mead's social and behavioral theory of the mind. Ethnomethodology, in contrast, is based on the phenomenology of Husserl and Schutz. These two philosophical positions lead to quite different kinds of social psychology. In Mead's pragmatism, on the one hand, the concept of *interaction* takes primacy over everything else. A person's world is seen as a series of interactions with other people and with objects in the world at large. The person is constituted by these interactions; therefore, subjects and objects cannot be separated in accounting for human conduct. Phenomenology, on the other hand, begins with the person as a psychological unit and proceeds to show how an individual's perceptions are framed collectively as well as personally.

1. The Situation: Two Definitions

The best statement of the difference between these two points of view has been given by Perinbanayagam (1974) in his discussion of the important concept of the *definition of the situation*. W. I. Thomas (1937), an early proponent of the interactionist position, argued that "situations defined as real are real in their consequences," and social psychologists have been struggling ever since to come to grips with the full importance of his observation. To the ethnomethodologist, proceeding from a phenomenological base, the definition of the situation is largely a product of the *intersubjectivity* of the actors. By this is meant simply that I have my viewpoint and you have yours, and together we attempt to reach some common grounds on which to act.

This common ground, which interactionists insist is the subject matter of social psychology, is more assumed than explained in ethnomethodology. The idea in phenomenology seems to be that definitions of situations are easily and effortlessly created. But Thomas noted that "there is always a rivalry between the spontaneous definitions of the situation made by the member of an organized society and the definitions which his society has provided for him" (Thomas, 1923, 42). Such common action, then, is a highly problematic interactional concern and not simply a straightforward psychological matter. Definitions of the situation are joint acts (as Blumer notes) and as a result must be negotiated between participants in a situation. Communication does not, then, according to the interactionist perspective, proceed through a process of intersubjectivity but rather through the process of interaction. Perinbanayagam points to the basic problem with phenomenology as a basis for *social* psychology when he says:

> The people in Schutz's world are alone and isolated in their personal facticity; they are strangers barely interested in even asking directions from the others in the situation, or *finding out* how the others are, by asking them, or listening to them, and certainly, according to all appearances, capable of taking care of themselves, of constituting the world all by themselves with never a moment of self-doubt or suspicion. . . . In other words, there is no intercommunication of interaction. The actions in Schutz's world are all one sided: one assumes a state of intersubjectivity, one assumes a reciprocity of perspectives, and one assumes the existence of the other. . . . The self is said to constitute the world and not *participate in its constitution with other people* [1974, 527].

Having a party does not consist merely of running down a bunch of people who already want to go to a party. It usually also involves persuading people to *be willing* to attend that party. Interactional strategies, not merely an exchange of perspectives, are what is at issue here. It may be easier to talk a woman into marrying you if she is already willing, but frequently a suitor is confronted with the additional problem of having to convince a person who is either neutral—or even unwilling—to be willing. Such negotiations are not easily dealt with in a perspective that assumes mutuality of existing perspectives as the basic framework of communication.

Despite these difficult issues and the nature of the criticism raised about ethnomethodology, researchers working from this theoretical stance have generated some important insights into human behavior and have offered a provocative new kind of social psychology. Their contributions will also be in evidence as we proceed in this book.

F. THE RESEARCH PROCESS

1. Puzzles and Solutions

How does the social psychologist now proceed, armed with questions and assumptions, perspectives and frameworks? Social psychologists do research to find out as much as they can about a given problem. But how is the problem derived? How do social psychologists know what to study? And, importantly, how do they know when they have found something important?

Our ways of thinking about these questions have undergone tremendous changes in the last 15 years or so, especially in the light of the publication of an important book in 1962 by Thomas Kuhn, *The Structure of Scientific Revolutions.* Kuhn is a natural scientist who came to question the traditional scientific explanation of how the research task develops. As important as his work was in placing scientific research within a fresh new framework, Kuhn's book also came to be an important source for rethinking social science (Ritzer, 1975; Friedrichs, 1970; Phillips, 1973).

One of Kuhn's most important points concerns the way in which changes come about in science. In the traditional way of looking at the matter, science grows in a progressive manner, with each advance building on those that precede it. Science, in this view, is a series of building blocks, slowly but inexorably moving us toward greater and greater levels of knowledge. Changes in scientific knowledge thus come slowly and in an incremental way. Kuhn believes that this point of view is false. He asserts that the conception of the history of science as the progressive accumulation of truth is largely an illusion, created when each generation of scientists rewrites its textbooks to give the impression that the current stage of knowledge is the apex of what has accumulated. In place of this incremental conception of science Kuhn advances the thesis that revolution marks the important changes in science. Truly major changes come about as a result of revolutions in the basic paradigms, or systems, of science.

Theory and research are interdependent.

2. What Is a Paradigm?

Kuhn offers, in effect, a sociological theory of science. He says that science takes the particular shape it does from the application of shared paradigms. A paradigm can be defined, in its simplest form, as "the entire constellation of beliefs, values, techniques, and theories shared by the members of a given scientific community" (Kuhn, 1970, 175). In other words a paradigm is a fundamental image held by members of the scientific community about the subject matter of science. Masterman (1970) notes that a paradigm does the following:

1. It defines what entities are (and are not) the concern of a particular scientific community.
2. It tells the scientist where to look (and where not to look) in order to find the entities of concern to him.
3. It tells the scientist what he can expect to discover when he finds and examines the entities of concern to his field [59].

Using these ideas, Ritzer (1975) offers a precise, technical definition of a paradigm:

A paradigm is a fundamental image of the subject matter within a science. It serves to define what should be studied, what questions should be asked, how they should be asked, and what rules should be followed in interpreting the answers obtained. The paradigm is the broadest unit of consensus within a science and serves to differentiate one scientific community (or subcommunity) from another. It subsumes, defines, and interrelates the exemplars, theories, and methods and instruments that exist within it [7].

What these interesting ideas mean is that theory and research blend in what Kuhn calls an "inextricable mixture" (1962, 108). There are, says Kuhn, no such things as "independent facts" or any other factors or standards that are independently true. The idea of what constitutes a fact is, instead, paradigm dependent, or a judgment rendered by scientists who apply one system or another. The competition that goes on between adherents of one paradigm and another is not the kind of battle that can be resolved by proof, because what constitutes proof is itself dependent on the application of one system or another. Furthermore, says Kuhn, we may have to give up the idea that changes of the prevailing paradigm carry scientists closer to the truth. Instead, they rearrange the criteria for accepting something as the truth.

3. Paradigms as Puzzles and Solutions

In all of science, including the science of social psychology, then, paradigms function to set puzzles and, at the same time, set the terms of their solution. When a machine is designed to manufacture jigsaw puzzles, the solution to the puzzle is built in. Once the machine is designed, there can be only one solution to the puzzle. From this point of view, explaining something satisfactorily is dependent on the whole scientific community's understanding of what it means to make a "satisfactory explanation" (Phillips, 1973). The facts to be explained and the very idea of an explanation are paradigm dependent. Changes in the prevailing paradigms of science come about because no paradigm can handle all of the possible puzzles the human mind is capable of devising. New paradigms arise to handle these problems, and, when a scientist gives up an old paradigm and embraces a new one, he undergoes a kind of conversion experience, for such a decision can only be made on faith (Phillips, 1973). When we speak, then, of "the facts," we are speaking about what people in a given social context (science) accept as the facts at any given time.

Science varies in its use of paradigms. Some sciences use a single paradigm that is dominant and holds a broad consensus among scholars in the field. In other sciences, such as social psychology, a number of paradigms all compete for the same subject matter. Adherents of one system are constantly questioning the assumptions of adherents of others, and intellectual blood flows in the streets as the battle rages. When there exists no dominant paradigm, practitioners spend a great deal of time defending their own favorite paradigm against attacks (Masterman, 1970).

Given this framework, social psychology, as well as all of the other social sciences, is a multiple-paradigm science (Ritzer, 1975). The perspectives, theories, and frameworks we have thus far sketched can all be viewed as paradigms competing for dominance in a large field of play.

We will not in this book try to be exhaustive in our treatment of all the possible systems in social psychology. Instead, we will talk about a few and then apply our analysis primarily to those that deal most fundamentally with the sociological side of social psychology. But it is important to note that social psychology is a living discipline that is constantly reassessing its prevailing systems of thought and method.

Keeping in mind, then, the close relationship between paradigm and method, we will examine some of the more important methodological techniques used by social psychologists and the paradigms from which they emerged. A multiple-paradigm science like social psychology will, of course, have multiple methodologies, too. We will discuss the major methodologies of sociologically based social psychology under four broad headings: 1) field research, 2) experimental research, 3) unobtrusive, or documentary, methods, and 4) interview and questionnaire (sometimes called survey) research.

G. FIELD RESEARCH

Studying behavior in the natural field of its occurrence is a fundamental contribution of sociologically based social psychologies to the larger discipline. The concept of *field* is a bit troublesome to students, because it seems to imply a sharply defined territory in which the researcher works. Actually, no such clear boundaries exist, for field researchers usually recognize very quickly that a field is necessarily continuous with other fields and that social processes have no absolute boundaries and no absolute beginnings or ends (Schatzman and Strauss, 1973, 2). For example, field research in a nursing home involves not only the setting of the nursing home itself as a physical place but also a clear understanding of the relationships between people who are confined to the home and those significant others outside whose decisions and continued presence affect life in the home (Gubrium, 1975).

The essence of field research is to immerse oneself in the actual setting in which the behavior under investigation occurs. The first task of field research, then, is an adequate description of social settings. The ability to see and then write in an accurate way about social relationships is in many ways more of an art than a science, but it is essential to good social psychology. The researcher begins much like a journalist or a detective (Sanders, 1976) trying to figure out what is going on. An adequate account of human behavior involves answers to the questions of who, what, where, when, why, and how. Above all, the researcher must be open to discovery and not dismiss the obvious as trivial, for much of social life involves dealing explicitly with what is easy to miss precisely because it *is* so obvious (Schatzman and Strauss, 1973).

1. Participant Observation

Participant observation is probably the best known technique of field research, and it has been most popular with social psychologists operating with the paradigm of symbolic interactionism. Researchers enter a setting they want to study and actually participate in the very scene they are observing, analyzing, and writing about. For social psychologists who are wed to the idea of process, this is an indispensible methodology, for it allows them to see life from the standpoint of the participants. Social psychologist Howard S. Becker's (1963) famous study of jazz musicians was conducted as participant observation, with Becker actually playing in the jazz group he was studying. In a highly controversial study Humphreys (1970), a social psychologist concerned with the sexual encounters of homosexuals in public restrooms, assumed the role of "watchqueen," a lookout who warned of the approach of "straights" or police. None of the participants in the sexual behavior under analysis doubted the watchqueen role played by the researcher, who did indeed give warning when necessary. Social psychologists who study deviant social worlds often find themselves in a position of playing a deviant role, although this is not absolutely necessary (Polsky, 1967). Because of the closeness of the researchers to the persons they are studying, however, participant observation often leads to various ethical dilemmas, although not necessarily more so than other techniques.

The essence of participant observation is to place oneself *within* the process without disrupting it and to take the perspective of the participant. From the standpoint of the paradigm of symbolic interactionism, taking the perspective of the participant demands that researchers construct an appropriate role affording the actual interaction with other participants. In a sense, researchers construct the social reality they want to describe. By actually participating, researchers can not only observe events from the standpoint of the people they are trying to understand but can also experience their emotions and concerns. These are the essential conditions defined by the symbolic interactionist paradigm that must be met by the methodology the researcher uses.

2. Nonparticipant Observation

Observation, which is the key to field research in social psychology, may also be of a nonparticipant nature. This means observing situations in terms of what can be understood as a neutral observer from the outside. Nonparticipant observation is almost always employed as an adjunct to participant observation. It is often used in the initial phases of a research project in order to determine many of the very practical elements of a social setting, such as the time when events occur, the physical arrangement of places and things, and the appearance of the participants. These elements can be ascertained best by simply being in a place and watching what goes on without a question being asked and even without the researcher being regarded as part of the setting by the participants. As an initial strategy nonparticipant observation can be indispensable, because it allows researchers time to discover the basic outlines of the field they are studying and to find out what kinds of questions and actions will help them find what they want to know. Such knowledge can prevent many disrupting errors when the researchers reach the point in a study when they actually join the group and begin to relate to it as participants.

H. EXPERIMENTAL RESEARCH

Many social psychologists, guided by a different paradigm, choose some form of experimental research. A paradigm in which experiments are required usually assumes that social situations have basic structures that determine the outcome of behavior occurring within them. This is a very different assumption from the previous comments about process made within the symbolic-interactionist framework. If one wishes to investigate social structures from this point of view, the careful *control*—rather than the nondisruption—of naturally occurring events will be the goal of the researcher. The experiment is uniquely suited to this type of structuralist paradigm. Experiments are usually of two types: the field experiment and the laboratory experiment.

1. The Field Experiment

Social psychologists sometimes use an ordinary social situation to check a theory. During the mid-1930s, when many hotels and restaurants excluded non-Whites, a sociologist had occasion to travel widely in the United States with a young Chinese student and his wife. They visited 184 restaurants and 66 hotels, and they were refused service only once. Then the sociologist wrote to each of these establishments and to a similar number that were not visited, to provide a basis for comparison. His question to each was: Will you accept members of the Chinese race as guests in your establishment? The responses are shown in Table 1-1. Nearly all said that they would not accept Chinese guests, although most had actually given satisfactory service to the Chinese couple when they appeared. The researcher experimentally established the difference between professed attitudes and situational behavior (LaPiere, 1934).

The nature of the field experiment is two-fold: 1) the study is done *in the field,* on the assumption that a minimum of tampering with the environment is necessary to minimize the effects of the experimenter's presence, and 2) the study is done by *experimenting* to allow the controlled manipulation of what are considered the crucial factors *producing* the outcomes observed. The es-

Table 1-1.   Willingness to accept Chinese guests

Response	Hotels Visited	Hotels Not Visited	Restaurants Visited	Restaurants Not Visited
No	43	30	75	78
Undecided	3	2	6	7
Yes	1	0	0	1

sential nature of the field experiment, then, is to compare outcomes (for example, behavior) produced in their natural environments but under two or more different sets of manipulated circumstances. The LaPiere study fits this definition in that the hotel and restaurant personnel were given two "natural" but different opportunities to respond to a request for service—by mail and in person. They gave, in most cases, two different kinds of behavior. Most responded verbally "no" through the mail or on the telephone under circumstances in which they did not have to act immediately in an embarrassing manner by evicting the Chinese couple, but responded "yes" when confronted more directly. The manipulation was the context of the request. By using a positivistic paradigm *and* a behavioral one, LaPiere was directed toward this type of methodology. The assumptions of the paradigms demand both the field setting of the study and the explicit control of the manipulated conditions, thus making the study an experiment.

2. The Laboratory Experiment

Laboratory experiments can be distinguished from field experiments in terms of the environment, or context, in which the manipulations are made. Both field and lab experiments are studies in which conditions relevant to the research objective are controlled by the researcher. The distinction between them is whether the theory being tested requires that the observed behavior occur within some "natural" environment or whether it could occur in a synthetic environment without jeopardizing the study. Both methodologies are dictated by the positivistic and behavioral paradigms, and the debate over the relative merits of each is simply in terms of the possible effects of an artificial laboratory setting on the behavior under study. Both types of methodologies are used primarily because of the felt necessity to control all extraneous variables and to manipulate a relative few in an effort to see their effects on behavior. Obviously, such a conception of control is the direct result of a structural paradigm, whereas the free and uncontrolled description of generic social processes is the result of a process paradigm.

Research by Asch (1952) on the effect of the group on perceptual judgment is perhaps the best illustration of laboratory experimentation on a social-psychological phenomenon. The object was to determine the effect of a unanimous group judgment on the judgment of a single individual. Seven laboratory controls were required. *First,* each of the 56 groups, consisting of up to 10 students plus the experimenter, were isolated in a small classroom for the duration of the experiment. *Second,* all individuals were asked to respond to an obvious judgmental task by stating aloud in the presence of the others which of three clearly different heavy, black, vertical lines on one card was equal in length to a vertical line on another card. *Third,* the researcher read the same instructions to all groups and conducted the experiment in the same uniform sequence. *Fourth,* the experimenter selected only one person to be uninformed. He was put in the dependent position where he always answered last, so that his judgment would be affected by the responses of all other students. This was arranged by putting him at the end of the table and always starting the responses from the other end of the table. *Fifth*, the researcher previously instructed all of the other students to pick a specific line, sometimes the short line and sometimes the long line, as the one equal to the comparison line, so that the dependent student was confronted with unanimous agreement on the wrong line at the time when he had to make his choice. The researcher rigged 31 groups to answer wrong unanimously and to do it in a matter-of-fact and convincing way. He also arranged with 25 other groups to answer correctly before the dependent student answered, to provide a basis for comparison of the effect of the rigged judgment. The *sixth* control was to keep complete and accurately labeled records of group identity and individual performance as the 56 repetitions of the experiment continued. The *seventh* control was for the experimenter to explain to the experimental students the method and purpose of the experiment and to answer any questions they might ask. This debriefing was clearly necessary because many of the experimental students had become uncomfortable, embarrassed, and uncertain when confronted with a unanimous set of wrong choices.

The results demonstrated a definite influence of erroneous judgments on the dependent students in the rigged groups. In a total of 392 judgments, there were 55% erroneous judgments when the influencing groups were instructed to answer wrong, compared with 33% erroneous judgments when the influencing groups were instructed to answer correctly. The distribution indicates that 19 of the experimental students resisted the pressure of unanimous wrong judgments, with an error rate substantially similar to that of the experimental students groups' attempt to answer correctly. But 12 of the groups showed a strong influence on unanimous erroneous judgments,

Table 1-2. Distribution of critical errors in experimental and control groups

Number of Errors	Control Group	Experimental Group
0	14	6
1	9	7
2	2	6
3	0	4
4	0	4
5	0	1
6	0	1
7	0	2
N	25	31
Mean errors	.5	2.3

Adapted from *Social Psychology*, by S. E. Asch. Copyright © 1952 by Prentice-Hall, Inc. Used by permission of Prentice-Hall, Inc., Englewood Cliffs, New Jersey.

and two of the control group's dependent students followed the erroneous lead consistently on all seven trials.

3. The Experimental Interview

The French psychologist Piaget investigated the judgmental, mental, and moral development of young children. He devised problems that required a selected response from children to indicate how they understood a relationship or a complex idea. Then he discussed the problem and asked the children to explain to him why they had chosen the explanation they had. Piaget or his coresearchers continued discussing the problem with the child until they were certain exactly how the children perceived the situation, repeating and asking test questions to verify full understanding. Piaget might put the same problem to 40 children, varying the ages from 4 years to 12. He was gradually able to trace the development of the ability to reason from the preschool age, when the child is first able to carry on abstract conversation, up to early adolescence. For example, 40 schoolboys from Geneva, Switzerland, aged 9 to 12 years were asked: "What is silly about this sentence? I have three brothers: Paul, Ernest, and myself." Only 13 of the boys solved the problem. The others had difficulty putting themselves in the place of the speaker. Several thought there would have to be four boys in the family for the speaker to have "myself" as a brother (Piaget, 1959a, 64).

Through this research strategy Piaget concluded that formal thought presupposes two factors. The first is social, involving the possibility of placing oneself at every point of view other than one's own. The second is psychological, involving the ability to assume a purely possible world as the province of logical deduction (Piaget, 1959a, 71). The experimental interview showed the process by which the developing child acquired an understanding of motion, acceleration, weight, social responsibility, moral "fairness," truthfulness, and the interrelation between different rules in a children's game such as marbles. These basic concepts and many others were explored, described, and tentatively explained (Piaget, 1965).

The experimental interview is a most appropriate device to deal with verbalized thinking. The questions and responses of the experimenter are of the same stuff as the responses of the subject. As is commonly assumed in other kinds of investigations, the question can be used as a suitable gauge of the response. It is likely to be successful if the experimenter has a well-defined objective and perseveres in testing the alternatives.

I. UNOBTRUSIVE MEASURES

A methodological middle ground exists between field and experimental research. Sometimes called *unobtrusive*, or *nonreactive*, measures, this form of research requires neither participation in the social world under investigation nor the manipulation of that world.

People, like other objects in the world at large, leave evidence of their presence. As a result the social psychologist can use these traces to find out various things about them. Process paradigms such as symbolic interactionism are especially suited to unobtrusive measures because the methodology is naturalistic; that is, the researchers do not intervene and change the natural processes they are studying as they might in the conduct of an experiment. For example, a great deal can be learned about a group of people by simply analyzing written material by or about the group. Probably the most important and popular unobtrusive measure is called *content analysis*. It is used to study the traces left by human behavior and relate them to the processes of that behavior.

An example of the use of content analysis is a study conducted in 1973 by Scully and Bart. These researchers, seeking evidence of the traditional male sex bias in the writings of some well-known gynecologists, analyzed the content of their standard textbooks (Scully and Bart, 1973). The frequency of certain topical themes indicated that the gynecologists did indeed show a male bias for which there is no basis in medical research. These themes included the assertions that most women are sexually frigid, that the male sex drive is stronger than the female's, that sex is primarily for reproduction, and that the vaginal orgasm rather than the clitoral orgasm is the "mature sexual response," an idea that has been disproved through clinical experimentation and observation (Masters, 1960).

In other words, a great deal of information about the social world can be got through various kinds of extensions of human beings: writings, art work, architecture, newspapers, books, stage productions, and so on. In fact, such evidence can sometimes be regarded as primary, especially when it consistently conflicts with people's direct responses about themselves in interviews or questionnaires. For example, if you ask people directly about their feelings about race, they frequently deny any racist attitudes. But if they belong to the National States Rights Party and subscribe to its publication, *The Thunderbolt*, a great deal of how they feel about race relations can be uncovered by simply analyzing the themes dealt with in that publication.

J. INTERVIEW AND QUESTIONNAIRE RESEARCH

Interviews and questionnaires have become standard research tools for many different paradigms in social psychology. Associated more with structural theories than process ones, these techniques are nevertheless used by a broad spectrum of social psychologists.

The difference between interviews and questionnaires lies in the role played by the researcher in the relationship with the respondents. An interview is conducted directly by the researcher, usually in a face-to-face situation. From the standpoint of process paradigms this is a preferable method, because the respondents can direct the researcher toward the precise meanings of their responses much more readily than questionnaires, which usually involve a response to fixed questions. The questionnaire is ordinarily used anonymously, is often mailed out and mailed in, and limits respondents in the kinds of responses they can give. Questionnaires are more useful when the information the researcher wants is reasonably cut and dried and can be answered in terms of discrete categories—yes and no, do you or don't you, how many times, and so forth.

The interview, on the other hand, is usually less structured than the questionnaire and can be usefully employed in conjunction with the observational techniques we have already discussed. Interviews tease out nuances of meaning in human behavior much more readily than do questionnaires. But they often involve more time and effort by the researcher, and the number of responses that can be realistically anticipated is much lower.

Interviews and questionnaires, as we have said, can be used in conjunction with many types of research strategies, but they are most widely associated with what has come to be known as *survey research*. Survey research is typically used to measure the distribution in a given population of some characteristic such as ownership of a particular product or, less reliably, the possession of a specific attitude.

K. PROBLEMS IN RESEARCH

There are numerous problems confronting the social psychologist who conducts basic research. The overriding problem resides in the paradox we began this chapter with: what we know about social behavior is dependent on our methods of studying it, while our methods of studying it are dependent on what we know about social behavior. Multiple paradigms generate multiple methods, which generate different findings. What this means, of course, is that bias is unavoidable but that by realizing the sources of bias the researcher can at least limit them as much as possible and, above all, admit the ones he has. A discussion of bias in social-psychological research can be organized around four typical problems: 1) investigator bias, 2) respondent bias, 3) the resistance of institutions to give up social data to researchers, and 4) resource limitations.

1. Investigator Bias

Investigator bias is one of the most serious stumbling blocks in the path of scientific research. The reader should recognize that social-science researchers work under the pressure of several forms of cultural bias. Ethnocentric bias may lead them to ignore contrary evidence from other cultural settings. The word *American* in sociological and psychological studies usually signifies ethnocentric bias, and a question such as "would you want your daughter to marry a Black man?" does not provide for the possibility that the person answering it may very well be Black. As we noted earlier in this chapter, little of what we think we know about the nature of human beings and society is based on empirical evidence.

Perhaps the dominant element in investigator bias is the researchers' powerful urge to prove themselves right with the least effort. Some reports are published from an experiment on a single unique sample, such as a psychology or sociology class for which the experimenter is also the professor. The investigator's role in a study is always a nagging question and a continual source of doubt.

2. Respondent Bias

People taking part in a social experiment may respond in ways that have little relation to their usual patterns of behavior. A researcher wanted to determine how long a student would work at a boring task. He had the subjects do two-column additions on sheets of paper filled with random numbers and then tear the completed sheet in 32 pieces and throw them away. These subjects stayed on the job for hours, apparently because of their belief that one had to endure anything for the sake of a "scientific experiment." The researcher called this the *demand characteristic* of the experimental situation (Orne, 1962).

Response acquiescence, or the tendency to answer "yes" regardless of the question, was shown when a researcher altered the wording of part of a question while leaving the rest unchanged. Thus, the respondents were presented with two contradictory statements: (1) it's hardly fair to bring children into the world the way things look for the future, and (2) this is a good time to bring children into the world the way things look for the future. The respondents agreed 62% of the time, regardless of the statement (Carr, 1971). This is *acquiescence bias.*

Another form of response bias is the tendency of subjects to put themselves in the most favorable light. Students who believed they were taking an ability test of some kind copied more telephone numbers than students who believed they were simply cooperating for the benefit of the experimenter (Sigall et al., 1970). In other words, the interview or questionnaire situation is itself part of a "definition of the situation," in which the responses given are part of a set of assumptions the respondent has. Response bias has also been demonstrated with already diagnosed mental patients, who tended to report only the more socially acceptable symptoms of mental illness when they were interviewed by telephone (Phillips and Clancy, 1970). Perhaps the greatest source of response bias is the often loose connection between verbalization and documentable fact. A man may say that he voted in the last election when the records show that he has not voted in the past four elections. He may assert an opinion on a subject he has never heard of and could not define. He may also misread, misunderstand, and mismark the questions. If there is a range of choices varying from low to high, many respondents consistently avoid the extreme values, even though an extreme might reflect their actual position on an issue.

Investigator and response bias are conspicuous features of many paradigms in social psychology. But response bias is more frequently associated with structural paradigms, which emphasize responses to interviews and questionnaires. And the biases of the investigator are usually associated more with process paradigms, which use observational techniques that depend on the categories and concepts used by the investigator. This traditional way of seeing the problem is not altogether true, however, for the biases of the investigator can slant the way an interview is conducted or a questionnaire is constructed.

3. Institutional Resistance

The leaders of an established institution are understandably reluctant to reveal information about its inner workings unless they can be reasonably sure that such information will be to their advantage. They worry about the novice investigator who may use his research information in a way that discredits the officers, workers, or clients of the institution. Even an institution that is already interested in taking part in a research project will show reluctance on the department level if labor union representatives, service personnel, or other persons feel confused or threatened as the research reaches their area. The investigators must take every precaution to inform others about the limits of the research and convince them that it will not embarrass them. The researchers should share interesting findings from previous research. If they can give evidence of a positive contribution to the organization, they will get better cooperation.

4. Resource Limitation

Social psychology is at best a developing discipline. As such, it has not reached much consensus about either its paradigms or its methods. Most of those who identify as social psychologists are primarily professors of psychology or sociology at the college level, and competing academic and professional duties limit their concentration on social psychology. Much of the research accomplished has centered on the classroom, using enrolled students as subjects and slight modifications of classroom facilities to create "laboratory conditions." There are relatively few professional journals that publish research findings in social psychology, at least when compared with a science like chemistry, which has many specialized branches supported by a number of journals in each branch. There has been relatively little financial support for research in social psychology, primarily because it has not been regarded as having very many practical applications. Later in this book we will show that this conception of the discipline is in error, and that social psychology has many exciting practical implications.

Such problems give social psychology a certain vitality and excitement, however, and there is abundant opportunity for any investigator to identify new areas of investigation, think up new puzzles to solve, and invent new research strategies for the task.

L. SUMMARY

Social psychology is an exciting series of puzzles and solutions about the most fascinating subject of all: human beings. Social psychology shows us how to focus our attention on everyday life in such a way as to reveal its features and characteristics.

Part of the difficulty of understanding social psychology is that the term encompasses a lot of territory. Social psychologists have studied attitudes, values, authority, control, deviance, respectability, personality, selves, identity, motivation, love, and hate. In fact, almost everything that people do and have, social psychologists have studied. In addition, social psychologists have studied all types of organisms: rats and pigeons, goldfish and people.

In this book social psychology is the study of human interaction. We are interested in the kinds of things that make people human. In a similar vein the book is oriented toward the social side of the field because of our insistence that interaction and relationships, rather than individual units, are the subject matter of social psychology.

In addition, social psychology deals with social processes. Time, change, ebb, and flow are all central features of human interaction and inescapable characteristics of human existence.

Social psychology has its roots in various ideas from the past. But it was specifically the rise of science in the 17th century that brought about new ways of thinking about the relationship between the individual and society that eventually emerged into modern social psychology. From a simplistic beginning, social psychology has evolved some extremely sophisticated ideas about the relationship between self and others. A continuing tendency, however, is either to reduce the individual to society (as Durkheim did), or to collapse all social processes into individual psychology. It is difficult to develop theories in social psychology that do not treat the individual and society dualistically.

For example, the personal perspective tends to view people egoistically. The person is the unit of analysis, and all action is reduced to processes that are going on within people. The social-contract theorists such as Locke and Rousseau took this point of view, seeing society as nothing more than a contract between individuals. Freud continued this line of inquiry with his conceptions of the personality as composed of the id, ego, and superego, as well as his discovery of the unconscious. Cognitive theories that locate the cause of overt behavior in the consciousness of the person have also become popular, especially among psychologically trained social psychologists.

Behavioral perspectives are at the opposite extreme from person-based theories, because they locate explanations of overt behavior not in the person but in past experiences that have conditioned that behavior to occur the way it does. B. F. Skinner has become the most influential scholar among the behaviorists.

The interactionist perspective, which arose primarily among sociologists, resists any attempt to separate the individual from society, arguing instead for their twin-born nature. This point of view originated in the work of George Herbert Mead, a pragmatic philosopher at the turn of this century, and Charles Horton Cooley, an early social psychologist. Herbert Blumer and Erving Goffman are two contemporary interactionist theorists who have kept the principles and tenets of this point of view in the forefront of modern social psychology. From the interactionist perspective, minds, selves, emotions, and meaning all arise as social acts in joint communication with other people.

A slightly different point of view is a new movement among sociologically based social psychologists called ethnomethodology. Based on phenomenology rather than pragmatism, ethnomethodology is similar to the personal perspective in that it begins with individual experience. But it moves quickly from there to the social nature of experience and constructs society as an outcome of that experience. The emphasis in ethnomethodology is on the background expectancies that govern and channel experience. The research method of this point of view consists of disrupting commonplace situations and then recording the reactions of subjects.

Social psychology consists of a series of puzzles about social life, and the research process is an attempt to find solutions to these puzzles. The process of thinking up puzzles (theory) and the process of finding solutions (methods) are not, however, independent. In an important book called *The Structure of Scientific Revolutions*, Thomas Kuhn offered us the concept of *paradigm* as a way of understanding the relationship between puzzles and solutions. He said that a paradigm involves a "fundamental image held by members of the scientific community about the subject matter of science." These paradigms come to set the term of questions and answers, telling us what constitutes a puzzle and what constitutes its solution. There is, according to Kuhn, no social or political vacuum within which "objectivity" is possible; instead, facts are paradigm dependent and therefore depend on what members of the scientific community at any given moment recognize as facts. This sociological view of science is equally applicable to social psychology, which is a multiple-paradigm science in that a number of different conceptions of what the puzzles are and what solutions are appropriate compete.

The major paradigms in social psychology have led practitioners toward the use of certain research methodologies. These include description, in which the researchers try to find out who, what, where, when, why, and how, and participant observation, in which researchers actually join a group that they want to know something about and then describe the world as it looks from within the group. The field experiment is another technique. Here the social psychologist uses an ordinary situation to check a theory, making up a test to fit the situation. The laboratory experiment is much more rigorous. Here the researcher tries to isolate some particular feature of social life and test it under highly controlled conditions in which extraneous factors are excluded. Rather than confronting his subjects directly, the social psychologist may use unobtrusive measures, which reveal things about the subject without requiring a face-to-face encounter. Indirect observation and content analysis of written material are two examples of unobtrusive measures. An interview may also be an experiment. More often than not, some combination of research strategies is used by social psychologists as they seek answers to the puzzles of the discipline.

Several problems emerge in social research. The investigator may have powerful biases that get in the way of understanding. While no investigator can be objective, strategies can be developed that minimize investigator bias. The respondents, moreover, may have biases that color findings, in the sense that they may act during an experiment or an interview in ways that are different from their everyday actions. This is one of the major difficulties with laboratory experiments. Other problems also emerge. Institutions are sometimes reluctant to assist with research using their facilities. Resources also limit. There is very little money for social-psychological research as compared with other kinds. Despite these problems, social psychology continues to be an exciting, vibrant form of inquiry that has in the past and will in the future yield fascinating insights about the nature of human interaction.

Language, Symbols, and Communication 2

A. INTRODUCTION

Language is perhaps the most important process in all of social psychology. When we stop to realize how much of our behavior consists of talk, it becomes clear that the ocean of words in which we are constantly swimming is essential to understand. Fortunately, social psychologists, linguists, anthropologists, semanticists, and even an occasional English professor have made important studies of the way language works. So we have a considerable body of research and writing about it. And the more we understand, the more significant language appears to be in our lives.

In addition, of course, human beings communicate with considerably more than words. In this chapter we will study the range and depth of communication, verbal or not.

B. LANGUAGE AS SYMBOLIC INTERACTION

Language is a system of verbal communication based on convention. It is not an object but a pattern of interaction. Language is probably as old as social interaction and thus goes back perhaps a million years. Its content is enormously flexible. And, judging from the wide diversity of vocabulary among the 2500 different languages in use in the world today, languages have been independently developed by even very small groups of people.

1. Human and Animal: Symbol versus Sign

There has been much debate in the literature of social psychology about the uniqueness of human symbolic language. Because we are interested in social psychology as the study of *human* interaction, the comparative question of whether this ability is unique is not as important for us as it might otherwise be. But we do believe that human beings are different from other kinds of creatures and that much of this difference has to do with their symbol-using capacities. Therefore, a major distinction is in order.

The distinction is between *natural signs* and *symbols*. All living things share the ability to pick up cues from their environment. Important experiments with dogs by Pavlov (1849–1936) showed that they become conditioned to signs and develop a sensitive capacity to read them. The sound of a bell, altogether unrelated to food, nonetheless comes to be associated with it. Cats, fish, chimpanzees, pigeons, and all other animals are sign readers. In fact, the behavior of animals is beginning to be studied as an advanced warning system against earthquakes, for their ability to read early tremors is considerably more advanced than that of humans.

Human beings also react to signs. Virtually any object, act, occurrence, or quality may function as a sign of something else (Lindesmith, Strauss, and Denzin, 1975, 118):

> The red glow of wood or metal indicates that it is hot; a gesture may reveal anger; a red light is a warning of danger; a pointer on a dial tells an aviator how high he is flying; and so on endlessly.

Natural signs, then, are all around us, and they involve some kind of physical stimulus. But even Pavlov, whose studies of animal sign reading advanced our understanding so greatly, never argued that the sign-conditioning process in nonhumans could be transferred directly as an adequate account of human behavior. For Pavlov recognized the existence of something else in human beings. For lack of a better phrase he referred to it as our "second signaling system." It seems to set us apart from other creatures in some fascinating ways (Pavlov, 1927, 407).

A dog's bared fangs constitute a natural sign that animals and human beings alike understand. (Photo by © George Rodger, Magnum Photos)

This second signaling system is the symbol. All animals engage in communication, but only human beings communicate with abstract symbols. Symbols are conventional signs that take on their meanings in social usage. There seems to be no exact counterpart in the animal world, as Leslie White has pointed out:

> It is impossible for a dog, horse, bird, or even an ape to have any understanding of the meaning of the sign of the cross to a Christian, or of the fact that black (white among the Chinese) is the color of mourning. No chimp or lab rat can appreciate the difference between holy water and distilled water, or grasp the meaning of Tuesday, [the number] 3, or sin. No animal save man can distinguish a cousin from an uncle, or a cross cousin from a parallel cousin. Only man can commit the crime of incest or adultery; only he can remember the Sabbath and keep it holy. It is not, as we well know, that the lower animals can do these things but to a lesser degree than ourselves; they cannot perform these acts of appreciation and distinction at all [1940, 23–24].

Symbols, then, come to stand for things during conventional usage. They are social creations in the sense that a solitary, unsocialized organism is incapable of producing them; they demand a social situation for their existence. Symbols are not particular, as signs are, but instead general and abstract. They are categorical distinctions that allow us to represent a whole range of events under a general term.

For animals the relationship in which one thing *stands for,* or *represents,* something else does not appear to exist except in a very elementary form. As S. I. Hayakawa has said:

> A chimpanzee can be taught to drive a car, but there is one thing wrong with its driving: its reactions are such that if a red light shows when it is halfway across a street, it will stop in the middle of the crossing, while if a green light shows while another car is stalled in its path, it will go ahead regardless of the consequences. In other words, so far as a chimpanzee is concerned, the red light can hardly be said to *stand for* stop; it *is* stop [1940, 26].

People sometimes act that way in cars, too, but their behavior is presumably a mistake and not something built into the way they act toward signs. To the chimp, a red light is a sign—that is, "a complete and invariable reaction which occurs whether or not the conditions warrant such a reaction (Hayakawa, 1940, 27). To the human being, however, the red light is a symbol, the meaning of which is conditional on the circumstances.

2. The Social Nature of Symbols

The concept of human behavior as symbolic interaction, as we have noted, was introduced into social psychology by George Herbert Mead. Mead noted that a gesture stands for an abstract idea and that the gesture arouses that idea in another individual. The response of the other person to the gesture is the meaning of that symbol. These symbolic exchanges may involve physical things, mental objects, actions, or even imaginary things.

Two conventional symbols are apparent in this classroom setting—the cross, which represents God, and the flag, which stands for country. (Photo by © Charles Harbutt, Magnum Photos)

Whatever meanings are transmitted, they arise out of the social interaction generated between people. We make continuing interpretations of the actions, gestures, and words encountered in our world.

At the beginning of an interaction two partners may have understandings of their relationship that are in conflict. In this case their conversation and gestures may not make sense until they realize that their definitions of each other and the situation are in disagreement. We can illustrate by the case of a young man who decided he wanted to marry the woman he was seeing, assumed that she would leap at the chance, and confided to mutual friends that they would be married in a few months. He had not considered it necessary to ask the woman in conventional English. At first she was puzzled by the actions and remarks of her boyfriend and their mutual friends, and they were equally puzzled by her peculiar responses. Because she had no intention of marrying the man, she was furious when she realized what had happened and before her departure told him off in extremely explicit English. Then, everyone understood.

The success of a speech act depends on whether or not the symbols mobilized by one party operate as a sign to the other (Henle, 1965). The symbols in language operate on different and quite discrete levels: as direct references, as in naming a simple object; as references to classes of objects; and as metaphors. We can show this expanding series of categories with the following sequence: the White House, white houses, houses, shelters, structures, buildings, property, real estate, economic assets, wealth, national wealth, global wealth. Metaphorical language communicates by defining one thing in terms of the properties associated with something else. For example: "The two teams battled to a tie" uses the terms of warfare to talk about sports. Similarly, "John was the life of the party" and "The Russian Bear dominates Northern Asia" express ideas metaphorically. Language is rich in metaphor, and the reader is invited to note the number of cases he or she encounters in which one thing is described or defined in terms of the imagery of something else.

The conventional, social nature of symbols is a point that cannot be overemphasized. Physical referents in the world at large do not force us to call them by any *particular* name. All it takes to make what Mead called a "significant symbol" is some agreement over its use. This is a hard point to remember at times, because the connection between convention and nature is so impressive in our experience. It takes a moment to figure out the error in the child's insistence that "pigs are called pigs because they're dirty."

If we are willing to endorse a new convention that is proposed, however, any number of possibilities exist for communication. The poet e e cummings (1894–1962), who used a minimum of capital letters when he wrote, is an example. The following poem of his may make little sense to the reader at first:*

anyone lived in a pretty how town
(with up so floating many bells down)
spring summer autumn winter
he sang his didn't he danced his did.

Women and men (both little and small)
cared for anyone not at all
they sowed their isn't they reaped their same
sun moon stars rain

children guessed (but only a few
and down they forgot as up they grew
autumn winter spring summer)
that noone loved him more by more

when by now and tree by leaf
she laughed his joy she cried his grief
bird by snow and stir by still
anyone's any was all to her

someones married their everyones
laughed their cryings and did their dance
(sleep wake hope and then) they
said their nevers they slept their dream

stars rain sun moon
(and only the snow can begin to explain
how children are apt to forget to remember
with up so floating many bells down)

one day anyone died i guess
and noone stopped to kiss his face
busy folk buried them side by side
little by little and was by was

all by all and deep by deep
and more by more they dream their sleep
noone and anyone earth by april
wish by spirit and if by yes.

Women and men (both dong and ding)
summer autumn winter spring
reaped their sowing and went their came
sun moon stars rain

But if we allow cummings a few idiosyncracies of language and "translate" his unusual ways of using words (a man is named "anyone" and a woman "noone"), the poem begins to communicate in some powerful and even universal ways about the life cycle. The reader's willingness to accept the proposed changes in conventional language creates the possibility of symbolic communication in an interesting new way. This is, of course, how language changes.

3. Meaning

Symbols have been called the directly observable data of meaning in social relationships (Duncan, 1968, 50). When a person expresses a significant symbol as communication to another person, the person is assuming that it has the same meaning for both of them. In conversation, then, there is a continuing need for affirmation that the messages are being received and understood in the sense in which they were intended. If the affirmation is not received by the sender, she or he will stop and attempt to clarify, perhaps first by repeating the symbol and then, if the symbol seems not to be understood, by transforming it into other words or explaining it through analogy or demonstration. We are forever explaining the meaning of new symbols or having others explain new symbols to us. This means that language is a dynamic system that is constantly undergoing modification and expansion.

Of course, the meaning of an object does not reside mysteriously within it but depends on how it is defined by the namer (Strauss, 1959, 18). As people shift their interest and focus of action, they redefine various objects, and reality shifts to accommodate to the new definitions. As Dewey put it, "Good things change and vanish not only with changes in the environing medium but with changes in ourselves" (Dewey, 1922, 86).

The concept of meaning has 16 definable applications, according to Ogden and Richards (1923, 186):

1. Meaning may be regarded as an intrinsic property of the referent of the significant symbol.
2. Meaning may be a unique relation of the object to some other object.
3. Meaning is commonly given by synonymous or related words, as in a dictionary.
4. Meaning may be taken as what a symbol implies, and this should be the same for the sender and the receiver.
5. Meaning is the essence of the object, or its true nature.
6. Meaning may be action projected onto an object, in the sense of what the object is used for.
7. The meaning may be taken as the event intended, as the volition, or that which is desired. Thus, the "meaning" of the student for the registrar may be to fill a chair in the classroom.
8. Meaning may refer to the place of something in a system.
9. Meaning may refer to the practical consequence of an object for the future, as in the meaning of a life-insurance policy.
10. The meaning of the object may be its theoretical consequence, as when a rising divorce rate is taken to mean a decline in family solidarity.

11. The meaning of a symbolic object may reside in its emotional consequence, as in gambling for excitement rather than to win.
12. The meaning of an object may be that which is actually related to it in a physical, temporal, or logical sense. The sunrise means a new day.
13. Meaning may refer to acquired associations, such as what is appropriate, intended, or suggested. Thus, a college may mean a campus, a library, social and cultural associations, a chance to maintain social status, or a chance to prepare for the future.
14. The meaning of the object may be that to which the user ought to refer.
15. Meaning may be what the user thinks he or she is referring to.
16. Finally, the meaning may be that to which the interpreter of the symbol refers; the speaker's meaning may or may not be the meaning applied by the listener.

This multiplicity of meanings of meaning demonstrates the enormous complexity of the problem.

4. Some Consequences of Symbols

Symbols make possible a whole range of human characteristics and activities that we take for granted. Religion, art, music, technology, war, morality, obscenity, and beauty are among the many human endeavors and qualities made possible by the symbol. Human beings, from the time they are socialized through this important instrument, are plunged into a symbolic environment from which they never again emerge. Human beings' responses to their world are largely through symbols, and all relationships are organized through the use of these devices.

Animals, on the other hand, may struggle with each other for food, for example, but they do not, as do human beings, struggle with each other for things that stand for, or represent, food. Money is mere paper with green ink on it until it is symbolically transformed in its use into the powerful medium of exchange for which people will cheat, steal, and even kill. Cassirer puts the case this way:

> Man lives in a symbolic universe . . . (He does not) confront reality immediately; he cannot see it, as if it were face-to-face . . . Instead of dealing with things themselves man is in a sense constantly conversing with himself. He has so enveloped himself in linguistic forms . . . that he cannot see or know anything except by the interposition of this artificial medium [1944, 25].

So symbols, as well as being devices that enable us to transcend ourselves and to experience many of the most magnificent areas of life, also present us with problems because they form a barrier between ourselves and the kind of direct experience of the world enjoyed by nonhumans. This means that the world of human beings is largely constructed by them through the available symbolic apparatuses.

Another less laudable side of language is the conflict it produces between people. It is difficult for us to realize that our way of talking and its particular way of defining reality are not the only possibilities. We are ethnocentric about our own language, and many problems and at least a war or two have been created in defense of the mother tongue. In Mark Twain's classic *The Adventures of Huckleberry Finn* there is a dialogue between Huck and Jim, the runaway slave, as they are floating down the Mississippi River on a raft. This conversation stands as a monument to the feeling that one's own way of talking is the only logical and decent way of doing so:

"Why, Huck, doan' de French people talk de same way we does?"

"No, Jim; you couldn't understand a word they said—not a single word."

"Well, now, I be ding-busted! How do dat come?"

"*I* don't know; but it's so. I got some of their jabber out of a book. S'pose a man was to come to you and say Polly-voo-franzy—what would you think?"

"I wouldn't think nuffin; I'd take en bust him over de head—dat is, if he warn't white."

"Shucks, it ain't calling you anything. It's only saying, do you know how to talk French?"

"Well, den, why couldn't he say it?"

"Why, he *is* a-saying it. That's a Frenchman's *way* of saying it."

"Well, it's a blame ridicklous way, en I doan' want to hear no mo' 'bout it. Dey ain' no sense in it."

"Looky here, Jim; does a cat talk like we do?"

"No, a cat don't."

"Well, does a cow?"

"No, a cow don't, nuther."

"Does a cat talk like a cow, or a cow talk like a cat?"

"No, dey don't."

"It's natural and right for 'em to talk different from each other, ain't it?"

"Course."

"And ain't it natural and right for a cat and a cow to talk different from us?"

"Why, mos' sholy it is."

"Well, then, why ain't it natural and right for a Frenchman to talk different from us? You answer me that."

"Is a cat a man, Huck?"

"No."

"Well, den, dey ain't no sense in a cat talkin' like a man. Is a cow a man?—er is a cow a cat?"

"No, she ain't either of them."

"Well, den, she ain't got no business to talk like either one er the yuther of 'em. Is a Frenchman a man?"

"Yes."

"*Well*, den! Dad blame it, why doan he *talk* like a man? You answer me *dat*!" [Twain, 1884, Chapter 14].

a. Naming and the construction of reality.   Symbols are not mere tags that we place on a preexisting reality; they enter fundamentally into the very nature of that reality. Ways of naming and describing the world become creations of that world. We do not tend first to see and then label, but to label and then see what the label calls for. Kenneth Burke (1965) has observed that we will never solve the problem of poverty in America until we decide what we are going to *call* poor people. Naming is an act of social placement that sets up ways of acting toward the object named. There is a difference between how people act toward an *alcoholic* and the way they act toward a *dirty drunk*, irrespective of how much liquor is in the person. Similarly, there is a fundamental difference between the social reality of a *homosexual* and that of a *perverted queer*. This is why various reform movements always seize first on language and attempt to change the very words people use toward them. Part of the civil rights movement of the 1960s was devoted to changing the language from *Negro* to *Black*. If you feel that these are merely different words for the same thing, we invite you to ponder what is meant by "the same thing."

5. Symbols and Thinking

Another of the continuing debates about language is over the role it plays in the process of thinking. Recalling Mead's theory of mind, it can be noted that language, as a representative of the social process, is an indispensible part of the mind. But the question of whether any thinking can occur without language and whether language determines the nature of thought is still an open one.

An influential theorist on this question was Benjamin Lee Whorf. Whorf was originally an insurance investigator, and he began to notice how important language is when he was studying fires. He noted in his investigations that how items in a building were named had something to do with the likelihood of their catching on fire. For example, a warehouse containing *empty* gasoline drums was more prone to blowing up than a warehouse containing *full* ones. The reason for this, he concluded, had to do with the kind of human behavior that tended to be mobilized around the term *empty*. *Empty* denotes *inert, neutral,* and by implication *safe*. Therefore, people were likely to be more careless with matches, cigarettes, and so forth around empty drums than they were around full ones. But this is misleading terminology, because the "empty" drums were far more hazardous than the full ones because of the explosive vapors they contained. Empty drums were more prone to exploding than full ones, a point that tended to be negated in the linguistic designation *empty*.

Moving from this original observation, Whorf, now in association with an anthropologist named Edward Sapir, began to explore the implications of linguistic designations. From these studies came what is known as the Whorf/Sapir hypothesis, which stated roughly that perception and thought are determined by the structure of language. What are typically regarded as cultural differences between peoples are really linguistic differences caused by the different structure of language itself. Western languages, emphasizing as they do a split between subject and predicate, lead to cause/effect types of logic. Substance, identity, and the *exclusion principle* (something either is or it isn't) are all a part of Western ways of thinking. In contrast, Eastern languages tend to stress the relational significance of properties. They operate not on an exclusion principle but on one that stresses the relationship between opposites (Whorf, 1956).

Whether all of our thought is determined by the nature of the language we work with is hardly the point. It is enough to say that most of our thinking does take place through the medium of language. And, although we might not want to go as far as Whorf does, there is nevertheless a certain sense in his assertion that agreement in human affairs is reached by linguistic processes if it is reached at all.

Although we may marvel at the complexity and richness of language, it is necessary to recognize that language is frequently awkward, uncertain, difficult, and inadequate. (Try communicating how much you love someone and see how inadequate language can be.) As Hugh Duncan so aptly puts it: "There is a certain anguish in communication" (Duncan, 1962).

C. THEORIES OF LANGUAGE

Despite all we know about language, there remains much that is mysterious. We do not, for example, have a very clear idea of how children acquire language, although they obviously do so very rapidly. The origins of language we know virtually nothing about. Given these mysteries, however, there are competing theories about the workings of language. We will now present a few of the more influential ones.

1. The Picture Theory

Language, according to one traditional view, consists of words, and each word has meaning only insofar as it stands for something else. One learns a language, from this point of view, by learning what each word refers to. Words are names for things, and to know a language is to know all the words for all the various things. This view of language—variously described as the naming theory, picture theory, correspondence theory, or denotative theory—is a traditional and still popular view of how language operates. Language, in this sense, is a kind of mirror of the world. The linguist and philosopher Alfred Korzybski used to speak of language as a "map" and reality as the "territory." A language was effective to the extent that it accurately portrayed the dimensions of the territory (Korzybski, 1933).

There have always been difficulties with this view. Connective words such as *the, a, like, and, with,* and so forth were usually excluded from this theory because they obviously have no referents but are conveniences within the language itself. In this view the meaning of a word is in the thing or object it denotes. But if this were true, would the word *Paris* have to change as the city increased or decreased in population? Such a view stretches credibility a bit too far. In addition, numbers do not seem to fit this theory very well. There are few *fives* to be found anywhere in the universe. Similarly, it is difficult to discover a real πR^2. What would a picture of "love" look like? Clearly, language is not simply a set of labels that refer to all of the things of the world.

2. The Game Theory

These ideas came to disturb the Austrian philosopher Ludwig Wittgenstein (1889–1951). His uneasiness with the picture theory was all the more ironic, because he had been in his early work the foremost proponent of this view and had argued it exceedingly well (Wittgenstein, 1922). But he later developed a wholly different theory of language.

The later Wittgenstein said that, instead of asking "What is this?" or "What is that?" the important question is how language functions or works. Wittgenstein insisted that we play games with language and that *the meaning of a word is its use in the language.* The naming, picture, or denotative game, which the picture theory had made so much of, is but one of an indefinite number of games that can be played with language. A word is not a name; a word can be used as a name, but it can also be used in a variety of other ways as well. For example, there are many words that do not mean what they say: "He has a heart of gold." "She let the cat out of the bag." "He kicked the bucket." "Don't beat around the bush." "We were scraping the bottom of the barrel."

Each of these so-called idiomatic expressions can be understood only if one knows what kind of game is being played. People who are native to a culture that plays these kinds of games with words will obviously pick them up very quickly. But the confusion of the foreigner (who may know formal English impeccably) when confronted with these expressions suggests the inadequacy of the denotative view of language. Furthermore, the meaning of a word depends on whom the audience for the words consists of. Consider, for example, the different meanings that are established by the same three little words, directed at different audiences: "I love you (girlfriend)." "I love you (mother)." "I love you (hot dogs or the New York Yankees)."

Words, then, have meaning only within the context of the social game that is being played with them. A dictionary, in this sense, is not a list of word referents but rather a list of conventional word usages. Dictionaries list various linguistic games and, when the games change, the dictionary will duly note it.

From this point of view it is clear that we could never teach a child language by pointing to all of the things in the world and calling them by their names. We may begin to teach language by playing the naming game with the child, but eventually the child learns the use of words in a game context. A child who asks where her mother is and is told "She went to a shower at Mrs. Peavy's house" may respond by asking "Why can't Mommy take a shower at our house?" The child simply has not yet learned all the games that can be played with the word *shower*.

Wittgenstein gave us, in effect, a sociological theory of language that stresses its social uses. Words are not tags for deeper things, for nothing can lie deeper. Instead, words are simple social conventions bound by rules and common usages. These usages can be talked about simply as games, and communication consists of a series of these games. When language changes it is because we have thought up new games to play with words and have secured agreement over the rules.

3. The Nativist Theory

In sharp contrast to either the picture theory or the game theory is the view held by linguist Noam Chomsky (1965). Chomsky's writings have had a profound impact on the science of linguistics, especially on developmental psychologists trying to explain the acquisition of language concepts in children. He argues that the ability to speak a language stems from innate sources and abilities. Fueling Chomsky's work is the fact that children acquire language very rapidly. Completely devoid of words at birth, children by the age of 5 have mastered thousands of words and phrases that a short time before they had never even heard. Chomsky believes that the same general principles underlie all human languages; they are universal regularities that govern the combinations of words. For Chomsky these language universals are genetically determined. Further, although environment is important in molding and pushing a child, the speed with which a person acquires language can be explained only by some innate facility.

Grammar and syntax are the focus of Chomsky's work, and he leaves rhetoric and specific linguistic content to social processes. This is a moderate position to take. Although there is clearly some kind of link between grammar and rhetoric, the specific relationship has never been satisfactorily worked out despite heroic efforts by some of the best minds to do so (Burke, 1945, 1950).

Chomsky is a controversial figure in social psychology, and his arguments are not well understood in the discipline. Many of his ideas are perhaps best understood when applied to persons such as aphasics, who for one organic reason or another have not acquired the basic tools with which to communicate symbolically. It is difficult to see how anything more than the very general capacity to acquire language could be translated into a genetic code—even the relationship between this capacity and the specific forms that language takes in thought and social action. The programming of innate ideas or universal principles is a notion that is filled with quandaries, and few sociologically oriented social psychologists accept Chomsky's views as anything more than an interesting working hypothesis.

D. VERBAL COMMUNICATION

Whichever theory of language finally prevails (and it is likely that no single theory will ever be universally accepted in social science), the point that language is primarily part of a social process will have to be retained. Talk takes place in a social situation, even when it all occurs within a single socialized person. The very process of thinking, as Mead pointed out, is an "internal conversation" that assumes that a person knows how to converse and does so with some anticipation of the presence of others. This section will deal, then, with the range and variety of verbal communication as it occurs in actual social situations.

1. The Communication Process

The interpretation of information varies with the social situation. When a 4-year-old girl was asked to tell a story from a series of pictures, she was expected to see the intended sequence of actions: a small boy reached for a toy truck, turned toward a little girl, and passed the toy truck into her hands. The last picture showed the little girl playing with the truck. But the 4-year-old interpreted each picture separately without reference to the others in the series. For the picture showing the boy putting the truck in the girl's hands, she said "They both were saying 'gimme, gimme, gimme.' " Her own experience of struggling for a toy gave a meaning that for her was implicit in the picture (Jennings and Jennings, 1974, 284).

On sociable occasions such as informal parties we may talk simply for the sake of talking (Duncan, 1962, 27). Conversation is the most general vehicle of sociability and a resource that people have in common. It offers an avenue for self-disclosure and for discovery of the social experience, ideas, and beliefs of the other. In what Simmel called *sociability*, the partners usually try to please each other and to sustain mutual interest in the conversation (Wolff, 1950). Pleasantry and good humor is generally in evidence. Each partner tends to be influenced to some extent by the information gained from the other, and there is usually some mutual shifting to a higher degree of consensus than they might otherwise have been inclined to give.

There are many specialized forms of conversational process through which relationships are carried out. The argument, for example, is built from a series of statements, explanations, pleas, threats, and emotional posturings in which the partners attempt to overcome differences of perception, purpose, and belief. Bargaining may include argument, but it usually depends on propositions for the exchange of services, property, and other things of value, based on mutual agreement and some form of mutual advantage. Punitive conversations occur when one partner has violated the expectations of the other. The offended partner scolds, criticizes, or reprimands the offender. If the perceived offense is mutual, the scolding and personal criticism go in both directions. These painful confrontations are effective in overcoming interpersonal conflict only if both partners value the relationship enough to endure the pain and are willing to make an adjustment in some workable direction.

A primary form of social conversation is the interaction that informs, one partner teaching or explaining something the other does not fully understand. Employers depend on their workers to tell them immediately when there is a problem or a serious loss in production. Children want to relate their successes, discoveries, and other experiences to parents, friends, and others who are willing to listen. Those who are in daily personal contact share information and ideas among themselves in order to maintain a degree of harmony and a common orientation. Narration, or story telling, serves both to inform and to amuse. Humorous, dramatic, and exciting stories give stimulation and pleasure to those who have not heard them, and the listener is enriched both by the new knowledge and by adding a story to her or his repertoire that can be passed on to someone else for pleasure and fun.

2. Grammatical Organization

The ordering of words is one of the determinants of their meaning. In the newspaper headline "Car hits tree," the word order shows that the first noun indicates the moving object and that the tree received the action. Rearranging the order to "Tree hits car" indicates that the tree was the moving object and that the car received the action. (This form of the sentence would be sufficient in many languages, but grammatical convention in English calls for the form "The car hit the tree.")

A speaker expressing word sequences through time makes decisions about which one of a variety of potential meanings are to be encoded in a given form (Rommetveit, 1971, 24). Thus, the word *only* has profoundly different meanings in the statement: "Only four people came to the meeting" and "Only a brain surgeon could save her." Hamlet's grim joke about the dead Polonius being found "at dinner" was explained by saying "It is not where he eats, but where he is eaten," by a body of "most politic worms." Polonius' political skills were subtly mocked by the indifferent worms, who made no distinction between "your lean beggar and your fat king."

Eight parts of speech are commonly identified in grammar: nouns, pronouns, adjectives, verbs, adverbs, prepositions, conjunctions, and interjections. Some words can readily shift from one part of speech to another. The word *heat* operates as a noun ("Blast furnaces generate heat"), verb ("Heat the mixture to boiling"), adjective ("He needed a heat treatment") and adverb ("She answered heatedly"). Pronouns are of particular interest, because they depend on the shifting viewpoint of the speaker. Children experience confusion at first in using and understanding the pronouns "you," "I," and "me." Self-reference shifts with the speaker, and, as children come to realize this, they begin to understand the position of other people in social relations (Chomsky, 1969). Carol Chomsky found that younger children were exceedingly bored with questions about who "he" is in sentences such as "Mickey told his mother he was hungry." Chomsky noted that older children can understand and enjoy this kind of problem.

3. Patterns of Face-to-Face Conversation

Dyadic talk, in which two persons converse more or less privately, is the earliest, the most intimate, and the most effective form of communication. Disagreement is tempered and toned down easily, and each partner recognizes the obligation to protect the self-reputation and interests of the other (Wilmot, 1975, 12–15). The conversational process depends on the continuing effort, attention, and response of both persons. The process produces a bond for a short period, and some increase in consensus or shared understanding often occurs. Conversation is a basic means of sharing in the social life of the community. And it provides the primary mechanism for all of the basic forms of direct social relations in cooperating, competing, entertaining, teaching, persuading, and loving.

Conversation is a creative process in which statements are generated in irregular sequence, sometimes from one partner and sometimes from the other. In natural conversation the length of utterance seems to be uncorrelated between the partners (Feldstein, 1972, 102). But a conversation is densely packed with these series of statements, while the listener provides an almost perfectly timed response in the form of a nod or an "uh-huh" or a "yes" at the end of each burst of phrases (Dittman, 1973). According to Dittman, children under the age of 10 have not attained skill in listening and do not provide dependable reactions, so that the adult speaker is never well assured that the child is listening. Children do conduct the transactions, explanations, and rivalries required in their play through meaningful verbal exchange. But they may all talk at once, with no one listening. The lack of response destroys the effect of the shrillest and most convincing arguments. Adults sometimes talk more effectively because they listen better.

4. Therapeutic Communication: Talk As Treatment

Talk is the circulating nutrient of social relations. Members of a social community *talk out* their problems. One who has suffered disappointment or a painful loss gets healing comfort by *talking over* the situation with a sympathetic friend. People *talk their way out* of trouble.

Courts solve legal problems through an elaborate pattern of oral discussion. Teachers, clergymen, and other professionals use lectures, sermons, and discussions to solve the problems of both groups and individuals. Workers of all kinds use conversation for argument, to solve problems, to correct errors, or to encourage coworkers. Children and the elderly may fail to solve personal problems because they cannot get the benefit of intelligent and helpful conversation with anyone other than persons of their own age. One of the most common complaints in marriage and divorce is that "he (or she) never talks to me."

The most common thread running through the process by which persons are labeled "mentally ill" is aberrant talk. The interactionist approach applied to problems of mental illness has during the last ten years shown clearly the linguistic basis of this interpersonal problem. Mead's theory of mind and self (discussed in detail in Chapters 1 and 6), which refuses to locate mental phenomena outside the social process, is a useful way of seeing the sociological roots of psychiatric disorder. An understanding of the *social* situation of persons labeled mentally ill (Goffman, 1961a) is often sufficient to understand their aberrant behavior clearly. (A detailed discussion of Goffman's work on mental illness is found in Chapter 12.)

"It's not my factory that's polluting the lake . . . . It's all those dead fish that're doing it."

People talk their way out of trouble, oversights, and errors.

The truly interpersonal origin of many seemingly personal problems was noted early by psychiatrist Harry Stack Sullivan (1892–1949). Using ideas that were in many ways compatible with Mead's understanding of the mind, Sullivan, as a result of observations in his clinical practice, described 15 of the most common "signs" of mental disorder taken by others as evidence of pathology:

1. Apathy indicates withdrawal, with indifference to the stimuli of normal questions, statements, and challenges.
2. Depression is shown by sadness, pessimism, and an expressed sense of futility.
3. Elation accompanied sometimes by sudden and drastic changes of interest is shown by superficial gaiety and continuing laughter without cause.
4. Overdramatization and extravagant use of superlatives indicates an unrealistic orientation.
5. Indecisiveness is shown by an inability to say "yes" or "no" to a straightforward question.
6. Habitual qualifying never permits the completion of a definite statement, because the patient can never change it enough to say quite what he or she means.
7. Tenseness during speech and abrupt movements show a precarious mental orientation.
8. Gross anxiety is reflected in expressed fears, irregular breathing, and faltering tone.
9. Some patients demonstrate psychopathic fluency, in which the verbal stream is continuing and superficial, jumping indifferently from one focus to another.
10. Some patients show extreme fatigue just from the effort to talk with the therapist.
11. The patient may be unable and unwilling to shift to a new topic, even though it is clearly appropriate to do so.
12. Some patients show autistic gestures and posturings that are unrelated to the conversation.
13. Patients often show a mental blank during a conversation that has been going smoothly, and there may be mental blocking of particular words.
14. Stereotyped expressions may be repeatedly inserted in the conversation without relevance.
15. Stereotyped gestures may be used without relevance (Sullivan, 1953, 183–195).

It should be obvious that these symptoms vary by time and among patients.

Laffal notes that schizophrenics may consistently reverse positive and negative assertions, putting "no" where "yes" is meant. Their speech is often disjointed and garbled, as in the following example: "Some day my forebears, my ancestors, will come, my, some day, my offspring will have great precocious hygienic precept, even more so than I" (Laffal, 1965, 137). It is not too much to say that what we call psychiatric disorder is most essentially a failure of words (Becker, 1962).

The psychiatrist uses conversation and discussion as the primary vehicle for reorienting the patient. According to Ruesch, 12 conversational techniques are used in the effort to reorient the patient: (1) pinpointing the problem with relevant details; (2) documentation of details from one consultation to the next, to gain consistency; (3) amplifying the facts with new information; (4) using concrete cases and general abstractions; (5) comparison; (6) contradiction of bad logic or incorrect statements; (7) confrontation; (8) argument; (9) acceptance of fact and identification of fantasy; (10) interjection of new material; (11) interpretation; and (12) analysis and synthesis for the patient to reintegrate his or her outlook (Ruesch, 1961, 188–200).

E. NONVERBAL COMMUNICATION

Much of the research on communication has historically suffered from a kind of "verbal bias," because it tended to focus primarily on language. In recent years, however, we have come to recognize formally what each of us perhaps already knows: that significant communication occurs even though no words are spoken.

1. People As Messengers

Human beings relate to one another through a complex system of communication, and during this process they use everything at their disposal: words, movements, gestures, eye contact, and much more. Much communication is implicit rather than explicit and connotative rather than denotative. The combination of the two makes for a more elaborate system than could possibly be provided by any single set of spoken symbols. When one person looks pointedly at another with a deep frown, it is clear to every observer that disapproval and hostility are being expressed. When two people laugh, they establish good feeling, relief, or amusement. If a man is trying to start a relationship with a woman (or vice-versa), all sorts of nonverbal forms of communication come into play. The simple act of arriving at a party conveys a host of things: acceptance of the invitation, establishing or renewing friendships, class and economic relationships, and so on.

Edward Hall, in one of the first systematic studies of nonverbal communication, talked about "the silent language" and worked out an elaborate series of studies to assess the meaning of speechless communication (Hall, 1959). An arm around another's shoulder conveys affection, friendship, or even power. In an interesting book entitled *Body Politics*, Henley (1977) presents some research suggesting that touching communicates considerable information about power and status relationships, especially between persons of the opposite sex. Men tend to touch women under some situational conditions in ways that communicate and confirm superior/inferior relationships. Other research confirms these observations. Summerhayes and Suchner (1978) provide experimental evidence suggesting that, when high-status men touch lower-status women, the power of the woman is perceived as diminished; however, when the lower-status woman touches the higher-status man, the man's status and perceived power are diminished, reducing the status difference between the two. These provocative studies illustrate merely a few of the raft of meanings surrounding the simple, nonverbal act of touching.

We understand nonverbal messages from animals, too, since those are the only kind we can get from them. One knows enough to avoid a growling dog and to open the door at the mewing of the family cat. In human interaction, signs of welcome, approval, interest, denial, rejection, and distrust are noted and responded to on every side, and they make up an important part of the human system of communication.

Much nonverbal communication is really more effective than talk, for others often take it to be "the real thing." It is hard to keep up a convincing pretense at a late hour—the fatigue somehow comes through. A mistimed yawn betrays a sleepy student in class, and the jaded lover may not be able to make a kiss convincing. Because we are constantly trying to maintain our relationships with others, we emit a stream of nonverbal cues that they read and interpret.

2. Varieties of Nonverbal Communication

Nonverbal cues vary widely by culture. These variations in what Edward Hall calls the silent language include time, space, attitude to work, play, and learning, and the language of behavior (Hall, 1959, 14). Failure to apply these nonverbal signals can frustrate or destroy attempts to influence and cooperate with persons from another culture. The courteous Japanese bows repeatedly to show respect for her associate, while the United States citizen would simply nod her head slightly to indicate recognition of the other person. An American Indian might hold his arm forward with the palm out and vertical to indicate greeting. An American policeman uses the same sign to tell a motorist to stop. The Japanese guest belches audibly to signal genuine appreciation of the host's dinner. The European suppresses the belch to avoid offending the host with boorish conduct. An American executive shows respect for an associate by keeping appointments promptly at the agreed time. The Latin-American executive is offended by insistence on such stern discipline and may keep her appointment within half an hour of the agreed time.

a. Gestures.   These consist of sequences of movements that consistently establish the same or similar meanings between the sender and the receiver. The gesture is a unit of communication that is complete in itself. When it is completed, it is sufficient either to elicit another gesture or some other form of message in response, or the sender and the receiver are both satisfied that the intended meaning is understood.

The hand gestures of beckoning, waving, and the stop signal are generally understood and answered with appropriate responses by young children,

How to Speak Arabic in Body Language

Right   **Wrong**

Normal conversational distance between Arabs is 13 to 14 inches, about half the distance Americans maintain. When approached this closely, we tend to laugh or flinch. Don't. Learn to like it.

Don't expect as much eye contact from Arabs. It's not shiftiness. It's just that they don't feel comfortable looking strangers in the eye.

Although Arabs consider the bone-crushing handshake uncouth, a firm grip is seen as a sign of good intent. Always shake on greeting or taking leave. Never offer your left hand. The left hand is not for shaking or passing or taking things; it is the "toilet hand." However, if you have somehow lost your right hand, a southpaw handshake is okay — but make it quick.

It is extremely rude to expose the soles of your feet. If you cross your legs, keep your uppers up.

Hands on the hips is considered an aggressive posture and is recommended only for troublemakers.

Backslapping is grounds for murder.

Arabs do not hold hands with women on the street, not even their wives, but they have nothing against your doing so. Just don't follow the Arab custom of holding hands with men.

(From **Esquire,** August 1975. Copyright 1975 by **Esquire** magazine. Reprinted by permission.)

even before they have developed verbal communication. The military salute is a precisely defined greeting sent from a subordinate to a superior officer or between military officers of equal rank. One can signal disgust by throwing up the hands or a loving welcome by opening the arms wide for an embrace. Thumbs up signal encouragement, and thumbs down signal denial or failure. Holding the hands with palms together and pointed upward before the chest indicates prayer or entreaty, and extending one or both hands forward with palms up suggests begging or the request that something be given. The young child soon learns to say "Please!" along with this gesture.

b. *Body messages.* Various body poses and actions communicate an attitude or relationship to others. Facing the body directly toward a partner with arms at the side and legs parallel constitutes an "open" position, indicating acceptance of the relationship and readiness to interact with the other. Crossing the legs and arms indicates resistance to some degree, because it involves closing oneself off from the other, at least in part. Orienting the body to either side, especially if the face and eyes are also turned away, is widely interpreted as avoidance and resistance and may lead to explicit demands by the other to "open up" and turn toward the other. Refusal to communicate is signaled by turning one's back toward the other, and, when it is deliberate and obvious, it is often taken as an insult and deeply resented.

c. *Portable personal objects as messages.* A girl carrying a softball bat is to some degree advertising interest and participation in the game. A man walking through the woods with a rifle or shotgun over his shoulder signals that he is in the process of hunting, not only to other persons but also to many gun-wise crows, coyotes, and squirrels. A soldier carrying a rifle or pistol signals that he is on duty. Construction and machinery workers wear hard hats when on the job, and the hat becomes a sign for being employed. For the criminal, the gun serves as a symbol of power and as a threat of death. When the bank teller recognizes the pistol pointed at him and the sack thrust in his cage, other explanations are not necessary. In hospitals, doctors carry prescription pads, nurses carry medical records, orderlies carry bedpans, and patients carry nothing.

What we are saying, of course, is that objects signal individual functions and statuses. Modern engineering students carry electronic calculators. Women signal different kinds of social orientation by "wearing" handbags that match their attire. Other personal objects that have served to signal the individual's social orientation include belts, fans, parasols, walking sticks, boas, kerchiefs, and headwear in great variety. Finally, wedding rings, class rings, and signet rings signal social identity; ribbons in the hair or on the person signal femininity; and earrings, neck beads, nose jewels, tattoos, and body paint proclaim a certain individuality that says "Look at me!"

d. *Face work.* The human face is like an animated bulletin board that continuously signals attitude, interest, awareness, emotional response, and readiness for other forms of social interaction. Goffman (1967a) refers to this as "face work." Nine facial features with their various possible positions are listed in Table 2-1. The possible combinations of the 38 positions indicated is 248,832, which approximates the figure of 250,000 given by Birdwhistell (1970, 164). Some of these combinations could not be observed (eyes up with lids closed), and some would be avoided (tongue extended with jaw clenched). But the variety of compounded expressions is enormous, and most active people emit rapid and extended sequences of facial expressions in interpersonal relations.

The hair is the least mobile feature, but it contributes substantially to the effect of facial behavior, to personal appearance, and to social presence. Women use a wide variety of hair styling, coloring, and arrangement. The hair may cling to the head, swing gently when the head is turned, or cascade and undulate with head and body movements. Volume, variety, and quick change may be increased by the use of wigs and hairpieces. With the return of the moustache and beard and the acceptance of long hair for men, a wide variation in appearance and identity is also available for them. A full-grown

Table 2-1.   Expressive positions for facial features

1 Hair	2 Head	3 Brows	4 Eyes	5 Lids	6 Nostrils	7 Lips	8 Tongue	9 Jaw
Styled	Straight	Normal	Straight	Normal	Normal	Relaxed	In	Relaxed
Augmented	Back	Raised	Up	Wide	Flared	Up	Tip out	Clenched
Unkempt	Forward	Lowered	Down	Narrow	Pinched	Down	Extended	Dropped
	Tilted		To side	Closed		Pressed		Extended
			Angled:			Pursed		
			Up			Open:		
			Down			Straight		
						Up		
						Down		

Adapted from *Interaction Ritual*, by E. Goffman. Copyright © 1967 by Erving Goffman. Used by permission of Doubleday & Company, Inc.

beard hides much of the face, and this may concentrate attention on the eyes and brows. The available stylings of beards allow creativity in shaping the face. By default, this confers some slight distinction on the clean-shaven or bald-headed man. An imposing or distinctive appearance increases the effect of impressions conveyed to others by facial behavior.

We will discuss four general types of facial behavior that create an expression by the compound position of the features. First is the neutral condition of the expressionless face, with all features in the "normal" position. The "deadpan" expression or "poker face" communicates a lack of response and serves to mask the emotions and intentions of the person. A person maintaining an unexpressive face may be treated as indifferent, alien, cold, or hostile. When a person is temporarily confronted with strangers and does not want to start a relationship, he or she may maintain a neutral expression and take no note of activities, looks, or minor cue signals that others send.

The second type of facial behavior is the smile—a positive facial activity that signals friendliness, warmth, and a happy, contented, or amused feeling. It often evokes an answering smile and some feeling of liking. Spontaneous and reactive smiles come and go according to the trend and content of social interaction. In the case of persons "on stage," who are trying to influence everyone positively, the smile may ironically become fixed and even frozen or artificial. But the habitual smile of the salesperson, the applicant, or the political candidate usually has a positive effect that helps in securing an audience.

The third and fourth types of facial behavior are eye contact and eye aversion.

Eye behavior communicates to others because it signals awareness and the direction of interest. Eye contact indicates mutual recognition. If it is sustained or repeated, eye contact signals strong interest and, potentially, a desire for other kinds of interaction. Awareness of being looked at changes a person's behavior.

Eye behavior is variously defined in different cultures; maintaining eye contact or averting one's eyes have different meanings in different settings. In the United States an innocent person is expected to look an accuser in the eye and to respond truthfully to questions. But Puerto Rican culture demands that an innocent girl should avoid looking boldly into the eyes of an accuser and that she should remain respectfully silent. A New York school principal, who did not understand this Puerto Rican definition, generated furious resentment when he interpreted such behavior by a 15-year-old girl as showing guilt (Fast, 1970, 136). When he realized what the girl's shy response meant, he apologized to her and to her parents, and peace was restored.

3. Nonverbal Symbols

Thus far we have discussed nonverbal communication as a series of signs. But it is important to note that symbols may be communicated nonverbally, too, and that much of our communication is of this type. For example, symbols of initiation help establish social relationships. The most elementary of these is the handshake.

Some cultures have a special ceremony to initiate a close personal friendship. In Germany men who wanted to become close friends traditionally performed the ceremony of *Brüderschaft* by linking elbows and drinking together from their beer steins. The ceremony meant that the two friends would thereafter call each other *"Du,"* the familiar form of "you," rather than the formal *"Sie."* In Italy and other southern European countries the blood brotherhood ceremony required each "brother" to draw a little blood in the palm of the hand and then to "mix" the blood in a close handpress with the other. This ceremony made the two blood brothers, with the same ties and obligations that are required of natural brothers. The same ceremony has been used in the United States for inducting outsiders into Mafia "families." Fraternity and sorority initiation ceremonies have very much the same function, although they may be less binding in practice.

The simple act of sending a greeting card of congratulations for a birthday helps to sustain interpersonal relations. A letter written by a child at summer camp to his or her parents has a symbolic value far beyond the simple "news" about the swimming and games. So it is with the occasional letter that the adult sends to a distant parent. The thought and love the letter symbolizes are deemed more important than the routine content of the letter.

Physical intimacies often symbolize personal relations (Argyle, 1969, 92). Touching another on the hands, arms, shoulders, and back symbolizes friendship and affection. The kiss with a relative symbolizes family solidity among Russians and the French, the kiss symbolizes affection between friends. The first sexual encounter between a woman and a man may symbolize personal surrender and the ultimate in "giving," although in casual sex there may be no such understanding. A marriage is said to be "unconsummate," or incomplete, until the couple have completed sexual intercourse.

a. Symbols of coercion.   Punishment is a symbol of force. For the young child, a spanking symbolizes power and authority. The prison sentence imposed on the convicted criminal symbolizes the authority of the criminal justice system and the community that sustains it. When the convict "serves time," in a symbolic sense he "pays a debt to society." Note that society gains nothing of material value either from the convict's "service" or from his "payment." The prison term is purely symbolic.

Behavior that symbolizes helplessness or desperation can be used to force others to give service. Although not much used in modern times, the "fainting fit," or "swoon," has been used by women to command attention in public places. The malingerer pretends to be sick to gain the indulgence and service that is morally owed to the incapacitated. A soldier who wants to avoid a long march suddenly reports a severe backache. In the battle area he may deliberately try to contract venereal disease in order to be sent to the hospital for treatment. Suicide attempts are often messages of desperation and serve to coerce attention and accommodation from others. Explaining his suicide attempt, a husband said he had fired his gun, but hadn't actually aimed it at himself. In this way he let his estranged wife know that he had intentions of suicide. He was successful in that he persuaded his wife to go to the reconciliation court through this message (Sachs, 1972, 56).

Coercion is also applied by withholding affection, privileges, food, or money, actions that may not be very damaging in themselves but that exert effective influence by what they imply. Refusal to talk or to communicate symbolizes rejection. The offending club member who is given the "silent treatment" usually feels forced to leave the organization. When mother resumes normal talking after several days of hurt silence, other family members are much relieved. Family intimates are a powerful source of frustration and pain (Goode, 1973, 148). This makes their symbolic behavior effective.

b. Symbols of termination.   These include the many forms of symbolic behavior that signify the threat or the fact of separation between two individuals who had been in a partnership or between an individual and a group in which he or she had been a member. If a wife threatens to "pack my bags," she is indicating a threat to leave her husband at least temporarily. If he then brings her bags in from the storage room, he is signaling acceptance of her proposal to leave! If she packs her clothes and her personal things, it is a sign she will leave. If she leaves no significant personal item behind, she may intend to leave permanently, and the observant husband will make this interpretation. If she neglects to take her handbag, identification, and cosmetic equipment, she is signaling that she will return for further negotiations. If the husband has them delivered to her he is signaling that further negotiations are not necessary. These nonverbal cues avoid the tension and pain of words and the difficulty of stating explicitly what, why, who, and how. At the same time they make the attitudes and intentions of both parties clear.

Regular employees who are being dismissed simply receive a blunt notice that their services will not be needed after a specific date, and the notice may not be received until that date. But with high-ranking company officers or players on major-league teams the situation may be too embarrassing or too delicate for a simple verbal notice. Then, nonverbal symbols are used to convey the message. The company officer learns that she has been "promoted" to a vice-presidency that has no managerial or policy-making functions. She may quietly move to her new pseudo-office and continue to accept a salary from the company, but she recognizes that she has lost her position of power in the company. The athlete may find his name omitted from the roster of players or that his locker has been reassigned to an area separated from those of the regular team.

This catalogue of nonverbal symbols is not exhaustive, but it is suggestive of the wide range of possibilities for symbolizing without words.

As symbolic creatures human beings seem to use their basic faculty—communication—in imaginative ways as they try, sometimes with great difficulty, to get their message across.

F. SUMMARY

Language and other forms of communication are all-important processes in the study of social psychology. Because people engage in communication in such a wide variety of ways, contemporary social psychologists have not limited themselves to an analysis of language but have also taken a close look at nonverbal forms of communication.

Language is not a thing or object but rather a pattern of interaction based on social conventions. Without language human societies would not be possible, for much of our humanity is tied up with symbolic processes. The ability to use symbols is one of the basic points of distinction between humans and nonhumans. All organic creatures seem to be capable of reacting to natural signs and cues from the environment, but human beings seem to be unique in their ability to manipulate abstract, representational symbols. Pavlov, the founding father of learning theories, made this distinction in his discussion of the "second signaling system" in human beings.

Language appears to be purely conventional. That is, physical referents in the world do not force us to call them by any particular name at all. Instead, people agree over words, and, when others respond to a symbol in terms of the same (or similar) meanings as those intended by the speaker, we have what Mead called "a significant symbol."

Symbols make possible much of the social world of human beings. Art, literature, music, religion, and technology are among the many things made possible by man's capacity to use symbols. People live, from the time they acquire language, in a symbolic as well as a physical environment. Symbols construct reality and do not simply reflect it, for they enter existentially into the social objects they name. Symbols also play a crucial role in the construction of human meaning and also in the very processes of thought. The work of Sapir and Whorf underscores the importance of symbols in the process of thought as well as action.

Three general theories of language have predominated: (1) the picture theory, which holds that words are maps of the "territory" of reality; (2) the game theory, which stresses the way language works in social games that people play with each other; and (3) innate, or nativist, theories, which hold that patterns of language are built into the genetic structure of human beings.

The communication process itself can take a host of forms. Sociability, in which persons talk simply for the sake of talking; arguments, in which people try to settle disputes; bargaining, in which exchanges are worked out; and punitive conversations, in which language is used to punish someone, are only a few of the possibilities. Indeed, language makes possible an enormous range of meanings and understandings.

The most common pattern of talk is probably dyadic talk, in which two persons converse. This is the most intimate and probably the most effective form of communication. Disagreements are easier to resolve in two-person groups than in larger groups, and both of the parties feel an obligation to save the face of the other.

Talk can also serve a variety of therapeutic functions and is one of the most widely used forms of treatment for problems in living. Talk gets us into difficulties, but it also gets us out. We regularly talk our way out of trouble, oversights, and errors and into jobs, marriages, and friendships. Courts of law, where much is on the line, consist primarily of talk. The process of education depends in large part on linguistic manipulations. If you suddenly took all the words out of a church, there would be little left except a building. Talk is primarily what people do during the course of a day. Indeed, the roots of psychiatric disorder are primarily aberrations of talk.

Talk is, however, accompanied by a wide range of nonverbal cues, signs, gestures, and expressions, all of which mix with language to provide for communication in the larger sense of the word. People are messengers, and they seem to be willing to do almost anything to get their message across. Humor, hostility, affection, friendship, love, sadness, and frustration are just a few of the emotions that are communicated and easily seen without any words being uttered.

Nonverbal communication varies from culture to culture, time to time, and place to place. Many hilarious or tragic episodes result from misunderstandings about the meaning of nonverbal communication.

Physical gestures, body messages, and physical objects are all used to establish meaning in social relationships without words. Much nonverbal communication among human beings centers in the face, which is like an animated bulletin board that continuously signals attitudes, awareness, interest, emotion, and readiness for other forms of interaction. In addition, hair style, racial characteristics, clothing, and virtually anything else that is visible can serve as an aspect of communication.

Gestures also function as symbols as well as signs. Handshakes symbolize friendship, kisses love, a spanking punishment, and silence withdrawal. These symbols open and close social relationships and are more often communicated nonverbally than in any other way.

Section Two

Socialization Processes

If the earth were struck by one of Mr. Wells' comets, and if, in consequence, every human being now alive were to lose all the knowledge and habits which he had acquired from the preceding generations (though retaining unchanged all his own powers of invention, memory, and habituation), nine tenths of the inhabitants of London or New York would be dead in six months . . . . They would have no language to express their thoughts, and no thoughts but vague reverie. They could not read notices, or drive motors or horses. They would wander about, led by the inarticulate cries of a few naturally dominant individuals, drowning themselves as thirst came on, in hundreds at the riverside landing places, looting those shops where the smell of decaying food attracted them, and perhaps, at the end, stumbling on the expedient of cannibalism.

Graham Wallas

Early Socialization 3

A. INTRODUCTION: A THEORETICAL APPROACH

Socialization is one of the most difficult concepts in social psychology to define. As a result, there are about as many definitions of the term as there are writers on the subject. Most definitions do, however, stress the developmental character of the process, and it is with this idea of socialization as lifelong and continuous that we will work in this and related chapters.

Socialization means the development of social functions and skills and the ability to relate to others. It is clear that human organisms have none of these things at birth. They are quite incapable of any of a thousand things that human beings do quite routinely after socialization has begun to work its magic. The emerging outcome of the process is a person recognizable as human who, while continuing to learn and be socialized throughout life, is capable enough to contribute to the socialization of others (Dager, 1964, 742).

The process of becoming human, however, does not simply make one a fully disciplined member of some kind of social mass. For, although saturated with conventional social material obtained from others, the individual continues to operate with some independence from social constraints and retains the capacity for further modification of his or her social environment (Wrong, 1961, 193). For this reason it is important to remember that sociological theories can never fully "explain" living human beings. The best that sociologists can do is describe and analyze the general features of life's social aspects. The social context of socialization is, however, extremely important.

Children usually have their first experiences with a family. Ritchie and Kohler (1964, 160) call the family "the nursery of socialization," which aptly suggests its importance for the child's initial acquaintance with attitudes, norms, values, and various kinds of social skills. In addition to parents, brothers and sisters or other relatives may provide additional sources of authority, competition, conflict, or security. It is not always easy to get along well in the middle of this mass of others, especially when you are only 2 years old!

The first objects in a newborn baby's world, then, are social objects. The band of family members gathered in the visiting room at the hospital offers us a portrait of the initial and continuing influence of other people on the newcomer's life.

1. The Person As Socializer of Society

Socialization, it must be noted again, is a two-way street. The broader implications of this statement are only beginning to be seen in the social psychology of socialization. They have been drawn out by the French social

"It's a girl!" The child is born into and has its first experiences with a family. (Photo by © Eve Arnold, Magnum Photos)

theorist Chombart de Lauwe. In his approach to the problem the idea of the individual's socialization cannot be separated from the broader view of the reciprocal relations between the individual, groups, and society. He calls attention to the way in which other people are continually redirecting their actions toward changes that occur in an individual. Parents do not simply socialize their children; their children also importantly socialize them. The coming of children to a family changes everything, and their presence teaches the parents a whole series of things that they have known before only vaguely, or perhaps not at all. Children put their stamp on the whole family and, through it, networks of relatives, friends, and neighbors (Chombart de Lauwe, 1966, 246).

Furthermore, larger and established social units also make adjustments that may build into massive shifts in custom and usage in response to the counterpressure of the young who are being socialized. The individual sometimes socializes a whole society, as when an inventor or innovator in the political, economic, or cultural field introduces techniques, terminology, and values that come to be widely accepted.

2. Dependency As a Socialization Process

The simple fact that infants are dependent on their parents presents possibilities for understanding the socialization process. Parsons and Bales (1955) have suggested that this dependency is one of the primary processes

Communication, the most important aspect of socialization, begins at a very early age. (Photo by © Eric Kroll, Taurus Photos)

through which socialization takes place. The infant gradually responds to the parent by adopting behavior that leads to a successful relationship with the mother and to the satisfaction of the baby's continuing needs.

As the infant comes to recognize the mother as distinct from itself, the social relationship between the two of them is defined in emotional terms, manifesting both love and rage. This love dependency provides an attachment the mother can use to influence the actions of the child. The relationship here is almost purely one of stimulus and response for a creature who has not yet learned language symbols and responds essentially at an organismic level. All of this will be transformed as language is acquired. But in these initial stages the mother socializes by stroking and by soothing talk or by disapproval and the withholding of affection.

Out of this initial relationship of dependency the child learns to interact in similar dependency relationships with other adults and, later, with peers. Thus, the father, other relatives, and a teacher can enter into the relationships with the child as socialization agents by using the dependency relationship.

3. The Components of Early Socialization

The elements that go into the socialization of the child do not simply pile up on top of one another but rather integrate into whole systems of social action. The simplest elements are learned first, and these then provide a basis for more complicated behavior. In general, the direction of this process is toward broader and more complex relationships with others. The rate of development and effectiveness of the process depend very much on the richness and variety of elements available to the child. For example, because blind infants do not see adult gestures and reactions, they are more self-centered and less expressive and attentive than sighted youngsters (Scott, 1969, 1032).

The first elements of socialization are simple motor skills and speech. As they develop through the early months of childhood, motor skills and speech become vehicles for socialization of the second order—through education, the learning of roles, and the acquisition of a self-concept. As children mature through the preschool stage, they begin to acquire the third-order elements of socialization. These include group membership, organized play, planning and projecting of social action, purposeful work, creativity, and social and economic exchange.

a. Motor skills.   Obviously, certain motor skills are basic to the participation of the human being in any more complex activity. For example, once children learn to walk, they can approach social or physical objects, seek out and engage others, and pursue or escape from a harried parent. Children can then, having acquired this basic skill, develop objectives, carry out plans, try out ideas, and interact with parents and playmates on more equal terms than if they could not move around at will. The young mother is soon socialized, too. She finds a new dimension in the challenge of child care when her firstborn learns to walk, because the year-old toddler can now initiate more kinds of action at a much more rapid rate. She must now contend with the child as a resourceful and even potentially dangerous individual.

The development of manual skills is also a vital element in early socialization. These skills begin with the simple business of being able to grab and release objects and develop later into the ability to control objects over a period of time. The infant begins by the sporadic manipulation of rattles and simple toys that others define as its property. Later, the child masters the more complex movements of holding a cup and eating with a spoon. Later, the child is able to employ toys as tools toward some organized goal such as completing a creative task with crayons, mastering a game of skill in which a score is kept, or constructing a finished object out of parts that must be coordinated or assembled. These skills are an essential element in the cooperative play of children in groups. The child playing alone often adds the missing social dimension by pretending that he or she is cooperating with a companion as the play proceeds.

b. Social identity.   Perhaps the most important aspect of the socialization process in early childhood is the acquisition of a social identity. A name is an act of social placement (Strauss, 1959). By constantly having their names affirmed in relations with other members of their family, children can then refer to themselves and can think of themselves as objects relative to other objects in the world at large. Thus, identity is developed through interactions with other identities, by acting in named roles, and by identifying themselves in complementary roles.

According to Mead (1934, 180), this self, which can be an object to itself, is a social process that arises in social experience. The social self of children develops, according to Mead, in three stages. First, there is a preparatory stage characterized by relatively meaningless imitation. Children take on and practice roles without knowing what they mean. Dressing like their mother in her high heels or putting on their father's tie, all the while mimicking what they have seen, represents such a stage in the process. Later, children will know what these roles mean, but at this point the entire charade is merely a preparation.

Next, the self is constituted directly by an organization of attitudes of others toward the child in particular social acts. Children come to see themselves from the standpoint of specific roles: friend, playmate, son, daughter. And, importantly, they know what these roles mean. In the final stage children begin to incorporate the attitudes of the group as a whole as a generalized, rather than a specific, other (Mead, 1934, 158). As the self develops, children begin to function as social persons. All of this begins with a certain egocentric logic and an egocentric view of the world. Through experience, however, children gradually discover that others do not think as they do and they make efforts to adapt to others. An egocentric logic is then replaced by a shared one created by the inexorable demands of the social world (Piaget, 1960, 301).

c. *Language as the key socializing factor.* Language is perhaps the most important element in the socialization process. This is true because its particular forms can come only from others and because it affords by far the most flexible and precise means of communicating with other persons. It is important to recognize that language is not an individual product. No one creates his or her own language but rather uses a conventional one acquired through interacting with others. Language makes possible a more extended development and refinement than any other form of social behavior. Most of the components of socialization we have discussed thus far are almost completely attained by early adolescence, but new vistas of language are continually opened throughout life.

Piaget has explored the development of language by children of various ages as a vehicle of socialization. On the basis of his landmark studies Piaget believes that children's language up to age 6 is largely egocentric and is used to verbalize personal experiences and self-impressions. Children organize their own actions and thoughts by putting them into words. After age 7 children begin to use language to explain and to learn from one another and to organize action. By this time self-directed, or egocentric, speech is down to about 25 per cent of the total output (Piaget, 1959, 49). Piaget also notes that

Socialization is a two-way street. (Photo by © Charles Harbutt, Magnum Photos)

at age 11 or 12 children shift in the course of their development from the authority of adults to the authority of peers, and this change is also associated with certain linguistic shifts.

4. The Importance of Play

Play is serious business. It is the reality for children, even though they may be aware that they are pretending (Vygotsky, 1939). Two girls, aged 5 and 7, may decide to pretend that they are sisters. They are able to manage their game accordingly until they decide to be something else. This ability to switch roles and to be who they don't think they are is an important stage in the development of children, for it sets the stage for any number of later roles that will be played.

Play is thus the process through which role taking occurs. Our previous discussion of Mead's work has shown the importance of this pervasive and far-reaching process. As the child takes on a variety of roles, various types of *anticipatory socialization* occur. Stone defines this concept in the following way: "The child plays many more roles than he will enact in later life, while the roles playfully rehearsed by the adult are generally those he firmly expects to enact later on" (Stone, 1962). Stone also notes a kind of *fantastic socialization*, in which the child may play roles such as cowboy or Superman

Activities such as feeding and bathing are accompanied by give and take. (Photo by © Richard Kalvar, Magnum Photos)

that are hardly anticipations of future roles. These rehearsals, either for roles that will be played or ones that will never be acted out, are important in children's development and constitute much of their life during the early phases of the socialization process.

B. INFANT SOCIALIZATION

1. The Prenatal Environment

Very little has been written about the socialization of infants, probably for good reason. Prior to the acquisition of language it is difficult to confirm any of our speculations about what is going on within the newborn child. Certain observations can be made, however. When we speak of the *prenatal environment* we are not, of course, talking about the womb of the mother, for little is going on there of a social nature. However, preparations for the arrival of the child have been taking place. The prospective mother and father begin to assume parental roles even before the child is born. Books on child-raising and the care of infants are purchased and read. Relatives are alerted, and a treasure house of materials begins to be gathered. If the sex of the child is either known beforehand or assumed (as in the case of parents who followed one of the various "recipes" for picking the sex of the child), adults begin to organize their behavior and remarks in terms of the anticipated social implications of one sex or the other.

During the neonatal period—roughly the first 12 weeks following birth—the main socialization process is from the infant to the mother. The process is most intense with the firstborn. In modern industrial society small nuclear families live independently, and girls have little opportunity to observe infant care at home. The young mother, confronted alone with her newborn, has little to sustain her beyond good intentions, indirect information, and a concern for her baby. Both mother and baby have few experiences and no established habits with which to cope with routine events that appear at first to be emergencies.

By the end of three months babies consistently respond to adults with distinctive variations in crying. They respond to the way they are answered in various calls for attention, promptly or tardily, gladly or grudgingly. Whether adults are patient or impatient, relaxed or rigid, gentle or rough in dealing with a baby will affect the pattern of his or her adjustment (Bettelheim, 1967, 17).

2. Adjustment of the Infant and Family

During the first week or two babies merely signal their discomfort by crying, but it is the baby who initiates the action and who evokes the reaction of others. It is the baby who starts crying and the baby who stops crying. The baby functions from the start as a socializing agent, and the other members of the family adjust their routine to conform to its needs.

The infant signals distress, hunger, pain, and rage by variations in crying. The initial adjustment and mutual accommodation between infant and mother constitute the first stage of socialization. Very soon, the baby is reacting to the quality of others' responses (Rheingold, 1969). Two persons—one barely born, the other adult—learn how to cooperate, how to react, and how to communicate needs and feelings to each other. At three months the infant's socialization is still at a rudimentary level, but it clearly exists and is oriented to the mother or other caring adult.

The usual objective of the mother is to satisfy her baby's needs. Babies at first are fed on demand, and modern pediatricians generally advise that babies know how much they need. When mothers spoon-feed their babies, there is evidence that they mentally put themselves in the baby's place, a classic role-taking relationship. Observations were made of 26 mothers as they fed babies from 3 to 12 months old. Each mother frequently opened her own mouth as she attempted to maneuver the loaded spoon into the baby's mouth. Mothers opened their own mouths independently of whether or when the babies opened their mouths.

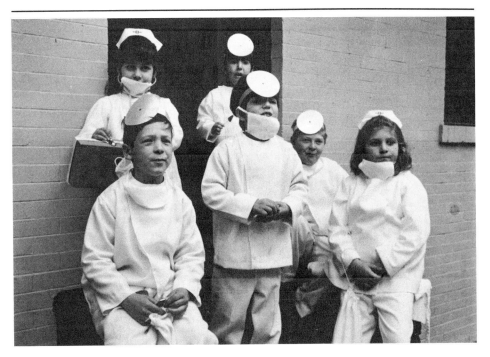

Play is the process through which role-taking occurs. Playing the role of doctor or nurse is an experience in anticipatory socialization. (Photo by © Abigail Heyman, Magnum Photos)

3. The Necessity of Love

Love, affection, closeness, and other social interaction seem to be essential to the development of the baby. In fact, the baby cannot develop and is not likely to survive unless it has the benefit of interaction with others.

In an interesting study conducted by Spitz (1945), two groups of infants were observed during their first year of life. One group of 69 infants was cared for by their mothers, who were serving prison terms. The mothers were allowed to be with their babies a few hours each day, during which time they lavished unrestrained love and attention on them. Conditions were not particularly sanitary, but these infants remained healthy and rapidly reached the toddler stage. The comparison group of 61 was cared for by eight busy nurses in a foundling hospital. These infants were isolated in cribs with sheets hung around the sides to prevent drafts. They received excellent care by medical standards, but the nurses attended only to their physical needs. These babies were quiet and inactive. They could see only the ceiling overhead. They had poor appetites and were underweight. At the end of the first year only five could walk unassisted. By the end of the second year 40 had died of infectious diseases, and the others failed to develop physically or socially. By contrast, all of the prison infants survived to a normal childhood. It is clear that physical maturation depends on continuing social relationships. It is as necessary to satisfy the child's hunger for human association as for food.

4. Early Language Development

Infants experience a more or less continuous flow of language during the first year of their life, but their own vocalization is confined to coos, gurgles, laughter, and cries. These vocal intonations seem to be indicative of contentment by 2 months, of pleasure by 3 months, and of specific desires by 7 months (Tonkova-Yampolskaya, 1968). It seems to be almost impossible for adults to speak to infants in the same tone of voice as they do to adults. Observation of mothers talking to year-old and 2-year-old children showed a clear pattern of simplification and redundancy that differed from that of ordinary speech. These children heard relatively simple grammatical structures with few subordinate clauses and complex verbs (Snow, 1972). It might be assumed that simplified speech facilitates the child's speech development. But it could be argued that children would develop more effective patterns of speech if they heard only usual adult speech. There is, however, little research on this point.

Russian children aged 12 to 13 months were involved in a simple experiment with an adult and an object that could be manipulated by a small child (Popova, 1968). Three experimental conditions varied the degree of adult involvement with the child. In the first condition the adult came near the child and manipulated the object while describing the object, the action, and the situation. In the second condition the adult initiated the same activity with the object; but the adult also actively involved the child in manipulating the object while talking about it and gave it to the child while describing it. In the third condition the adult gave the child the object to play with independently and alone. These actions were continued daily for five months—until the children were about 18 months old—with 24 children in three day nurseries.

The purpose of the research was to determine the effect of variation in the degree of contact with the adult on the child's vocal and verbal outputs. The results (see Table 3-1) indicated that active verbal involvement of adults with young children stimulated and accelerated speech behavior. The effect increased when the adult's activity was directed toward and shared with the child. The presence and verbal behavior of an adult are thus a major factor in the child's acquisition of language.

C. THE PRESCHOOL PERIOD

1. Language Development

Success in language development comes most rapidly during the period from 2½ years to 6 years of age. In early language attempts 2-year-old children can only partially express the words they hear. Still, most of their

Table 3-1. Effect of adult verbal stimulation on children 13 to 18 months of age

| | | Condition | |
Months	Adult talks, manipulates object near child	Adult talks, shares object with child	Adult leaves child alone with object
13–15	Forty to 50% of children silent, but listened to adult. Some children imitated and simplified words: *asha* for *rubashka* (shirt).	Throughout the period voluminous vocal activity. Many sounds and sound monologues.	Vocal activity very unstable, with 50 to 70% showing no vocal activity. Interest in toys varied extremely.
16–18	Most children uttered frequently heard words. Imitated many words they had heard. Ninety percent showed speech activity.	Eighty percent of children used individual words. Twenty-five percent used words independent of the experimenter. They averaged four words per period.	Positive change in attitude toward toys: exhilarated and fascinated. All expressed sounds and simplified words.

utterances are intelligible. There follows a massive growth of vocabulary combined with a rapid mastery of the ability to express thoughts in grammatically organized sets of words. Progress is so swift that by the age of 5 a child can discuss most conventional subjects successfully with an adult.

In the process of developing verbal proficiency, young children modify standard words. Sometimes they shorten them. Sometimes they substitute more familiar sounds for sounds they find difficult. For example, the word *mama* is an infantile version of the word *mother* in English and the word *mat* in Russian. The word *buh, bru'er,* or *bre'er* is sometimes rendered for brother, and *muh* for *milk.* One 3½-year-old child who was observed for six months developed 150 neologisms for standard Russian words, such as *lep* for *slepeno* (stuck together) and *davaiu* for *daiu* (I give) (Shurakova, 1969).

Children absorb new words readily, reaching a vocabulary of about 1000 words by age 3 and several thousand by age 5 (Shirley, 1938; Semenova, 1941; Hurlock, 1964). Their rapid development during this period of the ability to use complex language and sentence construction has also been documented (Montessori, 1967, 114). There is some evidence that children have recently increased the average length of their sentences, possibly due to the influence of television. Comparable samples of 4-year-olds had an average of 4.3 words per sentence in 1930 versus 5.3 words per sentence in 1957 (Mussen, 1969b, 295).

Whether from television or from face-to-face interaction, the child's primary source of language learning is adults. The process of correcting language use is illustrated from a recording of a 27-month-old boy named Adam who wanted to watch trucks passing by his house (Brown and Bellugi, 1964, 6):

> Adam: "See truck, Mommy! See truck!"
> Mother: "Did you see the truck?"
> Adam: "No I see truck."
> Mother: "No, you didn't see it. There goes one."
> Adam: "There go one."
> Mother: "Yes, there goes one."

The immediate correction of Adam's speech by his mother brings about, after some weeks or months, the appropriate improvements. This simple, direct style with short sentences has been called the *public language,* as contrasted to the *formal language* with its more elaborate syntax and more complete grammar (Bernstein, 1959).

By the time children reach age 5 their grammatical construction is about as good as that of the adults with whom they have associated (Todd and Hefferman, 1970, 387). However, children may be excessively literal in interpreting what has been said to them. A 5-year-old girl, Betty, was helping her mother by setting the table for company: "Mother: 'Betty, why didn't you put on a knife and fork for Mr. White?' Betty: 'Because I thought he didn't need them. Daddy said he ate like a horse' " (Chukovsky, 1963, 11). The child knows the difference between what is real and what she pretends but is inclined to assume that everything an adult says seriously is literally true.

2. Mother/Child Relations

The mother, often assisted by various helpers, is a primary source of socialization for preschool children. By repeated transactions with her, children learn to plan, carry out, and evaluate the basic kinds of social relations that tie two persons together in interaction. They develop autonomy as they learn to manage both themselves and their mother. They gain skill in securing and giving information and in gaining the interest and attention of others.

The following episode was recorded verbatim by an observer of parent/child interaction in a middle-class home (Maccoby and Masters, 1970, 145). It clearly illustrates the extent and limitations of socialization with a 3-year-old daughter.

Debbie (is upstairs):	Mother (is ironing downstairs):
"Mama, can you come upstairs?"	
	"What are you doing? Having a tea party?"
"Yes. Come."	
	"Do you want me to come upstairs for a tea party? In about ten minutes."
"It's ten minutes already."	
	"Okay. I'll come. But I have to come down and iron."
"Right now."	
	"Yes." (Finishes ironing piece, comes upstairs.) "Here's your party. Where am I supposed to sit?"
"Right there is where you go to sit."	
	"Is there enough room?"
"Okay. I forgot the coffee pot" (goes to get coffee pot).	
	"Does it have . . ."
"You pour. Oops!"	
	"It smells so good!"
"You have some cream for your coffee."	
	"Can I have a piece of toast too?"
"Yes. My friends have some too."	
	"Can I have a banana [candy in shape of fruit] too?"
"Yes."	

"Here's a tangerine with . . ."

"Here is some jelly."

"I'll have a triangle."

"The other day you did this again. You forgot to."

"Judy."

"Oscar. Sandra. I'll have to wash this."

"You know, I have mine done."

"At six."

"Yes."

"I'll do it."

"These are dirty."

"Bye" (washes dishes as mother leaves).

"Oh. They're fixed together. I'll take one off."

"No, thank you. I'll stay with my banana."

"I am going to cut it. A square?"

"I'll have a drink of coffee."

"Does your friend have a name?"

"Do you know who the other is?"

"That's good. Can I help? I have to run along. It's been fun, but I have to go home and iron."

"You're efficient. When did you get it done?"

"You got up early."

"Can I help with the dishes, or do you want to do it?"

"I'll put these here."

"Loved it. Bye!"

The child becomes progressively less dependent on her mother. At first she maintains strong interest in keeping close to her and in frequent physical contact. With the increase in confidences she becomes more interested in seeking attention and approval. There is also some shift in the target of action from the mother to other adults and to peers.

3. Sex-Role Differentiation

Sex identification begins in the behavior of the parents when the child is born. The child is given a name, and sex-specific pronouns are used to refer to the male and female members of the family. By the beginning of the pre-school period, between the ages of 2 and 3, most children show sex-orientation differences. They have begun to develop identification with the parent of their sex, if that parent is available for modeling (Mussen, 1969,

By the end of the preschool period, children are fully aware of their sex-role identification. (Photos by © Burk Uzzle, Magnum Photos, and © Abigail Heyman, Magnum Photos)

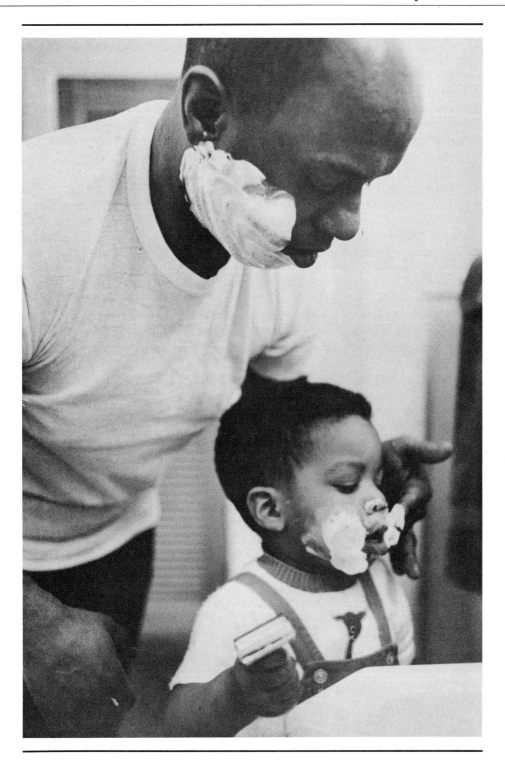

725). There are many props and reminders to assist sex identification—toys, clothing, and activities separately identified by sex. Boys are encouraged to be venturesome and independent, whereas girls are more restrained by parents and thus are more passive and obedient. The boy, by the time he is 5, realizes that he is expected to grow up and do something away from home. Here his fancy gets free rein, and he can realistically plan to become anything he can name, with acceptance and encouragement from his parents if it is acceptable for boys. The pathway to accomplishment, however, is not clear. For some boys this uncertainty of adult occupation may persist through high school and college.

The little girl by age 5 plans to become a mother when she grows up and usually has more or less well-tended dolls to legitimize her status as a mother. Many of her games are concerned with playing house, and her own mother provides a ready model. Feminine techniques of subordinate domination, enticement, and social maneuvering are explicitly rehearsed by the young girl, both with parents and with peers. Her world is more limited, but it is clearly in focus, and the objectives and routine are well known. In contrast, the boy can only grope toward his role models and typically does not avail himself of his father's job as an occupational model (Lynn, 1969, 43).

The boy's acting out of adult masculine roles includes props such as trucks, airplanes, and soldiers. As he becomes socialized in interaction, his role is not something he plays but something he *is* (Parsons and Bales, 1955, 100, 107). His audiences are not close and familiar figures, acting themselves, but imaginary foes, accomplices, or bystanders, carrying out some heroic part. For him the idea of expertise and adequacy is central to his action. Whatever the action, he must be successful, powerful, and resourceful (Parsons, 1964, 43).

Observation of 40 children averaging just under 5 years has indicated that communication between a boy and his mother contains significant levels of aggression. The mother's pressure on the boy for achievement in solving problems is also significantly greater than with girls (Hatfield, 1967). If the young boy does not have a father available, he is under strain to develop an adequate masculine orientation. To prove his maleness, he may show exaggerated social behavior reflecting toughness, violence, and aggressiveness that ill prepares him for ordinary adult roles in society (McCandless, 1969, 803). By the end of the preschool period children are fully aware of their sex-role identification, though they have a long way to go in working out how to play these roles successfully.

D. THE FIRST TWO YEARS OF SCHOOL

1. The Institutional Environment

When children enter the first grade at the age of 6 they find a new level of social autonomy and independence for which they should have been prepared. If they have been led to anticipate the adventures and discoveries of going to school and if going confers positive status in their mother's eyes, they will probably be enthusiastic and happy to make the transition. If they have received no preparation for the new status—particularly if they have been threatened with what might happen to them at school—they may enter with a sense of dread and disaster.

They acquire new property rights as they are assigned their own place in the classroom and the privilege of using school property in the building and on the playground. They enter two new groups, one with the teacher and one with the first-grade class. Within the class they have enormous latitude in selecting and changing playmates compared with the restricted choices at home (Yakovlyev, 1966). And they are judged by the teacher in terms of success in performing new kinds of assignments and taking their place as a member of a rather large group of peers.

At home much that matters in the world is out of children's reach, such as light switches, water faucets, cupboards, and the top shelves in closets. At the table, their plate is an inch under their chin, and their feet are 6 inches above the floor. At school it is more comfortable. The chair and desk fit children's proportions, for a change, and the blackboard is well within reach. They can get to the book racks and storage closets and somehow feel more at ease. At home they were outnumbered and overpowered by adults and other members of the family. At school, they gain a substantial standing as a member of a large class of students with which the teacher, the lone adult in the room, must come to terms. Each child in the class has a right to the attention and respect of all the others. This may be more than many of the children get at home.

In the school setting children make continued progress in socialization. Middle-class children are more attuned to the school experience, because they are more likely to have been positively prepared for it. Individual experience at home with books, pictures, and musical instruments—in addition to positive evaluations of education, reading, teaching, and learning—develops an anticipatory adjustment that eases the middle-class child's orientation to school. Some working-class children hear reading and education disparaged as a waste of time and a needless expense that must be endured because of the law. They may also hear negative remarks about the professions and occupations that are the goals of some educational programs.

Of a sample of 41 middle-class children and 24 working-class children interviewed five times over a period of three years, 76% of the middle-class children correctly developed the concept of the conservation of volume, compared with 29% of the working-class children. All of the middle-class children at the kindergarten stage were sufficiently skilled in language to be interviewed (Almy, 1966). It was suggested that many working-class children would benefit by special vocabulary training and help from children who understand. Working-class children's vocabulary is usually adequate for their language requirements at home, where much of the concern is for direct action and for immediately available objects. The theoretical, the conditional, and the possible appear to be much less significant for working-class children. Since these conceptual approaches are of the essence of academic work, it is to be expected that middle-class children will adjust more rapidly and will learn better. Such factors tend to preserve the differences between the two classes and therefore become a political issue.

In the class children learn to participate as an audience when the teacher is explaining or preparing them for some joint activity. They learn, after several reminders from the teacher, that they must not talk when this will interfere with the work or studies of others. They must learn to coordinate their efforts with those of their fellow students, whether their abilities in a particular endeavor are comparable to the others' or not. They may have to stop reading while a slow reader slashes through the strange tangle of words. Or they may not have a particular skill that others have. In either case they are under pressure to coordinate their speech and production with that of classmates and with them to follow the schedule of action set forth by the teacher. All of these functions are essential in children's socialization to prepare them to enter other kinds of groups. For this they need to establish a relation with the teacher that is friendly but impersonal. In most school systems they will have to adjust to a new teacher when they enter the second grade.

2. School and Power in the Socialization Process

On the playground the first-grade child begins to come under the influence of the peer group. A boy suddenly learns that sticking his finger in his mouth is "sissy" and that girls, when they bunch up, should be avoided. The first-grade girl learns the same thing about boys. Thus, sex segregation appears first on the schoolyard, sometimes by the voluntary arrangement of the two sexes and sometimes by arrangement of the school authorities. Girls may have their side of the classroom and the coatroom. Both groups accept the inviolable separation of rest rooms. This is an indirect manifestation of sexual power in which the distinctive rights of the sexes are asserted (Reese and Lipsitt, 1970).

From the position of the first-grader, the teacher has extensive power resources in several other categories. The teacher can comfort or praise, control and punish. And she is the arbiter of skills and technical knowledge. It is usual for the child to develop affection for the teacher, much of it related to his or her power.

Each child develops shared standards of skill in games, behavior in the presence of others, physical strength, and the limits for the treatment of others. One child becomes an expert for the group in a particular game, gains status, and may become a resource for teaching the game to newcomers to the school. Another becomes admired or avoided for the ability to fight.

3. Differences in the Social Characteristics of First- and Second-Graders

In the process of socialization during the first and second year in school, children make major strides in coping with secondary-group relations, as opposed to the primary-group relations involving the family and the home neighborhood. They learn, with somewhat variable success, to accept and apply relatively formal and impersonal relationships when they are carrying out "official" duties in the classroom. These duties include passing out work materials, acting as spokesman for a subgroup, or acting as a demonstration model for some new activity or technique.

Second-graders experience a distinct step upward in status relative to the first-grade "babies." The teacher reminds them that they are second-graders now and that a higher level of skills, interests, and conduct is expected. The grade hierarchy becomes explicit for second-graders through references by teachers, students, and family members. They may attempt to impress their higher status on individual first-graders, particularly if they have a younger brother or sister in the inferior status. With a full year of school experience behind them second-graders are better adjusted to the routines of classwork and may be more confident as new subjects are introduced. They are more often a participant and less often an onlooker in games, and in some games they may teach the rules and techniques to other children. They may receive or transmit bits of sex education.

The second-grade boy or girl is likely to develop a romantic attraction for another child of the opposite sex or for a teacher of the opposite sex. Evidence of this affection may appear on slips of paper passed or anonymously inscribed on sidewalks. These activities carry the child a step further toward eventual independence from parents and contribute to developing an adult and sexual orientation. Most children enter a close and continuing "chum" relation with a member of the same sex that involves talking, visiting, walking and playing together, and developing shared interests.

Children show symptoms of shame to an increasing degree from the age of 3 to 7 years. Soviet children of this age group in Kiev were observed for shame reactions under four experimental conditions: (1) playing with a toy after they were forbidden to; (2) peeking at blind man's bluff; (3) forgetting lines while reciting poetry to the group; and (4) making an error in a game. The results are shown in Table 3-2. Shame reactions consisted of blushing, admitting failure, hanging the head, withdrawing from the group, and showing confusion (Kulchitskaya, 1966). These reactions indicate concern for the judgment of the group or the superior and a clear understanding of the criteria of success. They constitute a primary motive for children to try their best and to solve new problems successfully in cooperation with classmates.

Table 3-2. Shame syndrome in children by age group (percent)

Condition	Younger (Age 3)	Middle (Age 5)	Older (Age 7)
1. Forbidden play	55	70	85
2. Peeking	50	65	75
3. Forgetting poetry	40	55	70
4. Error in game	—	50	60
(N = 95)			

4. Mother/Child Relations

The quality and range of adult orientation of the 6-year-old boy are illustrated by an excerpt of a dialogue between a boy and his mother. It was recorded in the family home as the mother was serving some ice cream to 6-year-old Norman and his two younger brothers (McBride, 1973):

Norman: "When I get married my wife is going to make me homemade ice cream just like Grandma's."

Mother: "She might not know how to make homemade ice cream."

Norman: "Wives are supposed to know how to fix ice cream and all kinds of food, like you and Grandma does."

Mother: "I don't know how to make ice cream, and your daddy still married me."

Norman: "I thought women was supposed to learn all that stuff to get married."

Mother: "It would be nice to know how to cook and make ice cream, but a lot of women don't know how. They meet somebody that loves them anyway, so they get married."

Norman: "Like I love Sharon?"

Mother: "Kind of. It's when you love a person a whole lot, and you want to spend all of your life with them."

Norman: "I love you like that, even though you fuss a whole bunch."

Mother: "Children are not supposed to love their mothers the same way they love their husband or wife. They can't marry their mother."

Norman: "If their daddy dies, then they can, can't they?"

Mother: "No."

Norman: "Mom, do you know why I like Sharon?"

Mother: "She is a nice little girl."

Norman: "No, that's not why. I like her because she acts like you do. She always brings me cookies to school, and she fusses all the time."

Mother: "Why does she fuss a lot?"

Norman: "She said I get on her nerves all the time because I don't know how to do anything right."

Mother: "Why do you like to be around somebody that says that all the time?"

Norman: "I don't know. I just do."*

The child's projection of himself to the adult married state and his stress on the similarity of the behavior pattern of his mother and his child sweetheart marks a major socialization pattern. The mother also socializes her son about the incest taboo by deflecting his marital proposal from herself outward to nonmembers of the family.

* Copyright 1973 by W. E. McBride. Reprinted by permission.

E. LATE-CHILDHOOD SOCIALIZATION

Between the ages of 8 and 12 the child undergoes extensive changes in patterns of thought, action, social relations, self-concepts, and interests. Children under 10 think of speed simply as hurrying, but children over 10 can think of speed in terms of its two components, time and distance (Piaget, 1971, 160). Small children assume that their thoughts are fully understood by adults and by other children, no matter how they have verbalized them. Older children are more sensitive to logical inconsistencies within and between assertions (Piaget, 1959, 25). This sensitivity has been found to double from age 7 to age 9.

1. The Use of Language

Children become much less egocentric in speech and hence more socially oriented in the later elementary-school years. This became evident in the analysis of children's references to peers in the first, third, and fifth grades. There was little change in the rate of egocentric (self-centered) references (Table 3-3), but there was a marked increase in nonegocentric references for both sexes—though greater for boys—by age 10. This means that the more mature children evince more recognition and concern for objects and ideas external to themselves. They are becoming more ready to deal with the world of other people.

Fourth-grade children habitually speak in longer sentences than second-graders though there is no difference in sentence complexity. Children of both ages who heard a model speaking in complex sentences did use more complex sentences a short time later (Harris and Hassemer, 1972).

When a sample of children from kindergarten, second grade, and fifth grade were given a series of memory tasks, the older children verbalized much more in rehearsing and naming, as an aid to memory (Flavell, 1966).

The ability to communicate verbally increases steadily with age. A sample of 74 boys from kindergarten and the first, third, and fifth grades

Table 3-3.   Relative increase in nonegocentric statements by grade level

| | Grade 1 | | Grade 3 | | Grade 5 | |
	Boys	Girls	Boys	Girls	Boys	Girls
Egocentric, we	.9	.2	1.0	.2	.8	.0
Egocentric, concrete	1.7	1.0	3.1	1.8	2.0	1.4
Nonegocentric, concrete	1.1	.8	1.9	1.5	3.2	2.4
Nonegocentric, abstract	.2	.3	1.4	.9	4.8	2.4
(N = 108 interview protocols)						

Adapted from "Children's Descriptions of Peers: A Wernerian Developmental Analysis," by H. H. Scarlett, A. H. Press, and W. H. Crockett, *Child Development*, 1971, *42*, 439–452. Copyright 1971 by The Society for Research in Child Development, Inc. Used by permission.

worked in pairs, with one partner explaining to the other from behind a screen how to arrange stacks of blocks. Their success increased consistently with age (Krauss and Glucksberg, 1969).

2. The Child's Self-Concept

Younger children tend to describe themselves in terms of sex, age, and various physical characteristics. Generally, they rate themselves as satisfactory. By the time they reach the fourth grade, some begin to rate themselves in terms of social criteria. At junior-high-school age they rate themselves in terms of comparison to others and may begin to see themselves as unsatisfactory (Kikuchi, 1968).

The sixth-grade child's self-concept appears to be affected by ability and home situation. Investigation of a sample of 159 children indicated that the self-concept for both sexes was positively related to high reading achievement and high arithmetic achievement. The child's self-concept was negatively related to family size and to birth order in the family and positively related to the degree of warmth shown by the mother and father (Sears, 1970).

Generally, the child's self-evaluation is dependent on others' overt evaluations. At first this depends on parental evaluations. As the child progresses in school, however, teacher evaluations and, later, peer evaluations begin to affect the overall evaluation of self (see Mead, 1934, Chapter 3). The self-concept is a conclusion that people draw from experiences in social interaction—how others respond to them and how they respond to the expressed images of others.

3. Adult Influence

It is generally recognized that adult behaviors and social interaction with adults provide the primary model for child socialization. If the parent provides guidance but allows children freedom to develop independent mastery and responsible decision making, they can develop self-reliance, competent judgment, and a questioning mind. Parental dominance may produce passivity, rebelliousness, and dependency (Elder, 1965). Children are likely to imitate the dominant mother regardless of the child's sex. If the father is the dominant parent, however, boys are much more likely to imitate the father and girls the mother (Hetherington, 1967).

Cross-cultural studies indicate that child rearing and mother/child relations have consistent effects on the child's anxiety level. The rural Japanese mother carries her infant, sleeps with it, and satisfies its needs almost instantly. Therefore, Japanese babies cry very little. French babies and United States babies are left more to themselves and experience more delays in gratification.

A cross-cultural comparison of a sample of 496 9-year-old boys and girls from France, Japan, and the United States showed large differences in children's level of anxiety and in their willingness to tell lies under various degrees of pressure (Iwawaki et al., 1967). In Table 3-4 the column labeled Mean Anxiety shows that Japanese boys and girls have an average anxiety score considerably lower than that of boys and girls from France and the United States. At the same time girls from all three countries have higher anxiety scores than boys from the same country. The differences are proportionately greater in the children's willingness to tell lies. Japanese boys are least willing to lie, and Japanese girls are not far above them on this test. But boys and girls from France and the United States show a relative readiness to tell lies. And the data from Table 3-4 suggest that there is a positive relation between the child's level of anxiety and willingness to tell lies.

The way parents socialize their children is thought to result from the way they were socialized by their own parents (Goode, 1964, 18). In the socialization process the adult reaches the child with messages, events, responses, and rewards. The adult must spend time and energy, resources and interest, and his or her own experience with the child. In cases where parents abuse, injure, or kill their children, the abusing parents were themselves abused or neglected as children (Spinetta and Rigler, 1972).

Family size has some negative effects on the amount of interaction be-

Table 3-4. Cross-cultural difference in anxiety and lying for 9-year-old children. (Figures in triangles are "small-t" measures of difference between means.)

	Japan Boys	Japan Girls	United States Boys	United States Girls	France Boys	France Girls	Mean Anxiety	Mean Lying	N
			Lying Difference						
Japan: Boys		-2.3	-2.8	-3.3	-3.4	-4.3	15.7	2.9	71
Girls	—		—	-1.9	-2.5	-2.7	16.0	3.7	84
U.S.: Boys	-3.5	-3.3		—	—	—	19.9	4.5	83
Girls	-6.6	-6.5	-3.0		—	—	23.7	4.8	86
France: Boys	-2.8	-2.6	—	4.2		—	18.8	5.1	66
Girls	-6.1	-6.0	-2.0	—	-3.3		22.2	5.2	66
			Anxiety Difference						

How to interpret the table: The small-t values in the triangles measure the size of the difference between the Anxiety Means (lower triangle) and the Lying Means (upper triangle). If the small-t is negative, then the column title mean is greater than the row title mean. Thus, Japanese girls in Column 2 have a higher lying score than Japanese boys, in Row 1. If the small-t value is greater than +1.9 or less than −1.9, with this many children, the difference between means is too great to occur in more than 5% of the research projects by chance.

Adapted from "Manifest Anxiety in French, Japanese, and United States Children," by S. K. Iwawaki et al., *Child Development*, 1967, *38*, 713–722. Copyright 1967 by The Society for Research in Child Development, Inc. Used by permission.

tween parents and children, and the combination of social class and sex of the child may increase this effect. Middle-class boys and lower-class girls see parents as less communicative and more controlling, more punitive, and less frequently praising than did other social classes in a study by Elder and Bowerman (Elder and Bowerman, 1963). One authority notes that the American child is often abandoned to the television set or to peer associations because of parental work patterns, the exclusion of relatives in the nuclear family's daily life, and the practice of age segregation. He dedicates a chapter of a book to "the unmaking of the American child" (Bronfenbrenner, 1970, Chapter 4).

In cross-cultural comparisons, German parents have been found to discipline their children more than American parents. But the German parents were also more affectionate, offered more help, and engaged in more joint activities (Devereux, 1962). A comparison of parental behavior in the United States and Sicily indicated that American parents pressured their children to fight and encouraged aggressive behavior in children to an extent that would be strongly deviant in other societies (Peterson and Migliorino, 1967).

However, no major differences were found in comparing the attitudes of sixth-grade British and American children toward their parents. In both countries, mother is favored over father by both sexes. Boys get more achievement demands and more punishment, and daughters get more household responsibility and more protection. In both countries, socio-economic status makes no difference (Devereux, 1969).

Goals toward which children strive are probably selected as a result of chance conversations regarding desirable occupations (Scanzoni, 1967). If this is the case, the mother's remarks should have more influence because children have more contact with her at home. Whatever the source, elementary-school children correlated very high with adults in their ranking of 15 jobs (Simmons and Rosenberg, 1971). Elementary children see all jobs as "good" but rate their father's job very high.

Children's aspirations are also affected by literature they read. Here, a strong bias against the feminine sex is in evidence. In 19th-century French literature for children male and female characters appear about equally. But in contemporary French children's literature boys' books have 86% male characters and girls' books have 57% male characters (Chombart de Lauwe, 1971). The picture is not greatly different in the United States, where children's literature also emphasizes the male role and includes females, if at all, as spectators, companions, and servants.

4. Peer Influence

The impact of peers increases gradually through the years of elementary school. It is not too much to say that, by the time adolescence is reached, the most important agency of socialization is not the family but the child's own peer group. From about the third grade boys and girls usually develop a close friendship with a person of the same age or a child slightly older. This close companion and other children in the peer group are essential. Peers provide confirmation and contradiction of self-judgments, competence, and self-esteem. Acceptance by peers is an index of social worth. Later, the peer group becomes the reference point for self-evaluation in the child's developing sexual orientation (McCandless, 1969, 808). Peers are an important source for teaching and learning, both in the schoolroom and on the playground. The slow child tries harder when confronted with a younger child who performs better in various school activities (Hamblin, 1971, 87).

Riesman talks about the peer influence as being a significant factor in the development of what he calls *other direction;* that is, children become socialized to the notion that the response of others is a significant element in their own actions. Other direction and its power can be seen in the response of a 12-year-old girl to the question "If you could be some type of super hero, which one would you be [Superman, Batman, the Green Hornet, and so forth]?"

> A. "I like Superman better than the others because they can't do everything Superman can do. Batman can't fly and that is very important."
> Q. "Would you like to be able to fly?"
> A. "I would like to be able to fly if everybody else did, but otherwise it would be kind of conspicuous" [Riesman, 1950, 83].

Other people should notice you, but not too much!

F. SUMMARY

Socialization is the lifelong process by which we acquire the knowledge and materials of interpersonal relationships. It is inherently developmental, going on literally from the cradle to the grave. Socialization occurs as much in nursing homes and work places as it does in nurseries and third-grade classrooms.

Social psychologists have been generally slow to recognize this continuous process and have concentrated instead on early-childhood socialization. As a result, we have slowly acquired a great deal of knowledge about how children are introduced to society and in the process become human themselves.

Much of our understanding of childhood socialization has been based on the assumption that it is the family that socializes the child. However, we are beginning to see that socialization is a fully *interactive* process. Children socialize others to new roles, norms, skills, and values as much as they themselves are socialized to these things.

The newborn child is nevertheless very much the dependent member in relationships with the family, and this dependency seems to provide the possibility for socialization in the first place. The fact that children can be molded into social objects as they interact with others is due in part to their dependent status.

The elements that go into the socialization of children—manual skills, physical dexterity, social identity, and the acquisition of language—integrate rather than simply accumulate. This integration of similar materials in different ways is what accounts for much of what we often call "individual differences." Of the elements that go into the socialization process, language is generally considered to be the most important. Mead showed in a classic discussion the way in which language gives rise to the self. And Piaget studied the development of a shared, conventional language out of an initially egocentric one. These are just two examples of the many studies that have focused on the indispensability of language in the socialization process.

Very little has been written about the socialization of infants, because it is difficult to confirm what might be going on within the newborn child. It is reasonable to assume, however, that socialization begins from the very moment of birth and that communication between the infant and the world starts at once.

Whereas infancy is characterized by nonverbal communication, from the ages of 2 to 6 there is a massive growth in the vocabulary of the child, and verbal skills are attained with a proficiency that is truly amazing. Between the ages of 3 and 5 sex roles begin to be differentiated as the child increasingly interacts with others as male or female. From the age of 5 on the child shifts to the institutional environment of the school, and profound changes begin to manifest themselves. The child is no longer the center of attention in a family but rather one of many clamoring for the attention of the teacher. The elementary school years are profound ones for the socialization process. Many of the materials needed for life in mass society are acquired during this time.

Whereas the early-childhood years are characterized by the acquisition of specific and concrete skills, the later years are given more to the acquisition of the ability to abstract and generalize. For example, children under the age of 10 tend to think of the concept of *speed* as simply hurrying or going fast. But children over the age of 10 are capable of thinking of speed in terms of its two components, time and distance. Children's self-concept is elaborated considerably in later childhood as they begin to rate themselves in comparison with other children. Parental evaluations are initially important, but later the ratings of peers take on prime significance. "Other" rather than "inner" direction becomes the main standard against which self-evaluations are made.

Adolescent Socialization 4

A. INTRODUCTION: TEENAGERS IN AN ADULT WORLD

Society is largely the product of adults. The officially approved norms, values, and goals sanctioned for adolescents have been conceived, pursued, and established by adults. Peter Manning and Marcello Truzzi (1972), recognizing this reality, wrote: "The category of youth in the context of American society is a social creation, not a mere product of biology. Since adults in society possess the power to create and apply labels, youth comes into being when it is defined by the older generation" (22).

Thus, the very concepts *youth* and *adolescence* are in many ways creations of the adult world. The establishment of right and wrong, normal and abnormal, good and bad are all judgments rendered largely by adults. In spite of the fact that socialization is always a reciprocal process, the power held by adults over adolescents is one of the primary social realities we must keep in mind as we attempt to understand this important stage in the development of human beings.

1. Identifying Adolescence

What is adolescence? What differentiates this period of development from other periods? The term *adolescent* is of relatively recent vintage. Coined in 1916 by psychologist Stanley Hall, it was defined as having the following attributes: (1) dependence on persons in positions of authority, (2) prepubescence (the period prior to puberty), (3) sexual learning, and (4) prelegal preparation for responsible social roles. At least two of these characteristics appear in earlier periods of socialization: dependence and sexual learning. But the intense dependency of infancy and childhood is beginning to taper off in adolescence, and the introductory sexual learning of childhood is becoming more intense.

Moving beyond Hall's early attempt to identify adolescence, three important characteristics come to mind. Adolescence can be identified as a function of age, of physical and physiological changes in the body, and of changing social roles. We will try now to assess the significance of each of these characteristics.

a. Age.   All human societies apparently use age as a basis for defining the various social characteristics, potentialities, and possibilities for human beings (Eisenstadt, 1961). This can no doubt be attributed to the relationship between age and physical, mental, and social development. As an individual becomes older, physical strength increases, the ability to communicate with others is enhanced, and greater quantities of knowledge are usually absorbed. It is not surprising, then, that age would be a common identifying characteristic among people everywhere.

However, the relationship between age and development is not a simple one. If we could establish a pattern for physical, mental, and social development in human beings, we could identify significant points in development with some certainty by merely identifying a particular age. However, it is difficult to tell where infancy ends and childhood begins. We know that a 2-month-old baby is an infant and that a 5-year-old child is not. Similarly, we are inclined to view a 16-year-old as an adolescent rather than a child. But the transition from one growth phase to the next is so gradual that we cannot identify adolescence absolutely with age.

b. Bodily changes.   Psychologists generally define adolescence according to physical criteria, concluding that the beginning of menstruation in girls and the appearance of pubic hair in boys marks its onset (Levine, 1963). According to this definition, about 50% of girls reach puberty between the ages of 12 and 15, while 50% of boys do so a bit later, between 14 and 16. Other key factors in adolescence, from this point of view, are first ejaculations in boys and changing body contours in girls (Simon and Gagnon, 1969; Rothchild, 1969; Levine, 1963). In keeping with these definitions, van Gennep (1960) aptly identifies adolescence as that phase in which an individual passes from an asexual to a sexual world. Although identifying adolescence purely in physical terms would be a mistake, there is little doubt that sexual changes are powerful, especially when coupled with the highly significant social definitions that accompany such transformations.

c. Changing social roles.   Even more important than age and physical development for an understanding of adolescence are the changes that occur in a person's social roles. The adolescent slowly moves from being a child, with few responsibilities besides going to school, to a kind of anticipatory adulthood. Besides education, the adolescent's concerns begin to embrace occupation, the enormous and worrisome contingencies of the sexual world, and the prospect of becoming independent of a parental authority. In short, adolescence can be characterized and understood in terms of the process by which some roles are terminated and others are initiated.

2. The Psychological and Sociological Approaches

Berger (1963) identifies two approaches to the study of adolescence: the psychological and the sociological. The psychological approach focuses on adolescence as a transitional state between childhood and adulthood. It is a period of conflict and tension resulting from accelerated physical and cultural growth and the withholding of certain adult rights, opportunities, and responsibilities. Conceptualized as a transitional stage, adolescence is viewed as a time of awkwardness and pain. It is a stage through which rapid passage is perceived to be desirable.

Out of this perspective has emerged a second perspective—that of adolescence as a subculture. This sociological approach views adolescence as a way of life sometimes apart from the adult world and functioning with a set of values often in opposition to those of adult society.

In comparing the two approaches, Berger writes that "the subcultural view suggests nothing inherently transitional except in the sense that all experience is transitional, representing as it does, the passage from what one was to what one is about to become" (1963, 52). The transitional approach minimizes the permanent influences of the adolescent experience. Adolescence discussed in subcultural terms does not carry this implication. Both approaches help us understand the adolescent period. We will view adolescence as a transitional period out of which subcultures emerge. Although the initiation and termination of adolescence may be abrupt and dramatic, it is the transition and subcultural affiliations that characterize these years.

B. ADOLESCENCE AS A PROCESS OF TRANSITION

David M. Smith (1970) characterizes adolescents as people who are chronologically, physically, mentally, and emotionally caught in a twilight world between childhood and adulthood. The adolescent is expected not to act like a child but is denied the responsibilities of adulthood. Miller (1970) supports Smith's position, asserting that early adolescence is a time of severe turmoil. As individuals undergo physical changes, they find themselves simultaneously seeking emancipation from family relations and increased identification with peer groups.

Both of these writers have captured the restlessness and transitoriness of the adolescent years. Adolescents are thinking and feeling human beings. Entry into the adolescent world initiates for them a journey of self-discovery and self-identity. It is during these years that they begin to gain an understanding of themselves and their relation to the world around them. Guardo and Bohan (1971) recognize four areas in which awareness occurs:

1. A sense of humanity, which involves an awareness that one's capabilities, limitations, and experiences are distinctively *human*.
2. *Sexuality*, which is knowledge of one's maleness or femaleness and behaviors that derive therefrom.
3. A sense of *individuality*, which gives one the assurance that one is a unique being with an identity of one's own.
4. Continuity, the notion that one's past experience is connected to the present and future.

Though these awarenesses begin to flourish in middle childhood, they blossom even more fully in adolescence. Teenagers begin to gain an awareness of their own autonomy. They identify a world outside the family for themselves. In Eisenstadt's (1961) words: "The adolescent is developing personal identity, psychological autonomy, and self regulation. He is attempting to link personal temporary transition to general cultural images and to cosmic rhythms and to link psychological maturity to the emulation of definite role models" (p. 17).

1. The Identity Crisis

In an important book Erik Erikson (1958) has called the major crisis of adolescence the identity crisis. It is in this period of development that the individual begins to focus on the meaning of self. A young child focuses primarily on the present. If he or she does focus on the past or the future, it is the immediate past or immediate future. The one exception might be the child's usually frivolous responses to the question "What are you going to be when you grow up?" As the individual enters adolescence, the past and the future become more meaningful. The individual has a past on which to focus. He or she also sees a future and the possibility of serious career options, marriage, and children. This serious focus on the future stimulates serious thought on the past and present. The boy or girl considers such questions as "Who am I?" "What do I want to become?" "What are my interests?" "What kinds of potential do I have?"

In searching for an identity, individuals are searching for their humanness, uniqueness, and worth. They are beginning to face the responsibilities of growing up. Adolescence is that time when individuals realize that they must at last *commit* themselves to an identity. As Erikson puts it, it is the time when identity becomes crystallized.

Examining the adolescent experience of identity, Douvan and Adelson (1970) noted two important factors that have affected the formation of identity: sex and social class. The importance of the sex factor is in the distinctly different directions in which it has traditionally routed males and females in their search for identity. Douvan and Adelson noted that boys tended to construct their identity around their vocational choices. In most cases girls did not. Anchoring identity in the vocational choice tended to give a young man the feeling that his identity was in his own hands. For the young woman this has not been true. Generally, the young woman's identity has been bound up not so much in what *she is* as in what *her husband will be.* This has forced her identity to remain obscure. In Douvan and Adelson's words:

> Someone has spoken of marriage as a "mutual mobility bet." We may add that for the girl it is equally an identity bet. It is for this reason that the girl, unless she is one of the rare ones who remain committed to a work ideal, seems unrealistic and romantic, often foolishly so, when asked to imagine a future life for herself. She tends to retreat into stereotyped notions of the future, imagining a life of suburban idyl. She seems more comfortable in the present; her vision of the future is necessarily dim; and . . . identity formation (so far as it depends on an anchorage to the future) is likely to remain incomplete [1970, 25].

We may also note that social class, or status, is a central component of the adolescent's identity. The adolescent period is, perhaps, more class conscious than any other. Adolescents' appraisal of others involves any number of important dimensions, the most important of which is social class. It is not just their present social status that is paramount to their identity but also their future social status. "Identity encompasses both the past-in-present ('What I am through what my parents are') and the leap from present to future ('What I deeply hope to be, what I deeply dread being')" (Douvan and Adelson, 1970, 26).

2. The Adolescent's Self-Perception

How do adolescents see themselves? What are the most important identifications for males and females in our society? Gecas, Thomas, and Weigert (1973) attempted to answer this question by administering the Twenty-Statements Test to high-school students in three societies: the United States, Puerto Rico, and Mexico.* The researchers explored four identities in terms of importance and frequency: (1) gender, (2) religion, (3) family, and (4) peer influence. Gecas and his colleagues used the concept of *identity* to refer to the location of an individual in social space. They suggested that the individual selectively integrates elements from this space to form a self-concept. The researchers hypothesized that religion and family identities would have a greater impact on Latin Americans. They also expected masculine and feminine roles to be more central in Latin Americans than in Anglo-Americans. And they hypothesized that peer influence would be more central to Anglo-Americans.

---

*The Twenty-Statements Test is a classic means of measuring identity. Developed by Kuhn and McPartland, this instrument simply asks a person to answer the question "Who am I?" 20 times. The responses are then analyzed to see what the most important identities in a person's life are.

Data were collected from two distinct studies conducted at approximately the same time. The first study involved middle-class Catholic adolescents attending co-educational high schools in New York, St. Paul, San Juan, Puerto Rico, and Merida, Mexico. All of these adolescents were approximately 16 years old. The second study was conducted in the Minneapolis area and involved lower-class Protestant students in public school.

Data analysis of the first sample indicates that the most striking pattern is the consistently high importance and frequency of gender identity. Adolescents are very much aware of their sexual identity. Analysis also revealed that *peer* identities have a more prominent position in the identity hierarchies of males, whereas *religion* and *family* are more prominent for females. Differentiating between Anglo-Americans and Latin Americans (both Catholic), the importance of hierarchies appears as follows:

Anglo-American	*Latin American*
1. Gender	1. Gender
2. Religion	2. Religion
3. Peer	3. Family
4. Family	4. Peer

No doubt much of the similarity here can be attributed to the fact that both groups are Catholic.

A somewhat different pattern emerged for the Minneapolis sample. Again, gender was the most important factor for both males and females. Unlike the Catholic adolescents, though, the Protestant youth ranked peer identities second. Family was ranked third by both males and females. Surprisingly, both ranked religion last. This may be an indication of Protestant Anglo confusion and uncertainty about religion. It is interesting to note that regardless of culture the most important identity within adolescence is that of sex.

In a 1969 study for CBS news, Daniel Yankelovich indirectly asked college-age youth to characterize themselves by responding to the statement: "The main trouble with the younger generation _____ (free response)." The youth were characterized as college and noncollege. Their responses are shown in Table 4-1. The percentages tend to reflect the restlessness and transitoriness felt by youth. The frustration experienced in the search for identity becomes apparent in their characterizations. By the same token, it may not be too unrealistic to suggest that their characterizations are in part those assimilated from the adult culture.

3. Adult Perceptions of Adolescents

How do adults view adolescents? Do they stereotype them? Do they apply ready-made images to anyone bearing the label? What do they expect of adolescents? First, we would be somewhat naive to believe that the label

Table 4-1. College-age youth rate their faults

	Total Youth	College	Noncollege
Immature	21%	25%	20%
Too impatient	13	16	12
Intolerant and close-minded	10	12	10
No respect for authority or parents	10	7	11
Self-centered and lack responsibility	10	8	11
Doesn't try to communicate with older people	10	11	10
Has too much freedom	9	4	10
Nothing—there is no trouble	9	4	5

adolescent did not conjure up certain concrete images in the adult's mind. Adults do apply the label, and the end result might sometimes be noted as a self-fulfilling prophecy (particularly if youth assimilate these labels).

Smith (1970) asserted that information concerning adolescents is derived from three main sources: (1) direct experience of behavior, (2) interaction with other adults, and (3) the mass media. Information funneled through these sources has created an image of the adolescent. In 1958, Dwight McDonald depicted this image:

> Adolescents are people who spend an hour a day listening to disc jockeys; they are the most assiduous movie goers in the nation, preferring especially films about monsters, rock and roll music, and teenagers like themselves. More than half of them "go steady" and practice the proto-sexual intimacies implied by that phrase. The boys are very car conscious and spend a good deal of their leisure time reading about, talking about, and working on hot rods. They read *Mad* and its imitators *Frenzy* and *Thimk*. They don't read the Bible, don't go to church regularly, are bored by politics, ignorant of the Bill of Rights and so on [44].

Today we might modify this characterization slightly. Monster films have been replaced with sex-oriented films. Rock and roll has evolved. *Mad*, *Frenzy*, and *Thimk* have had to share their popularity with *Playboy*, *Playgirl*, and *Viva*. The boredom of politics has been alleviated by nationwide scandals. However, adolescents are still thought to be irresponsible. To most adults, they are individuals who dress strangely and sport distinctive hair fashions. They are still preoccupied with sex and are consistently engaging in deviant behavior. They still go steady, though their feelings for members of the opposite sex are thought to be unstable puppy love. Adolescents are thought to be restlessly groping for the mechanisms by which they can regulate and control their lives.

Yankelovich captured the attitude of adults as they characterized adolescents in his 1969 survey. He asked parents of college-age youth what it was about the younger generation that bothered them the most (free response). The replies are shown in Table 4-2.

These percentages show a tendency on the part of the adults to stereotype youth on the basis of their dress. The frequent reoccurrence of so few different responses tends to reinforce the stereotype. As a biological, social, and psychological category, adolescence is subject to labels applied by adults. In part, it is this stereotyped image against which adolescents rebel.

What seems most apparent in this discussion of the adolescent's self-perception and the adult's perception of the adolescent is the clash of viewpoint. Adolescents see themselves as emerging from the world of the family. There is a recognition of autonomy. The initiation into independence is just enough to stir a desire to obtain more. They are restless and somewhat impatient. Lacking experience with life, they are not familiar with all alternatives. In experimenting with life, they may step outside what adults consider proper. Adolescents simply call this experimentation. Adults term it rebellion. It is not surprising that the opposing viewpoints of parents and youth serve as a catalyst for what is frequently called the *generation gap*.

That phrase has been tossed about freely by youth and adults alike. The emancipation of the adolescent from the home and the assimilation of youth into subcultures has helped to create a series of conflicts between parents and children. Parents, having adapted to one value system, find it difficult to

Table 4-2. Parents rate the faults of youth

	Total Parents	Parents of College Youth	Parents of Noncollege Youth
Grooming and appearance	21%	14%	23%
No respect for authority of their elders	20	17	20
Nothing—the majority are good kids	14	16	13
Self-centered and lack responsibility	11	10	12
Immature and naive	11	10	11
Rebellious—want too much freedom	10	8	10
Use drugs	11	9	12

understand their child's resistance to conformity. The adolescent, having been made aware of a world of alternatives, cannot comprehend the parents' inability to entertain them. So communication frequently collapses.

4. Sources of Conflict: Two Examples

In the mid-1960s a very popular singing group emerged from England. They had a long line of smash hits, the first of which was "I Want to Hold Your Hand." This group called themselves the Beatles, and they changed the face of American youth. One distinctive feature of the Beatles was their long hair, and it was not long before many other musical groups also began growing their hair long. This craze moved from the music world into the general population of youth. Hair was the "in" thing. Even a musical was written about hair.

It may seem impossible that such a simple thing as hair could create conflict between adolescents and adults, but it did. The military had virtually institutionalized short hair for men. The growing popularity of long hair led school officials and employers to establish hair rules. Fathers literally walked their sons into barber shops to ensure that their hair got cut. Long hair was

Hair is a continuing means of establishing one's identity in adolescence and provides a constant source of conflict between parents and teenagers. (Photo by © Eric Kroll, Taurus Photos)

identified with the "hippie" movement. Males with long hair were stereotyped as deviant, radical, boisterous, and troublemaking. Hair became a symbol of rebellion.

About this same time, women's fashions experienced a radical change. Fashion designers came out with a little number that became very popular among young women—the "mini." Mothers became distraught. School officials showed their distress. Regulations regarding the length of dresses and skirts were put into effect. Such clothing was perceived as too sensual and suggestive. Girls who insisted on wearing their skirts so short were perceived as being loose or immoral.

5. Factors in the Parent/Youth Conflict

Though both long hair and short dresses came to be accepted (and even adopted) by adults, these examples imply that youth have a greater willingness to entertain change. To suggest that this is always so would probably be incorrect. But if there is a period of time in life when conflict within the family is more likely, it is probably adolescence. Kingsley Davis (1940), writing on the sociology of parent/youth conflict, cited a number of reasons for this fact.

a. *The pace of social change.*   The first important variable cited by Davis is the rapidity of the change that creates the gap between generations. Parents are labeled old-fashioned or traditional; youth are found too modern and free. The result is conflict.

b. *Differing rates of socialization.*   Davis noted that rapid social change would have no power to produce conflict if it were not for the differing rates of socialization of the parents and child. The family is not a static entity but a process in time. When rapid social change occurs, the family is instrumental in helping members make an adjustment. Davis notes that the family would have no trouble adjusting if it were not for the fact that youth is the time when socialization occurs most swiftly. The result is that cultural content that has been absorbed by the parents is different from that being absorbed by the child—producing a cultural lag on the part of parents. The parents in socializing the child try to apply the content given them when they were at that stage. But this content is inappropriate, and the parents cannot modernize their point of view because they are the product of their experiences. Adolescents see adults as looking at the world through a rear-view mirror.

c. *Physiological differences.*   Davis also asserted that, though the disparity in chronological age remains constant through life, the precise physiological differences between parents and offspring vary radically from one period to another. The organic differences between a parent and an infant are far different from the differences between a parent and an adolescent. At adolescence, the contrast is between an organism just reaching its full powers and one just losing them. However, Davis cautions that these differences exist in all cultures and cannot be used independently to explain the parent/youth conflict in our culture.

d. *Psychosocial differences: adult realism versus youthful idealism.* Though parents and youth both profess to be seeking the truth, the old are more conservatively realistic than the young. Utopian ideals are taken less seriously. Practical ideas are taken more for granted. There is a tendency for an older person to gravitate toward the status quo. Adults may be bothered by the inconsistencies of ideals and more concerned with the practicality of them.

Youth, on the other hand, have been protected from many social experiences. They have not been suffocated by cynicism and despair, and consequently their ideals soar nobly upward. The failure on the part of society to embrace youthful ideals often creates cynicism. Conflict may be the end product.

e. *Sociological differences: parental authority.* It is important to note that our society establishes different social positions for parents and youth. This status differential is inherent in the makeup of families. But it does not, in itself, produce conflict. It may even help to prevent it. Our society has focused little attention on institutionalizing the progressive readjustments of authority between parent and child. In our society separation from the family occurs in adolescence through education, work, marriage, and change of residence. Parents are concerned about the activities of their children, and their own social identity is somehow tied up in their offspring. They know they must let go, and yet they are reluctant to do so. Davis asserted that it is only with a definite system of institutional controls that the resultant conflicts can be neutralized.

f. *Concentration within the small family.* The family is a unique system in that it manifests a "paradoxical combination of concentration and dispersion." The smallness of the family induces intense feelings. At the same time, most activities take place outside the family. These close kinship relations become paramount to one's emotional life. Yet the diversity of activities threatens this emotional union and thus can be viewed as a potential source of conflict. Protective parents often cannot let go!

g. *Open competition for socioeconomic position.* The occupational future of an individual comes into question in adolescence as the young person considers a number of occupations that he or she could follow. Parents often try to help young people make this decision. And parents generally have high aspirations for their children. The proverbial example is that of a father who wants his son to follow in his footsteps and the son who is not interested in that line of work.

h. Sex.   At adolescence the individual first experiences his or her full sexual capability. But sexual enjoyment is denied. The adolescent is instructed to channel his or her energies in more appropriate and accepted directions. As Davis put it, "The parent with respect to the child's behavior represents morality, while the offspring reflects morality plus his organic cravings." The stage is thereby set for conflict, evasion, and deceit. For the majority of parents toleration is never possible. For the majority of adolescents sublimation is never sufficient. Given prevailing concepts of morality among adults about children, conflict seems well nigh inevitable.

6. The Adolescent as a Marginal Individual

Sociologists use the term *marginal man* to refer to individuals caught between two cultures. These people are not truly a part of either. Certain aspects of their life-style are a part of one culture. Other aspects belong to the second culture. They are caught between the two without maintaining full membership in either. By analogy, at least, we may perceive adolescents as marginal individuals. They, too, are caught between two worlds: the world of the child and the world of the adult. During this transitional period they are

Adolescence is that time in life when a person is virtually at the peak of his or her sexual capacity. (Photo by © Magnum Photos)

thought to be too old to enact the roles of children and yet too young to play the roles of an adult. Neither world seems to fit them well.

Friendenberg (1963) characterizes adolescents as second-class citizens. Legally, they come close to having no basic rights. The minority status afforded them results in discrimination. Adolescence is viewed by adults as a period when gratification is deferred in favor of education and training.

Winch (1967), in discussing the principle of deferred gratification, identified two alternatives that might reduce the stress and intergenerational conflict of adolescence:

1. Socializing adolescents to accept deferred gratification as a reasonable arrangement.
2. Minimizing the consequences of adolescence and its very existence.

He identified three conditions that have bearing on the first alternative:

1. Acceptance by the adolescent of the goals for which the period of education and training is designed.
2. Acceptance of the idea that such goals are achievable at the cost of a reasonable expenditure of effort.
3. Acceptance of the ethic of deferred gratification.

Three conditions bearing on the second alternative are:

1. Acceptance by parents and employers that higher education is not required for a considerably greater number of occupations than currently seems to be believed.
2. Willingness of parents and other adults for adolescents to have "adult privileges" (sexual freedom, marriage, parenthood) and to make such "privileges" financially possible.
3. Acceptance by parents and other adults of adolescents' insistence on their own values (for example, social concern and altruism, immediate rather than deferred gratification) and their rejection of their parents' values (for example, competitive achievement, upward mobility).

Realization of these conditions would involve compromises and a greater degree of permissiveness (one for the other) on the part of both parents and adolescents. The complexity of society, resulting from industrialization, urbanization, and increased emphasis on education, has helped to prolong the adolescent period. When this complexity is coupled with the rapidity of social change, a certain amount of stress and intergenerational conflict seems inevitable. However, we might note that this is not necessarily to the detriment of others. To the contrary, such differences can become catalysts for social change. Down through history, youth have left their mark on all the rest of us.

C. ADOLESCENCE AS A PERIOD OF SUBCULTURAL AFFILIATIONS

We have characterized adolescence as that period in life when the individual seeks to expand personal relations outside the realm of the family. From the time children enter school, they are aware of individuals outside their family. In the early grades, though they enjoy the company of such persons, their family is always paramount. At adolescence the family clearly begins to play the secondary role, with peers stepping into the forefront. No doubt our educational structure is largely responsible for this phenomenon. Young people are placed in an academic setting for a good part of the year. Their primary social contacts are with their peers. The adult segment verbalizes the importance of an education, emphasizing the desirability of high academic performance. Mothers (especially middle-class ones), in addition to echoing educators, stress the importance of being physically attractive. Adolescents are encouraged to develop heterosexual relationships. Likewise, fathers may impress upon their sons the importance of athletics for recognition and respect. Consequently, the adolescent seeking acceptance is taking an essential step in the formation of his or her self-concept. The formation of peer-group relations is also the foundation for various subcultural affiliations.

1. Functions of the Peer Group

Wagner (1971) identifies three important functions of the peer group. First, it reinforces the set of individual characteristics shaped by parents and the early preadolescent environment; but it also presents alternative values and concepts. Adolescents are placed in a decision-making position. They must decide which alternative is appropriate in any given situation. Second, the peer group offers adolescents an opportunity to try on roles until they eventually adopt the ones best suited to them. Peers are used as a sounding board as adolescents experiment with various adult roles. Third and most prevalent, according to Wagner, is the teaching of adolescents to get along with others. These social relationships help adolescents develop a social identity.

College youth are the group to which the term *generation gap* best applies. Collegians, on the whole, tended (at least in the '60s) to be less conservative. However, even among them, differing needs exist.

Thornberg (1971) further characterized college youth on the basis of three differing orientations: (1) those academically oriented, (2) those vocationally oriented, and (3) those socially oriented. College youth select peer-group relations whose values accommodate their orientation. Those academically oriented tend to hold the least traditional values. The vocationally oriented hold values similar to the noncollege group. The socially oriented hold values that fulfill their needs for socializing and competition.

Wagner and Thornberg would agree that peer-group relations work to establish the adolescent's self-image and social development in a stage when identity is crucial. The peer group affords structure and stability. The status of the individual is defined. Experimentation with roles is found acceptable. Thus, peer-group relations offer an individual a real sense of security in these critical years, probably even more than the family, from whom emancipation is sought.

2. Dating

The peer-group relationship known as dating begins, for most individuals, in adolescence. The most socially approved mode at this time is multiple dating. In the North American system adolescent boys are expected to pursue any number of girls for a date. The girls can accept as many as they like with no moral stigma attached, provided they use restraints in their dealings with the persons involved.

There are a number of viewpoints regarding dating patterns in North American society. Some look on dating as a positive and healthy activity. Others take a more critical view. Burgess and Locke (1953) saw adolescent dating as a maximization of fun with no other concern than pleasure for the two involved. Dating relationships among adolescents are not thought to be love relationships. They are simply means of obtaining social approval (resulting from several dates) and attention from the partner. Dating is a form of entertainment that helps to alleviate loneliness and to enhance one's self-worth.

Willard Waller (1937), a major critic of the dating system, took a more critical view, citing multiple dating as the primary cause of moral decay in our society. He suggested that it fosters thrill-seeking, exploitative relationships in which women are seeking expensive amusements at the man's expense and the man is seeking only sex. C. T. Husbands (1971) also criticized the multiple dating system, not for its exploitative nature but for its superficiality. Dating has a gamelike character, and the two persons involved must learn the rules of the game. The rules stipulate the roles to be played. How well one plays the role will in some cases help to determine how frequently he or she dates.

The dating relationship for the adolescent is meant to be an investment in self-worth. But sometimes it yields just the opposite. In playing the roles understood to be appropriate in the dating environment, individuals may inhibit their spontaneity and self-expression. The person may feel that stepping out of the role would create tension. Consequently, though adolescents may go out with many members of the opposite sex, they are not necessarily well equipped to make assessments of character from their experiences. The result may be that the dating experience does not provide much positive development of the self-concept. In fact it may be detrimental, in that individuals may have reservations about being someone they are not. Secondly, the premium placed on dating is such that those not dating (for whatever reason) will consider themselves less valuable than their peers.

Adolescents entering college are usually well versed in the ritual of dating. It is here that their dating activities will probably take on a more serious perspective as they begin to look for a future mate. Becker (1964) observed that the dating system and the round of formal and informal social functions provide an excellent training ground for this purpose. Fraternities and, especially, sororities place a great deal of emphasis on dating. In fact, some pledges are required to have a minimum number of dates per month, and most students will feel some pressure to date. This was substantiated by Larson and Leslie (1968), who conducted a study on the dating patterns of sorority and fraternity members at a U.S. university. Two members of each fraternity and sorority were selected to rank the 25 fraternities and 11 sororities on campus. The fraternities were divided into four categories: four were ranked very best, five very good, eight good, and eight average. The sororities were given one of three designations: excellent (three), good (five), and average (three). Agreement among members doing the ranking was substantial, therefore creating no real problems in formulating levels of prestige.

Information on serious dating patterns was collected from the "Social Swirl," a listing of involvements published in the campus daily newspaper between October 1, 1966, and March 31, 1967. These listings were fairly accurate, because each sorority and fraternity had a social chairman whose responsibility it was to place these dating relationships in the paper. Three categorical relationships were considered: (1) "dropped," (2) "pinned," and (3) engaged. The three levels of increasing commitment were symbolized by a piece of jewelry donated by the male and worn publicly by the female: (1) a pendant, or "drop," worn on a neck chain; (2) the male's fraternity pin worn on the breast; and (3) a diamond engagement ring.

Of the 1,477 fraternity members, about 20% were classified as either dropped, pinned, or engaged. Of these 302, 63% dated sorority women. Of the 533 sorority women, 47%, or 249, were either dropped, pinned, or engaged. Of these 249, 82% dated fraternity men. The larger percentage of sorority women dating fraternity men was explained by their greater emphasis on dating fraternity members.

Of those fraternity men coming from the "very best" groups, 44% dated women from the "excellent" sorority group. Another 37% of the men from this group dated from the "good," or middle, group. In those sororities ranked excellent, 41.3% of the women dated men from the very best fraternities. Twenty percent of the women from sororities ranked excellent dated men from other campuses. Members of the lower-ranked fraternities and sororities were relegated to dating within the appropriate levels of ranking or with independents. The pecking order of such systems is obvious. Varying levels of status are attached to sororities and fraternities. Such organizations are valued by peers, and to gain acceptance, therefore, one shows interest.

Dating, then, is a training ground for adult roles. It also provides reward or gratification to participating individuals. In many cases the frequency and quality (based on peer-group evaluations) of dates is a determinant of popularity. In this respect dating is extremely crucial to self-esteem and self-worth. It becomes a key factor in helping the adolescent form an identity.

3. The Adolescent Subculture: Fact or Fiction?

The question of whether an adolescent subculture exists is an extremely controversial one. Parsons (1942), Davis (1944), and Green (1968) all testify to its existence. Elkin and Westley (1955) are leading antagonists to this position.

Sebald (1968) noted that arguments favoring the existence of a subculture assume that the typical adolescent is beset by socially caused "storm and stress." The storm and stress are the result of insecurities over occupational choice, identity, generational conflicts, and sexual frustrations resulting from conflict between physiological maturation and social prohibitions. Advocates of the subculture concept contend that the peer culture is a compensation providing a sense of security and a feeling of belonging during this period of adolescent discontinuity. This assumes that identity is highly dependent on a relatively stable position in a social order. Adolescents alleviate their uncertainty over a structured place in society by seeking a clear status among peers, according to this argument.

Elkin and Westley challenged these assumptions, suggesting that the adolescent subculture is an unjustified myth. After interviewing a sample of 20 adolescents and their parents and studying life-history material of 20 others, they concluded that the generation gap is nonexistent. Rather, family ties are close, consensus within the family is high, and parent/child interaction is more than adequate, they found. They reported that the patterns of adolescents' social life are similar to those of their parents and that in many cases adolescents accepted responsible and adult perspectives (Elkin and Westley, 1955).

The findings of this study are questionable because of the small sample size. It is difficult to generalize to a population from a small data base whose representativeness is also in question. The bulk of work in this area seems to favor the conclusions reached by Parsons, Davis, Coleman, and Green—the adolescent subculture does exist and is a useful way of looking at the problem of growing up in society.

4. Subcultural Spirit

Paul Goodman, in an important piece of work (1964), characterized the adolescent subculture as a "resistance to the interruption of growing up further" and a "resistance to the pressure to excel in 'their way.'" The contents of the adolescent subculture include "cars, games, sex, simple music, and being popular." But Goodman conjectured that conscious fixation on such rudimentary objects is inevitably both against adults and imitative of them. In fact, Goodman asserted, there is nothing authentic in the youth subculture except its youthful vitality, its disappointment in being cut off from the adult world, and its spite against adults' demands. In the background of this rebellion is the "organized system" to which most adolescents eventually conform. In Goodman's words "the importance of the youth culture is its protest that adults are alien and they are not worth growing up to" (1964, 27).

Keniston echoed Goodman's thesis: "The real token of a generation gap . . . is not overt and visible rebellion against the previous generation, but a vision of parents and those of their generation as irrelevant" (1970, 52). These feelings of dissatisfaction with the adult culture lead adolescents to establish subcultural memberships that meet their needs. How do adolescents organize and describe their feelings about how they are to live? How conforming or deviant are they with respect to the expectations of others?

These questions were posed in a study conducted by Norman Goodman (1969), in which 1300 sophomores, juniors, and seniors in the Northeastern United States were questioned. A wide variance in social class, intelligence, and other characteristics was obtained. Self-characteristics were assessed by means of a questionnaire. Participants were asked what they expected of themselves and what they thought their mother, father, friends, and best-liked teacher expected of them. Persons were also asked to assess how they and the significant people around them viewed their actual behavior as compared with their expectations. Three adolescent roles were evaluated: (1) the role of family member, (2) the role of peer-group member, and (3) the role of student. Though each individual was asked to respond to how each significant person (mother, father, friend, and teacher) would react in certain situations, only the mother and father were considered in evaluating the family role, only the friends were used to evaluate the peer-group role, and only the teacher's feelings were considered in the student role.

Goodman noted that the most prominent finding in his study was adolescents' tendency to organize their behavior differently in various situations. When they are with family, they engage in certain behavior patterns. When they are with friends, these behavior patterns may be modified slightly. Within the academic setting, still other behavior patterns may be viewed as more appropriate. Additionally, adolescents see greater internal consistency within a specific role than they see across roles.

Of particular importance was the question of conformity, because the assertion of autonomy (as earlier suggested) is extremely acute in adolescence. Not surprisingly, Goodman found that the adolescent conforms more to the rules of friends than to parents' but more to the rules of parents than teachers'. (These findings are somewhat contradictory to those of James Coleman [1960], who asked of adolescents "Whose disapproval would be hardest to take?" Fifty-three percent responded "parents," 43% responded "peers," and 3% responded "teachers.")

The adolescent's tendency to conform more to friends than to parents and teachers helps to position the individual in the youth subculture. The adolescent subculture may be viewed as a compromise between the adult's demands for conformity and the self's demands for autonomy. The adolescent subculture attempts to incorporate the best of two worlds: the novelty and curiosity of youth mixed with the freedom and independence of adulthood.

5. The Subculture Defined

What are the recurrent and basic features of a subculture? Very simply, *culture* has been defined as a blueprint for behavior of a total society. Subculture, then, might refer to a blueprint for behavior of a smaller group within the society. As Sebald put it, a subculture is "a special blueprint that accommodates a number of people whose needs and desires are not provided for by the main and overall blueprint of the society." Subcultures can be developed for almost any group—including adolescents. Sebald noted that subcultures are frequently defined by delineating their functions. He listed seven important characteristics (Sebald, 1968):

1. Common values and norms.
2. A specific language not shared with the larger culture, expressing what is of particular significance to the participant.
3. A common style of behavior, including the observance of fads.
4. Standards specifying the right appearance in terms of dress, grooming, makeup, and the like.
5. A feeling of belonging, thinking of one's peer group in terms of "we" instead of they.
6. An understanding of status relations—for example, the existence of a working order of social positions that, at the minimum, clarifies leader/follower relationships.
7. Gratification of specific needs for which the larger culture does not provide.

In assessing each of these functions, Sebald writes,

(1) Adolescents derive from [the subculture] a peculiar *set of values* that consists neither of adult nor of child standards. (2) They speak an *argot* that is often only partially understood and approved by adults. (3) Teenagers cultivate relatively *independent vogues and fads,* for example, rock 'n roll dancing, which they do not enjoy sharing with adults. In fact, they are prone to change to new styles once adults approve and adopt a teen-age fad. (4) They observe independent *standards of grooming and clothing.* Deviation from the accepted mode may be punished in various ways, ranging from sneering and name-calling to physical violence or ostracism. (5) They acquire a *primary-group* belonging in which they

are accepted as total individuals. This primary-group involvement functions as a partial and progressively increasing substitute for the teenager's family of orientation, which he leaves gradually. In a sense, the adolescent peer group aids young individuals in their strides toward emancipation from parental control. (6) They derive *status relationships* that enable them to engage in predictable and consistent interaction with their peers and that ameliorate the disorientation and lack of social stability during the change from child to adult frame of reference. (7) Teenagers find in the peer subculture an environment that facilitates *evasion of adult control* and, in a sense, forms a solid front in combating adult authority. The subculture allows the adolescent to immerse himself in a peer group that is psychologically as well as physically remote from adult overview. Teenagers are provided with opportunities for increasing *heterosexual contacts and adolescent sex behavior.* In other words, the typical teenage dating syndrome, inclusive of sexual experimentation, is facilitated and promoted by the teenage subculture [1968, 33].*

Therefore, we might suggest that adolescents use the subculture to compensate for what they believe are the inadequacies of the overall adult culture. It provides a workable alternative as they cope with the transition years.

6. The Educational Subculture

Next to the family, the educational system probably participates more than any other agency in the socialization of the child. At school the individual is exposed to new knowledge. Possible career choices are identified. Peer-group relationships that are crucial to this formation of identity are developed. The integration of the school system into the adolescent's life is so complete that the educational environment itself forms the basis for a subculture.

The literature regarding the value and validity of the educational subculture establishes two opposing viewpoints. The first suggests that the system provides a microcosm in which the individual can rehearse the roles thrust on him or her in adulthood. The second declares that it unnecessarily prolongs the adolescent years.

Becker (1964) upheld the positive viewpoint, contending that the educational subculture is a preparatory ground for learning adult roles. In assessing the college subculture, Becker wrote:

Going away to college provides a rehearsal for the real thing, an opportunity to be away from home and friends, to make a new life among strangers, while still retaining the possibilities of affiliation with the old. In the dormitory, and even more so in the fraternity and sorority, one finds himself on his own but at the same time surrounded by strangers who may become friends. One has the ex-

*From *Adolescence: A Sociological Analysis*, by H. Sebald. Copyright © 1968 by Appleton-Century-Crofts. Reprinted by permission of Prentice-Hall, Inc., Englewood Cliffs, New Jersey.

perience of learning to shift for oneself and making friends among strangers
[p. 14].

Aside from the adult marriage and career roles, Becker noted, the college subculture tries to teach "institutional motivation." Students must
learn to want only those things the institution says are worth wanting. The
college teaches them to want a degree, and they must endure what the university asks in order to get it. It may well be that this motivation is the most
important acquisition in the college setting, for better or worse.

Ralston and Thomas (1972) asserted that, if there is one aspect of North
American society that has extended adolescence, it is the educational system.
They traced this emphasis on education to four primary influences:

1. The American myth that education is the key to success.
2. Parental desire for their children to have a better education than they themselves.
3. The use of education as an alternative to military service.
4. The level of education sought by businesses for prospective employees.

Today's values hold that a bachelor's degree is desirable. Acquisition of
this goal places the individual in a period of limbo lasting from age 12 or 13
to age 21 or 22. Ralston and Thomas suggested that an exaggerated value of
education has resulted in the crowding of universities with students who
have neither the desire nor the potential for study. These authors suggested
that students are a fertile field, therefore, for radical movements and are
likely to protest their marginal existence by striking out at the society that is
the cause of their dilemma. Ralston and Thomas suggested that the youth
involvement in social issues, experimentation with sex and drugs, and the
creation of countercultures are all attempts by young people to communicate
to society that they, too, are adults.

D. YOUTH MOVEMENTS

Howard (1974) wrote that "adult glorification of youth rests, in part, on
the fact that adults see youth as a period when one has energy for sin and no
time for sorrow." Youth is seen as a time when one can live a life that is not
serious. As earlier suggested, young people who resist adult efforts to
socialize them are seen as deviants or rule breakers. Howard makes an important distinction between two types of deviance: (1) vertical and (2) lateral.
Vertical deviance occurs when persons in a subordinate rank attempt to
enjoy the privileges and prerogatives of a superior rank. The 12-year-old
child who runs behind the barn to smoke a cigarette is engaging in vertical
deviance. Lateral deviance occurs when persons "in a subordinate rank develop their own standards and norms apart from and opposed to those of
persons in a superior rank." The teenager who smokes marijuana rather than

tobacco is engaging in lateral deviance. Vertical deviance is characterized by value consensus. Lateral deviance is characterized by a conflict over values.

Howard notes that the youth movements of the 1960s and 1970s have drawn their following primarily from the middle class. Traditionally, middle-class youth have reacted to their questionable status by engaging in vertical deviance, concerning themselves with such adult prerogatives as sex, cigarettes, and liquor. More recently, reactions stemming from marginal status have taken the form of lateral deviance. The discontent of middle-class youth has found its expression in various youth movements and, consequently, the rise of countercultures. These movements include the drug culture, the hippie movement, communal living, the Jesus movement, and various political movements.

1. Drug Use

The drug subculture is recently a phenomenon of middle-class youth. Howard (1974), theorizing on this point, reasoned that the socialization experience of middle-class youth probably gives them a sense of "divided self." There is the "public" self, bounded by the laws of society and functioning in prescribed roles. And there is an "inner" self, which is more joyous, free, and innocent. In coming to grips with this duality, the individual finds the traditional "establishment" disillusioning. Feeling stifled by the society and by "unfair" laws and restrictions, a person may react by seeking freedom from conformity and by searching for new experiences.

The drug subculture offers an escape from this conformity, although in other ways it merely changes what is being conformed to. It is also said to offer the individual a new experience. The drug user may ascend or descend to levels of reality that are not ordinarily perceived.

Whether lower-class people feel this division of self is not entirely clear. Using a Freudian metaphor, Bensman (1973) wrote that "the middle classes have traditionally been characterized as highly emotional and incapable of impulse control. It is the rules of impulse control which the 'new' freedom of the middle classes is rejecting" (p. 63).

a. The marijuana user. Suchman (1968), in a study of drug use in academia, noted that marijuana is the most frequently used of the illegal drugs. In characterizing the marijuana user, he found that males are three times as likely as females to smoke marijuana, upper-income groups twice as likely as lower-income groups, single students four times as likely as married students (although engaged students used it the most), and atheists and "other religious affiliations" more likely than Protestants, Catholics, or Jews.

Tec (1970) questioned 1,704 high-school boys and girls in a well-to-do Eastern suburb about marijuana use. He found it to be influenced by three factors: (1) the presence and quality of parental models for behavior, (2) the extent to which associations within the family are defined as rewarding and

Vertical deviancy occurs when persons in a subordinate rank attempt to enjoy the privileges and prerogatives of a superior rank. (Photo by © Richard Kabar, Magnum Photos)

meaningful by its members, and (3) the presence of parental controls or indifference. Youth coming from broken homes are more likely to use marijuana than those coming from homes that are intact. Adolescents whose parents (especially the mother) drink hard liquor or use a generous supply of tranquilizers or sleeping pills are more prone to use marijuana than adolescents whose parents do not. Adolescents who receive recognition and respect from family members are less likely to smoke marijuana. Adolescents who perceive family demands to be unfair and excessive are more likely to use marijuana.

b. *Reasons for drug use.* As mentioned earlier, the theoretical perspective surrounding the drug culture seems to suggest that drug use is a social act engaged in to express distance between the user and others. Affiliation with the drug subculture implies dissatisfaction on the part of members. The reason or reasons for this dissatisfaction and accompanying drug use may not always be clear. Winick (1973) listed ten possible ones:

First, since World War II, North America has, for the most part, experienced prosperity. This continuous prosperity has made many youth insensitive to the idea of doing themselves gradual harm. They experiment with drugs because they feel, if they do get into trouble, they will be given a second and sometimes even a third chance.

Second, adolescence is the time when sexual identity becomes most crucial. Yet masculinity and femininity are now likely to be blurred. The feminist movement is a recent and well-known example of efforts to place men and women on the same footing. Drugs tend to minimize gender in an individual. Consequently, drug use may involve an escape from conventional sex-role expectations.

Third, Arnold van Gennep (1960) noted that most societies provide rites of passage, or ritualistic behavior for individuals passing from one status to another. In North America, where rites of passage are so rare and where adolescence offers instability in status, the ritual associated with drug experimentation might seem very appealing.

Fourth, Winick noted that drug use among middle-class youth peaked in the mid- and late '60s, during the United States' major involvement in Southeast Asia. Faced with the possibility of serving military time in Vietnam, many young men chose the gratification received from drugs over the conventional deferred-gratification pattern.

Fifth, the public acknowledgement of drugs and their value on the part of a number of popular recording artists was extremely influential in sparking the drug movement. Jimi Hendricks, Janis Joplin, Bob Dylan, and the Beatles were advocates of drug use. Though Dylan and the Beatles have since disavowed their earlier writings advocating drugs, these writings were influential in creating a favorable attitude toward drugs.

Sixth, the average elementary-school child views three hours of television a day. The programs are frequently interrupted by commercials, many of which deal with prescribed medication for alleviating pain. Winick suggested that such exposure could create an atmosphere of expectation about "better living through chemistry."

Seventh, rationality as a tool for coping with life has proven in the eyes of some adolescents to be a broken dream. Rationality applied to national and international affairs has often led to disaster. Drugs are thought to be a shortcut to the nonrational, out of which new lifestyles may emerge.

Eighth, with over 50% of our population under 27 years of age, young people are very aware of competition. Increased emphasis on higher education has bred a generation of professionals. Many youth, rather than dealing with competition, prefer to drop out of the rat race and escape through drugs.

Ninth, the ill in our society often receive indulgence and gratification. The sick person is coddled back to good health. Thus, experimentation with drugs may simply be a means of seeking rewards.

Tenth, for some youth drug experimentation is attractive because it offers so many risks—health hazards and the possibility of arrest among them. Some youth may simply be seeking the excitement that comes with challenges whether legal or illegal.

2. The "Hippies"

A second counterculture to develop in the 1960s was the "hippie" movement. It rejected both the traditional goals of North American society and the conventional means of achieving those goals. The hippie philosophy perceived success to be defined largely in terms of having money and a certain standard of living. The hippies believed that the means by which this standard of living was achieved is either meaningless or demeaning. They contended that the rewards of the system are not intrinsically satisfying.

In some respects hippies simply inverted traditional values. Rather than working and investing their money in a "good" life-style, they chose to be relatively free souls living in voluntary poverty. Hippies perceived the average citizen to be somewhat less than a human being, programmed into a life-style that teaches the benefits of material possessions. People adopting this life-style choose as one of their major goals the obtaining of material wealth. It is "good" to live in a nice house, drive a new car, own a color television set, take annual vacations, and add regularly to a savings account. The hippie contended that such people have no true identity. They are mere robots of society.

Howard (1974), in his discussion of hippies, identified four types: (1) visionaries, (2) "freaks" and "heads," (3) "marginal freaks," and (4) "midnight hippies" and "plastic hippies."

a. Visionaries.   Howard credited the visionaries with having given birth to the movement. These individuals had a vision of people "growing together," and it was their goal to remove those things that posed barriers—property, prejudice, and preconceptions about what is moral and immoral.

Free stores were opened. Free clinics were established. Free shelter for runaways and persons on bad trips was provided. People were encouraged to "do their own thing" because that is what yields the "good life."

b. *"Freaks" and "heads."*   Though the visionaries used drugs, drugs were not the focal point of their behavior. "Freaks" and "heads" are differentiated from the visionaries by their heavy emphasis on drugs. The two terms differ in that *freaks* has a negative connotation, but *heads* does not. The freak was a compulsive, sustained drug user. The head used drugs to experience a euphoric feeling. Drugs used included marijuana, hashish, methedrine, and LSD, to name only a few. Individuals were searching for enriched meaning to their lives, for a richer reality. The use of drugs to achieve this end might be compared to the use of sensitivity groups to find one's true self. Human-potential groups are also means of breaking out of a life-style in an effort to give new meaning to life (Howard, 1970).

c. *"Marginal freaks."*   The spreading popularity of the hippie movement attracted a number of persons who were only vaguely aware of its philosophy. Though their awareness was greater than that of the plastic hippies (see below), they were unable or unwilling to commit their whole lives to the experience. Marginal freaks included runaways, high-school dropouts, and college dropouts experimenting with the new life-style.

d. *"Plastic hippies" and "midnight hippies."*   Plastic hippies can be credited with giving the movement a pop impact. The identifying marks of a hippie (love beads, headbands, Benjamin Franklin glasses, leather shirts) became salable items. For some the movement simply became a fad characterized by certain styles. These individuals were plastic hippies. They were not committed to the value of the hippie movement. In one respect, though, their values were congruent with those of the true hippies—many were users of marijuana. This increased demand for marijuana, and the resulting shortage was largely responsible for the sense of demoralization in the hippie community (Winick, 1973).

The majority of hippies were in their teens or early 20s. However, there were a number of older persons who shared the hippie philosophy but who were integrated into the "straight" world. And whereas the average person would pay little heed to the visionaries and freaks, the midnight hippies were listened to. Their relative social acceptance allowed them to articulate and justify the hippie viewpoint with at least some possibility of being believed.

The decline in popularity of the hippie movement can be attributed in part to its exploitation by some individuals. For some it became a vehicle for self-aggrandizement and antisocial ends. "The counter-culture's vocabulary of spontaneity and openness became a weapon used by men seeking to exploit women sexually" (Howard, 1974, 195). Drug pushers also took advantage of the movement. It was gradually replaced by alternatives considered more viable.

3. Communal Living

The decline in popularity of the hippie movement was followed quickly by a rise in the popularity of communal living. Community living was an effort to return to a simple life. Many of the individuals coming out of the hippie movement still held firmly to its values. They were looking for another vehicle through which those values could be expressed. Communal living shunned materialism and differential status based on wealth. Property was frequently held in common. Individuals shared the work load. Food was divided equally among all. Life was simple. This simple life-style, though, was not without its problems. The community-living arrangement raised several questions in the minds of followers. Howard (1974) identified six questions:

1. Who can be a member?
2. To what extent should there be explicit rules about the division of labor?
3. To what extent are elements of a private, noncommunal identity permitted? (In other words, can people retain personal and private possessions? Is monogamy permitted?)
4. How are decisions made? Are they made communally, by a select few, or by one person?
5. How does the commune support itself economically?
6. How does it maintain nonhostile relations with the outside world?

These and similar questions became the foundation for two basic philosophical stances governing communal-living arrangements. The first position suggests that structure works against community. People are perceived to be inherently good but corrupted by society. Society is generally defined as any social setting with rules, including the home, the classroom, the business. From this perspective came communes void of structure. Anyone was welcome to join. No one was asked to leave.

A second philosophical stance recognizes the value of structure without differing statuses. Everyone is perceived as equal. Specific tasks and responsibilities are assigned, but generally on a rotating basis. Decision making follows a formalized set of rules. Individuals desiring membership in the commune are screened to ensure that the values of those who enter are congruent with those living in the commune.

Fairfield and Sardonval (1972), after conducting a national survey on communes, formulated a number of principles they theorize are necessary if a commune is to survive. Here are three:

1. The more people, the more organizational structure is needed.
2. The less thoroughly members know and understand each other, the more structure is needed.
3. The less time members spend together, the more structure is needed.

Though communal living has always held a certain amount of interest for a small number of people (Harmonites, Oneidans), the movement has never been very popular. Today, the movement as perceived by youth has for the most part climaxed in interest, and most young people have moved on to new interests.

4. The Jesus Movement

The United States has always been characterized as a basically Christian nation. Its founding is rooted deep in religious tradition. However, recent writings about religion in the lives of Americans suggest a decline in commitment, specifically on the part of youth. Glock and Stark (1968) noted, in fact, that the decline in religious commitment was greater among young people than among their parents. Hastings and Hoge (1970) surveyed changes in religious commitment among college students between 1948 and 1967. Their findings suggested diminished traditional religious commitment (accompanied by liberalized beliefs), reduced religious activity, more and earlier questioning of religion during adolescence, and fewer designations of religious preference. Gecas, Thomas, and Weigert (1973) noted that among Protestant youth religion is the least important factor in identity formation. These studies seem to support the notion that youth are not attracted to the church. The traditional religious principles adopted by the older factions of the church are set aside by young people. Youth reject what they regard as the plastic and hypocritical image that they see draped around the church today. Many young people perceive the church to be caught up in materialism.

Though formalized religion is unattractive to youth, we cannot infer from this a lack of religious commitment and involvement. Support for this notion lies in the various religious movements that swept the nation in the 1970s. One of the most widely known and publicized is the Jesus movement. Plowman (1971) wrote that the movement consists for the most part of converts from the drug, radical, and occult scenes. The philosophy of this movement is expressed in such slogans as "Turn on to Jesus" and "Get high on Jesus." The informal services are characterized by high levels of emotional involvement. Adherents openly express a love and happiness and inner peace resulting from their experience.

Howard (1974) said the Jesus movement "provides a way for dissident youth to be reintegrated into society" (207). Though "Jesus people" have the external style of hippies, their basic values include cleanliness, wholesomeness, faith in God, love of country, and obedience to those in authority. The embracing of Establishment values suggests that the Jesus movement may provide a means by which people can estrange themselves from the behavior of the counterculture. Affiliation with these fundamentalist groups may help refugees from the countercultures to regain middle-class status.

If the Jesus movement offers any real danger to the individual, it is probably what Don Williams (Plowman, 1971) calls a "sociological cop-out by Jesus People looking for Christ's soon return." Rejection of the world system sometimes leads to rejection of the world and to an unloving attitude toward its people. A second danger arises from an oversimplified trust that Williams labels supersubjectivism (Christ gives the highest high). An individual may harbor false hopes in attempting to cope with life's problems. If the problems remain unsolved, the individual may become disillusioned and cynical.

The Jesus movement, like the drug, hippie, and communal movements, reflects a restlessness and disenchantment on the part of youth for the Establishment. The Jesus movement differs from the former three movements in that its philosophy is not in opposition to the rules of the larger culture. Where the drug, hippie, and communal-living movements are seen as countercultures, the Jesus movement is not. It is an avenue by which one can divorce oneself from the countercultures and reenter the larger culture.

5. Political Movements

The disillusionment of youth and their quest for self-expression have also been channeled with enormous amounts of energy into political movements. Political rebellion on the part of youth has long been a part of history. In a society that upholds democracy and equality, however, such behavior seems unlikely. Richard Flacks (1970) attributes much of the rebellion on the part of youth to this society's extensive educational system. Government support of higher education has made it possible for many individuals to obtain an advanced education, thus greatly expanding the middle class. By the same token, social benefits anticipated from this development have not been forthcoming. In Flacks' words, "Liberal politics have not eradicated gross social inequality, have not improved the quality of public life, and perhaps above all have not created a pacifist, internationalist global posture on the part of the American Government" (1970, 344). Ironically enough, to the middle-class, educated person society is likely to appear increasingly chaotic and deteriorating. It was this disillusionment that stimulated youthful involvement in the early '60s.

The escalation of the Vietnam War only magnified this disillusionment. The use of the draft to continue the war, the failure of the war on poverty, and the transformation of the Black movement's tactics from integration efforts to a more radical struggle for liberation and economic equality all helped to project a United States that was largely reactionary, authoritarian, and repressive. The Watergate scandal in the 1970s only reinforced these feelings of disillusionment. The result was that young people were looking for a United States that was humane, intellectual, and democratic. Flacks summarizes the political youth movements:

> The expansion of higher education in our society has produced a social stratum which tends to rear its children with values and character structures which are at some variance with the dominant culture. Affluence and secure status further

weaken the potency of conventional incentives and undermine motivations for upward mobility. The outcome of these processes is a new social type or subculture among American youth—humanist youth. Such youth are especially sensitized to injustice and authoritarianism, are repelled by acquisitive, militaristic, and anti-nationalistic values, and strive for a vocational situation in which autonomy and self-expression can be maximized. They have been politicized and radicalized by their experiences in relation to the racial and international crises, and by the failure of established agencies of renewal and reform, including the universities, to alleviate these crises. They also sense the possibility that opportunities for autonomy and individuality may be drying up in advanced technological societies. One of the reasons that their political expression has taken generational form is that older ideologies of opposition to capitalism and authoritarianism have failed in practice [1970, 345].*

Robert M. Kahn and William J. Bowers (1970) conducted a research project in which they attempted to characterize the individuals involved in student political movements. From the literature in this area they developed four hypotheses:

1. Activist students come from high-status families.
2. They have a strong academic commitment.
3. They major in the social sciences and humanities.
4. They have a strong intellectual orientation.

Data were obtained from a nationwide survey of college students in 1966. As had been predicted, the data indicated that student activists do tend to come from high-status backgrounds. However, school quality appears to be an important factor. That is, when school quality is controlled, the relationship between socioeconomic status and student political activism largely disappears. Kahn and Bowers summarized by writing: "Thus the higher rate of activism among students from high status families is primarily a result of the fact that they are concentrated in the higher quality schools" (1970, 40). It is this concentration that may encourage the emergence of a student-activist subculture. Such behavior is reinforced by the colleges and universities themselves.

The relationship between academic commitment and student activism was also confirmed. However, when school quality was controlled, academic performance was found to be unrelated to student activism at the lower quality school. At these schools relatively few students are activists regardless of their academic commitments. At the higher quality schools the relationship holds—the more academically committed students are more prone to student activism.

*From "Social and Cultural Meanings of Student Revolt: Some Informal Comparative Observations," by R. Flacks, *Social Problems*, Winter 1970, *17* (3), 354. Copyright 1970 by The Society for the Study of Social Problems. Reprinted by permission.

The third hypothesis—that activist students are more common among social-science and humanities majors than among those in the physical sciences and preprofessional programs—was also substantiated. Again, differences vary consistently with the academic quality of the institution. The social sciences and humanities presumably encourage a critical appraisal of contemporary society. However, tendencies to convert these critical perspectives into social and political action are enhanced by the quality of the educational institution attended.

The fourth hypothesis—that there is a direct relationship between intellectual orientation and student activism—was confirmed without qualification. At all levels of educational institutions, students who were intellectually oriented were substantially more likely to be activists than were their classmates. Kahn and Bowers interpreted this as suggesting that students who think of themselves as intellectuals may feel that they should participate actively in contemporary social and political issues.

The most compelling findings of their research relate to the importance of the quality of the school itself. Kahn and Bowers summarize in this way:

> Clearly, there is something apart from a student's social background, his academic commitment, his field of study, or his intellectual orientation that promotes activist involvement at the better quality colleges and universities. The top ranking schools, in particular, somehow encourage activism among their most able and intellectually oriented students. Thus, the determinants of student political activism, rather than merely being characteristic of individual activist students themselves, are also to be found in the quality of the educational institutions that they attend [1970, 55].

The high-quality educational institutions are pacesetters. They are influential in educational, social, and political reform. In other words these schools may in effect stimulate protest by providing a supportive climate and a symbolic and strategic target for the student activist.

E. SUMMARY

Adolescence is a social phenomenon. It is a stage created and labeled by adult generations. Its beginning is perhaps best identified by *physical and physiological changes* in the body. Its end is better identified by *age*. At 18, an individual is legally an adult. The stage of adolescence, though, is perhaps best characterized by the *changing role structure*. It is that period when individuals begin to experiment with various roles that will eventually go with them into young adulthood.

Adolescence has been approached from two academic perspectives. The psychologist has viewed it as a transitional period of frustration, restlessness, and conflict that the individual must simply endure. Individuals are described as hanging in limbo until their passage into adult life. The sociologist has viewed adolescence as a period involving subcultural affiliations. Youth emancipate themselves from familial relations and seek identity and positive reinforcement from peer-group relations within various subcultures. Both perspectives offer insight into the adolescent years. The youth subcultures may be viewed as a reaction to the transition through which the adolescent must go.

In viewing adolescence as a transition stage, primary focus is on the individual's identity. The major crisis of adolescence has been labeled the identity crisis. It is a time when youth are seeking to determine who they are and what they want to become. Research has shown that the most salient factor in identity formation is gender. Additionally, self-reflections focus on a sense of frustration and restlessness. Whether or not this results from adolescents' assimilating adult images is not known. We do know that the adult image of youth reflects this same frustration and restlessness. Adults view adolescents as unkempt, disrespectful, self-centered, irresponsible, immature, and somewhat rebellious.

These differing viewpoints are in part responsible for what has come to be known as the generation gap. Davis, addressing himself to this parent/ youth conflict, cited eight reasons for its existence: (1) the pace of social change, (2) differing rates of socialization, (3) physiological differences, (4) psychosocial differences: adult realism versus youth idealism, (5) sociological differences: parental authority, (6) concentration within the small family, (7) open competition for socioeconomic position, and (8) sexual tension.

Winch offers two alternatives to youth's marginal status resulting from the principle of deferred gratification. The first alternative involves socializing the adolescent to accept deferred gratification as a reasonable arrangement. The second involves minimization of the consequences of adolescence. The first alternative places the primary burden on the adult. No doubt the final solution will involve a compromise on the part of both youth and adults. We should not infer from this line of reasoning, though, that adolescent stress and conflict are totally dysfunctional to a society. On the contrary, they can be the catalyst for social change.

In viewing adolescence as a period of subcultural affiliations, primary focus is on peer-group relations, dating as a special type of interaction, the evolving of subcultures out of peer relationships, and social movements. The peer group might be viewed as the prime agent of socialization within the adolescent years. It offers the individual structure and stability, a well-defined status, and an opportunity for role experimentation. Thus, the peer group affords the individual a sense of security at a critical period in life.

Dating is a special type of interaction that evolves naturally out of peer-group relations. For the most part, dating is a means of enhancing one's self-worth and social identity.

Though there is controversy over whether the adolescent subculture is fact or fiction, most sociologists agree that it is an empirical reality. Sebald asserts that the adolescent subculture is a reaction to the individual's shaky status in the adult world. The subculture helps the adolescent adjust to the transitoriness of this stage of life.

Several sociologists have expressed the opinion that the adolescent period is merely the product of our prolonged educational system. This educational subculture thus becomes a breeding ground for frustration and unrest, resulting in social movements meant to strike out at the adult world. These movements reflect what Howard labels lateral deviance.

Three social movements (drug, hippie, and communal living) resulted in the development of countercultures. Each of these movements embraced a philosophy that rejected the Establishment. Each perceived the Establishment as upholding the empty and worthless goals of materialism and the acquisition of wealth. Members of the drug culture, the hippie subculture, and the communal-living subculture all sought release from the "unfair" laws of society. They wanted to be free to seek new experiences. These three movements were reacting to status-quo keepers.

The Jesus movement also reflects a sense of restlessness on the part of youth. However, the values of this subculture are more in line with the values of the larger culture. The Jesus movement consists primarily of converts from the drug, radical, and occult scenes. Howard views this movement as a concerted effort on the part of youth to reenter the larger adult culture. Membership in this subculture provides a means by which individuals can divorce themselves from the behavior of countercultures.

Like the movements already mentioned, political movements are quests for self-expression. Disenchantment with the establishment resulting from the escalation of the Vietnam War, the use of the draft to continue the war, the failure of the war on poverty, the transformation of the Black movement, and the Watergate scandal have helped spark political activism.

Adult Socialization 5

A. INTRODUCTION: LIFE AS A SERIES OF PASSAGES

In an enormously successful book based on the developmental social psychology of a number of scholars, Gail Sheehy (1976) characterizes adult life as a series of passages marked by crises. The term *crisis* does not necessarily denote a catastrophe, but rather a turning point after which one's past recedes and one's future is changed. The unparalleled success of *Passages* is testimony to a glaring deficiency in social psychology—the tendency to look on socialization as a process that ends largely with childhood or, certainly, adolescence.

Psychologists have gone over virtually every aspect of childhood socialization, and we have a fairly coherent picture of the changes that occur in children throughout infancy and childhood. However, much of Freudian theory has been based on the assumption that personality is more or less set by the time a person is 5 years old, a doctrine challenged by Charles Bolton:

> The almost universal locating of the basic determinants of personality differentiation in infancy and early childhood betrays the same bias of avoiding the alternative-producing conditions of human conduct. . . . It is an illusion that personality development, in the sense of differentiation, slows down after childhood is passed. One has only to reflect upon the shock felt at reunions with once bosom college friends to recognize the truth of [Nelson] Foote's statement that "ten close friends fan out far more in the individualization of their identities between, let us say, ages 30 and 40 than between 10 and 20." We are constantly assured that personality is stabilized by the end of childhood and merely unravels in adulthood. But where is the evidence for these assertions? For the most part, the point is merely assumed" [1963, 6].

Much of the newer literature and research in social psychology is now beginning to emerge from the shadow cast by Freud and is taking seriously the idea of socialization as a lifelong process. Persons do not emerge from adolescence like wind-up dolls, socialized to deal with the world correctly from then until they die. Socialization is, instead, a continuous process of relating the self to others and of acquiring the shifting and transitory tools with which to deal with the changing contingencies of life. It is with this understanding that we turn to the socialization of adults.

1. The Stages of Adulthood

As people move through life, profound changes occur as a result of their experiences and relationships. These stages have been documented recently in the work of Roger Gould (1978), who uses age categories as a rough benchmark against which to describe fundamental changes in adulthood.

Ages 16–22. Between these ages, emerging adults are still tied primarily to their parents. Enormous demands are placed on the parents, who are expected to be devoted to their children. Emerging sexuality means that a person must come to grips with the body that is now being repossessed from the parents.

Ages 22–28. Early adulthood is characterized by a movement away from direct dependence on the parents. However, self-identity remains a problematic issue, for most adults during this period are still directed enough by their parents so that excursions away from values and attitudes learned at home often come at a high price in self-esteem.

Ages 28–34. Reaching a certain level of maturity and independence, adults during this period typically try very hard to be the master of their own destinies, often feeling that nothing can shake the hard-won independence of finally being one's own person.

Ages 34–45. Life is now defined increasingly in terms of work, which provides both a sense of power and purpose. For men, marriages are likely to fall victim to careers. Women, having seen their children grow to a level of independence, want to branch out from the confines of the mother role.

These stages are ideal typologies, and not everyone goes through them in exactly the same way. But Gould's research is beginning to add up enough cases to give us a meaningful profile of the changes of adulthood. The point is that the years of being adult are not static at all but a dynamic period of change (Gould, 1978).

These stages are only the beginning of our understanding of adult socialization. Naturally life does not end and change does not terminate at age 45, but the best research we have available has been on these years of adulthood. We will have more to say later about older age groups, and even about how people are socialized for death and dying.

2. Overview

The idea of stages of adulthood gives us a way of talking about adult life in dynamic terms, not as a state but as a process of continual growth and change. It should not surprise us to discover that adulthood is dynamic. We typically notice as we get older that many things decline in importance while other interests and needs become paramount. What we eat and drink, our definitions of beauty and comfort, the meaning we give to money, and the value we place on work, recreation, entertainment, friends, and family all may change as we move through life.

This chapter explores these changes, as well as many other processes that characterize adulthood. Rather than a time when people come to "have it made" (an endearing fantasy of the young), adulthood is best seen as a time when many of the most crucial and far-reaching decisions of life are made, watersheds are reached, and the inevitable decline into old age and death are perceived as imminent realities. These aspects of adulthood lead us to the view that this stage of our lives and the socialization processes that occur within it are as precarious and problematic as those occurring within any other stage of life.

B. THE NATURE OF ADULT SOCIALIZATION

1. The Varying Character of Adult Life

Perhaps the biggest change on entering adulthood is the confusing variety of alternatives that is suddenly available to a person. A separate residence must often be established and a new job or school faced. Instead of the fixed curriculum offered by the high school, college freshmen often face a listing of 3000 to 5000 courses, from which they may select only 40 to 60 for their next four years of schooling. In the world of work there is a choice to be made among more than 30,000 jobs. This sheer variety of choices is often overwhelming. Clarity of perspective becomes submerged in the richness of the view. The need to change the routine, skills, social networks, and orientation of the individual repeatedly throughout adult life constitutes the basis for much adult socialization. Old dogs may not be able to learn new tricks, but human beings *must* be able to.

2. A Give-and-Take Process

a. Reference groups.   Socialization is always a two-way street. The self a person has acquired before becoming an adult must be integrated in some workable fashion with other people's in a given social situation. One of the most important set of others is known in social psychology as the *reference group*. Reference groups are those persons whom an individual utilizes as a frame of reference for his or her behavior. The new lawyer imagines what the men and women of the legal profession expect, and behavior is oriented toward these persons. Taking on and playing to reference groups is an important adult activity.

Reference groups operate in the socialization process in three ways. First, normative groups specify roles, direct attention to them, and set the major bounds for conformity and deviance by defining—always in a given situation—the latitude of variation permitted in the role. Second, the comparison reference group shows how the role is to be played. Third, the audience group responds to a person's specific performance and either applauds or boos one's "act."

These three functions may be carried out by the same person or by different persons (Kemper, 1968, 35). For example, a newly employed secre-

A business office—a normative organization. (Photo by Godrey, Magnum Photos)

tary is usually expected to have good typing skills (unless she works in Washington), regular work habits, a good knowledge of language, the ability to handle correspondence, and so on. These are normative requirements. Other secretaries, either observed or imagined, provide the reference group for comparison with the new secretary's work. Supervisors and others in the office constitute the audience that observes and evaluates the performance.

   b. *Resistance to socialization.*   Because socialization is a two-sided process, persons may resist the attempts of organizations to fit them into a mold. Such patterns of resistance may be highly effective because employees, for example, may form various alliances in their attempt to deal with a socialization system. Howard Becker notes that students in a medical school he studied developed an alliance of their own in which they found ways to reduce the work load and circumvent the teachers (1970, 295). Cadets in a military academy often conspire to hide one another's violations of academy rules from the inspectors, just as government officials in the White House did during the Watergate affair. College students may agree to try to talk a professor out of giving a final examination. Employees may resist the regulations and demands of the work place by concealing one another's failures and oversights. Such examples are living proof that socialization is a two-sided affair, especially for adults.

C. SOCIALIZATION IN THE FAMILY

For adults as well as for children, the family usually is the most important socializing agency. When a married couple begin living together, they must attempt to cooperate in many joint activities without any very complete experience. As Berger and Kellner (1964) have suggested, marriage is essentially the union of two strangers. No matter how long they have known each other before, the couple have never known each other *in the marriage relationship.* Understandings must be reached in terms of their new identities as married persons, and this often involves the liquidation of old friends of the husband and old friends of the wife who now, *because they are not married,* constitute a threat to the new relationship. Instead, new friends who are themselves married are taken on because they are in a unique position to validate the new selves being constructed by the husband and wife.

Many of the changes that adults are called on to make stem from the complex new relationships that are required when a person marries and begins to produce a family. The demands on a person begin with marriage and become increasingly complex as children are born, members of the family die, relatives join the family and live for a while, and divorce or

Marriage is essentially the union of two strangers. (Photo by © Eric Kroll, Taurus Photos)

remarriage occur. Brim suggests that families, like persons, have stages with which socialization is correlated, and these stages are tied to the ages of the members. One must first adjust to a spouse and then to children as infants, later as adolescents, and still later as adults. A new relationship has to be established with the spouse after the children have left home. And finally, the person must learn to live alone or to rebuild life after becoming a widow or widower (Brim, 1968, 205).

The birth of the first child has a heavy impact on the social psychology of most families, especially in the typical case where infant care suddenly becomes the full-time occupation of (usually) the wife. She may have no experience at all with the needs of an infant and is usually quite unprepared for the 24-hour day often associated with the loud and insistent newcomer to the family. If the wife concentrates fully on the care of the baby, her relationship with both her husband and with friends is profoundly altered. Dyer (1963) found that more than half of the mothers in his study saw the birth of their first child as an extensive or severe crisis, promoting enormous changes in their lives. The presence of the child caused an inordinate amount of work, loss of freedom, and fatigue. Little time was left for the husband. Other research has shown that husbands still give very little help with the new baby, leaving most of the work to the wife.

1. Value Socialization

The family is often seen as a cradle of value socialization for children. But it may well be that in the modern world children are more socialized to the values of their peers and that the most important socialization to values occurs in adults. The socialization that does occur seems more *within* generations of the family than between generations. Bengston (1975) studied the distribution of four values in 256 family groups, including adults, children, parents, and grandparents. The four values were (1) humanism, (2) materialism, (3) collectivism, and (4) individualism. Humanist values include service to others, equality, personal ethics, and world peace. Materialist values include money, possessions, attractive appearance, and social recognition. Collective values include religious participation, loyalty, and patriotism. And individual values include skills, excitement, personal freedom, and a sense of accomplishment.

Bengston found an ongoing process of socialization within the family that is bilateral, in that it goes both from parent to child and from child to parent. However, there was more agreement on values within the grandparent, parent, and child generations than there was between generations within the family (Bengston, 1975). The direct parent/child socialization will produce values in the child, but not necessarily those of the parent. The difference between parent and child values comes partly from the social environment and partly from collective relations in peer groups.

2. Peer Socialization

Peers influence adults as much as they do children and adolescents. Modern technological society calls for relatively frequent moves because of changes in job. Each of these changes enhances the role played by peer groups in an adult's decisions.

People we work with contribute to our socialization in various ways. Regular patterns of interaction, relationships with supervisors, systems of rules, and standards of production all involve the giving and receiving of assistance from persons who are at the same level as ourselves. New employees go through a considerable period of informal training that is provided by fellow workers. The new worker gets to know colleagues and comes to count on them for help on the job. The success or failure of a person in the work setting is often directly related to the quality of relationships with peers.

In China, even personal crises are formally decided by a court of peers. Two Chinese workers, a man and his wife, went to court in Peking to secure a divorce. The wife charged that the husband had struck her and that he was unrepentant about his adultery six years before. The judge held a trial at the factory, and the other workers who knew each of them joined in making the decision. The other workers concluded that the divorce should be denied. But they agreed that the husband had erred seriously and that he should repent. Such a situation seems absurd in our culture. And yet frequently a husband and wife rely on informal networks of peers to make a decision on such an important matter as divorce (Lubman, 1973).

A second example of the socializing influence of peers also comes from China. Visiting there in 1975, an American journalist asked a social scientist about the "child-abuse" problem in China. When the Chinese scientist could not understand the question, the American journalist explained that in the United States a small proportion of parents get so enraged that they beat their children severely enough to require hospitalization or, in some cases, severely enough to kill the child. The Chinese scientist was incredulous. He said that he did not think this could happen in China because the neighbors would never allow it. Although such a statement does not settle the question about child abuse in China, it does point to the powerful influence of peers in well-integrated neighborhoods.

D. SOCIALIZATION AT WORK

1. Professional Socialization

Many adults spend a substantial number of years preparing for professional careers. Such preparation usually includes an intensive period of technical training, contact with other professionals in the field, and the attempt to master an elaborate body of knowledge. Professions are different from other lines of work in that there is usually the feeling that a lifelong commitment is being made.

Many professional careers have a certain desperation about them. The training itself is, of course, rigorous. But even after one has achieved a professional credential such as a Ph.D. or medical degree, there is the compulsion to "make one's mark" and the feeling sometimes that, if that mark is not made early, it will not be made at all. Socialization among professionals is also a lifetime process. Continued acceptance in a career depends on sustained performance, and advancement in the field requires increased levels of application and productivity. Two fields that demonstrate the inexorable demands of a continuing socialization process are the academic professional and the professional military person.

a. The academic professional.   Reaching the top in the academic area normally requires from 10 to 20 years of effort after the completion of a four-year college degree. During this period of time, four or five years are needed to complete the requirements for the doctoral degree, but this is only the beginning. Reading, writing, teaching, and research are heavily concentrated within a field of specialization. After a doctoral degree is obtained, research, writing, teaching, and other duties are started at the lowest level, the assistant professor. The scholar may continue in this rank from five to ten years until his or her productivity is thought sufficient to justify advancement to the rank of associate professor. Advancement to the rank of full professor may require another ten years or more, plus a professionally recognized major contribution, such as an invention, theory, or book.

Throughout the grind that constitutes graduate school, socialization processes are at work. For young academicians to get through their education they will have to be caught up in the "mentor syndrome" (Sheehy, 1974, 77), a process in which a person attaches himself or herself to an older (and presumably more recognized) scholar who guides, directs, and legitimates the younger scholar's work. The term "assistant professor" can mean just that; for the assistant professor to rise through the ranks, he or she must show proper deference to the values, attitudes, and conventions of academia as much as the aspiring executive or the bank teller who wishes to someday be vice-president.

b. The professional soldier.   The military professional must also continue education, study, and self-development throughout a career. The officer is minutely evaluated each year by the immediate superior, and the entries on the efficiency report determine in large part whether and when the officer advances in rank or assignment. If the report is negative or shows any other mediocre qualities, the officer is likely to be dismissed from the service. In addition, the socialization process involves acquiring closely controlled standards of personal appearance, including uniforms, grooming, posture, and movement. The daily schedule of the cadet who is just learning the ropes includes an intricate system of social relationships among the various classes of military personnel.

The socialization process in the military academy is deliberately rigorous, and its purpose is either to convert the cadet to acceptance of military values, orientations, behaviors, and technical skills or to get the cadet to withdraw from the academy. The U.S. Coast Guard Academy has lost about 46% of the entering class in the first year of training in recent years. First-year cadets are closely confined to the academy in the early months of training, and they are harshly disciplined by upper classmen (Rootman, 1972). The situation is not very different for cadets at the other academies. Rootman found that the cadets who withdrew from the Coast Guard Academy were influenced to do so when they decided that they could not fit the personal roles demanded by their superiors. If the actual interpersonal fit between cadets and the others in their training section was poor, they were transferred to another section. As the cadets realized that they had a poor fit within the system, they would talk over withdrawing from the academy, both with outsiders and with other cadets. Withdrawal was voluntary, and it was not resisted by academy officers. When the decision was accepted, the withdrawing cadets were isolated from others and relieved of normal duties for the time required to release them from the school. Rootman suggested that similar models of total socialization may apply in religious seminaries, convents, and nursing schools.

2. The Woman's Career

The traditional career for a North American woman is to marry, bear children, and "keep house." The girl's childhood and adolescent years continue to be filled with a stress on the ideals of romance, marriage, maternity, and being a housewife. As the girl grows up, there is increasing emphasis on her need to be sexually attractive.

Neither in an economic nor in a social sense does the home-bound wife have genuine equality with her husband. Weitzman believes that the socialization literature has considerably overestimated the effectiveness of the socialization process in the case of women. If the process were working completely, women would presumably be fulfilled within their role. However, nearly every major study of women's satisfaction has shown that those who conform most closely to the traditional female role are those least fulfilled (Weitzman, 1975, 137). Weitzman's observations demonstrate that socialization is *not* a process that is ever completed, for reassessment of one's role seems to be a continuous process in which a person is making constant modifications, if not of one's behavior at least of the rationales and feelings that support it.

a. Changing definitions of women's roles.   Although we take up the question more exhaustively in Chapter 13, it should be noted here that the feminist movement has been perhaps the most far-reaching socialization agency in the reassessment of women's roles in North American society. The women's movement has socialized by calling into question a whole series of traditional assumptions about the purpose of women's identities in relation to work, family, men, politics, recreation, sexuality, and virtually every other aspect of life.

As with most movements, at first those who argued the precepts of women's liberation were on the defensive. Later it was the traditionalists who had to justify their refusal to validate those same precepts. Many women began to question their status, identity, and behavior. When these doubts arose, other agencies of socialization could be looked to for support. Other women who had undergone the transition from passive housewife to active feminist, magazines such as *Ms.* and *The New Woman*, television programs depicting women in nonstereotyped roles, and even cigarettes ("You've come a long way, baby") all supported and enhanced the questions that had been raised earlier. Voluntary groups such as the National Organization for Women were available to be joined, and political causes such as the equal rights amendment were vehicles through which one's new freedom could be established and sustained. All of these factors show just *how* the socialization process took place, often in adult women who had previously possessed entirely different outlooks on these matters. Suddenly, women were no longer living exclusively in a manmade world.

This is not to say, of course, that countervailing forces were not also at work. Indeed, one of the dilemmas of socialization is that the person must select, out of a multitude of socializing influences, which to incorporate into life and which to ignore. Traditional definitions of what it means to be a woman also have their adherents, and there are avenues of support for women who want to assume traditional roles.

It has been generally assumed in American culture that a wife's primary achievement is to make her husband happy, although he may have more important things to do than make her happy (Greer, 1971, 271). Greer contended that women are loathed, mocked, despised, used, and sexually abused by men. Several years earlier, Maccoby asked whether a woman really needs to be passive and dependent in order to be sexually attractive to men. She noted that the social and economic role of women is necessarily a dependent one during the child-bearing years, but she asked whether our whole definition of femininity should prepare her for this segment of her life as opposed to others (Maccoby, 1963, 36). Here is at least the suggestion that a woman's career could have some content other than reproduction and child rearing.

Another sociologist notes that the mother's working outside the home is voluntary and not obligatory (Bernard, 1975). It is acceptable for a mother to work to *supplement* a father's income, but her job is likely to be any one that fits the family schedule, not a career. It is the husband's job that is important and that is presumed to fix the family's social status. Women may be advised to break their career into three stages, including (1) full-time work right out of school, (2) little or no work while the children are young, and (3) increasing school and work until they are back to a full-time career in middle life (Bird, 1974, 130). This is the traditional approach, and it is a part of women's socialization in that it continues to persuade many women that they must be full-time mothers while their children are in the preschool years. When the mother does resume work, her new job is sandwiched among her other duties. Her husband may continue to assume that his only duty is to perform his job and bring in the primary income.

With respect to a career, the working wife is at a serious disadvantage. First, often she has not expected and has not been trained for a primary career outside the home, and she may well have taken little serious interest in the opportunities available for career training. Second, she may lose six to ten years of experience and career development during the time she is caring for preschool children at home. Third, she may not be able to concentrate on her outside job as readily as a man if she maintains a heavy load of responsibility for home services to her husband and children.

Further, many working women consider themselves as secondary, both as providers of income and as workers on the job. The majority of women have been content to remain in subordinate service positions. Generally, their status as workers has been low, doubtful, and unstable (Cole and Lejeune, 1972). Women may assume that they are entering the job market only temporarily. On that basis they may not seek opportunities for upgrading their skills or be as aggressive as men in seeking advancements in salary and position. The combined effect of late and low-level participation in employment, coupled with job discrimination, is that women average only about 60% as much pay on full-time jobs as men doing the same kind of work. On the job they are likely to defer or be forced to defer both to supervisors and to male workers on matters of pay and promotion.

b. Women in professional careers. Generally, women in professional careers have had to overcome major obstacles to get established. In some cases this has included a struggle with a mother during adolescence. Sometimes, the budding professional woman rebels against the passive image of the "nice girl" who enters dating with a view to marriage and maternity. This rebellion against female dependency can entail an obsessive devotion to technical success, high performance in academic subjects, and often an early choice of profession.

Professor Margaret Hennig (1970) studied the career patterns of 35 high-level women executives in the United States. They were officers of a corporation and supervised male executives and technicians, along with other duties. They had left college with baccalaureate degrees with the aim

The types of occupations available to women have increased dramatically in the last few years. (Photo by © Abigail Heyman, Magnum Photos)

of developing a full career in business. They started at small jobs at $20 or so a week, frequently given by friends of their fathers just to humor them. They dressed plainly and concentrated on the job. They learned the business thoroughly and soon became knowledgeable sources for the solution of operational problems. Many became assistants to promising young executives and followed them up within the corporation. These women executives were careful to avoid personal relations with superiors, subordinates, and co-workers. If an important client suggested sex, it was never "yes" and never "no" but always "maybe." In 30 to 40 years, each of them reached a position at or near the top of the corporation.

They had made it a point always to be fully informed regarding the business. They took special courses when these would be directly helpful to the job. About half of them eventually married, but only past age 35 or 40 to a man well established in the business world and about ten years older. In the early stages of their careers they had to "think like a man, work like a dog, and act like a lady." They were under constant tension and had a feeling of planning every word and act. They had a feeling of having to try hardest in everything, with absolute commitment to one company in a pattern of high-level corporation socialization. In the latter stage of the career they were able to relax and enjoy a sense of well-earned security. However, none of them dared to bring a woman protégée up the career ladder after them. They fought a long, lonely battle and succeeded through giving superior service to their company.

E. GROUP SOCIALIZATION

1. Voluntary Associations

As children and even to a certain extent as adolescents, people have many of their decisions about what organizations to join, what friendships to maintain, and what rules to live under imposed by others. But as adults, people must make these decisions themselves. The choice to join, whether it be a church group, fraternal organization, public-service group, or even deviant subculture, is filled with many contingencies. The issue here is that a person *chooses* to accept, in effect, a type of socialization. This voluntary submission to the socialization process is done because these groups confer status, recognition, and self-esteem.

Some of the more fascinating forms of voluntary association are those that are not publicly approved but nevertheless are joined and do require new forms of socialization. Henshel (1973), for example, studied 25 married women, each of whom was a participant in a swinging sex group consisting of two or more married couples that exchanged partners among themselves. The processes of socialization required to become a member of such a group were clearly revealed in his study. First, the decision to enter was usually the result of an arduous process of negotiation, with the husband usually being the one more insistent on getting into the group. After joining, however, both partners soon learned that swinging gives more sexual gratification to wives than to husbands and that the practice is a more important avenue to sexual freedom for women than for men. Afterward, it was usually up to the wife to try to persuade her husband to stay with the group. In other words, the newcomers to the group socialized each other as well as being socialized by the whole group.

Many things must be learned if one is going to be a swinger. Swingers generally have strict codes of conduct despite their reputation for "anything goes," and the new couple must be socialized to a large array of expectations and understandings about proper conduct while swinging. For example, swinging groups may specify either closed or open swinging. In the former, couples exchange partners and then go to private settings for sexual activities. The latter means that sexual activity takes place openly in front of everyone in the group. Couples are usually expected to swing only when their spouse is also present, and for this reason singles are often not permitted to join. Cleanliness is usually mandated carefully, and a couple may not be invited to more parties if they do not strictly maintain standards. Almost all swingers insist that couples be married. These rules are communicated to newcomers by veterans to the scene who are knowledgeable about the practices, values, and standards of the swinging world (Bartell, 1971).

Homosexuality serves as another example of socialization to voluntary groups. A study by Dank (1974) shows that there is an interval of approximately six years between people's first awareness of sexual preference and their identification of themselves as homosexual. This process of self-identification is socialized in the sense that one's "coming out" into open homosexuality is usually the result of being urged by other homosexuals to attend gay parties and dances and of frequenting gay bars. In addition, magazines and newspapers seem to play a role in the socialization of many "closet" gays to adopt an open stance about their sexual preference. Many of the respondents said they felt relieved and encouraged when they realized that there were so many others like themselves, and they were happy to enter the gay world.

Socialization to the homosexual world continues after the person formally comes out, for other homosexuals increasingly become the point of reference as heterosexual friends fall away after learning that a person is gay. What we can see in the example of homosexuality is that socialization is a process of both "pushing" and "pulling." People's experiences in a new social world both increase their ability to participate in the new scene and simultaneously push them away from older worlds of experience.

2. Total Institutions

Perhaps the most poignant opposite of a voluntary association is the total institution, which is as involuntary as any setting could possibly be. A total institution has been defined as "a place of residence and work where a large number of like-situated individuals, cut off from the wider society for an appreciable period of time, together lead an enclosed, formally administered round of life" (Goffman, 1961a, xiii). Examples of such institutions include prisons, mental hospitals, military academies, and religious cloisters, and many adults spend at least part of their lives in such places. Professional supervisors have authority to control and classify the inmates and to prescribe treatment, work, training, and duty assignments for them. When large numbers of inmates are crowded into an institution, they are likely to be processed as identification numbers rather than as persons and to be treated simply as physical objects by the staff. Whatever the degree of effectiveness of an institution, the inmates do try to find ways to reduce the authority and the control of the professional supervisors.

a. *Prisons.* In U.S. prisons the staff is only moderately effective in maintaining confinement of inmates and is mainly concerned with meeting the legal requirements of recording and housing them and accounting for funds. In some prisons and mental hospitals, where staff turnover may exceed inmate turnover, the organizations are literally run by the inmates (Brim and Wheeler, 1967, 63).

Prison socialization is generally in the hands of the inmates. According to Wheeler, there are three dominant features. First, the normative order opposes the staff and stresses loyalty to inmates. Second, there is informal social ranking that places inmates most hostile to the staff at the top and those most cooperative with prison staff at the bottom. Third, there is a struggle among inmates for power, including control over homosexual relations and drugs. And there is a great deal of physical violence, including the murder of inmates (Wheeler, 1969, 1008). As a result of inmate domination of daily life in the prisons, the resocialization that does occur is mainly in the direction of making the inmate a more dedicated criminal. The person is effectively pressured by the most primitive means into maintaining a close association after he or she leaves prison. The result is that younger prisoners are very likely to continue in crime.

Some of the effects of time spent in prison were carefully measured by an American criminologist, Sandhu, while serving as officer in charge of a prison in the Indian state of Punjab. He found that three months' confinement produced a significant degradation of personality characteristics as measured by the Gough California Personality Inventory. Testing of 200 prisoners indicated an increase in hostility, critical values, and delinquency potential and a decrease in home adjustment and vocational adjustment (Sandhu, 1968, 68, 120). He concluded that counseling and other therapeu-

Prison—a coercive organization. (Photo by © Danny Lyon, Magnum Photos)

tic means could have a favorable effect only if they were given in the early weeks of imprisonment, before the influence of other inmates could alienate the new prisoner. Treatment attempted after three months' imprisonment was very unlikely to have any measurable or observable effect. According to Sandhu, the most helpful effect for the prisoner is his preprison socialization, and this is notably strengthened if the inmate maintains primary contacts with his immediate family (Sandhu, 1974, 142).

Wheeler found important cultural differences in his study of Scandinavian prisoners. There was no violence and very little resistance to prison staff. Prisoners made more reference to life outside prison and generally had little association with other inmates. In Norway only 500 prisoners were serving sentences longer than six months. He believed that the most important element in Norway was a virtual absence of a subculture of violence and antagonism (Wheeler, 1969, 1013). The rate of imprisonment in Norway was 14 per 100,000 population, compared to 116 per 100,000 population in California, where the average sentence served was a little less than two years.

b. Mental hospitals. Goffman has summarized the "moral career of the mental patient" in terms of a perceived betrayal by a close and formerly trusted relative. The patient then proceeds through a series of events that strips away freedom, property, customary routine, and the respect and cooperation that had formerly been received from others (Goffman, 1961a, 124). The prepatient period is marked by lapses of behavior that gradually become so disruptive of conventional social relations that someone such as a supervisor, teacher, physician, or relative decides that the individual must be put under medical treatment. The exact nature of the problem may be unknown both to the victim and to others.

At this point a relative takes responsibility and has the person admitted to a hospital as a psychiatric patient. If the patient resists, the police may be called to assist in the commitment. The patient may believe that he or she has been betrayed and abandoned by a spouse, parent, or child and may temporarily withdraw from all communication. The patient usually has clothing and personal possessions taken away and during the diagnostic period may wear a hospital gown and be confined to a bed in the psychiatric ward. If the psychiatrist decides that treatment in a mental hospital is required, a sanity hearing must be held by the court so that a commitment order can be issued by the judge. The patient then becomes legally incompetent to enter into contracts, vote, write checks, or undertake other responsible acts expected of an adult.

The mental-hospital patient is usually confined first in a locked ward. The ward is often bare and sparsely furnished with simple cots and benches. The inmate has no personal possessions. There is little to do except sit, and the patient may stay alone, silent, and unresponsive when called by name. After a time the patient usually becomes more active, begins to talk to other patients, and begins to cooperate more with the staff. This improvement is rewarded with a transfer to a better ward, where the furnishings are better, games and writing materials may be had, and there is some provision for recreation. If the patient continues to improve in outlook and behavior, a further reward is given by a transfer to an open ward, with the privilege of going out on the hospital grounds or to town, usually in the company of other patients. Improper behavior or refusal to cooperate with the staff is punished by a return to the less favorable wards and by withdrawal of privileges. This system of transferring patients either upwards or downwards in the hospital-ward organization serves to resocialize them in a sort of "social hothouse" (Goffman, 1961a, 163).

Professional staff members interview each patient about once a week after reading through the patient's hospital file. The staff member confronts the patient with the facts of past behavior, which may be ridiculous and embarrassing, in an attempt to break down defenses and rationalizations. When the patient is able to "face reality" and maintain an acceptable pattern of behavior, the responsible relative or spouse may be called to accept custody of the patient for a trial visit home. If the trial visit is successful, the relative may accept permanent responsibility for the patient until the medical authorities decide that the patient has recovered. Then there is a sanity hearing in court, and, if the evidence is adequate as presented by the doctors and by the custodian, the patient may be legally restored to competency.

c. Religious orders.   Most of the major religions provide forms of total institutions in which the members withdraw and devote themselves exclusively to the religious life. These holy orders may be rigidly segregated by sex and are often built in remote areas, where intrusion from the secular world is unlikely. The novice, on entering, usually gives up all personal possessions, including conventional clothing, and his or her secular identity. A new name is conferred, and the novice dresses in the costume of the order. An extremely taxing schedule of devotions, prayers, and services, mixed with various forms of physical and mental labor, begins early and ends late.

The rules of the order often forbid close personal friendships between members as well as any form of personal intimacy. In rejecting worldly pleasures, the order may require simplicity and poverty not only for individual members but also for the order. Because the order must be self-sustaining, the members labor to produce food, clothing, buildings, tools, services, and other requirements. It is not uncommon to forbid personal communication, either during certain periods of time or permanently. The Roman Catholic order of Trappists requires permanent silence and abstinence along with confinement within the monastery. Such an institution represents almost complete resocialization for a very distinctive form of social life.

The reader can see, then, how these seemingly diverse social worlds—prisons, mental hospitals, and religious orders—share a number of similarities when looked at from the vantage point of social psychology. Prisoners and nuns are both socialized. And, though the purpose of the socialization is different, many of the processes are the same. Shutting a person off from the outside world accomplishes many of the same things, even when the reasons for doing it are vastly different. The major advantage of the total institution, at least from the standpoint of its administrators, is that control can be maximized and socialization can therefore be speeded up.

F. SOCIALIZATION IN LATER YEARS

New problems of socialization for adults come when the individual can no longer maintain the adult career pattern because of incapacity or retirement from work. For top management and the self-employed, the time of retirement from work is voluntary and somewhat easier to accept. For middle managers and the working class, it is involuntary and often requires a difficult adjustment (Hochschild, 1975). Retired workers may not realize that they are missing the routine of going to work, the social interaction with workmates, and the familiar burden of contending with supervisors. The sudden sharp reduction of income, made worse by steadily rising prices, may contribute to a sense of dread about the future. The individual may not have identified these specific problems, but they may produce a feeling of frustration and despair that make it difficult to maintain positive social relations with other members of the family. They also call for a redefinition of the individual's position in the family and in the community that the person may resist or try to ignore.

The retired couple may cling to a lifestyle they can no longer support and to social relations that are no longer suitable to their needs and interests. The retired man may find it impossible to understand that he no longer fits in with his old friends at work. The active and alert widow may be astonished and hurt that married friends, so cordial and close before she lost her husband, no longer call or invite her to their gatherings. These are examples of the social-psychological problems of social disengagement that can accompany retirement and aging. The individual has the genuine and often painful problem of learning how to live socially under the new conditions.

Socialization for withdrawal from former roles must include substitution and acceptance of adequate new roles. Otherwise, people's enforced retreat from active participation in society no longer supports approval from themselves or others and leads to frustration (Riley, Foner, Hess, and Toby, 1969).

1. The Nursing Home

Nursing homes are specialized institutions providing for the care of elderly persons who can no longer live at home. In the better maintained nursing homes physical comforts are well provided. Nursing care and medical assistance are available, special diets can be provided as required, and physical therapy is used. A social worker usually conducts recreational and social activities, and clergymen come by to conduct religious services. Lighting, plumbing, and temperature control are generally of high quality. The nursing home gives the impression of being pleasant, comfortable, and socially supportive. However, the patient may find the adjustment quite difficult, even in the well-conducted nursing home, particularly if he or she has led a sheltered life previously.

Such was the case with one widow, who somewhat impulsively turned all her assets over to a nursing home in return for care for the rest of her life (Hughes, 1974). By the terms of the agreement she brought her own bedroom furniture, drapes, a scatter rug, and a few books from her home. After a few weeks she suggested that the nursing home provide a record player, and she secured some records to brighten up the time. But the staff resented the extra work required to clean around her special furniture. They also appeared to resent her making suggestions, which could intrude on the prerogatives of the social worker.

Patients are expected to receive care passively and gratefully. They are not expected to offer suggestions or to take any kind of leading role. Some nursing-home staff members may encourage patients to show initiative, but others are very likely to discourage the patient's participation in any role other than that of an object of treatment. In short, the staff is organized and trained to provide physical care and housing, and it only incidentally faces the need for meeting the individual and social requirements of patients. One of the reasons for this is obviously the role age plays in North American culture generally. In a culture oriented toward the values of production, consumption, wealth, vitality, and the future, the elderly may simply have no clear place. This neglect is often coupled with our tendency to deny death (Becker, 1974). As a result the aged are often shuttled to the side, either because they are not useful in a material, practical way or because they remind younger persons of their own mortality.

The answers to the problems suggested in this discussion of the nursing home are not easy, but our general proposition that socialization be viewed as a lifelong, continuous process seems to offer some suggestions. We usually mark a person's life off in terms of distinctive stages: childhood, adolescence, preparation for work, work, and retirement. It may well be that the general acceptance of this developmental career pattern needs to be challenged. If life were seen more as a continuous whole, the question of what to do with the elderly would cease to exist in its present form. Training people to live their lives rather than simply orienting them toward mak-

Nursing homes are total institutions that care for persons no longer able to care for themselves. (Photo by Abigail Heyman, Magnum Photos)

ing their livings would have the consequence of moving us toward a lifelong place for everyone, not simply for those who are useful or practical in an economic sense. Recent changes that seem to be moving the society away from any type of arbitrary retirement age would seem to be in the general direction we are suggesting.

2. Death and Dying

It may seem ironic to talk of socialization for death and dying. But Elizabeth Kübler-Ross, a Swiss-born doctor, found a serious need to study this social phenomenon, and she has created a new dimension of medical and hospital treatment for it (Kübler-Ross, 1969). If socialization is indeed a lifelong process, then a consideration of how to die and the meaning of death could begin very early in life. We know, for example, that children have conceptions of death. These ideas occur early and in association with quite naturally occurring events such as the death of a pet or the change of seasons (Kübler-Ross, 1975). There is little reason why socialization for death and dying as a necessary part of life could not take place very early. Indeed, we know that such socialization actually does take place, although it typically does so in a very negative way. Children may be barred from the places where death occurs, shielded from discussions of death, or have death euphemized in a variety of ways ("Grandpa is asleep," "Daddy has gone away," and so on). Such strategies teach children that death is a topic not to be discussed. This means that the implications of this highly important human phenomenon must be picked up later in life, often after patterns of denial have already been established.

In addition, death and dying have become increasingly institutionalized. Rather than dying at home, as used to be the case 100 years ago, people now typically die in hospitals or nursing homes, often out of both sight and consideration of those still involved in the routines of everyday life. The primary problem is that the dying patient tends to be rejected and ignored by both doctors and nurses. If the case is hopeless, medical personnel are likely to find other things to do. They may deny that the dying patient is at all capable of responding, experiencing, or even talking, or that any kind of attention might be necessary. The family of the dying patient often alters the pattern of behavior by becoming strained, uncommunicative, tense, and awkward. Most patients realize by these many gross signs, whether they are told or not, that their end is considered certain and possibly very near.

Conditions vary widely, and the patient may realize that the illness is terminal months before the end actually comes. Particularly in the case of many forms of cancer, there is considerable time for the patient to contend with his or her social situation before death. Kübler-Ross studied the problem by conducting a seminar for personnel in the helping professions, including nurses, doctors, social workers, clergymen, and psychologists. She found that dying patients who were still well able to talk were quite willing to be interviewed in front of the seminar. In three years she interviewed more than 200 terminally ill patients. She explicitly discussed with them their approaching death, their feelings about it, and the problems they were encountering with themselves, the medical and service personnel, and their families.

The dying patients were articulate, rational, matter of fact, and socially responsive. Primarily, they wanted to be treated like living human beings, socially as well as physically, while they were still alive. They wanted social exchange that would be normal for other patients, and they were particularly grateful for the opportunity to have serious talks with doctors, nurses, clergy, and members of their families.

At first the hospital staff were resistant and hostile to the seminar. Only one nurse in 12 felt that the dying patient really needed nursing care. In the case of physicians, the more training they had the less willing they were to get involved in such work. The hospital staff exhibited to Kübler-Ross a desperate need to deny the very existence of the dying patient. They seemed not to know how to cope with such a situation and to assume that there was nothing to be done. This compounded the difficult problems of the patient, who keenly felt this abandonment and denial. As a result of the seminars and writings on the subject the helping professions are turning back to the dying patient with better understanding and more sympathy.

Patients go through five basic stages of adjustment on learning that there is a terminal illness. After the initial shock the first stage is denial. Patients refuse to believe what they inwardly know is true. They think of miracles, confused X rays, wrong diagnoses, and other possible escapes. The second stage is anger that such a thing could come to them rather than to someone else who could be "more readily spared." The third stage is depression, in which patients become bitter, hopeless, and despairing. Then there is a stage of bargaining for a little more time and for special concessions. The final stage is acceptance, in a peaceful and positive way. Throughout these stages of adjustment the patients need help, social contact, and professional assistance.

The surprising thing is that one treatment session can relieve the dying patient of a tremendous burden, and a simple, open question can readily elicit the individual's needs (Kübler-Ross, 1969, 270, 276). Finally, the dying patient sinks into a "decathexis," or desensitized period, in which there is simply a need for a human presence, in a "silence that goes beyond words." The time of death is a moment that is neither frightening nor painful but a peaceful cessation of the functioning of the body.

It should be stressed that socialization with the dying patient also includes those immediately responsible, either as members of the helping profession or as members of the patient's family. Death brings a termination of social relations, and all those involved need to learn how to communicate and cooperate among themselves. It makes an impossible situation for the dying patient if others pretend that the condition does not exist. It is deeply insulting to assume that the patient can be left uninformed and not consulted about the expectation of death when everyone else knows about it, particularly when an abrupt change in the behavior of doctors, nurses, social workers, clergymen, family members, and friends makes the facts obvious to anyone. The patient does need help, a continuation of regular care and visitation, and the chance to visit and talk things over. The patient needs the kindly indulgence and assistance of friends and attendants as he or she goes through the social and emotional strain of adjustment to the immediacy of death.

G. SUMMARY

Adult socialization has, until recently, been largely ignored by social psychologists enamored of childhood and operating on the assumption that socialization is a process that ends when a person becomes an adult. However, recent work indicates that all of life is a series of passages, marked by movements from one status and stage to another.

Adult life is perhaps distinguished best by noting its varying character. The adolescent who becomes an adult suddenly finds himself or herself confronted by a bewildering array of alternatives now available.

Much of adult socialization involves coming to grips with life in various kinds of organizational settings, including normative organizations such as a business, utilitarian organizations such as a factory, and coercive organizations such as a prison.

Other people influence adults as much as they do children. By the time a person gets to be an adult, he or she has usually established some kind of "reference group" that guides behavior and acts as a point of contrast. Because socialization is a reciprocal process, people may resist attempts by others to fit them into a mold. Alliances with similarly situated people are also an effective way to deal with socialization attempts, especially within large institutional settings.

Much adult socialization occurs in the context of voluntary associations. Indeed, one of the major differences between being a child and being an adult is the large number of voluntary as opposed to involuntary groups to which a person may choose to belong. Rather than having parents tell the person what groups he or she is going to be a member of, the adult is now in a position to decide independently.

Socialization may also occur in total institutions. Some adults spend at least part of their lives in the confines of prisons, mental hospitals, and other such places where the person is regarded as an inmate and leads a formally administered life. Although these institutions differ in the scope of control, they by no means depart from our general assertion that socialization is a two-sided process. There is much evidence that the inmates of prisons and mental hospitals, for example, do as much to socialize their keepers as vice versa.

The socialization of adults also continues to be very much a socialization to various primary, face-to-face groups. Work, marriage, religion, and family relationships continue to be relatively small settings, and their influence and significance for the person seem if anything to have increased as our society has grown larger.

Adults are also continually socialized to values. Such values as humanism, materialism, collectivism, and individualism show a continuous socialization from childhood through adulthood. Social interaction is a more or less constant stream of value statements, value inculcations, and value socialization from birth to life. If anything, what values they are to be socialized to is a more important question for adults than it is for children.

As a continuous process, socialization can even be seen in old age and death. The preparation for old age begins to occur in the latter stages of adulthood as the realization that retirement from work is a passage in life that signals decline and death as much as continued life (at least in the Western World). The literature on nursing homes similarly supports the idea that socialization processes are at work there, both in terms of how to live in this new surrounding, and also how to die there.

Self and Others

Nothing is judged more carelessly than people's characters, and yet there is nothing about which we should be more cautious. I have always found that the so-called bad people gain when we get to know them more closely, and the good ones lose.

Georg Lichtenberg

The Social Self 6

A. INTRODUCTION

We have seen how a person acquires some of the basic material out of which a life is built. Socialization, from infancy to death, is only a prologue to the actual performances a person gives in relating to others. It is important to understand that there is a difference between learning and acting, between what people know and what they do. Cuzzort (1976) discussed the matter this way:

> It is much too simple to try to account for . . . behavior by saying it is learned. The concept of learning and its related concept of socialization have been popular ideas for handling the problem of why people behave. Simple and apparently obvious though these concepts are, they nonetheless are incapable of dealing with the problem of action. They can help account for *what* has been learned, but they do not necessarily account for the ways in which that learning will be put into action. That is, learning and socialization help account for the form of behavior, but not for the act of behaving itself. One can, for example, learn and know the doctrines of Quakerism or Nazism without being disposed to behave in its terms. Whether an action will be engaged in depends, finally, on an "artful" judgement by the actor, who must evaluate the complexities in a way which is *something more* than a mechanical or machinelike learned response [297 – 298].*

In other words a theory of the self is important in social science because it is the acting organism who links impulse to action, contingency to performance. It is in this context that we want to discuss the somewhat controversial, but nevertheless indispensible, concept of the self.

B. THEORIES OF THE SELF

How the concept of self is handled is one way in which psychology and sociology have contributed differently to an understanding of the person. There has been a long-standing argument between psychologists and

*From *Humanity and Modern Social Thought,* Second Edition, by R. Cuzzort and E. W. King. Copyright 1976 by Holt, Rinehart and Winston, Inc. Reprinted by permission.

sociologists over this matter. Most psychologists prefer the term *personality*, and most sociologists prefer the term *self* (Stone, 1970). The debate has revolved around several orienting issues (Gordon and Gergen, 1968):

1. The self as fact versus the self as construct.
2. The self as subject versus the self as object.
3. The self as structure versus the self as process.
4. The self as single versus the self as multiple.

In general, psychological treatments of self have taken the first position on these issues, and sociological treatments have taken the second. We will discuss each issue briefly.

1. The Self as Fact versus the Self as Construct

Is the self a *thing* located in time and space? Many of those who have written on the self speak of it as an actual fact, a thing located somewhere. The self is assumed to have real-world properties, no different in the final analysis from any other thing available to perception. This mode of thinking has created serious problems in thinking about the self. It has led many social scientists to ignore a large number of human phenomena that are not open to such a literal interpretation.

The other side on this issue views the self as a hypothetical construction of human beings who believe sincerely in their own constructions. The self in this sense is real in the same sense that Santa Claus is real at Christmas time. The reality of the self in this view lies not in its location in time and space but in the fact that human beings act *as if* there were a self located inside themselves and inside others.

2. The Self as Subject versus the Self as Object

What do we experience when we experience the self? Psychologists, as well as ordinary folk, often think of the self as a subject, or a *subjective thing*. The problem, of course, is that even the act of thinking about the self in this way transforms it into an object, thereby removing its subjective qualities. Descartes (1596–1650), the founder of modern psychology, set the stage for thinking about the self as a subjective phenomenon with his famous statement "I think, therefore I am." If the self is truly subjective, then of course it transcends the possibility of ever getting at it or giving it a location. The problem of locating the subjective self has been ruminated over by Bierstedt:

> If I do not know what I am, can I not at least say where I am? This too is difficult. I think that I am somewhere behind my eyes—at least I have the impression that I look through them when I see—but now that I have put the words down on paper the notion seems a bit ridiculous. I know the eyes are mine (the left one, for example, has been nearsighted for years), but now I am confused again about what the "mine" might refer to. Modern surgical tech-

niques could transfer them to someone else. But nothing could transfer the I that now owns them to someone else, and if it could be done then I would probably no longer be me but rather someone else. . . .

I think it is time to stop this speculation about me. You have the same problem too, or at least I think you do. What are you, anyway? I don't mean what is your name, what is your street address, what is the color of your hair, or whether you are tall or short or fat or thin. I mean, who are you? Do you also have an I that baffles you when you try to explain your being to your self? Have you ever been tempted to think that you might have had another body than the one you have, say a body of a different color or a different age? Isn't it curious, when you stop to think about it, that you are you today and that there has never been another you in any period of history? How strange that you should be you, and I I, and that there is no confusion of identities between us. Suppose the arrangements of life and consciousness and existence were such that when we became dissatisfied with our body we could thrust ourselves into another and then continue both to be ourselves and to have ourselves permanently, through all of future time? Would we then be able to know more about this ineffable self that refers to itself as I? [1970, 185–186].*

Such thinking about the self is fascinating but in the end a bit nonsensical. A self that is no more than a subject cannot be named, held, talked about, or even thought of except subjectively! The subjective self is mine, or yours, and that is all we can say. It is like Kafka's Castle, heavily fortified but by parties unknown. As soon as we begin talking or thinking about it, it loses its private dimensions and becomes an object in our experience, and the terms belong to a public universe of discourse, not a private one.

In contrast, sociologists have generally taken the position that the self arises as an object in our social experience. The self is not a subject in us when we are born but a social object that develops or emerges out of our interaction with others (Mead, 1932).

3. The Self as Structure versus the Self as Process

In keeping with the implications of the two preceding controversies, there is a debate in social psychology centering on the view of self as structure. Psychologists from Descartes to Skinner have used a structural model of human beings that is mechanical in nature. The self is viewed as a system of mechanical parts with psychological processes as outcomes of the workings of the parts. (The reader has undoubtedly seen cartoons of a human head composed of cogs, gears, chains, and pulleys.) Psychoanalytic theories of the self, rooted in the ideas of Sigmund Freud, see the ego as an organization or structure that mediates the behavior of the acting organism.

A different way of looking at the self emphasizes process over structure. In this view the self is a certain type of process or series of relation-

---

*This and all other quotations from this source are from *The Social Order*, Third Edition, by R. Bierstedt. Copyright 1970 by McGraw-Hill, Inc. Reprinted by permission.

ships that occurs when human beings interact, not a structural entity located anywhere in the organism (Mead, 1934). In this sense the self is like a moving stream. The whole is seen, rather than the parts, and change is stressed over permanence.

4. The Self as Single versus the Self as Multiple

The final issue is whether *self* is a singular or plural concept. Do we have basically one self, which organizes and directs our behavior? Or is a person many different selves in the course of a lifetime? The question usually arises in an effort to deal with two disparate but fundamental observations about human beings. First, there is a certain stability to a person's life that seems to require a single-self concept to explain it. We experience ourselves often as containing a unity even though we do many different things and play many different parts during the course of our lives. The self in this sense is seen as a unity or at least as an organizer of the many experiences that come through it.

Second, the literature of social psychology is replete with observations and research that imply that the self is multiple in character—that there are many selves that vary considerably in their influence during the course of a lifetime or even during a single day (James, 1890; Sullivan, 1953; Goffman, 1959). This view is bolstered by the observation that a person's behavior is not only highly variable from one situation to another but is at times even inconsistent (Deutscher, 1973). Are we the same person at 2 that we are at 65? Are we the same person in church that we are in a dance hall on Saturday night? Are we the same with ourselves as we are with others? These fascinating questions tend to lead to the observation that, even though we experience a certain unity at times, we also experience and see enormous transformation occurring during the course of our lives.

The problem of single versus multiple selves helps us to clarify some of the implications of the three disagreements discussed earlier. To determine whether there is a single self or multiple ones, one must be able to decide whether different expressions of the self are *the same* or *different*. Each of these controversies revolves around this distinction. It may very well be that the controversies about the self we have cited are actually ways of disagreeing about the same thing. Is human behavior to be viewed as a series of structures acting on each other, or is it to be viewed as an emergent process? Can permanence and change be handled in the same conceptual framework?

As we have indicated, sociology and psychology are generally distinguishable on the basis of how they handle these four issues. Psychology most often sees the self as a fact, as a subject, as a structure, and as basically singular. Sociologically oriented social psychologists are more likely to view the self as construct, as object, as process, and as multiple. These issues are all embedded in the work of several influential theorists, to whose work we now turn.

C. THEORISTS OF THE SELF

1. George Herbert Mead

The common-sense view of the self is usually the psychological one. Much of the time, when we think of the self, we think of it as an antecedent to action. That is, a person has a self first, and that self directs the person's behavior. This common-sense view seems logical, but George Herbert Mead (1863–1931) disagreed with it strenuously. Mead was a philosopher at the University of Chicago in the early 1900s. He taught a course on social psychology that came to have so much influence that his students collected his lectures and published them in book form after his death (Strauss, 1964). In these lectures Mead asserted that previous theories of the self were inadequate because they needed a self to get the process of behavior started. Thus, the self was assumed rather than explained. Mead sought instead to demonstrate how selves arise in the course of behavior (Desmonde, 1970). Children are not born with selves but develop them later in interaction with others, he contended. This process in which selves arise in social relationships occurs in the context of three sequential stages, which Mead termed *play, game,* and *the generalized other.*

a. Play.   Since the self is not literally a thing, but rather a relationship between the individual and others, the only way a child can acquire an understanding of the self is to take the role of another person. After an initial series of meaningless imitations, according to Mead, the first stage in the development of the self is spontaneous play. In play the child is unable to take more than one role at a time. Mead likened this to playing hide-and-go-seek. The child tries to play his or her role by taking on the role of one specific other person (the one who is "it" or the person who is not "it"). The child then "hides" or "seeks" in terms of where he or she might be hiding or seeking *if he or she were the other person.* In play, then, the role of one specific other is taken on, and things are seen from the standpoint of that one other person. Mead saw the development of this ability to take the role of another as a crucial skill in acquiring a self that can be shared, related, and communicated to others.

b. Game.   The second stage in the development of self Mead likened to a game. The person still acquires a sense of self from others, but the surroundings and circumstances are more complicated. In a game the person has to play his or her role in contrast not to just one other role but to a whole series of roles. Baseball is different from hide-and-go-seek. A catcher who does not know what the other members of the team are doing cannot play his or her own role correctly. *Games require the ability to coordinate several roles and relate them to the one you are playing.* The child, then, begins to relate a single role to a whole series of other roles in the context of whatever it is that is going on.

In play, the role of a specific other is taken on. (Photo by © Bruce Davidson, Magnum Photos)

c. *The generalized other.* The final stage of self-development involves what Mead called the generalized other. Mead notes that a person acquires a self in contrast not only to a single role and to multiple roles but also to a kind of general role in, let's say, a whole community. This generalized other can be very important to one's sense of self. The concept of *Southerner,* for example, is a very significant symbol that suggests far more than a simple geographical location. It implies a general set of others that a person can use as a reference point—either positively or negatively—in defining the self.

As we can now see, the self develops in society rather than existing previously. In each of Mead's phases the child is progressively better able to differentiate self from other. In the play stage only one role formed the reference point for the self. In the game stage several roles provided this reference. And in the generalized-other stage a whole constellation of others provided the vantage point from which to define the self. Mead, then, saw the self as always a social artifact, an outcome of the interactions and relationships one has with others.

d. *I and me.* Mead spoke of the phases of action through which the self emerges as the *I* and the *me.* The I is spontaneous, undefined, subjective, and personal; it is that phase of people's existence that they often speak of as "having" and that they jealously guard from the intrusion of others. The I, simply put, is the process of action. The me, however, emerges out of the appraisals that others make of oneself. One has a me only by virtue of interaction with others, and it is the me that is by far the most important self or series of selves that a person experiences in the course of many social careers. The subjective nature of the "I," however, keeps the self from being totally determined. We cannot be absolutely sure of the outcome of any social encounter, in large measure because of the I.

As phases of social action, the I and me relate to each other in interaction. A me is an I that used to be. And the I is not a thing at all, but a capacity the organism has for seeing itself as an object of its own experience, of defining itself from the standpoint of others. The I is formulator, the me formulated (Stone and Farberman, 1970). Mead's view of the self can be summarized in the following quotation from *Mind, Self, and Society:*

> It is impossible to conceive of a self arising outside of social experience. When it has arisen we can think of a person in solitary confinement for the rest of his life, but who still has himself as a companion, and is able to think and to converse with himself as he had communicated with others [1932, 140].

e. *Language as the mechanism for self-development.* Language provides the mechanism by which selves emerge, Mead argued. The concepts of *I* and *me,* although they seem vague, in fact point to very precise linguistic actions. Children's self-development can be traced directly to their ability to manipulate these two phrases. And it is consistent with Mead's theory of the self that children refer to the self as a me before referring to it as an I. In other words the concept of oneself as object arises prior to the conception of oneself as subject.

Language is also important because it demonstrates preeminently how the self is social. Language clearly belongs to a public and social world, not to a private, psychological one (Wittgenstein, 1958). In this sense language and society precede the individual and provide the material from which the self develops. Children learn about themselves by seeing and relating with other selves, and the tools through which this development takes place are largely linguistic.

2. William James

William James (1842–1910) was one of the most important and wide-ranging thinkers in history. He came from perhaps the most intellectually productive family ever known. His father was a jurist of some reknown, and his brother, Henry, was an important literary figure. William James made important contributions in three fields: psychology, religion, and philosophy.

James's writings on the self in his monumental *Principles of Psychology* (1890) formed the basis for many of the social ideas about the self that developed afterward. He actually was the first to make reference to the aforementioned concepts of the *I* and the *me*. The stream of consciousness that we call the self is both known and knower, partly object and partly subject. James called these aspects the me and the I and then discussed the me as being of three types.

The *material me* is composed of all the "things" that people claim, such as bodies, clothes, houses, cars—indeed everything within the category of personal possessions. It is important to see just how much of what we call the self is in fact composed of such things. To see what happens to a person whose dearly beloved sports car is demolished in a traffic accident, even if he or she emerges uninjured, is to see the significance that material objects have for our sense of self. Children are known to cry, indeed even mourn, the loss of a favorite doll or toy. The body itself is well known as a depository for the self, and this is one reason why a mastectomy performed on a woman is such a trauma—part of the self has been cut away (Quint, 1963). Without material objects the self would be impoverished indeed, and it was James who first noted this significant fact and related it to a social-psychological understanding of the person.

Next comes what James referred to as the *social me*, or social self. This is the recognition one gets from others. James put the case this way and we might note his clear alliance with the view of self as multiple:

> Properly speaking, a man has as many social selves as there are individuals who recognize him and carry an image of him in their mind. To wound any

one of these images is to wound him. But as the individuals who carry the images fall naturally into classes, we may practically say that he has as many different social selves as there are distinct groups of persons about whose opinion he cares. He generally shows a different side of himself to each of these different groups. Many a youth who is demure enough before his parents and teachers, swears and swaggers like a pirate among his "tough" young friends. We do not show ourselves to our children as to our club companions, to our customers as to the laborers we employ, to our own masters and employers as to our intimate friends. From this there results what practically is a division of the man into several selves; and this may be a discordant splitting, as where one is afraid to let one set of his acquaintances know him as he is elsewhere; or it may be a perfectly harmonious division of labor, as where one is tender to his children and stern to the soldiers or prisoners under his command [1890, 294].

Indeed, Hitler, the monster of our age, is said to have been gentle, sensitive, loving, and undemanding when in the presence of his personal secretary (Speer, 1970).

A good example of a social me is the image held about you by somebody you love. Love, with all of its emotional investment, also involves an investment of the self. And when that self is not held in high esteem, the impact on the person may be enormous. Further research on self-esteem and the importance of reference groups (Cohen, 1959; Hyman, 1942; Kemper, 1968) can be traced directly to James's pioneering work. Self-esteem is influenced positively or negatively only if the I cares about the me under consideration. As James personally pointed out:

> I, who for the time has staked my all on being a psychologist, am mortified if others know much more psychology than I. But I am content to wallow in the grossest ignorance of Greek. My deficiencies there give me no personal humiliation at all. Had I pretensions to be a linguist, it would have been just the reverse. So we have the paradox of a man shamed to death because he is only the second best pugilist or the second best oarsman in the world. That he is able to beat the whole population of the globe minus one is nothing; he has "pitted" himself to beat that one; and as long as he doesn't do that, nothing else counts. He is to his own regard as if he were not, indeed, he *is* not [1890, 310].

Finally, James recognizes a *spiritual me*, which is a collection of one's stages of consciousness and psychic faculties. This is the vaguest and least sociologically satisfying of the three mes. But his discussion of the spiritual me does point to one of the most important contributions James made to theories of the self: his reconceptualization of *consciousness* as a process. What we call *states of mind* are merely momentary incidents in a process. By considering consciousness as a process and not as a structure in the brain, James opened up new vistas for studying the self.

3. Charles Horton Cooley

Charles Horton Cooley (1864–1929) was an early American social psychologist, a contemporary of both Mead and James who made significant contributions to a sociological view of the self. We discussed his interactionist assumptions in the first chapter, and now we turn to his ideas about the self.

Cooley, in a series of books on self and society (1899, 1902, 1918), argued against the classic dualism of individual and society. As we have already indicated, to Cooley they were "twin-born"—one does not exist without the other. "The imaginations people have of each other," said Cooley, "are the solid facts of society." Furthermore, "society exists in my mind as the contract and reciprocal influence of certain ideas named 'I,' Thomas, Henry, Susan, Bridget, and so on. It exists in your mind as a similar group, and so on in every mind" (1902, 84).

Cooley likened the self to a "looking glass," arising reflectively out of the reactions and opinions of others. It has, as we have previously stated, three elements: (1) the imagination of our appearance to the other person, (2) the imagination of the other's judgment of that appearance, and (3) some sort of feeling about it, such as being proud or being horrified. In Cooley's sense, "I am not what I think I am. I am not what you think I am. I am what I think you think I am."

This formulation is a restatement of James's idea of the social self, but Cooley went beyond the "looking-glass self" to develop a general theory of society based on the smallest kinds of social-psychological relations (Martindale, 1960). As self emerges in a process going on between the person and others, the first group arising in and out of that relationship is what Cooley spoke of as the "primary group." Primary groups are "characterized by intimate face-to-face association and cooperation" (Cooley, 1909). Examples include the family, the work group, a coffee klatch, and even two lovers by the lake. The primary group is not only the first association the human being forms but also the most lasting. For no matter how complex, institutionalized, and bureaucratized one's associations become, there always exist primary groups that sustain and develop a more personal sense of self. It is appropriate, then, that Bierstedt (1970) speaks of the primary group as the most indestructible of all human groups.

D. THE SELF-CONCEPT

Much of the research generated by the idea of self has been directed at the conceptions people hold of themselves. The idea has been that, in order to understand people's behavior, it is necessary to know something of what they think of themselves. Much of this research has been stimulated by the pioneering work of Manford H. Kuhn and his associates at the University of

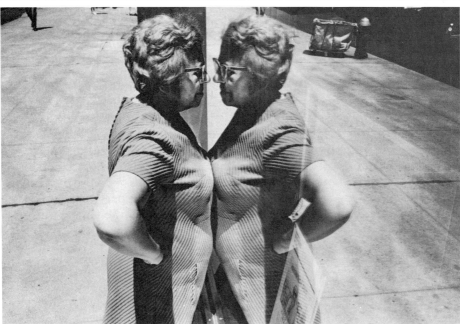

Cooley likened the self to a looking glass that reflects the reactions and opinions of others. (Photos by © Susan Meiselas, Magnum Photos, and © Richard Kalvar, Magnum Photos)

Iowa, who developed an instrument designed to measure self-conceptions. The instrument, called the Twenty-Statements Test, consists of answers to the question "Who Am I?" asked 20 times. The answers a person gives on the test constitute, in the order they are given, the person's key self-conceptions. This procedure "operationalizes" the self, defining it in terms of a series of procedures by which the researcher defines the self (Kuhn and McPartland, 1954).

Not surprisingly, answers to the question "Who Am I?" cluster around important social identities. Examples include "student," "girl," "husband," "Baptist," "daughter," "oldest child," "happy," "bored," "good wife," and so on.

Self-conception theory wants to know just how the behavior of an individual is consistent and stable. What are the reference points people use in defining themselves? How is behavior consistent from situation to situation? How do people go about organizing conduct? These questions inevitably lead to some such ideas as self-conception. Because these are difficult questions, not all social scientists have been willing to take them up. To Shibutani, this reluctance to tackle the questions associated with the study of the self is regrettable:

> To be sure, the study of what a person experiences as himself is difficult, but it is paradoxical that . . . scholars in their capacity as investigators should ignore such phenomena, when in their daily lives they are never so foolish. If a psychologist were confronted by a powerful drunk who insisted that he could "lick anybody in the house," he probably would not challenge the contention by claiming that self-images cannot be measured with precision. Should he go home and find his wife in the arms of a strange man who insisted he was her husband, it is unlikely that he would shrug his shoulders and say that personal identity has never been demonstrated to be important. Many of the difficulties in the study of these phenomena begin when a search is made for some physical object located somewhere in the body, when the concepts of self-image and self-conception refer to complex forms of behavior. Each person can imagine what he has done, what he is doing, what he is able to do, or what he proposes to do and can respond to his own imagination. These concepts refer, then, not to some part of the human body, but to uniformities in behavior [1971, 216].*

1. Origins of Self-Concepts

Research on the origins of self-concepts has consistently indicated that they arise in our interactions with others. Whether we see ourselves as good, bad, fat, thin, intelligent, stupid, capable, or incompetent; or whether we are self-assured, self-doubting, self-loving, or self-hating depends very much on the development of these ideas out of direct and continuous associations with others.

*This and all other quotations from this source are from *Society and Personality*, by T. Shibutani. Copyright 1971 by Prentice-Hall, Inc. Reprinted by permission.

Miyamoto and Dornbusch (1956) tested the idea of self-conceptions. They concluded that the response of others is indeed related to self-conception, and they also found support for some of Cooley's earlier ideas that a person's self-conception is even more closely related to his or her own perceptions of others' responses. As far as self-concepts are concerned, we seem to be not actually what others think we are but what we think others think we are, just as Cooley suggested.

Although our self-concepts clearly have their origins in the responses of others, it is not always easy to say just where people have got the particular conception of self that they have. The recent notoriety of transsexuals has pointed out a number of intriguing ideas about self-conceptions. Most of us obtain our original sexual identity from the responses that parents, friends, and peers make toward us. We label baby boys with blue ribbons and baby girls with pink ones even before they have left the hospital. People respond to them in terms of these basic human identities, and most children dutifully come to see themselves in the same terms. However, reports from transsexuals indicate that this response of others can be rejected, the person coming to feel self as being the opposite sex from the one imputed both by nature and by others (Morris, 1975). The celebrated transsexual tennis star, Renée Richards, claims to have vivid memories of herself as really being a girl even at the age of 4 (Kopkind, 1976). The arbitrariness and social origin of sexual self-conceptions can clearly be seen, and the question of what sexual identity really is increasingly comes to be answerable only in consensual, social terms.

2. Self-Esteem

The basic questions of identity, as we have seen, are answered by others. Similarly, how we *feel* about ourselves—that is, our level of *self-esteem*—arises also out of our interpersonal behavior. While self-concepts refer to our image of ourselves, self-esteem speaks to Cooley's third criterion in the looking-glass idea, how we feel about that image.

Self-esteem is crucial in our attempt to understand human behavior. In one way or another human beings tend to organize their lives around ways to enhance their feelings about themselves. Ernest Becker suggested the concept of an "inner newsreel" to get at the process by which people review the symbols that give self-esteem and make them feel important and good. "We are constantly testing and rehearsing whether we *really* are somebody, in a scenario where the most minor events are recorded, and the most subtle gradations assume an immense importance" (Becker, 1962, 68).

Naturally, people attain self-esteem by performing the roles that a particular society provides: doctor, lawyer, teacher, business executive, engineer, and so on. These tangible and widely held criteria of success are the benchmarks against which we measure our sense of worth. To lose a job, then, can be a shattering experience. One realizes that the work was more than a way of making money and supporting oneself; it was, from the standpoint of self-esteem, at least, life itself. "Almost all of one's inner life, when he is not absorbed in some active task, is a traffic in images of self-worth" (Becker, 1962, 68).

If the means by which a person attains a feeling of self-worth are created in society by playing social roles, it is not surprising that women and men, occupying as they do different roles in virtually all societies, attain their sense of worth from different things. For a man, the loss of a job, retirement, or some other occupationally related change of situation may be accompanied by a diminishment of his sense of value. For a woman, however, the loss of a role connected with the home may have greater impact. Thus, we note that, when a woman's children leave home, when the process of maternal loss symbolized by the onset of menopause takes place, or when some other kind of role loss occurs that reminds a person of just how much of herself was wrapped up in a set of relationships, depression and a diminished sense of worth often result (Henry, 1973). Here the relevance of Cooley's formulations can be seen clearly, for his work anticipated the increasingly recognized fact that women suffer from too narrow a definition of roles connected with the home and that men suffer equally from the narrowness of the roles they play and the self-conceptions they have.

E. ERVING GOFFMAN AND THE DRAMATURGICAL SELF

The early social psychologists we have discussed in this chapter—Mead, Cooley, and James—as well as many we have not spoken directly of—Freud, Sullivan, Erickson, and Fromm—have all in some sense pointed to the basic property of the self: it is a social production. People are dependent on one another for their identities. In this sense people make a pact with society in the creation and preservation of the self.

Much of social psychology has failed to recognize, however, that the process of building up human identities is a continuous and lifelong process that can be seen in every single social encounter in which people participate. Human actors must create and maintain a self each time they come into contact with one another. This awareness of the fragile, staged nature of the self has been captured nicely in the work of a contemporary social psychologist, Erving Goffman.

Goffman, in a major work entitled *The Presentation of Self in Everyday Life* (1959), used the metaphor of the theater to express the process by which selves arise, live, and may die in everyday life. In this *dramaturgical perspective* the self is seen as a staged production, a series of masks that people present to audiences of various kinds who review their performances. The self is the result of this interaction between actor and audience. Rather than being tied to a given personality, it is a continuously shared, interactive phenomenon. The dramaturgical dimensions of the self were first described by Park:

It is probably no mere historical accident that the word person, in its first meaning, is ... mask. It is rather a recognition of the fact that everyone is always and everywhere, more or less consciously, playing a role.... It is in these roles that we know each other; it is in these roles that we know ourselves [1950, 249].

1. The Self As Image

We will recall Cooley's idea that "the imaginations people have of each other are the solid facts of society" (1902, 84). In Goffman's dramaturgy this idea is taken quite literally. What we know of another person we know as an image that he or she has presented to us. When people enter one another's presence, they have many reasons to present, have validated, and maintain a certain image of themselves. They do this, according to Goffman, by establishing an *impression*. This is done by manipulating two types of *expressions: expressions given* and *expressions given off*. Expressions given are speech—communication in the traditional sense of the word. Expressions given off are an entire range of communications that have little or nothing to do with words: facial expressions, gestures, hair style, clothing, tone of voice. Through a person's use of both verbal and nonverbal expressions, audiences (others) come to hold an image about him or her.

2. Impression Management

Viewing the self as a performed character means that the self a person has in any situation will be the product of an interaction between the performance he or she is giving and the response the audience makes to it.The self as a dramaturgical production is nicely described by Goffman in the conclusion to his book:

In this report the performed self was seen as some kind of image, usually creditable, which the individual on stage and in character effectively attempts to induce others to hold in regard to him.While this image is entertained *concerning* the individual, so that a self is imputed to him, this self itself does not derive from its possessor, but from the whole scene of his action.... A correctly staged and performed scene leads the audience to impute a self to a performed character, but this imputation—this self—is a *product* of a scene that comes off, and is not a *cause* of it [1959, 252].

Since the self is an image established socially in the presence of crucial audiences, it is obviously open to considerable manipulation. In Cooley's looking-glass self we attempt to control impressions by a judicious and detailed attention to appearances. This attempt by the actor to control the impression that others come to have of him or her is referred to by Goffman as *impression management*.

3. Appearance and the Self

In Goffman, the self appears the way a character in a play appears. The image an audience comes to hold will depend on what it sees. The self, then, is established in appearances. And in the dramaturgical sense, appearance constitutes reality because audiences can act only on what is placed before them. Actors, recognizing this, establish a self before others primarily by controlling how they appear before those others.

The most careful dramaturgical analysis of the self has been conducted by Gregory Stone (1962). Stone asserted that the process of identifying someone as a self typically involves two related processes: (1) identification *of* and (2) identification *with*. Identification with a person was previously discussed in our treatment of role taking. We identify with a person by taking their role. Thus, children acquire a sense of the roles of mother and father by taking these roles and by seeing themselves in their terms. Identification *of* another person, however, necessarily precedes identification with them, for it is necessary to know *who* a person is before we can possibly take their role, thus identifying with them.

A major means of identifying persons, Stone noted, is by looking at their clothing. Clothes (Goffman might say costumes) are a major means by which people come to see themselves and others as distinctive selves. Sexual identities, for example, are almost always established by appearing in female or male dress. Our previous discussion of transsexuals demonstrated just how easy it is for biological males to be taken socially for females simply by being in control of how they appear. Clothing virtually constitutes our "second skin" (Horn, 1975). And advertising constantly alerts people to the ritual significance of clothing in social relationships ("Clothes make the man").

Stone also noted that in worlds of work a change in title typically demands a change of dress. Respondents in his study were presented with the following story:

> John had an excellent record as foreman in an automobile factory. Eventually, he and two other foremen were promoted to the position of division head. John was happy to get the job, because of the increase in pay. However, he continued to wear his old foreman's vest and work clothes to the office. This went on for several months until the division heads he had been promoted with began to avoid him at lunch and various social gatherings. They had dressed from the beginning in business suits and had mingled more and more with older managerial employees. John found himself without friends in the office [Stone, 1962, 95–96].

When asked "What finally happened to John?" about 80% of the people interviewed in Stone's study predicted dismissal, demotion, or, at the very least, no further promotion. One informant quite seriously suggested that

John was a potential suicide! In common-sense terms it would seem ridiculous that a person might commit suicide because of a clothing decision. And yet a careful understanding of the social psychology of the self begins to point to its being built up out of just such seemingly trivial material. To lose a self is to lose certain responses that are mobilized toward a person, and these responses of others are predicated on just such appearances as those provided by clothes.

If the social psychology of clothing sounds trivial, one might examine the case of trials in courtrooms. Surely judges, jurors, and attorneys know better. But the following news story shows differently:

Attorney D.C. Thomas took one look at his client and knew he was in big trouble.

He had told her to "dress dignified" for her day in court. . . . But here it was 15 minutes before court was to begin, and she was standing there in mini-skirt and low-cut blouse that "left little to the imagination." "I just nearly fainted. . . . I almost had a heart attack," Thomas recalls.

There was no way Thomas—or any other attorney—was going to let her appear before a jury in that sexy get-up, so he sent her home to change clothes. She returned a while later wearing a far more "dignified" skirt and jacket. . . .

Philosophers say clothes don't make the man, but just try convincing an attorney whose client or chief witness is about to make an appearance before a jury.

Attorneys representing defendants in damage suits advise their clients not to wear flashy, expensive clothing or jewelry in order to present a simple and not well-to-do image.

Attractive women, like the one in Thomas' story, are told to "dress down" in an effort to present an appearance more likely to meet with the approval of envious female jurors. . . .

Young male defendants sporting long hair or beards are sometimes actually marched to the barber shop by their attorneys to make them more presentable to middle-aged and older male jurors. . . .

[Attorney Bill] Berry said he advises both his clients and their witnesses "to dress in a manner in keeping with their station in society."

That means . . . that a truck driver should wear khakis and a shirt, a banker should look like a banker, and a housewife should look like a housewife.*

Furthermore, it may be noted that those factors that qualify a presentation of self—such as values, moods, attitudes, and identities—are themselves established in appearances. The kind of self we have in a social relationship is dependent on a set of appearances presented by the actor (Stone calls this a "program of appearance") and also the response that others make to this program (the audience's "review of appearance"). In other words, we show our values by our appearance and at the same time

*From *The Daily Oklahoman,* October 11, 1976. Reprinted by permission.

are appraised by others in terms of them. The priest's collar shows a whole system of religious values. Moods are expressed, and hopefully are appreciated by audiences. When we see a group of people crying, we are not likely to try out a new practical joke on them. *Their* mood might not allow them to *appreciate* the joke. Finally, we propose our attitudes and announce our identities through appearances, which others then use to anticipate our future behavior.

This scheme gives us a wholly distinctive and quite sociological way of viewing the self. Selves are products and presentations that the conscious organism presents to others, *whose responses are indispensible to the creation of a socially viable self.*

4. Dramaturgical Teams

The self as a set of performances that an actor gives to others who review them still suggests a kind of solitary individual presenting the self to a single audience. This two-way model is itself too limited to permit an understanding of the many situations in which people act in everyday life. Goffman notes that our selves are very often acted out as members of teams—that is, two or more persons who cooperate in staging a performance.

For example, when husbands and wives appear before others, they usually present themselves as virtually three different selves simultaneously. They first want others to hold an impression of them as a couple, a married team that possesses a collective and shared identity. In fact, we often refer to couples as the Smiths or the McDougals. Then there are the separate identities, Susan and Jim. But they are not really separate, because each of the marital partners may act to shore up and support the individual self presented by the other. The wife may show more deference, respect, and subordination to her husband in public than she would ever think of showing him when they are by themselves. Similarly, the husband may support his wife's presentations of her skill as a housewife, club member, or even fellow professional in ways that he might not do when they are with each other alone. Marriage and other kinds of sexual alliances represent the merger of individuals into a team of players who will have an interest in protecting and supporting the selves of their teammates.

How do teammates support each other's presentations of self? Goffman points to three important defensive attributes and practices engaged in by members of dramaturgical teams: (1) dramaturgical loyalty, (2) dramaturgical discipline, and (3) dramaturgical circumspection.

a. *Dramaturgical loyalty.* Teams are established when dramaturgical loyalty is given. We tend to accept as members of a team persons who we have come to believe will contribute to the performance we are giving to others. Conversely, we tend to reject as teammates persons who might give the show away. Wives, husbands, friends, workmates, and even members of our same sex, age, or racial or religious group may effectively aid us in the performances we are giving to others.

In contrast, children tend to be notoriously bad teammates. A child has not yet acquired the defensive practices and symbolic intricacies of social life. Adults are therefore likely to exclude a younger child from certain conversations, because one can never be sure to whom the child will communicate the secrets of the team.

b. *Dramaturgical discipline.* Teammates who are assisting in the giving of a show will have to exercise some control and discipline in the part they are playing. Embarrassment occurs when people communicate out of character—that is, when they communicate things that are discrepant with the role they are supposed to be performing. If the surgeon stops in the middle of a delicate operation, takes off his or her gloves, and begins reading a comic book, all parties to the operation are likely to experience the most acute embarrassment over the failure of the actor to exercise the kind of discipline and control ordinarily associated with the role of surgeon.

c. *Dramaturgical circumspection.* A great deal of care must be exercised when a performance is being given. There are many ways in which a show can be given away, thereby destroying the selves that had been so painstakingly built up. Dramaturgical circumspection simply means the exercise of this care. Teammates, for example, often find it necessary to "keep up appearances" when others are present. Goffman notes that on Pacific islands during World War II surprise military inspections by U.S. officers were not very likely to occur, so the impression the soldiers tried to give to their superiors could be relaxed. When a signal was given, however, that an important audience was about to arise on the scene, frantic activity often resulted as the participants tried desperately to get all the appearances back in order (Goffman, 1959). College students can appreciate this example by noting the unusually frenetic activity that results at a dorm room or apartment when a student's parents are coming for a visit.

Teammates know these dramaturgical requirements of everyday life, and we rely on them to exercise due care in the presentations the team is giving.

5. Regions, Region Behavior, and the Self

The kind of self people present and how that self is likely to be taken depend on where the performance takes place. The critical significance of place for the social psychology of the self will be evident in our discussion.

A region may be defined simply as any place that is bounded by barriers to perception (Goffman, 1959, 106). In this sense, personal psychology is always social in the sense that it occurs in an environmental setting (Barker, 1968). How we act—and who we are—depends on where our activity is occurring. People are often taken to be certain kinds of individuals merely by virtue of where they appear. A man's presence in a house of ill repute may be hard to explain away as an effort to save the women's souls! Individuals have a self imputed to them by others quite simply on the basis of where they are seen. For this reason, actors ordinarily exercise care about where their presentations take place. Goffman notes two types of stages on which selves are performed: front and back.

Front-stage regions are places where performances are given, and back stages are where they are prepared for. Because of the incongruities in the types of actions that take place in these two areas, care will usually be taken so that audiences who see a performer front stage will not see him or her in preparation for the same performance backstage. The meaning of a given performance may be diluted, if not destroyed altogether, if audiences see it being prepared for.

For example, those who have worked in the kitchen of a restaurant (even a fashionable one) may not find the food quite as delectable as those who consume it out front at the tables. Similarly, a woman's date for the senior prom may be carefully shielded from seeing her in curlers and cold cream before he picks her up at 7:30. To have seen the careful preparations that go into a front-stage act might modify in the eyes of the audience the essentials of that very performance. This is one reason why husbands and wives, who know each other backstage all the time, may silently smile when they see their spouses performing to others in ways that are incongruent with information they have imparted to them backstage.

Backstage and front-stage language vary considerably. Airline crews may cordially welcome passengers to Flight 509 over the loudspeaker while privately referring to them as "pigeons" when the microphone switch is turned off. Funeral directors refer to the corpse as "the loved one" or "Mr. Smith" when with the bereaved family. But in the embalming room they may make reference to the body as a "floater" (drowning victim) or "an HR" (human remains) (Turner and Edgley, 1976).

Actors can stop giving expressions, but they cannot stop giving them off as long as they are in the awareness context of others (Glaser and Strauss, 1967). This is one of the reasons why regions are so useful to human beings. They provide physical barriers that stop others from seeing the person in a performing role, as well as serving as a stage where people can purposely violate their front-stage performances as a way of relieving tension. In this sense back stages are not only places where performances are prepared for but also places where a very different kind of performance can be given. Back stages, then, provide the actor with a region where the oppressive demands of front-stage performing can be relieved, if only for a short period of time.

North American culture is divided into a whole series of regions with an eye to this performing nature of self-presentations. Bathrooms are usually built toward the rear of a house rather than adjoining the living room. Bedrooms, similarly, are not ordinarily located close to entertainment areas. And, not surprisingly, bathrooms and bedrooms usually have locks on the door, while kitchens and broom closets usually don't. The dramaturgical functions of such circumstances are obvious.

6. Reality and Contrivance

This way of talking about the self conflicts sharply with most of the common-sense assumptions that people in the Western world tend to make about the relationship between themselves and their behavior. As we have mentioned, Westerners tend to think of the self as a core, an organization of behavior, rather than as an ever-shifting result of what we are doing before others at any given time. The extent to which we are capable of controlling the way we come off to others is often largely denied by people. In the usual common-sense way of thinking about the matter, selves exist and direct people's behavior, and what a person basically is cannot be changed or altered and certainly will come through in his acts.

In similar fashion a person's behavior is usually seen as being either real, sincere, and honest or a fabrication that can ordinarily be seen through. Goffman shocks us by turning the matter of self and performance around, putting the performance first and having the self as an outcome of a successful production. Because successful performances can be contrived (indeed, they must always be *put on*), the relationship between reality and contrivance is far more complicated than the usual common-sense manner of thinking would suppose. In fact:

> There are not many French cooks who are really Russian spies, and perhaps there are not many women who play the part of wife to one man and mistress to another; but these duplicities do occur, often being sustained successfully for long periods of time. This suggests that while persons usually are what they appear to be, such appearances could still have been managed. There is, then, a statistical relation between appearances and reality, not an intrinsic or necessary one [Goffman, 1959, 71].

For Goffman, whether people believe sincerely in the parts they are playing is only one—perhaps even a minor—attribute of the performance being given. The key issue is the actor's success in getting *others* to believe that he or she believes in the part being played.

7. The Moral Nature of the Self

Part of the fascination in Goffman's ideas stems from his success in linking the self to others in a moral chain. The self is part of the moral apparatus by which society maintains itself. The idea that societies keep themselves in business by constructing symbols of right and wrong and then ask, cajole, or coerce their members to go along with their definitions is as old as human thought about the nature of social order. What Goffman added to this set of ideas, however, is an insistence that the basic moral claim made on people is that they impress others and in turn be impressed by them. As both object and image, the self has many of the attributes of any other object: it can be manipulated, presented in various lights, and bought and sold. But it is also taken to be crucially *mine* in a subjective sense. For this reason the defense of one's presented self is a serious business. Given this intense and emotional meaning the self has for people, Goffman said, society must have certain agreements and rules over how people are to treat each other's self-presentations. Two such agreements and rules stand out: demeanor and deference (Goffman, 1967a).

Demeanor is the obligation to present oneself to others. When we encounter a person who behaves badly, we are simply noting that his self-presentations are not up to par. The person has not constructed a performance in such a way that the audience can easily and unembarrassingly identify with it. The recluse, the egomaniac, the schizophrenic, and—on occasion at least—all the rest of us present ourselves so that the audiences find it difficult to identify with a performer's acts in anything other than symptomatic terms (Wilkenson, 1974).

Such a moral obligation to present oneself well places an unbelievably large burden on the actor. Demeanor is serious business, and parents spend much of their time trying to teach their children proper decorum. Indeed, the process of socialization we have discussed in this book is in large measure given over to instilling in children not only skills with which to perform but also the moral willingness to do so.

However, such a burden clearly could not be borne by the actor alone, for no one can perform with proper demeanor and give convincing performances all the time. The dramaturgical approach to self recognizes that mistakes, gaffes, *faux pas*, breakdowns in an actor's command over his lines, and other embarrassments are always going to occur in social life. Therefore, the second half of the dramaturgical equation—deference—becomes the means by which audiences save the faces of those whose performances go awry. The deference conventions by which the audience saves poor performances might be called *face rituals*. If our faces *are* our selves, as Goffman contends (remember that the original meaning of the word *person* is *mask*), it will be imperative that audiences protect these faces in the social encounters in which they are presented. For, as Becker noted: "In the social encounter each member exposes for public scrutiny, and possible intolerable undermining, the one thing he needs most: the positive self-valuation he has so laboriously fashioned. With stakes of this magnitude there can be nothing routine about social life. Each social encounter is a hallowed event" (1962, 88).

Understanding this "serious business" of the presentation of self, we begin to see just why apologies, excuses, and an outright willingness to look the other way during a poor performance are so prevalent in social life. To do anything else would be to undermine the self so intolerably that relationships would be impossible. Society seems to be based on a tacit, but nevertheless important, moral agreement: try to give convincing performances, and try not to be too hard on others when their performances break down. They will in turn try to do the same thing, and together we will all get on with the business of living.

8. Mental Disorder As Moral Delinquency

Clearly, the agreement we have discussed has limits. If a person claims to be God, it will be very difficult for his audiences to overcome this gross breach of the requirements of demeanor. No matter how much the audience would like to look the other way (and there is considerable evidence that they usually try for a long time), it is finally impossible because there is simply no social framework except a psychiatric one in which that kind of performance can be placed (Mechanic, 1962; Sampson et al., 1962; Szasz, 1970; Scheff, 1966). Labeling a person mentally ill and dispatching him or her to a mental hospital becomes simply an audience's way of dealing with performances that are so incompetent that no audience, regardless of how sympathetic it may be, is finally able to validate them. The psychiatric self that is imputed to such a performer, then, is a way of dealing with the actor's breach of what Goffman believes to be the essential moral demand of social life.

F. SUMMARY

The concept of self, although having a controversial past, seems indispensible to social psychology. Some kind of linkage is necessary between what people know and what they do, between socialization and acts. The link between these concerns is provided by the concept of self.

Theories of the self have centered on four orienting issues: (1) the self as fact versus the self as constructs, (2) the self as subject versus the self as object, (3) the self as structure versus the self as process, (4) the self as singular versus the self as multiple. In general, psychological treatments of the self are defined in terms of the first proposition in each of these issues, and sociological treatments are couched in terms of the second.

Interest in the idea of self received much of its impetus from the ideas of the American pragmatists James, Mead, and Cooley. Each of these theorists sought to overcome both antecedent and organismically based assumptions about the self. And all three developed theories that lodged the self in social processes. Mead's formulation was probably the most adequate sociologically, for it specified the social mechanism of language as the device specifically making the emergence of selves possible.

Much of the research on the social psychology of the self has revolved around the idea of self-conceptions. Kuhn and others have sought to operationalize the idea of self, centering it in ideas the person has developed in his or her associations with others. What one thinks of self-conceptions is the idea of self-esteem—a person's positive feelings about self. Much of our behavior seems to be grounded in a desire to enhance ourselves in the eyes of others.

Clearly, the most radical theory of the self is that proposed by Erving Goffman and the dramaturgical school of social psychology. In this view people are defined as characters involved in a theatrical production before audiences that review their performances, validating or rejecting the presented self. In Goffman's view the self is an image that is open to considerable manipulation because its substance lies in the management of appearances. Goffman's ideas offer a clear sociological alternative to psychologically based theories of the self that speak of it as a structure or organization of ideas located within the solitary organism.

Social Motives 7

A. INTRODUCTION

Why do people do the things they do? This simple question has haunted social psychology (as well as you and me) for decades. And it has been the basis of a flood of research and writing, much of it confused by the very nature of the question asked. The problem of motivational research, as Lindesmith and Strauss (1956) pointed out, is that people, unlike any other objects of scientific study, have ideas of their own about why they act as they do. When we impute motives to people, they have the disconcerting habit of talking back to us. They often tell us that the motives we have selected as the mainsprings of their actions really have nothing to do with their behavior at all.

In this chapter we will concern ourselves with the concept of motivation as applied to human conduct. It poses some of the most vexing and controversial questions dealt with in social psychology.

B. TRADITIONAL VIEWS OF MOTIVES

Traditionally, motives have been viewed as either internal or external forces that push or pull the essentially passive human organism into action (Brissett and Edgley, 1975). People are viewed as fundamentally at rest, waiting to be activated by the operation of one of these two motivational forces.

1. Internal Motives

Internal-motivational schemes view human behavior as caused by drives, instincts, needs, or reflexes. Hunger, sex, self-preservation, tension reduction and self-actualization (Maslow, 1954) are all viewed by psychologists as basic internal motives that energize human action from the inside out.

While these internal-motivational schemes seeking to explain human behavior have had great currency in social psychology, they have always suffered from serious inadequacies.

Much of the literature explaining human behavior in terms of internal motives has been biologically reductionist. In other words, it has sought to explain complex *social* behavior by referring to internal, or bodily, states. There is little doubt that bodily conditions are associated with everything people do. The body, as Scott and Lyman (1968) suggested, is always present and therefore always available to be used as a motive. It is a mistake, however, to view any physical condition as the entire motive, or cause, for any action. The reason is that bodily conditions do not necessarily lead to any given social behavior unless and until those conditions have been defined and interpreted by the acting organism. For example, a pain one identifies and interprets is very different from a mere organic feeling—it lays the basis for doing something. To be aware that one is hungry is different from merely "being" hungry (Blumer, 1969).

In fact, hunger serves as an excellent illustration of the inadequacy of biological motive schemes. Although everyone needs to eat and has basically the same kind of body, eating behavior varies considerably around the world. As Bierstedt pointed out:

> Some [people] subsist on fish; others on berries and roots. Some drink milk; others abhor the thought of it. Europeans, in fact, are frequently astonished to learn that American men drink this white fluid product of the cow even after they have grown up. The French look upon water as a liquid good only for washing. Snakes, scorpions, feathers, worms, monkeys, frogs, lizards, lice, wasps, bees, beetles, snails, and even clay and rotten wood and canned peaches can be found among the foodstuffs of various peoples. No Eskimo has more pride than the one who can offer his guest a mixture of caribou eyes, auk slime, ptarmigan dung, and fermented brain of bear, the whole thoroughly pre-chewed by the host to make it soft and palatable. In this department . . . there is no doubt whatever that one society's meat is another society's poison [1970, 133].

Furthermore, the speed with which a person eats, the places and circumstances surrounding eating (McDonald's versus Maxim's), and even whether a person feels hunger or revulsion at a particular food depends not on biological factors but on social ones. One of the authors once had the experience of participating in a practical joke at a party. He and a couple of collaborators went to a specialty shop and purchased several cans of quite edible but bizarre epicurean delights: fried grasshoppers, chocolate-covered ants, braised agave worms, and baby bees. We arranged them on an hors d'oeuvre tray amid the Fritos and chip dip and awaited the arrival of our guests. When they came, each of them sampled some of our delicacies and several commented on how good they were. One girl, particularly enamored of the fried grasshoppers ("They're so crunchy!") insisted that we tell her what they were. We finally relented and, on naming them, watched with increasing alarm as she turned several colors, put her hand over her mouth, and fled for the bathroom.

Such observations suggest that the motives for eating are not rooted in biology at all but in the various conventions surrounding the act of eating. In fact, whether a person eats or starves to death depends on the meaning involved in the social act of eating. Prisoners sometimes go on hunger strikes. It has been repeatedly noted that devout Hindus may choose to starve to death rather than eat beef because of the meaning that act would have for them. In fact, a starving person is reported to feel no hunger after the first few days without food. All of these examples serve to illustrate that biological conditions, on their own, are quite insufficient to account for complex social behavior.

Many of the same observations can be made about that highly touted internal motive, sex. Since the time of Freud (and probably for a long time before) human beings have accounted for much behavior on the basis of sexual motives. Sex is seen as the driving force behind even the most non-sexual acts. Once again, however, we discover that biological apparatuses associated with sexuality are insufficient to explain the social act of sex. Sex is typically overlaid with a variety of symbolic meanings, interpretations, definitions, and classifications. Most of the difficulties people have with sex are interpersonal, social, and symbolic, not biological. If an animal is having difficulty with sexual functioning, you can bet that there is something wrong with its body. But human impotence and frigidity, for example, are almost never caused by bodily disorders. In addition, we may note that some people choose to be celibate because of religious beliefs, and the so-called sex drive may cease to have much significance in their lives.

None of this is to say, of course, that sex is insignificant. Rather, its significance far transcends any attempt to ground it in simple biological processes. Freud's most enduring contribution to our understanding of human behavior lies not in his biologically based theories of sexuality but instead in his observation that everything a person does is potentially symbolic—that is, people may make something of it. As a biological urge sex is insufficient to explain social behavior. But as a gesture that the self and others take to be meaningful, sex is a powerful and important element in human conduct (Swanson, 1967).

2. External Motives

Much of social science has fostered the idea that the essential motive forces that explain action are external to the organism, playing on it and producing its behavior. External-motivational schemes are found in various environmental determinisms: Marxian economics, organizational and structural determinism, and the stimulus/response theories of writers such as B. F. Skinner.

In these schemes, once again, is implied the idea that human beings are passive and are moved to action only by the operation of "conditioning" forces. Prior learning, the economic system, or organizational constraints of one kind or another are seen as the causes of human activity. In many ways the environment is like the body—it is always present and is available to be specified as the activating force behind social behavior. For example, Marxist economic determinism sees the important motivations as stemming from the economic structure of a society. According to this view, all ideas, art, values, attitudes, beliefs, and even music and popular culture stem from and are determined by the basic economic structure of that society. The individual is powerless to do very much about it. Indeed, if people act against their own economic interests, they are guilty of what the Marxists term "false consciousness." All of society is seen as a continuing struggle between classes to elevate their position and further their own economic concerns.

In the case of Skinner human beings are considered even more radically passive, human acts being reduced to the status of conditioned reactions quite determined by prior episodes of learning. In the following section we will make some important distinctions that will help us understand the social side of the problem of motivation and give us a different way of viewing human behavior.

C. MOTIVES AND CAUSES

In both internal- and external-motivational schemes some antecedent circumstance is regarded as a cause and the person's act as an effect. At first glance this seems like an eminently reasonable way to account for human behavior. After all, don't people have needs, and can't their behavior be seen as an attempt to satisfy internal states? Furthermore, hasn't our understanding of external social forces pointed to the fact that people *are* stimulated to action by various kinds of structural conditions? Although such attempts to account for human behavior seem reasonable enough, a closer examination of both the assumptions and the actual practice of such explanations reveals glaring deficiencies that we must seek to overcome.

1. Problems with the Concept of Cause

First, there are problems with the concept of causality itself. If we see motives as basically "causes" of behavior, therefore, we will be saddled with the same difficulties. As Cuzzort (1976) suggested, Western culture developed the concept of cause to help people understand the events of the world around them. But it was, and remains, an awkward idea, mainly because it is based on a mechanical and physical view of the world. Whatever human beings are, they are not simply mechanical and physical things.

Nevertheless, there has probably never been developed by the human mind a better way of understanding the operation of physical things than the idea of causality. When we see a car moving down the road, we can be sure that the movement of the car is the result of certain operations going on inside. Gears are turning, spark plugs are firing. And the car, taken as a whole, is not controlling these forces at all. So, with non-human things cause is a useful way of understanding their movement in time and space. The car is clearly reacting only to forces that are playing on it. It is not self-consciously reaching out and interacting with those same forces.

When we attempt to apply this common-sense scheme to human behavior, however, we are confronted immediately with problems. For human behavior is in the realm of action and purpose, not simply in the realm of movement and position (Burke, 1965). To put the case most simply, causes have a backward orientation. They point to antecedent conditions as an explanation for observable events. Motivation theories, to the extent that they have construed motives as synonymous with cause, have focused on these antecedent conditions. This leaves open, however, a whole realm of distinctly human activity oriented around motives not as causes but as purposes, not as antecedents but as anticipations. When we speak of human behavior, we are inevitably drawn into a discussion of intentions, goals, purposes, consequences, and reasons, all of which occupy a different logical realm than does a discussion of causes (Peters, 1958).

We can see the inadequacy of the concept of cause by noting the following example:

> We are told that a juvenile has stolen an automobile. What made him do that? That is, what *caused* him to do that? We answer that he wanted to be a big shot with his friends. Why did he want to be a big shot? Because our culture rewards aggression and assertion of self. Why does our culture reward aggression and assertion of self? Because individuals who are assertive and aggressive are useful to a cultural system engaged in a quest for profit and progress. Why did profit and progress become important? Because there were certain prior ideologies that were congenial to the development of such interests. . . . Why? Because. Why? Because. There is no end to the causal implications that come from even the simplest social movements [Cuzzort, 1976, 295–296].

The concept of cause, when applied to human affairs, leads us to an infinite regression. Everything that happens is presumed to have a cause, and the cause had a cause, *ad infinitum*. We are stuck with a great chain of events, all leading in a circle back to their starting point. We are in the same dilemma that Mark Twain was when he tried to explain why he became a writer. The great American humorist wound up tracing the cause of his decision back to Caesar's crossing of the Rubicon in 49 B.C. (Twain, 1935). On further reflection, Twain even decided that he hadn't pushed his analysis back far enough. If Eve had not been tempted by the serpent and in turn tempted Adam, the entire history of the human race would have been different. In fact, if God had put Martin Luther and Joan of Arc in the Garden of Eden instead of Adam and Eve, everything would have turned out differently, for *nothing* would have got *them* to eat the apple.

Even in the physical world the concept of cause has its problems, for every explanation tendered by human beings sets up a counterexplanation that is at least as plausible. Stouffer related the now-famous Parable of the Dead Duck to make his point. A duck is flying over a marsh in the middle of Michigan, when a hunter jumps up and shoots him. What causes the duck to die? The hunter's shot? Are you sure?

> Well, there is a physiological explanation. The duck died because of a hemorrhage, which left the heart no blood to pump. And there is a psychological explanation. The duck died because the hunter was the kind of person he was—if he had had different frustrations in his youth, he might not have be-

come a bird killer. We might take a psychoanalytic dive into this one, but let's skip it. And there is an ideological explanation. If the culture of Michigan were like that of parts of India, the killing of the duck, or of any other animal, for that matter, would be reprehensible. And there is a geographical explanation. Note that the duck died in a marsh. No hunter probably would have been waiting for him on top of the hill. Finally, consider a technological explanation, the gun that killed him, a product of technical progress in the manufacture of lethal hardware [Stouffer, 1958, 173].

2. A Noncausal Definition of Motives

Apart from difficulties with the idea that behavior is "caused," another problem already mentioned is that human beings "explain" their own and other people's behavior to themselves and to one another. Following this observation, sociologist C. Wright Mills suggested the notion of motives as devices that people use to explain their behavior to other people when they are called on to do so.

At first glance this conception of motivation seems outrageous. It turns motives from causes of behavior into mere words or other communications that people use to give others the sense of why they are doing what they are doing. One reason this conception seems so radical is that both the Freudian (internal) and the Marxist (external) motivational schemes have convinced us that the accounts people give to each other are not the "real" reasons for their behavior at all. In the case of the Marxist, a person's own statements are only cover-ups for his or her class ideology. Freudians discount a person's own accounts as mere "rationalizations."

For the social psychologist, however, the accounts that people give to one another and that are routinely acted on in social relationships offer us a powerful tool for understanding the empirical reality of the social world. For when people act toward one another, they do not have direct access to the metaphysical "reality" that Freudians and Marxists refer to. Instead, people in everyday life must necessarily deal with one another's behavior, communications, signs, and signals (Goffman, 1959). Motives, in this sense, offer a key to understanding social organization by linking one person's acts to another person's understanding.

Unlike causes, which have a backward, antecedent reference in time, motives look forward to the future consequences of behavior. They are the devices by which human actors communicate their intentions, reasons, explanations, justifications, excuses, accounts, apologies, requests, and disclaimers to others. John Dewey offered us the beginnings of a social approach to motivation with the proposition that *man is naturally active* (Dewey, 1922). From the beginning of our lives until our deaths, we are given to action quite naturally. Motives, in this sense, do not rest in our minds and guide our behavior. They are a crucial part of our behavior and exist only in interaction with others or with ourselves. Whitehead captured this point nicely when he said: "We cannot think first and act afterwards.

From the moment of birth we are immersed in action and can only fitfully guide it by taking thought" (1922, 17).

Dewey's proposition preempts all attempts to explain why people act in the first place. If people are quite naturally active as opposed to passive, the question is not what causes action but how it is that an act takes this form or that, a turn this way or a turn that way. Dewey's position is that people observing an act evaluate it. If they think it is fine, they do not question it as to motive at all. If the audience to a particular act finds problems with it, however, the members may try to get the actor to reassess his or her actions from their point of view. Challenge and reassessment are the basis of all infant and childhood socialization. And, as we shall see, this double process continues throughout life. The challenging audience (which, of course, may be oneself) has some idea of an acceptable alternative to the problematic act. And if the audience can specify the desirable consequences flowing from the more acceptable alternatives, it may well succeed in getting the act redirected (Stone, 1970). Dewey shifts the problem of motivation from the purely psychological to the social by showing how motives are used as a form of social control.

So motives have to do not with past events but rather with the patterning, timing, and direction of immediate behavior (Hebb, 1949). As social psychologists we are not concerned with the direction of all human activity but rather with the conduct of a person who is participating in a specific interactional episode (Shibutani, 1961). Our understanding of a human action, then, is considerably enhanced by an analysis of how people use motives in the construction of their actions with others and how these motives change.

3. Vocabularies of Motive

Mills, whose ground-breaking article on the social psychology of motives we referred to earlier, suggested that motives arise only under certain circumstances. When, then, are motives likely to emerge? The typical motive situation involves the interruption of some line of action. This interruption takes the form of one person challenging the behavior of another. Mills said that "men live in immediate acts of experience and their attentions are directed outside themselves until acts are in some way frustrated. It is then that awareness of self and of motive occur" (1940, 905).

Motives, then, arise when an act is questionable. In response to the challenge, a person gives a motive, the function of which is to satisfy the questioner, usually about the goals, purpose, end, or intention of his or her act. If the challenger is satisfied, the challenge is removed. In this sense motives can be regarded as "unquestioned answers to questions" regarding social conduct.

Another question implied in a discussion of motives is why some motives are given and not others. The answer lies in the analysis of different social circles. Motives are organized into "vocabularies" that are accepted because they have currency in a particular social setting. "Motives are of no value apart from delimited societal situations for which they are appropriate vocabularies. They must be situated. . . . Motives vary in content and character with historical epochs and societal structures" (Mills, 1940, 907). The motives people use are learned during socialization. Thus, they are given to people by their society just as are all of the other tools and resources we reviewed during our discussion of socialization.

As we can see, people do not have motives and then act. They first act and then, during the course of their relationships with others, learn the appropriate vocabularies of motive with which to justify their participation in that act. When people join a group, they typically also have provided for them the appropriate vocabulary of motives for that group. The decision to join may have been based on a variety of factors—opportunity, inclination, and the like. But once people have joined, they often find themselves taking on the same motives that other members of the group use. As Weber pointed out in an early discussion of the problem of motive: "The motives which induce people to work vary with different social classes. . . . When a man changes rank, he switches from one set of motives to another" (1963, 316–317).

In other words, agreement among any group of people concerning the motives of another person merely tells us something about the common terminology with which they operate. In fact, it would be surprising indeed if people who used the same vocabulary of motives did not arrive at the same judgments about why people do the things they do. We may question psychoanalysis in this regard, because it imputes motives to people that they themselves do not possess. "To explain one's conduct by the vocabulary of motives current among one's group is about as self-deceptive as giving the area of a field in the accepted terms of measurement" (Burke, 1965, 21).

Often there is a considerable difference between the motives people impute to themselves and the ones others impute to them. Motives thus may be both avowed by an individual and imputed by others (Blum and McHugh, 1971). The fact that disparities exist only suggests that persons may typically try to use vocabularies of motive that are not only efficacious but also put the best possible face on the conduct in question. This is why we are uncomfortable when people are telling us why we are doing what we are doing. And it explains how it is that people come to try to control the motives that others impute to them.

Motives vary not only from group to group but also from time to time. In North American culture today, individualistic, hedonistic, and economic motives are generally regarded as plausible motives. So it is difficult for us to realize that such motives have not always enjoyed the currency they do now. For example, if a man says that he took another job because the new one paid more money than the old one, few people will continue to ask

Is the motive for this person's behavior apparent? (Photo by Bob Adelman, Magnum Photos)

about his motives. Similarly, if a woman says that she did something because it was in her own individual interests to do so or because she did it to have fun, her audience is unlikely to believe that they have not been told the "real" reasons for her action. But if a man is asked why he did something and responds by saying that "God told me to do it," the articulation of such religious vocabularies of motive is likely to be questioned seriously, sometimes even psychiatrically (Edgley, 1970).

We may say, then, that the motive vocabularies people accept do vary from time to time and place to place. For example:

> During the middle ages, a monk who found a sick woman at the monastery gates, violated the rules of his order by taking her inside, and then nursed her back to health, could insist that he was only carrying out God's will; his explanation would probably have been accepted by many people. Today, however, it would be suspected that the monk was actually struck by the woman's beauty, but being pious, he repressed and sublimated his erotic impulses, thereby deceiving himself into believing that he was an instrument of divine purpose [Shibutani, 1961, 183].

But can we be sure that our current vocabularies of motive are the authentic ones and that everybody else's are mere "rationalizations" and cover-ups? We are exceedingly ethnocentric about our motives, often insisting that our vocabularies are the real ones. A catalog of various kinds of historically situated motive vocabularies does not exist at the present time. But we can, as just noted, see the rise and fall of various motive currency. Even as recently as the 1960s college students rejected economic vocabularies of motive in favor of humanistic ones (Reich, 1970). A scant ten years later, however, although humanistic vocabularies of motive had not lost all of their saliency, pecuniary motives were showing a resurgence in the vocabularies of college students.

D. THE INTERPERSONAL USE OF MOTIVES

1. Accounts

Sociologically oriented social psychologists have been relatively slow to adopt the view of motives we have just sketched, primarily due to the continuing use of causal models in social-science research. However, the empirical utility of the concept has recently come to be appreciated. And we are beginning to see that the use of motives in interpersonal settings offers us a powerful tool for understanding the linkage between social-structural concerns and interpersonal ones. Sociologists Scott and Lyman (1968), as part of a general recognition that sociologists were neglecting the dimension of talk as a social process, provided a cataloguing of types of motives that people typically use in their relationships with one another. They defined an *account* in the way that Burke, Mills, and Weber defined a motive: as a statement made by a social actor to explain unanticipated or untoward behavior. They noted, in the same way their predecessors did, that accounts are called for not when people engage in routine, common-sense behavior but only when uncommon, unconventional, nonroutine, or even aberrant behavior occurs. In other words, accounts are more than simply "explanations," because there is the added implication, as we have noted, that the behavior might well be unacceptable or wrong.

Next, Scott and Lyman divided accounts into two types—justifications and excuses—on the basis of whether the actor accepts responsibility for his or her behavior.

a. Justifications.   To justify an act is to accept responsibility for having done it but to deny the negative implications associated with it by the challenging audience. Soldiers, for example, may accept the charge that they have killed others but deny that killing is immoral under those circumstances.

Justifications, in other words, are socially approved vocabularies of motive that defend an act in the face of some claim that it is or might be wrong. Capital punishment is an act that is often justified by its advocates. They may admit that killing is indeed wrong, but not if the person being

"Did she get to the part about tearin' off the bumper yet?"

Accounts are called for primarily when people engage in uncommon, unconventional, non-routine or even aberrant behavior.

killed has killed others. The American judicial system is clearly not an absolute system of prohibited acts but rather a place where the meaning of acts is negotiated according to various standards of responsibility (Scheff, 1968).

Research by Sykes and Matza (1957) on motives used by juvenile delinquents to neutralize their deviant behavior is taken by Scott and Lyman to be an excellent list of justifications. These motives include "denial of injury," "denial of victim," "condemnation of condemners," and "appeal to loyalties."

In *denial of injury* the actor admits that he or she did a particular act but asserts that it was permissible to do that act because no one was injured by it or it had negligible consequences. Thus, people calling for motives are said to be really making a lot out of nothing.

Denial of the victim is a different sort of justification. In this case the actor states that the act in question was justified because the victim deserved whatever he or she got. Various kinds of people are sometimes seen as deserving victims: people who have injured those the actor is now being accused of having injured; people who occupy deviant roles (for example, whores, pimps, and homosexuals); members of racial and ethnic minorities; and distant foes such as Communists or politicians.

In *condemnation of the condemners,* the actor challenges or attempts to discredit those very persons or their surrogates who are challenging him or her. The person admits having performed the act in question but contends that the challengers have done much worse and are hardly worthy of asserting any challenge. Challenges to challengers are sometimes instigated on the basis that, inasmuch as the act in question is commonplace, why is the person being singled out for a challenge? Why not others? Such an appeal is sometimes very effective.

Another technique of justification is an *appeal to loyalties.* Here the actor asserts that the action in question was correct because it was in the interests of one whom he owes allegiance. Persons routinely lie, for example, in order to protect a friend or relative. Although lying is usually seen as wrong, many people are moved by this motive, and it is routinely regarded as justified behavior. In courts of law, spouses cannot be forced to testify against each other, presumably because the appeal to loyalty would obviate any attempt to get them to tell the truth if it were damaging. Similarly, political radicals often appeal to a "higher" loyalty than that of the state when confronted with a challenge.

"Let's move to the back seat . . . my eyes hurt if I sit too close to the screen!"

The accounts people give to one another offer a powerful tool for understanding the reality of the social world.

Two final justifications are discussed by Scott and Lyman: "sad tales" and "self-fulfillment." In the sad tale, the actor accounts for his or her aberrant behavior by pulling out a series of past incidents, using them to justify his or her present behavior. In self-fulfillment, various participants in deviant behavior, especially drug- and sex-related deviance, account for their behavior by saying that they did it in order to enhance themselves, expand their consciousness, or fulfill themselves sexually.

b. Excuses. Excuses are accounts that admit that the act in question is wrong (and by implication that the challenge to it is correct) but deny full responsibility for having done it. The soldier who admits that killing is wrong but argues that he was ordered to kill is conceding the wrongfulness of his act but arguing that he "had no choice." Such motives were used after the My Lai incident in Vietnam.

Excuses, then, are socially approved vocabularies of motive that mitigate responsibility by placing part of the blame on something or someone else. Scott and Lyman identify four major types: "appeal to accident," "appeal to defeasibility," "appeal to biological drives," and "scapegoating."

"Look, Mom . . .
I can juggle THREE
EGGS at once!"

"You shouldn't have
YELLED like that!"

Excuses are socially approved vocabularies of motive that mitigate responsibility by placing part of the blame on something or someone else.

An *appeal to accident* admits that what the person did was wrong, or bad, but that he or she is not responsible because the whole thing was an accident. Accidents are effective motives because they appeal to the universal idea that the very environment in which we live is hazardous and that people cannot always control either themselves or the objects they manipulate. Appeals to accidents are able to work only if they are used infrequently. If accidents tend to happen to the same people frequently, others are likely to see them as clumsy or to discount their appeals on the grounds that they are making them up.

Appeals to defeasibility are the social version of the debate over free will versus determinism in philosophy. The mind of a person is taken to be made up of two elements, knowledge and will, and an excuse for challenged behavior can therefore be that a person did something against his or her will or didn't know. "I didn't know" is an appeal that distinguishes between intentions and consequences. This distinction forms the basis for many legal appeals as well as a host of motive exchanges in everyday life. Such an appeal recognizes that the consequences of an act were very bad but denies responsibility on the ground that the person did not mean to do the act.

Another type of defeasibility excuse is an appeal to biological drives. Biological motives are perhaps the most universal of all the types we have mentioned, precisely because everybody has a body. For example, illness in our culture (as in many others) is commonly recognized as an excuse for not fulfilling various social obligations such as work or school. Again, the timing of and repeated use of this vocabulary of motives may reduce its acceptability for a given actor, but its status as a generally accepted excuse remains.

Similarly, appeals to other biological drives serve as an adequate excuse for questioned conduct. Scott and Lyman note that among traditional Italians "uncontrollable sexual desire" is often accepted by the wives of unfaithful husbands as an excuse for extramarital intercourse. The wife does not condone her husband's affairs but accepts his excuse that he couldn't, after all, "help it." Finally, married couples who choose voluntarily to remain childless have often found it to their advantage when challenged about not having children to say that something is "wrong" with either the husband or the wife. This biological motive seems less troublesome than having to explain their decision in other terms (Kiser, 1979).

Scapegoating is the last type of excuse Scott and Lyman consider. This is perhaps the classic form of excuse giving, with roots in antiquity. In scapegoating a person contends that his or her own behavior was forced by the behavior or attitudes of others (Adorno, 1950). De Hoyos and de Hoyos in an article on the Mexican family system (1966) show the way a teenager explains why he got into trouble. The girl he truly loved was not available to him, so "because of Antonia, I began to stay away from home. It was one of the main reasons I started to go on the bum, looking for trouble."

The phenomenon of scapegoating is also engaged in collectively. Disasters, for example, are often an occasion for scapegoating. The grief and anger over loss lead people to believe that *someone* must be to blame. In the Cocoanut Grove fire of 1942, in which 488 persons burned to death, no fewer than five separate scapegoats were blamed for the disaster in the weeks after the fire. "If only it had not been for the busboy who struck a match, a prankster who removed the light bulb the busboy was trying to replace, the fire department who had approved the club as safe the week before the fire, other city officials, and the owners of the club, all of those people would still be alive" (Veltfort and Lee, 1943). "If only" is the basic logic of scapegoating.

2. Honoring Others' Motives

This typology of motives serves to catalog some of the primary strategies by which people excuse and justify their actions to others when called on to do so. But audiences as well as actors have a hand in the motive process. Just as we may be expected to *give* motives when called on to do so, we are expected to *honor* the motives of others when they give them, at least under certain circumstances.

Motives given by the actor can either be honored or not honored. If they are accepted as an adequate account of the conduct in question, the relationship that has been interrupted continues. If they are not honored, further challenges may be forthcoming until an adequate motive is either given by the actor or imputed by the audience. The most common circumstance in which a motive is accepted is when it is conventional in the social circle in which it is given. Social circles may be seen as *universes of discourse* (Mead, 1934), language areas in which some kinds of motives are perfectly routine and others bizarre or unacceptable. Heroin addicts may be able to justify their habit in a drug-using subculture but find it very difficult to get middle-class suburbanites or Southern Baptists to accept any motive as acceptable at all.

Scott and Lyman argue that whether or not an account is accepted depends on certain background expectancies held by the persons in an interaction. By *background expectancies* they mean "those acts of taken-for-granted ideas that permit the interactants to interpret remarks as accounts in the first place" (Scott and Lyman, 1968). In this sense there are certain rules governing interaction, among which are rules about accepting other people's motives. A person asked why he or she is depressed may answer simply by referring to "family problems." This remark, at least in our part of the world, will almost always be taken as an adequate motive for acting depressed, because "everyone knows" that "family problems" are a cause of depression.

In fact, given the background expectancies of the universe of discourse called North American culture, "I'm having family problems" can be seen as virtually an all-purpose motive. It is likely to be accepted as either a justification or an excuse for a wide variety of behavioral aberrations. It is often accepted as a motive for drinking heavily, missing work, the failure to pay bills, and being mentally ill (MacAndrew and Edgerton, 1969; Scheff, 1966). There are other motives that seem to fit this category. For example, illness in our society is an all-purpose motive that is accepted for a host of deviations. We may note here that while persons do come to be "ill" in the sense that they have certain bodily conditions that show physical symptoms, people first see their "illness" not as an illness at all but as social deviance (Freidson, 1970). We tend to encounter illness in others first as "missed work," "not being up to par," and so on. Only later do we account for these deviations as being due to illness. We also use virtually the same procedures that are used in courts of law to decide how serious an illness is and whether the social deviation that "causes" the illness is conditionally legitimate, unconditionally legitimate, or completely illegitimate and subject to stigmatization. The following table, taken from Freidson's research, shows the way in which we impute the motive of illness as a justification for social misconduct:

Table 7-1. Types of deviance for which the individual is not held responsible, by imputed legitimacy and seriousness *(contemporary U.S. middle-class societal reaction)*

Imputed Seriousness	Illegitimate (Stigmatized)	Conditionally Legitimate	Unconditionally Legitimate
Minor Deviation	Cell 1. "Stammer" Partial suspension of some ordinary obligations; few or no new privileges; adoption of a few new obligations.	Cell 2. "A Cold" Temporary suspension of few ordinary obligations; temporary enhancement of ordinary privileges. Obligation to get well.	Cell 3. "Pockmarks" No special change in obligations or privileges.
Serious Deviation	Cell 4. "Epilepsy" Suspension of some ordinary obligations; adoption of new obligations; few or no new privileges.	Cell 5. "Pneumonia" Temporary release from ordinary obligations; addition to ordinary privileges. Obligation to cooperate and seek help in treatment.	Cell 6. "Cancer" Permanent suspension of many ordinary obligations; marked addition to privileges.

The process of socialization, then, provides us with a whole series of understandings about the conditions that are likely to call for accounts, what kinds are given, and the circumstances under which the accounts of others are to be honored or rejected.

3. Verbal and Apparent Motives

As forms of communication motives may be verbal, apparent, or—usually—some combination of both. Whether or not an account is honored depends on the particular way it is given and the mixture of verbal and nonverbal elements in the giving of it. If a girl is asked by her parents why she was late in getting home from a date and answers by saying that the movie lasted longer than it was supposed to, her motive may be rejected if her clothes are in disarray, her lipstick is smeared, and her hair is mussed. The parents may reject her offered verbal motive and impute the apparent one: she was parking with her boyfriend. Similarly, many of the motives of mental illness that are imputed to a person who is acting strangely depend not on what he says but on the appearance of his eyes, face, and gestures while he is saying it (Scheff, 1966; Edgley, 1970).

People seem to know that talk and appearances go together, so that they typically pay some attention to their appearance while they are giving an account of their conduct. The communicative style of the account may be *intimate*, as in close relationships; *casual*, as among members of a group;

"Could I use some of your perfume, Mommy? I've got a big favor to ask Daddy."

Persons seem to know that talk and appearance go together; they typically pay some attention to their appearance while they are giving an account of their conduct.

formal, as in bureaucratic meetings; and *frozen,* which we often hear from telephone operators. The style plays a large role in determining whether the account will be accepted or not (Scott and Lyman, 1968).

4. Avoiding Motive Situations

When motives are called for, there is always the implication that a person may have done something wrong (Peters, 1958). Therefore, people frequently attempt to avoid the whole matter. In other words, when a call for motives is given, it places the actor on the defensive right away. Not surprisingly, then, hierarchies are often set up. Certain statuses and identities are thus shielded from having their behavior challenged, at least by subordinates. Privates do not ordinarily challenge the conduct of generals (at least to their face), and generals don't usually give motives to privates (Stone and Farberman, 1970). In addition, people may employ other techniques as strategies for avoiding motive situations. Scott and Lyman mention three: *mystification, referral,* and *identity switching.*

In mystification, people concede that they are not doing what they are supposed to be doing, point out that there are reasons for their unexpected actions, but say that they cannot tell the challenger what the reasons are. "It's a long story" is often sufficient to avoid the whole matter. People can also mystify the challenger by asserting that secret information exists of which the challenger is unaware.

In referral, actors simply refer the challenger to someone else for an explanation of their untoward behavior. Motives can be referred to doctors, lawyers, former lovers, psychiatrists, social workers—almost anyone who is known to have information of a privileged or expert nature.

Identity switching is a strategy in which people say that they are not whom the challenger believes they are. Given the situational nature of identities, it may be easy for a person to contend that the challenger has the right body but the wrong person. If a person is caught bending over another man who has been seriously injured in a knife fight, he or she may be challenged with "what are you doing!" The person may then avoid the challenge by answering "You don't understand, I'm a doctor and this man's been hurt."

In fact, it is well to point out here that the negotiation of identities ("Who are you?") is really the basic problem motives seek to deal with. There are very few questions about behavior that cannot be answered with the appropriate identity. And there are, conversely, very few acts that will be correct and proper for all identities (Foote, 1951).

5. Disclaimers

A variant of the motive situation has been identified by Hewitt and Stokes (1975). Their influential article noted that problematic events of varying seriousness occur all of the time in everyday life. The role of motives, as we have seen, is to smooth these problems over and to make interactions that have broken down work again for the participants. When rules are broken and expectations are not met, people do try to repair the damage and restore the meaning.

Motives, as we have seen, operate retrospectively; that is, they are used by actors *after* a break in interaction has occurred. But do actors ever try to set up situations so that a potential break will *not* occur? Obviously they often do. Hewitt and Stokes introduced and defined a concept that deals directly with this phenomenon of dealing with possible breaks in interaction *prospectively*. This concept they termed the *disclaimer*.

Hewitt and Stokes noted that in interaction people try to fit the events of behavior to some situational theme, usually a theme that is conventional, well known, or generally accepted. In other words, actors well know that their acts serve as the basis for categorizing them in the eyes of others and that their behavior will be taken by their audiences as symptomatic of them. As we noted in the chapter on the self, people appear in guises that others take to be them. Their doing is taken as their being (Burke, 1965). Hence, modifications in conduct are likely to occur:

> Put another way, as the individual anticipates the response to his conduct, he may see it either as in line with an established identity or as somehow discrepant, in which case it may be taken as a cue for some new typification, possibly a negative one, possibly a more favorable one [Hewitt and Stokes, 1975, 3].

Knowing they will be categorized and finding themselves in some situations without any certain way of anticipating the response, people are likely to invoke disclaimers. The disclaimer is, then, "a verbal device employed to ward off and defeat in advance doubts and negative typifications which may result from intended conduct. Disclaimers seek to define forthcoming conduct as not relevant to the kind of identity-challenge or re-typification for which it might ordinarily serve as the basis" (Hewitt and Stokes, 1975, 2).

In short, disclaimers are prospective attempts on the part of people to control, short-circuit, or otherwise ward off possible challenges and other responses from others. Examples are all around us: "I know this sounds stupid, but. . ." "I don't want you to think I'm prejudiced against blacks, but I did hear this funny story I'm dying to tell you. . . ." "I haven't thought this through, but it seems to me that. . . ." "This is going to make you unhappy, but you do realize that. . . ."

The preface to the actor's remarks *disclaims* that what is about to follow should be used as the basis for a challenge to either identity or motive. Clearly, the hope of a person who articulates a disclaimer is that his or her intended act will not become the basis for either a challenge or a negative categorization.

There are several types of disclaimers that actors use to accomplish these ends. For example:

a. *Hedging.*   The hedge operates as a minimal commitment to what is about to follow. The person is saying two things: that what he or she is about to say is tentative and that the response to this tentative statement could be serious. For example: "I'm not sure this is going to work, but let's give it a try anyway." Challenges to identity are warded off in the hedge, because the person is not claiming an identity to go with his or her statement. Of course, as Hewitt and Stokes pointed out, if a person holds an identity that makes the hedge suspect, he or she will have to use other kinds of hedges. The chairman of the Nuclear Regulatory Commission cannot preface an answer to a question about the safety of nuclear power by saying: "Of course, I'm no expert, but. . . ." Therefore, an expert may hedge a statement by appealing to faulty memory, misunderstanding, or misquoting in order to ward off being relabeled as incompetent. This tactic is used often by politicians.

b. *Credentialing.*   The exactly opposite kind of disclaimer may also be effective. If people know that others will respond negatively to their intended act but are nevertheless strongly committed to it, they may well try to claim special credentials, qualifications, or exemptions. "I'm not prejudiced—some of my best friends are Jews—but. . . ." This man knows that he is about to be classified as prejudiced but claims that, because he has friends of the type of person that he is seeming to be prejudiced against, this puts him in a special category. In fact, this kind of statement is a classic statement of credentialing and is used all of the time to claim a special privilege for acting in an arbitrary, capricious, or prejudicial way about a group or category of persons.

c. *Sin licenses.*   Presented identities are often challenged, and motives are often called for under circumstances in which rules are broken (Peters, 1958). Therefore, if people are going to break a rule, it may be to their advantage to say that they know what they are doing and do not fear the negative classification that others are about to make of them. "We realize that you will probably think this is wrong, but. . . ." This statement appeals to a common sentiment in social life: the notion that rules are often broken with good reason and that rule violators are not necessarily deviant. In fact, the whole business of breaking rules is overlaid with a complex system of understanding in which it is often not only acceptable but even required (Douglas, 1970). A pilot whose plane develops engine trouble violates every rule of traffic safety by setting the plane down on an interstate highway. But others, although recognizing that landing an aircraft on a highway is against the rules, may applaud the pilot for getting it down safely. By invoking the sin disclaimer, people stipulate in advance that they know that the rule they are breaking is a rule but that there are extenuating circumstances for violating it. Sin licenses "pay due respect to the rules even while establishing the conditions under which they may be broken" (Hewitt and Stokes, 1975, 5).

d. *Cognitive disclaimers.* People generally know that others will respond to their acts easily if they fit common definitions of situations. Therefore, it will be to their advantage, if their behavior does not fit such an easily assigned definition, to prospectively set up a framework in which it can be dealt with. So we discover that a lot of behavior is prefaced with remarks such as "We know this sounds crazy. . . ." By anticipating doubt, the actors seek to reassure others that there is nothing wrong with them and that they, like their audience, recognize the ostensibly bizarre character of their behavior. Indeed, it may be a kind of index of how far we have gotten from one another in terms of common frameworks of understanding to note how often these types of disclaimers are used in social interaction.

e. *Appeals for the suspension of judgment.* Responses to statements and acts are often immediate and powerful. All it takes are a few words or gestures, and audiences frequently make a quick judgment and respond in terms of what they believe is forthcoming. Actors frequently attempt to take this into account by beginning their act with a disclaimer that asks the audience in advance to wait on them until they are able to set up a context in which the judgment will be more favorable or accurate. "I don't want to make you angry by saying this, but. . . ." This example recognizes a fact about communication of which Thomas Szasz has spoken so eloquently: that persons who are successful in defining the situation are often the ones who "win" in relations with others, and that this is an important aspect of social life:

> The struggle for definition is veritably the struggle for life itself. In the typical Western two men fight desperately for the possession of a gun that has been thrown to the ground; whoever reaches the weapon first, shoots and lives; his adversary is shot and dies. In ordinary life, the struggle is not for guns, but for words; whoever first defines the situation is the victor; his adversary, the victim [Szasz, 1973, 21–22].

Appeals for the suspension of judgment are a way of winning the battle by getting to the definitional apparatus first.

E. MOTIVES AND SOCIAL PROCESSES

1. Motives and the Self

If the self is a social process that revolves around personal things (Sullivan, 1953), then being in command of motives is one way actors establish themselves as distinctive selves in social dramas. Self-concepts are often predicated on the existence of various rationales (Foote, 1951). "I am not the type of person who does things for reasons like that" offers a number of insights into the importance of motives for a person's concept of himself or herself. Similarly, people often act or don't act on the simple basis of whether they have a self-enhancing reason or not. The selves people hold in any given situation can be seen as a function of the motives they are able to give to sustain the action in which they are engaged.

2. Motives and Social Change

In addition to having important interpersonal functions in social relationships, motives as we have sketched them in this chapter offer a powerful way of understanding a number of larger-scale problems traditionally dealt with in sociology.

For example, theories of social change have sought to deal with the question of how societies change by pointing to changes in various structural conditions such as technology (Ogburn, 1946), the economic factor (Marx and Engels, 1930), ideology (Mannheim, 1936), and many others. These theories suffer from a common problem, however. They do not sufficiently show how some structural condition becomes involved in people's interpersonal behavior. The concept of motive vocabularies offers a way of providing this linkage.

Mills, for example, argued that motives exist as situated vocabularies held in some social circles (Mills, 1940). But how did these circles come to be? The answer lies in Stone's trenchant observation that "every social change requires a convincing rationale" (1970). People do not accept wholesale changes in their society without some talk, negotiation, and even argument and conflict. They must come to feel that a proposed change is for the better, or at least that it is necessary (perhaps a necessary evil). This is the interpersonal dynamic of change. The ordeal of change (Hoffer, 1956) comes from seeing one's own rationales rejected. The best single analysis of a particular social change and its underlying roots in motive vocabularies is the classic study by Max Weber, *The Protestant Ethic and the Spirit of Capitalism* (1930).

Weber's thesis is well known. It is, simply stated, that religion had a functional relationship to the rise of capitalism and that certain features of Calvinist doctrine formed the basis for its development. But did Calvinist Protestantism simply "cause" capitalism to happen? Obviously not, and it is important to underscore that Weber was speaking both implicitly and explicitly about human beliefs and attitudes that resulted in certain forms of behavior. In other words, as Perinbanayagam (1967) has shown, Protestantism provided a new vocabulary of motives, a fresh rhetoric for existence and, especially, for wealth.

The relationship between religion and economic action can then be explained simply: Calvinists believed that people were "called" by God to certain work and would experience either success or failure. Once the call has been received, it is people's responsibility to labor long and well in their calling. Furthermore, should they gain wealth and affluence as a result of their labors, this wealth should be regarded as a trust, and that trust should be held for times of trouble ("saving for a rainy day"). The fortune is merely a sign of God's grace and a promise of salvation. Such ideas became wide-spread in Western Europe after the Reformation. These beliefs—and a group of people who practiced them fervently—became the basis for an economic system called capitalism that required the willingness of people to save money, live frugally, and plan for the economic future. In other words, acting out the Protestant rationale provided the necessary "capital" for the development of a wholly new economic system.

This short sketch shows that the traditional problems of sociology are certainly amenable to a social-psychological interpretation. Indeed, such an analysis is necessary in order to show the linkage between structural concerns and personal behavior. Other examples that could be given include the social transformations wrought by Lenin and Trotsky in Russia, Hitler in Germany, Gandhi in India, and even John Kennedy in this country ("Ask not what your country can do for you; ask what you can do for your country").

3. Motives and Mental Disorder

The concept of motive vocabularies also offers us a way of understanding certain problems of deviance and mental disorder. If motives form a basis for social order by providing a way by which people can understand and communicate with one another, it follows that, when motives are not forthcoming or the wrong kind are given, definitions of deviance are likely to be made.

In this social sense it is important to recognize that what we call "mental illness" is a way people have of explaining behavior that they cannot understand or deal with in any other terms. Mental illness serves as a kind of residual explanation (Scheff, 1966) that people employ to fill in gaps in their understanding left by bizarre, mystifying, or incomprehensible conduct. So, if people are defined as mentally ill when their behavior "makes no sense," and if the function of motives is to put people in communication with one another about the "sense" of what they are doing, then it follows that mental disorder may well be a label we put on people when we do not understand their motives (Edgley, 1970). We say that mental patients do not "reason logically," but this very conception presupposes that there exist standards for determining just what constitutes "logical reasoning." Such standards do exist, and they are created and maintained socially (Mannheim, 1936).

The circumstances under which people come to be defined as mentally ill indicate that motives play a key role in the process. Two research studies (Clausen and Yarrow, 1955; Schwartz, 1955) indicate the following about the responses people make to behavior that is later termed "mentally ill":

1. There is an elaborate imputation of motives to deviants in order to rationalize their behavior in some acceptable way.
2. The length of time in which audiences have been engaged in this motive

imputation is a factor in determining the point at which a definition of mental illness is made.

3. Situational, personal, cultural, and referential factors all play important roles in the definition of deviance.

4. Intermittent, rather than continuous, episodes of misconduct increase the likelihood of audiences' rationalizing the behavior of another acceptably. Continuous displays of bizarre behavior are much more difficult to explain away and increase the probability of a definition of mental disorder being made.

5. Audiences typically accommodate improper behavior by adapting themselves to it ... symptomatic reactions that are intensifications of long-standing response patterns become part of the fabric of everyday life, thus making it even more difficult to disentangle that which is "symptomatic" from that which is "normal."

6. Behavior is normalized, justified, excused, explained, or made acceptable by assuring oneself that the behavior seen in another is also present in oneself or that it is widely seen in those who are not ill.

7. When behavior cannot be normalized through the use of these motives, it can be made to seem less severe to outsiders by supplying motives for the person's behavior.

8. Hospitalization for mental illness does not necessarily decrease the tendency for relevant audiences to continue normalizing, rationalizing, or denying a person's disorder.

This summary indicates that there are strong indications that motives play a key role in the social definition of mental illness. In other words, definitions of someone's mental illness are made not simply when interpersonal rules are broken but also—and more importantly—when no normalizing motives are offered to explain the violation. There is little in the way of personal conduct that cannot be "explained away," at least for the time being. Conversely, there may be little that is acceptable if we do not understand the reasons why people are acting the way they are.

The three major mental disorders—schizophrenia, paranoia, and depression—can be understood at least tentatively in terms of the view of motives we have given in this chapter. For example, in schizophrenia we clearly have an interpersonal case where a person not only acts strangely but also gives the most bizarre kind of motives when called to account for his or her conduct. "Why were you late?" might be answered "Because it's the Fourth of July." Such a statement makes no sense, especially if it is given on the third of January. So the schizophrenic not only engages in bizarre behavior but—more importantly—gives the most bizarre, illogical, and nonsensical motives.

In paranoia, the motive problem seems not so much that the person gives the wrong kind of motives but that he or she is a motive imputer. The person imputes the grossest and most conspiratorial motives to others. A man who believes his neighbors are trying to kill him or that the milkman is trying to steal his wife may create tremendous difficulties for others in social relationships, especially if such charges are false. Lemert (1962) has pointed out the self-fulfilling nature of such motive imputations; his research can be summarized in the idea that paranoids have real enemies. In other words, paranoids create a real (as opposed to a fictional) set of enemies by imputing unsavory motives to others.

Clinical depression seems to be defined on the basis of a different kind of motive problem. Depressed people may well seem not to give any motives at all in contexts where their behavior clearly calls for them. Some explanation will usually be called for if a person continually stares at walls, feels sad all of the time, and is completely uninterested in others or in social life.

Obviously, these tentative statements about the relationship between motives and mental disorder and that between motives and social change may be faulty. But they do demonstrate the compelling significance of the problem. In the future the concept of motive vocabularies as socially defined and executed rhetorics will offer some of the most intriguing and provocative research opportunities in social psychology.

F. SUMMARY

Motives have traditionally been construed in social science as causes of behavior, giving much of the research in social psychology a highly determinative cast with little sense of either personal freedom or a personal link to society. Recently, however, the concept of motives as purposes, reasons, justifications, and excuses has been introduced to the literature of social psychology. It seems to offer a powerful way of linking individual acts to social processes.

Motives, in this sense, do not compel people to act. They enable them to act by giving them a reason for what they do. By understanding how reasons are themselves made in and by society, we can see that motives have a social as opposed to a psychological or biological base. Motives are "unquestioned answers to questions" concerning social conduct. Their function is to repair disruptions in social relationships by putting others in communication with us about the sense of why we are doing what we are doing.

This idea of motives as purposes provides us with a link between individual behavior and social processes and offers a powerful way of understanding such important social processes as the self, social change, and mental disorder. In the future, the concept of motive vocabularies will be one of the most heavily researched and most interesting ideas in social psychology.

Social Roles 8

A. INTRODUCTION: THE NATURE AND THEORY
OF THE SOCIAL ROLE

1. A Necessary Concept

It is difficult to analyze a person's diverse patterns of action in daily life without a concept that defines his or her organized performances in relation to others. The concept that social psychologists commonly use for this purpose is the *social role*.

In examining the implications of the concept of role, we will draw on insights from the fields of sociology, anthropology, and psychology. Znaniecki, an early social psychologist, tried for 30 years to develop a common conceptual approach to individuals, not as psychological entities but as participants in social life (1965, 202). He needed a term that could apply to such widely different kinds of people as little girls, medieval knights, modern capitalists, rulers, serfs, priests, poets, lawyers, scientists, politicians, wealthy women, and factory workers. He found the dramatic term *role* most useful for the purpose.

Leading role theorists, in turn, have given a broad range of definitions to the concept of role. Linton (1936), for example, offered a cultural definition. He described roles as the sum of behavioral patterns associated with a particular status, including the attitudes, values, and behavior ascribed by the culture to all persons occupying the status.

Kelvin offered a more focused definition. "Roles consist of norms and expectations associated with positions in a social structure; with the position as such, independent of any particular individual who may hold the position" (Kelvin, 1970, 145).

Goffman, in a less structural and more situational vein, defined role as the response of individuals in a particular position. He said we usually bind our interest to the situation of some kind of person in a place and time, as in the factory during working hours or the home during nonworking hours. In other words, it is not so much that there *are* roles in the abstract sense of the previous two definitions. Rather, people structure their acts *as if* there were roles. In any event, the concept of role gives us a way of understanding the individual and others in terms that are not dualistic.

Goffman's goal was to adapt the concept of role for use in close observations of moment-by-moment behavior. Goffman cited the carnival merry-go-round. For the small child every ride can be viewed as an instance of a somewhat closed, self-realized situation. The 3-year-old demonstrates bravery and self-control; the 8-year-old shows his or her ability as a rider; the 12-year-old may show disdain for the role and achieve distance from it by ignoring the horse, riding backwards, or leaning sideward at a ridiculous angle (Goffman, 1961b, 97–99).

For the person, then, at some particular place and time, the successful performance of a role requires some fairly complex sequences of actions in cooperation with other role players. These roles are often performed in the direct presence of others such as teachers, coaches, friends, or rivals, all of whom impose some evaluation on the performance.

It is impossible to overemphasize the social nature of the role. The roles of one person always emerge in relation to the roles of others. Roles require two or more actors tied together by the context of their acts. For example, there is no role of wife without the corresponding role of husband, no role of child without the role of parent, and so on. Each role is enacted through time in joint play with a partner, and some kind of social action is ordinarily accomplished as a result of this engagement of roles.

2. Role Theory and Research

Although the concept of role has been widely used in the behavioral sciences, role theory has only gradually taken on definitive form. Even now there remains a good deal of ambiguity about the term. Historically, the idea of role has served as a link between psychology and sociology, suggesting as it does a psychological component to the sociologist and a sociological component to the psychologist. We are not, however, clear in either discipline on just what roles refer to. Role has been used to talk about an organization, or pattern, or behavior, but it is not clear what the content of this pattern is. Sometimes role is talked about as an organization of rights and privileges associated with a position in society. At other times it is referred to as a pattern of behavior. And it has been defined as a structure of attitudes and expectations.

Brissett and Edgley described some of the consequences of this disagreement:

> In the face of this lack of agreement, and perhaps because of it, social psychologists have employed the term in discussing nearly every facet of social life. Indeed, if one takes seriously the idea of sexual roles in marriage, it can be said that the human organism encounters a jungle of roles from the moment of conception until sometime after death. According to social psychologists, the shadows cast by roles are visible throughout the life cycle—one's parents, one's friends, one's spouse, one's children, one's lover, one's failure, one's occupation, and one's own selves are but a few of the roles with which a person is said to deal during a lifetime. Add to this the burden of having roles "ascribed" to oneself, "achieving" roles, "taking roles," "playing" roles and, in cases of mis-

fortune, experiencing "role conflict" and "role stress," and we have a formidable array of role-related activities for each individual [1975, 106].*

Despite its many ambiguities, however, the concept of role has been used extensively and profitably in research. We will note several examples here.

An investigation of the rights of the *sick role* showed that the extent to which people accord it legitimacy is inversely related to family size, regardless of socioeconomic status. The larger the family, the less willingness there was to tolerate the sick role (Petroni, 1969).

The effect of explicit instructions was much greater on female college students in the *leader role* than it was on male students, who were much more likely to ignore instructions (Sashkin and Maier, 1971). A study in which student actors simulated the relations between supervisor and clerk indicated that supervisors yield more to the clerk's pressure to overlook the rules if the clerk will later be rating the supervisor (Simmons, 1968).

An attempt to demonstrate the *chivalric male-protector role* when the female is threatened was totally unsuccessful, even though the aggression simulation was so realistic that one female victim suffered cracked ribs when a male aggressor threw her across the room (see Table 8-1). The case of a male onlooker protecting a female from male aggression simply did not occur, although males offered help about half of the time in the other combinations. Female onlookers offered no help to male victims, and only two offered help to female victims (Borofsky et al., 1971).

Table 8-1. The relation of sex and protection during physical assault

Aggression Pattern		Male Onlooker		Female Onlooker	
Attacker	Victim	Helped	Didn't Help	Helped	Didn't Help
Male	Male	4	1	0	5
Male	Female	0	6	1	3
Female	Male	2	1	0	7
Female	Female	4	3	1	4

Chi square = 5.75; $p < .05$

From "Sex Differences in Bystander Reactions to Physical Assault," by G. N. Borofsky, G. E. Stollock, and L. A. Messe, *Journal of Experimental Social Psychology*, 1971, 7, 313–318. Copyright 1971 by Academic Press, Inc. Reprinted by permission.

*This and all other quotations from this source are from *Life as Theater: A Dramaturgical Sourcebook*, by D. Brissett and C. Edgley. Copyright 1975 by Aldine Publishing Company. Reprinted by permission of Walter DeGruyter, Inc.

In 49 cases of *mother/child interaction* involving play with puzzles, mothers initiated action 27 times with the first-born child and five times with later-born children. First-born children were rewarded with demonstrated love significantly more often than later-born children if they succeeded with the puzzle, but not if they failed (Hilton, 1967).

In marriage it appears that the degree of segregation of the roles of husband and wife varies directly with the closeness of the couple to their own families (Bott, 1955). If a husband or wife continues close social involvement with his or her own family, there is much less shared action between the couple. If the couple moves away from both families, the amount of shared interaction increases. A study of 106 families in England (Turner, 1967) strongly supports this finding, as shown in Table 8-2. This is of special interest to role research, because it begins to identify interaction between various kinds of roles.

These examples show that the concept of roles can be a useful focus of research. Although ambiguity still bedevils the notion of roles, we can bring some order to the theoretical confusion by differentiating among types of roles, studying their observable properties, and looking at how people come to acquire and manage their various roles.

B. CHARACTERISTICS OF ROLES

1. Types of Roles

Of the multitude of roles people find themselves playing, we will suggest two general types that increase our understanding of their social nature. On the one hand, some roles are *ascribed*. We have them by virtue of the application of a social category based on a personal condition such as age or sex. One is a brother or sister or is 14 or 40 pretty much without choice. The role is, in effect, thrust on the actor. On the other hand, some roles are *achieved* by the actor's developing a skill to the point at which he or she can perform a given task.

The ascribed role depends on some widely shared characteristic of the person that is conventionally or even arbitrarily used by others to define the

Table 8-2. Conjugal roles and social networks

Conjugal Role Relation	*Interconnectedness of Social Networks*		
	Close-Knit	*Medium*	*Loose-Knit*
Segregated	42	10	4
Intermediate	13	0	7
Joint	8	8	14

Chi square = 26.9; $p < .001$ df = 4

From "Conjugal Roles and Social Networks," by C. Turner, *Human Relations*, May 1967, 121–130. Copyright 1967 by Plenum Publishing Corporation. Reprinted by permission.

individual's position. Age, sex, and kinship roles are commonly cited as ascriptive roles. One often discovers that one's identity as teenager, son, and male come from others almost entirely apart from the matter of personal choice. These ascriptive roles, furthermore, must be incorporated into more clearly achieved ones. Airline pilots must dress, perform their duties, and relate to others in a way that is consistent with their sex and age, in addition to their technical role. The male pilot who dresses in drag for the flight will probably discover from the reaction of others that his technical competence is not nearly enough to bring off the role acceptably!

Ascribed roles used to be regarded as those we had no choice over at all, such as the aforementioned examples of age and sex. But now it seems that even these basic human identities are open to modification. The example of transsexuals indicates that male and female are not immutably ascriptive, although they may be virtually so. The cult of youth—in which age is apparently, if not chronologically, turned back—likewise suggests the control people may exercise over even the most basic roles they play.

The achieved role may include a broad variety of behaviors appropriate to a particular social function. The role of a police officer must be achieved by reaching certain levels of training and education, being appointed by a government agency, and meeting criteria of age, health, and citizenship. The role calls for continuous performance of duty on a daily basis over an extended career. But individuals filling this role have a wide variety of behaviors that may be appropriate to law enforcement. Police officers choose from many career alternatives within the general category of the role, including security, investigation, traffic control, police administration, training, and emergency work. Thousands of generalized occupational roles can be identified as achieved roles.

2. Properties of Roles

Although more than a hundred terms have been applied to role phenomena, we will condense the terminology to four labels that designate the most important observable properties of roles. This discussion is heavily dependent upon Biddle and Thomas (1966).

a. Role extension.   Roles may be extended to incorporate several kinds of action. For example, a cashier at a movie box office has a relatively narrow role that involves receiving money, making change, and dispensing the appropriate number of tickets in exactly the same manner for all patrons. A building contractor has a much more extended role that includes dealing with suppliers, hiring workers, dealing with bank officials and government agencies, and buying and selling real estate.

b. Engagement and disengagement.   Roles are born, they live awhile, and then they die. *Engagement* and *disengagement* are terms that suggest this development. The ability to disengage one role and to engage another is essential to the actor in varying social situations. Role engagement sometimes involves well-marked indicators that a role is in play or that it is terminated. The shopkeeper ends his or her role for the day by turning off the lights and locking the door. Departing party guests may experience painful delay in disengaging their guest role at the door on a wintery evening, because they must appear reluctant to end the happy time had with the shivering host.

The enactment and continuation of any role require a measurable segment of time. As the variety of roles multiplies for a particular actor, he or she may experience increasing conflicts in allocating the time spent in action with different role partners.

c. Role tasks.   Social roles vary in the complexity of the tasks performed. For example, the mechanic's role might involve not only the replacement of the parts in a carburetor and the adjustment of the engine until it runs smoothly but also the filling out of necessary paper work and the necessity of engaging in a broad range of relationships with the supervisor of the shop, the parts manager, and the mechanic's apprentice. Contrast this with the role of independent newspaper carrier, which involves a much less complex task and a narrower range of relationships.

d. Role playing and role taking.   The actual playing of roles involves the taking of others' roles, too (Mead, 1934). By the social psychologist's convention, role taking refers to the actor's putting himself or herself in the place of someone else and imagining how an action would be interpreted by the other. O'Toole and Dubin (1968) observed that mothers, when spoon-feeding their babies, appear to put themselves in the infant's place because the mother frequently opens her own mouth as she attempts to maneuver the loaded spoon into the baby's mouth. A therapist working with a troubled spouse may ask a husband to put himself in the wife's place and imagine how his behavior must appear to her.

C. HOW ROLES MESH IN SOCIAL SITUATIONS

1. Linking the Actor to Others

As we have seen, role is the concept that links one person's acts to another's in the context of a social situation. What is sometimes described as social structure is defined by the distinctions people make in their role relations. The actor uses only a limited portion of his or her behavioral resources to play the roles associated with a specific social position. He or she plays a reserved part by agreement and in cooperation with other players in the same situation. For the person, the badge of acceptance in various well-defined niches in society is his or her ability to play the different kinds of roles required in different contexts. At the same time, each actor is profoundly dependent on other actors in sustaining social relations. Since roles are born in relationships, it is up to the continuing efforts of the participants to keep them going.

Viewed on a day-to-day basis, society appears to be relatively stable. But this appearance belies the considerable effort often necessary by actors to enact their roles in such a way as to perform competently. Human beings spend the bulk of their waking hours engaging and reengaging in roles in the course of an active day. In each of these engagements actors meet the basic expectations of their fellows and yet manage to inject novel elements into the detailed exchange. Since each actor must sustain multiple roles with different sets of individuals, he or she can engage in only a few at a time. Interaction is a focused process, and it is difficult to enact large numbers of roles at the same time. Consequently, many settings for roles are vacant much of the time. The downtown area of large cities is mostly vacant after 5 P.M., and the suburbs are vacant much of the day. The same sort of thing is true of theaters, churches, cafeterias, amusement parks, classrooms, hotels, and passenger vehicles. These settings are constructed in order to elicit only a few of the multitude of roles that a person performs in the course of any given day.

The roles of one person always emerge in relation to the roles of others. (Photo by © Elinor S. Beckwith, Taurus Photos)

In a broader sense, there is a massive transition of actors who periodically enter and leave behavioral settings. They pass through the educational system, vacation periods, occupations, residences, and family and personal associations. A primary characteristic of modern social life is rapid change, constant adjustment, and the repeated problem of mastering the behavior associated with new roles. As our society has become more specialized and fragmented, the range of discrete roles required of each member has increased. This has presented a larger number of problems for which the performer must devise a solution. Who could have foreseen 50 years ago, for example, the solutions devised by husbands and wives to keep those roles intact while pursuing individual work careers, sometimes at long distances from each other?

2. The Dynamics of Social Roles

The static concept of role may imply that the role is always in effect, in some sense, and that the role fully occupies the actor during engagement. In real life, however, both assumptions are too generalized to be accurate. There is a vast difference in the interplay of mother and child at 5 months of age and at 5 decades. In the latter case the maternal role is more historic than real. For the individual actors there may be very little carryover from one role relation to another. Their actual involvement in some roles may be so reduced that others perceive them as defaulting on the role. Many actors throw themselves wholeheartedly into a role they think "important" and neglect less important roles. If Dr. Dough, the plastic surgeon, spends 80 hours a week at the hospital, his wife may say he does well as a doctor but poorly as a husband and father. Others recognize an acceptable range of investment for a specific role. If actors fall short of the required range of investment, they are considered negligent. If they exceed it, like Dr. Dough, they may be considered to be obsessed or overdedicated.

3. Commitment to Role

Actors vary in the extent to which they are committed to the roles they play. Commitment and belief in the part one is playing do not seem to be as much a requirement of social life as the actual competent playing of the role itself. In our society, furthermore, basic ascribed roles can be combined with a greater variety of specialized roles, and there can be greater independence between roles (Banton, 1965, 52). Within occupations the orientation of commitment varies. Professors are often more oriented to their occupation and to colleagues than to students. Lawyers may be more client oriented. Engineers tend to be more oriented toward the corporation that employs them than to the engineering profession as a whole. It is not unheard of to find third-grade teachers who double at night as call girls. Although this last example may be rare, it does suggest that even the technically competent playing of a role does not assure that the actor is committed to it exclusive of all others, even some seemingly antithetical ones.

In modern industrial societies the necessity of having flexibility within and between roles does not seem to fit the rigid kinship systems that other societies in other places and at other times defined as appropriate. Commitment to the work role depends very much on personal advantage and status enhancement. For example, quitting the firm often costs the actor status, pay, rewards, and seniority. A study of 3045 U.S. Catholic priests indicated that celibacy was the principal cost of commitment to the role. Many saw the restriction on marriage as so costly that they were ready to leave the clergy. More than one-eighth of the clergy did leave for other careers from 1966 through 1972 (Schoenherr and Greeley, 1974).

4. The Role Set

A role set may be defined as the array of role partners with whom an actor must be involved in performing a particular social role (Merton, 1957, 369). The role set of a schoolteacher includes all of those audiences that he or she plays to at one time or another in the enactment of the role: school principal, secretaries and custodial personnel, other teachers, and students. Because of this variety of audiences, the actor needs a considerable amount of interpersonal dexterity to bring the roles off adequately. One of the major challenges of roles is to schedule and control relationships with sometimes conflicting sets of others. Each actor usually has several specific role sets, each of which imposes delicate problems of organization, scheduling, and negotiation. When serious problems of management arise, the actor adjusts schedules, talks things over with others in the set, or even tries to restructure the set. (A divorce is a reorganization of the role set.) Because social settings are relatively stable, it is usually possible for people to find new audiences and new sets of roles when the old ones do not work. Finding a new audience for one's role performances is one of the most typical solutions to the problem of interpersonal conflict.

Roles do, however, require a good deal of competence in their performance. A person with limited verbal or academic skills is likely to be confined to a low-paying job in the middle-class world. But a person well endowed with these skills may have a difficult time getting along in the ghetto.

5. The Interdependence of Roles

The multitude of separate roles a person plays are tied together in time and space because the person transfers some of the values and experiences from one set to another. The actors in each set acknowledge the competing requirements of related social roles. Families surrender routine family functions in deference to a child who has an important part in the school play.

The employer temporarily releases a family man from his work duties when there is a sudden disaster at home. (The same understanding is not always shown the working woman—hence the recent controversy over maternity leaves with pay for mothers.) The children's play group will accommodate itself to mother's restrictions and demands and to changes introduced by community agencies in the neighborhood. Public roles may exert weight on making the "proper" marriage, relating to the right friends, determining the neighborhood of residence, and adopting a workable mixture of public roles (Heine, 1971, 107).

Much of the organization and institutionalization of social process has arisen from the necessity of ordering, accommodating, and coordinating the relations between different roles. Parsons notes that the mother role is anchored between the adult level of the family and the mother/child role, whereas the father role permits a great deal of interchange and transit between the family and the rest of the world (1955, 81). This observation, of course, has also been made by many women these days, and they are rapidly changing the situation!

The adult-female sex role is in a process of change in most Western industrial societies. It is slowly being transformed from the traditional inferiority and dependence on a husband to a position of general equality with men. Female equality is coming to be recognized in legislation and courts, but custom and convention continue to establish female subordination to the male. As one sociologist put the case, women have already been damaged through socialization by the time they get married. They have been trained to accept second best, not to strive, and to accept the fact that they are unworthy of more than low-status, low-paying jobs and must serve their husbands as domestic workers without pay and as compulsory sex partners (Gillespie, 1971).

The female-subordination theme is well entrenched—for example, in children's readers. Little girls are continually depicted as invisible, passive, waiting, and doll-like in appearance and as the prize of the hero's activity. The boy speaks, acts, solves, and triumphs; the girl pleases, helps, serves, smiles, and stays at home. In 18 children's readers surveyed by content analysis in one study, not one woman had a job or a profession (Weitzman, 1972). College textbooks on marriage and the family are similar in regarding "women's place." The female is viewed by the male sociologist as one who belongs at home ministering to her husband and children, forswearing all other interests (Ehrlich, 1971).

Perhaps the best that can be said for confining women to the home/wife/mother role is that it serves gloriously the interest of men. But women are deprived of the more challenging aspects of the female role early in life, when their children reach mid-adolescence. If the women's role is to be broadened, upgraded, and made equal to that of the man, it is likely to come about only if women insist on it. Apparently, many are insisting on it, and doing so with considerable success.

A large repertoire of roles gives the person flexibility, competence, and status among others. Accumulating a large number of roles is apparently more gratifying than stressful, in spite of the fact that such a repertoire requires more complex organization of time and resources than a limited number would involve. Each role carries with it privileges and rewards. Multiple roles provide alternatives, bargaining power, and trade-offs. The expansion of the number of roles one can play affords security, emoluments, and leverage in relation to partners and other actors as well.

D. ACTOR MANAGEMENT OF ROLES

Thus far we have spoken of roles more or less externally. However, it is necessary to note that human beings exercise considerable control over the roles they play through a variety of management techniques.

Perhaps the most intricate and far-reaching technique is the individual's sense of dramaturgy. Using this technique, actors are able to present themselves convincingly and continuously in a specific social guise. This requires that they monitor their own behavior so as to exclude invalidating acts, thoughts, gestures, and malapropisms that would weaken their act. At the same time they must keep up behavioral appearances that sustain the action and stimulate the partner. Actors must maintain face and not communicate out of character. But the difficulty arises when we note that actors must maintain a different face to the many sets of others that they relate to. Indeed, different masks are worn by actors as they play roles toward peers, subordinates, superiors, work mates, and playmates. Interpersonal dramaturgy means that actors are aware of the necessity of employing selectively such factors as secrecy, deception, privacy, and honesty if they are to bring the role off (Sprey, 1969; Goffman, 1959).

Intricate motor skills are also an important part of the success of many roles. They may constitute the main stumbling blocks to successful role performance. Any number of performances have gone awry because of dropped props, stumbling actors, or falling scenery.

1. Role Conflict

Role conflict arises when the same actor attempts to play two incompatible roles. This experience is a hallmark of Western society, as the following examples indicate. The embezzler posing as the honest bank officer and the married minister who supports a clandestine love affair experience conflict because the moral contradiction threatens their professional status. The playing of some roles obviously conflicts with the playing of others!

Law schools have found it difficult to place female graduates with male lawyers because their wives would experience role conflict with such a partnership (Epstein, 1970). Male seniors of an Ivy League college indicated sex-role inadequacy in relation with women in such matters as assertiveness, determination, decision, courage, independence, aggressiveness, and stability under stress (Komarovsky, 1973). It is difficult to meet the requirements for superiority of the male role when faced with female students who are in fact equal.

Role conflict is also induced when the actor attempts two disparate roles at the same time, like babysitting with two vigorous children while studying mathematics. Finally, role conflict results when too many separate role performances are required of an actor (Snoek, 1966).

2. Fitting the Role to the Person

Most actors try out alternate approaches in the process of becoming expert in a role. Flexibility is essential in successful role performance, as the actor shifts from the tasks associated with the performance of a very formal role (such as, let's say, sitting on the Supreme Court) to the performance of very informal roles (such as bantering with close friends). People often relieve the strain of one role by shifting to another. The homemaker may leave household chores to become a customer in a dress shop.

One of the most important techniques used by actors to fit roles to themselves is what Goffman calls *role distance* (Goffman, 1961b; Coser, 1966). Role distance is a technique by which performers separate themselves from the role they are playing. They may do this for several reasons. First, they may want to stave off becoming completely engulfed in a role. Secondly, they may need to assert some independence from the role. And finally, role distance is a useful way of demonstrating to others complete mastery over the role they are playing. Surgeons, for example, may display humor during a delicate operation in order to relieve tension and put their assistants more at ease. Workmen on a job may play pranks on newly hired workers as a means of dramatizing some aspect of the work, such as its complexity. The prankster may substitute a piece of the wrong size on the assembly line and then laugh with the others when the victim struggles to make it fit (Lundberg, 1969).

Actors may put distance between themselves and the role to repudiate the role either temporarily or permanently. In this case the person may burlesque the role or perform it in an exaggerated way that is directly contrary to that usually required. The highly disciplined petty officer on shore leave may mimic naval procedure among his fellows or become boisterously intoxicated. And the newly retired laborer may go out of her way to flaunt her travel exploits to her former work mates.

Role distance, then, is a way by which people separate themselves from their roles—or at least from what their roles imply about them. Role distance is not really a denial of roles, for roles must be continually created in order to smooth relations with others. However, role distance is a way of expressing that the role is not playing the person. In this sense role distance is an affirmation of personal worth (Brissett and Edgley, 1975).

Roles may be played sincerely or cynically—that is, on the basis of morality or expedience (Goffman, 1959). The moral, or sincere, orientation centers on the officially approved demands of the role. The role is performed "as it should be," regardless of sanctions. The expedient orientation maximizes rewards and minimizes costs. A third type combines morality and expedience, seeking the best compromise.

The use of demonstration models to help other people learn the requirements of roles is a familiar means of teaching role requirements. The incidence of willingness to help motorists in difficulty, for example, seems to be significantly increased if other motorists observe someone receiving help with a flat tire before they encounter another motorist who obviously needs help (Bryan and Test, 1967). A role model may also operate negatively. Second-born college men with an older sister scored lower on a femininity scale and showed more interest in typically masculine outdoor activity than did second-born men with older brothers (Leventhal, 1970). Acting out the sick role seems to be a mode of adjustment when coping is particularly difficult. The student who displayed more stress in the form of anxiety, discomfort, and emotional tension had a higher frequency of visits to the school medical clinic in one study (Mechanic and Volkart, 1961). Physical disability that is officially or medically recognized offers a means of altering one's behavior by suspending the usual requirements of a role with official approval.

3. Acquiring Knowledge of Social Roles

a. Stages of role acquisition. The capable actor does not emerge full blown, as the goddess Athena did from the head of Zeus. Developing actors must learn the role behaviors that will satisfy the expectations of more experienced role partners. Equally important, they must learn to avoid behavior that others define as inconsistent and contradictory to a required role, or else develop strategies for changing their minds about just what constitutes the role.

Four stages of role acquisition have been identified: (1) anticipatory, (2) formal, (3) informal, and (4) personal (Thornton and Nardi, 1975). The anticipatory stage includes orientation and preparation, using hearsay, fantasy, and learning about the content of the role. In the formal stage others specify the role, teach the beginners, and correct their mistakes in performance. In the informal stage the actors have some mastery of the role and can begin to apply the rules as they see fit. In the final stage, when the actors have full mastery of the role, they may mold it in their own individual way.

Parsons (1964, 42) illustrated role development with the emergence of the sex role. Young children gradually learn to differentiate the role of female or male from the more generalized role of the child member of the family. The prototype of sex-role differentiation for the children is that of the male and female parent in relation to each other and in relation to

"C'mon over, Dennis! I think
I learned how to make fudge."   "Diff'rent, huh? I use
garlic instead of vanilla."

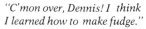

Newcomers to a role often make mistakes in trying to play it.

them. They learn that boys do not cry and that girls do not fight with their fists. They learn that boys will someday be expected to function in the world of work, commerce, industry, and government, whereas girls are required to keep house and care for children. Boys should be active, resourceful, and aggressive in their role behavior. Girls need not extend their primary interests beyond the immediate confines of the family and home in this simple model, and their most appropriate role-relevant games involve playing "house" or "hostess." Learning either the male or the female sex-role behavior requires renunciation of previously permitted infantile behaviors, avoidance of behaviors specific to the opposite sex, and convincing performance of role-relevant behavior.

In late adolescence the erotic attachment implicit in the adult sex role is permitted, this time outside the family (Parsons, 1964, 45). Throughout, the female role calls for passivity, cooperation, and personal service. The male role calls for aggressiveness and self-assertion in childhood play relations and for dominating masculinity, typically exemplified in organized athletics and in the exercise of power, in adult life (Wyer and Weatherley, 1965). It can be shown experimentally that women tend to maneuver men into the leadership position when there is a choice. When high-dominance female students were paired with low-dominance male students in performing a sexually neutral type of clerical task, the females suggested that the male be the leader (Megargee, 1969). The efforts of feminist groups to change these roles suggest the dynamic and interactive nature of them.

b. *The natural history of the role.*   The actor passes through many distinct roles during his or her social experience. Each of these, regardless of duration, has a continuity to it, manifesting a fairly consistent developmental sequence that is important in assessing role phenomena. We might call this sequence the natural history of the role. This history begins with orientation to the content of the role. This orientation process may be quite deliberate, as in the case of being trained to do a specific task. Or it may be the result of chance associations, as when the individual becomes interested, let's say, in a new hobby. The orientation often includes a *role model*—that is, a fellow actor whom the newcomer is able to imitate in some respects. Commitment and self-involvement begin to emerge in a little-understood transition from the orientation phase. The actor presumably begins to see himself or herself in the role and to want to perform it. Some abstract training occurs through the role partner, as the actor attempts to develop better insights and skills, objectives, and purposes.

In this initial phase the newcomer to the role often evidences uncertainty, awkwardness, and hesitation. The role partner may be permissive and encouraging, easily overlooking mistakes and gently making corrections. With practice and experience the actor achieves some mastery in the competent performance of the role and may then teach and share the behavior with new role partners. The final phase is one of retirement and relinquishment of the role, as the actor moves on to new ones. This final phase is often accompanied by considerable social reorganization for the role partners. Relinquishment of roles occurs at all stages of life, as when the small child surrenders the baby role, the maturing adolescent leaves school, or a middle-aged player gives up golf. Leaving a role is one of life's most poignant moments.

4. Behavior's Relation to Role

Specific kinds of behavior are closely related to particular roles and have a decisive effect on the success of the role. For example, the social caseworker is expected to establish and maintain an accepting relationship with each client. But he or she frequently plays the role of a rejecting parent when the client is unwilling to cooperate by the rules (Stream, 1968, 282). There are no exact prescriptions for incorporating the truly human behaviors associated with amusement, nervousness, fascination, and concentration in the performance of roles. But such elements do stamp the role performance as genuine, and the lack of them may lead the audience to impute phoniness to the role.

The demands of performing a role are so potent that they can easily lead to delusion. Undergraduate students tasting distilled water in 50 trials were asked to report each time whether it was salted or unsalted. Although a few subjects never reported tasting salt, 24% of all responses reported salt (Juhasz and Sarbin, 1966). The students' assumption that the experimental-subject role would include the salt experience led them to believe they had tasted salt when there was none.

The emotions involved in a role have a measurable effect on behavior. Fromme and Schmidt (1972) instructed college students to work themselves into a state of fear, anger, sorrow, or neutral feelings toward a strange student who was sitting passively at a table some distance away. They were then told simply to approach the student, look at him and then return. The mean proximity of approach in the fear condition was 32 inches, compared with 15 inches in the other three conditions. In the sorrow condition, subjects maintained eye contact 24% of the time, as compared with 48% in the other conditions.

It is possible to perform various social roles under extreme restrictions if verbal contact can be maintained. A polio patient paralyzed from the shoulders down and confined to a respirator tank continued to be an excellent mother. Her children came to the tank each morning so she could tell that they were properly fed and dressed for the day. When the children returned from school each child told the mother of the day's activities (Coser, 1966). She was able to maintain the mother role even under such conditions!

As the actor gains proficiency in a role, more and more control is taken on even though the person may be working under close supervision and exact job specifications in a rigid bureaucratic system. The more professionally oriented manager, for example, looks more to outside opinion and to the judgment of colleagues outside the organization in determining his or her own policies and procedures. He or she does this in spite of the efforts of superiors to apply rules and controls. The more professional manager thus gains autonomy and independence in the exercise of authority by looking to external reference groups, peers, and the "invisible college" of the profession (Haga et al., 1974). Kipnis's work *The Powerholders* also shows a relaxation of supervision and the use of differential control measures when a person is playing a role proficiently (Kipnis, 1976). In contrast, the less professional manager follows the bureaucratic prescriptions more closely and is not so much influenced by external professional standards.

5. Parallel Roles

Parallel roles are a social psychologist's way of designating behavior that occurs when individuals perform similarly with no need to interact among themselves. Customers in a market, for example, generally ignore one another as they go about doing pretty much the same thing: getting their groceries. Individual members of an audience at a rock concert find themselves in an integrated role relationship with the performers, ushers, and ticket takers, but in a parallel relationship with other members of the audience. Brothers and sisters in the same family are likewise in a parallel relationship with respect to their own roles. A mother or father has relatively specific performance obligations toward each child. But there are no equally specific role-performance demands between siblings, except in the case where the older child is asked to take care of his little brother. In this circumstance both children may challenge the relationship as fraudulent and resent the forced relationship that deprives them of their usual parallel relationship.

6. Integrating Roles

Role playing is a cooperative enterprise—we usually help one another play roles. When one partner has more knowledge and experience with a role, the process of interaction usually includes a great deal of transfer in which expectations, norms, and techniques are exchanged between those who are new to the role and those who are veterans. This tutoring aspect of social relationships is most apparent in the teacher/student and parent/child interaction. But the attempt to equalize an understanding of how roles are played is to be found in virtually any relationship in which one person has more knowledge of a role than the other. If both partners lack experience, the relationship may develop on a quite arbitrary basis, with some conventional parts of the role being omitted. Research on the sharing of household tasks among retired couples has indicated that the retired husband tends to take over certain household tasks from the wife. These tasks are not shared but, rather, divided between the couple (Ballweg, 1967).

Sex is a part of the role of husband and wife but, incredible as it seems, it is possible for a married couple to omit altogether this aspect of the role and carry on a marriage while preserving the virginity of the wife. One thousand such couples located through medical clinics in New York City ranged in the duration of their sexless marriages from one year to 21 years, with an average of eight years. The reasons for the omission of coital intercourse included fear, revulsion, and resistance to pregnancy on the part of the wife (Blazer, 1964).

7. Audience Effects

People play their roles to audiences that review them. If the audience to a person's role changes, the role itself may well change. Videotaped records of parent/child interaction in 40 families revealed a significant difference in the smiling behavior of fathers and mothers. Fathers smiled at their children when the content of their speech was friendly, whereas mothers smiled at their children regardless of the content of their speech. Both parents smiled frequently when they knew they were being observed and much more rarely when they supposed they were unobserved (Bugenthal et al., 1971). This illustrates the difference between what is often called public and private behavior. If there is no audience other than the primary participants, the role performer is free to develop his or her performance solely in terms of the actions of the partner. If an audience of persons outside the primary role relation is present, the action may be profoundly modified to include the perceived expectations of the audience and may disregard some of the ordinary expectations of the partner.

Whether or not a role relation is generated may depend on the perceived characteristics of the actors. Plainly dressed black or white college women were instructed to drop groceries from a broken bag approximately 10 feet from another shopper in front of a supermarket in various black or white neighborhoods. The goal was to determine what proportion of subjects would perform the helping role in the presence of other shoppers. The subjects of the experiment were differentiated by race and sex, as shown in Table 8-3 (Wispe and Freshley, 1971).

Help was offered in only 20% of the cases, primarily by males. Black females offered no help, and white females were more willing to help a white female than a black female. Males seemed affected by the conventional male helping role, offering help in 34% of the cases. People in supermarkets in black neighborhoods were more friendly, and black men offering help seemed to enjoy doing so. White helpers did so under strain and seemed to be embarrassed. In this case there was only a 20% probability that the role of helper would be enacted. The simple, brief relationship imposes differential responses by type of helper.

The response rate of people doing manual tasks is increased if others are watching them. If the majority of all responses are correct, then the effect of an audience is to increase output. If the task is difficult and most attempts are errors, then the effect is to reduce the success rate. This is because the pressure to act faster makes the dominant and erroneous response more likely (Zajonc, 1965).

8. Controlling and Manipulating Roles

Several controls are typically applied in the performance of social roles in order to maintain boundaries, restrict the action, or prevent interference between phases of action. Goffman points to the need for civil inat-

Table 8-3. Percentage of passers-by who helped a female shopper with a broken grocery bag

Helper Shopper	Black Male		Black Female		White Male		White Female	
	Black	White	Black	White	Black	White	Black	White
Percent helping	41	36	0	0	23	36	5	18
N	22	22	22	22	22	22	22	22

Total percent helping: 20

From "Race, Sex, and Sympathetic Helping Behavior: The Broken Bag Caper," by L. G. Wispe and H. B. Freshley, *Journal of Personality and Social Psychology*, 1971, *17*, 59–65. Copyright 1971 by the American Psychological Association. Reprinted by permission of the author and publisher.

tention in situations where it is not appropriate to enter role relationships with strangers who happen to pass by (1963b, 84). For example, in public places such as train stations, elevators, and doorways the trick is to acknowledge other people's presence while not acting as though they were objects of undue curiosity by, for instance, staring at them.

Role performance is also made easier by inattention to slips and errors or to potentially embarrassing accidents and incapacities. One simply overlooks potential disruptions in the stream of action in the same way that one attempts to filter out other forms of interference. Some roles may be too tightly or too loosely structured for a particular actor to tolerate them (Goffman, 1959). Some actors are incapable of maintaining the precision and accuracy demanded of an accountant or a cashier. Others might be equally uncomfortable at a Boy Scout summer camp.

The successful performance of a role requires attentive staging, acceptance by the partners, and well-timed supportive responses. When a wife asks her husband's assurance that he loves her, a moment's hesitation in answering or the appearance of doubt can shatter the situation. Roles may even require deception or withholding information about other parts that some of the actors are also performing. The traitor or spy carefully maintains a seemingly legitimate role with one set of superiors who are deceived about his relationship to the enemy. Double agents deceive both sets of superiors. Similarly, surprise presents and surprise parties also require collusion and deceit. The role of a mistress is likewise concealed by a married man with a job to protect.

Generally, there is a need to restrict information that is shared between role partners exactly to that scope of knowledge most conducive to the success of the particular role relation. The relation can be jeopardized by insufficient information about the partners, by information that is discrediting to the relation, or by too much irrelevant information. For this reason there are well-established techniques for concealing errors and dirty work involved in the performance of roles. The hostess may not permit dinner guests to see the kitchen. Lawyers generally try to conceal facts that would prejudice their case. Finally, actors sometimes find that several social roles are being stripped from them through the collusion of others who have been their role partners. A business partner may disappear with all of the funds and terminate a business operation. A wife may strip her husband of professional and recreational roles, reducing him to an invalid role because he has suffered a heart attack.

9. Limits on the Range of Action in Role Performance

The behavioral content of many roles is rather precisely specified. Specific ranges of acceptable actions, gestures, and topics of conversation are often well established, particularly where there is a formal organization (Argyle, 1969, 273). Generally, role clarity improves role performance, and role ambiguity degrades performance. Role clarity is less for brides than for grooms, particularly if the bride is not working and has only a small apartment to care for and no children. Under such conditions the bride is likely to be uncomfortable and dissatisfied with her ambiguous and unaccustomed role (Sarbin and Allen, 1968, 506).

Nowhere are role expectations more nicely under control than in the dental office. Observation of 114 patients disclosed full and immediate cooperation when the dentist politely requested patients to open their mouth, hold a piece of equipment, rinse, spit, or turn a bit more to the right. The dentist tended to repeat his statements more for children, but interaction was brisk and efficient for all patients (Linn, 1967).

The quality of interaction between supervisors and subordinates who come from autocratic families is more likely to be autocratic. Fathers who occupied low-status work roles experienced coercion by supervisors at the work setting and related in a similar manner to their sons (Elder, 1965).

E. SUMMARY

The concept of role is one of the most durable in all of social psychology. It has, historically, been a link between psychology and sociology, a term that could bridge the gap and be used by both disciplines with profit. Many different definitions of role exist, but all focus on the organized performances of a person as he or she acts in relation to others.

There are a multitude of roles a person plays in his lifetime. There are ascribed roles, achieved roles, sex roles, age roles, political roles, economic roles, and occupational roles, to mention only a few.

The basic idea of the role is that it provides a way of linking the acts of one person to the acts of another. What is usually seen by the sociologist as "social structure" can be seen by the social psychologist simply as distinctions of a certain type that people make in their role relationships. Many of the satisfactions, frustrations, and achievements of life arise in the context of role playing.

Roles are not static; they are dynamic components of social relationships. Roles are played and played at, usually with some considerable investment on the part of the actor. Roles must be carried off; they do not automatically enact themselves. Therefore, deciding which role to play and how to play it occupies considerable time during the course of a single day.

Actors, of course, vary in the extent to which they are committed to the roles they play. Modern industrial society seems to require the playing of such a multiplicity of roles that it would be unrealistic to assume that the actor was equally committed to all of them. Rather, it seems that Western societies, at least, put more stress on the competent playing of the role required in a situation rather than insisting that the actor fully believe any given part being played.

An important point in the understanding of roles is that actors manage the roles they play rather than the role managing them. Although some types of roles may seem to the actor to be relatively involuntary (such as sex roles), there are few roles that are not elaborated and altered by the efforts of the actor playing them. A considerable amount of dramaturgical dexterity may be required in juggling and fitting together the large number of roles required in modern society.

Roles are also played out against the context of the roles of others. Social psychologists sometimes speak of a role set such as student/teacher, parent/child, and husband/wife. One role exists only in relation to the other role.

Role conflict arises when the actor attempts to play incompatible roles. Western society seems to have created a whole series of situations in which role conflict might arise.

Actors attempt to fit the roles they play to themselves. In this sense roles are made as much as taken on, and one of the most important techniques by which this is accomplished is role distance. Performers expressly separate themselves from the roles they are playing for a variety of reasons.

Knowledge of social roles must be acquired in social relationships with other role players. We do not know how to play roles at birth, but acquire the skill during the process of socialization.

Some roles are hierarchically arranged, whereas others are parallel. A mother is in a hierarchical relationship to her child, but two customers in a store are in a parallel relationship to each other. There is frequently conflict when a parallel role is turned into a hierarchical role by one of the actors.

There is a considerable tutoring aspect to the playing of roles. People teach each other roles as they are interacting, and the process of learning and acquiring a particular role is continuous throughout life.

Despite the ambiguities in the idea of a social role, the notion remains popular among both sociologists and psychologists. Because it offers such a clear link between the concerns of the two disciplines, the concept may be expected to remain a vital part of social psychology.

Small Groups 9

A. INTRODUCTION

1. Definitions

John Donne's observation that no man is an island has special significance for social psychologists. The group is fascinating to us because it displays so many properties that help us understand what an individually oriented psychology has difficulty explaining. For example, groups outlive their
individual members, so patterns of recruitment and socialization are important. They also transcend their individual members in the sense that they
often act in ways that a majority of their members might individually repudiate. In short, groups seem to be, in many respects, more than the sum of
their parts.

A small social group has few enough members that each is able to
communicate with all the others face to face (Homans, 1950). Such groups do
not become social realities immediately when people assemble. Rather, they
develop gradually through a series of interactions among the members. At
first, individuals who are beginning to form a group try various subjects of
conversation. Thibaut and Kelley (1959) talk about this as "exploring the
matrix of possible outcomes." Because most people have an extensive range
of interests and capacities, the process of exploration in any group usually
touches only a small fraction of the potential range of relationships and
activities the group could develop.

One of the most important characteristics of a group is its size. Variations in size make enormous differences in the activity, organization, and
quality of a group. Georg Simmel (1950) did early theoretical work on the
significance of group size. His suggestion that social scientists investigate the
geometry of the relations among group members led to major lines of development for what came to be known as *field theory*, the major proponent of
which has been Kurt Lewin. Simmel focused particular attention on the
"dyad," or two-person group. In the most profound sense the dyad is basic to
all social relations, because it is the most intimate and concentrated of all
groups. It is important to note, as Simmel did, that a dyad has features that
transcend the membership of the individuals who compose it. Anyone who
has ever invited a third party into a dyad and then had to deal with the
resulting conflict can well appreciate the extraindividual quality of the two-
person versus three-person group.

2. Primary Groups

The primary group, of which the dyad is an example, has five defining
characteristics: (1) it is a direct, face-to-face relationship; (2) it is un-
specialized; (3) it is relatively permanent; (4) it includes a small number of
persons; and (5) the association is relatively intimate (Cooley, 1933). These
are relationships with members of our family, close personal friends, or col-

The dyad is basic to all social relations because it provides the most intimate and concentrated relationship one human being can have with another. (Photo by © Burk Uzzle, Magnum Photos)

leagues with whom we interact on a regular basis. Within the primary group persons develop understanding, affection, and mutual support. Primary groups, of necessity, deal with the whole person. They are not specialized, but deal with their members across a wide range of interests and concerns. Close friends in a primary group play games, solve problems, work on projects, make plans, pool resources, discuss, argue, reach agreement, and depend on one another. Primary groups are relatively permanent and are built on a base of continuous and prolonged association. They may endure for several years or even a lifetime. The members think of the relationship as stable and dependable, not as something that must be renegotiated each time they come together. Primary groups are usually small because the necessary level of intimacy they involve tends to be difficult to sustain in a larger group. However, a person may be a member of several primary groups.

The intimate aspect of primary relationships includes affection, physical contact, the ability to share the most damaging secrets, and the mutual security and satisfaction that comes from the feeling that one is loved and cared for. The intimacy afforded in primary groups is one of the reasons the primary group has been called "the most indestructible of all human groups" (Bierstedt, 1970). Whatever heights of success and power people might reach or whatever depths to which they might fall, there is usually a primary group of loved ones who provide a base of support. Most people regularly go back to the support of a family or friends as a relief from the impersonality of work and the formality of the world of public and semipublic places. The primary group is powerful, immediate, and basic; it is the foundation for all levels of social organization and for all other types of social processes.

B. GROUP INFLUENCES

1. Willingness to Accept Risk

Individuals in experimental settings have frequently accepted a greater risk after discussion in a group than they would when alone (Clark, 1971). For example, French women students were more conservative in risking bets of .2 francs and .6 francs (about 5 cents and 15 cents) when making the decision alone but shifted to a greater level of risk for themselves when they were in a group (Zaleska and Kogan, 1971). French male students also shifted as did male students from the United States.

Similar results were found when the "risk" was imaginary. These tests were conducted in England, New Zealand, Germany, and Israel. An imaginary risk is illustrated by the question: "Which job would you select: (1) a position with average salary, lifelong security, and a guaranteed pension or (2) a high-paying position with good opportunity for success but without pension provisions and entirely dependent on your ability to perform?" Of course, the second choice is the "riskier," but the respondent is not really taking any risk to choose it and may do so simply to make a good impression.

The triad is more complicated and holds far more potential for conflict than the dyad. Can you see possibilities for conflict in this picture? (Photo by © Eric Kroll, Taurus Photos)

2. Patterned Relations among Group Members

Sociometry is a technique generally used to establish through diagrams the relations among group members, following the theory and technique of the pioneering psychiatrist Jacob Moreno (Moreno, 1934; Borgatta, 1975). Moreno viewed the socialized person as a social atom who can fill a more or less predefined position in relation to other social atoms. The result is a social group with molecular structure. He devised a graphic method using points to represent persons and lines and arrows to show their combined relations. This method identifies central persons (marked by many communicating lines), triads, dyads, and isolates. The total picture helps to identify the poorly integrated group, and it also shows clusters of effective members in well-integrated groups.

The principle can best be illustrated with a communication sociogram of a small group. In Figure 9-1 the odd-numbered circles represent boys in an elementary-school class, and the even-numbered circles represent girls. The figure is a "directed graph" because the arrows graph the action in either direction or in both directions. One boy, No. 9, had no contact with the other children during the period of observation. The boys talked very little among themselves, and they approached the girls more often than they approached each other. Nearly half of the verbal interaction occurred among the girls, and this centered heavily on No. 2. She was approached by all of the other girls and by none of the boys. Because five arrows concentrate on No. 2 (counting the double arrow from No. 6 twice), she was the sociometric star of the group. No. 1 was the center of action on the boys' side, but he was approached by only one boy and one girl and was linked to less active persons. The girls appear to have been more communicative and more socially oriented from the evidence in these graphs.

Analysis of this kind can be very helpful in analyzing the quality and pattern of relationships in small groups. If the group is larger than 15 persons, the pattern formed by the directional arrows becomes very complex and difficult to represent by a sociogram. However, groups of 50 or more can readily be represented in a metric table (Table 9-1), where the rows represent action given and the columns represent action received. A series of such graphs recorded at regular intervals over a period of time could show numerous relational developments in the group and could give evidence of the quality of action among the group members.

3. A Sociogram Analysis of a Work Group

Close observation over several months at a Western Electric plant revealed that work groups established internal controls over their own output that were far more effective than incentives or supervisory control applied by management (Roethlisberger and Dickson, 1939). Workers in the bank-wiring room made telephone switching devices, each of which required 3000 electrical connections. The prescribed rate was 914 connections to be wired each hour, or 7312 per eight-hour day. A fast, steady worker could exceed this

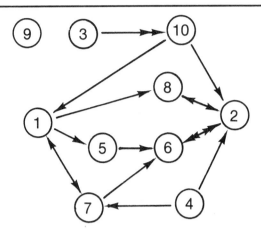

Figure 9-1. Sociogram for small elementary-school class. (Adapted from *Classroom Group Behavior,* by M. Bany and L. Johnson. Copyright © 1964 by Macmillan Publishing Co., Inc. Used by permission.)

Table 9-1. Communication in a small elementary-school class

		To Boys						To Girls						Sum
		1	3	5	7	9		2	4	6	8	10		
From Boys	*1*			1	1						1			3
	3											2		2
	5									1				1
	7	1								1				2
	9					(.17)						(.28)		0
From Girls	*2*									2	1			3
	4			1				1						2
	6							2						2
	8							1						1
	10	1				(.11)		1				(.44)		2
	Sum	2	0	1	2	0		5	0	4	2	2		18

standard by 5% to 10%, and all of the nine wiremen in the bank-wiring room could reach it at a moderate working pace. However, the group developed a lower norm: two devices per wireman per day. Since an experienced wireman could complete at least 10% more than two devices per day, it was necessary to hold back the workers who were exceeding the group norm. When a worker was completing too many connections, other workers tried to persuade him to slow down. If he ignored their wishes, they criticized and threatened. They also punished him physically by "binging" him on the upper arm. The "bing" was a single hard blow on the muscle. Stronger punishment might also include two or three bings. This punishment was conventional in the group, accepted by all members, and effective for enforcing group norms.

The patterns of association in the 12-man work group in the bank-wiring room are diagramed in Table 9-2 for four kinds of relationships, determined through observation and by interviews with each worker. Helping occurred after a faster worker completed his own "fair day's work" of two devices; he filled out the time by helping a slower worker with his wiring. The game-playing relation consisted of cards and other games during the lunch period and "binging," which could also serve as a playful exchange, during the day. There was also shared recreation, such as bowling after working hours. Table 9-2 reveals a cluster of interaction among workmen 1 through 6 and a second cluster of workmen 7 through 11. Number 12 was an isolate who had very little relation to his workmates. Although these workers were in the same room, they also made up two distinct subgroups of four workers each densely bound in mutual friendship, plus one group of four workers claiming no friendship within the work place.

The giving of help was fully distributed through the work group. Each worker was sometimes helpful to someone else, although three workers did not receive help from others. Of these, No. 1 scored highest in interaction with five of his fellow workers; No. 6 was antagonistic to most other workers; and No. 12 received antagonism from only one other person and no other form of interaction from anyone else. No. 12 was the only worker who did not participate in the game playing. All others played in games with an average of four other workers. Nine workers maintained antagonistic relations with one or more others, and only three workers were not hostile to anyone else in the work group. The total of antagonistic relations was only slightly lower than the number of friendly relations. This mixture of four kinds of social relations and the resulting two well-distinguished subgroups seemed to be compatible with the basic function of the bank-wiring work group—namely, the steady production of telephone-switching equipment. The pattern of selective pairing for friendship, helping, game playing, and antagonism appears to have supported the structuring of work relations. From a combination of his own and others' choices, each worker developed a group of associates with whom he worked effectively and either avoided or ignored the remainder. All workers except the isolated No. 12 showed a capacity for positive relationships with about five other workers. These two subgroups of four to six workers were closely knit in friendship, helping, and games. There was, however, relatively little interaction between the two subgroups, and most of that was negative and antagonistic.

For small groups, the sociogram and the sociomatrix help to show the internal dynamics of interpersonal relationships. They can be used extensively by teachers to learn about the social psychology of their classes, by people in work settings, and even by people who would simply like to

Table 9-2. Friendship (F), helping (H), game partnership (G), and antagonism (A) in a work group: Four variables in a sociomatrix

From \ To	1	2	3	4	5	6	7	8	9	10	11	12	F	H	G	A	Sum
1		G	FHG	FG	FHG	G			A	A			3	2	5	0	10
2			HG	HG	HG	G		A	A	A			0	3	4	-3	4
3				FG	FG	GA	H						3	1	5	0	9
4					FG	GA							3	2	5	-1	9
5						GA		FH					4	1	5	-1	9
6							A	GA	A	A		A	0	1	5	-7	-1
7								HGA	HG	HG			0	4	3	-2	5
8					FH	GA	GA		FG	FG	G		3	1	5	-3	6
9						A	HG	FHG		FHG	FG		3	3	4	-2	8
10						A	G	FG	FG		FG		3	1	4	-2	6
11							H					FHG	2	2	3	0	7
12								H					0	1	0	-1	0
Totals																	
F	3	0	3	3	4	0	0	3	3	3	2	0	24				
H	0	4	2	2	3	0	3	3	2	2	1	0		22			
G	5	4	5	5	5	5	3	5	4	4	3	0			48		
A	0	-3	0	-1	-1	-7	-2	-3	-2	-2	0	-1				-22	
Sum	8	5	10	9	11	-2	4	8	7	7	6	-1					72

From *Management and the Worker*, by F. J. Roethlisberger and W. J. Dickson. Harvard University Press, Copyright © 1939, 1967 by the President and Fellows of Harvard College. Reprinted by permission of the publishers.

know something about the interpersonal networks existing in their own neighborhood.

C. GROUP RESPONSES TO SOCIAL FACTORS

Groups are as influenced by social factors and situations as individuals are. For example, a group transported to another culture finds itself as bewildered as a single individual would, with one important exception. Having the group available tends to intensify interpersonal relationships, even among strangers. This effect was shown in a group of 34 young Jewish counselors from the United States who were spending a year in Israel (Herman and Schild, 1961). Although the members did not know one another before the trip, the group became a powerful reference point because of the unfamiliarity of the foreign culture.

Wives' perceptions of their husbands appear to be influenced by their own association either with individual friends or with a clique of several friends with whom they are in frequent contact as a group (Nelson, 1966). Wives who associated primarily with individual friends were more likely to describe their husbands in emotional and social terms, with emphasis on personal qualities, considerateness, and attention to individuals in the family. The wives who were associating with several friends in cliques emphasized the instrumental qualities of their husbands, mentioning their abilities, skills, job standing, and prospects for the future.

The meaning of Nelson's interesting study is that one-on-one, individual relationships produce different kinds of consequences than do relationships in groups. Groups are adept at bringing out the actor in all of us. And when people play to a larger audience, they seem to be more concerned with making an impression (Goffman, 1959).

In one of the most famous studies of a small group, Homans (1953) found that failure to recognize differences in the difficulty of work and the experience of members of a work group tends to produce dissatisfaction and subsequent refusal to move into more demanding jobs. In a billing office ten young women were working as "cash posters," entering cash receipts in the records and crediting customers' accounts in a simple mechanical operation. There were also 20 older women, who had years of seniority, working as "ledger clerks." They were responsible for reviewing and correcting the ledgers and for bringing them into agreement with other records. However, the company gave the same pay for both jobs and often transferred the ledger clerks down to cash posting whenever the cash posters got behind. Since the supervisors gave neither pay nor status recognition to the more difficult job, the cash posters declined a "promotion" to ledger clerk. The company's refusal to acknowledge differences in status, performance, and seniority that the workers could see very clearly created dissatisfaction and lack of interest in the work group.

1. Effects of Status on the Rating of Group Workers

Beliefs about status in the group consistently affect the way members rate other members and themselves on performance of both group and individual activities. In a sample of 250 students in 50 groups that averaged five members each, individual members tended to rate all other members of the group collectively as slightly below average in participation, ideas, guidance, and leadership (Gustafson and Gaumnitz, 1972). Individuals tended to rate themselves significantly above average for the group on all of these measures.

In Whyte's study of a boys' gang (1955), there was an attempt to pressure gang members to attain bowling scores consistent with their status in the gang. If a low-status member was bowling too well, others would try to distract him with calls and shouts and would withhold approval if he scored well. If a high-status member was bowling, the others would keep everyone quiet so as not to distract him and would give loud approval of his successes, with encouragement and reassurance when he bowled poorly.

Four groups totaling 29 boys in summer camp in Canada demonstrated this tendency to estimate their individual performance on canoeing, rifle firing, and height judging consistent with the status of their group (Koslin et al., 1968). In another test, boys throwing balls at a scored target were organized in two groups and received status rankings at ten levels in each group (Sherif et al., 1955). There was a difference of 2.5 levels between status and rating of observed performance by the peers in the group. High-status boys were ranked higher than their actual performance and low-status boys lower, although there was a very low correlation between status and performance in one group and none in the other. These pressures within groups and the effort of group members to perceive actions and outcomes consistently with group goals are one of the most interesting facets in the life of groups and their members.

2. The Mirror Effect

In the initial stages of group task performance, small groups seem to be inhibited by observing television playbacks of their own work as a group (Walter, 1975). Fifty groups of students with five to seven members each were assigned two problems to work out as a group. After the first problem the groups were organized in sets of ten for five experimental treatments: (1) no treatment; (2) a brief discussion; (3) a video replay of the first group session solving the first problem; (4) showing a model group solving a similar problem on television; and (5) a playback of the first session plus the video presentation of the model group. Those groups that saw the replay of their own problem solving were consistently inhibited, relative to other groups, when they went to work on the second problem. It should be noted that these were newly formed experimental groups. It is not likely that continued viewing of television playbacks would inhibit group performance, because professional athletes and teams improve their performance through careful analysis of their errors on video replays.

3. Encounter Groups and Training Groups

Carl Rogers defines the encounter group as "a planned, intensive group experience" using interactional processes and group influence to help people improve their social and relational skills (Rogers, 1970, 1). He traces the movement in group training to Kurt Lewin, who had discovered that it was easier to persuade entire groups to undertake new activities than it was to persuade individual members of those same groups. Since 1947, when the first of the modern training groups was formed, many kinds of these groups have worked to influence their participants in such areas as personal communication, managerial skills, problem solving, sensory awareness, dancing, creativity, artistic work, and the escape from alcoholism and drug addiction (Rogers, 1970, 5).

A training group usually meets for at least several hours—more often, for several days—to develop the group process and to allow time for the participants to begin making the desired adjustments. There is a gradual buildup of communication among group members after an initial period of informal milling and chance contacts. As positive feelings come to be realized and expressed, a closeness develops in the group, along with various behavior changes. For a time, at least, after their experience with an encounter group, participants show more understanding of others and more skill in communicating and relating with them (Rogers, 1970).

Training groups are designed to make the members more sensitive to the significant behavior, needs, and overt communications of others. Managers and specialists in business who have gone through sensitivity training in an encounter group have shown improved skills in relating to both individuals and groups. They have shown increased skill in communication and greater tolerance and consideration for others in the training group and at work. These changes last for some time after training, but may fade out after about 12 months (Cooper and Mangham, 1971, 10). Managers have better understanding and more skill in dealing with peers and subordinates. The fact that frankness, openness, and full communication are not habitual and not encouraged at work may account for the rather complete dissipation of long-term effects. For this reason it is argued that the positive effects of training groups will endure longer if entire work groups go through sensitivity training.

It has been shown that heterogeneous groups reach training objectives more successfully than homogeneous groups (Harrison and Lubin, 1965, 168). In homogeneous groups the members support one another too readily and are unwilling to confront one another realistically. Heterogeneous groups seem to have built-in conflict that facilitates a more vigorous attack on interpersonal problems and more success in reaching solutions and consensus. Trainees who were assigned to heterogeneous groups for morning sessions and to homogeneous groups for afternoon sessions learned more in the heterogeneous groups.

D. DYNAMIC PROPERTIES OF GROUPS

Although small groups are generally described in terms of action and process, there is a persistent tendency within social psychology to treat the group as if it were a stable structure, fixed in its internal relations among members. Simmel, ordinarily a process theorist of the first order, fell into this trap when he suggested that the three-person group would tend to degenerate into a coalition of two members as a power unit to control the third (Simmel, 1950). Actually, six possible combinations of relative power can be identified for three-person groups consisting of members A, B, and C: (1) $A = B = C$; (2) $A > B$, $B = C$, and $A < (B + C)$; (3) $A < B$ and $B = C$; (4) $A > (B + C)$ and $B = C$; (5) $A > B > C$ and $A < (B + C)$; and (6) $A > B > C$ and $A > (B + C)$.

This formidable-looking sequence can be simply illustrated. With a mother and two small children, the mother usually has greater power than that of the two children combined, while the power of the two children is about equal, as in relationship 4. When these children become teenagers, this situation may change to power relationship 2, where the mother has more power than either one of the children but less than their combined power (Burhans, 1973). When faced with two insistent teenage children, a parent often feels outnumbered and understaffed!

1. The Distribution of Communication

As organizational patterns develop in groups, the process of generating and directing communication must be selective. Following the theorizing of Mayhew and Levinger (1976), once a sequence of conversation occurs, there is a higher probability that a later, related sequence will occur between the same actors. These operating sequences tend to suppress potentially rival sequences in order to avoid confusion.

In the limited time of any group meeting the person who starts speaking will probably need to add more to what he or she has said. And others who respond may cause the first person to add further remarks. This leaves less time and opportunity for others in the group to speak. The longer any one member waits to get into the conversational chain, the less opportunity will be available to him or her later. Table 9-3 shows a fairly typical pattern of the declining participation among the six members of a series of task groups who discussed and decided on a solution to a problem in 45 minutes. The most active member generated 431 acts per 1000, which was more than

Table 9-3.   Communication by frequency rank of actors (rate per 1000 acts for 21,311 acts by 18 six-man groups)

		To 1	2	3	4	5	6	Person	Group	Total
	Rank									
From	1		58	45	26	21	15	165	266	431
	2	82		21	15	9	5	130	57	187
	3	64	19		14	6	3	107	35	142
	4	45	15	13		4	2	79	32	111
	5	31	11	7	4		1	52	21	73
	6	22	6	5	3	2		38	18	56
Total		244	109	91	61	41	27	573	427	1000

Adapted from *Working Papers in the Theory of Action*, by T. Parsons, R. F. Bales, and E. Shils. Copyright 1953 by The Free Press. Used by permission. (Contains errors of rounding.)

twice the level of output for the second most active member and about eight times the output level of the least active member. The most active member directed more than half of his or her remarks to the group as a whole. And he or she directed more remarks to each other member than other members directed to one another (Bales, 1953, 129).

This illustrates the pattern by which the action in a small group becomes organized and concentrated through one dominant member, with the cooperation, response and support of other members on a declining scale. This patterning seems to be a necessary part of the process of group action. Someone in the group must initiate action and concentrate the attention of members of the group on the problem at hand. Which member serves this function depends on the nature of the task, the interest of the various members, and their willingness to cooperate. All of these factors, of course, vary through time with particular groups and particular situations.

2. Interaction Processes in Small Groups

To sustain the process of interaction in a small face-to-face group, the members must develop a system for linking one another's acts in such a way that desired goals are carried out. Robert Bales (1970, 92) developed a theoretical design to describe this process (see Figure 9-2).

Bales theorized that, before the group can work on the task, the members must develop and establish social and emotional relations among themselves. They must recognize each other as persons, work out a coordinated system of responding to one another, and maintain a focus of thought and interest. The "social/emotional area," as shown in Figure 9-2, is divided into a positive region and a negative region, each containing three parts: friendly or unfriendly behavior, dramatizing or tense behavior, and agreeing or disagreeing. This outer region must be established and maintained before the inner "task area" can be operated (Bales, 1950). In the task area the members concentrate on the problem by three kinds of communicative behavior: the giving or asking of suggestions, opinions, and information.

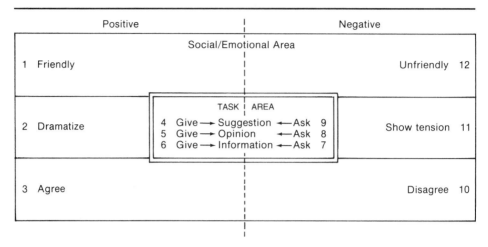

Figure 9-2. Interaction process space for small groups. (Adapted from *Personality and Interpersonal Behavior*, by R. F. Bales. Copyright © 1970 by Holt, Rinehart and Winston. Used by permission.

Logically, the information defining the problem and the related facts must come before other kinds of action. As the information accumulates and the members develop a joint understanding and concensus on definitions and the scope of the problem, they begin to give opinions and to evaluate and rank the facts in order of importance. As this process continues, some members begin to reach tentative conclusions, and they suggest solutions to the problem. As these suggestions come to be shared and accepted, they begin to take the form of decisions and to operate as a mechanism of control.

As the members of the group discuss and attempt to persuade each other, they begin to strain and degrade the social/emotional foundation for their cooperative work. Resentments and frustrations begin to build up, and they become too irritated to continue work on the task. As this happens, they must go back to the social/emotional region to repair and restore positive interpersonal relations. For this purpose, the group may develop a specialized social/emotional leader who can give members positive emotional support, soothe hurt feelings, and reduce hostility (a "stroker," in contemporary language). He or she is less interested in accomplishing the group task than in keeping everyone happy. The social/emotional leader is a pleasant, likable, and jocular person who cares more about you than about what you do. This leader jokes and dramatizes the situation to relieve tension but shows little concern about the task. If no one brings the group back to the task area, the social/emotional leader may joke and play with other members, and the task may go undone. The task leader is skilled in moving the group toward a decision and conclusion on the task, but he or she needs the social/emotional leader to restore the good humor of the group.

Bales has devised a three-dimensional system for plotting the position of each member and the group as a unit along the dimensions of dominating and subordinating behavior, positive and negative emotional actions, and working toward or away from the solution of the group task and goals (Bales, 1970). For the group to stay together and to make progress toward solving the problem, the members must generally stay on the positive side in emotional relations. To work out the group task, it is necessary to have more members spend more time in positive accomplishments. As fatigue and frustration accumulate, shifts must be made backward away from group goals and in a more positive direction toward emotional satisfaction before members can resume the coordinated effort for the group task.

Long-term groups, such as a small school class, move through several phases during the academic year. As an example, an experimental class in small-group relations was left unstructured to afford it the opportunity of observing and analyzing its own social development as the class objective (Dunphy, 1968). The members felt disorganized and uncomfortable in the early weeks of the class, because they were uncertain about how they could relate to the instructor, who gave very little guidance. The relationships turned negative and hostile in the middle of the two-semester class, and in mid-spring the class thought the instructor was cold, rejecting, and evil. In the next month, near the end of the school year, the class began to feel more secure and to regard the instructor in a positive way (maybe because grades were due). Members of the class also changed their parts and influence in the class. An aggressor who was negative and critical was eventually thrown out of the group.

3. System Boundaries

Every system requires well-established and recognizable boundaries. Sometimes the boundary is distinguished by the fact that people on one side of the boundary behave very differently from those on the other side (Phillips and Converse, 1972). Doctors, orderlies, interns, and nurses may look very much alike and mix among themselves on duty in the hospital. But the patterns of behavior among them demonstrate clear social and professional boundaries. Doctors give orders to nurses; nurses do not give orders to doctors. Doctors come and go very freely; interns are more closely confined to the hospital. Orderlies take orders from doctors, nurses, and other hospital staff but may exert slight authority over patients. Patients take orders from everyone in white and have no clearly defined rights. Thus, behavior patterns and reciprocal relations clearly mark the boundaries between these five types of persons maintaining social relations as a group in a hospital.

System boundaries of a social group may be marked by number. Exactly five team members must be on the basketball court for each of the two opposing teams during play. Physical barriers such as walls, doors, and dividers and file drawers may mark the boundary of an office work team. Social boundaries are established for a work group by *assignment* to a particular recognized group, by *enlistment* on the payroll, and by *membership* in the organization. The member may be pushed outside the boundary by being dismissed from the job and having his or her name removed from the payroll. Symbolic markers also indicate boundaries. These include distinctive uniforms, name and title badges, and names for occupational functions, such as "clerk," "cashier," "general manager." Customers and visitors who mingle with them are excluded from the work group.

Dunphy defined the open system as "one with a boundary sufficient to maintain a certain degree of inner integrity and distinctiveness, yet sufficiently flexible and permeable to be able to use the environment in maintaining its own existence" (1972, 91). Social groups receive members from the outside society, and, when they lose members, those departing from one group typically shift into some other group. The same group members may maintain radically different relations with other members in the group. In a family group, the mother maintains a marital relation to the father, and a parental relation to her son and daughter. The same two members in a group may be partners in one game, and rivals in another game. The same group may maintain one set of specialized relations as a singing group, another set of relations in an athletic game, and still another regarding property ownership, money, and loan obligations. It is these different kinds of relations that give order to the interaction process within the group. The success of the group requires organization and control of the interaction processes and exchanges between and among group members in their many kinds of relationships. Success also requires control and efficiency in directing transactions with the social and physical environment. A work group that loses a member needs to recruit and train a new member to replace the lost member. If some new kind of activity is undertaken, members of the group may need to secure supplies and equipment from the outside environment. Work groups, by definition, relate to the outer environment by contributing some service or product either to other parts of the company or organization or to the external society. In treating the small social group as a social system, the members are usually the elements. The many kinds of possible organized social relations may be analyzed in the system, either one by one or by connected sets of relations.

An athletic team is a good example of a small social group as a social system. A team may be defined as a set of two or more persons who cooperate in the staging of a performance. The athletic team as a social system is most fully apparent while the team is in play and strongly competing with another team in a standard game. The team is identified by colored uniforms, its position on the playing court, and the closely regulated pattern of interaction among the players.

4. Change and Equilibrium

All social groups are subject to change from without and within. In the first place, they are open to exchanges of various kinds with the physical and social environment. Each of these transactions causes some increase or decrease in the relative influence of individual group members, in member satisfaction, and in the adequacy of resources of time, money, supplies, or other requirements of the group. Within a certain range the group can continue to function. It may be said to be in *equilibrium* when there is a balance between the resources and abilities of the group and the work or interaction it must carry out. If the group loses members through transfers, dismissals, disability, or resignation, there is a state of *disequilibrium*, or unbalance, until the membership is restored with adequate replacements. If supplies are exhausted, if customers are lacking, or if cash funds are not available for current operations, the group is also in disequilibrium. The group cannot operate successfully until all of the necessary resources are brought back into balance.

If a single member of a well-integrated group were to change goals or methods of operation while the others made no such change, it would throw the group into disequilibrium. For this reason, each member will resist a change that violates group standards or group requirements. Since the group is organized and integrated for working cooperatively, it is easier for the entire group to make a change (Lewin, 1951, 228). If it is desired to change a group, two conditions are required, according to Lewin (233). The first requirement is that the members of the group become *motivated* to make the change. It is easier for them to achieve motivation through established processes of discussion within the group than it is to become motivated as individuals. The second requirement is that the group reach a *decision* to make the change. The decision is also reached through interaction processes established within the group. In short, if members of a group reach decisions collectively, they are more likely as individuals to be committed to the decision reached.

E. GROUP LEADERSHIP FUNCTIONS

1. Group Requirements

The social group is an interaction system, and it must sustain the action in order to sustain the group. According to Stogdill, "Leadership is without meaning except as it serves the function of group performance or survival" (1974, 428). As the action shifts, the requirement for leader behavior shifts. The group member most able and interested in getting the group task performed will generally start the action, ask the questions, suggest decisions, and enforce rules that maintain action in the group operations. Where task and performance needs are primary, the instrumental leaders have the most influence and the most acceptance, as was the case with student nurses rotating among psychiatric hospital wards in the course of a year (Turk, 1961).

As time is spent on the group task, tension mounts to the point where it begins to interfere with the task, and the group requires reduction of tension. At this time the task leader may merely aggravate the situation, and the social/emotional leader must become the group clown and bring tension release through joking and laughter. Other members may briefly take the stage by telling stories or by interacting playfully with other members. Breaks for refreshments and sociable conversation may be used to ease tension and get the group relaxed enough to resume work.

The social situation determines the leadership requirements of the group, and the leader is usually sensitive to these requirements. Sherif was testing the proposition that the latitude of acceptable behavior, as defined by the norms of the group, varies according to the importance of the activity to the members (Sherif, 1964, 179). One successful group leader often fouled other members of the group in intragroup games, but he was very sportsmanlike in observing the rules when his group team was playing against other teams. He was supporting the norms selectively, depending on the situation.

In investigating the status systems in ten high schools, Coleman (1960) found that the schools were dominated heavily by extramural athletic competitions. Virtually no recognition was given to academic functions. Therefore, there was no leader for academically inclined students or faculty. The leaders were all either male stars on the school athletic teams or females who had the heady honor of "going with" the male athletic stars. Other studies have shown that athletic coaches tend to predominate in influence among high-school faculty and have a higher probability of rising to administrative positions.

2. Leader Functions

In summarizing leadership studies, Luft noted that there are no special characteristics of leaders and that there is a distribution of the leader function in the group. But the leader function does include the empathic ability of the member to sense what goes on in himself or herself and in the other members of the group (Luft, 1970, 44). The leader may sometimes be required to serve as a scapegoat for the group or may push another member into the scapegoat position to drain hostility away from himself or herself (Gallagher and Burke, 1974). Shaw defined effective leaders as "task-able, sociable, and motivated to lead" (1971, 286). However, this definition does not prevent the leader function from circulating among several members of the group. The circulation of information and the relevant discussion of group problems and adjustments is the responsibility of all members of the group, but the place where it centers marks the group leader. She or he is at the center of the web of interaction. But the leadership function is also identified by the fact that the suggestions, information, and requests are in agreement with group needs (Homans, 1950, 418). The leader is also marked by a sense of awareness and concern for the inclusion of all group members, from the first to the last (Jennings, 1950, 212). The leader is more observant of the group as a whole, whereas the nonleading members may consistently ignore some of the other members.

3. Leader Limits

The opportunity to act as leader is strongly affected by social and situational variations. Laborers tended to be chosen as jury foremen only half as often as proprietors (Strodtbeck et al., 1957). Primary-group support for the leader may affect support for larger groups. U.S. infantrymen in World War II fought to support their immediate buddies in the infantry squad, not for the war objectives (Verba, 1961, 57). In cross-cultural comparison, the Japanese and Soviet expectations of personal loyalty are opposed. The Japanese is expected to put private obligations, both social and moral, before his public obligations. The Soviet individual is required to put obligations to the society and the nation first (Verba, 1961, 47ff). These conditions limit the leaders' relations to members.

Juvenile-gang "leaders" are severely limited by the willingness of gang members to accept their ideas and continue to spend time and resources with the group. The gang leader must often be surprisingly conciliatory in relations with other gang members (Short and Strodtbeck, 1963). The member can easily resist the pressure of the leader by the threat of breaking away from the gang. Therefore, leaders must dominate through stimulating suggestions, and they can succeed only if the outcome is not a failure. One delinquent gang called the Dons was observed over a period of five years (Jansyn, 1966). Two leaders were identified. The task leader was more formal, more neutral, and fair to all. He was more active in the legitimate operations of the gang, such as games and recreation, in which a large portion of the gang was usually engaged. The "delinquent leader" was more impulsive, personal, and self-indulging. He operated with a smaller group of three or four other boys in stealing and fighting and was more accepted among the boys for whom delinquent behavior was routine.

F. SUMMARY

Small social groups are important parts of our lives, and social psychologists have paid a great deal of attention to them. Groups vary by size and complexity. When a group gets too large, its qualities begin to change significantly.

Groups allow us to see processes that are purely social and cannot be accounted for with reference to individual psychology alone. The difference between a two-person group and a three-person group seems to be related to form and not the content or makeup of the group.

Among the more important groups in which we live out our lives as social beings is the primary group. This small, intimate, interpersonal form of interaction is characterized by closeness and a great deal of face-to-face association. One enters a primary group as a whole person, not just as a role or position.

Groups have influences on both the individual and on other groups. Social psychologists have conducted numerous experiments showing how individuals are significantly influenced by their groups. Examples include taking risks, making decisions, and even inflicting pain on others.

Such studies of group effects have developed methods of diagraming interaction patterns among members of the group. Moreno's technique called the sociogram is perhaps the best known. It can be a useful device for establishing the dynamics within a group.

Groups are as responsive to social factors as individuals are. Cross-cultural associations, perceptions of others, and satisfaction among workers are all related to the nature of the group dynamic. The way in which individuals are perceived by other members of the group seems also to be related to their status within the group.

Encounter and training groups have enjoyed something of a vogue in North American society. These groups are designed to improve people's interpersonal skills or help them overcome a problem such as drug addiction or alcoholism. These groups do seem to allow a person to transcend difficulties in ways that would be difficult acting alone.

Although social psychology has tended to see groups in structural terms, this chapter has emphasized the dynamic processes around which all groups revolve. Power and constraint within groups are dynamic processes, rather than static, structural relationships.

The processes of interaction within small groups have been explored for a number of years by Harvard sociologist Robert Bales. He has developed an elaborate system for understanding how groups facilitate and occasionally interfere with the tasks and goals they set for themselves. Bales' work emphasizes the interrelatedness of group processes and the types of system boundaries that are established as identity and control mechanisms for members of a group. Using a functional model, Bales wants to know how balances are maintained or disequilibriums occur. His work also tries to understand the role of a leader within a small group and how effectiveness is either enhanced or diminished. Although Bales has been criticized for his theoretical treatment of small groups, his research continues to stimulate additional research in this fascinating and provocative subject.

Attitudes 10

A. INTRODUCTION

All of us, at some point in life, stop to question our behavior and our reasons for engaging in it. We want to know not only who we are but also what the factors are that go into making us who we are. Why did we believe in Santa Claus so intensely yesterday but completely discredit his existence today? How is it that we hated members of the opposite sex only a few short months ago but can't live without them now? Why is it that crew cuts for boys were so popular just a few years ago but are so rare now? Why is there frequently a wide gap between what people say and what they do? The answers to these questions, as well as many other intriguing ones, lie partially in an area sociologists and psychologists have been studying for years: social attitudes.

In 1935 Gordon Allport wrote, "The concept of attitude is probably the most distinctive and indispensable concept in contemporary American social psychology. No other term appears more frequently in the experimental and theoretical literature" (Allport, 1935, 3). Half a century later, the term still remains prominent in the field, although its popularity has suffered from time to time. We will address this question of changing fashions in attitude research later.

1. A Short History of the Idea of Attitude

The initial use of the term *attitude* was by Herbert Spencer (1862), who used the word to refer to a mental state of the person. Later, in 1888, Lange used the concept in a laboratory experiment. He instructed one group of subjects to concentrate on being ready to press a key at the onset of some stimulus. Another group of subjects was told to concentrate on the incoming stimulus itself rather than the key. He found that those asked to concentrate on the key responded more rapidly. He concluded that the response was at least a part of a "set" within the individual that he labeled the subject's *aufgabe*, or task attitude. The idea that an attitude contains both mental and behavioral elements has remained intact in most of the definitions in use today, although there are serious difficulties with this conception, a point we will take up in detail later.

Historically, the concept of attitude has enjoyed popularity among both sociologists and psychologists. (It is perhaps one of the few concepts the two camps have been able to agree on.) Because the term is elastic enough to apply either to the disposition of single, isolated, individual characteristics or to broader patterns of culture and society, psychologists and sociologists have found it a meeting ground for discussion and research.

For psychologists, interest in attitude seems to be rooted in their fascination with individual differences (Kiesler et al., 1969). Why is it that different individuals behave differently in the same situation? For the most part, this phenomenon has been explained in terms of attitudes.

For the sociologist, the concept has been used in a different way. Allport (1935) wrote that sociologists had sought for a number of years to supplement their cultural and societal concepts with a psychology that might express in concrete terms the mechanisms through which culture is carried. As we have noted, early explanations by sociologists were couched in terms of instinct, imitation, and suggestion. Bagehot, Tarde, and Baldwin were all leading advocates of this position. In fact, one of the first textbooks in social psychology used the theme of imitation/suggestion (Ross, 1908). However, it soon became evident that the term *instinct of imitation* was circular and tended to discredit the importance of custom, convention, and environment, all concepts sociologists have traditionally relied on in their explanations of social conduct. As a result, instinct and imitation were gradually replaced by the concept of attitude.

This evolution in the acceptance of the concept of attitude by sociologically oriented social psychologists reached its apex in 1918, when Thomas and Znaniecki argued that social psychology *is* the scientific study of attitudes. They said it is not enough to look at the objective sociological conditions impinging on a person but it is also necessary to consider concrete differences between individuals in order to understand social and cultural phenomena. For sociologists since that time the concept of attitude has become a major means of explaining social and cultural change.

2. Toward a Definition of Attitude

As might be expected of an idea that finds itself at home in both sociology and psychology, little consensus exists about just what attitudes are. Berkowitz (1972) notes that over 30 different definitions of *attitude* exist. We will now turn to an examination of at least a few of these definitions.

The aforementioned Thomas and Znaniecki (1918) defined an attitude as a "process of individual consciousness which determines real or possible activities of the individual in the social world" (22). Attitudes represent a primary means of explaining individual differences in socially significant situations. LaPierre (1934) defined an attitude as "a behavior pattern, anticipatory set or tendency, predisposition to specific adjustment to designated social situations, or, more simply, a conditioned response to social stimuli" (230). Stated somewhat differently, Deutscher (1973) suggested that a social attitude is a verbal response to a symbolic situation.

Despite this proliferation of definitions, Berkowitz (1972) proposed that most definitions be placed in one of three basic categories. The first school of thought perceives as the predominant element in attitude the individual's evaluation of a reaction. A person's attitude toward an object or issue can be viewed as the favorableness or unfavorableness of his or her feelings toward the object or issue. Thurstone (1928) and Likert (1932), both of whom pioneered in the area of attitude measurement, supported this definition. A second group of definitions characterizes an attitude as a readiness to respond in a particular way with regard to an object. Chave (1928), Bogardus (1931), Allport (1935), and Mead (1934) all defined attitude in this way. A third group of definitions employs a triadic scheme of cognitive, affective, and behavioral components. Secord and Backman (1964) favored this type of definition, defining an attitude as "certain regularities of an individual's feelings, thoughts, and predispositions to act toward some aspect of his environment" (97).

The view that attitudes do involve three components—affective, cognitive, and behavioral—seems to be the most acceptable position today. The *affective* component refers to the emotional dimension of an attitude. For example, if people say they like money they are describing their feelings about money. The *cognitive* component refers to knowledge based on information. People know that money is valuable, because they see its worth in their day-to-day interactions. The *behavioral* component involves one's predisposition to act. Because money is valuable, people like it and they prepare themselves to earn some amount of it.

It is also useful to differentiate among the terms *value*, *attitude*, and *opinion*. Although the terms are often used interchangeably in the literature, they are not totally equivalent in meaning.

Value is a broad disposition. Values are generally considered to be deeply ingrained and therefore relatively lasting. Rokeach (1974), evaluating change and stability in the U.S. value system, noted that certain values always remain steadfast within the population. For example, adult Americans perceive themselves as peace loving, freedom loving, family oriented, honest, hard working, and responsible. They do not see themselves as hedonistic, aesthetic, intellectual, or concerned with status. Rokeach viewed these perceptions as indicators of Americans' values, which appear to be relatively stable. Those changes that have occurred are related to changes in the economic structure and the emergence of various issues concerning war and peace, racism, sexism, and ecology. These issues seem to become most important when various subgroups of adult Americans become dissatisfied with some segment of the system. We will pay greater attention to this topic in our discussion of social movements.

Attitudes seem to be generated in part from values. Whereas values are generally quite broad, attitudes are usually more specific. Although attitudes are considered to be relatively enduring, they may not be as permanent as values. The love of freedom, for example, is a value identified by Rokeach (1974). A specific aspect of freedom loving might involve one's attitude toward wiretapping. Family orientation is also viewed as a value. A family-oriented person, then, will hold specific attitudes toward child rearing.

Opinions, when differentiated from attitudes, are viewed as even narrower expressions. Although we sometimes distinguish between specific and general attitudes, the term *opinion* is more frequently applied (Schuman,

1970). We might say that, whereas values are established in attitudes, attitudes are established in opinions. A woman may be a freedom-loving person and hold generally negative attitudes about wiretapping. However, under certain circumstances she may approve of wiretapping. If she feels her own privacy is being invaded or threatened, she may even allow her own phone to be tapped. Because opinions are situational, they reflect the short haul and are therefore easier to change than attitudes or values.

The reason for differentiating between these three terms is to give us a better understanding of the complexity and multifaceted nature of the concept of attitude.

B. ATTITUDES AND BEHAVIOR

Most of the definitions of attitude we have discussed support a common assumption found in virtually every area of attitude study. That assumption is that there is some close connection between attitudes and behavior. This assumption is supported in the definitions of attitude that recognize "tendency to act," as well as Mead's symbolic interactionist conception of attitudes as the "beginning of the act" (1934).

However, the body of research that has sought to link attitudes and behavior has been notoriously unsuccessful. Either there exists little relationship at all between people's professed attitudes and their behavior or, if there is a relationship, in many instances it is negative (Deutscher, 1973). This diversity of research findings led Warner and DeFleur (1969) to identify three broad views on the relationship between attitudes and behavior: the postulate of consistency, the postulate of independent variation, and the postulate of contingent consistency.

1. *The postulate of consistency* suggests that verbal attitudes provide reasonably accurate guides for predicting what people would do if they were confronted with the object of their attitude. In other words, there is a direct relationship between attitudes and behavior. Given an attitudinal position, behavior can be accurately predicted.

2. *The postulate of independent variation* argues that there is no reason to assume that attitudes and behavior are consistently related. They are two separate and distinct dimensions of an individual. Thus, just as attitudes may vary independently of one another, they may also vary independently of behavior. Knowledge of attitudes does not presume knowledge of behavior.

3. *The postulate of contingent consistency* suggests that the relationship between attitudes and behavior is dependent on certain situational factors. Norms, roles, group membership, reference groups, and subcultures pose contingent conditions that can modify the relationship between attitude and action. Consequently, predictability may be good in certain situations but less than adequate in others.

1. The Postulate of Consistency

Strong evidence for the postulate of consistency can often be found in the behavior patterns of individuals who are known to have extreme attitudes on a particular issue. Prejudice scales, for example, are frequently validated by administering them to groups of Northern and Southern Whites—although even this does not always produce consistency (Merton, 1940). With emphasis on changing sex roles, attitude scales dealing with traditional and nontraditional women can demonstrate attitude/behavior consistency when administered to a feminist group and to antifeminist individuals. Selection of subjects from the extreme ends of an attitudinal continuum produces an effect that is more dramatic than that produced by a random sample representative of the entire continuum. This might suggest, then, that the postulate of consistency is effective only when we are dealing with extreme attitudes.

Brannon and his coworkers (1973) were able to demonstrate consistency between attitudes and subsequent behavior on the subject of open housing. They interviewed 640 White Detroit residents and found that 82% preferred the statement that the homeowner has the right to decide to whom he or she would sell a house; 16% preferred the statement that the homeowner cannot refuse to sell because of the race of the buyer. Three months later, using other interviewers, Brannon approached the same respondents with a request to sign a petition and to authorize the listing of their names in the newspaper in support of the petition. More than 70% of those asked to sign a petition consistent with their earlier choices were willing to sign, and 58% authorized listing their names in the paper.

One of the better known studies dealing empirically with attitude/behavior consistency was conducted by DeFleur and Westie (1958). White subjects were taken into an interview room in which they were presented with a variety of questions designed to assess their feelings about Blacks. Their answers were operationalized as a measure of attitude. After completion of the questionnaire, subjects were shown a number of color slides in which males and females were interracially paired. In some slides a well-dressed, nice-looking Black male was paired with a young, well-dressed, nice-looking White female. In other slides a White male was similarly paired with a Black female. The couples were sitting beside each other in separate chairs in a room that could have been a living room or dormitory lounge. They were looking at each other with pleasant facial expressions.

After viewing the slides, the subjects were told that another set of slides was needed for research. Each subject was asked if he or she would be willing to be photographed with a Black person of the opposite sex. The subject was then given a mimeographed form and told that this was a "standard photograph release agreement, which is necessary in any situation where a photograph of an individual is to be used in any manner." The agreement consisted of a graded series of uses to which the photograph would be put, ranging from laboratory experiments to a nationwide publicity campaign advocating racial integration. Subjects were asked to sign their names to each use they would permit. "In America, the affixing of one's signature to a document is a particularly significant act. The signing of checks, contracts, agreements, and the like is clearly understood to indicate a binding obligation on the part of the signer to abide by the provisions of the document" (DeFleur and Westie, 1958, 669–670).

The results are presented in Table 10-1. The relationship between attitude and behavior is primarily consistent. It is interesting to note, though, that 14 of the 46 subjects (approximately 30%) did not behave consistently. Nine of these indicated low verbal prejudice but gave a low number of permissions. The other five appeared to be highly prejudiced from the verbal measure but gave a large number of permissions.

These inconsistencies should not significantly detract from the importance of the research. The attitude/behavior consistency postulate can, of course, never hope for perfection (100% in prediction). Still, this approach finds very little support in the literature. We will consider why this is so shortly.

2. The Postulate of Independent Variation

The postulate of independent variation can be seen operating in a classic study conducted by LaPierre (1934). His study dealt with the inconsistency of motel and restaurant proprietors who had indicated by letter that they would turn away Chinese guests but did actually serve a Chinese couple when they appeared in person. Driving approximately 10,000 miles around the United States, LaPierre and the Chinese couple were refused service only once out of all hotels, motels, and restaurants at which they stopped. LaPierre interpreted the responses received by letter to indicate attitude. The actions of the desk clerks and waitresses toward the Chinese couple were taken to signify behavior. The question asked in the mailed questionnaire was "Will you accept members of the Chinese race as guests in your establishment?" Ninety-two percent of the restaurants and cafes

Table 10-1. Relationship between Whites' race attitudes and willingness to sign permissions to be photographed with a Black

| | Subject Attitude | |
Behavioral Measure	Prejudice	Lack of Prejudice
Few permissions	18	9
Many permissions	5	14

From "Verbal Attitudes and Overt Acts: An Experiment on Salience of Attitudes," by M. L. DeFleur and F. R. Westie, *American Sociological Review*, 1958, *23*, 667–673. Copyright 1958 by the American Sociological Association. Reprinted by permission.

and 91% of the hotels, auto camps, and tourist homes replied "no." The remainder replied "uncertain" or "it depends upon the circumstances."

LaPierre's study has been criticized for its definition of attitude. Kiesler, Collins, and Miller (1969), for example, reasoned that a response of "yes," "no," or "uncertain" in a letter should be considered a behavioral act. In those terms, LaPierre was simply comparing one behavior to another. If this is true, however, we might also reason that written answers to any test or any standardized scale might be interpreted as behavior. Then, any such attempt to make an attitude public becomes behavior, and we are hard pressed to identify what we mean by attitude. Although LaPierre's study has its limitations, this is probably not its major fault.

Campbell has criticized the study as not demonstrating a true inconsistency.

> He [LaPierre] and the Chinese couple were refused accommodations in .4 percent of places stopped. The mailed questionnaire reported 92.5 percent refusal of Chinese. The first thing we note is that the two diagnostic situations have very different thresholds. Apparently it is very hard to refuse a well-dressed Chinese couple traveling with a European in a face-to-face setting, and very easy to refuse the Chinese as a race in the mailed questionnaire. . . . But this is not evidence of inconsistency. Inconsistency would be represented if those who refused face-to-face accepted by questionnaire, or if those who accepted by questionnaire refused face-to-face. There is no report that such cases occurred [1963, 160].

The LaPierre study might be considered the first in a long series of studies relating attitudes to behavior. The postulate of independent variation has been tenable more times than not. It would seem, then, that the leading question should not be "Why are attitudes related to behavior?" or "Why are attitudes not related to behavior?" but rather "When are attitudes related to behavior?" Raab and Lipset's (1962) definition of an attitude reflects this conditional relationship to behavior: "An attitude is not a thing, it is a process; it is an interaction. It is an interaction involving not only the person and the object, but all other factors that are present in any situation" (23). They suggest that, in order to predict behavior from attitudes, some measure of all situation variables would have to be devised. LaPierre was not far afield from this position in 1934. He wrote: "If social attitudes are to be conceptualized as partially integrated habit sets which will become operative under specific circumstances and lead to a particular pattern of adjustment they must, in the main, be derived from a study of humans' behavior in actual social situations" (26).

3. The Postulate of Contingent Consistency

The failure to find uniform consistency between attitudes and behavior served, then, as a springboard for this new area of attitudinal research—the identification of those situations and conditions in which attitudes and behavior are related. Frideres, Warner, and Albrecht (1971) made a case for the postulate of contingent consistency in their examination of situational variables as a means of explaining consistency between attitudes and behavior. The authors selected four attitudinal topics: (1) war in Vietnam, (2) gun control, (3) legalization of marijuana, and (4) Black-White relations. These researchers were interested in the subjects' overt acts toward the attitude object and the degree to which these acts were consistent with the individual's attitudes. Four hypotheses were tested:

1. There will be a positive association between the subject's initial attitude expressed toward the attitude object and his overt behavior emitted toward that same object.
2. When the overt behavior of the individual is disclosed, the consistency between his attitude and his subsequent overt behavior will decrease.
3. As the amount of social participation increases, the degree of consistency between attitude and overt behavior will decrease.
4. As the situation changes from one in which the individual's attitude is incongruent with that of his immediate group to one in which his attitude is congruent (toward some particular attitude object) the degree of consistency between the attitude and overt behavior will increase.

Frideres and his colleagues found 80% of their subjects willing to participate in the overt act that was consistent with their previously measured attitude. Consistency of behavior with attitudes was less in private situations than public situations. Social participation was not a significant variable. Predictability for those individuals whose attitudes were congruent with their immediate group was good. Predictability of behavior when one's attitude was incongruent with the group was low. This study did support the postulate of contingent consistency. Behavior appears to be more consistent with attitude when the individual's attitude is the same as the group of which he or she is a part.

4. Factors Linking Attitudes and Actions

a. Constraint and distance. Warner and DeFleur (1969) examined social constraints and social distance as intervening variables between attitudes and behavior. *Social constraint* was defined as pressure to act in accordance with what others are perceived to feel as appropriate and desirable conduct in their presence or in the actor's definition of the situation. High social constraint signifies a high probability that significant others will know. Low social constraint refers to anonymity (no one will know). The meaning of *social distance* was based on the sociological considerations of status positions and role expectations in a social relationship. In other words, how much distance does a person place between himself or herself and various kinds of social groups? The attitude in question was prejudice toward Blacks.

Subjects were mailed a letter that asked them to sign a pledge to be returned to the sender by mail. The pledge committed the subjects to engage in one of several varieties of behavior involving Blacks, ranging from dating to making an anonymous contribution to a Black education charity. A subject's signature on the pledge was considered overt behavior. Verbal attitudes were collected independently by a scale. For those individuals least prejudiced, attitudes and action tended to be most consistent when they were not exposed to the responses of others unfavorable toward integration. Attitudes and action tended to correspond under situations where there was low social constraint (anonymity protected) and where social distance was maintained. Less consistency was found when these subjects were asked to behave favorably toward Blacks in situations in which they would be directly disclosing their acts to others. For those individuals most prejudiced, the greatest consistency was found under conditions of high social constraint and for those acts that are normatively prohibited (reduction of social distance). The authors concluded, though, that other factors need to be examined, including reference groups, significant others, voluntary organizations, peers, roles, and subcultures.

b. *Situational and personality factors.* Albrecht and Warner (1973) supported the postulate of contingent consistency in their research on situational and personality factors affecting attitude/action consistency. The situational factor examined was *disclosure*: whether the attitude is made public or remains private. The two personality variables considered were *need for approval* and *inner/other directedness.* Albrecht and Warner hypothesized a more consistent relationship between attitudes and behavior for inner-directed people, who are more likely to look to themselves and their own values for directives in their response to behavioral situations. Other-directed people are more likely to look outside of themselves for such directives. Situational factors, such as having one's attitudes disclosed, should thus have more effect on the person who is other directed. Albrecht and Warner make the same arguments for the "need-for-approval" index, suggesting that it and other directedness may be getting at the same thing.

Two hundred and four students from introductory sociology courses were given a questionnaire by their class instructor. The instrument was designed to obtain extensive background information. It also included several attitude indexes to measure the subjects' need for approval and their inner/outer directedness, as well as several items requesting reference-group information. Upper and lower quartiles were established for this instrument, and subjects falling in the extremes were later invited to participate in a "voting study." Each subject participating was subjected along with two confederates to one of several experimental conditions. These included two conditions of disclosure (public or private), two conditions of attitudinal congruence (the two others present could take a position that was either congruent or incongruent with that of the subject), and three conditions of social participation (anonymous-no participation, anonymous-participation, and face-to-face participation).

Albrecht and Warner found no significant relationship between disclosure and attitude/action consistency. In fact, there was a slight tendency for attitudes and action to be more consistent in public than in private. The hypotheses linking attitude/action consistency and the two personality factors were supported. Other-directed subjects exhibited lower attitude/action consistency when their behavior was disclosed to an audience that was perceived as feeling strongly contrary to their own position. Consistency was maintained when the behavior was to remain strictly private.

c. *Multiple beliefs versus single belief.* Bruwold (1972) also found evidence for the postulate of contingent consistency in his search for attitude/action consistency. He began by defining an attitude as the emotional reaction to an object or proposition. Behavior was defined as observable activity of the individual that can be described. Belief was also sorted out, and was defined as an assertion accepted as true by the individual. Consistency was defined as congruence of attitude with belief or behavior.

Bruwold thought that the relationship between attitudes toward a specific object and beliefs and behavior regarding that object would show significant consistency in people for whom the attitude object is important. The research dealt with the topic of reclaimed water in a San Diego suburb. Bruwold felt that users of a community swimming pool supplied with reclaimed water should have more positive attitudes toward such water use than nonusers. He also felt that individuals who believe that California faces an imminent water shortage should have more positive attitudes toward reclaimed water than individuals who do not hold this belief. And he hypothesized that individuals who believe that the scientific methods of water purification are superior to natural methods should have more positive attitudes toward reclaimed water for swimming than individuals who believe that the natural methods are superior.

Twenty-five respondents were selected from the suburb. Attitudes were measured with a standard scale. Knowledge of the respondents' behavior was obtained through a structured interview that dealt with the use of facilities. Beliefs were also assessed in the interview through a set of semistructured questions. The study was then conducted a second time, using 100 respondents. The basic research design was not changed.

Neither study produced significant results. Bruwold concluded that, although specific attitude/belief and attitude/behavior consistencies were not always significant, there was evidence for such consistency when more than one belief or more than one type of behavior were considered together. In other words, when a single belief is involved, attitudes may not be consistent; when a number of beliefs are involved, attitudes are more likely to remain consistent.

d. Social factors. Social factors have a major impact on attitudes, which in turn provide some of the basis for social behavior. The understanding of large-scale social phenomena depends on the attitudinal effects these phenomena exert on individuals. Perhaps the influence of *public opinion* is best illustrated in political reactions, such as party preference and voting behavior. Public attitudes are also brought to bear on consumer goods, property ownership, employment, social services, and cultural affairs. One person's attitude carries little weight from a broad social perspective. But when the same attitude is shared by a large fraction of the community, it can be significant for maintaining stability or for inducing change. Widely shared attitudes are the basis of public opinion.

Dickson's (1968) research on *social class* and dental care showed differences between middle- and working-class British respondents. Of the middle-class respondents, 91% said they would have their teeth filled to prevent decay, compared with 53% of working-class respondents. In this sample, 72% of the middle-class adults said they visited their dentist regularly, compared with 27% of the working class. Other studies have shown that middle-class persons have more positive attitudes toward medical service and health care. The more positive attitude results in more effective medical treatment.

Attitudes widely shared by people may shift over time. In the case of racial attitudes, there was far less difference between manual and nonmanual workers in the 1970s than in the 1950s, and the South became more like the rest of the United States in attitudes on the rights of minorities (Glenn, 1974).

Another social factor that can affect attitude/action consistency is the *orientation* of the individual to the community in which he or she lives. The *cosmopolitan* type does not need to depend solely on the community of residence for employment and social resources. Thus, medical, scientific, and other professional people and many kinds of skilled workers readily change from one community to another for improvements in job, income, and lifestyle. The *local* type has no resources outside the community where he or she lives. Therefore, "locals" are more under the influence of persons in the home community, whereas "cosmopolitans" are more responsive to the influence of the wider society.

Does the local or cosmopolitan origin affect college students' consistency between their shared political-party preference and their ideological beliefs? A study by Nelson and Tallman (1969) indicates that cosmopolitan students are more likely to maintain consistency between political ideology and party preference. As Table 10-2 shows, the local student is more likely to maintain consistency with his or her father's political preference. The degree of authoritarianism also appears to affect consistency between humanitarian attitudes and helping behavior. In a study by Fischer (1973), persons low on authoritarianism showed more consistency than those who were less tolerant of homosexuality, illegitimacy, prostitution, and abortion, which indicated high authoritarianism.

C. ATTITUDE/ACTION CONSISTENCY: REASONS FOR FAILURE

The three postulates that try to explain the relationship between attitudes and actions all make one basic assumption: behavior is a function of attitude. Surprisingly enough, research that supports a relationship between attitude and behavior indicates that people bring their attitudes in line with their behavior rather than the opposite (Cohen, 1960; Gerard, 1965; Landy, 1966). Lauer (1971) summarized this failure of congruency. Rather than reasoning in terms of the three postulates, he suggested that the problem lies "in our failure to create research designs that reflect the complexity of the problem and in the tendency to exalt the importance of the proximate causes of overt behavior" (247). He posited that it is the "publish or perish" syndrome that has forced us into a simplistic and unrealistic research design.[1] Lauer suggested that attitude research that takes account of the complexity of attitudes themselves, as well as the complex manner in which attitudes interact with other social phenomena, must consider the following six characteristics.

1. Attitudes Are Interdependent

A typical research approach to the relation between attitudes and action is to identify attitude as the independent variable and behavior as the dependent variable. Any overt act involves not a single attitude but a number of attitudes. Attitudes are mental phenomena and cannot be separated from one another for experimental purposes. Lauer agreed that behav-

Table 10-2. Percentage of students whose political views agreed with those of their fathers

Type of Student	Conservative	Middle	Liberal
Cosmopolitan	18	26	53
Local	37	47	69

From "Local and Cosmopolitan Perceptions of Political Conformity," by J. I. Nelson and I. Tallman, *American Journal of Sociology*, 1969, 75, 193–207. Copyright 1969 by The University of Chicago Press. Reprinted by permission.

[1] Fishbein (1967) presented an argument diametrically opposed to Lauer's. He viewed an attitude as a relatively simple, unidimensional concept referring to the amount of emotion for or against an object. Our inability to obtain a strong relationship between attitude and behavior has spurred a growth from a simple, unidimensional concept to a complex, multidimensional concept.

ior is organized in terms of attitudes, but always in terms of a plurality of attitudes. Therefore, he suggested that it is reasonable to assume that a minimum of two attitudes will be necessary to obtain a significant correlation between attitudes and behavior. In many cases, more than two might be required. Byrne and McGraw (1969) found that persons low in prejudice respond similarly to both Black and White strangers. However, a prejudiced individual's response to a Black stranger is dependent on the degree to which they share similar attitudes. The more similar the attitudes, the more positive their behavior to the Black stranger.

2. Attitudes Are Multidimensional

Katz and Stotland (1959) and Secord and Backman (1964) identified three components of attitudes: affective, cognitive, and behavioral. And, not all of these components imply behavior. Albrecht and Warner (1973) wrote: "Behavior that is predicted by taking into account only a single variable, such as attitude, may have relatively weak predictive value since the behavior is the result of the interaction of multiple forces" (16). In Wiessburg's terms, "An attitude, no matter how conceived, is simply one of the terms in the complex equation we use to predict behavior: we cannot expect it to do too much (1965, 424). Lauer wrote that, although most social psychologists agree that the affective and cognitive components are present, most would agree that the behavioral component may be missing. Fishbein went much further: "Rather than viewing beliefs and behavioral intentions as a part of attitude, I prefer to define them independently, and to view them as phenomena that are related to attitudes" (1967, 478). The argument is well taken, in that most instruments constructed to measure attitudes include only the evaluative, or affective, component. Though an attitude is said to include three components, it is only the affective component that is measured and treated by researchers as the essence of the attitude.

3. Attitudes Are Extrapolated or Existential

Lauer defined an extrapolated attitude as one that is projected into an imaginary situation. An existential attitude is one that arises out of an actual situation. The "failure" to predict behavior can be traced to extrapolated attitudes. Lauer was not suggesting that extrapolated attitudes are of no value. Their value, however, lies in the ability of researchers to replicate their findings in the actual situation and in the ability of subjects to apprehend the actual situation in their imagination. Crespi (1971) concurred with this evaluation, contending that improving behavioral prediction requires test items having properties similar to those present in the actual situation. Opinion polls dealing with actual situations, for example, have had good success predicting three kinds of behavior: voting preference, movie attendance, and consumer brand preference.

4. Attitudes Are Central or Peripheral

Lauer perceived the organization of attitudes to be a network of inter-locking attitudes. Any single attitude is more or less central or peripheral in this system. The more central the attitude, the greater the number of other attitudes with which it is linked and, consequently, the more likely it is to influence behavior. Attitudes with fewer links are more likely to be subservient to situational factors. A mother's attitude toward her child, for example, will probably be quite central. Other attitudes, such as volunteer work and career plans, may be more peripheral in this system.

5. Attitudes Are Primary or Secondary

Lauer identified primary attitudes as those that are crucial to people's selfhood—their values, self-concept, and ideology. Jones (1964) and Veevers (1971) have presented evidence that subjects may be incapable of making accurate judgments in matters that bear on their self-concepts. Therefore, it is considerably more difficult to tap primary attitudes. Lauer was suspicious of attempts to measure primary attitudes from simple pencil-and-paper tests deriving attitudes from anticipated behavior in hypothetical situations. The individual is less vulnerable in imagined situations. Similarly, a real situation might arouse protective defenses not aroused in an imagined situation. Kiesler, Collins, and Miller (1969) also recognized this problem. They wrote: "We can expect a high correlation between pencil and paper measures of attitude and behavior responses only when both behaviors are elicited by the same object" (166).

6. Attitudes Operate in Specific Social Contexts

Behavior is an interaction between dispositions and situations. This particular point supports the postulate of contingent consistency, suggesting that not only the attitude but also the factors surrounding a given situation affect the relationship between behavior and attitudes. Triandis (1964) conducted a study that provides evidence for this position. White, Protestant, male undergraduates at the University of Illinois were asked to indicate how they would behave toward certain persons, including a 50-year-old Black, Roman Catholic, male physician and a 20-year-old White, Jewish, female soda-fountain clerk. Behavior to which the subjects responded included admiring the character of, being commanded by, physically loving, kissing the hand of, going fishing with, stopping from voting, discussing moral issues with, losing a game to, and treating as a subordinate. With the student sample, five separate factors were found:

1. Admiring the character of
2. Falling in love with
3. Being partners in an athletic game with

4. Doing a favor for
5. Treating as a subordinate

Consequently, knowledge about admiration does not allow us to predict who a person might choose as a partner in an athletic match. The situations are separate and distinct, and knowledge of one does not help us to predict another.

7. Conclusions

The postulate of contingent consistency seems to offer the most logical and feasible explanation for the relationship between attitudes and behaviors. The fine line between our definitions of values, attitudes, and opinions also lends support to this postulate. Social psychologists' ways of getting at values and opinions differ very little from their procedures for measuring attitudes. Consequently, what we define (using scaling procedures, for example) as attitude might just as accurately be defined as value or opinion.

If we accept the position that attitudes are symbolic responses to symbolic situations, then we are giving credence to the importance of the situation. We are recognizing that attitudes cannot be described as analogous to fixed personality traits. Instead, they must be viewed as having a flexibility, or elasticity. A given attitude does not provide us with perfect or even close-to-perfect predictive power. An attitude arising in the context of a social situation may be guided by certain values, but it is subject to variability.

An attitude, then, is a spontaneous response to one's perception of the social situation in which he or she is interacting. In the terminology of rocketry, spacecraft's attitude is its position in flight. Similarly, a person's attitude is his or her position at a particular point in life.

D. THE VALUE OF ATTITUDE RESEARCH

1. Six Values of Attitude Research

The inconsistency between attitudes and actions should not cause us to totally disregard the value of attitude research. The following discussion will be largely dependent on Lauer (1971), who identified six major values of attitude research.

1. *Attitudes influence psychological processes.* Both perception and learning are affected by attitudes. Perception of any phenomenon tends to be congruent with existing attitudes. Similarly, it is more difficult to learn or retain material that is incongruent with attitudes. Studies dealing with prejudices towards Jews and identification of Jews in a series of photographs (Scodel and Austrin, 1957; Himmelfarb, 1966) suggested that anti-Semitic judges tend to identify a larger number of photographs as being of Jewish persons, even though many of these identifications are incorrect.

2. *Attitudes function as an ecological variable.* Lauer cited Shibutani (1971, 279) as arguing that three factors affect the individual's behavior: how the situation is defined, the individual's self-concept, and the reference group. In other words, individuals function within the context of an attitudinal ecology. And their understanding of the attitudes of those significant others who compose their reference groups will bear directly on behavior. Albrecht and Warner (1973) supported this contention, particularly for individuals who are other directed. Knowledge of people's attitudes may give us insight into their self-concept and their significant others.

3. *Attitudes help define groups.* Other things being equal, individuals tend to choose to interact with those who have attitudes similar to their own. Newcomb (1961) developed and tested the theory that people with similar attitudes are attracted to one another. Newcomb's proposition was based on the premise that in every individual there is a need for consensual validation. In other words, people order their environment. But their interpretation of the order is no guarantee that this order is correct. Consequently, in order to reinforce their interpretation, they seek others whose interpretation of that order are similar to their own. Thus, knowledge of people's attitudes gives us insight into the kind of other people they find most attractive.

4. *Attitudes inhibit certain behavior.* Although a great deal of research attention has been given to the relation between attitudes and behavior, little attention has been paid to the significance of attitudes in inhibiting certain kinds of behavior. Myrdal (1968) posited that attitudes as well as institutions make up a significant barrier to social change.

5. *Attitudes affect their objects.* Rosenthal and Jacobson (1968) demonstrated the effect of teacher attitude on pupil performance. Notice that it is the behavior of the attitude object and not the subject that is affected.

6. *Attitudes are formed out of behavior.* Returning to a point made earlier, researchers have had difficulty in establishing causal links between attitudes as the independent variable and behavior as the dependent variable. As we have indicated, the same has not been true for establishing a link between behavior as the independent variable and attitudes as the dependent variable. Lauer cited several research efforts that have found this link:

   a. Lieberman (1956): A change of roles brings about a change of attitudes.
   b. Hyman and Sheatsley (1964): Changing discriminatory practices leads to a change of discriminatory attitudes.
   c. Breer and Locke (1965): Attitudes may shift as a result of participating in various task groups.
   d. Colombotos (1969): Legislation may change attitudes even before behavior changes.

The implication is that measurement of attitude is one way of measuring social change. Emergence of an attitude, then, may serve to legitimate and therefore perpetuate the new behavior patterns. When attitudes and behavior are inconsistent, we can predict that one or the other will change.

2. Looking Back

Irwin Deutscher (1973), in evaluating 31 years of attitude/action studies, concluded that we have suffered a "methodological regression" because we have not gotten much closer to predicting actions from attitudes. Such a theoretical perception holds to the position that there should be a fixed attitudinal stance. A methodological regression—no! A theoretical regression—quite possible! Because research finds its beginning within a theoretical framework, it would seem that the cyclical nature of the research process has not been functioning properly. We begin with a theoretical position: attitudes and actions are related; given one's attitude, behavior can be predicted. When our methodologies fail to support this theoretical position, the logic of the research process dictates theoretical alterations. Instead, we have relied mostly on methodological alterations, holding fast to the original theoretical position. Now it seems that such a theoretical position is much too simplistic. We cannot ignore the importance of the social situation. Just as a thermometer registers a slightly different temperature when moved from room to room, so does an individual register a somewhat different attitude when moving from situation to situation. A new and different theoretical perspective seems long overdue.

E. SUMMARY

The study of attitudes is perhaps the single most important concept in the field of social psychology. The term was first used by Herbert Spencer to refer to a mental state. With little delay the term soon became very popular in both sociology and psychology. Psychologists were looking for a concept to help explain individual differences. Sociologists were looking for a concept to explain the mechanisms through which culture is carried. Perhaps the biggest stimulus to the study of attitudes came from the field of sociology, specifically from Thomas and Znaniecki, who defined social psychology as the scientific study of attitudes.

The concept of attitude has been defined in a number of ways. Berkowitz placed the bulk of the definitions into three basic categories. The first of the schools of thought perceives the evaluation of a feeling reaction as predominant. A second group conceives of an attitude as a readiness to respond in a particular way with regard to an attitude object. The third approach employs a triadic scheme of cognitive, affective, and behavioral components. It has been criticized for its failure to establish a causal link between the three components. Even to date this link has not been satisfactorily established.

One of the major concerns of social psychologists has been the relationship between attitudes and action. Three postulates explaining this relationship were discussed. The postulate of consistency suggests a positive relationship between attitude and action. That is, knowledge of an individual's attitude allows us to predict his or her behavior. This position was supported through the research of DeFleur and Westie (1958), which examined the relationship between prejudice towards Blacks and one's decision to be photographed with a Black. The postulate of independent variation posits no direct relationship between attitudes and action. Attitudes and action are thought to vary independently of each other: knowledge of one's attitude does not allow us to predict behavior. Research supporting this postulate was conducted by LaPierre (1934) on hotel, motel, and restaurant owners' prejudices toward Chinese. The postulate of contingent consistency suggests that the relationship between attitudes and actions is dependent on intervening variables. That is, in certain situations we can expect attitudes and actions to be related. In other situations the relationship may not exist. Research supporting the postulate of contingent consistency has isolated such intervening variables as social constraint, social distance, situational factors, and personality factors.

The inability to find a positive relationship between attitudes and actions has created concern among researchers. Fishbein cited this discrepancy as a major reason for the shift of the concept of attitude from simple and unidimensional to complex and multidimensional. Lauer, in contrast, postulated that our inability to observe a one-to-one relationship between attitudes and action is the result of our efforts to oversimplify the concept. He cited six major reasons for the failure to observe attitude/action consistency:

1. Attitudes are interdependent.
2. Attitudes are multidimensional.
3. Extrapolated attitudes must be distinguished from existential attitudes.
4. Attitudes may be central or peripheral.
5. Attitudes may be primary or secondary.
6. Attitudes become factors in behavior in specific social contexts, interacting with other variables in that context.

Despite this lack of consistency between attitudes and actions, Lauer argued that attitude research is still of tremendous value. He cited a number of values, but perhaps most important for the sociologist is the use of attitudes for perceiving social change. Attitudes serve as a type of individual and social thermometer for measuring and identifying individual and societal responses in various social situations.

Interpersonal Attraction 11

A. INTRODUCTION

Have you ever thought how much easier it is to talk and act when you are around people you know and like? Similarly, when we are around strangers or foes, interaction may be strained and difficult. What accounts for these feelings? What processes are involved in the common-sense experience of simply liking, being attracted to, or loving someone else, and what is involved when we are repulsed or feel hatred? Many of the processes we have discussed in this book may have little to do with whether a person likes or dislikes another person, but there are many other situations in which liking, loving, and hating are central concerns.

If you have ever planned a party, you know that interpersonal attraction will be a critical matter. It is a question not only of whom you like but also of what kinds of attractions exist among the people you invite. A close look at people's conversation during the course of a day would probably reveal that much of it is devoted to who likes whom and who doesn't. As our society becomes increasingly anonymous and dependent upon appearances (Riesman, 1950), those relationships based on attraction become all the more important.

In some types of relationships, of course, attraction is irrelevant. For example, status seeking ("keeping up with the Joneses") may have little to do with liking and virtually nothing to do with loving. We are reminded of a cartoon that shows a husband figuring up the bank balance and saying with some frustration to his wife: "Mildred, tell me something. Why do we spend money we don't have, to buy things we don't need, just to keep up with people we can't stand the sight of?" Nevertheless, liking, loving, friendships, and other intimate relations have become among the most important forces in contemporary society. Therefore, it is vital to try to find out how a person comes to like others, what attractiveness means, and other related matters.

B. THEORIES OF ATTRACTION

Attraction is an easy process to experience but a difficult one to explain. Three different theoretical orientations have been prominent, and each is based on a different way of viewing behavior. These three approaches are generally termed in the literature the *cognitive*, *reinforcement*, and *interactionist* perspectives. We will discuss each in turn, showing how they have contributed in different ways to an understanding of the process of attraction.

1. Cognitive Theories

Cognitive theories emphasize thought processes as the basic determinant of all behavior. The human being is viewed as a mind trying to deal in a rational way with the complex issues of the world around it. Social behavior is seen as an outcome, or consequence, of the processes of the mind. By placing the explanation for behavior outside the individual actor, cognitive theories are the least sociological. However, since much of the literature on interpersonal attraction has used this approach, we will describe it and demonstrate some of the insights that can be gained from looking at the problem in this way. Then we will go on to more sociological points of view.

One such cognitive approach is the *balance theory* of social psychologist Theodore Newcomb (1961). We have discussed this theory in general terms elsewhere. It finds a tendency to organize conceptions about others, oneself, and things in the environment in a "harmonious, balanced, or symmetrical way." Certain relationships are more satisfying than others. If one person likes another and if they both dislike liver and onions, a balanced state is said to exist in their relationship. A good interpersonal relationship is characterized by basic agreement and a similarity of viewpoints about other people, places, and things. Therefore, political parties may originate when two per-

"I'll tell you why you're a liberal! Because I'm a conservative!"

Balance versus imbalance.

sons decide that they hold similar beliefs, both about the things they like and the things they deplore. In other words, the attractiveness of someone else may depend simply on what you and he or she agree to dislike. Following this theory, it is not surprising at all to learn that much of the dialogue between two people, especially during the initial stages of establishing a relationship, has to do with putting together likes and dislikes. "Oh, you like the Beatles too!"

The most unsatisfactory relationships, said Newcomb, stem from a lack of balance between agreements and disagreements. Friendships that have been cemented on the basis of a mutual appreciation of football, a breed of dog, or what constitutes a beautiful woman may suddenly fall apart when the friends discover that they disagree about the existence of God. When an imbalance occurs, one person may try to move the relationship back to a balanced state by trying to convince the other to change. Or balance can be attained by changing one's own mind. Finally, the person may resolve the situation by simply not admitting that an imbalance exists. ("He says he doesn't believe in God, but he *really* does.")

Newcomb's balance theory, along with a similar formulation advanced by Fritz Heider (1958), has generated a great deal of research, all of which has borne out many of the fundamental propositions discussed above (Miller and Geller, 1972; Price, Harburg, and Newcomb, 1966). Problems do exist, however. Birds of a feather may flock together, but opposites may also attract. People do seem to have the capacity to "agree to disagree," although certainly the majority of our most intimate relationships seem to involve basic agreement.

2. Reinforcement Theory

Reinforcement, or stimulus/response, theories have their roots in learning theory and interpret attraction as a learned response. Instead of focusing on the mental processes by which people work out likes and dislikes, reinforcement theory seeks to discover how attraction came to be established initially. The basic propositions of this theory are quite simple. People are attracted by rewarding things and repelled by punishing ones. All circumstances of interpersonal attraction are explained in terms of a person's learning to associate positively with rewarding people and things and negatively with punishing stimuli. We are more likely to be attracted to people who compliment us and give us gifts than to people who criticize our acts or spit on us.

Demonstration of the reinforcement theory has been done by Lott and Lott (1965). They placed children in a group to play a game in which some received toys from the experimenter and others received no reward. Those who received the rewards liked not only the experimenter but also their fellow group members better than those who did not. Rewards create an attraction not only toward the person giving the reward but also toward other aspects of the environment.

The problem with this theory of attraction lies in its inadequate explanation of what is usually the case: rewards and punishments are often combined in a relationship with the same person. How do we account for the fact that we do maintain strong attractions for people who punish us? For example, the relationship between parent and child is usually a very strong one even though the parent dispenses punishments. Reinforcement theory has only one answer: that in these cases the ratio of rewards to behavior is greater than that of punishment (Baron, Byrne, and Griffitt, 1974). There may exist, however, strong attractions to persons with whom the "punishments" far outweigh the "rewards," at least numerically.

Much of the more recent work in reinforcement theory as a way of understanding interpersonal attraction has taken place under the rubric of *exchange theory* (Thibault and Kelley, 1959; Homans, 1961; Blau, 1964). Although there are technical differences between exchange theory and other types of reinforcement theories and although sociological social psychologists have more commonly embraced the former, many common difficulties remain. In exchange theory attractions are based on punishments and rewards translated into the economic terms of *cost* and *reward*. All relationships—friendship, marriage, work, and so on—are explained in terms of a ratio in which the costs are lower than the rewards.

3. Interactionist Theory

The two preceding theories regard attraction as a process that has to do with individual persons. In the cognitive theory attraction is a decision that takes place in the mind. In the reinforcement theory each person is stimulated to like another person on the basis of prior conditioning. Under exchange theory a relationship will presumably break down when the exchange is perceived as uneven or unfair by either of the participants. People do not stay married because they "love" each other or because of a sense of responsibility, commitment, or obligation but because the rewards of the relationship are greater than the costs. When the costs start to outweigh the rewards, the relationship will end (Blau, 1964).

Interactionist theory, in contrast, sees attraction as being an *interpersonal*, not a *personal*, process. It is not so much a cognitive decision or learned response as it is a *mutual* definition of a situation. Interactionist ideas have developed not from laboratory studies of attraction, in which a subject responds to a stranger on the basis of various kinds of information, but in naturalistic settings where a decision is always connected to the social situation in which the participants find themselves. Levinger and Snoek (1972), for example, pointed out that laboratory studies tend to be superficial. They deal with first impressions rather than with long-term relationships and with interpersonal attraction as a one-time event rather than a continuous process. Levinger and Snoek emphasized in their research that the important factors in a relationship differ from time to time. A husband may have been attracted to his wife initially because of her shapely figure and beautiful face but later find that these things are not sufficient to sustain a marriage. He may discover that he continues to be attracted to her on the basis of other attributes.

In other words, interactionists contend that theories of interpersonal attraction have not sufficiently focused on relationships as having *careers* (Becker, 1964). Similarity and mutuality may be more developmental and descriptive concepts than explanatory ones. Interactionist theory, however, has only recently paid attention to interpersonal attraction as a concept to be investigated. The entire matter has been more studied by psychologists using laboratory methods than by social psychologists using interactionist theories and naturalistic methods. The basic concepts of an interactionist approach to attraction are, however, clear; we now turn to a discussion of these concepts.

C. PHYSICAL APPEARANCE

1. The Social Significance of Appearance

Physical appearance is one of the most socially significant determinants of attraction. Differences in appearance form the basis for a host of social definitions—some extremely positive, some neutral, and some tragic. Such characteristics as beauty, skin color, weight, height, hair length, facial hair, and mammary glands are but a few of the elements that people make so much of in interaction. Beauty may only be skin deep, but people pay a lot of attention to skin. Erving Goffman noted in an important book on the difficulties of persons with physical stigmas the difference between elements that are internal and those that are external:

> A person with carcinoma [cancer] of the bladder can die with more grace and apparent normalcy than a harelip can order a piece of apple pie [1971b, 353].

Stone and Farberman (1970) wrote that physical appearance is part of a process of "symbolic transformation." Physical characteristics are at base neutral, but they become elements in the symbolic world of human beings and, as such, are transformed into meaningful objects that are not at all neutral in their consequences.

Consider the social significance of skin color. Pigmentation is determined by a person's genetic skin code and has nothing to do with his or her inherent capabilities. However, as a result of certain symbolic transformations skin color turns out to determine quite a lot. Marriage, work, leisure, housing, and even friendship all come to be predicated, at least in part, on this arbitrarily assigned physical characteristic. The large body of literature developed by social psychologists on prejudice and discrimination all points to these patterns of interaction as being absolutely dependent on the existence of physically perceivable differences in appearance.

Standards of physical beauty are relative from culture to culture, but all cultures apparently make distinctions between people who are beautiful and those who are ugly (Linton, 1936). As Bierstedt pointed out:

> In certain parts of Africa, for example, the most desirable females are the fattest ones. When the girls reach the marriageable stage their mothers take them away from the tribal encampment, stuff them with rich and heavy foods, and rub them with butter, which they use as a cosmetic rather than as a food. If the young lady gains so much weight that she can hardly walk, the regimen is considered a success and she has no trouble finding suitors when she returns to the tribe. Indeed, the story is told of a talented and internationally famous American actress who, at a ceremonial dinner in London, captivated all of the guests with her personal charm and grace and wit. She managed also to chat amiably with the guest at her left, an African chief, who, at the conclusion of the dinner, said to her in his impeccable Oxford accent, "I could easily fall in love with you if only you were black and fat" [1970, 142].

It is, of course, not necessary to go to another culture to discover that standards of beauty in both males and females are relative to time, place, and situations. This is why the pinup girl from World War II looks so strange and anachronistic to us today. She was undoubtedly pretty, but she looked very little like the fold-outs we see in *Playboy* and *Penthouse*.

Although standards of beauty and handsomeness are subject to some change over time, in the Western world slimness has in general been valued over fatness, a full head of hair in men over baldness, and large breasts in women over small ones. In addition, the size and shape of the nose, mouth, and ears are factors in people's assessment of just what constitutes good looks. And a vast array of products has been sold so that people can put on a socially acceptable appearance or cover up one that is less than perfect. Advertisers tell us that we can attract others only if we are physically appealing, and they give us examples of both the appealing and the appalling. Add to this the large amounts of money that are spent for cosmetic surgery to increase the size of the breasts, change the shape or size of the nose, remove wrinkles from the skin, and bring protruding ears back into line, and you have what might be called the appearance and attraction industry.

One of these elements, odor, has a particular social significance. Odor, of course, cannot be seen, but it can definitely "appear" (Largey and Watson, 1972). Odor is also culturally relative rather than absolute in its meaning, but in North American culture it may be noted that we tend to define any unmasked body odor as offensive. In other words, if in social relationships a person can smell the other's body as opposed to his or her mouthwash, toothpaste, perfume, after-shave lotion, or deodorant, this is defined negatively. The only two situational exceptions seem to be during and after athletic competition and during sexual relations.

2. Opposite-Sex Relationships

Studies clearly indicate that whether we like a member of the opposite sex depends in large measure on how attractive he or she is (Walster, Aronson, Abrahams, and Rottman, 1966). Courtship and dating are social rituals based very much on attractiveness. "Blind" dates are problematic for that very reason. It is difficult to define and initiate a relationship when you don't know what the other person looks like, especially when you are dealing with a member of the opposite sex.

Despite this important and sometimes brutal aspect of the social psychology of physical attractiveness, most persons do manage to find others to whom they are both attracted and attractive. This is in part a defensive strategy, for the symbols that define beauty are so important in society that they are often defended strongly against change. An extremely attractive person who chooses to marry someone much less attractive may find that their relationship is always seen by others as "odd" and that they are the object of much talk. This kind of talk may indeed be a factor in the couple's own relationship after a while. We are geared to wanting the most

What does she see in him? What does he see in her? (Photo by © Dennis Stock, Magnum Photos)

attractive person possible, but we are also willing to accept a person who is much more like ourselves (Berscheid et al., 1971). This is due not only to our own feelings about the matter but also to the expectations and sanctions of others.

3. Same-Sex Relationships

The observations we have made thus far have their greatest significance in opposite-sex relationships. But it should also be pointed out that physical attractiveness is of great importance even when we are dealing with a person of the same sex. For student subjects, at least, popularity and liking seemed to depend greatly on physical appearance (Byrne et al., 1968), even when the object of liking was a member of the same sex. In business and politics same-sex relationships may well be based on the same features of physical attractiveness that we have pointed out as being so crucial in opposite-sex relationships (Lerner and Gellert, 1969; Holstein et al., 1971).

4. Stereotyping

Physical appearance also forms the basis for stereotyping people and dealing with them in prejudicial and discriminatory ways. The term *stereotype* is derived from the Greek word *stereos*, which means rigid, firm, or hard. The term was introduced into wide usage by Walter Lippmann, who described in a book on public opinion how people "for the most part . . . do not see and then define, [but] define first and then see" (1922).

In social life we frequently discover that we must act on the basis of categorical information. We know only that the person we are dealing with is a Catholic, a Democrat, a businessman, a military officer, or a schoolteacher, and we form our judgments about him or her on the basis of what we know about those categories. When a person is being interviewed for a job, the interviewer can know very little except what the categories of appearance show. The person may well get the job on the basis of whether or not the interviewer "likes his looks." Despite the seeming unfairness of it all, it would probably be impossible for us to get rid of this element of interaction altogether. For example, Alfred Schutz defended the usefulness of these categorical perceptions, calling them *typifications:*

> Typifications of human individuals . . . of their motives and goals . . . were formed in the main by others, . . . predecessors or contemporaries, as appropriate tools for coming to terms with things and men, accepted as such by the group into which [a person is] born. . . .
>
> The sum-total of these various typifications constitutes a frame of reference in terms of which not only the sociocultural, but also the physical world has to be interpreted, a frame of reference that, in spite of its inconsistencies and its inherent opaqueness, is nonetheless sufficiently integrated and transparent to be used for solving part of the practical problems at hand [1964, 232].

What Schutz is saying is that stereotyping is virtually inevitable because of the utter impossibility of dealing with other people in all of their uniqueness and individuality. We stereotype races, ethnic groups, political preferences, occupational groups, sexual identities and preferences, social classes, and religious groups, to mention only a few. Stereotypical imagery is built up in jokes, stories, and slurs.

The patterns of attraction and repulsion that are to be found in stereotyping are basically symbolic. That is, concepts or names come to stand for the race or group as a whole. A classic study by Katz and Brady (1947) demonstrated that persons saw people with black skin as superstitious, lazy, happy-go-lucky, ignorant, musical, and stupid. Jews were seen as being shrewd, mercenary, industrious, grasping, intelligent, sly, and clannish. Turks were viewed as cruel, treacherous, sensual, dirty, deceitful, and revengeful. Although this study is now dated and although there has been an increased public awareness about stereotypes, these conceptions continue to exist, especially when one deals with groups that are farther removed from actual physical and social contact. A high-level Cabinet officer in the administration of former President Gerald Ford was forced to resign over publicity about a highly stereotyped racial joke he told.

Stereotypes can be positive as well as negative. While negative ones seem to create the most stir, dealing with people categorically on the basis of positive stereotypes is also prevalent. The teacher who expects his or her Black student to excel in basketball and music is operating on the basis of stereotype as much as the teacher who expects these same Blacks to be below average in mathematics and English. The stereotypes, to the extent that they are acted out, may of course lead in a self-fulfilling way to exactly these characteristics being demonstrated by the group they are attributed to.

Once a stereotype has been accepted, its categorical effects can even transcend physical characteristics and distinctions. This point has never been captured with more poignancy than in the writing of Langston Hughes, who commented on "that powerful drop":

> Leaning on the lamp post in front of the barber shop, Simple was holding up a copy of the *Chicago Defender* and reading about how a man who looks white had just been declared officially colored by an Alabama court.
> "It's powerful," he said.
> "What?"
> "That one drop of Negro blood—because just *one* drop of black blood makes a man colored. *One* drop—you are Negro! Now, why is that? Why is Negro blood so much more powerful than any other kind of blood in the world? If a man has Irish blood in him, people will say, 'He's part Irish.' If he has a little Jewish blood in him, they'll say, 'He's *half Jewish.*' But if he has just a small bit of colored blood in him, BAM!—'He's Negro!' Now, that is what I do

not understand—why our *one* drop is so powerful. Take paint—white will not make black *white*. But black will make white *black*. One drop of black in white paint—and the white ain't white no more! Black is powerful. You can have ninety-nine drops of white blood in your veins down South—but if that other *one* drop is black, shame on you! Even if you look white, you're black. That drop is really powerful. Explain it to me. You're colleged."

"It has no basis in science," I said, "so there's no logical explanation" [1958, 26].

The explanation, of course, does not lie in biological science. It lies in the social processes of stereotyping, prejudice, and categorical judgment.

Social psychologists have used the idea of stereotype more in studies of intergroup conflict than in any other area. But the concept is beginning to be used increasingly to study more general processes of interpersonal attraction and repulsion.

The attractiveness of a particular social category may have virtually nothing to do with incidents of actual contact with members of the category. This point was brought home dramatically in a social-distance study by Hartley (1946). Persons were shown a list of racial, ethnic, and religious groups and asked questions dealing with how close they were willing to be to them—live next door to, have for friends, have for marital partners, and the like. To the predictable list of Blacks, Indians, Chinese, and Jews Hartley added three fictitious groups—the Danerians, the Pirenians, and the Wallonians. Sure enough, those persons who did not want any Blacks or Indians living next door didn't want any Danerians or Wallonians on their block either. Some went so far as to say that they had known or worked with Danerians and Pirenians and knew them to be lazy and untrustworthy. In other words, the processes of stereotyping have to do with attraction, purely and simply. Those persons who answered in this way simply did not want to be around persons who were not like them.

Much stereotyping is on the basis of in-group and out-group patterns. Those groups to which we belong are described differently than those groups to which we do not belong, *even in terms of the same attributes.* The attribute of *loyalty*, highly valued among members of our own group, becomes defined as *clannishness* when describing Jews. Group pride may become *elitism* when looking at others. And *standing up for one's rights* becomes sheer *belligerence* when the object of inquiry is another group.

Since most people belong to multiple categories, the process of stereotyping is extremely complicated. For this reason social psychologists have noted that stereotypes tend to be more intense around certain *master statuses* a person has (Hughes, 1958). Such social identities as Black, homosexual, and mental patient are overriding in their significance of stereotyping. Whatever else a person may be, such master statuses become a filter through which other persons see them.

5. Stigma

A good example of both the overriding significance of some social categories and the importance of physical appearance is the process by which people are stigmatized. The term *stigma* is of Greek derivation and meant originally a mark carved or burned into the skin to identify miscreants. The Greeks strongly felt that negative moral status needed to be advertised, and slaves, criminals, and traitors were branded so they could be identified as persons to be avoided (Goffman, 1963b). Stigma has now been expanded to refer to any person who is negatively identified on the basis of some physical or informational characteristic.

The basis of stigma is social identification. A person is *identified* by others in terms of various sorts of attributes. The repulsions associated with stigma are inevitably tied up with these presentations. Goffman distinguished between discredited identities and those that are merely discreditable. The difference is important, even though a stigmatized person will probably experience both. In the case of *discredited identities*, people have already been defined negatively by others. *Discreditable identities* involve information about the person that must be controlled lest it lead to discrediting.

Some stigmatized persons are immediately known. They are visible through physical signs of their difference: polio victims, other types of cripples, deformed persons, persons with horribly visible scars, burn victims, and amputees. We are not attracted to these people because they are grossly unattractive given the ordinary definitions of how human beings ought to look. Their stigma cannot be removed, is difficult to cover up, and must usually be simply lived with. For "normal" people the person with a visible stigma tends to stand out and support the prevailing definition of normality by contrast (Douglas, 1970). By making distinctions in this way, we of course imply that the stigmatized person is not quite human. Acting out this assumption, people typically exercise a wide variety of discriminations (Goffman, 1963b). Various terms associated with stigma are often used in everyday language without thought to their original meanings: *cripple, bastard, idiot, crazy.*

Given this general attitude, those with a physical stigma never know what the attitude of a new acquaintance will be and whether they will be accepted or rejected (Barker, 1948). Even when they are accepted by others, an additional problem may be that they do not know whether the acceptance was given completely or only half-heartedly and whether it was motivated by a genuine egalitarianism or by a sense of pity. In this sense, undue attention can be as difficult as rejection. An amputee, for example, talks about her experience in sports:

> "Whenever I fell, out swarmed the women in droves, clucking and fretting like a bunch of bereft mother hens. It was kind of them, and in retrospect I ap-

preciate their solicitude, but at the time I resented and was greatly embarrassed by their interference. For they assumed that no routine hazard to skating—no stick or stone—upset my flying wheels. It was a foregone conclusion that I fell because I was a poor, helpless cripple" [22].

For the stigmatized, the ordinary rewards and punishments can no longer be unthinkingly attributed to attributes of the self. Rather, there is always the suspicion that they might have been given on the basis of the stigma. The entire matter of interpersonal attraction is thrown into chaos.

D. NONPHYSICAL STIGMAS

Whereas the illustrations in the previous section deal with stigmas that are immediately visible, there are many other factors affecting attraction that are not physical at all. There are persons who, even though they may have been discredited on numerous occasions, hold identities that are by and large only discreditable. Mental patients, persons with criminal records, homosexuals, alcoholics, drug addicts, persons who have attempted suicide, and even—on a milder scale—persons who have been discharged from jobs or have gotten divorces all represent examples of discreditable identities.

In each of these cases, individuals know that information about them exists that will discredit them should it come into play. When a person with a discreditable identity interacts with others, then, the question is whether to display the information or not to display it, to tell or not to tell, to let on or not to let on, to lie or not to lie.

An excellent case in point is the person who has a psychiatric history. Because mental illness does not exist as a "thing" (Szasz, 1961) but rather as a conception attributed to people who have certain kinds of problems in their lives (Rosenhan, 1973), the crucial issue is whether or how this information about the person's former status comes into play. While in a mental hospital a man will be regarded as sane or insane, well or sick, depending on a variety of contingencies having to do with his own presentations, the responses of others, the circumstances and surroundings, and so on (Goffman, 1961a). But once out of the hospital the man's problems are quite different. In the hospital the man was clearly discredited by virtue of being there. But outside, because mental illness cannot be seen as can the scars of polio, his identity is only discreditable. It is not so much that the person must face prejudice against himself, but rather that he "must face an unwitting acceptance of himself by individuals who are prejudiced against the kind of person he can be revealed to be" (Goffman, 1963b).

The former mental patient, then, faces two problems: (1) whether or how to keep his former status secret and (2) if the information does come into play, how to manage it in the least damaging way. If the information does become known, the person may have to overcompensate. Former mental patients sometimes complain that they have to be "twice as sensible as normal people" (Freeman and Simmons, 1961). However, when a discreditable identity becomes known, it may or may not be discredited. Part of the ex-patient's dilemma, then, will be how to keep discreditable identities from becoming discredited ones. One technique, investigated by Fred Davis (1961), is called "deviance disavowal." For example, the former mental patient may assert that hospitalization was for a physical and not a mental disorder. Or the ex-patient may say that the problem was a relatively "normal" one and not as deviant as is being implied. Such tactics are taken up in more detail in Chapter 13 in a discussion of motive vocabularies.

One of the things people fear about a stigma is its shared quality. Those around the stigmatized person, such as family members, friends, or members of a work group, often find that they must deal with the stigma. To some extent they, too, are discredited. This is one reason why such stigmatic relationships tend to be avoided (Schwartz, C. G., 1957). In fact, hospitalization for mental illness is in many states a ground for divorce.

E. FRIENDSHIP

1. The Social Nature of Friendship

Friendship is a purely social concept; you can't have a friend all by yourself. Friendship demands both the existence of others and a set of interactions with which to maintain itself. The literature we have previously discussed points out that people tend to like one another when they share certain similarities. However, we know little about friendship as a social institution that fits into the general pattern of whole societies and fulfills social functions (Suttles, 1970).

In many respects friendship has grown as a significant feature of American life as our society has become more anonymous (Riesman, 1950). In a society that has been described as "a world of strangers" (Lofland, 1973), where our contacts are increasingly sporadic, specific, exchange based, and structured, the significance of friendship has increased. Friendship fills a void where other institutions fail to provide close interpersonal ties.

This is not to say, of course, that friendship exists only in complex, industrial societies. It is only to say that in such societies friendship has a special significance. In most societies friendship provides the same general functions, allowing persons to go beyond institutional and status relationships to more meaningful, intimate, and lasting ones.

2. Friendship and Friendly Relations

Studies of interpersonal attraction, although they have gotten at many of the external factors that go into the making of friends, have generally not given an adequate account of friendship. This is primarily because of the failure to distinguish between friendships and friendly relations. According to social psychologist Suzanne Kurth, *friendship* is an "intimate interpersonal relationship involving each individual as a personal entity." *Friendly relations* are "outgrowths of a formal role relationship and a preliminary stage in the development of a friendship" (1970, 136).

Friendly relations are more or less required in our society. The ability to "get along" with others is not simply a nicety, it is positively a necessity of life in modern society. We establish friendly relationships with fellow workers, for example, not simply because it is nice to be friendly with people we work with but also because we might well lose our jobs if we do not get along.

Despite the general desirability of friendship, having a lot of friends poses its own problems. Since friendships demand a high level of intimacy and a considerable investment of both time and the self, too many friendships may be a luxury few people can afford. As Simmel noted, "Such complete intimacy becomes more and more difficult as differentiation among men increases. Modern man possibly has too much to hide to sustain a friendship in the ancient sense" (1950, 326). Because of this consuming characteristic of friendship, friendly relations may be safer. Friendships may cost us much more than friendly relations, and, although the rewards may be concomitantly higher, in many cases people feel it is simply not worth it. Friendly relations can develop into friendships; in fact, being friendly with someone is usually seen as a preparatory stage to establishing a friendship. Much of the time we are committed to a whole series of friendships, almost to the point where our "calendar is full." We simply do not have the time or the emotional currency with which to engage another friend or to transform an existing friendly relation into a full-fledged friendship.

Friendships and friendly relationships have a number of characteristics in common, although each of the common characteristics shows important qualitative distinctions. For example, both friendships and friendly relationships require in some measure that the interaction be defined as "voluntary," but this is much more important in friendships than it is in friendly relations. Friendships are "unambiguously voluntary" (Kurth, 1970), whereas friendly relations may also carry the implication that "as long as we have to work together, we might as well be friends." In other words, our willingness to be friendly with other people is often contingent on their presence in social situations that are not entirely voluntary. Friendliness, in this sense, is often a defense against conflict, boredom, and ambivalence, whereas friendships tend to be established for their own sake.

Friendly relations also lack the sense of uniqueness and individuality that are the hallmark of friendships. We are generally friendly with our neighbors because, among other things, it would be dangerous not to be. But if neighbors who are also close friends move from the neighborhood, the new family who buy the house—although we would probably be friendly to them—might not be the close friends the others were. This is because of the relative uniqueness of friendships. They are, as we noted previously, "irreplaceable." Similarly, many social organizations involve a whole network of friendly relations, and yet few if any of the participants may be close friends.

Friendships and friendly relations differ considerably in the degree of closeness and intimacy among the participants. Friendly relations are decidedly not *close;* if they become so, they are transformed into friendship and the participants do not regard themselves any longer as merely "friendly." All friendships involve a level of intimacy that friendly relations do not, but it is interesting to notice that persons also make hierarchies of their friends. They sort their friends into "close friends," "best friends," "former friends," and even "almost friends" (Jourard, 1958). This means that the simple concept of friendship may well be inadequate to cover the vast range and intensity of the kinds of relationships that fall under it.

Like all other relational careers, friendships must be maintained in order to survive. Friendships, like everything else, are born, live awhile, and may die (Becker, 1962). Friendly relations are a prelude to and a beginning point for friendships. Once people, for whatever reason—including some obligatory ones—find that they like each other, they may then decide to form a friendship. Undoubtedly there are cost/reward factors involved in the decision to become friends, but if that is the case it must necessarily be concealed.

As people size each other up with an eye toward friendship, several processes take place. Waller (1937), as well as others, has noted that individuals often throw out "lines" that others may or may not accept. There exist many structured and conventional settings for the exchange of such approaches. Parties, "mixers," dances, cocktail lounges, and other such places serve as stages on which lines can be given and persons can freely react, either accepting the line or rejecting it and moving on to someone else. Bars and other liquor-serving establishments are standard places for these types of exchanges and have been studied extensively by social psychologists (Cavan, 1966). Lines are useful in that a person may accept the line, acting as if it is not a line at all, or reject it as "merely a line" without any particular penalty.

The lines men give women for establishing a sexual relationship are well known and are illustrated here with an Ann Landers column. But many other lines can be identified as well. "We'll have to have you over sometime," "Sometime soon we'll have to get together," and "I sure would like to get to know you better" are all serviceable lines that can either be mutually seized or passed off as merely a line.

After a line has been accepted, the individuals involved will have to move from what is expected or required to what is freely given and voluntary. The moves they make will have to be interpreted as movements toward friendship. Many kinds of moves have been identified: tentative by Ann Landers

Girls Reveal
Sexual Come-ons

DEAR FRIENDS: Recently I asked my female teenage readers what "lines" the boys were using these days to break down their resistance. The response was staggering. Would you believe over 18,000 letters? To my surprise (although I should have learned long ago never to be surprised at what turns up on my desk) I received a handful of letters from boys telling me what "lines" the girls had used on THEM.

I received a few critical letters admonishing me for putting out a "how-to" list for beginners. "Young boys are plenty aggressive these days," wrote a mother of three daughters in Wheeling, West Virginia. "It's foolish to supply them with alternate 'lines' should theirs fail."

I hastened to inform "Wheeling mother" that the purpose of printing the "lines" was to wise up the naive and vulnerable who, too often, are snowed by cool cats on the make. Hopefully, if the girls see it in print, they will recognize it for what it is — just a line. And a fairly standard one at that.

I promised to share my findings with you. Here they are:

SHARON, PA.: "COME ON. WHAT are you afraid of? Don't be a baby. It's just part of growing up."

Louisville, Ky.: "If you really loved me you would. That's the way people express their true feelings. It's been going on since the world began."

Honolulu: "It's very painful for a guy to be in this condition and not get relief. You got me all heated up; now if you're any kind of a woman you'll take care of me."

Marshalltown, Iowa: "It will be good for your complexion. You should have seen my face before I did it. Honest. It's better than any medicine."

Carbondale, Ill.: "You're the most excit-ing chick I've ever met in my whole life. I have never wanted anybody the way I want you."

Fort Lauderdale: "Life is so uncertain. Who knows whether you'll be alive tomorrow? It would be awful if you died in an accident or something without experiencing the greatest thrill of all."

Mexico City: "You're awfully uptight. Sex is a great tension-breaker. It will make you feel relaxed."

Gatineau, Quebec: "I want to marry you someday. Now we have to find out if we are sexually compatible."

ROCHESTER, N.Y.: "I'VE HEARD rumors that you're 'lezzie.' If you aren't, prove it."

Nassau, The Bahamas: "I promise we won't go all the way unless you want to. We'll stop whenever you say."

Harrisburg, Pa.: "You have nothing to worry about, I'm sterile."

Toronto, Canada: "I know you want it as much as I do but you're afraid of your reputation. I swear I will never tell anybody. It will be our secret."

Shrewsbury, N.J.: "It isn't sex I'm after. I'm already in love with you. If you get pregnant I'll marry you right away."

Durham, N.C.: "You have the body of a woman. Mother Nature meant for you to have sex. You're ready for it."

And now that most unique approach in the handful of letters from boys who had been propositioned by girls: From Greenwich, Conn.: "I have a terrible time with cramps every month. The doctor said I should have sexual intercourse. Of all the guys I know, you're the one I want to help me with this medical problem." (P.S. The guy said no.)

Figure 11-1. Examples of "lines." (From "Ann Landers," *Tulsa Daily World*, November 23, 1976. Copyright © 1976 by Field Newspaper Syndicate. Reprinted by permission.)

moves, positive moves, formal moves, informal moves, and so forth. The significant point, however, is that each move is taken by the other as an indication that transformations in a friendly relation are forthcoming and that the person making them wants to make their relationship into something besides what it already is. Gifts, for example, are ordinarily taken to be something more than simply an expression of friendliness, as anyone with a Christmas gift list knows. (But we may well give a Christmas card to a list of persons with whom we are merely friendly, often for reasons that have more to do with power and constraint than with voluntariness [Johnson, 1971]). Even though gifts may be given insincerely, this must be proven. It is difficult to turn a gift down and even more difficult to maintain a stance of ambivalence toward a person who has given you a gift (Mauss, 1954). Indeed, gifts are perhaps the best way to initiate a relationship of friendship and to generate an identity that did not exist before (Schwartz, B., 1967).

After a relationship is established, various issues will assert themselves. For example, even though a friendship is voluntary and supposedly transcends economic considerations, a person will often be concerned that a friend is not "holding up his end of the relationship." Tests may be devised to make sure that the relationship is kept on a relatively equal plane. In romantic relationships, for example, the participants may be concerned if one person is becoming more deeply involved and committed than the other (Waller, 1938). The kinds of conflict that can result from friendships and their accompanying emotions of anger, hate, love, rejection, and the like are substantial indeed. It is easy to see how friendly relations are sometimes more attractive than friendships.

3. Characteristics of Friendship

Suttles (1970) has provided the most comprehensive sociological definition of friendship. He defined friendship in terms of four primary elements:

1. Friends value each other *as persons* rather than for incidental advantages that may accrue as a result of their friendship. In other words, although the friendship may have all kinds of secondary advantages, its establishment is primarily based on liking and caring for the other person, not on what he or she can do for you. Therefore, it is considered inappropriate and insincere if a person is opportunistic in selecting friends, picking only those who can do him or her the most good. As a result, any sign of exploitation is felt to discredit a relationship founded on friendship.

2. Although it is acceptable to appreciate the objective qualities of a friend, friendship as a relationship is not supposed to be based on these qualities. To like a person because of his or her hair, good looks, money, or automobile is not to like the *person* but only those *things*. To suggest that one's friendship with another would cease if the friend lost his or her job, looks, or social standing is usually felt to disclose that the friendship was built on a fraudulent base. Indeed, one is not supposed to like friends because of the faces they present, but because of an intimate knowledge of their "real selves."

Displaying "real self" behavior to another person is one way of establishing friendship. (Photo by © Eric Kroll, Taurus Photos)

3. The exchange of objects between friends is not supposed to be based on their economic value or public status but only on the preferences, wishes, desires, and knowledge of the friend. Therefore, it is quite inappropriate to give a hospitalized friend the monetary equivalent of a vase of flowers, even though it would be appropriate to loan a needy friend money. Furthermore, the concept of reciprocity is at least momentarily suspended with friends; when a gift is given, one need not be immediately returned. Friends "freely give" without any expectation of return.

4. Finally, friends are appreciated in terms of their uniqueness, not as an instance of a particular category. Friends are supposed to be "irreplace-able" because they are recognized as unique. Friends are not to be abandoned because one has found another "just as good." Friendship is a primary relationship in the most genuine sense of the word (Cooley, 1902), and its abiding characteristics are intimacy, individuality, and loyalty.

4. Establishing and Developing Friendships

These four elements must be brought into play when one establishes a friendship with someone else. How is this done? First, a person must offer to another a display of his or her "real self," often by contrasting one presentation with others that are more conventional or routine (Suttles, 1970). In other words, friendships are established by displaying something to the potential friend that one might routinely withhold from the view of others. Secrets, formally out-of-character talk and gestures, and intimate details of one's life and problems are all ways of initiating a friendship. Coupled with this is the idea of doing something for someone without any thought or expectation of remuneration.

Individual displays of unconventional, "real-self" behavior to another person are one way of establishing friendship. Another is what Suttles calls "collective remissions." In a collective remission one is confronted with a situation in which friendship is virtually demanded, and some type of intimate, "real-self" behavior is the norm. Examples include cocktail parties —where formal, "stuffy" persons are expected to "let their hair down," "feel free," "swing," or do something "outrageously out-of-character" (MacAndrew and Edgerton, 1969)—orgies, stag parties, masked balls, and the like. In these situations, one is expected to show others a violation of propriety as evidence of a substantive self that lies "behind the facade." Not to do so is likely to mean that one will be labeled a "wet blanket," "party pooper," or "square" and will not be invited to subsequent gatherings. The reciprocal disclosure of potentially damaging or embarrassing information about oneself serves to assure that "everyone will be friends."

The repeated failure of the law to close down places and activities that serve as scenes for the exchange of such proprietary violations is testimony to the power and necessity of friendship in modern society. It is the aged, the divorced, the ugly, and the deformed who often find themselves without friends because they do not have a stage on which to present even their shortcomings (Edgerton, 1967). Not surprisingly, we have heard loud complaints in recent years from these very groups, and there has been an attempt to establish places and situations where they, too, can establish friendships.

Friendship seems to be so important in modern society that it is even a commercial property. The rise of professional encounter-group therapists, sometimes hired by professionals, bosses, and members of the business community, suggests the attempt to create situations in which friendships can more readily be established. However, these ventures are not always successful, because they violate one of the most important elements of friendships: that it not be encumbered by considerations of monetary gain. To hire a person to help everybody be friends seems to be a contradiction in terms.

5. Friendship and Privacy

Friendship depends on the ability of persons to maintain a certain private self that is available to be shown only to their friends. If people are unable to separate their social and public selves from what they construe to be their private and real ones, they will have no currency with which to establish a friendship. There are many circumstances (to be taken up in more detail in Chapter 13) in which this privacy is taken away. In prisons, mental hospitals, and the armed services (at least before recent changes), such a "mortification" of the self was mandatory as a prelude to the making of an institutional self (Goffman, 1961a). However, with perhaps the exception of mental hospitals, inmates of total institutions have been surprisingly ingenious in developing ways of keeping things from their keepers. The guidelines for such associations are provided by the individuals themselves out of whatever material they can find, and not by the organization itself.

As a matter of fact, the making of friendship out of informally derived materials is the norm, for formal society finds friendship to be a somewhat deviant enterprise. For example, when friendship rather than formalized decision making dictates what happens in business or government, many people find the process reprehensible. They feel that a "buddy-buddy" system and not agreed-on policies formed the basis of important decisions. It is widely felt, for instance, that jobs, promotions, salary increases, and the like go to people on the basis of a kind of illegitimate friendship. This is not to say that friendship doesn't have rules but simply that these rules are often at variance with official expectations about what ought to be going on.

Suttles (1970) went so far as to say that deviation is a major basis of friendship: "The logic of friendship is a simple transformation of the rules of public propriety into their opposite." Friends can touch each other, whereas strangers cannot. Friends can taunt, yell, ridicule, and even throw racial epithets at each other in ways that would lead strangers to blows. Indeed, Suttles offered the observation that "if, tomorrow, it became publicly proper for strangers to spit upon meeting one another, friends would probably assume that they have the right to neglect this duty" (116).

However, as a social institution friendship involves a definite series of rules and expectations that are quite conventional. Once friendships have been formed, they are guided by a whole host of compelling and serious emotions. To "go back" on a friend is not only damaging to the relationship with the friend but is also likely to seriously damage relationships with others who feel that the person has proven to be untrustworthy. Just as other people find it difficult to stay completely out of the breakup of a friend's marriage, they also find it difficult to keep silent when a friend is ending a relationship with another friend. So, although friendships seem to be established in deviation, their major functions for society are exactly the opposite.

6. Friendship and Exposures of the Self

It is commonly assumed that friendship has to do with the exchange of private and secret information. The disclosure of secrets is part of the making of a friendship. However, the issue of friendship is considerably more complicated than such exposure. A more complex theory of the self must include the fact that there are many circumstances in which we exchange information of an exceedingly private nature to total strangers. In fact, as

Simmel (1950) pointed out, friends and strangers have a great deal in common in *relationships*.

In other words, when exposures of the self are made, they must be made with some care. Therefore, if discretion is to be assured, the exposures must be made either to a close friend, who will guard the secret, or to a stranger—either a total one or one designated in society for the explicit purpose of inquiring in an unthreatening and confidential way into the private character of another. Doctors, lawyers, psychiatrists, clerical persons, counselors, and teachers are all persons to whom the self is exposed in ways that could be approached only with the closest of friends, and sometimes not even with them. The relationship between a person and this special group of "strangers" tells us a great deal about the properties of friendship. The reason professionals can be told such intimate details about the self is because certain safeguards are built into the nature of the relationship. Doctors, lawyers, and the other groups we have mentioned respond to the person's disclosures only in a limited, circumscribed way. If a patient were to tell her doctor a series of lurid stories about her sexual fantasies, the doctor would be seriously out of line if he responded that he too had thought of similar fantasies and suggested that the two of them meet for a sexual encounter. No, the doctor is supposed to respond in a professional, detached, and objective way. Not to do so would be to break the careful shield that guards the presentation of intimate details under professional circumstances.

In addition, exposures of the self to specially designated, professional persons involves the expectation that, because they do not know you personally, they may be less inclined (both by social distance and ethical constraint) to tell others the secrets. This is why people may actually be reluctant to take such personal problems to a professional if that doctor or lawyer is also a close personal friend. The things we tell to friends, professionals, and total strangers are those that we hold as most cherished and feel must be allowed only in the safest hands. This trust is one of the reasons why the mentioned occupations are held in such high status and esteem (Hodge et al., 1964).

It should also be pointed out, however, that the information given to professionals in guarded settings is on occasion so valuable that attempts are made to erode the confidentiality and privilege of the relationship in order to obtain the exchanged secrets. Even with doctors and lawyers, there is an occasional attempt to force them to reveal private information. And with the less hallowed positions of social worker, prison guard, and even psychiatrist (Szasz, 1970), the professional person may well prove to be the agent of someone else, so that even communications with seemingly trustworthy guarantees may be problematic. These cases underscore the significance and importance of "true friendship" in our society, where information, especially of the secret variety, is increasingly a commodity to be bought and sold.

F. LIKING AND LOVING

Studies of interpersonal attraction have generally been stymied by both the simplicity and the complexity of the problem. Liking, attraction, closeness, and love, despite their ubiquity, are surprisingly resistant to generalization. We are attracted to and may even "love" a whole series of people, places, and things that do not seem to be equal at all, either in terms of their properties or of what we mean when we speak of liking and loving them. For surely there is a difference in saying that a man loves his mother and saying that he loves hot dogs, apple pie, baseball, and Chevrolets. Attraction, liking, and loving may apply in some sense to all of these relations, but not in the same way. Careful distinctions are called for.

Much of the literature on the topic of attraction has concerned itself with the idea that people tend to prefer others who are physically close. Marriages, for example, more often occur between persons who live near each other (Bossard, 1932). Propinquity, however, is surely the minimal condition for attraction and liking, because there are far more people to whom we are physically close than people we transform into friends or marital partners. We need to know, in short, not how close people are physically but how they develop social and psychological closeness. For example, is a trans-Atlantic telephone conversation between two persons a physically close relationship? In many respects it is. Similarly, we may maintain close ties with a friend, a lover, or even a spouse through nothing more physical than the letters carried by a third party called the postman. Once again, the fact of these matters does not seem to be as important as their definition within the bounds of a particular relationship. Students of propinquity as an element in attraction have probably made the mistake of thinking they were dealing with absolute properties, when in fact they were dealing with defined properties (Scott, 1970).

1. Love Is Something Special

Be that as it may, one of the most important forms of interpersonal attraction has, until very recently, escaped much attention in social psychology. This is the elusive relationship called love. This inattention has traditionally stemmed from the fact that liking seemed to fit traditional social-psychological methodologies better than love did. Furthermore, when social psychologists did turn their attention to love, they usually regarded it as simply an intense form of liking. This is unfortunate. As Rubin (1970) has shown, qualitative differences do exist between the two concepts, and love can be understood as distinct from mere liking. People who merely liked each other tended to use phrases such as "I think that _____ is a very good person" and "I have great confidence in _____'s judgment." When people spoke of those they were "in love with," however, the very terms of their conversation changed. "I would do anything and go anywhere for _____."

"If I could never be with _____, I would feel miserable." "One of my primary concerns is for _____'s welfare." These responses suggest that, although intensity is obviously greater for people who are in love, the very *terms* of their discourse are different from relationships of liking (Rubin, 1970).

Much work remains to be done, however, on the phenomenon of love; the brevity of this section is reflective of the paucity of research on the topic. Once we discover the basic dimensions of love, social psychologists will be in a position to investigate how it develops in various kinds of relationships. Important distinctions need to be drawn, for example, between love as it exists over time. Some research already done seems to indicate that in the initial stages of adolescent love its intensity is directly related to the amount of parental interference in the relationship. Later, love seems to be more defined in terms of factors such as trust and companionship (Driscoll et al., 1972). Studies of how love develops at various stages of a person's life, how it changes over time, and how it dies promise to hold some of the most profound insights for the social-psychological investigation of human interaction.

Love is one of the most important forms of interpersonal attraction. (Photo by © Mary Ellen Mark, Magnum Photos)

2. Ending Relationships

Sometimes friends or lovers feel that a relationship that was once close must be broken off. Since people are usually ambivalent in their resolve to end a relationship, this can be a time-consuming and difficult process, sometimes taking several years. And relationships may be partially maintained. For example, a husband and wife who choose to divorce may want to preserve some kind of amicable relationship. Since persons have invested a great deal of themselves in the initiation and maintenance of a relationship, ending it is almost tantamount to suicide. Part of oneself dies along with the relationship. Trial separations and offers to see each other again soon are testimony to the difficulty people have in making clean breaks with each other, even when they see such a termination as the only sensible alternative.

G. SUMMARY

Attraction, liking, friendship, and love are major processes in the lives of human beings. These processes help to explain all sorts of behaviors. Many of the important decisions of everyday life, including who gets the job, who is elected to the office, and who goes to jail depend finally on who likes whom. This observation, and much of the research we have pointed to in this chapter, strikes at the heart of many of our feelings about inequity in everyday life. Yet we know of no way by which we could remove such considerations. Indeed, we know that in most important respects the processes of attraction are exceedingly positive.

Various theories have been proposed by social psychologists to deal with the empirical reality of interpersonal attraction. Cognitive theories see attraction as a decision accomplished in the mind. They focus their attention on the way in which that decision is made. Reinforcement theory believes, in contrast, that attraction is a learned response, much like learning to drive a car or play golf. We learn what to like, primarily on the basis of rewards and punishments. Interactionist theory, although only recently developing, sees both of the preceding ideas as overly psychological and *personal*. Attraction is viewed as the result of various interpersonal processes.

Physical appearance is one of the most socially significant categories with which social psychologists deal. Although physical attraction is profoundly relative to culture, virtually every human group makes important decisions based on some definition of beauty and ugliness. Opposite-sex relationships and even same-sex relationships are altered in important ways by the definition of physical appearance. In addition, stereotyping and scapegoating have their basis in people's physical distinctions between groups of people. Such typifications have both positive and negative features, and every human group seems to make them. Stigmas of various kinds demonstrate the symbolic significance of physically based distinctions in society.

In addition, there are many nonphysical forms of stigma. Information of a negative nature can be the basis of differential treatment of human beings and change the nature of attraction. Attractions can be destroyed if information of certain kinds is revealed.

One of the most important categories of interpersonal attraction, especially in modern society, is friendship. As industrialization and urbanization create a mass society in which relationships are increasingly entered into anonymously, the necessity of friendship rises. Friendship includes such attributes as valuing the friend as a person rather than for advantages that might accrue; liking another person because of what he or she *is*, as opposed to what he or she *has;* basing economic exchanges only on the worth and value of the relationship rather than the object exchanged; and making friends on the basis of unique and individual properties the friend has.

Friendship is also distinguishable from friendly relationships. Friendships are initiated through the use of various procedures, are maintained, and may later die if the qualities that went into the relationship are transformed in their meaning.

Liking and loving may also be conceptually distinguished. Important contributions can be made to the social psychology of interpersonal attraction by studies of how loving differs from mere liking.

Section Four

Applications

The Scholar-Scientist is in acute danger of being caught, in the words of one of Auden's poems,

"Lecturing on Navigation while the ship is going down."

Robert S. Lynd

Morality in 12
Social Relations

A. INTRODUCTION: MORAL RELATIVITY

Consider the following story:

> Once upon a time there was a woman named Abigail who was in love with a man named Gregory. Gregory lived on the shore of a river. Abigail lived on the opposite shore of the river. The river that separated the two lovers was teeming with alligators. Abigail wanted to cross the river to be with Gregory. Unfortunately, the bridge had been washed out. So, she went to ask Sinbad, a riverboat captain, to take her across. He said he would be glad to if she would consent to go to bed with him preceding the voyage. She promptly refused and went to a friend named Ivan to explain her plight. Ivan did not want to be involved at all in the situation. Abigail felt her only alternative was to accept Sinbad's terms. Sinbad fulfilled his promise to Abigail and delivered her into the arms of Gregory.
>
> But when she told Gregory about her amorous escapade in order to cross the river, Gregory cast her aside with disdain. Heartsick and dejected, Abigail turned to Slug with her tale of woe. Slug, feeling compassion for Abigail, sought out Gregory and beat him brutally. Abigail was overjoyed at the sight of Gregory getting his due. As the sun sets on the horizon, we hear Abigail laughing at Gregory.

We meet in this cheerful little allegory five characters: Abigail, Gregory, Sinbad, Ivan, and Slug. If you were asked to rank these five on a scale of one to five from least liked to most liked, how would you respond? The way we rank these five individuals is a clue to our notions about moral standards. We might, for example, like Abigail for her honesty in telling Gregory what she had done in order to get across the river to him. We might just as easily dislike her for her guilt about the whole matter. We might like Gregory for his high moral principles. But then we might dislike him for his self-righteous indignation and inability to forgive. Although Ivan is neutral about the whole thing, our feelings toward him might be quite intense. We might like him a lot for minding his own business. We might strongly dislike him for not feeling any sense of social responsibility. Our feelings for Slug might be strongly tied to our ideas about violence. If we believe in violence and what it can accomplish, we might probably rank him high. If we do not, we might rank him much lower. Sinbad seems to be one of the more interesting characters in the story. If we don't like him, it is possibly because we see him as one who uses people. If we like him, we probably admire his honesty, directness, and calculating mind. After all, he could have taken Abigail halfway across the river before bargaining with her!

The story points to many of the concepts and issues in any discussion of the social psychology of moral behavior. How does a "conscience" develop? How do rules concerning morality influence our behavior? Is the norm of reciprocity ("You scratch my back and I'll scratch yours") stronger than the norm of social responsibility? How does a sense of morality develop in children? In adults? Does individual morality differ from social morality? Can something be right for me but wrong for everyone else? Out of what kinds of social processes does morality emerge? These are some of the issues we will be addressing in this chapter.

B. THE DEVELOPMENT OF MORALITY IN INDIVIDUALS: PSYCHOLOGICAL VIEWS

Morality can be defined as "patterns of behavior, principles, concepts, and rules employed by individuals and groups in dealing with the issue of right versus wrong" (Simpson, 1974, 82). Although it is virtually impossible to define right and wrong in an absolute sense, we know that every society constructs such definitions and applies them. Our own conception of morality is strongly tied to religious principles (Rubin, 1975). For example, in the Judeo-Christian tradition the Ten Commandments represent a moral code. Those who do right will be rewarded (in heaven), and those who sin will be punished (in hell). The importance of these simple religious principles appears central to the development of morality, for they are a crucial part of the process by which the individual acquires a sense of right and wrong.

Much of what we know about the social psychology of moral development has been the result of research conducted by psychologically oriented social psychologists. Sociologists, perhaps because of their views on cultural relativity, have been reluctant to become involved with the concept of morality. The importance of the idea in any discussion of human behavior, however, is so compelling that social psychologists of differing theoretical preferences and backgrounds are now beginning to take a close look at this important concept. We will begin our discussion with a review of pioneering research in the area.

1. Sigmund Freud

Freud, the founder of psychoanalysis, believed that the acquisition of morality in children is strongly linked to sexual aggressiveness. These are the events of childhood from which morality emerges (Freud, 1924):

1. Young children are attracted sexually to the parent of the opposite sex.
2. These feelings result in conflict with the parent of the same sex.
3. In order to avoid jealous retaliation by a stronger adult and to avoid displeasing the same-sex parent, who is also loved, the child suppresses his or her feelings.
4. The child then internalizes the image of both mother and father, accepting his or her parents as parents.

Hogan has summarized Freud's position on moral development as follows:

These internalized images [mother and father] serve as guides to conduct. Moreover, because the demands of both the instincts and society are relentless, the individual is doomed to a life of internal conflict. Too much animal makes a sick society, too much society makes a sick animal [1973, 111].

This entire process Freud labeled the *Oedipus complex*. He believed that adult morality forms out of a sense of guilt that is the product of the oedipal situation. To explain the process of moral development, Freud relied on the aforementioned three-compartment self: the id, ego, and superego. The id consists of selfish, primitive, biological impulses, which seek immediate gratification regardless of the consequences. The superego, as the reader will recall, is the conscience of the person—society's rules internalized. The ego is the conscious, defensive part of the self, mediating disputes between instinct on the one hand and moral codes on the other. According to Freud, morality develops as a result of this internal struggle taking place within the individual.

Because the Oedipus complex occurs very early in life (before the age of 5), the superego, or conscience, also begins to develop early. Therefore, Freud concluded, the process of moral development as well occurs quite early.

In summary, Freud viewed morality as the result of the interplay between impulse and conscience. Individual behavior is molded in such a way as to avoid a guilty conscience. Questions remain about Freud's conception, however. Is guilt contained within the individual, as Freud would have us believe? Or is the nature of the social situation in which people find themselves likely to have something to do with moral behavior? The Swiss psychologist Jean Piaget addressed these issues.

2. Jean Piaget

The pioneering work of Jean Piaget on moral development has been the impetus for a whole series of other studies now concerned with this important process. Piaget (1965) described moral development as a two-stage process. At Stage 1, the *heteronomous stage*, the child develops a "morality of constraint." He or she simply accepts parental dictates as moral absolutes. "The morality of an act is judged in terms of its consequences rather than in terms of the actor's intentions, and justice is equated with whatever the authority demands" (Hogan, 1974, 112–113). At Stage 2, the *autonomous stage*, the morality of constraint is replaced by a "morality of cooperation." The child develops a sense of the relativity of moral rules. "The morality of an act is judged in terms of the actor's intentions, and justice is seen in terms of equality and equity" (Hogan, 1974, 113).

Piaget's theoretical position on individual moral development evolved out of his research with children. For example, he asked children to compare two stories. The first was about a boy who accidentally broke 15 teacups that had been left out of sight behind a door. The second was about a boy who broke a single cup while trying to steal jam from a cupboard.

After hearing the stories, children were asked to indicate which child they would punish the most. With astonishing consistency, children 7 and under elected to punish the boy who had caused the greatest damage. For young children it was the absolute act, not the intentions of the actor, that defined the moral quality of what was done. With children 8 and over the reverse was true. The harshest punishment was meted out to the jam thief. This decision was based on the older children's ability to evaluate the intent as well as the act itself. Thus, younger children tend to make primitive judgments, ignoring intentions, whereas older children, like adults, weigh intent quite heavily.

The important implication of this experiment is that the child is learning to differentiate between authority and justice. In other words, the question of fairness becomes independent of the source of authority from which the rule originated (Ross and DiTecco, 1975). Piaget's work has stimulated a great deal of research, much of which has substantiated his basic premises (Bandura and McDonald, 1963; Lerner, 1974; Arbuthnot, 1973). The sense of fairness has been demonstrated in McGhee's (1974) research on moral development and children's appreciation of humor. Second-graders at both the heteronomous and autonomous levels of moral development were told one version of the following story:

> (Unintentional high damage) Helen was only a little girl and had never baked a cake before. But she decided she would surprise her mother by baking a delicious cake for her mother's birthday. When Helen's sister came into the kitchen, she found Helen beating her hands up and down on a bunch of eggs. She had made a big mess with eggs and shells splattered all over. Helen turned to her sister and said innocently, "I'm baking a cake and the recipe said to beat the eggs."

> (Intentional low damage) Helen was only a little girl who didn't get along well with her mother. Her mother always made her dry the dishes and she didn't like drying dishes. One day when her mother asked her to help with the dishes, she got mad and decided to mess up the table. When her sister walked in, Helen gave a sly smile and said, "I'm baking a cake and the recipe said to beat the eggs" [517].

After reading a story, the children were asked to rate it for funniness according to a five-point scale ranging from not funny at all to very funny. The results of these studies showed that heteronomous children consistently found stories with highly damaging outcomes funnier than stories with less damaging results. For autonomous children this trend was found only when the damage occurred unintentionally. In general, autonomous children found accidentally damaging outcomes funnier than intentional ones.

Piaget's work and the further research it has spawned are not without problems. Gutkin (1973) posed a logical extension and criticism, suggesting that moral intentions are a part of the more general problem of social responsibility:

> The problem is to know for what we are entitled to hold a person responsible. In turn, the question of whether the person intended the consequences which his action brought about suggests itself as an important consideration in judging his responsibility [372].

Gutkin went on to assert that the perspective of intentional versus unintentional is grossly oversimplified. In fact, Gutkin (1973) and Walster (1966) have both provided evidence that adults and adolescents can be influenced by the seriousness of the consequences quite apart from considerations of intention and responsibility. In other words, the damage-centered moral view of childhood may never be entirely outgrown by adults. Under some circumstances it may even reassert itself. This relationship between individual and social responsibility is one that the psychological research has never satisfactorily addressed, and we will return to it shortly.

3. Lawrence Kohlberg

Psychologist Lawrence Kohlberg (1969) has attempted to extend Piaget's theoretical position, believing that mature moral judgment develops even further than Piaget's morality of reciprocal cooperation. Kohlberg identified three main levels of development, each having two stages:

1. Preconventional (premoral)
   A. Stage 1: Goodness is defined in terms of physical consequences resulting from actions.
   B. Stage 2: Goodness is defined through instrumental actions because, through reciprocity, they supply what is wanted from others.
2. Conventional (morality of conventional role conformity)
   A. Stage 3: Good behavior is defined as that which is pleasing to others and approved by them.
   B. Stage 4: Goodness is viewed as a law-and-order orientation—respect for authority and the belief that social order should be maintained.
3. Postconventional (principle reasoning—morality viewed as independent of authority)
   A. Stage 5: What is "right" is defined by social contract or agreement and may be changed if viewed useful.
   B. Stage 6: Morality is based on the autonomous functioning of conscience in accordance with abstract principles of justice, equality, and reciprocity. Dignity of human beings as individuals is respected.

Building on Piaget's (1965) work on the developmental process through which morality is acquired, Kohlberg believes he has isolated the *structure* of morality from its content. This structure is represented in his three levels and six stages. In keeping with Piaget's practice, Kohlberg presented experimental subjects with dilemmas having moral implications:

> In Europe a woman was near death from a special kind of cancer. There was one drug that the doctors thought might save her; it was a form of radium that a druggist in the same town had recently discovered. The drug was expensive to make, but the druggist was charging ten times what the drug cost him to make. He paid $200 for the radium and charged $2,000 for a small dose of the drug. The sick woman's husband, Heinz, went to everyone he knew to borrow the money, but he could only get together about $1,000, which is half of what it cost. He told the druggist that his wife was dying and asked him to sell it cheaper or let him pay later. But the druggist said, "No, I discovered the drug and I'm going to make money from it." So Heinz got desperate and broke into the man's store to steal the drug for his wife. Should Heinz have done that? [1958, 22].

Kohlberg's research revealed that the first, or preconventional, level clearly dominates at age 7. Seven-year-olds define goodness in terms of physical consequences and instrumental acts that help them obtain what they want from others. By age 10 the second level is beginning to emerge, and children become concerned with conforming to seek approval. It is at this level that they become aware of political rights, social responsibilities, and conformity to social roles (Mitchell, 1974). For Kohlberg moral judgment is the result of natural processes operating through the institutions of society (family, church, school, government). As individuals pass through each stage, they become increasingly aware of this moral structure.

Kohlberg's research has been criticized by Simpson (1974) for its ethnocentric character. As noted by Nader (1975), "All societies that we know anything about have accepted ideas as to what is just and fair ... [but] ethnocentrism in all societies probably reigns supreme in the area of justice" (163). Whereas Kohlberg argued that his six stages of moral development are universally applicable, Simpson suggested that they are, in fact, culturally relative. Simpson noted that this bias was clearly delineated by Rest (1974), who defined Kohlberg's stages as sociological rather than philosophical. Rest reviewed each stage as a new conception of the social arrangements that a given society has agreed on:

> Stage 4 supports the known and established social arrangements of one's own society by default because "it" has no criteria for weighing competing social orders or rule systems. By definition, Stage 5 occurs only in a democracy and a constitutional democracy at that: (1) The individual agrees to be bound by the laws of the society he lives in. (2) He recognizes the functional need for

agreed-upon law as distinct from the need for repression of evil and violence. . . . Stage 6 is equally culture-bound. . . . Law and social authority are
seen as limited by prior natural human rights [1974, 499].

The influence of culture on moral development is, of course, one of the
major areas of debate between psychological and sociological views of morality. Psychologists are usually interested in trying to locate the source of
moral development in absolute conceptions of fairness, equity, or justice
within the person, regardless of cultural influence. Sociologists, on the other
hand, believe that morality, like all other aspects of human behavior, develops in association with others in a social or cultural relationship. An
interesting study by Denney and Duffy (1974) attempted to find the relationship between a mother's level of moral reasoning and her child's. The
subjects in the study included 17 6-year-olds, 17 10-year-olds, and 17 14-
year-olds, as well as their mothers. The children and their mothers were
interviewed separately. Each child was asked 11 questions that required a
moral judgment; one of the stories was the following:

> Kathy's parents told her that if she didn't do well in school she would be
> punished. On the next big test Kathy didn't know many of the answers. When
> the teacher wasn't looking, Kathy copied someone else's answers. Kathy got a
> good grade on the test. Kathy's mother was so happy that Kathy got a good
> grade on the test that she took her out for an ice cream sundae. Was Kathy
> right to copy the answers? Why? [Denney and Duffy, 1974, 279].

Each mother was asked 15 questions that were designed to get at the
moral principles mothers convey to their children. For example:

> If you found that [child's name] had stolen something from a department store,
> but did not get caught, what would you say or do? [272].

The results indicated that, as the age of the children increased, both
their level of moral reasoning and the level of moral reasoning implied in
the mothers' treatment of them increased. This study lends support to the
possibility that cultural changes (as reflected in the mother's treatment of
the child) may be influencing the appearance of stages in the child's development of moral reasoning. Other studies indicate that moral judgment is
influenced both by opinion agreement and the extent to which other people
support one's own reasoning. Individuals, when trying to resolve a moral
dilemma, do seem to seek the advice of others (Keasey, 1974; Rest, 1974).

C. THE SOCIAL-PSYCHOLOGICAL PERSPECTIVE ON MORALITY

Whereas the psychologist focuses on the development of morality in
individuals and the sociologist emphasizes conceptions of morality as the
preserver of the social order, the social psychologist is interested in moral

behavior in interpersonal situations. In many ways the social-psychological view of morality can be described as a microscopic examination of the norm of reciprocity, defined as the expectation that something done to one person will be responded to in kind (Adams, 1965; Homans, 1961; Sampson, 1969; Walster et al., 1973). In other words, social psychology seeks "to understand how persons' selfish appetites have been curbed in their business relationships, harm-doing or exploitative relationships, help-giving relationships, and even loving relationships" (Sampson, 1975, 47).

1. Distributive Justice: Two Solutions

One of the major components of this social-exchange theory of morality is the concept of distributive justice. According to this concept, the participants in an exchange relationship are aware of the justice of the relationship and will try to maintain its justice (Schafer and Kloglan, 1974). Homans (1961) has been credited with having first introduced the rule of distributive justice: "A man in an exchange relation with another will expect that the rewards of each man will be proportional to his costs—the greater the rewards, the greater the costs—and that the net rewards, or profit, of each man will be proportional to his investments—the greater the investments, the greater the profits (17)."

Homan's theory of distributive justice boils down to an equity solution. Resources (wealth, income, status) are divided according to defined contributions (ability, intelligence, hard work). Some people are seen to deserve more of available resources because, compared with others, they have more invested (Schafer and Kloglan, 1974).

A contrasting solution to the problem of distributive justice is to develop a theory of equality based on dividing resources equally, instead of proportionally. All persons receive the same, regardless of age, sex, race, skill, or training (Walster and Walster, 1975). This is the classic Marxian solution to economic morality, and it has not met with much success.

There is a growing body of literature that can aid us in assessing this problem. Sampson (1975) noted that this literature identifies four key factors that influence whether the equity principle or the equality principle will be followed (52–57).*

1. *The person's interaction goals.* An equity choice suggests that one's goals are person oriented. It suggests maximizing one's own personal gain even at the expense of others. An equality choice suggests that one's goals are interperson oriented. It represents a desire to create positive interpersonal relationships. Thus, we might characterize interaction goals as either instrumental or interpersonal.

*The following material is adapted from "On Justice As Equality," by E. F. Sampson, *Journal of Social Issues*, 1975, *31*, 45–64. Copyright 1975 by the Society for the Psychological Study of Social Issues. Used by permission.

2. *The person's basic orientations.* We might describe an individual's orientation as one of two types: (1) Competitive or equity solution in which the person strives to benefit self at others' expense (Kelley and Stahelski, 1970), or (2) *equality* solution to the distributive problem which stresses cooperation. An equity solution to the distributive problem stresses competition.

3. *The person's situated identity.* Situated identity suggests that a person's behavior be examined from the impressions it causes other people to form. Goffman's (1959) work on self-presentation offers a good documentation and analysis of this phenomenon in everyday life. For example, we might say that "to be cooperative, interpersonally concerned, and equality oriented is to call for a situated identity of 'feminine,' whereas to be competitive, instrumentally concerned, and equity oriented is to call for a situated identity of 'masculine'" (Sampson, 1975, 55).

4. *The person's sex-role orientation.* There is a growing body of literature that asserts that females tend toward equality and males tend toward equity (Bond and Vinacke, 1961; Uesugi and Vinacke, 1963; Vinacke, 1959; Leventhal and Lane, 1970; Benton, 1971). The findings of Blumstein and Weinstein (1969) and Leventhal and Anderson (1970), for example, led them to conclude that there is a tendency for males to redress distributive justice, whereas females do not. Studies of coalition formation in triads (Vinacke, 1959; Bond and Vinacke, 1961; Uesugi and Vinacke, 1963; Vinacke and Gulickson, 1964; Wahba, 1972) indicated that females adopt accommodative rather than competitive behavior in transactions with their group. This behavior is presumably designed to preserve harmonious interpersonal relationships for the maintenance of the welfare of all the group members (Wahba, 1972). Male subjects, in contrast, adopt a more competitive strategy in their transactions with group members. Their major concerns appear to be protection of self-interests. Thus, we might say that accommodative and competitive behavior are normative feminine and masculine strategies, respectively (Wahba, 1972).

Sampson's analysis strongly suggests that neither equity nor equality is an innate and natural solution to the distributive-justice problem. Each has merit that arises in social relationships.

2. Hogan's Five Dimensions of Moral Development

A comprehensive view of moral development was offered by Robert Hogan (1973). He viewed moral development in terms of five dimensions, each of which must be taken into account.

The first is moral *knowledge.* A person must have some notion of the "rules of the game." This is presumably why young children and newcomers are not generally held as accountable as those who have been in a situation longer. Ignorance of the rules is usually held to be a motive for misconduct, at least a few times.

The second dimension of moral conduct is *socialization*. This is more difficult, for it involves not only the social existence of rules but also to what extent a person recognizes them as binding.

The third dimension is *empathy*, which, according to Hogan, allows a person to think in terms of the spirit rather than the letter of the law. Empathy has two components. The first is the ability to play roles in interaction with others. The second is the ability to take the role of others, or imagine how one would feel in someone else's shoes.

The fourth element in moral development is *autonomy*, or "the degree to which one's moral decisions are free from the influence of peer group pressures and prestige factors." Hogan readily concedes that autonomy is a troublesome concept because it lacks precise definition. Furthermore, everyone is influenced to a degree by the ideas of others, especially peers (Riesman, 1950). Nevertheless, the concept is important, for it points to the fact that some people are much more easily influenced than others.

The last dimension in Hogan's scheme concerns the degree of *instrumental value* in established rules and procedures.

One end of this dimension is defined by those who prefer to make decisions on the basis of personal and intuitive moral feelings; these judgments, which are based on the dictates of conscience, may often conflict with established procedures. The opposite pole of this dimension is defined by persons who distrust

The experience of serving on a jury often changes people's minds about concepts such as justice and morality.

moral intuitions and prefer instead to rely on conventions, contracts, and formal agreements as a means for regulating social affairs [114].

Hogan suggests that individuals at either end of the continuum are less than socially mature, a value judgment of the first order. The extreme intuitionist has little regard for the rights and privileges of others. The extreme instrumentalist defends the status quo. And the debate goes on.

D. THE SOCIOLOGICAL PERSPECTIVE: NORMS

1. Defining the Social Norm

Among the many definitions of the social norm offered by sociologists, one of the more comprehensive is that of Roland Hawkes (1975). A norm may be described loosely as a rule, a standard, or a prescription for behavior, according to Hawkes. Essential to the notion of a norm are the requirements that it is in some way enforced and that violations of it have consequences.

Parsons describes the norm as a verbal description of a concrete course of action—thus regarded as desirable—combined with an injunction to make future actions conform to this course (Parsons, 1949, 75). As rules of behavior, social norms carry a sense of "oughtness" with them (Nisbet, 1970, 226). This is apparent when a disinterested person expresses moral indignation at the violation of a social norm (Merton, 1957).

The social norm is a rule, usually stated in a few words, to require or control specific actions by persons in society. For example, there is a general norm that motorists must obey traffic regulations wherever they drive. A no-parking sign expresses the norm for that location. Although there is no mention of what the punishment will be if the sign is ignored, the experienced driver knows that the police may remove and impound the car or impose a fine on the offender. This means that any necessary force may be applied to compel obedience to the norm requirements. The threat of force and punishment by the police makes the norm "stick." But most mature members of society believe that every driver "ought" to obey the traffic rules, whether or not a police officer is there to enforce them.

2. Norm Hierarchies

Although any social norm can be stated separately, norms are generally organized into systems of rules that are graded and ranked in order of importance (Scott, 1971, 79). Differences in the degree and amount of punishment for violating norms indicate their position in the hierarchy. In the traffic codes, "nonmoving violations" are less serious and bring about lighter penalties than "moving violations." If two norms come in conflict, the less important rule may be violated. The norm of keeping quiet in the library may be ignored to give a loud warning if a fire is discovered. In time of war the law that forbids all normal commercial exchange with the enemy overrules the ordinary requirement to send back money for goods that have been delivered. Announcing the state of war does not cancel the debt, but it suspends the debt for the duration of hostilities. When peace is restored, the creditor may demand payment, and the claim will be recognized.

3. Norms for Maintaining Social Order

Social norms apply not only to individuals but also to groups and organizations. There are many thousands of federal, state, and local laws in the United States, for example, which control the activities of commercial, institutional, and social organizations. Bankers are required to know, understand, and apply the rules of banking, and the bank's customers no doubt believe that officers "ought" to conform to the banking regulations. Teachers "ought" to meet their professional obligations in teaching and "ought" to educate students as fully as possible in the announced subject matter. A minister "ought" to obey the rules and requirements of the ministry and the denomination and "ought" to set an example for the community by obeying all of its norms. These dos and don'ts are ingrained in the fabric of society and thus provide it with an orderly and dependable structure (Sartorius, 1972).

4. The Norm of Social Responsibility

The norm of social responsibility refers to mutual expectations that constitute the unwritten contracts between persons, describing their obligations and privileges (Nettler, 1972). It is expected, for example, that people will help others in need (Berkowitz and Daniels, 1963). The norm of social responsibility addresses the issues of accountability and answerability (Blatz, 1972). A business official who has entered into a purchasing or sales contract is responsible to the contracting party and may be forced to carry out the agreement by court action if the terms are not met voluntarily. Of course, every official "ought" to meet the requirements of duty without having to be forced. Consider the case of former President Richard Nixon.

In the summer of 1968 Republican party officials were caught breaking into the Democratic headquarters. The incident was played down until after the presidential elections. For some two years, the media reported new and astonishing information on the Watergate break-in. During the course of this two-year period, President Nixon made several television appearances before the American public to avow his innocence. In the spring and summer of 1970 Nixon's innocence became highly questionable due to information uncovered through the White House tapes. Nixon was forced to resign.

In the eyes of the majority of American people, President Nixon was not immune to official accountability, as he appeared to assume. On the contrary, as the first officer of the U.S. government, he carried the highest

The idea of social responsibility addresses itself to the issues of accountability and answerability. (Photo by © Marc Ribaud, Magnum Photos)

responsibility to uphold and enforce the nation's laws. Every citizen has a moral responsibility to obey and uphold the laws of the society and a moral obligation to report violations of the law. In some countries, such as the Soviet Union, each citizen is required by law to report any violation of law and may be formally charged, convicted, and punished for failing to do so.

The norm of social responsibility has become of increasing concern to the social psychologist since the brutal murder of Kitty Genovese in New York City in 1964. She was returning home from work at 3 A.M. when she was repeatedly stabbed and raped by a young man. Her screams brought 38 of her neighbors to their windows to see what was happening (Rosenthal, 1964). Each saw some part of the incident. Many saw the murder. But no one went to her aid. No one called the police until she had already been dead for 30 minutes.

This incident served as a catalyst for many social psychologists concerned with the issue of *bystander apathy*. One of the early experiments designed to investigate this problem was conducted by Latane and Rodin (1969). Subjects were telephoned and asked to participate in market research. They were told that they would be evaluating games and puzzles and were given a location to which they were to go. Upon arrival, subjects were greeted by a young woman who asked each person to fill out a questionnaire. Then the woman went next door to her office. Very shortly a loud crash was heard and the woman was heard moaning.

Similar experiments carried out by Latane and Darley (1969) include:

1. Issuing smoke through a wall vent while a subject completes a questionnaire.
2. Having customers in a discount beer store witness a staged theft of a case of beer.
3. Having a subject speak via intercom to another person who suddenly seems to have a violent seizure.   .

For each of these situations, the experimental conditions were varied. Sometimes the subjects were placed in a room alone. Sometimes they were placed with an apathetic stooge. Sometimes they were placed with another naive subject with whom they were strangers. And some of the time they were placed with a friend.

The findings were consistent across experimental settings. When subjects were alone and viewed distress signals, approximately 70% helped. When subjects were seated with an apathetic stooge, only 7% assisted. The naive subjects seemed to model the stooges' behaviors. When subjects were seated with a naive stranger, approximately 40% assisted. And when subjects were seated with a friend, in 70% of the cases at least one person moved to help.

The predominant finding from these experiments was that an individual is more likely to offer assistance when in the company of a friend than when in the company of a stranger. Additionally, the tendency to act when in the company of a friend does not really differ from the tendency to act alone. Latane and Darley extended their findings to explain incidents similar to the Kitty Genovese murder:

> When an emergency occurs in a large city, many people are likely to be present. The people are likely to be strangers. It is likely that no one will be acquainted with the victim. The bystanders may be unfamiliar with the locale of the emergency. These are exactly the conditions that make helping least likely in our experiment [127].

We cannot say that the norm of social responsibility is inoperative. There may even, at times, be other social norms keeping it in check.

5. The Norm of Reciprocity

"You scratch my back and I'll scratch yours." Everyone has heard this familiar cliché. Its message harmonizes with another familiar saying: "You can't get something for nothing."

In any social interaction where human services are extended, we expect to be rewarded (Homans, 1961). When we give a Christmas gift to a friend, we usually expect to get one in return. Many people send Christmas cards only to those from whom they have received cards. Certainly the norm of reciprocity addresses the issue of cooperative behavior as a basis for maintaining social order and structure. Gouldner (1960) gave a precise definition. A norm of reciprocity in its universal form makes two interrelated minimal demands: (1) people should help those who have helped them, and (2) people should not injure those who have helped them.

Gouldner's remarks were based in part on theories developed by the anthropologist Malinowski more than 30 years earlier. He had spent many months living among the natives of the Trobriand Islands, about 700 miles northeast of the northern tip of Australia. Some of the Trobrianders specialized in fishing, and some specialized in farming. Each fisherman had a farmer for a trading partner, and each partner was expected to supply the other, either with fish or with yams. In this exchange generosity was appreciated and admired. Stinginess was condemned and resented. The punishment of the stingy fisherman or farmer was loss of his trading partner. Losing the partner meant losing half of one's diet. And one could meet personal obligations only with food. In Malinowski's words:

> What perhaps is most remarkable in the legal nature of social relations is that reciprocity, the give-and-take principle, reigns supreme also within the clan, nay, within the nearest group of kinsmen. The relations between the maternal uncle and his nephews, nay, the most unselfish relation of all, that between a man and his sister, are all and one founded on mutuality and the repayment of services [1959, 47].

As elsewhere in the world, the Trobriand Islander tried to keep his creditors, whether trading partner or kinsperson, reasonably satisfied without being too hard on himself. He gained credit by meeting his obligations well and lost credit by meeting them poorly. There were, of course, laws and restrictions to control individual behavior. Many of these community laws were "not only occasionally broken, but systematically circumvented by well-established methods, and there can be no question about spontaneous obedience to the law" (Malinowski, 1959, 81). If two Trobrianders carried on an illicit love affair secretly and decorously and if no one stirred up trouble, there might be gossip, but no demand for punishment. But if a scandal broke out, the whole community turned against the guilty ones, and one or the other might be driven to suicide.

6. The Norm of Equity

This norm refers to equitable distribution in interpersonal dealing. A more familiar equivalent for this norm is fairness. It is not fair to take advantage in a game by breaking the rules. When food, money, and other desirable things are distributed among a group, each one should receive a "fair share," and it is unfair to leave anyone out. In discussing the obligations of the good manager, a business leader said that "the manager's ultimate success is not based on 'getting more' for any one group but rather on his or her ability to see that the efforts and the resources of all who contribute to the business are effectively integrated and equitably rewarded" (Parker, 1960). Research has shown that people who are cheated in one exchange tend to compensate for the loss in the next exchange if they have the power of choice. In this the subjects tend to seek equity with the world, not with specific partners (Austin and Walster, 1975). It may be a mistake to deal with a person who has just been cheated.

E. THE SOCIOLOGICAL PERSPECTIVE: MORALITY

1. Questions of Moral Theory

The sociologist's concern with morality deals primarily with the relation between moral standards and social order. Given the egocentric nature of humans, the sociologist wants to know how they set aside selfish interests in pursuit of cooperative goals. Such cooperative efforts keep society working, and moral norms provide the means for persons and groups to relate to one another in complex ways for long periods of time. Sociologists have largely accounted for this social order by the process of norm formation. "The normative approach suggests that the unbridled exercise of egoism can be checked by changing man's nature through the inculcation of norms" (Black and Tanur, 1974).

a. Society as a moral order: Durkheim.   Emile Durkheim (1858–1917), the French sociologist, postulated that "every society is a moral order" (1933, 228). And the moral rules are simply the outward expression of principles of social organization. Moral rules provide the basis for social solidarity.

> Everything which is a source of solidarity is moral; everything which forces man to take account of other men is moral; everything which forces him to regulate his conduct through something other than the striving of his ego is moral; and morality is as solid as these ties are numerous and strong [Durkheim, 1933, 398].

For Durkheim, the basis of solidarity and moral rule is the *industrial division of labor*. The units of solidarity that make up "moral communities" are occupational associations. The idea that formulates and regulates these relationships is *professional ethics* (Wolf, 1970). Thus, with Durkheim we might very well view moral rules, rights and wrongs, or oughts and ought nots as culture bound and culture generated. Stated another way, morality might be viewed as "the set of standards prescribing right conduct within the social-cultural organization" (Weinstein, 1973).

b. Structural components of social morality: Parsons.   Talcott Parsons has divided the public or societal system of morality into four functional subsystems, which he labeled (1) pattern maintenance, (2) integration, (3) goal attainment, and (4) adaptation (Parsons, 1969). Like Durkheim's, Parsons's view is that morality strives to maximize cohesion and order. The subsystem of cultural or pattern maintenance, for example, maintains the major standards or values governing social and cultural organizations. This is usually accomplished through value commitments or through the ability to create obligation. Integration, or the societal community, functions to keep the various social roles within a meaningful framework. Goal attainment channels one's energies toward socially recognized goals. Adaptation, or economy, transforms the nonsocial environment in accord with social goals. The public morality described by Parsons has been identified as the code of moderate organizational leaders in the United States (Weinstein, 1973). It is often this kind of morality that leads men to oscillate between obedience and revolution (Frazier, 1972).

2. Culture and the Formalization of Moral Assessments

Max Weber (1864–1930) believed that cultural development involves an increase in normative organization. He identified four principal developments: (1) the increasing quality and power of orderly legislation within large and pacified political groupings; (2) the increasing scope of rational comprehension of an external, enduring, and orderly cosmos; (3) the increasing regulation of ever-new types of human relationships by conventional rules, and the increasing dependence of people on the observance of these rules in their interactions with one another; and (4) the growth in social and economic importance of the reliability of the given word—whether of friends, vassals, partners in exchange, debtors, or anyone else (Weber, 1963, 35).

The growth of economic, political, social, and cultural organizations within and between societies called forth a constant development of formal and informal systems of morality. The formal side of these moral systems was revealed in legislatures, courts, and a vast collection of civil and criminal laws and enforcement agencies. The informal side was revealed by the conventional standards of interpersonal relations in manners, customs, and social standards. Although the extent and content of the total moral system is approximately the same in all large industrial societies, each system is unique and fully operative only within its own singular society. A person who has committed a crime in Italy has not violated English criminal law, even though both the criminal and the victim may have been citizens (or "subjects") of the government of England. The reason is that only Italian judicial agencies have authority and responsibility in Italy. Yet most of the laws and statutes in force in Italy are also to be found in England.

A universal tendency toward mutual aid was identified by Kropotkin, particularly among the lowly, the poor, and the powerless. He called these "standing institutions of mutual aid and support" (Kropotkin, 1960). Mutual aid seems to arise spontaneously and naturally in face-to-face association, both within children's play groups and among adults. It appears to depend on simple compassion and a desire to be helpful when danger or misfortune strikes any of the individuals in the group. For example, young children may compete vigorously and maintain personal hostilities among themselves. But if one is hurt, the others run and call loudly for help. Housewives in a neighborhood baby-sit for one another's children, help with cooking and housework in time of sickness, run errands, and give personal services, and they do this in a generous spirit with little concern for the cost to themselves. It is an expression of goodwill and a willingness to extend help to the neighbor or to the stranger who is in a helpless situation. Kropotkin believed that this human concern for others nearby is a natural element of social morality.

Since any society is an active, dynamic system of process and exchange, there is a constant process of adjustment in applying social norms to real-life interaction. Gouldner said that:

> Due to the very fact that different parts have different degrees of commitment to a given social system, they are differentially committed—some more, some less—to the system's moral code. Second, the moral rules themselves are not given automatic and mechanical conformity simply because they "exist"; the varying degrees of conformity given by different system parts are a function of different parts' bargaining positions. Conformity is not so much given as *negotiated* [1960, 217].

A new employee who is anxious to keep a job usually expects—and is expected—to comply closely with the rules of punctuality and performance. The new employee arrives on time and does not leave early. But the well-established and highly capable secretary may extend the lunch hour or sometimes, for personal convenience, leave early. And the manager may call in to announce that he or she will be out of town on business for "two or three days." Position makes a difference in the application of rules.

Nonperformance of duty may be "legitimized" by the proper authority (Haber and Smith, 1971). If a person falls ill and a doctor orders confinement to bed or to the hospital, then being away from work or other social duties is fully legitimate, perhaps for an extended period. If a police officer shoots a person who is resisting arrest, a formal hearing may be held to forestall later charges by the resister, and the process works to legitimate the officer's action. If a bank official makes an "honest mistake" in accepting an obviously forged check, superior officials may agree for the bank to accept the loss and to excuse the erroneous action.

The moral character of a society may also be indicated by the common attitude to violation of the norms. Menninger noted that the once-familiar concept of sin seems to have vanished in the United States. He defined sin as the failure to realize in conduct and character the moral ideal, at least as fully as possible, under existing circumstances. It is a failure to do as one ought to one's fellow man (Menninger, 1973, 18). In highly religious communities there is deep and continuing concern to overcome temptations to sin, to confess and express sorrow and contrition for sins already committed, and to improve one's moral character, until a high state of ethics is achieved.

This concern with being a "good person" is not confined to religious bodies, however. It may also be found in schools, in dedicated political organizations, and in military and professional organizations. German prisoners of war, feeling guilt about letting themselves be captured, used to ask: "Do you think I have been a good soldier?" When duties and norms are well defined and are frequently stressed, the quality of performance is usually plain, both to the actor and to observers. If there are no such definitions, it may be impossible to gauge the quality of compliance and performance.

3. Cultural Changes in Moral Climate

The moral climate of a society shifts noticeably with time and circumstance. One evidence of this is the increase in domestic violence as a result of war. In analyzing criminal statistics for 110 countries, Archer and Gartner found a consistent increase in criminal violence that appeared to relate primarily to the legitimation of violence by the top authorities of the nation. This increase was not affected by economic depression, disorganization within the country, or victory or defeat in the war (Archer and Gartner, 1976). Angell has demonstrated similar effects in a study of 40 major U.S. cities. He found they were becoming more homogeneous and that their moral integration was declining, based on crime statistics comparing data from the years 1940 and 1970. The standard crime index showed a marked increase in the 30-year period, and the greatest increase in crime was found in Northeastern cities (Angell, 1974).

Most major societies are torn by moral conflicts that vary in intensity. The most difficult of these conflicts is experienced in time of civil war, when individuals are forced to choose between support of the established government and the revolutionary group. Or the moral conflict may be long enduring. Myrdal diagnosed the United States as a moralistic nation that was suffering because of the conflict between the high democratic ideals of freedom, liberty, and equal justice under law and the denial, segregation, oppression, and confinement imposed on the Black minority. He was careful to point out that this moral struggle was going on not merely between different segments of the population, but also within the hearts and minds of individuals (Myrdal, 1958, 58). Since Myrdal published his monumental study, *An American Dilemma*, much has been done to improve public and institutional treatment of Black Americans.

National groups may demonstrate marked differences in attitudes toward work and their own position in life. A comparison of attitudes of about

1000 French and U.S. workers indicated that the French workers had significantly lower morale. More than two-thirds of the French workers said they felt powerless, compared to about half of the American respondents, and about twice as large a proportion of French workers had a feeling of normlessness (Seeman, 1972). The French worker seemed to feel much less autonomy and self-confidence than the comparable American worker.

Milgram has assessed Norwegians from a rather different viewpoint. Based on personal observations, he was impressed by the Norwegians' high degree of social responsibility and their consideration for one another (Milgram, 1977, 171). They expressed extreme democratic conformism and carried out political disputes and debates with great patience. It would violate Norwegian ethical standards and would show very bad manners to show oneself as better or wiser or more capable than the next man. Even the schoolchildren were impressed with this ethical value, and were discouraged from raising their hands in class too often. "Don't try to appear better than us" is a widely accepted social norm in Norway.

F. MORAL ISSUES

1. Legislating Morality

"You can't legislate morality" rings as true today as it did more than 50 years ago when prohibition of the sale and distribution of alcoholic beverages was the foremost moral issue of the day. Although it was against the Constitution, as amended, to sell alcohol, drinking and drunkenness continued throughout the United States. And a thriving outlaw industry sprang up to brew, distill, and distribute the forbidden products. A very similar situation exists today with respect to the distribution and sale of marijuana. Moralistic laws to control and prevent sexual behavior such as adultery, fornication (heterosexual intercourse by unmarried persons), homosexual relations, and even masturbation have proved generally ineffective. Most of these behaviors have been performed habitually by a very large portion of the general population.

Issues concerning life and death have also been difficult to resolve by legislation. Many believe that capital punishment is an effective deterrent to crime, and legislators seem eager to write laws acceptable to the U.S. Supreme Court so that the death penalty can be imposed for certain crimes. The rub is that it has been almost impossible to apply such penalties fairly and justly, regardless of the crime and the criminal. The Black male teenager who is accused of murder is far more likely to pay the extreme penalty than the mature White businessman accused of the same crime.

The legalization of abortion has incensed those who believe that life begins the moment of conception. These opponents of abortion define a deliberate abortion as "murder." When abortion was illegal, however, it was not "murder" that was charged but simply violation of the abortion law.

And charges were not brought against the woman who aborted herself or against the woman who paid an abortionist to operate on her. Instead, the criminal action was brought against the doctor or medically untrained abortionist. Finally, those who wish to prohibit abortion by law may be violating the person and the rights of the pregnant female who is unable or unwilling to continue her pregnancy. Does she have any right to control her own life and her own body? Should her private condition be a public concern? Whatever the outcome, pregnant women who are unwilling to give birth will get abortions, simply because legal agencies are not capable of controlling them.

The case of Karen Quinlan brought another important moral issue into public awareness. Karen went into a coma resulting from a combination of drugs and alcohol. For more than a year she was kept alive by means of a respirator and other special life-support equipment. When she failed to regain consciousness and medical tests indicated severe brain damage, her parents sought authority from the courts to remove the life-support equipment and allow her the right to die. They won this case and set a legal precedent. But the comatose patient continued breathing when the support equipment was removed. This case raised the moral issue of whether a dying individual has the right to reject extreme medical measures to prolong life.

2. Some Conventional Moral Orientations

The moral orientation of a society depends on the dominant institutions of the time. Legislatures in the United States have long been preoccupied with the personal habits of the individual. They have tried through laws and enforcement campaigns to prevent prostitution, gambling, drug abuse, drinking, and homosexual relations. These victimless "crimes" have been very costly to judicial and enforcement agencies and have had relatively little success in reducing the numbers or proportion of those who practice these behaviors. In contrast, property offenses, particularly misappropriation of large funds by corporation officers and employees of financial institutions, are rather lightly punished. Judicial treatment tends to be more favorable for the middle-class and professional offender.

Violence may constitute a positive social value, sufficient to create a strong public demand for it in the entertainment media (Gerson, 1968). Violence may be a persistent part of our fantasy lives, and a national sample of U.S. males showed that 80% of them had been punched or physically attacked or had made such attacks on others (Ball-Rokeach, 1973). Violence is an integral part of the criminal's plans in the television script, and the police or intelligence agents are ready to respond with more effective violence. The tools of violence include handguns, hunting weapons, knives, and explosives, all directed at the opponent's body. Automobile chases and dramatic wrecks add to the excitement, and at least one life is usually sacrificed in the encounter. Such entertainment makes murder and destruction a familiar experience and desensitizes the viewers of all ages to death and suffering. Perhaps it is not surprising that American motorists will speed past injured persons on the highway without stopping to give aid or even calling in to report the accident, considering the brutality and barbarism of their television and movie viewing experience. Our heroes are ruthless men who kill without hesitation and, at least in fiction, rarely have any pity or concern for the wounded and dying.

In cultures where religious functions are dominant, primary moral concerns center on religious relationships and religious behavior. Sacrilege, or failure to respect religious objects, buildings, and ceremonies, is a serious crime and is severely punished. Heresy, or the utterance of beliefs that reject or deny major beliefs of the religion, may easily bring on the death penalty, if religious authorities have the power and if they feel that the community is threatened. The heroic figures in the religious community are the church founders and the leading church officers. Their moral leadership is expressed in service to the church and perhaps a heroic level of sacrifice for the faith. Conversion, repentance, prayer, ordination, sanctification, and confirmation become morally significant social events in the community.

Societies dominated by political movements manifest primary concern with loyalty and service to the party. When a revolutionary party is newly installed in power, it is particularly sensitive to the threat of rival parties and to defections. Often, the party doctrine is recast from the more idealistic formulas of the revolutionary period to more practical tenets. Resistance to the leaders results in branding with treason, usually to the nation. Virtue is identified as devotion to the party. In some major Communist countries intense indoctrination in party dogma and policy is used to develop a "socialist conscience." The loyal member is expected to review his or her own actions, searching for mistakes and misdeeds. At periodic meetings the members publicly confess their errors, both voluntarily and in response to criticism from other party members. The way in which these criticisms are given and received has much to do with the member's advance or decline in the party. The good member, as a matter of moral principle, is expected to sacrifice personal interests for the benefit and protection of the party. In this sense the party is not its membership, but rather its program and the purpose. The party thus achieves the social value accorded to the church, the nation, or the king, for which the sacrifice of human life and the dedication of wealth and property are completely and unquestioningly justified. Such an entity becomes the highest moral object in the society.

In time of war military morals become dominant. In some societies such values and a warlike state may become a relatively permanent way of life. Members of a military organization are rigorously trained to put the success of the military mission above everything else. A good soldier does not ask questions, except to be sure that the military orders are correctly understood. The soldier or officer sacrifices his or her own life and those of the entire combat unit if necessary. It should be noted that, with the atomic weapons of the age of mass destruction, all members of the warring nation are equally vulnerable to destruction, regardless of age or sex. The soldier is not concerned with long-range moral objectives, such as preservation of the nation or ultimate victory. This is the concern of the higher commanders. For this reason, strict discipline is required. Authority is absolute, and willful failure to follow orders may be punished by death. In many military organizations, cowardice or desertion in the face of the enemy may be punished by death. On the positive side, those who perform combat missions successfully are rewarded with praise, increased authority, and military honors. Personal courage and bravery during combat are the most highly honored moral characteristics. This military morality can be illustrated by an incident in the Soviet infantry during World War II. Two soldiers were ordered to attack an enemy position. The junior of the two turned and said: "I can't do it. I am afraid. Go ahead and shoot me, but don't tell the others. Let them think I died fighting." The senior soldier said: "No. I am going to shoot you, and I am going to tell the others!"

The morality of science requires at least a mention. The primary goal of scientific work is to discover new knowledge and to gain an improved understanding of natural processes, including social processes among human beings. Scientific and public honors go to the researcher who can make such discoveries. These rewards take the form of appointments to research positions, grants and awards to fund research, and—in exceptional cases—certificates and medals similar to those awarded to military achievers. Perhaps fame or, at a minimum, a respected "name" is the most important reward for the struggling scientist. The scientist is expected to be absolutely honest in the treatment and reporting of data. He or she must check and recheck articles to be published in scientific or scholarly journals to ensure their accuracy. The scientist does not omit or forget to mention awkward or anomalous elements in the findings, even though they cast doubt on what the scientist is trying to prove. Of course, the scientist gets credit for a discovery or a theory by being the first to publish it. It is in this area that the scientist's morality falters. A three-year study of the Apollo moon mission indicated that the scientists were anything but objective and disinterested. Each was passionately committed to one of a set of opposing theories, and each was likely to reject and ignore evidence that opposed the favored theory. Moreover, they could not trust one another with their newly developed information. As one scientist put it: "It is only when I began to do something significant and important that people began to steal from me. When I began to manage a big research program, and all the big important people began to visit me, they would rush home and try to outdo our results. You know you're doing something important when people want to steal it" (Mitroff, 1974). The problem is acute in the exact sciences, where several very capable researchers may be in a race to complete the same precise experiment first.

G. SUMMARY

Though moral behavior limits one's freedom and though it is sometimes inconsistent with self-interests, people usually do what they ought to do. In other words, people do learn to differentiate between "right" and "wrong" and to act accordingly. Our concern in this chapter has been with why this happens and how it happens. Freud addressed the question of why, postulating that moral development results from the child's need to suppress his or her strong sexual feelings for the parent of the opposite sex. Freud labeled this phenomenon the Oedipus complex and believed that it occurs before 5 years of age.

Jean Piaget and Lawrence Kohlberg, for the most part, assumed the origin of morality and simply proceeded to describe its development. Piaget viewed the development of morality as taking place in two stages: heteronomous and autonomous. The heteronomous stage is characterized by a morality of constraint. The child's views reflect strict adherence to parental authority. The autonomous stage is characterized by a morality of cooperation. The child's views reflect his or her ability to judge intentions as well as consequences. Kohlberg developed what he considers to be a logical extension of the Piagetian model. Kohlberg's research has attempted to isolate moral structure from its content. Three levels of moral development are identified, each having two stages: (1) preconventional, where goodness is defined in terms of physical consequences (Stage 1) and in terms of instrumental value (Stage 2); (2) conventional, where goodness is defined in terms of what is pleasing to others (Stage 3) and in terms of law and order (Stage 4); (3) postconventional, where "right" is defined by social contract (Stage 5) and where morality is based on the autonomous functioning of conscience (Stage 6). Each of these models focuses on the individual. Concern is for the development of morality within the individual.

The sociological perspective on morality has taken the emphasis off the individual and placed it at a broad structural level. The question to be answered is the Hobbesian question of social order and cohesion: "How is it that in pursuit of their own self-interests persons do not so relate to others, likewise pursuing their own interests, that society disintegrates into a war of all against all with benefit to none?" Durkheim and Parsons both addressed this issue. Durkheim suggested that "the moral basis of advanced societies is the group basis of advanced societies." In other words, moral rules provide the basis for social solidarity. In a somewhat similar vein, Parsons suggested that public morality functions to maximize social cohesion and order.

Moral standards to which we adhere usually take the form of social norms. Two such norms that have strong moral tones are the norm of social responsibility and the norm of reciprocity. The norm of social responsibility addresses the question "Am I my brother's keeper?" The norm of reciprocity addresses the issue of receiving something in return for investments made.

The field of social psychology has addressed both of these issues under the guise of distributive-justice theory. The rule of distributive justice, first introduced by Homans, suggests that "a man in an exchange relation will expect that the rewards of each man will be proportional to his costs—the greater the rewards, the greater the costs—and that the net rewards, or profit of each man will be proportional to his investments—the greater the investments, the greater the profits." Homans' discussion of distributive justice provides an equity (reciprocal) solution to the distributive problem. An alternative is an equality solution. Sampson, in evaluating current research, noted that there are four key factors influencing whether the equity or equality principle will be followed: (1) the person's interaction goals, (2) the person's basic orientation, (3) the person's situated identity, and (4) the person's sex-role orientation. The rule of distributive justice provides a personal-level view of the norm of reciprocity and the norm of social responsibility in action.

Robert Hogan has provided a comprehensive view of moral development in terms of five relatively independent dimensions: (1) moral knowledge, (2) socialization, (3) empathy, (4) autonomy, and (5) instrumental value in established rules and procedures. Hogan conceded some difficulty with precise conceptualization of autonomy. He also characterized the two poles of his final dimension. At one end are those whose decisions result from the dictates of conscience. At the other end are those whose decisions result from formalized contracts. According to Hogan, each of these is less than socially mature.

The development of individual and societal morality has resulted in raising a number of issues with strong moral undertones. A few of these, including capital punishment, abortion, and infanticide, deal with a basic moral issue: the value of human life. Others, including prostitution, gambling, and legalization of drugs, deal with basic human rights.

Each perspective on morality (psychological, sociological, social-psychological) indirectly addresses the basic desire to survive, both individually and collectively.

Deviance, Control, and Total Institutions 13

A. INTRODUCTION

The concepts and processes we have discussed thus far have applied, for the most part, to social situations that are relatively open and to people who are "nondeviant." The other side of social life is the ever-present deviant world, which people often attempt to conceal, and social settings that are relatively closed. It is to these phenomena that we turn in this chapter, for social psychology has a great deal to offer to an understanding of them.

B. THREE CONCEPTIONS OF DEVIANCE

In social science the way we view a phenomenon has something to do with what it is. To call a rock a rock is not to change the nature of the rock. But to call a human being a paranoid or a felon is to do something fundamental to his or her social as well as personal identity. Therefore, the conceptions of deviant behavior and social control held both by social scientists and by individual persons are very important.

There has been a significant change in recent years in the prevailing conceptions of deviant behavior, deviants, and their control as a process in society (Gibbs, 1966). In this section we will discuss these changing conceptions in order to focus on the fundamental issues involved when people recognize, define, and deal with one another's deviant behavior.

1. Deviance in the Actor

Probably the oldest attempt to explain deviant behavior—and one that is still popular—is the assertion that the deviant is either biologically or psychologically distinctive and that this distinction is the "cause" of the person's deviant behavior. This explanation was part of a general trend following the publication of Darwin's *Origin of Species* in 1859 to apply biology to human behavior (Sagarin, 1975, 78). Biological explanations took such forms as the widespread idea that certain people had an inborn tendency to become deviants and that under the proper circumstances this tendency would become manifest in their behavior. Some scientists saw in the deviant such types as the "born criminal" and the "bad seed." Biological theories have waned at times, but they always seem to come back. Much of this work has been devoted to explaining crime and criminal behavior.

a. Biological theories.   The earliest attempt to trace crime to biological sources is usually credited to Cesare Lombroso (1836–1909). A physician who was inclined to look at phenomena biologically, Lombroso believed that humans have evolved beyond their original nature, which was primitive, wild, antisocial, and aggressive. Criminals, therefore, are genetic throwbacks to this earlier stage. Lombroso worked out all manner of physical and physiological differences between convicts and a control group of ordinary citizens. Criminals are more likely to have darker skin, jutting jaws, hairy bodies, shifty eyes, a strong muscular structure, and additional characteristics that distinguish them from the normal population, he contended. Lombroso did not argue that all criminals are of this type. But he asserted that a large proportion of them are, to use his phrase, "born criminals" (Lombroso, 1912).

European scientists were not the only scholars to promulgate biological theories of deviant behavior. In the United States the work of an anthropologist named Earnest Hooton (1887–1954) was attracting attention. Hooton tried to show that convicts are physiologically different from persons who have never been convicted of a crime. In addition, he found specific types of bodies to be correlated with specific types of crimes. Hooton believed that tall, thin men are more likely to murder and steal, whereas tall and heavy men not only murder but also commit a lot of forgery and fraud. Small, thin men burglarize; short, heavy men are rapists; and men with a "mediocre" build break the law without any particular preferences (Hooton, 1939). On the basis of his research, Hooton also argued in favor of the "born-criminal" theory. Because criminals could not "help themselves," it would be necessary to confine them in permanent prison colonies or perhaps even to execute them all. Because of the extreme determinism of Hooton's conclusions and some deficiencies in the conduct of his research, his work was severely criticized and is referred to now only as an example of the extreme biological lengths to which scholars have gone in a desperate attempt to explain crime and deviance.

While Hooton's research was rejected, the whole biological strain of thought about deviance was not. The most famous study was made by a physician and psychologist, William Sheldon (Sheldon et al., 1940). He believed that the body-type approach was basically correct and identified three such types in his research, the now-famous ectomorph, endomorph, and mesomorph. Sheldon described these types as follows:

> When *endomorphy* predominates, the digestive viscera are highly developed, while the somatic structures are relatively weak and underdeveloped.

"Born criminals"

Endomorphs are of low specific gravity. They float high in the water ... are usually fat but they are sometimes emaciated. In the latter event they do not change into mesomorphs or ectomorphs any more than a starved mastiff will change into a spaniel or a collie. They become simply emaciated endomorphs.

When *mesomorphy* predominates, the somatic structures (bone, muscle, and connective tissue) are in the ascendancy. The mesomorphic physique is high in specific gravity and is hard, firm, upright, and relatively strong and tough. The skin is relatively thick, with large pores, and it is heavily reinforced with underlying connective tissues. The hallmark of mesomorphy is uprightness and sturdiness of structure, as the hallmark of endomorphy is softness and sphericity.

Ectomorphy means fragility, linearity, flatness of the chest, and delicacy throughout the body. There is relatively slight development of both the visceral and somatic structures. The ectomorph has long, slender, poorly muscled extremities with delicate, pipestem bones, and he has relative to his mass, the greatest surface area and hence the greatest sensory exposure to the outside world [Sheldon et al., 1940, 7–8].*

Sheldon saw the individual as a mixture of the three types, and their importance lay in how *predominant* one was over the other two in a given person. A careful measuring scale produced what he called a *somatotype*— that is, an average for a particular individual. Sheldon, on the basis of a study of juvenile delinquents, believed that mesomorphs were more likely to be represented among lawbreakers and that because of their superior muscular structure they were in a better position to engage in violent crimes (Sheldon et al., 1940).

Sheldon's work, because it argued from the point of view of both physiology and psychology and because it was based on probability rather than determinism, attracted more scientific interest than its predecessors. It stimulated the longitudinal research undertaken beginning in the 1930s by Eleanor and Sheldon Glueck, who studied a large number of factors in juvenile delinquents, including body type and hereditary patterns (Glueck and Glueck, 1950). Following a careful methodology, the Gluecks concluded that biological factors, combined with many others, do have some role to play in the creation of juvenile delinquency.

Research that tries to trace deviance to elements that are internal to the person rises and falls. There have been attempts to explain deviant behavior in terms not only of body type, but also of brain deterioration, glandular disturbances, bumps on and shape of the head, and even genital pathologies and the number of tooth cavities (Box, 1971)! The most recent resurrection of biological theories of deviance came during the 1960s, when a widely reported study asserted that aggressive crime is much more likely among men who have an extra Y chromosome—an XYY as opposed to the normal XY pattern (Price and Whatmore, 1967). Men with an extra Y

---

*From *The Varieties of Human Physique*, by W. H. Sheldon, S. S. Stevens, and W. P. Tucker. Copyright 1940 by Harper & Row, Publishers, Inc. Reprinted by permission of Dorothy I. Paschal, Executor of the estate of the late Dr. Sheldon, Ph.D., M.D.

Sheldon believed that mesomorphs, because of their superior muscular structure, are in a better position to engage in violent crimes than are people with other body types. (Photo by © Bernard P. Wolff, Magnum Photos)

chromosome, it was argued, are biologically more prone to violence, a lack of self-control, and certain physical characteristics such as a tall, lean frame and acne. Most recently, biological theories have surfaced again in the work of Konrad Lorenz and other animal ethologists and even in the learning theories of some psychologists (Clinard, 1974).

b. *Psychological theories.* Another popular way of looking at deviance as a characteristic of the actor is to trace deviant behavior to psychological, as opposed to biological, sources. In this way of thinking personality, temperament, and past experiences have somehow left a deviant mark on the person, making him or her more prone to the commission of deviant acts. These theories are also quite deterministic. The actor is usually seen as one who can be rehabilitated through the use of such techniques as psychotherapy or behavior modification. In other words, the deterministic processes that forced deviance in the first place can be reversed by replacing them with other processes that force respectable behavior. The idea that the deviant is a "degenerate" or has a "pathological" or "sociopathic" personality is the current version of a way of thinking that goes back to the earliest periods of the study of deviance, when scholars spoke of "moral insanity" and "moral imbecility" (Sagarin, 1975, 89).

With the rise of modern psychiatry much deviance is explained in this way, both by scientists and by persons in everyday life. The deviant is seen as someone who is "sick," the underlying "sickness" being seen as a "cause" of the deviant behavior. These ideas have their roots in a number of strongly held beliefs concerning the primacy of the individual. The proponents of a psychiatric, or medical, model have ideas that can be summarized in the following way:*

1. All deviant behavior is a product of something in the individual, such as personal disorganization or "maladjusted" personality. Deviants are individuals who are psychologically "sick" persons. Culture is seen not as a determinant of deviant and conforming behavior but rather as the context within which these tendencies are expressed.
2. All persons at birth have certain inherent needs, in particular the need for emotional security.
3. Depriving the young child of universal needs leads to the formation of particular personality types. Childhood experiences such as emotional conflicts largely but not exclusively determine personality structure and the pattern of behavior in later life. The degree of conflict, disorder, retardation, or injury to the personality will vary directly with the degree of deprivation.
4. A child's experiences in the family, by affecting his or her personality structure, largely determine behavior in later life, whether deviant or non-

*Adapted from "A Sociological Critique of Psychiatric Theories of Crime," by J. Hankin. In Marshall B. Clinard (Ed.), *Sociology of Deviant Behavior.* Copyright © 1957 by Marshall B. Clinard. Copyright © 1963, 1968, 1974 by Holt, Rinehart and Winston. Reprinted by permission of Holt, Rinehart and Winston.

deviant. The need for the mother to provide maternal affection is particularly stressed.

5. A high degree of certain so-called general personality traits—such as emotional insecurity, immaturity, feelings of inadequacy, inability to display affection, and aggression—characterizes the deviant but not the nondeviant. Such traits are the product of early-childhood experiences in the family. Deviant behavior is often a way of dealing successfully with such personality traits; for example, so-called immature or emotionally insecure persons may commit crimes or may drink excessively and become alcoholics.

These basic propositions are used by many people, scientists and citizens alike, to explain a wide variety of behavioral aberrations. Crime, delinquency, drug addiction, suicide, mental illness itself, sex offenses, alcoholism, homosexuality, and even gambling and visiting prostitutes have been explained with reference to these ideas.

These psychological theories are often intertwined with psychoanalytic ones. Following the enormous intellectual and cultural edifice created by the work of Sigmund Freud, many psychiatric and psychological personnel who work in the area of deviance use Freud's ideas in explaining and treating deviants.

As our discussion of Freud's ideas in the first chapter indicated, the human personality is conceived of in three parts. The *id* is the primitive, animalistic, often sexual series of urges that compels the organism. It is unconscious, or largely so. The id is supposedly involved in everything people do. The *ego*, on the other hand, is a structure that operates on the level of consciousness and is a defense mechanism to ward off various assaults on the self. The ego is basically a mediator between the id and the third part of the self, the *superego*, which is composed of partly conscious and partly unconscious elements and represents the oppressive attempt on the part of society to control people through the development of such things as a conscience, which inhibits people's behavior through the mechanism of guilt. The id and the superego are more or less in conflict with each other. The id is saying yes and the superego is saying no. Neuroses, psychoses, and their accompanying behavioral disorders (such as deviant behavior) are all seen as the result of the struggle going on between the id and superego. Deviance results from a weak ego that is unsuccessful in controlling that conflict (Freud, 1929).

c. A critique.   The inadequacies of perspectives that see deviance as an inherent characteristic of the actor are numerous.

Biological theories of crime and deviance fall prey to several difficulties. First, after decades of research no biological characteristic that distinguishes deviants from nondeviants, criminals from noncriminals, has ever been discovered (Gibbs, 1966). As a result, very few social psychologists now entertain very seriously the idea that deviants are atavistic, defective, or mentally inferior to the rest of the population. Even in the case of the extra Y chromosome, it is worthwhile noting that even the original researchers pointed out that the majority of persons with an extra chromosome are *not* criminals. Furthermore, as Gibbs noted, even casual observation and common sense seem to cast doubt on the notion that criminals and deviants are so by virtue of biology. "Since legislators are not geneticists, it is difficult to see how they can pass laws in such a way as to create 'born criminals.' Equally important, since most if not all 'normal' persons have violated a law at one time or another, the assertion that criminals are that way by virtue of heredity now appears most questionable" (Gibbs, 1966, 11).

Another, more serious, shortcoming of biological explanations of crime and deviance seems to be that, because deviance (of all sorts) is socially defined, it is questionable just how it can be biologically determined. As Austin Turk (1964) has pointed out, "There is apparently no pattern of behavior which has not been at least tolerated in some normative structure." Although there appear to be some reasonably universal general categories of norms, such as limitations on the use of violence, there is no specific social rule that has ever been shown to be present in all human societies. Even the infamous incest taboo, while it exists as a general prohibition in all societies, is so variably defined that it is difficult to discuss without reference to the specific definitions, understandings, and conditions under which it is invoked. In other words, biology is a relatively constant factor in human social life, whereas the social rules whose violation constitutes deviance are enormously variable.

Similarly, psychological theories that place deviance inside the actor are deficient in that they fail to show a link between any general condition and the commission of a particular act. Such factors as low self-esteem, an "antisocial temperament," repressed fears, and unconscious drives are, given the assumptions of psychology, resident in many people, not simply those who commit crime or engage in deviant behavior.

In addition, theories that place deviance within the actor have been created on the basis of research that is questionable because of seriously biased sampling procedures. If, for example, our research interest is in the commission of *crime* but we take as our subjects only legally identified *criminals*, we may come to be confused by fundamental differences between these two categories. Studies of crime that use criminals as a research sample deal only with criminal failures. They do not deal with the majority of crime, which is not reported, not solved, and consequently gotten away with. Therefore, trying to draw conclusions about crime, for example, from studying convicted criminals may be about as valid as drawing conclusions about college students by studying those who have dropped out of college (Simmons, J. L., 1969).

Furthermore, by using in our studies institutionalized populations, we do not know whether we are studying the process of deviance or the results of the processes of institutionalization. The early work we discussed by

Lombroso, Hooton, and Sheldon all dealt with institutionalized populations. Similarly, the Gluecks' studies used legally identified juvenile delinquents. One wonders, therefore, if their conclusions are conclusions about the propensity to commit crime or about the propensity for getting caught committing crime, two things of obviously different significance.

These problems of methodology are even more acute when evaluating psychological research on deviants. Most psychological studies, obviously, deal with persons who are in treatment, either voluntarily or involuntarily, so that drawing conclusions about their psychological characteristics and imputing those attributes to the rest of the deviant population is questionable. Methodological problems are made even more acute by definitional difficulties. Personality factors, traits, and so on are very difficult to isolate and measure. When a person represents some extreme case, consensus may be easy. But for most deviants agreeing about whether they have pathological or integrated personalities is most difficult.

Finally, with regard to the widely held idea that deviants are "sick," numerous problems can be cited that tend to cast doubt on its validity. The concept of illness applied to behavior is obviously an analogy (Szasz, 1961). Bodies can be sick because there is widespread consensus about what constitutes a healthy body. Teams of physicians from various social and cultural backgrounds can be called together and immediately reach a consensus that a patient's leg is broken. This is because a broken leg is a physical happening, not a social act. The distinction is important, for if deviance is a mere happening like a broken leg, then responsibility for it can no longer be placed on the deviant, any more than we would expect a person to be responsible for having a broken leg. In this sense biological and psychological interpretations of deviant behavior tend to regard deviance as a kind of accident for which the person cannot properly be held accountable. Thus, conceptions of deviance have important implications for social, legal, and judicial policy. It is, however, much more difficult to reach a consensus about just what constitutes "healthy" behavior. The problem has to do not so much with medicine as with values. This is one reason why the rules whose violation constitutes deviance are so variable. Because people at different times and places have held such highly conflicting values regarding how to live and what to do, they have instituted an extremely wide range of laws, norms, and expectations.

However, unless the norm is specified, the concept of illness makes no sense. And when the norms are social ones rather than medical ones, the judgment seems to be more a political act than an objective and scientific one. Thomas Szasz (1974) has been the most persistent critic of the medical approach to deviance, especially to those forms of deviance subsumed under the heading of "mental illness." He stated the basics of this problem well:

> Starting with such things as syphilis, tuberculosis, typhoid fever and carcinomas and fractures, we have created the class "illness." At first, this class was composed of only a few items, all of which shared the common feature of

reference to a state of disordered structure or function of the human body as a physio-chemical machine. As time went on, additional items were added to this class. They were not added, however, because they were newly discovered bodily disorders. The physician's attention had been deflected from this criterion and had become focused instead on disability and suffering as new criteria for selection. Thus, at first slowly, such things as hysteria, hypochondriasis, obsessive-compulsive neurosis, and depression were added to the category of illness. Then, with increasing zeal, physicians and especially psychiatrists began to call "illness" (that is, of course, "mental illness") anything and everything in which they could detect any sign of malfunctioning, based on no matter what norm. Hence, agoraphobia is illness because one should not be afraid of open spaces. Homosexuality is illness because heterosexuality is the social norm. Divorce is illness because it signals failure of marriage. Crime, art, undesired political leadership, participation in social affairs, or withdrawal from such participation—all these and many more have been said to be signs of mental illness [1974, 44–45].[*]

Nevertheless, the translation of behavioral problems into psychological and medical terms has had great currency, possibly because it deflects attention from the processes and persons who are involved in the making of social norms (Stone and Farberman, 1970). If deviant behavior is certified as having come from some medical pathology, the questions raised by the deviance are suddenly neutralized. Therefore, there is now a general consensus that "Hitler was paranoid, De Gaulle senile, Castro mad, Goldwater unstable, and Johnson egomaniacal" (Stone and Farberman, 1970). This mode of thinking tends to obscure the very real questions of power and constraint, leadership, authority, and decision making that flowed from each of those leaders. For if their behavior was only a "symptom" of some underlying medical pathology, then the behavior itself is passed off as only a secondary matter. These problems cast considerable doubt on the use of illness as a metaphor for understanding deviant behavior.

2. Deviance in the Act

If the conception of deviance as a characteristic of the individual deviant is faulty in so many respects, what about the view of deviance as a characteristic inherent in certain types of acts themselves? This conception assumes that deviant acts will have enough in common to form the basis for an understanding and explanation of deviance. Some acts are deviant because they are highly injurious to society. For example, murder is almost universally condemned, along with theft, rape, and a host of other acts. This point of view has most often been associated with the sociological theory called functionalism (Parsons, 1951; Merton, 1957). In this view some acts are functional—that is, they contribute to the maintenance of society—and some are *dysfunctional*—that is, they act to tear society down.

The problem with this conception lies in the fact that, although it is very easy in the abstract to say what kinds of acts are "injurious to society," in actual practice it is much more difficult. If all of us went around murdering one another, we presumably would not have a society for very long. At the same time, the United States as a society is trying to decide whether murder by execution should be one of its policies.

Austin Turk (1964) called the functionalist conception even further into question by asking if crime is a category of behavioral act at all. He noted, as we have, that the history of criminology is the history of a search starting from criminal types—biological, psychological, and sociological—in an effort to develop scientific explanations for why persons deviate from "legal norms." However, these cumulative efforts have rather forced us to the point where it might be necessary to question whether there are *any* significant differences between the overwhelming majority of legally identified criminals and the rest of the relevant general population. The working assumption has been that *crime* and *not-crime*, deviance and nondeviance, are classes of behavior instead of simply classifications associated with the process by which individuals come to occupy the ascribed statuses of *criminal* and *noncriminal*. Turk offered eight types of evidence against the proposition that deviance and nondeviance are behavioral categories.

1. As we mentioned above, there is apparently no pattern of human behavior that has not been tolerated in some place at some time. Anthropology, comparative history, and research into subcultural differences all show that it is virtually impossible to compile a list of acts that are deviant everywhere.

2. The behavioral elements of an illegal or deviant act are not specific to those acts. Activities of the human organism do not automatically sort themselves into deviant and nondeviant categories. The sorting is a matter of cultural definition and the willingness to apply those definitions to some individual or group. In other words, the things deviants do, the needs they have for doing them, and their values, goals, and attitudes are not unique; therefore, explanations cannot be made in terms of them.

3. Definitions of other people as deviant can involve a great deal of selective perception, in which we notice only those things about them that are most damaging. In addition, our recall and classification of events are affected by our concerns in a given situation. In this way we take the raw data and organize them as a criminal or deviant act.

4. The behavior of all individuals contains many more acceptable than unacceptable actions, objectives, and relationships. If a person were completely vicious and treacherous and posed a continual threat to all the people around him, he would not be tolerated in any human group. The fact is that even the most antisocial human beings (including presumably those with extra chromosomes) engage in far more behavior that is quite conven-

Law enforcement has not succeeded in eliminating prostitution, "the world's oldest profession." (Photo by Elliott Erwitt, Magnum Photos)

tional. The stories of famous deviants often include sketches of how warm and gentle they were with friends or children. If most individuals identified as deviants are indistinguishable from nondeviants in their behavior most of the time, certainly the idea that there are fundamental differences between the two categories is questionable.

5. Criminal and deviant acts attributed to the same individual vary from time to time. The highly specialized deviant who is predictable in terms of timing, locale, types of acts, and the like is a rarity. If there is no "career line" in the records of most deviants, there is little reason to assume that theories of criminality based on the characteristics of acts can tell us very much.

6. Most criminal acts do not become known and recorded. Studies of self-reported offenses (Porterfield, 1946), studies of offenses known to public and private organizations but not to the police (Schwartz, 1945), and Sutherland's (1949) famous study of white-collar crime indicate that there are far more deviant acts being committed at any given time than is usually acknowledged. Savitz (1962) has spoken of the "nondelinquent" majority as being nondelinquent only because it hasn't been caught yet. Deviant acts are so numerous within the population at large that any attempt to compare a sample of institutionalized deviants and a control group of the "nondeviant" majority is extremely suspect. The difference between the two groups may well be that one was caught committing a deviant act and the other was not. If most people engage in deviant acts, it is highly questionable to explain the difference between criminal and noncriminal on the basis of any set of differences correlated with such acts.

7. Not all people known to have violated the law are punished for their violation. There is a selective factor in every aspect of the process by which people come to be identified as deviant. Discretion is the rule, rather than the exception (Cicourel, 1967). If all of the people who are *known* to the authorities to have committed criminal or deviant acts are not formally identified as deviants, then the more appropriate question is "Why is one person who engaged in a certain behavior given the status of criminal while another who engaged in the same behavior is not?" This question obviates the usual "Why do criminals engage in criminal behavior?"

8. For most categories of crime the rates are relatively high for lower-class, minority-group, young, male, transient, urban populations. Sociological analysis of these differences indicates that higher crime rates are associated with subordinate positions within the social structure, not with the commission of particular acts.

Given Turk's persuasive analysis, it is difficult to conclude that it would be possible to compile a list of acts that were deviant either universally or specifically. The simple observation that a person is driving off in a car does not tell us whether this is a deviant or a nondeviant act. We would have to inquire whether the car was his and, if not, whether he had the permission of the owner to use it. Even if he did not have permission, an emergency condition or other mitigating circumstance might argue against classifying his behavior as "car theft." It is similarly difficult to know when a rape has occurred, because rape is a definitional and relational category, not a behavioral one. This is to say that there is nothing that goes on in rape of a behavioral nature that does not also go on in voluntary sexual intercourse. To know that the person is struggling or that the sex act is particularly "violent" is not to know that a "rape" has been committed. Knowledge of rape ultimately depends on an analysis of the definition of the relationship between the two persons involved, not the overt "behaviors" they have engaged in.

Furthermore, the idea that rules are social creations takes us away from scientific classifications and toward social, legal, and political ones. Whatever these classifications might be, they are most certainly not usually scientific ones. Norms and values are based on nonscientific criteria for the most part, and it is clear that people have defined all sorts of acts as deviant, including some that are so humorous as to border on the ridiculous. The following examples of outdated and absurd laws demonstrate the problem:

Alabama: The State Court of Appeals once ruled that it is illegal to call anyone a skunk or Adolf Hitler.

California: A Los Angeles ordinance forbids young people to dance together unless they are married.

Georgia: State law provides that it is a misdemeanor for citizens to attend church on Sunday unless they are equipped with a loaded rifle. In Atlanta, shop owners are required by law to pull down a shade during the robing and disrobing of their mannequins.

Indiana: Men who habitually kiss human beings are not allowed to wear mustaches.

Iowa: Women are not allowed to wear corsets. (When this law was first passed years ago, men were appointed as corset inspectors; their duty was to poke women in the ribs to see whether they were wearing them.)

Massachusetts: In Winchester, a young girl may not be employed to dance on a tightrope except in church.

Nebraska: A woman may use profane language before a man, but a man may not use profane language before a woman.

New Jersey: A person can be arrested for slurping soup.

Virginia: In Roanoke, it is against the law to advertise on tombstones.

Undoubtedly, many of the acts that these laws tried at one time to regulate were thought to be of some importance. But the fact that they are still legal violations indicates that behavior that breaks rules does not necessarily brand a person as deviant. The basic problem is not to identify characteristics of either acts or actors but rather to explain and deal with the criminality and deviance of behavior, not the behavior itself (Sutherland, 1949).

3. Deviance in Interaction Process

Both of the previous conceptions take deviance to be a matter of fact. The deviance that is assumed is taken to be nonproblematic in its occurrence; when it happens, we see it. The third point of view takes neither the deviant nor deviance to be a matter of fact, but rather the result of a process—an interaction between what a person does and how others are responding to him or her about it. Variously known as *labeling theory*, the *audience-reaction* approach to deviance, and *neo-interactionism*, this approach flatly rejects the assumption that social deviations are the result of anything intrinsic to either deviants or their deviations. Rather, it is during the course of interaction that acts come to be defined as deviations and people come to be classified (or labeled) as deviants.

The roots of this approach lie in the early work of George Herbert Mead that we have already discussed and—especially—in the writings of Edwin Lemert (1951). In an important but mistitled book, *Social Pathology*, Lemert distinguished between what he called *primary* deviance and *secondary* deviance. Primary deviance is the act of breaking social rules. Secondary deviance, however, is what happens in the process by which others respond to the primary deviation. Lemert noted, as we have, that deviance cannot occur without a social context. He saw this context as a way in which initial acts of deviation come to be stabilized into deviant careers. The person, in part because of the response of others, may take on the role of deviant and begin to use it in his or her self-conception. When this occurs, deviance is likely to continue, because it has been incorporated as part of the self-system.

It is indeed possible for persons to break rules (that is, engage in primary deviance) while continuing to occupy quite conventional statuses and roles. For example, white-collar crime depends on playing conventional roles (Sutherland, 1949). By the same token, fee splitting and ghost surgery among physicians, bribes on the part of politicians, neuroses of professors, and concealed homosexuality all may be covered by a cloak of conventionality. In contrast, secondary deviance occurs when the person's participation in deviance is taken on as a role itself, often at the expense of more conventional ones. When a homosexual comes "out of the closet" or a drug addict joins a group of users, we have a situation that is qualitatively different—the person has incorporated deviance as a social role. In Lemert's analysis, secondary deviance can occur either voluntarily or involuntarily, but the audience-reaction approach has focused primarily on the involuntary aspects of the social role of deviant.

In other words, whether people consider themselves to be deviant or not is an important factor in understanding deviant behavior. Executives who are arrested for white-collar crime are sometimes surprised to discover that anyone would consider them criminals for what they did. The rapid rise of massage parlors across the country has enabled a number of re-

The rapid rise of massage parlors has enabled a number of women to make a living for themselves or augment their husbands' salaries through commercial sex without having to regard themselves as "whores." (Photo by © Bob Adelman, Magnum Photos)

spectable women to make a living or augment their husband's salary through commercial sex without having to regard themselves as "whores" (Verlarde and Warlick, 1973). People may engage in homosexual acts, sometimes for years, without regarding themselves as homosexual at all (Humphreys, 1970). A person may be a heavy drinker and yet not play the role of alcoholic. In fact, the most successful organization for dealing with drinking problems, Alcoholics Anonymous, recognizes this distinction and will not take people unless they are prepared to regard themselves as alcoholics. Secondary deviance is important because, as the deviant develops a role involving other deviants and acquires knowledge and skill in avoiding detection and arrest, his or her commitment to the role becomes more intense. A web of commitments begins to build up around the role. Coupled with the increasing exclusion from more conventional roles, it leaves the deviant with essentially one alternative: to continue participation in what is the only social circle now left. To be sure, the deviant could choose some other line of action, but the point is that this is very difficult to do once a deviant role has been embraced. Therefore, as Robert Stebbins suggested:

Commitment is the belief on the part of the committed individual that he is trapped in his deviant role by the force of penalties that appear when he tries to establish himself in nondeviant circles. Recognition of these penalties marks a major turning point in his deviant career; one where his realization of the forces both for and against continued deviance is especially acute [1971, xvi].

Obviously, commitment to the role has some positive benefits for the deviant. Years of keeping a secret may have taken its toll in anxiety, fear, depression, and guilt. For the secret homosexual the decision to "come out" may be, for all of its problems, the most liberating experience of his or her life. No longer does the person have to assume the responsibilities of living a respectable life in addition to the deviant one. This same experience is reported by many different kinds of deviants, from homosexuals and prostitutes to professional criminals and alcoholics (McCaghy et al., 1974).

The interactionist approach to deviance, then, assumes that the responses of others are a key factor in the social creation of a deviant identity. What a person does primarily is an important factor, but only a single one, in the process by which persons come to be categorized as deviant. Several classic statements from the literature serve to make the point:

Forms of behavior *per se* do not differentiate deviants from non-deviants; it is the responses of the conventional and conforming members of the society who identify and interpret behavior as deviant which sociologically transform persons into deviants [Kitsuse, 1962, 253].

From this point of view, deviance is not a quality of the act a person commits, but rather a consequence of the application by others of rules and sanctions to an "offender." The deviant is one to whom that label has successfully been applied; deviant behavior is behavior that people so label [Becker, H. S., 1963, 9].

From a sociological standpoint, deviance can be defined as conduct which is generally thought to require the attention of social control agencies—that is conduct about which it is felt "something should be done." Deviance is not a property *inherent* in certain forms of behavior; it is a property *conferred upon* these forms by the audiences which directly or indirectly witness them. Sociologically, then, the critical variable in the study of deviance is the social *audience* rather than the individual person, since it is the audience which eventually decides whether or not any given action or actions will become a visible cause of deviation [Erikson, K., 1962, 308].

A person can commit any number of primary deviations and not have these translated into the terms of deviance, either because other persons are not aware or because they choose not to make an issue of it. Using our previous discussion of the biological view of deviance as an example, we can see that, even if Lombroso, Hooton, and Sheldon had been correct in their view that criminals are biologically distinctive, the biological factor neither identifies criminals nor (importantly) explains their criminality. Perhaps biology could conceivably explain why certain acts occur, but it could by no means explain why these acts are criminal. The explanation, then, for the criminality of behavior, its deviant qualities, lies in the process of interaction that takes place between the actor and the responding audience. How, then, do we account for the deviance of deviant behavior, the criminality of crime, and the intense negative feeling associated with these categories? This is the key problem of the social psychology of deviant behavior. It is to this question that we turn in the following section.

C. DEVIANCE AND RESPECTABILITY

1. Two Worlds

For centuries deviance of all sorts has been construed as a matter of fact. There were two rigidly conceived worlds—deviant and respectable, separate and unequal—and the only question to be answered was how to account for why some persons deviated and others did not (Brissett and Edgley, 1975, 257). From this common-sense set of assumptions flowed explanations of various kinds, as we have already seen. The study of deviance became a battle ground for various theories. People deviate because of some aberration of their bodies, said the biologists. No, said the psychologists, deviation results from psychological deficiencies, maladjusted personalities, psychopathic tendencies, emotional disturbances, and the like. But no, said the sociologists, deviation results from poor environments, social disorganization, "anomie," and wear and tear in the social machine.

2. The Necessity of Moral Opposites

The questions raised by these perspectives center on the motivations of the deviant. What factors moved this person to the commission of a deviant act? It is clear now that this sort of inquiry has been partially misplaced, because it has overlooked the necessary relationship that exists between deviance and respectability (Douglas, 1970). Such an assertion is not simply an arbitrary or capricious abstraction invented by social scientists. It is taken from close analysis and observation of people interacting in everyday life. If we observe people and hear them talk about these matters, we come to notice that the social meanings of either deviance or respectability can be understood only in terms of the reference point provided by their opposite. Several examples should make the point. The concept of God as ultimate good makes sense only in terms of the concept of Satan as ultimate evil. Good and evil are linked in a moral chain, each requiring the other for its definition. Similarly, the existence of a social category called *beautiful woman* depends necessarily on the coexistence of a category called *ugly woman.*

"The Cabinet? *I thought homosexuals were only in the closet!"*

Many types of deviance are found in surprising places.

Why is this so? No one knows for sure. It may well be that the nature of language forces us to look at things in these oppositional terms, although this thesis has been severely criticized (Whorf, 1956; Sapir, 1964). For whatever reason, this moral fact of human social existence is a necessary and powerful tool in understanding both the existence and relative permanence of deviant behavior and all of the attempts human beings make to control it. The most important consequence is that we will always have deviance at the same time and precisely because we have respectability (Douglas, 1970). It may even be that, the more intensely the conceptions of deviance are held, the more intense will be the attacks on respectability, and vice-versa. We know that ages of saints also turn out to be ages of demons, and that in the middle of the Victorian Era with all of its repression of sexuality there existed some of the most incredible sexual deviancy that has perhaps ever existed.

At any rate, what we have here is a conception of deviance that roots the phenomenon in fundamentally social processes. As long as human societies persist in the construction of categories of respectability, they will of necessity create categories of deviance. This point may appear to be overly pessimistic, but it actually means two rather optimistic things. First, because human beings are collectively in control of the categories that constitute deviance, they can change them if they wish, although they will always need some. This is, in fact, occurring. The categories of rules whose violation constitutes deviance are constantly changing. There are numerous behaviors for which we would have locked people up a hundred years ago that now hardly warrant a passing yawn. Conversely, many things that formerly were looked on as positive are now regarded as quite negative—for example, having ten children. Secondly, and more importantly, deviance has positive uses in society.

3. The Social Uses of Deviance

At the risk of being irreverent, one could almost say of deviance what Voltaire said about God: it is such a useful idea that, if it did not exist, someone would have to invent it. Perhaps the most important use of deviant categories is the already mentioned function of providing a contrast for the social construction of categories of respectability. This is an important function, for, if moral people are to have respectability, they must have a point of immoral contrast. Deviant groups—prostitutes, pimps, homosexuals, thieves, bootleggers, murderers, and even bums, hobos, and tramps—perform this function nicely. This accounts in part for why many people are reluctant to give up such highly moral terms as *whores, queers, perverts, degenerates,* and *fornicators* in favor of a terminology that is more neutral in its moral tone.

Various groups that have been the target of stigmatizing labels of deviance provided, as long as they were labeled deviant, a cheap and regular supply of labor. Poverty is the best example of this. Herbert Gans has pointed out a long list of functions that poverty performs, including the moral one of generating a disreputable, deviant category in order to clearly identify the boundaries of respectability:

> The poor can be identified and punished as alleged or real deviants in order to uphold the legitimacy of dominant norms. The defenders of the desirability of hard work, thrift, honesty, and monogamy need people who can be accused of being lazy, spendthrift, dishonest, and promiscuous to justify these norms [1972, 279].

By far the most positive use of deviance is economic. If all forms of deviant behavior were to stop abruptly, the economy might well collapse, for so many people make their living off of administering deviance and deviants. Sagarin estimated that there are more than a half-million people involved in police work, tens of thousands of judges, corrections officers, criminal lawyers, politicians, social workers, psychologists, sociologists, and other people whose livelihood depends directly on the existence of a stable and dependable supply of deviants (1975, 370). This does not mean, of course, that alternative work could not be found, but it does suggest the extent to which our present society is dependent economically on deviant behavior and its products. A car thief, undoubtedly attempting to justify his own behavior, nevertheless put his finger on a major point when he said:

"Look, who do I hurt? I tell you, I don't hurt nobody. The people whose cars are stolen, they're insured, and they get money and buy new cars. The insurance companies are making plenty, and if cars weren't stolen, they wouldn't have the business they got, they couldn't charge these prices for insurance, and they wouldn't make this profit. I give people employment, not only demolishing these cars, but guys in the factories making new cars. Detectives, cops, all sorts of people get work because I'm in business. I tell you, nobody gets hurt" [Sagarin, 1975, 369].

Without accepting this point to the extreme that any behavior could be justified, it is nevertheless noteworthy that deviance and its control are an important economic enterprise. This point serves to validate our previous assertion concerning the close connection between deviance and respectability.

D. THE INTERPERSONAL CREATION OF DEVIANTS

If deviance is created in and by society, then it is necessary to know something of how this process occurs. Even if deviants were born, there would still have to be some process by which they were recognized. People are not automatically labeled deviant; instead, there is a ritual process they go through on the way to becoming identified as deviant.

1. Degradation Ceremonies

Harold Garfinkel (1956) precisely articulated the steps a person goes through in becoming identified by others as deviant. A degradation ceremony is "any communicative work between persons whereby the public identity of an actor is transformed into something lower." The identities that are thereby created will then be "motivational" rather than simply "behavioral." In other words, in order for the label to stick, people must see the person not simply as someone who has done something bad but also as a bad person who is given to do bad things. During the degradation ceremony people publicly deliver a kind of moral curse, calling upon everyone to bear witness that the miscreant is not what he or she appears to be but is something altogether different. Such moral indignation serves to ritually transform the self by destroying the old one and creating a new one. Persons who have been shamed report just such feelings on being degraded publicly. "I could have sunk right through the floor," "I wanted to run away and hide," "I wanted the earth to open up and swallow me" are all sentiments felt by those who have undergone such a degradation. The importance of degradations to the social psychology of the self is simply that the ceremony serves to testify that the new identity is not just an overhaul of the former one. It is a genuine transformation, one kind of identity being replaced with another of an entirely different kind. Garfinkel suggested that eight steps are involved:

1. Both the event and the perpetrator must be removed from the realm of everyday character and be made "out of the ordinary." What the person did can in no sense be seen as an accident. Not only must the event be seen as intentional, but the fact that it could have been accidental must also be made to seem inconceivable. An offender may short-circuit the process here if he or she is successful in making it appear to have been an accident or effectively argues that "everyone's doing it."

2. A good/evil dichotomy must be set up so that the perpetrator and the event are assigned to the morally negative category. The negative category must be made to be seen as not only preferred but also morally required. Alternatives are posed to the audience in such a way that not choosing to degrade the person will be seen by others as condoning his or her behavior.

3. The denouncer (the person who is leading the degradation ceremony) must be seen as a public, not a private, figure. The denouncer is acting for all, not out of any vested interest or personal vendetta. This is why some persons are better denouncers than others. If a friend can be recruited to lead the ceremony, it will be more effective. Others will see the friend as acting out of nothing other than a public sense of responsibility.

4. The denouncer makes the dignity of public values accessible to view and delivers the denunciation in their name. ("Surely you parents do not want homosexuals teaching in our schools!")

5. The denouncer is invested with the right to speak for all. He or she has the authority to denounce.

6. The denouncer must be defined by witnesses as a supporter of the public values from which the denunciation is being launched. Persons who are themselves tainted cannot speak. Therefore, persons who are known to have engaged in the same behavior as the offender are not effective denouncers, because they are open to the charge "why, you've done the very same thing."

7. For a degradation ceremony to be a success, social distance must be created between the denouncer and the denounced. People will begin to think of the denounced in terms of "how could you have done such a thing?"

8. The denounced person must be ritually separated from the legitimate order. He or she is placed outside the group and made to seem strange, alien and bizarre.

Few readers will not have been on one side or the other of a degradation ceremony.

2. Deviant Careers

It is important to recognize that deviance does not simply happen, it develops. An act begun for one reason may continue for quite another, and additional acts may be required as the pressure of the situation leads the person from one type of behavior to another. The fatal flaw in most theories of deviance is that they often do not recognize this simple fact. People begin various kinds of deviance for vastly different reasons, and how their career develops depends on factors that are often situational. Cohen has captured this situational character of the development of deviance nicely:

> For example, a person might set out to burglarize a house. Quite unexpectedly, the householder may come home and attack the burglar with a deadly weapon. The burglar, to save his own life, kills the attacker. What started out as a burglary might end up as murder, due to a circumstance that was not necessarily implicit in the earlier stage of the act. However, although the arrival of the householder was a separately determined event, unforeseen and perhaps unforeseeable, the situation as a whole is partly a product of the actor's own doing [1966, 103].

What this means is that deviant acts, like all others, are built up in the course of their execution. Simply focusing on the intent or background of the deviant is not likely to take into account just how he or she came to be involved in the behavior in question.

The question of deviance often revolves around the motivations of the deviant. But, as Becker has pointed out, most people have had deviant impulses at times, at least in fantasy. Thus, one might as easily ask why ordinary people do not follow through on their impulses and engage in deviant behavior (Becker, H. S., 1963, 26–27). Becker believed that the reason they don't has to do with their being committed to a network of conventional careers—marriage, work, family, community—that an escapade of deviance might well end. This is a very compelling argument, especially in light of the fact that, as soon as a former category of deviance becomes somewhat respectable, all sorts of conventional people are then likely to indulge in it. The use of marijuana is a prime example. Some types of drugs, such as alcohol, are associated with quite conventional and respectable careers. Others, such as heroin, are seen as part of the most deviant kinds of lifestyles (Szasz, 1974). Given the fact that it may be difficult to hold down a job if your neighbors know you use heroin, this is not surprising. People become progressively committed to careers, either conventional or deviant, and it is necessary to understand how this sequence of commitment occurs if we are to understand deviance.

3. Simultaneous and Sequential Models

Given this view of deviance as a progressively occurring process, a model that deals with sequence rather than simultaneity is required. Many of the statistical models currently in use in social science assume that the factors making up a particular behavior occur all at once. However, as Becker's (1963) analysis of the marijuana user has shown, a sequence is involved. What this means is that we may need different types of explanations to account for a person's behavior at various stages of the deviant career. For example, in the case of the marijuana user we may need one kind of explanation to account for how he or she came into a situation where marijuana was available. We may need another explanation to account for how, given the availability, the person decided to try it. And yet another type may be needed to explain how, given an initial use of the substance, a person joined a subculture and continued its use. Each stage is a necessary condition of the next, and each requires analysis of its own features. A sequential model, then, will be required for a proper analysis of any kind of deviant career: the drug user, alcoholic, criminal, delinquent, and even the suicide. Such sequential career analysis is now being done, generally by social psychologists using interactionist models and research strategies.

Most types of deviance have a corresponding corrective institution. Because deviance presents social problems, there is a concerted attempt to control it by identifying deviants, dealing with them, and discharging them back into society. Therefore, in each case of deviance we are confronted with questions concerning how institutions come to identify deviants, what they do with them after they have been identified, and what happens to them after they have been released from the institution. The first question we dealt with in the preceding section. The second question we turn to now in a discussion of what have been called "total institutions."

E. TOTAL INSTITUTIONS

Obviously, not all types of deviance are considered so serious that they require institutionalization. However, those that are offer us a fascinating look at the lengths to which a society feels it must go in order to control certain forms of behavior.

1. What Is a Total Institution?

The most comprehensive analysis of total institutions has been conducted by sociologist Erving Goffman, who defined them in the following terms:

> A total institution may be defined as a place of residence and work where a large number of like-situated individuals, cut off from the wider society for an appreciable period of time, together lead an enclosed, formally administered round of life [1961, xiii].

Prisons provide the classic example, but Goffman identified five different types of institutions: (1) those designed to care for persons felt to be incapable and harmless—homes for the blind, aged, and orphaned; (2) those places established to take care of people who are incapable of taking care of themselves and are a threat to the community: sanitariums, mental hospitals, and—in some parts of the world—leper colonies; (3) institutions designed to protect the community against intentional threats against it: jails, prisons, prisoner-of-war camps, and concentration camps; (4) institutions established to accomplish some specific purposes: army barracks, boarding schools, ships, and the like; and (5) institutions designed as retreats from the world: monasteries and convents.

Each of these places has a common link with the others, despite numerous differences. They are all enclosed from the outside world in such a way that interaction with other people is difficult if not impossible.

2. Total Institutions and the Self

Total institutions are always designed for some purpose. They may be custodial in the sense that their major function is to warehouse human beings for some period of time for some reason. Or they may be rehabilitative in that they actively seek to change those who are recruited as a population. In either case the materials out of which a person builds a self will be in direct relation to the institution itself, since the inmate cannot easily leave. Goffman asserted that this results in the "mortification of the self." No matter how benevolent the institution may be, changes in the self occur by virtue of the person's being there for an extended period:

> The recruit comes into the establishment with a conception of himself made possible by certain stable social arrangements in his home world. Upon entrance, he is immediately stripped of the support provided by these arrangements. In the accurate language of some of our oldest total institutions, he begins a series of abasements, degradations, humiliations, and profanations of self. His self is systematically, if often unintentionally, mortified. He begins some radical shifts in his *moral career*, a career composed of the progressive changes that occur in the beliefs that he has concerning himself and significant others [1961, 14].

The key question here is the issue of how normal people know they are normal. It turns out that conceptions of normality are made possible by a stable environment of objects and persons that continues to validate us in the terms that we appropriate for ourselves (Stone, 1962). For example, people ordinarily expect to exercise some control over the guise in which they appear before others. In order to do this, various kinds of materials are necessary: a wardrobe, cosmetics, toilet items, and the like. In total institutions, however, these things are often removed completely, and institutional items are supplied in their stead. As a result something as personal as appearance can be controlled by the institution, a profound occurrence for the self. Prisons replace names with numbers. The military gives everyone a *uniform* designed, among other things, to make all selves correspond to the categories desired by the institution. The idea is to strip the individual as quickly as possible of his or her old self and to substitute an institutionally approved one.

There are, of course, many rationales for this. In many total institutions the self that is being stripped away is regarded as so problematic that it was what got the inmate to the institution in the first place. So no real loss is felt—although to the person the loss may be profound.

Another artifact that tends to give people a stable view of themselves is their location (Birenbaum and Sagarin, 1973). Freedom of movement means that, if people are being treated in ways that violate their own sense of who they are, they have the option of leaving and going somewhere else. In total institutions this is obviously not possible, so that people must deal with the self as it is dealt with in the setting in which they find themselves. This circular relationship between self and location is one of the most profoundly significant observations made in contemporary social psychology, and it has been brought home time and again when research is conducted in total institutions. In addition, the person's very presence in a prison or a mental hospital means that he or she is in contact with people in disrepute in a setting that is virtually defined as contaminating.

There may also be an assault on the self that stems from the fact that people are no longer able to control information about themselves. In ordinary social relationships people are usually able to exercise some control over what others come to learn about them. But in total institutions such control is almost impossible. In mental hospitals, for example, various facts about the inmate's past behavior, especially those that are most discrediting, regularly come into play; indeed, they are the basis for admission. These facts are collected and recorded in a dossier that is available to the staff and, on occasion, to outsiders. On these occasions, the inmates have to expose facts and feelings about themselves to audiences they might not want to interact with at all. In addition, ordinary information may come to look quite extraordinary when it is given about a person who is an inmate at a total institution.

3. Exposure and the Self

It is somewhat ironic, then, that the most significant impact of life in a total institution stems not from inmates' being isolated from others but rather from their being totally exposed to others. Being kept under 24-hour surveillance, even for one's own good, is likely to have an enormous impact on the self. Ordinary rituals of modesty, such as the right to privacy when using the toilet, may be suspended. In effect, people in a total institution may come to feel that they are being contaminated by a forced social relationship, just as much as the rapist's victim is.

This problem of contamination and exposure may be made even more troublesome by the inmates' attempts to keep themselves away from other inmates. In mental hospitals, for example, it is likely that new patients may feel that they are innocent and have been locked up unfairly. As a result, they may avoid talking with anyone, stay to themselves, and try to avoid ratifying any interaction that would open them to the scrutiny of others.

Because this strategy only serves to validate the conception of the patients as mentally ill, it is both self-defeating and finally impossible to carry out.

Coupled with the feeling of involuntary exposure may be a profound sense of betrayal. Mental hospitals routinely gain their authority to lock people up from those whom we usually turn to in time of trouble, the family. This interesting structural fact about our society means that, when involuntarily committed patients find themselves in a mental hospital, they may discover that those they thought would help them are exactly the people who put them there. This may lead the inmates to the astounding realization that the closeness of a relationship tells you nothing about its trustworthiness. No matter how justified mental hospitalization may have been, the stay is likely to bring with it feelings of abandonment and betrayal. This is frequently the case with other total institutions as well.

4. Being Sane in Insane Places

Mental hospitals offer one of the best examples of the social-psychological processes at work in total institutions. One such process that has devastating impact on the self is what Rosenhan (1973) called the problem of "being sane in insane places." The problem is that when people are hospitalized for mental illness, virtually everything they do is seen as a symptom that confirms their illness. Rosenhan documented this dilemma with a cleverly conceived experiment in which he had eight perfectly sane "pseudopatients" admitted to several mental hospitals. The pseudopatients told only one lie: that at a prior time in their lives they had heard "voices." They said that they were not hearing them now and were having no other problems. After that, the pseudopatients acted as normally as possible and told the truth when questioned about their past lives.

Despite their public show of sanity within the institution, none of the pseudopatients was discovered to be an imposter by the psychiatric staff. Seven of the eight were admitted with a diagnosis of "schizophrenia in remission" and stayed in the hospital between seven and 52 days before release. Several of the patients suspected that they were frauds, but the staff did not. To the contrary, the staff routinely read their behavior while in the mental hospital as symptomatic of their mental illness. When patients became upset about happenings within the mental hospital, the staff assumed that the upset stemmed from their underlying pathology, not from their present interactions. Patients who walked around the floor a lot because they were bored and had nothing better to do were assumed to be doing that because they were nervous and anxiety ridden. The past histories of the pseudopatients were reinterpreted from the standpoint of their psychiatric label, and their present behavior was continually read in light of their presence in a mental hospital.

The experiment was later reversed after officials at one mental hospital, having heard of Rosenhan's finding, protested that he had conducted his experiment at a hospital whose staff was not as highly trained as it should have been. Rosenhan then told them that during the next three months, one or more pseudopatients would attempt to be admitted to their hospital. Each staff member would rate each patient who arrived according to the likelihood that he or she was a pseudopatient. Judgments were obtained on 193 patients who were admitted for psychiatric treatment. Forty-one patients were alleged, with high confidence, to be pseudopatients by at least one member of the staff. But actually, Rosenhan presented *no* pseudopatients to the psychiatric staff for admission. This second experiment is instructive because it shows the overwhelming tendency to see others in the light of some previously held conception. Believing they were in the presence of mental illness, staff members saw pseudopatients as mentally ill. But believing themselves to be in the presence of sanity, they saw that in many places, too.

Rosenhan's astonishing findings demonstrate the power of institutional settings to generate their own conceptual logic, and the author was clearly upset by his own conclusions when he wrote:

> The needs for diagnosis and remediation of behavioral and emotional problems are enormous. But rather than acknowledge that we are just embarking on understanding, we continue to label patients "schizophrenic," "manic-depressive" and "insane," as if in those words we had captured the essence of understanding. The facts of the matter are that we have known for a long time that diagnoses are often not useful or reliable, but we have nevertheless continued to use them. We now know that we cannot distinguish insanity from sanity. It is depressing to consider how that information will be used.... A diagnosis of cancer that has been found to be in error is cause for celebration. But psychiatric diagnoses are rarely found to be in error. The label sticks, a mark of inadequacy forever [1973, 258].

5. The Staff World

Total institutions obviously do not intend to "mortify" the self, lock people up unfairly, or engage in many of the activities and processes we have discussed in this section. They present themselves, instead, as rational, humanitarian organizations designed to accomplish a few socially approved ends (Goffman, 1961a). The official objective of total institutions is the reformation of their inmates in some ideal direction. However, as with all official ends, contradictions occur between what the institution does and what its officials say it does, and this forms the basic context of the staff's daily activity.

Because the products of total institutions are human beings, the occupational prejudices that ordinarily exist have a special significance. Just as an airplane mechanic may not like to work on certain types of aircraft, the staff of total institutions may not like to deal with certain types of people. These prejudices are aggravated by the fact that the contamination felt by the inmate is often transferred to the staff. Therefore, prison guards and sanitarium workers often find themselves to be the objects of the same kind of prejudice that is directed toward inmates. Just as idealism meets its fate in medical school (Becker, H. S., Geer, and Hughes, 1961), the humanitarian ideals of new staff members in total institutions are often eroded by the day-to-day exposure to the realities of the ward or the cell block.

Total institutions have responsibilities to society that make their impact on patients even more devastating. In exchange for taking patients' or convicts' civil liberties away, the institution is supposed to guarantee their safety and well-being while they are in the institution. This means that certain kinds of technically unnecessary standards must be maintained when the products of an institution are human beings. For example, both prison officials and the staff of mental hospitals are often obliged to thwart the suicidal efforts of inmates, even if it means placing them in straitjackets.

Finally, the staff members of total institutions require a rationale to justify the hardships they see themselves as sponsoring every day of their work. Such rationales usually involve the idea that they are necessary to society's welfare—"someone must do this work." In the case of mental hospitals, the medical view of the patient as sick serves to legitimize many forms of treatment that might be suspect if the patient were not regarded as ill (Belknap, 1956).

F. SUMMARY

Deviance and control are ever-present parts of human social relationships, and social science has made a series of efforts to establish the nature of the problems and modes of treatment.

In recent years there has been a significant change in the prevailing conceptions of deviance and control. The oldest and most popular attempt to explain deviant behavior lodges the "cause" of a person's deviance somewhere within him or her. Widespread attempts were made to explain deviance in terms of biological factors that predisposed a person toward deviant behavior. Such factors as body type, shape of the head, genetic and hereditary patterns, and constitutional deficiencies were sought as an explanation for deviant behavior. Added to this were attempts to explain deviance in terms of psychological factors such as early childhood experiences, mood states, sexual conflicts and the like.

These theories that saw deviance as an inherent attribute of the deviant proved to be inadequate because they sought a biologically or psychologically determined explanation to account for conduct whose meaning depends entirely on social definition.

The conception of deviance as a characteristic of certain types of people has been augmented by the view that deviance is a characteristic of certain types of acts. In this view certain acts are inherently deviant because they tend to destroy the society in which they occur. This view suffers from the difficulty of deciding just what acts are injurious to society and which are not. This determination seems to be more political, social, and legal than it is scientific.

A final conception suggests that deviance is part of an interaction process in which not only the act but also the nature of the response to the act must be taken into account. This point of view distinguishes between *primary* and *secondary* deviance—between the initial rule-breaking behavior and the process by which it is seen, reacted to, and incorporated into the role of the deviant.

In addition, an understanding of deviance must take into account the dialectical relationship between deviance and respectability. Deviance exists in part because it is necessary to the definition of respectability. The necessity of moral opposites demonstrates that categories of deviance, while not absolute in their content, must always exist in some form. In addition, deviance has certain social uses, such as economic ones, that mitigate against its eradication.

As a social creation, deviance is made through the exercise of certain social-psychological processes, including degradation ceremonies. Degradation ceremonies may be part of the process by which a person is launched on a deviant career, which includes changes in his or her self-concept. The career develops in a sequential fashion, with different types of explanations being required to account for deviance at different stages of the career.

After a person has been identified as a deviant, he or she may be placed in a total institution and forced to lead a formally administered round of life. Total institutions have a particular relationship to and impact on the self. The person is systematically stripped of his or her old, problematic self, and an attempt is made to replace it with a new, institutionally derived one. This process has serious and profound consequences, especially in mental hospitals, where the patient's behavior tends to be understood in the light of the presumption of mental illness.

The world of the staff is also contaminated by the conception of total institutions in our society. Members are able to sustain their presence on the basis of a rationale that they are doing necessary societal work.

Collective Behavior and Social Movements 14

A. INTRODUCTION

There is no known utopian society. All societies are perceived by their members as having both strengths and weaknesses. And these aspects are actually part of a complicated social process, with the eyes of the beholders as important elements. Attributes of a society that are seen as strengths by some are terrible weaknesses to another. And efforts to overcome the weaknesses and replace them with strengths take many different forms. One of the most dynamic forms of collective behavior is participation in social movements.

All social movements are the result of some form of collective behavior, although not all examples of collective behavior involve social movements. For example, the Woodstock rock festival during the summer of 1969, the occasional fad of swallowing goldfish, and the fashion of wearing zoot suits or raccoon coats are all instances of collective behavior—spontaneous and short-lived behavior engaged in collectively—but none ever became organized into a full-fledged social movement. Social movements, rather, are commonly seen as "collective enterprises to establish a new order of life" (Blumer, 1946, 199) or "socially shared activities and beliefs directed toward the demand for change in some aspect of the social order" (Gusfield, 1970, 2).

The social movement is by no means a new force in society. It has probably been a part of history for as long as human beings have claimed uniqueness and for as long as existence has required the cooperation of other human beings. Today, movements remain an important part of a society. In this chapter we will examine the origin of social movements, their nature, and their characteristics. What purposes do they serve? What kinds of individuals join social movements and why? We will apply this theoretical knowledge to three specific movements: (1) the Black liberation movement, (2) the women's liberation movement, and (3) the gay liberation movement.

B. THEORETICAL PERSPECTIVES ON SOCIAL MOVEMENTS

We might define a social movement as an organization or cluster of organizations whose purpose is changing the established social structure (Orum, 1974; Stallings, 1973). A social movement is, by definition, a dynamic phenomenon and cannot be adequately studied within a static conceptual framework (Lauer, 1972). Theoretical formulations, though, have not always emphasized this dynamic character. On the contrary, structural approaches have sought to identify those factors that initiate a movement (Watson, 1973; Zygmunt, 1972). These approaches seem to fail, however, for at any time we could probably identify factors in society that contribute to unrest. However, it is the *process* that is necessary in order to turn this unrest into a full-scale social movement.

Interactionist theories, although concerned with unrest and social disorganization, generally give more explicit attention to collective processes through which movements arise, develop, maintain themselves, and change. From this perspective, social movements have been viewed as dynamic processes passing through at least four stages: (1) a time of intensified individual stress, (2) a time of cultural and social disorganization, (3) a time of revitalization, and (4) the resultant new order (Dawson and Gettys, 1929).

Within the context of these two broad theoretical perspectives—structural and interactionist—five specific theories have evolved. Each offers a different explanation for the origin and development of social movements: (1) status inconsistency, (2) cumulative deprivation, (3) relative deprivation, (4) rising expectations, and (5) isolation.

1. One-Dimensional Theories

a. Status inconsistency. Consider the following example:

Mrs. Jones is an average North American homemaker. At 30, she has been married eight years to a successful lawyer. They have two children, ages 5 and 7. Although Mrs. Jones has a bachelor's degree in business, she has never worked. At 30, with her family completed and both children in school, she decides to embark on a career. After several unsuccessful interviews Mrs. Jones reluctantly concludes that it is not going to be easy to break into the business world. Additionally, her husband is somewhat distraught with her decision to go to work. Consequently, Mrs. Jones finds herself at a crossroads, feeling intense frustration.

Mrs. Jones is typical of many women who have experienced what Gerhard Lenski (1954) called "status inconsistency." The status-inconsistency thesis has been summarized by Treiman (1966, 651–652):

Social status is multidimensional and hierarchal. Individuals are located in social space in terms of their positions on a variety of dimensions of status—occupation, education, income, ethnicity, etc. Each person occupies a particular status configuration, determined by his location on each of the component dimensions. Thus, some status sets will be "crystallized" in the sense that all of the component statuses give rise to similar values and expectations while others will not. The theory argues that those individuals whose positions on the different dimensions are not crystallized—those whose status memberships give rise to conflicting values and expectations—are likely to experience more strain and tensions than people whose status sets are crystallized.

In more specific terms, Orum (1974) suggested that certain patterns of status inconsistency are more likely to produce psychological tension.

Recognizing the potential usefulness of the theory, Geschwender (1967) proposed that people experiencing status in consistency might seek to end this conflict by committing themselves to radical movements. By aligning themselves with a movement, people hope either to clarify their statuses, thus reducing conflict, or to alter their statuses in concert with the new possibilities offered by the movement. We will see how this can happen in our discussion of the women's liberation movement later in this chapter.

Status inconsistency as a theoretical explanation for the existence of social movements has received some support in the social-psychological literature (Rush, 1967; Hofstadter, 1963; Kelly and Chambliss, 1966; Kenkel, 1956). These explanations generally follow the pattern of showing that members of a social movement experienced status inconsistency before joining and that the movement held out hopes of reducing it. However, the motives for joining a social movement are complex, and generalizations about the relationship between status inconsistency and social movements are premature (Orum, 1974). Before greater claims are made, much more research will have to be done.

b. *Cumulative deprivation.*   Let us return to Mrs. Jones and her search for a job.

> After much persuading, Mrs. Jones finally convinces her husband of her need to work. Through much concerted effort she also finds a job in public relations with a local advertising firm. After a year of work Mrs. Jones has not received a promotion. Furthermore, her salary increases have not been proportional to cost-of-living increases. Needless to say, Mrs. Jones is frustrated.

Cumulative deprivation as a theoretical perspective on social movements suggests that progressive economic impoverishment will eventually create the dissatisfaction necessary to induce participation in social movements. According to this theory, when a person's economic position moves from poor to even poorer, dissatisfaction and discomfort will be experienced. This dissatisfaction will eventually culminate in a full-blown social movement. Union movements can be explained within the context of the cumulative-deprivation theory. In fact, economic insecurity might be cited as a major motive for striking.

Although there is some support for the cumulative-deprivation theory (Zeitlin, 1966; Leggett, 1964), it is quite limited. It is enough to say that the cumulative-deprivation theory appears to be the least popular of the five theoretical perspectives.

c. *Relative deprivation.*

> Mrs. Jones, in her frustration, begins to examine her position in the firm in relation to others. One notable difference is immediately perceived. Most of the

men who began at the same time and in the same position as she have been promoted.

The relative-deprivation thesis suggests that there is an increasing gap between what individuals feel they should get and what they actually get (Geschwender, 1968). In many ways the relative-deprivation perspective can be viewed as similar to cumulative deprivation and status inconsistency. All three imply less-than-ideal conditions. However, cumulative deprivation implies self-assessments based on a comparison of one's own position at various times, whereas relative deprivation results from self-assessment based on comparison with others at various times. And status inconsistency simply seeks to explain the origin of the deprivation, cumulative or relative.

Karl Marx unknowingly introduced the relative-deprivation thesis when he wrote:

> A house may be large or small; as long as the surrounding houses are small it satisfies all social demands for a dwelling. But let a palace arise beside the little house, and it shrinks from a little house to a hut [quoted in Ladd, 1966, 24].

The Black liberation movement has been explained in terms of relative deprivation (Ladd, 1966; Pettigrew, 1964). Searles and Williams (1962), studying the civil rights movement, found that a disproportionate number of participants came from Black, middle-class homes. They speculated that the desire to participate resulted from the deprivation middle-class Black students felt when they compared themselves with middle-class White students.

Not all research has supported the relative-deprivation hypothesis. Orum and Orum (1968), for example, found that Black students from high-education/low-income families were no more likely to participate than other Black students. Thus, before greater credence is given to the relative-deprivation hypothesis, research will have to examine the concept more sensitively.

d. Rising expectations.

Give him an inch and he'll take a mile.

This expression gives the gist of the rising-expectations thesis. The thesis suggests that, if, "because of a partial fulfillment of their ambitions, people are subject to heightened aspirations, they may then become disenchanted by the too gradual improvement of their lot, and channel their discontent in a [political] protest movement" (Orum, 1974, 188). The Black liberation movement has been explained within the framework of rising expectations. Desegregation of schools did not automatically ensure desegregation of housing or equal employment opportunities. Amendment of

Title VII to include sex did not ensure the abolition of sexual discrimination on the job (Bird, 1974). After these changes, Blacks and women were expecting further gains, which did not come as quickly as expected. Thus, the decision to form and participate in a social movement was made.

Although the rising-expectations thesis has been quite popular in the literature, it has received little systematic and intense empirical attention. Certainly, more empirical research is needed.

e. Isolation.   You've heard the old saying "Woman's place is in the home." In many ways this candid opinion reflects the isolation thesis. Isolation may be viewed as the social separation of an individual or group of individuals from others. Kornhauser (1959), in discussing the thesis, noted that social isolation produces an availability for participation in social movements. In other words, a person who is isolated is, by definition, one whose time is not encumbered with very many other group or organizational affiliations and who presumably has the time to participate in a social movement.

Of the five theoretical perspectives the isolation thesis has the least support in the empirical literature. Perhaps it, along with earlier mentioned points of view, could be used to explain the newly formed gray liberation movement. Older persons, with time on their hands and many dissatisfactions, formed a movement to protect their social, political, and economic interests. Until more research is conducted, however, there will remain little verification for this point of view.

2. Toward a Social-Psychological Synthesis

None of the five perspectives we have just discussed has dominated research on social movements. Each has strengths and weaknesses that help it explain some social movements but not others. The theories are not mutually exclusive, which means that researchers must use them carefully, integrating them as they attempt to understand various movements.

a. Orum's synthesis.   Anthony Orum (1974) has done considerable work on social movements. He has synthesized parts of the five theories into an integrated model. According to Orum, four separate mechanisms lead to participation in social movements, each corresponding to a major strand of research.

The first strand is socialization; the mechanism arising out of it is social affinity. People join social movements for one of two reasons: (1) because the espoused purposes of the movement are congruent with their own values and (2) because their friends or associates are drawn into the movement. This particular aspect or segment of the model usually represents the earliest joiners.

The second strand Orum labels the deprivation strand, encompassing cumulative and relative deprivation and rising expectations. People brought into the movement through this mechanism—the relatively deprived—have experienced some setback in life and are looking for new avenues through which their goals can be achieved.

The third strand is derived from the psychopolitical school of research into political behavior. Within political movements, one frequently finds those who are politically effectual: "people who feel they can affect the political system, largely because they have affected it in the past through a variety of channels, particularly through their involvement in political and quasi-political organizations" (Orum, 1974, 196).

The fourth strand is the mass-society perspective; it is useful in identifying the fourth critical segment in protest movements, the periodically unengaged. The basic premise here is that most social movements would never have gotten started without people who had considerable time on their hands.

Orum provided a diagram of this perspective that traces participation in social movements. The model is composed of seven variables (197–199):

1. *Participation* (X_1). This variable refers to the amount of time, activity, or money contributed to a movement.
2. *Political trust* (X_2). This variable refers to a person's belief that the political system is performing its task satisfactorily.
3. *Political efficacy* (X_3). This variable refers to the belief that one can affect what happens in the political system—for example, by joining voluntary associations or writing to one's congressional representatives.
4. *Unstructured work routine* (X_4). This variable designates the amount of flexibility one has in determining when one will work.
5. *Subjective dissatisfaction* (X_5). This variable refers to the belief that one is in some respects deprived. Most often this refers to a discrepancy between one's current situation and one's expectations; sometimes it refers to the belief that one's future will not measure up to one's hopes for it.
6. *Subgroup identification* (X_6). This variable refers to a more or less conscious identification with the subgroup in whose name a political movement, in effect, acts.
7. *Self-esteem* (X_7). This variable refers to a person's sense of self-regard.

Figure 14-1 shows the operation of these seven variables in Orum's four mechanisms leading to participation. The first of these mechanisms, social affinity, is seen to operate through two main lines of influence. The first is indirect, through the formation of political attitudes $(X_6–X_2–X_1)$. The second is direct, through contact with "significant others" $(X_6–X_1)$. The indirect path suggests that some people participate in social movements because they identify with the values of the movement's subgroup. This leads to low political trust, which in turn increases the likelihood that one will participate in a social movement.

The second main route to participation stems from deprivation. Orum hypothesized that subjective dissatisfaction (the operational term for relative deprivation) leads to a low level of political trust, which in turn leads to movement participation $(X_5-X_2-X_1)$.

The third main route to movement participation stems from those who are politically effective, represented by Orum as self-esteem (X_7) and political efficacy (X_3). Persons high in self-esteem sometimes translate this personal attribute into high degrees of political efficacy, which in turn leads to participation in social movements $(X_7-X_3-X_1)$.

The fourth main route to movement participation is direct. People with relatively unstructured work schedules are more apt to become involved in social movements primarily because they have more time (X_4-X_1).

Orum's synthesis makes an important contribution in explaining the origin and development of social movements. His multidimensional theory provides us with a much broader understanding of movement phenomena.

b. *Geschwender's synthesis.* Geschwender offered a somewhat different social-psychological perspective of social movements. He combined Homans' (1950) theory of distributive justice and Festinger's (1957) theory of

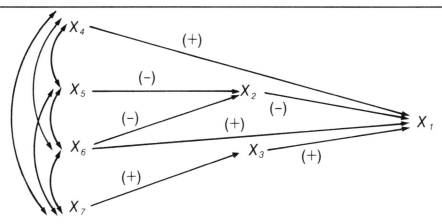

X_1 = Participation
X_2 = Political trust
X_3 = Political efficacy
X_4 = Unstructured work routine
X_5 = Subjective dissatisfaction
X_6 = Subgroup identification
X_7 = Self-esteem

Figure 14-1. A causal model of the antecedents of participation. (From "On Participation in Political Protest Movements," by A. M. Orum. Reproduced by special permission from *The Journal of Applied Behavioral Science*, 1974, *10*, No. 2, Fig. 1, p. 198, NTL Institute for Applied Behavioral Science.

cognitive dissonance to provide a more complete and integrated perspective having seven basic assumptions (Geschwender, 1968, 132):

1. All individuals hold sets of cognitions, including some that are reality based, some that are definitional, and some that are normative.
2. Reality-based cognitions include perceptions of one's status in the educational, occupational, income, and ethnic hierarchies. Definitional cognitions include the definition of ethnicity as an ascribed investment, education as an achieved investment, occupation as a social reward, and income as a material reward. Normative cognitions include the belief that rewards received should be proportional to investments.
3. Any set of cognitions may stand in a relation of dissonance, consonance, or irrelevance, depending on the internal relations that hold among reality-based and normative cognitions. If the conjunction of a reality-based and a normative cognition implies the negation of another reality-based cognition, then a state of dissonance exists.
4. Dissonance is an upsetting state and produces tension for the individual. This tension leads to an attempt to reduce dissonance by altering cognitions or deleting old ones. Attempts to alter reality-based cognitions involve attempting to change the real world.
5. Those with inconsistent statuses who receive rewards less than they believe to be proper for their investments feel anger. Those whose rewards exceed investments feel guilt. Anger is a sharper form of dissonance than guilt. The intensity of dissonance-reducing behavior is directly proportional to the sharpness of dissonance.
6. Dissonance-reducing attempts take the form of coping responses—attempts to change the real world when possible.
7. Dissonance-reducing attempts move from the simple to the complex. The most complex form of attempting to change reality is attempting to alter society.

Using these assumptions, Geschwender derived several predictions concerning the effect of temporal changes in socioeconomic conditions on the origin of social movements:

1. Reality-based cognitions will include perceptions of present socioeconomic circumstances and time lapse between past and present. A higher level of socioeconomic circumstances will be defined as preferable to a lower level of socioeconomic circumstances.
2. Individuals whose present socioeconomic circumstances are at a higher level than past circumstances will be aware of the fact that they have experienced improvement and will define further improvement as possible or desirable. The discrepancy between anticipated future circumstances and present circumstances will produce dissonance. Anticipation of future rate of progress will be determined by rate of past progress (time-lapse cognition).
3. Reality-based cognitions will include perceptions of present and past socioeconomic statuses of relevant reference groups. Comparisons will be

made between rates of progress of self and relevant reference groups. Discrepancies between perceived rates of progress will produce dissonance.

4. Individuals whose present socioeconomic circumstances are at a lower level than past circumstances will be aware that they have experienced a worsening of conditions and will be fearful of further deterioration. A comparison of present circumstances and past circumstances will produce dissonance.

5. Attempts to reduce dissonance will take the form of attempting to change society when it is believed that sufficient power is or can be harnessed to bring this about. They will take a rightist direction when present circumstances are at a lower level than past circumstances and a leftist direction when present circumstances are at a higher level than past circumstances.

6. The intensity of dissonance experienced will be inversely proportional to the time span during which the discrepancies developed and will be directly proportional to the size of the discrepancies. The intensity of attempts at change will be directly proportional to the intensity of dissonance.

7. Change-oriented, dissonance-reducing attempts on the part of those whose statuses are consistent will take a rightist orientation when high ethnic status is combined with lower levels of occupation or income. They will take a leftist orientation when high educational status is combined with a lower level of occupation or income.*

Thus, by synthesizing status inconsistency, dissonance theory, and social-exchange theory, we can provide a somewhat different theoretical perspective of social movements. This perspective is perhaps weakest in its prediction of movement participation as the means of alleviating dissonance. Although it is retrospectively simple to view dissonance as an antecedent to movement participation, it is not so simple to predict at the time that acts of dissonance will result in movement participation. Nonetheless, the theory does provide us with another social-psychological perspective on movement participation.

c. *Zygmunt's motivation model.*   A somewhat different approach to the social psychology of social movements has been offered by Zygmunt (1972). Although not rejecting the structural and interactionist approaches, he contended that more fundamental questions can be answered using motivational analysis. Motivational analysis, as an explanatory perspective of social movements, has focused mainly on the recruitment problem—why people join social movements. Zygmunt wrote that "motivational analysis has primarily taken the form of attempts to establish psychofunctional connections between the properties of social movements (usually construed as 'appeals'), on the one hand, and the social-psychological characteristics of

* Adapted from "Explorations in the Theory of Social Movements and Revolutions," by J. A. Geschwender, *Social Issues*, 1968, 47, 127–135. Copyright © 1968 by The University of North Carolina Press. Used by permission.

potential or actual recruits (generally construed as motivational predispositions), on the other" (451). Zygmunt believed that, for motivational analysis
to be most useful, it must be grounded in several generic properties of
movements (453–454):

1. Social movements originate within concrete historical contexts and are
   conditioned in their development by the sociocultural systems within which
   they seek to operate.
2. Social movements tend to flourish under conditions of social disorganization. Such conditions are likely to be accompanied by or to produce some
   degree of psychological disturbance within individuals and groups in the
   form of alienation, disorientation, deranged motivations, and the like.
3. Social movements have a set of distinctly collective dimensions. Although
   they vary greatly in degree of coordination, they have interindividual, relational, and interactional properties that cannot be reduced to purely intra-
   individual terms.
4. If they are to endure and operate effectively, social movements are obliged
   to develop some kind of organizational structure. They also need a symbolic
   system to coordinate their operations and to maintain continuity.
5. Social movements seek change. Although showing considerable diversity in
   both the explicitness and the content of their goal structures, they typically
   seek, in however groping a fashion, to bring about modification in prevailing institutions, practices, or views.
6. Social movements live and operate in time and are subject to transformations in their ideological and structural designs, as well as in their relations
   to the broader society.*

Additionally, Zygmunt proposed that the use of motivational analysis
to evaluate the recruitment process must be grounded in an adequate
theory of (1) alienation, (2) attraction, (3) conversion, and (4) membership
management. Because a social movement is negatively disposed toward the
prevailing sociocultural system to some degree, a background of alienation
is an important common denominator of all potential recruits. Although
alienation is necessary, it is not sufficient. Therefore, some theory of attraction is also required. Since movement characteristics become appeals, those
individuals exposed to them are motivationally predisposed to perceive,
evaluate, and respond to them directly. Although in the broader sense alienation and attraction involve conversion, a more specific meaning must be
applied to this concept. The process of conversion means resocializing individuals and shaping their predispositions to meet the movement's own organizational requirements. Membership management refers to keeping a
close watch on individuals to ascertain what kind of members they become
or continue to be. Thus, Zygmunt proposed a study of social movements

placed within the context of the broader recruitment process, recognizing the movement's sociocultural context, its interactional character, and its longitudinal span.

Each of these theoretical perspectives offers a somewhat different mode of analysis. Consequently, each gives us a somewhat different view of a social movement. Let us now turn to the application of these theoretical perspectives by examining three movements: (1) the Black liberation movement, (2) the women's liberation movement, and (3) the gay liberation movement.

C. BLACK LIBERATION MOVEMENT

1. Historical Background

Throughout history, Blacks have been the target of prejudice and discrimination. Slaves were imported into the Americas as early as 1501. The treatment of slaves by Whites implied that they were less than human. Whites were human and Blacks were simply slaves. And it was the White man's task to see that this was remembered. This attitude was reflected by a Georgia sheriff less than two decades ago (Way, 1964, 13): "There's nothing like fear to keep the niggers in line."

Although the Civil War brought an end to slavery, it did not bring an end to this kind of prejudice and oppression. Approximately 100 years after the war this prejudice and oppression were exemplified by separate restrooms for Blacks and Whites, separate drinking fountains, separate schools, and job discrimination. It was this deep-rooted prejudice and primarily this oppressive behavior that Blacks were determined to confront. Out of their frustrations and determinations the civil rights movement was born (Nelson, 1974). This movement was the forerunner of the Black liberation movement and has been characterized as the most significant social movement of the 1960s (Nelson, 1971).

2. Origin of the Movement

The beginning of the civil rights movement dates back to the U.S. Supreme Court's decision to desegregate the schools in 1954. In 1964 further hope was offered to the Blacks with the passage of a strong federal Civil Rights Act. But even these did not alleviate the discrimination. As late as 1964 numerous schools remained separate and unequal. As a result, unrest rose. Consequently, the late 1950s and the early 1960s were characterized by many nonviolent marches and sit-ins. One of the leading advocates of nonviolence was the late Dr. Martin Luther King, Jr., leader of the Southern Christian Leadership Conference. With his violent death, restlessness increased. For many, progress was simply too slow and the price was too high. They could not see Dr. King's dream becoming a reality. Thus, they talked more of revolutionary changes and retaliatory violence. The movement continued but with a new name—the Black liberation movement. Its leaders and followers are, today, committed to fighting for Blacks' freedom and rights.

Thus, we can characterize the Blacks' drive for freedom as two distinct movements (Skolnick, 1969). The civil rights movement began in the 1950s and continued to the mid-1960s. The Black liberation movement began in the mid-1960s and continues to the present. In comparing the two movements, Skolnick (1969) noted four major differences:

1. The civil rights movement was directed at Southern legal and social practices. The Black liberation movement concentrates on the Black slums of big cities.
2. The civil rights movement opposed those facets of racism ingrained in culture (separatism). The liberation movement focuses on more stubborn and firmly rooted sources of racism. It stresses independence instead of integration.
3. The civil rights movement was composed primarily of middle-class Blacks and Whites. The Black liberation movement has rejected White leadership and has tried to attract lower- as well as middle-class Blacks.
4. The civil rights movement was dedicated to nonviolence. The Black liberation movement advocates self-defense and attainment of freedom by any means.*

3. Organizations in the Movement

The first of several organizations formed to aid the Blacks in their quest for freedom was the National Association for the Advancement of Colored People (1910). This organization was largely the result of W. E. B. Du Bois's efforts to champion freedom for Blacks. Du Bois (1868–1963) embraced the "Black is beautiful" theme and sought to encourage and develop pride among Blacks. Other civil rights organizations formed since include the Congress of Racial Equality, the National Urban League, the Student Nonviolent Coordinating Committee, the Southern Christian Leadership Conference, and People United to Save Humanity.

4. Discussion

Having seen how this social movement evolved, we will now examine it in light of the earlier mentioned theoretical perspectives.

Beginning with status inconsistency, we might look at two important characteristics: race and education. When educated Blacks are unable to obtain jobs for which they are qualified, simply because they are Black, we can expect status inconsistency to develop. When Blacks compare their po-

*From *Politics and Protest*, by J. H. Skolnick. Copyright 1969 by Simon & Schuster, Inc. Reprinted by permission.

Dr. Martin Luther King was a leading advocate of non-violence. (Photo © Wide World Photos)

sitions in life to those of their White counterparts, we can expect the resulting perception to be one of relative deprivation. Cumulative deprivation could very well be perceived when Blacks compare their own positions in life over a period of years. Isolation is exemplified in the segregation or separatism that was the watchword of the 1950s and early '60s. But with the Supreme Court's 1954 decision, Blacks were given some hope (rising expectations). Unfortunately, things did not happen as quickly as anticipated. Thus, Blacks were very ready for a social movement.

Orum's model can also be applied to the Black liberation movement. We might reason that Du Bois's "Black is beautiful" theme was internalized by many Blacks through the process of socialization. However, the theme seemed to directly contradict the perceptions of White culture (relative deprivation). Thus, middle-class Blacks (more likely to be unstructured in their work schedules) initiated a movement to destroy this injustice. These Blacks were joined by many who identified with the values of the movement.

Geschwender's model offers us a somewhat different perspective of the movement. Blacks, like Whites, are socialized to believe in the American Dream. After all, the Declaration of Independence does declare all men to be created equal. Since, in reality, there is little equality, dissonance is created. To alleviate this dissonance, Blacks have organized to change reality, thus giving birth to a social movement.

Zygmunt's motivational model offers us some insight into the recruitment process. The U.S. was ripe for a Black social movement. In the 1950s, the culture was dominated by Whites; Blacks were alienated from that culture. As Dr. Martin Luther King, Jr. wrote from his jail cell, how do you explain to a tearful little girl why she cannot go to the local amusement park? The movement was attractive because it provided Blacks with a new philosophy and a new positive identity. Blacks were resocialized to believe "Black is beautiful." The success of the movement is perhaps best demonstrated by the fact that it has proved to be the prototype of many other social movements (Johnson, 1974).

As you can see, these theories are neither mutually exclusive nor logically exhaustive. Each provides us with a somewhat different perspective of the Black movement as we attempt to view and understand its role in society.

D. WOMEN'S LIBERATION MOVEMENT

1. Historical Background

The historical inequality of the sexes is expressed in the following characterization: "Men are defined by their achievements and associations outside of the home. Women are defined by their men or absence of men."

Freud depicted the inequality of the sexes in his classic view of femininity (Wesley, 1975, 120):

1. *Anatomy is destiny:* Woman's nature is determined solely by her anatomy, specifically by the fact that she does not have a penis. Thus, the formation of the female's personality is influenced by her ability to reproduce. The psychologically normal woman is concerned chiefly with the roles of wife and mother.

2. *Penis envy:* Because she does not have a penis, the female child considers herself defective and is therefore naturally envious of the male. The woman's clitoris is inadequate to provide libidinal gratification, and this loss is only partially compensated for by the possibility of giving birth to a male child.

3. *Faulty development of the superego:* Just as the feminine castration complex pushes the girl away from her mother into an Oedipal attachment with her father, the male castration complex pushes the boy away from his father and to his mother. Because the girl has more difficulty resolving the Oedipal conflict, she has a lesser capacity for sublimation.

4. *Masochism and passivity:* As a result of the woman's general feelings of inferiority and inadequacy, aggressiveness is focused inward, which results in a masochistic personality. Furthermore, because of her sexual role as a receptor, the woman naturally develops passive tendencies in all social roles.*

For Freud, woman was the "abnormal" sex (Slaby and Sealy, 1973). And this biologically rooted inferiority seemed to confirm women's social inferiority. This inferiority is quite apparent in the writings of Edwin Aderman, who during a tour in North Carolina in 1889 wrote that "the idea largely prevails here that women need no education, that they were intended for house-work" (Eaton, 1974, 188). Women were designed for procreation, and they were to stay home and dutifully carry out this role. Women were to refrain from speaking out in public. They were to be submissive to their husbands' authority. So oppressive was the woman's position in life that her fate has been described as analogous to that of Blacks.

2. Origin of the Movement

The contemporary women's liberation movement can be traced to two rather timely events: (1) the publication of Betty Friedan's (1963) book *The Feminine Mystique* and (2) the addition of the word *sex* to Title VII of the 1964 Civil Rights Act (Freeman, 1973). The importance of these two events was realized on June 30, 1966:

> The occasion was the last day of the Third National Conference of [state] Commissions on the Status of Women, ironically titled "Targets for Action." ... The opportunity came with a refusal by conference officials to bring to the floor a proposed resolution that urged the EEOC [Equal Employment Opportunity Commission] to give equal enforcement to the sex provision of Title VII

*From "The Women's Movement and Psychotherapy," by C. Wesley, *Social Work*, 1975, *20*, 120–124. Copyright 1975 by the National Association of Social Workers. Reprinted by permission.

as was given to the race provision. Despite the fact that these state commissions were not federal agencies, officials replied that one government agency could not be allowed to pressure another. The small group of women who had desired the resolution had met the night before in a hotel room to discuss the possibility of a civil rights organization for women. Not convinced of its need, they chose instead to propose the resolution. When the resolution was vetoed, the women held a whispered conversation over lunch and agreed to form an action organization "to bring women into full participation in the mainstream of American Society now, assuming all the privileges and responsibilities thereof in truly equal participation with men." The name NOW [National Organization for Women] was coined by Friedan, who was at the conference researching her second book. Before the day was over, 28 women paid $5.00 each to join [Freeman, 1973, 798–799].*

Carolyn Stoloff has accurately captured the theme of the movement, and this theme is corroborated by Ryckman and colleagues (1972) and Mahoney (1975):

Women's liberation is a political and social movement founded *by* women *for* women. . . . The movement seeks a redefinition of femininity and masculinity to denote not what men and women are expected to be, but what they are capable of becoming when freed from the traditional sex-linked roles which limit their potential for full emotional and intellectual development. . . . It critically examines existing patterns of social order, such as monogamous marriage, the nuclear family, and the capitalistic structure of the economy, and proposes radical alternatives [Stoloff, 1973, 325–326].

3. Organizations in the Movement

One of the first organizations formed to help alleviate the oppression of women was the Woman's Christian Temperance Union (WCTU). This organization was directed under the able leadership of Frances Willard, who worked for obtaining the vote for women as a means of abolishing the saloons. The WCTU was followed by a surge of similar organizations also fighting for women's suffrage: the League of Women Voters, the National Consumers League, and the General Federation of Women's Clubs. Acquisition of the right to vote saw a waning of the movement. In the 1960s, though, the movement was revitalized.

The contemporary women's liberation movement does not have tightly knit organizations. On the contrary, the new movement manifests itself in an almost infinite variety of groups, styles, and organizations. This diversity is reflected in the two major branches of the movement, often called "reform" and "radical," or "women's rights" and "women's liberation" (Hole and Levine, 1971). The reform branch, which is concerned primarily with

*From "The Origins of the Women's Liberation Movement," by J. Freeman, *American Journal of Sociology*, 1973, *78*, 792–811. Copyright 1973 by The University of Chicago Press. Reprinted by permission.

the problems of working women, is represented organizationally by NOW. The style of organization tends to be traditionally formal, with elected officers, boards of directors, bylaws, and other elements of the democratic procedure. The radical group consists of numerous small groups (for example, WITCH—Women's International Terrorist Conspiracy from Hell) engaged in a variety of activities (Laudicina, 1973). Basically abhorring the idea of leadership, they convey the message of everyone's doing her own thing.

4. Who Joins Women's Liberation?

Several studies have attempted to characterize women who join the movement (Cherniss, 1972; Goldschmidt et al., 1974; Stoloff, 1973). Stoloff succinctly described them:

> The Women's Liberation Movement members studied appeared to be outgoing, politically and socially gregarious women from relatively nonreligious, middle or upper-middle class, urban or suburban backgrounds, in whose homes liberal political opinion was given frequent expression. They tend to place high valuation on humanitarianism and personal autonomy and are strongly motivated to create conditions under which it will be possible for them to lead full

The women's movement has involved women of all ages. (Photo by © Eric Kroll, Taurus Photos)

and productive lives. Moreover, far from being sexually frustrated, antagonistic, and man-hating, most movement women studied appear to be sexually liberated persons who do not feel it necessary to offend men in order to defend women. While acknowledging their need for men, they do not deny their own needs and aspirations, nor undermine those attributes and personal characteristics which run counter to traditional definitions of femininity but on which are founded their self-respect and self-acceptance [338–339].*

5. Discussion

Status inconsistency, as a theoretical perspective, offers the same explanatory effectiveness for women as for Blacks. Again, we are dealing with both an ascribed characteristic (sex) and an achieved characteristic (education). When females are denied equal employment opportunities, simply because they are female, frustrations develop. In many cases women holding the same jobs as men are paid less (relative deprivation). And while men are being promoted and advanced to higher salaries, women are frequently left unacknowledged (cumulative deprivation). Social isolation is also experienced by women, though not as severely as by Blacks. Universities and clubs have admitted males exclusively. This sense of separatism might be viewed as a motivating force of the movement. With the passage of Title VII, women's hopes and aspirations were raised. However, progress was slow, providing another motivating force.

Using motivational analysis, we might reason that the alienation of women from equality with men in a predominantly man's world helped to spur the movement's birth. The appeal of the organization to women was its emphasis on equality. Women who joined were resocialized to believe in the humanity (not maleness or femaleness) of every individual. The movement maintains its membership in part through consciousness-raising groups (Wesley, 1975; Barrett et al., 1974).

Let us now turn to a social movement that is quite different from either the Black movement or the women's movement—the gay liberation movement.

E. GAY LIBERATION MOVEMENT

1. Historical Background

The gay subculture presents a contrast to the Black subculture and the female subculture. Being Black or female simply reflects one's biological makeup. Being gay is much more complex. There is no biological characteristic that determines the appropriateness of this label. Rather, it is based upon one's behavior patterns—a sexual preference for one's own sex.

In a traditionally heterosexual society, homosexuality poses a threat to the conservative and narrow-minded "straight" person (Killinger, 1971). In a society founded on Christian principles that teach procreation as the purpose for sexual relations, homosexuality seems without purpose. Consequently, homosexuals have been viewed as deviant individuals who are psychologically sick (Lyons, 1973). They have been counseled to seek psychiatric aid to help them redefine their sexual preferences. The prejudice facing this group has been so vast that, in the past, gays have preferred to remain anonymous (closet homosexuals). Since the late 1960s and early '70s, though, gays have been stepping out of their closets to make their sexual preferences known. By doing this, they hope to eradicate the prejudice and stigma surrounding the name *homosexual*.

2. Origin of the Movement

The gay liberation movement was founded in San Francisco in the late 1960s by Gale Whittington and Leo Laurence (Killinger, 1971). Its history has been stormy. One of the calmer events of the movement occurred in 1968, when the Reverend Troy Perry, a fundamentalist preacher, and a small group of friends met in Los Angeles and decided to form a church to minister largely to the homosexual community (Enroth, 1974). This group formed a quasi-denominational structure known as the Universal Fellowship of Metropolitan Community Churches.

The gay movement was not readily accepted by traditionalists—certainly not by the police, who provided frequent harassment. By 1969, though, gays were no longer quietly tolerant of such treatment. New York City gays, as well as straights who lived in the area, turned on the police and attacked them when they came to investigate a neighborhood bar (the Stonewall riots). In that same year a number of male homosexuals, members of the Gay Liberation Front, announced their intent to settle in Alpine County, California, and take over the government. Thus, they reasoned, they would no longer be subject to discrimination and legal sanctions. Local residents, including the county sheriff, vowed this would never happen. They expressed the opinion that homosexuals are immoral, unsavory characters who would be a threat to the basic values of the inhabitants (Dressler, 1973). Local resistance and, perhaps, the inherent impracticality of the project, led to its ultimate failure, but it was a significant event in the history of the movement.

The year 1969 also saw the publication of the Gay Manifesto, which accurately addressed the repressions to which gays had been submitting. The publication stressed the need for gay individuals to exorcise their guilt. It concluded with the following challenge (Killinger, 1971, 716):

1. Free ourselves; come out everywhere; initiate self-defense and political activity; initiate counter community institutions.

2. Turn other gay people on; talk all the time; understand; forgive; accept.
3. Free the homosexual in everyone; we'll be getting a good bit of shit from threatened latents; be gentle and keep talking and acting free.
4. We've been playing an act for a long time, so we're consummate actors. Now we can begin to *be* and it'll be a good show.

Killinger (1971) summarized the movement's perspective (716): "The development of this new life style entails new ways of looking at self and world, and therefore signals the development of new attitudes toward the problems of repression that have hounded the gay community throughout recent history."

3. Organizations in the Movement

The gay liberation movement is represented by such organizations as Mattachine, Gay Activist, and Gay Liberation Front (Ivey, 1972). Across the United States on endless college campuses, gays have applied for charters. However, the issue of a gay organization on campus remains quite controversial. At the University of Missouri, for example, gays were refused a charter. When challenged in the courts, the university's decision was upheld. When the University of Tennessee's refusal to administer a charter was challenged, however, the court ruled in favor of the gay liberationists and ordered the university to grant a charter.

Perhaps the most legitimizing forces for the movement are the religious organizations. There are more than 40 Metropolitan Community Church congregations in the United States. The group has organized its own seminary in Los Angeles, and it has assisted a Jewish group in the establishment of a gay synagogue—the Metropolitan Community Temple. Roman Catholics have also organized a gay religious group, known as Dignity. Perhaps surprisingly, religion seems to be a central force in gays' decision to reveal their "secret."

4. Discussion

Let us attempt to view the gay liberation movement within the context of the theoretical perspectives discussed earlier. We can begin by eliminating status-inconsistency theory, because there is no ascribed status involved. One variable that we must be concerned with in applying movement theories to gay liberation is visibility. Blacks are visible. Women are visible. They can be identified immediately. Gay people are not so easily identified. And it is not until they are identified that prejudice and discrimination become overt. For gays who make their sexual preferences public, job discrimination is a central problem (cumulative deprivation and relative deprivation). They are also ostracized by the majority of heterosexuals (isolation).

Do male or female homosexuals generate more hostility toward their cause? Why? (Photos by © Ian Berry, Magnum Photos, and by © Alex Webb, Magnum Photos)

Using Geschwender's model, we might use the following line of reasoning. Heterosexuals view homosexuals as sick. In contrast, homosexuals view themselves as normal. They simply reason that sexual preferences do not make one either sick or normal. Consequently, cognitive dissonance is experienced. Alleviation of this dissonance has taken the form of the gay liberation movement. One of the movement's slogans, "Free the sister in ourselves," expresses the need to dissolve dissonance (Keith, 1974). This slogan stresses the need for each individual to liberate all of himself or herself, thus eradicating the notion of sick or normal.

Zygmunt's motivational-analysis model also provides a viable explanation of the recruitment process. Both closet and public homosexuals are alienated individuals. They are socially and psychologically ostracized. A part of this isolation may be self-induced and result from low self-worth, because these individuals have been taught to believe they are "different." The appeal of the organization is restored positive self-worth. This appeal is quite apparent in the Reverend Troy Perry's favorite slogan, "God loves me, too" (Perry, 1972). Those attracted to the movement are resocialized (converted) to believe in their own self-worth and to be proud of their gayness. "Say it out loud" has become the watchword of young people who have learned to express their sexual preferences openly. These good feelings are frequently reinforced through consciousness-raising groups (Chesebro et al., 1973).

F. SUMMARY

No society exists in a perfect state. No doubt this is largely due to the fact that individuals are different. What might be considered perfect for one would be imperfect for another. These perceived imperfections cause some individuals to seek change. Such efforts frequently take the form of social movements.

Numerous theories have been set forth to explain social movements. Among the earlier and simpler perspectives, five seem most prominent: (1) status inconsistency, (2) cumulative deprivation, (3) relative deprivation, (4) rising expectations, and (5) isolation. Status-inconsistency theory rests on the premise that incongruence between an ascribed and an achieved status will result in dissonance. Cumulative-deprivation theory suggests that progressive economic impoverishment will eventually create the dissatisfaction necessary to induce participation in a social movement. The relative-deprivation thesis suggests that there is an increasing gap between what individuals feel they should get and what they actually get. According to the rising-expectations theory, if ambitions are partially fulfilled, individuals may become disenchanted with the too-gradual fulfillment of their lot, thus setting the scene for a social movement. Isolation—the separatism of a group of individuals from others—produces an availability for participation in a social movement.

These five theoretical perspectives provide us with simplistic, one-dimensional explanations of social-movement phenomena. In an effort to overcome the explanatory limitations of this simplicity, Orum and Geschwender proposed independent and somewhat different models that attempt to integrate the simpler perspectives. Using a somewhat different approach, Zygmunt proposed a motivational model incorporating alienation, attraction, conversion, and membership management to explain the broader recruitment process.

Applying these various theoretical perspectives, three current social movements were examined: (1) the Black liberation movement, (2) the women's liberation movement, and (3) the gay liberation movement.

The roots of the Black liberation movement can be found in the time of slavery. The exploitation and oppression of Blacks had been loathed not only by Blacks but by many Whites. The freeing of slaves following the Civil War did not end this oppression. One hundred years later, Whites were still discriminating against Blacks. The Supreme Court's 1954 decision to end segregation in the schools did not prove to be immediately successful. Neither did the Civil Rights Act of 1964. Consequently, Blacks were left little recourse but to fight, both nonviolently and violently, for their human rights.

The women's liberation movement bears some similarity to the Black movement. Whereas Blacks faced discrimination because of their color, females faced discrimination because of their sex. The contemporary women's movement originated in June 1966. A group of women attending the Third National Conference of Commissions on the Status of Women was seeking enforcement of the sex provision of the 1964 Civil Rights Act. When their resolution was vetoed, they decided to form a formal group—the National Organization for Women. Today, women's liberation has two main factions, reform and radical. The reform branch strives for the advancement of women's rights, and the radical branch espouses a do-your-own-thing philosophy.

Gay liberationists differ from Black liberationists and women's liberationists in one very important respect: visibility. Whereas Blacks are easily distinguished by their color and women are easily distinguished by their sex, gays have no distinguishing biological characteristics. They are simply individuals, both males and females, whose sexual preferences are for members of their own sex. Until the late 1960s such sexual practices were usually kept secret because of prejudice and discrimination. In the late 1960s, though, the gay subculture came to reject the notion that a homosexual is a sick person. Rather, it espoused the position that the homosexual is an individual whose sexual preferences run counter to the average (as opposed to the term *normal*). They professed their self-worth in the eyes of God and man as they set about to reeducate the public on homosexuality.

Such movements are vital sources of social change in society. Through them, people are able to effect rapid change—change that might otherwise be evolutionary instead of revolutionary. We might reason, as did Gamson (1974), that fighting gets you where you want to go. Social movements keep us continuously aware of the uniqueness of human beings in a dynamic society.

Section Five

Overview

But the world is not just <u>in fact</u> immeasurably more complicated than the laboratory; the complexity is a condition of any life we would think worth living.

A. R. Louch

Social Psychology: Problems and Promises 15

A. INTRODUCTION: A DIVIDED FIELD

As the Latin dramatist Terence put it, "nothing human is foreign to me." This is the stance taken by social psychologists as they approach human conduct. Like every other line of human endeavor, social psychology operates   389 in an atmosphere filled with problems. Many of the statements we have made in the text are problematic. They represent the best available knowledge and interpretation at a given time, but other possibilities are always on the horizon. In this last chapter we want to take a look at some of the problems in and with social psychology. We will then offer a discussion of the promises of the discipline and trace some of the future directions it might take.

Social psychology has had and, we suspect, will continue to have a difficult time carving out a distinct professional identity. Born as a bridge between psychology and sociology, it now has a home in both academic departments. And the assumptions, theories, and methods it uses may still bear the stamp of those parent disciplines. There remain two types of social psychology—psychological and sociological—and there may be little overlap or interaction between the two. In fact, one of the more interesting encounters a teaching social psychologist has is when he or she confronts the dean to justify a student's receiving credit for a social-psychology course in sociology when the student has had a course with the same title in the psychology department. The two courses often bear little resemblance to each other.

The problem of a consistent identity for social psychology is also, however, the basis of much of the vibrance and intellectual ferment in the field. Social psychology's diversity means that a wide range of theoretical propositions, assumptions, methods, and concerns are available to the working researchers. When one is trying to understand social behavior, having too many different ideas is much less troublesome than not having enough. As it turns out, many of the conflicts between sociologically and psychologically oriented social psychologists are really a matter of terminology, a point we will discuss in detail momentarily.

B. PROBLEMS OF THEORY

1. Multiplicity

The largest single problem social psychologists deal with is the welter of theoretical orientations to be sorted out within the discipline. Brissett and Edgley stated the problem this way:

> To many people, the most bewildering aspect of the field stems from the great many theoretical orientations encompassed by the term "social psychology." Owing much to the interdisciplinary character of the field, theoretical orientations have proliferated. Social psychology has become a "no-man's land" in which scholars from sociology, psychology, anthropology, and elsewhere have tried their hands at constructing their own unique version of reality. As a result, the student is confronted with a rather remarkable range of "truth." Too often it appears that a valid explanation by one social psychologist is dismissed as irrelevant trivia by another [1975, 1].

The problem of proliferation of orientations, as we have said, is caused partly by the complexity of the subject matter. Another factor, however, is the multiple-paradigm status of social psychology. Multiple paradigms, such as those we have discussed in this text, generate different kinds of observations and interpretations, often making it difficult or even impossible to compare observations across paradigms. Nevertheless, there are distinct advantages to a multiple-paradigm approach.

The existence of multiple theories suggests that science is a social process in which findings represent the application of assumptions and the comparison of empirical results within the framework of those assumptions. For example, in our discussion of theories of deviance in Chapter 13, we contrasted psychological and biological theories with social ones. However, these comparisons were all made from a particular point of view (the interactionist perspective). Therefore, if we applied a different paradigm, different conclusions might well be the result. Let us say that we assume (from political research) that legislators make laws primarily as a function of political pressure that is independent of any evaluation of the need to control aberrant behavior. It is reasonable to assume, therefore, that no biological or psychological determinants of the aberrant behavior could have caused the legislation. However, we might assume that the legislative process is based on biased perceptions of the need to control certain kinds of behavior. It would then be not at all unreasonable to expect that the laws that are passed might very well correlate with the biological/psychological nature of persons committing those acts. This is but one of many examples we could use to show that theoretical controversies within social psychology are primarily the result of differing assumptions about both subject matter and human nature in general (Wrightsman, 1974).

2. Relevance

One of the reasons why theory is so important is that it is the business of asking questions, and the questions we ask establish the relevance of our observations (Stone and Farberman, 1970). The problem of question asking in social-psychological theory is that social "reality" is really inexhaustible, a point made persuasively by studies in anthropology. The nature of our questions inevitably gives rise to particular kinds of answers, so that our questions must be selected with great care. The very objects of our inquiry are brought into being by the kinds of questions we formulate.

The relevance of a particular observation, then, will be established by the nature of the question asked, and the conceptualization made. Whether people even see a particular object (physical or social) can be related to whether or not they see any relevant relationship between themselves and the object. Stone demonstrated this by asking students in his social-psychology course to write letters to friends in which they listed the three most important features of their classroom. Three weeks later they were asked to imagine that they were now social psychologists and to write a letter to another social psychologist about what was in the room. The objects of their observations changed radically. In the first series of letters, to friends, virtually all of the students described various physical objects in the room (lights, windows, blackboards). In the second series of letters many more students observed various kinds of human behavior going on in that same room. "Behavior was observed only after it became relevant to the student" (Stone and Farberman, 1970).

Additional questions about relevance are often asked. Questions of validity aside, some people simply do not feel that an understanding of social psychology contributes anything of importance to their comprehension of everyday life. These questions of relevance center on several themes. First, the charge is often made that social psychology is not really generalizable, or at least not on a par with the laws of physical science. Secondly, it is alleged that there has not been very much progress in social psychology, for what we know about human behavior now is not substantially different from what some perceptive observers knew 400 years ago.

These are difficult charges to address, because relevance is such an intensely personal matter. However, it is relatively easy to show that social psychology can yield some highly significant and even profound observations, even if it does not always do so. Admittedly, social psychology is not on a par with the physical and natural sciences in the number of "laws" that it can enumerate. This is due to several dilemmas, not the least of which is the fact that social psychology has not had nearly as much time as the rest of science to develop its theory and methodology. In addition, as this book should have proved, social psychology is in many ways far more complex than natural science. Imagine how different geology and botany would be if rocks and trees had their own ideas about why they do the things they do. The fact that human beings are self-reflective changes the equation dramatically and makes the scientific study of them considerably more complicated.

Another variation of the charge that social psychology is not very relevant is that its observations tend to be nothing more than "what everybody already knows anyway." Since the objects of social psychology have to do with everyday life, many of its statements and conclusions are naturally going to be recognizable to almost anyone—as opposed to organic chemistry, whose double helix is still comprehensible only to a few. Because social psychology can communicate its findings in terms that are understandable to anyone in reasonable command of a common language does not mean that its findings are irrelevant, unless we mean that relevance must necessarily be esoteric! We might add that many concepts in social psychology that are now readily accepted were not nearly so well understood when they were first articulated. Much of the Freudian perspective was rejected by the lay public as nonsense when it first came on the scene but is seen as quite reasonable now, even by those who have had little education (Seeley, 1967). In fact, one of the continuing problems in social psychology is how to redress the inadequacies in a theoretical perspective such as Freudianism after it has been so pervasively accepted by the lay public.

Despite what we have just said in response to these charges of irrelevance, we must admit that there is a continuous struggle within social psychology over applied versus pure research. Many of the perspectives and theories we have discussed in this book remain somewhat abstract and difficult to apply directly to such everyday concerns as poverty, war, racism, or even how to make a dime or win a spouse. Applied research is directed toward the solution to some particular problem, whereas pure research is more concerned with the delineation of general processes without any necessary interest in application. What must be stressed, however, is the interrelationship between applied and theoretical pursuits. Every concrete, applied project in social psychology must be grounded in a theoretical base that exists, usually, because someone was free to work on the theory unencumbered by immediate, practical needs. In any case, applications can hardly be reached in a theoretical void. Theoretical ignorance does not usually breed adequate solutions.

C. PROBLEMS OF METHODOLOGY

As we have argued throughout this book, methodological problems cannot really be separated from theoretical ones. The two intertwine in the researcher's attempt to find out about the social world. Nonetheless, rather specific questions about technique continually arise. These questions, concerning how the researcher went about doing the studies that generated particular observations and conclusions, tend to center on the general question of *validity*.

1. Criteria of Validity

While technical discussions of validity have traditionally been confined to social psychologists, such controversies are beginning to spill over and are now taking place among well-educated lay persons. Borrowing from Stone and Farberman (1970), we may note that debates over validity generally center on three conventional criteria for establishing the validity of a social-psychological statement. The three are universality, logical coherence, and consensus of the competent. None of these is being adequately met at the present time.

a. *Universality.* The criterion of universality requires that statements made hold true (that is, can be reestablished by replication) from one time to another and one place to another. Therefore, in order to be valid, a statement made by a social psychologist ought to apply both cross-culturally and historically. Such a statement is, obviously, very difficult to make. While many cross-cultural studies exist, many have been predicated on the basis of questions that are not strictly those of social psychology. Those that have been social-psychological in their emphasis have not shown that universality can be realistically achieved (Stone and Farberman, 1970).

And if it is difficult to show that social psychology has validity cross-culturally, our attempts to show that our statements apply historically present problems that are overwhelming. In the first place, recorded history constitutes only a fraction of all history, so "historical" data are really very recent data. Secondly, the further we go back in recorded history, the more specialized do accounts of human conduct become. This is because in early recorded history only the economically and socially privileged classes were able to write. We know very little about how the rest of society lived except what the higher classes tell us. More importantly, meanings change drastically from period to period. And social psychologists, like other scholars who make use of historical data, fall prey to imputing current meanings and interpretations to past events. As Stone asked, for example, how can we arrive at historically valid generalizations about the socialization of children when there is reason to believe that the social notion *child* did not even exist until certain events in 17th-century Europe brought it about? Similarly, when we impute contemporary motives to historical figures, are we not really deluding ourselves (Stone and Farberman, 1970)?

The fact that universality will probably never be achieved by social psychology does not, of course, mean that we ought to abandon it as an ideal. The quest for universals encourages both historical and cross-cultural study that, at its best, enlarges the horizons in which our observations might apply. More importantly, it also serves as a check on observations that are culturally and historically biased.

b. *Logical coherence.*   Another criterion of validity is that statements should not contradict each other. They should be logical. Once again, social psychology, as well as most other scientific endeavors, is deficient on at least two counts. First, logical contradictions can be found in most scientific work. Physical science and social science are both riddled with logical inconsistencies. In fact it seems that, the more compelling a piece of scientific work is, the more likely it is to be rejected (at least initially) as logically absurd. Certainly Einstein's version of science was seen in this way by the Newtonians at the turn of the century. The reason for this seems to be that all logic is based on a set of linguistic rules, or grammar. Therefore, statements that depart from these rules or follow a different set will be seen as illogical.

The entire idea of a logic seems in many ways to be an ethnocentric bias on the part of the user. To be logical is to use one particular type of grammar consistently. The problem, however, lies in the fact that there are many other grammars than our own. Why should Greek grammar—the one we know best in this part of the world—be exclusively used when other logical grammars not only exist but also seem superior in many ways to our own? Ideas of cause and effect, subject and object, appearance and reality—all important dualisms in Western thought—seem to stem directly from the imperatives of language and seem logical only by virtue of the use of those languages. To say, then, that a statement is "logical" means only that it adheres to the rules laid down by a particular grammar.

c. *Consensus of the competent.*   The final criterion of validity is that those who should know about a statement agree it is valid. This is the criterion most often used, and it is perhaps the least satisfying. In human affairs what is finally valid in any situation depends on who lines up in support of a statement. Those who are skilled, trained, or experts are generally believed when statements are made, rather than those who are unskilled or untrained. This criterion of validity can clearly be seen operating in natural and physical science, and Kuhn's work that we discussed in the first chapter offers ample evidence that this is the case (Kuhn, 1960). The consensus that exists about certain matters in the physical sciences, however, seems almost universal (although of course it isn't) compared with the level of consensus that can be found in the social sciences.

In social psychology, as we have shown throughout this book, there are various perspectives concerning the interpretation of human behavior. As a result there is little, if any, consensus about the validity of a particular statement. What seems to be a profound and valid statement to one social psychologist is often dismissed as useless trivia by another. There do exist pockets of consensus (typically called schools of thought) within social psychology, but there does not exist any overriding, basic consensus among social psychologists. Therefore, any statement made is open to question, and all statements are validated in terms of some particular framework of interpretation. This means that there is a political dimension to truth, consensus being something that is struggled over, won or lost, momentary, never fixed (Stone and Farberman, 1970). For all of these reasons, validity in social psychology is a fleeting matter.

2. Deficiencies in Subject or Experimenter

There are additional problems with the validity of social psychology. Much of the field has an experimental cast. That is, statements are made and conclusions are reached on the basis of experiments conducted by the social psychologist using human subjects. Aside from the ethical issues raised by such experimentation (a subject we will address later in this chapter) many questions of validity can also be raised concerning these studies. As Schneider (1976) has pointed out, the typical subject for much of the research reported in the literature of social psychology is a naive college sophomore. Most social psychologists are also college professors, and their research is conducted not with extensive funding but more often on a shoe-string. Therefore, practical considerations often dictate that students be used for experiments later reported in the literature as social-psychological truth. The college sophomore is ideal because he or she is not likely to question the purpose of the experiment, doing it merely as part of a course being taken.

Obviously, college students represent a terribly biased sample. They have been found to be much more likely than the general population to be smart, rich, first-born, middle class, White, and prone to cooperate. Moreover, many of the variables that social psychologists point out as influencing human behavior—such as mood, color, tone, definition of the situation, and even the temperature and humidity of the room in which the experiment is carried out—are often ignored when social psychologists conduct their own experiments about the attitudes and behavior of their own subjects.

In addition, as we pointed out in the first chapter, experimenter bias continues to be an important issue in social psychology. There is the feeling, justified or not, that social psychologists too often find what they want to find, conducting their experiments in such a way as to gather evidence confirming their own hypotheses. The way an experimenter puts questions to subjects, the expectations he or she has of them, and the presentation of the experimenter's self all may be seen as influencing the behavior of subjects. Martin Orne (1962) has called this the "demand characteristic," and it remains a troublesome and unresolved issue in social psychology. All of this is to say that there is a social psychology of social-psychology experiments. Many of the same observations social psychologists make of other situations and relationships in human behavior also apply to their own experimental situations. This is, of course, inevitable, for if social psychology is to be valid, surely its observations about others also apply to itself.

Perhaps the best way to summarize the questions of validity and relevance in social psychology is by stressing that it is a multiparadigm discipline. What is judged as valid depends on the assumptions brought to a study, and what is judged relevant depends on the uses to which the ideas are to be put and the understanding people have about their applicability. While seemingly a drawback of social psychology, this diversity may actually be one of its most positive features.

D. PROBLEMS OF ETHICS

John Jung has dramatized one ethical problem in social psychology in the following way:

> Let us consider an imaginary but not too implausible day in the life of a commuter in a big American city. As usual, your train was late so you grab a taxi to make up time. Traffic is slow because some woman has a flat tire and

everyone is slowing down to watch some gallant male motorist change it for her. No sooner does the traffic clear than you pass another lady in distress with a flat tire. Strange coincidence, you think to yourself.

Finally you arrive at your destination, but as you get out of the taxi you notice a small gift-wrapped parcel on the seat that must have been left behind by the previous passenger. You are tempted to take it but you finally control yourself.

Just before getting to your office, you notice a stamped but unmailed letter lying on the sidewalk that is addressed to the Black Panther party. Someone must have dropped it, and you debate whether or not to drop it in the corner mailbox. But since you're already late for work, you decide against it.

You have a long but otherwise uneventful day at the office. Now it is time to go home but since you can't find a taxi, you decide to take the subway. You are engrossed in reading the newspaper when you hear a scream. Looking up quickly, you notice an apparently drunk young man falling to the floor of the compartment. Bum, you think to yourself and resume reading.

Before getting on the train, you decide to stop at the corner liquor store for cigarettes. While you are there, two men come in asking for a rare imported brand of beer. After the storekeeper goes into the back of the store, the pair grab a case of beer and dash out without paying. Not wanting to get involved, you do not report the "theft" when the proprietor returns. Finally you get home, happy to have survived another day in the big city! [1977, 2]*

As you probably guessed, although all of these incidents could have been authentic, they could also have been rigged. Each incident described has, in fact, been staged by social psychologists.

As one of a number of research strategies in their arsenal, social psychologists have increasingly been using the natural experiment, in which unwitting participants are used to test a theory. Permission of the subjects is, of course, not secured either before or after the experiment takes place. The illustration above describes several natural experiments conducted in such a fashion by social psychologists. With each of these procedures, ethical issues are involved.

A distinction is usually drawn in the discipline between naturalistic *observations* and naturalistic *experiments*. In the first case, the experimenter does not ordinarily tamper with the usual behavior of the people studied. He or she is, as we have said in other places, a *participant observer* who tries to fit into a situation with as little disruption as possible. Although naturalistic observations—especially those that involve disguises or some other kind of deception in order to gain access to a social situation—raise questions (which we will deal with later), our concern here is with the naturalistic experiment.

*From "Snoopology," by J. Jung, *Human Behavior*, October 1975. Reprinted by permission.

1. Naturalistic Experiments

The ethical question at issue is this: do social psychologists have the right to conduct experiments in which persons are manipulated without their knowledge? Two absolutist views will be stated in order to show the extremes of the question. On the one hand we have those who say that such experimentation is never justified. We must always obtain permission from people in order to study them experimentally. On the other hand are those who argue that such experiments are always justified (at least if no one is harmed) because it is the right of social psychologists to search for truth and knowledge. Some version of the latter position has been used for years to justify much of the research that we have used in the compilation of this book.

The major issue here is deception. Most moral codes condemn lying and deception as destructive of mutual trust. However, deception is a common strategy in much social-science research (Warwick, 1975). Strategies range from outright lies, in which experimental subjects are given false information, to the use of confederates who appear to be part of the group of experimental subjects. For example, one of the most widely reported studies in social psychology was based on lies. Rosenthal and Jacobson, in order to find out how much teacher expectations affect student performance, deceived a number of elementary schoolteachers. They told them that certain children in their classes would do well academically and that others probably would not. They said these predictions were based on a test of "intellectual blooming." In fact, there were no significant differences in the children. At the completion of the school year the two researchers found what they had predicted: the children who were expected to achieve did so and those who were not did not. They called this the "Pygmalion effect," and it has since been repeated in over 200 separate studies, all of which have used essentially the same deceptive methodology.

Studies based on deception are difficult for social psychologists to give up. For one thing they have a dramatic effect and receive widespread publicity when reported. In addition, many social psychologists do not feel that valid information about various kinds of behavior can be obtained if subjects know the purpose of the experiment. In other words, a Pygmalion effect exists in most human affairs. If people know the purpose of the experiment, they are likely to play to it or try to subvert it. In either case the naturalistic situation the researchers have tried to create is destroyed.

More importantly, perhaps, is that people are often furious when they discover that they have been used as guinea pigs—particularly if children fail in a classroom setting because the teacher was set up by a social psychologist with false information about them. Experimental social psychology, conducted often by psychologists, is most often guilty of this type of deception. However, sociologically oriented social psychologists have increasingly been using similar research strategies. For example, ethnomethodology, discussed earlier in the book, tries to validate its propositions by intentionally breaking the rules of social situations in order to observe the responses of people in those situations.

2. Naturalistic Observations

Sociologically oriented social psychologists are not as likely to set up experiments, relying instead on various forms of participant observation or survey research to obtain information. But these strategies can also be questioned ethically. The most visible example is the controversy raised by the research of Laud Humphreys (1970). Humphreys conducted no experiments, either naturalistically or of the laboratory variety, but he did push the ethics of naturalistic observation in an interesting way. Humphreys was interested in a particular kind of homosexual behavior, that occurring in public rest rooms, often called "tea rooms" in gay argot. In order to obtain information on those who frequented tea rooms, Humphreys himself posed as a "watch queen." He both observed impersonal sex acts between consenting homosexuals while at the same time faithfully signaling the participants if police or "straights" were about to enter the rest room.

Later, Humphreys did engage in deception by following up with a survey of the participants. Having gotten their license-plate numbers while serving as watch queen, he went to their homes doing a "market survey" in order actually to collect social and demographic data about them. He did not tell them that he was doing a study of homosexual behavior, of course, did not reveal that he knew that they were homosexuals, and maintained their anonymity by never revealing who they were. By doing his work in a public place, Humphreys minimized the deception to a certain extent. He also was a valid participant as well as an observer in the sense that he performed the role of watch queen competently. However, had his research interests been revealed, his work would have been much more difficult. And, although he was clearly sympathetic to the situation of the homosexuals, he still deceived them. A proponent of the absolutist position on the ethics of deception could clearly fault him.

Humphreys's work set off a hailstorm of criticism and debate, both within the fraternity of social scientists and from without. In a celebrated exchange between defenders of social science and journalistic critics, Horowitz and Rainwater defended Humphreys, and columnist Nicholas Von Hoffman castigated his work as an example of the bad ethics rampant in the field (Horowitz and Rainwater, 1970; Von Hoffman, 1970).

Horowitz and Rainwater defended Humphreys on two grounds. First, they said, he was sympathetic toward the plight of homosexuals and used his research in an effort to show that their behavior was harmless and did not warrant the police-state tactics being used to stop them. Second, such a strategy provided intimate knowledge of the homosexual world that social scientists previously did not have. Von Hoffman countered by saying that lofty ends do not justify snooping into the private lives of people by social scientists any more than by the CIA or the FBI. The battle is still raging.

3. Laboratory Manipulation

While naturalistic studies present ethical problems, perhaps the most dramatic moral dilemmas of social science have come to the fore as a result of the research of Stanley Milgram. In one of the most famous laboratory studies of our time, *Obedience to Authority*, Milgram (1975) used confederates who faked receiving an electric shock. His aim was to test whether ordinary citizens would engage in behavior that they thought was injuring someone if they were told that some high authority approved it. A student of Solomon Asch, whose studies of how groups pressure people into conformity are now classics, Milgram set up the following laboratory situation:

A naive experimental subject is told that he is taking part in a study of "learning" with another subject (who is secretly a confederate of the researcher). The two draw to see who is "teacher" and who is "subject," but the drawing is rigged so that the experimental subject will be the teacher and the confederate the learner. The subject watches as electrodes are pasted to the confederate's arm. The confederate says he is not sure about this procedure because of an earlier heart condition, but the experimenter assures him that everything is all right—the experiment might be painful to him, but not harmful. All of this is done for the benefit of the experimental subject, who now understands that his supposed partner has a heart condition and will suffer some pain. The subject is then given a series of word pairs such as "nice–day," "fat–neck," and so on to read to the confederate. The list is then repeated, with the subject reading the first word and the confederate—who is now behind a partition—answering from a list of four multiple-choice options. The learner pushes a button. If his answer is correct, the experimental subject goes on. If he is wrong, the subject pushes a switch that buzzes and gives him an electric shock.

The experiment begins with what the subject thinks is a 15-volt shock, and the voltage increases with each wrong answer. The control board goes from 15 to 450 volts, and it also has verbal descriptions of the shock levels, ranging from "slight shock" to "danger: severe shock." If at any point the subject hesitates to push the button, the experimenter calmly tells him to go on. The idea of the study is to find the shock level beyond which the subject will refuse to push the button. A recording coming from behind the partition simulates resistance from the confederate. The objections start with a grunt at 75 volts and build up to a "hey, that really hurts" at 125 volts. The voice becomes desperate with "I can't stand the pain, don't do that!" at 180 volts, complains of heart trouble at 195, gives an agonized scream at 285, refuses to answer at 315, and then is silent (Milgram, 1974).

The results were devastating. Believing at first that few people would go all the way through the board to the "dangerous" levels, Milgram found that virtually all the subjects would, especially if they were encouraged by the authority of the experimenter. On the basis of these studies, Milgram concluded a number of things about obedience to authority. Among them was the opinion that, if Nazi-like extermination camps were set up around the country, there would be little difficulty in recruiting ordinary citizens to staff them.

This is perhaps the most ingenious scheme of deception ever devised by a social psychologist, and Milgram has established a high academic reputation on the basis of it. The justification for it is the same: in the name of science such deception is justified because it helps us understand more about our own behavior. Despite "debriefings" that sometimes tell the subjects the actual purpose of the experiment, the procedures used are still the subject of intense controversy in the social sciences.

4. Possible Solutions

How do we resolve the doubts about our own research? Several solutions have been offered. Jung suggested a time-consuming and expensive procedure in which a representative sample of a group about to be studied would be contacted to review the experimental procedures and advise what they considered to be ethical problems (Jung, 1975). The American Psychological Association advocates the use of a risk/benefit principle to see whether the potential benefits of a study employing deception or other questionable procedures outweigh its drawbacks. Such a judgment is left to the individual investigator, who, of course, is likely to see the benefits more than the risks.

Erikson, in a comment on the use of disguised observation in sociology, proposed that the following principle be adopted: "It is unethical for a sociologist to *deliberately misrepresent* his identity for the purpose of entering a private domain *to which he is not otherwise eligible*"; and "that it is unethical for a sociologist to *deliberately misrepresent* the character of the research in which he is engaged" (1967, 372).

Yet another reason for being concerned about such research strategies was offered by Erikson. "It seems to me that any attempt to use masquerades in social research betrays an extraordinary disrespect for the complexities of human interaction, and for this reason can only lead to bad science" (373).

E. THE PROMISE OF SOCIAL PSYCHOLOGY

Despite—and perhaps even to a certain extent because of—the problems we have discussed, social psychology remains for us a dynamic and useful enterprise. Many of the problems are more characteristic of our time and of a scientific era than they are peculiar to social psychology. At the same time, social psychology offers the promise of achieving in the future two important goals, both of which are already being realized in certain respects: understanding and application.

1. The Goal of Understanding

To understand the social world around us is one of the promises of social psychology. Even if the discipline never develops a systematic group of laws and predictive relationships in the way that natural science has, it will still generate insights into the human condition that enlarge our horizon as we attempt to understand questions about ourselves and our interdependent relationships to one another. In fact, if human behavior is ever positively tied to a series of absolute laws, the political implications will be devastating. If human behavior is controlled by processes that are unchangeable, what are the prospects for human freedom? While one psychologist, B. F. Skinner, has already proposed such a circumstance (Skinner, 1971), others (Roszak, 1969) have raised serious questions about both the possibility of accomplishing such a task and the ethics of trying. As an experiential as well as an objective science, social psychology finds itself in the position of being a critical part of the very processes it studies. To aid people in understanding better their relationships to one another is no small accomplishment in a complex and sometimes inscrutable world.

It is difficult at times to know whether a social psychologist has merely analyzed an existing condition or helped create it. For example, it was only after Erik Erikson's idea of the identity crisis gained some notoriety that students began to go through one. Before Erikson, people were more likely to say that they were simply under a lot of pressure or that they felt confused about their goal (Cuzzort and King, 1976, 324). One could speak of any number of similar cases in which social-psychological research has passed into the public domain and become part of a common vocabulary. Certainly much of Freudian thinking occupies such a status in the Western world (Seeley, 1967). There is no question that social psychology, as well as many of the other social sciences, has become an influence on the way people think about themselves and the environment around them. Not only are hundreds of thousands of dollars worth of tax money spent on research projects, but also people in everyday life often turn to sociologists, anthropologists, social psychologists, and psychologists for light on the way we now live. *Psychology Today*, a magazine the reader has probably seen on many a supermarket newsstand, sits alongside *Popular Mechanics* and *Field and Stream*. If you want to know about your car, you read *PM*. If you want to know about trout fishing, you read *F&S*. And if you want to know more about human behavior, you may pick up *PT*. A relatively small number of people read *The Journal of Social Psychology*, but the research findings published there regularly filter into the public domain and become part of general knowledge. It may be that, just as we once turned to novelists and other literary figures for comment on the times, we now increasingly look to social science for such commentary.

2. The Goal of Application

To understand something is not necessarily to be able to do anything about it. If we *are* to be able to change the conditions of our lives, however, understanding is an important prerequisite. As the social and political problems of the 20th century have accumulated, so has the call for help in solving them. Increasingly, much of this appeal has gone to social science. George Miller, in his 1969 presidential address to the American Psychological Association, said "I can imagine nothing we could do that could be more relevant to human welfare, and nothing that could pose a greater challenge to the next generation of psychologists, than to discover how to give psychology away" (Miller, G., 1970, 21). This goal has been echoed in virtually all the social sciences—to get social science out of the researcher's private domain and into a public universe of discourse where its findings, understandings, and expertise can be used for public benefit.

Social psychologists have not systematically tried to apply what they know about social processes. Young (1972) suggested several reasons for this state of affairs, including: (1) social psychologists simply do not want to, (2) they believe there is not enough knowledge to be applied with confidence, (3) the idea of applying knowledge has never really occurred to them, and (4) they do not know how to apply what they know. Indeed, the problems of applied research seem at first glance so formidable as to dissuade anyone from trying. Applied research has all the problems inherent in basic research, along with many additional ones. The problems peculiar to applied social psychology are largely ethical and political. Research can be conducted with impunity about noncontroversial matters or on groups and people who have little political power. But the repercussions that may come from studying controversial matters such as prejudice, discrimination, how children should be reared, social deviants, and questions of morality are often more than most social psychologists are willing to endure.

There is also the nagging question of to whom social psychology is useful. In whose interest and for what purposes is a research study conducted? In the kind of climate in which social psychology operates, it is clear that vested interests are involved when a researcher is hired to conduct a study. As McKee (1969) has pointed out, the independence to pursue a set of problems and publish the results may be met quite satisfactorily. But if this freedom is exercised only *after* research problems have been selected and designed from the standpoint of the interests of a sponsoring agency, then a study may be in serious jeopardy. Because not everyone in our society has equal access to a social psychologist's skills, the discipline may become simply an intellectual servant of various power interests in society. The question of whom social psychology is to serve is a basic and perplexing one.

There is also the problem that prediction and explanation can go hand in hand with social control. To the extent that social psychologists can explain and predict the behavior of human beings, this information can be used by agencies in society to manipulate the citizenry. One has only to look at the uses to which social psychology is put in the Soviet Union, where political dissent is defined as mental illness, to see the problem. It is, of course, easier to see the manipulation of social scientists in the Soviet Union than it is to see it in the United States, but sponsoring agencies armed with money often have control as the basic goal of their studies. This is why all social psychologists must understand the historical context of their society and their research problems. Seeing oneself as a part of the problem under study and seeing the research act in its social, political, and economic context are a major part of assessing the ethics of a particular piece of applied research.

The potential negative impact of applied research can also be reduced by clarifying the possible frameworks of interpretation within which a set of data can be understood. This is why it is so important to realize that multiple meanings are generated by multiple paradigms in social psychology. Social science is not a process of discovery so much as a process of invention in which the selection of a framework of interpretation cannot be separated from the "facts" a researcher "discovers." What we need here is a *reflexive* social psychology that is knowledgeable about itself, its context, and its relationship to all who play a role in its formulation (Gouldner, 1970).

Despite all of these difficulties the last several years have seen an exponential increase in the intensity of the debate over the question of application, and it seems that the sentiment for practical use is strong. There are a number of ways in which the concepts, theories, and methods of social psychology could be useful in a world full of problems.

First, rapid social changes that have occurred in the past 25 years have left serious marks on the personal lives of many people. Questions of self and identity have become paramount in ways that our great-grandfathers could not have understood. Sociological and anthropological theories often need the personal linkage supplied by social psychology. How do changes in the structure of our societies change the circumstances of our personal lives? What kinds of identities are available in a given society? How are these identities dramatized? How do they arise? How do they sustain themselves? How do they change? These are relevant questions that social psychology can raise and then try to answer.

Social psychology has also been one of the stronger academic disciplines in showing a number of areas in which our assumptions are not congruent with the facts of a situation. Descriptive research is study that tries to show just what a particular set of facts is in a social situation. For example, studies in social psychology first showed the utterly irrational basis of racial prejudice. Discrimination based on race may result in a self-fulfilling prophecy, so that Blacks (or other minority groups) continue to occupy the bottom rungs of society because they are expected to do so and forced to remain there, not because of anything inherent in their capabilities. Many of the time-worn assumptions about social life that have become crystallized in our thinking as facts can be shown to have no factual basis at all. Much of the research on socialization we reported in the three chapters on the life cycle are living examples of the way in which social psychology can serve as a continual reminder that the world is not always what common sense would make of it.

Besides descriptive studies, much of the research in social psychology offers the reader a way of understanding relationships between classes of events in new and potentially liberating ways. The entire section of the text on "Self and Others" offers a way of seeing oneself in an entirely different way than a simple stance of individualism allows. To know that one's self, one's motives, one's roles, and one's appearances are all a part of interactive, shared social processes does not have to be depressing. Indeed, it can point the way to more effective uses of these parts of life. Without being manipulative or cynical, social psychology can lead to an understanding of one's relationships with others that offers the possibility of both more meaningful encounters and better feelings about the encounters one has. In an age in which self-esteem is so important, but so difficult to achieve without the help of other people, such understanding can be liberating indeed.

Such considerations as these have really been secondary, however, as we have written this book. Our primary concern has been to help you see what an exciting and intellectually stimulating field of inquiry social psychology really is. For, despite applications of the discipline on the broadest conceivable scale, social psychology, like all other intellectual pursuits, in the last analysis serves primarily as a personal form of enlightenment.

Glossary

Account: A type of motive, or a statement made by a social actor to explain unanticipated or untoward behavior.

Achieved roles: Roles earned as a result of developing a skill to the point at which one can perform a particular social function.

Actor, social: The self as it emerges in face-to-face interaction.

Adolescence: A developmental period of early adulthood with (1) continued dependence on authority, (2) early sex development, (3) sexual learning, and (4) preparation for fully adult roles.

Adolescent subculture: Adolescence viewed as a way of life, somewhat apart from the adult world and functioning with a set of values often in opposition to adult society.

Alienation: Estrangement from the self and others.

Anomie: A state of normlessness, occurring when societal norms fail to function or when an individual enters a new social environment where the norms are not understood or applied.

Anticipatory socialization: The playing and practice of certain social roles in preparation for the actual performance of such roles in later life. Most forms of training fall in this category.

Appeal to defeasibility: An excuse for behavior that suggests that a person did something against his or her will or did not know the situation.

Ascribed roles: Roles given by virtue of the application of a social category independent of behavior, based on a condition such as age or sex.

Associationism: The notion that the primary units of the mind are associated with external behavior.

Attitude: Certain regularities of an individual's feelings, thoughts, and dispositions to act toward some aspect of the environment.

Audience: In dramaturgical analysis, those persons who observe and respond to an actor's performance.

Audience segregation: A technique by which the actor attempts to prevent certain audiences from seeing certain performances.

Autonomous stage: According to Piaget, the second and final stage of moral development, in which the child develops a "morality of cooperation" based on internal controls.

Balance theory: A cognitive approach suggesting that there is a tendency to organize conceptions about others, oneself, and objects in the environment harmoniously, in a positive way.

Behaviorism: The notion that behavior is the basic subject matter of social psychology and that research should deal only with observable behavior.

Behavior perspective: The view that external conditions are the source of all action.

Black liberation movement: A struggle by Black people in the United States for full equality.

Body messages: Nonverbal meanings inferred from various body poses and actions.

Civil rights movement: Protests in the 1950s and 1960s, strongly supported by Black people of the United States, against the racial discrimination that deprived them of equal opportunity in education, culture, occupation, health care, and public facilities.

Coercive organizations: Organizations that impose a high degree of control over the behavior of individuals. For example, prisons and mental hospitals.

Cognitive disclaimer: Setting up by the actor of a framework within which his or her behavior can be dealt with if it does not fit an easily assigned definition.

Cognitive theory: A constellation of ideas that emphasize the mental system of the actor as the basic source of all external behavior.

Cognitive theory of attraction: Emphasis on the thought processes as the basic determinants of attraction to others.

Collective behavior: The study of behavior and meanings that emerge in interaction and bring formerly disparate individuals into a collectivity. Examples include crowds and mobs.

Communal living movement: A return to the simple life. Materialism and differential status based on wealth are shunned. Property is frequently held in common. The work load is shared, and food and other benefits are divided equally.

Conditioning theory: Suggests that present behavior is a product of past episodes of learning and that the task of social psychology is to discover the "contingencies of reinforcement" that are most likely associated with behavior. The stimulus/response perspective.

Conflict theory: Asserts that conflict rather than consensus is the fundamental quality of social life.

Conformity: The use of approved social means of pursuing approved social goals.

Consensus of the competent: A criterion of acceptability: the validity of a scientific statement depends on who joins in support of it.

Content analysis: Systematic measurement of written material to identify characteristics not directly presented or intended.

Conventional morality: According to Kohlberg, the second of three main levels of moral development. Doing what the conventional role demands.

Credentialling: A type of disclaimer. The actor claims special credentials, qualifications, or exceptions.

Crisis: Used by Sheehy in discussing adult socialization. Indicates a turning point after which one's past recedes and one's future is drastically changed.

Culture: A blueprint of the behavior of a society, including ideas, beliefs, technology, conventional ways of doing tasks, and all systems of communication.

Cumulative deprivation: A theory suggesting that cumulative economic impoverishment will eventually create the dissatisfaction necessary to lead individuals into social movements.

Definition of the situation: A series of acts that serve to represent or define a situation for both self and others.

Demand characteristic: Data provided to a researcher based on what the respondent thinks the researcher expects, rather than what is correct.

Disclaimer: A term used by Hewitt and Stokes to refer to situations in which actors attempt to head off negative responses by giving an account of why their conduct may appear unusual.

Discreditable identity: One that would be discredited if degrading or disgraceful facts were known.

Discredited identity: A consequence of the negative definition of a person by others, as of a person convicted of a repulsive crime.

Distributive justice: The belief that someone in an exchange relation with another will expect their rewards to be proportional to the costs. The net rewards for each should be proportional to net investment.

Dramaturgical circumspection: Goffman's term for the exercise of care when a performance is given to avoid destroying the selves that have been so painstakingly built up.

Dramaturgical discipline: Goffman's term for the control actors must exercise in the parts they are playing.

Dramaturgical loyalty: Goffman's term for the acceptance of persons as team members who we believe will contribute to the performance the team is giving for others.

Dramaturgical perspective: Views the self as a staged production, or a series of masks that people present to audiences.

Dualism: The idea that an entity can be rationally separated into two parts—for example, mind and body, society and the individual.

Dyad: A two-person group, usually in some pattern of sustained interaction and exchange.

Ectomorphy: One of Sheldon's three body types: flat chest, slight development of the visceral and somatic structure, and long, slender, poorly muscled extremities.

Ego: Freud's mediator between the id and the superego. A self-structure that operates on the level of consciousness. A defense mechanism to ward off various assaults on the self.

Egocentrism: The perception of self as the center of all experience, to the exclusion or neglect of others.

Egoism: The tendency to pursue self-interests in disregard of equivalent interests of others.

Empirical data: Information derived from sense perceptions of the external world.

Encounter group: A planned, intensive experience using interactional processes and group influence to help people improve their social and relational skills.

Endomorphy: One of Sheldon's three body types: large, highly developed digestive viscera (belly) and relatively weak body structure. Generally fat, but may be emaciated.

Ethnocentrism: Viewing one's own life-style and culture as the most appropriate and proper way to live. Denial of the equality or acceptability of other cultures.

Ethnomethodology: Study of the ways in which people make sense out of social situations. Investigation of how common sense is applied in everyday life, from the viewpoint of different actors.

Exchange theory: Views human behavior as a response to the relation between rewards and costs. Individuals are motivated to maximize rewards and to minimize costs.

Exclusion principle: The belief that something must be true, to the exclusion of all evidence to the contrary.

Excuse: A type of motive that admits that an act was wrong but denies full responsibility for it.

Experiment: Research in which the social psychologist manipulates certain variables in order to observe their effects on concrete behavior.

External motivational schemes: The view that human behavior can be explained by actions external to the organism.

Face ritual: Goffman's term for the arrangement and sustaining of a role performance that allows one to reveal some things and conceal others.

Face work: Goffman's term for the process of sustaining a particular social presence and action required for a given situation by maintaining "face" in the presence of others.

Fantastic socialization: A child's playing of roles that can hardly be conceived as feasible future roles, such as Superman, Wonder Woman, or a ghost.

Field research: Distinguished from laboratory research in that it is accomplished in the natural settings in which social behavior occurs. See participant observation.

Field theory: Proposed by Kurt Lewin, it suggests that one's behavior is not simply a function of attitudes and personality but is also a function of a distributed area of the personality called *life-space,* within which the individual can move about.

Front: Any fixed part of a person's performance that serves to define the self for audiences.

Game theory: Developed by Neuman and Morgenstern, it explains the system of strategy and choice for the players in an interactive game. Choices of alternatives, taken by turns, lead to winning or losing outcomes.

Gay liberation movement: Founded by homosexuals seeking to attain equal rights in employment—and in society in general—without being forced to conceal their life-style.

Generalized other: Abstract social audience, such as the society or community, internalized and incorporated into a person's act.

Generation gap: Conflict between parents and youth, frequently causing a collapse in communication.

Gestalt psychology: Holds that an individual does not respond to discrete stimuli but rather to their total configuration.

Glossing: In ethnomethodology, the use of words as a shorthand to express more complex and generally understood meanings.

Hedging: A type of disclaimer. An actor is saying two things: that what he or she is about to say is tentative and that the response to the statement could be serious.

Heteronomous stage: According to Piaget, the first stage of moral development. The child develops a "morality of constraint" based on approval or disapproval by others.

Hippie movement: It rejected the traditional goals of society and the conventional means of achieving them. The Hippies preferred to be "free" souls in voluntary poverty.

I: Used by Mead to refer to the part of self that is spontaneous, undefined, subjective, and personal. The *I* is the source and the process of action.

Id: Freud's term for that asocial part of the self (usually associated with the body) that seeks simple gratification without concern for others.

Identity crisis: Erik Erikson's term for that time, sometimes associated with a sudden social conversion of status, when one comes to question who one is and what one is to become.

Identity switching: Strategy for avoiding motive situations. The actor asserts that he or she is not the person whom the challenger intends to confront.

Impression management: Goffman's phrase for actors' attempts to control the impression that others have of them. The quality of performance must be sustained to maintain a social status.

Interactionist perspective: Stresses the reciprocal relation between individuals and between the individual and society as the source of all action.

Interactionist theory of attraction: Views attraction as an interpersonal process in which individuals are attracted to each other because they share mutual definitions of the situation.

Internal motivational scheme: The view that human behavior can be explained by drives, instincts, needs, or reflexes.

Interview: A research tool for acquiring information through direct questions asked by a trained interviewer. It is usually less structured and more informal than a questionnaire.

Investigator bias: Distortion resulting from the researcher's reaching a desired conclusion not supported by the evidence.

Isolation: A theory suggesting that the separation of an individual from others or the separation of a group from the rest of society may create dissatisfaction that leads to participation in social movements.

Jesus movement: It provided a means by which dissident youth could be reintegrated into society. Embraced the basic values of cleanliness, wholesomeness, faith in God, love of country, and obedience to those in authority.

Justification: A type of motive that defends an act in the face of some claim that the act is, or might be, wrong.

Laboratory experiment: Research conducted in an artificial and more or less precisely controlled setting.

La morale: Used by Comte to refer to a new, true, and final science of society that would deal with the "individual unity of man."

Language: A system of verbal communication based on convention. A pattern or system of interaction, rather than an object.

Lateral deviance: That which occurs when persons in a subordinate rank develop their own standards and norms apart from and opposed to those of persons in superior ranks.

Logical coherence: A criterion of validity holding that statements within a scientific study must be consistent with one another.

Looking-glass self: Used by Cooley to suggest that self and society are mere reflections of each other. The self arises reflectively in reaction with (1) the imagination of one's appearance to another person, (2) one's imagination of the other's judgment of that appearance, and (3) a resultant self-feeling of pride or humiliation.

Marginal freaks: Individuals who were only partly aware of the hippie philosophy and who were unwilling to commit their whole lives to the experience.

Material me: Used by James to refer to all the "things" that a person claims for himself or herself as property, especially personal property such as clothes, home, cars.

Me: Used by Mead to refer to the part of self that emerges from the appraisals of others. The *me* is the product and the object of action.

Mesomorphy: One of Sheldon's three body types: somatic structures of bone, muscle, and connective tissue are well developed; the physique is hard, upright, and relatively strong. Generally an athletic type.

Midnight hippies: Individuals who shared the hippie philosophy but who were integrated into the conventional world.

Moral career: Used by Goffman to indicate the progressive change that occurs in one's beliefs about oneself, as in the social conversion of entering a total institution.

Morality: Patterns of behavior, principles, concepts, and rules employed by individuals and groups in dealing with the social issue of right versus wrong.

Morality of constraint: Judgments are made in terms of an act's consequences, rather than in terms of the actor's intentions. Justice is equated with whatever authority demands.

Morality of cooperation: Judgments are made in terms of the actor's intentions. Justice is seen in terms of equality and equity, or "fairness."

Motivational analysis: An explanatory perspective of social movements, focusing on the recruitment process and explaining why people join.

Mystification: Strategy for avoiding motive situations. Actors admit not doing as they should and point out that there are secret reasons that would justify them that cannot be told.

Natural experiment: Research in which changes in the independent variable occur without the manipulation of the experimenter.

Nonverbal communication: Use of gestures, physical signals, positions, and postures, without the use of words.

Norm: A rule, a standard, or a prescription for behavior. It controls specific actions by persons in society.

Normative organization: One that is bureaucratically structured. Both professional training and on-the-job development frequently require highly specialized work. Individuals have a great amount of autonomy and large responsibility.

Norm of equity: The idea of fairness, taking into consideration all surrounding circumstances and the interests of all parties.

Norm of reciprocity: Cooperative behavior as a basis for maintaining social order and structure. People should help those who have helped them and should not injure those who have helped them.

Norm of social responsibility: The mutual expectations between persons, describing their obligations and privileges. Includes the issue of accountability and answerability.

Oedipus complex: Used by Freud to refer to excessive emotional attachment of a son to his mother, with either conscious or unconscious sexual desires.

Opinion: Specific judgment on an issue that reflects a given orientation.

Paradigm: A pattern for arranging and relating concepts, parts of a system, or components of an object.

Parallel roles: Those played by individuals who are performing similar behavior but who do not need to interact among themselves, such as customers in a store.

Participant observation: A technique of field research by which researchers enter a natural setting and participate physically in the scene they are observing, analyzing, and describing.

Peers: Individuals of approximately the same age, educational level, and social standing—equal in power and influence.

Person perspective: The view that the individual is the source and center of all action.

Phenomenology: A philosophical perspective on everyday life that provides the theoretical assumptions for ethnomethodology and some aspects of dramaturgical analysis.

Picture theory: Suggests that language consists of words and that each word has meaning only insofar as it stands for something else.

Plastic hippies: Individuals who wore the identifying marks of the hippies, such as love beads, head bands, Ben Franklin glasses, and leather shirts, without being part of the movement.

Positivism: A philosophical position holding that the methods and techniques that have proven their worth in natural science should be applied to social science.

Postconventional morality: According to Kohlberg, the final level of the three main levels of moral development. Morality is internal and is independent of external authority. An honest person needs no warden.

Postulate of consistency: Suggests that verbal attitudes provide a reasonably accurate guide for predicting what people will do when confronted with an object of their attitude.

Postulate of contingent consistency: Suggests that the relationship between attitudes and behavior depends on certain situational factors such as norms, roles, group membership, and the social environment.

Postulate of independent variation: Argues that there is no reason to assume that attitudes and behavior are consistently related.

Power: The ability to change the responses of others without their consent.

Pragmatism: The belief that ideas have value only in terms of their practical consequences.

Preconventional morality: According to Kohlberg, the first of three main levels of moral development, which is a premoral stage.

Prejudice: Any prejudgment of the individual based on social criteria such as race or sex.

Primary deviance: Used by Lemert to mean the act of breaking social rules.

Primary group: Defined by Cooley as characterized by (1) face-to-face association among the members, (2) no special or formal goals, (3) relative permanence, (4) small size, and (5) relative intimacy among members.

Program of appearance: Used by Stone to refer to the set of appearances that the actor presents, in sequence, to an audience.

Psychology: The study of the mind of the individual as it influences human behavior.

Pygmalion effect: The notion that knowledge of what is expected results in affirmation of these expectations.

Questionnaire: A research tool for acquiring information about subjects. It is usually self-administered, and the subjects usually remain anonymous.

Reference groups: Those persons an individual has in mind for guiding his or her own behavior, ideals, and goals.

Referral: Strategy for avoiding explanation of motive situations. The actor refers the challenger to someone else for an explanation of his or her questionable behavior.

Reinforcement theory: Assumes that animals, including human beings, consistently repeat certain specific behaviors as a result of experiencing either rewarding or punishing stimuli in association with those behaviors.

Reinforcement theories of attraction: Rooted in learning theory, they attempt to interpret interpersonal attraction as a learned response.

Relative deprivation: A theory suggesting that an increasing gap between what individuals feel they should get and what they actually get will create the dissatisfaction necessary to induce participation in social movements.

Respondent bias: Distortion resulting from respondents' giving what they desire rather than what is correct information.

Response acquiescence: A tendency for the respondent to be agreeable and to answer "yes" regardless of the question.

Review of appearance: Used by Stone to refer to the response that an audience makes to an actor's program of appearance.

Rising expectations: A theory suggesting that a partial fulfillment of deprived people's ambitions leads to higher aspirations. When frustrated by overly slow improvement, such people may join a protest movement.

Rite of passage: A phrase credited to Arnold Van Gennep, referring to rituals performed when individuals pass from one social status to another. The wedding ceremony is one.

Role conflict: The problem that arises when an actor attempts to play two incompatible roles at the same time.

Role disengagement: Terminating the action and withdrawing from the setting that a role performance established.

Role distance: A technique whereby performers expressively separate themselves from the role they are playing. Thus, a supervisor playing softball at the office picnic says "I'm no athlete!" to avoid damaging his or her image for poor performance.

Role engagement: Entering into the action required by a social role.

Role set: The array of partners with whom an actor must be involved in performing a particular social role.

Role extension: The expansion of a role to include a number of specialized tasks.

Role tasks: The activities and jobs that must be performed as a part of the role.

Scapegoating: A type of excuse for behavior in which people contend that their own behavior is only a result of the behavior or attitude of others.

Secondary deviance: Used by Lemert to mean a deviant life-style or identity. It is often the result of having one's primary deviance responded to and labeled as deviant by others.

Self-concept: The ideas and beliefs that one has of oneself.

Self-esteem: The feelings one has about oneself in relation to others and in relation to society or special elements of society.

Self-fulfilling prophecy: The idea that what one expects will influence what one does and what will actually happen. The player who thinks "I will probably lose" may slack off and cause a loss that need not have been.

Sex roles: Behavior as it is influenced by an ascribed characteristic of sex; for example, someone may behave as wife, husband, bride, or homosexual.

Significant other: Used by Harry Stack Sullivan to refer to an important audience in a person's life.

Sin license: A type of disclaimer. Actors contend that they know they are about to break a rule but that they do not fear the negative classification that others may apply to them.

Small social group: A number of persons who communicate with one another and are few enough so that each person is able to deal directly with each of the others face to face.

Social act: Behavior given meaning in a social situation.

Social behaviorism: Proposed by George H. Mead to mean that human acts must be taken as social responses, not as mere organic movements. Renamed *symbolic interactionism* by Blumer.

Social class: Used to refer to a person's standing in a community, generally based on education, occupation, income, or wealth.

Social determinism: The view that the society shapes and molds the individual.

Social-emotional group leader: The individual who attempts to establish, restore, and maintain positive interpersonal relations among the members of a group.

Social identity: The distinct characteristics an individual acquires as social self-awareness through social experience.

Socialization: The development of functions, skills, understandings, and abilities to relate to others in social connections. It is the process of becoming capable in social relationships and is continuous and lifelong.

Social me: Used by James to refer to the recognition one gets from others through social relations.

Social movements: Socially shared activities and beliefs directed toward the demand for change in some aspect of the social order.

Social process: The continuous flow of action, interaction, and development of persons and groups.

Social psychology: The study of human interaction. The discipline studies the individual in social context and the continuing relationship between self and others.

Social roles: The organized performances of a person in relation to others in a social relationship or setting.

Sociogram: A pictorial or graphic representation of the relations among all of the individuals of a group.

Sociology: The study of society, working through groups, organizations and institutions, and its effects on human behavior.

Sociometric matrix: A digital representation of the relation among all of the members of a group, laid out in rows and columns. A *1* where row 2 crosses column 3 indicates that member 2 likes member 3. A *0* indicates no relation.

Sociometry: A technique for diagraming the relations among all individuals in a relatively small group, such as members of a social club.

Somatotype: Used by Sheldon in reference to the general form of the human body.

Spiritual me: Used by James to refer to the collection of one's stages of consciousness and psychic faculties.

Stereotype: An oversimplified generalization about objects, persons or situations that are to some degree false.

Stigma: Any physical or social characteristic that results in a negative identification of a person, often resulting in social avoidance or uncomplimentary treatment.

Subculture: A blueprint for the behavior of a smaller group, sometimes at odds with the larger society.

Superego: Used by Freud to mean a part of the self composed of partly conscious and partly unconscious elements. It is formed by society's systems of rules and constraints that attempt to hold self-centered human beings in check.

Survey research: A strategy using a questionnaire with a large number of respondents to measure the distribution of some characteristic in a sample of a larger population.

Symbol: A conventional sign that acquires meaning in social usage. Represents something other than itself.

Symbolic interactionism: Emphasizes man's unique ability to use symbols. Social action between individuals, accordingly, is mediated through symbols in conventional systems of language and signs.

Symbolic transformation: The transformation of neutral objects into meaningful objects. Examples are sacred objects, trophies, and skin color.

Sympathetic introspection: Used by Cooley to describe a research technique in which social psychologists look into their own internal processes and lives.

Task leader: Individual who takes the initiative in solving the problems of an organization.

Total institution: A place of residence and work where a large number of like-situated people lead an enclosed, formally administered life. A prison, convent, or military camp.

Training group: One that works to improve participants' personal communication, growth with others, managerial skills, or problem solving.

Transsexual: A person who has had a sex-change operation.

Transvestite: A person who dresses in the clothing of the opposite sex.

Universality: A criterion of validity requiring that statements made about a subject hold true at all times and in all places when the same test is applied.

Unobtrusive measures: Nonreactive measures of social reality that do not involve the awareness of observation or measurement by the participants.

Utilitarian organizations: Those where the workers are less specialized in training, have less autonomy in determining the organization of their work, and have less freedom in interpreting and applying rules in the system.

Utopia: An ideal society operating on fully rational principles of law, commerce, and technology.

Validity: The degree to which a scientific study has measured what it intended to measure.

Value: What a person or a society considers worthwhile in either attitudes or actions.

Vertical deviance: That which occurs when persons in a subordinate rank attempt to enjoy the privileges of a superior rank.

Visionaries: Hippies who had a vision of people growing together. It was their goal to remove barriers such as property, prejudice, and preconceptions about what is moral and immoral.

White-collar crime: Offences committed by persons of social respectability and status, usually in connection with their occupation—for example, embezzlement and fraud.

Women's liberation movement: Founded by women for women to enable them to reach full equality in economic, educational, and political institutions.

References

Abelson, R. P. Computers, polls, and public opinion—some puzzles and paradoxes. In E. Aronson and R. Helmreich (Eds.), *Social Psychology*. New York: Van Nostrand Reinhold, 1973, 270–278.

Abramson, M. *Interpersonal Accommodation*. New York: Van Nostrand Reinhold, 1966.

Acock, A., & LeFleur, L. A configurational approach to contingent consistency in the attitude/behavior relationship. *American Sociology Review*, 1972, *37*, 714–706.

Adams, J. S. Inequity in social exchange. In L. Berkowitz (Ed.), *Advances in Experimental Social Psychology* (Vol. 2). New York: Academic Press, 1965.

Addeo, E. G., & Burger, R. E. *EgoSpeak: Why No One Listens to You*. Radnor, Pa.: Chilton, 1973.

Adorno, T. *The Authoritarian Personality*. New York: Harper & Row, 1950.

Aiello, J. R., & Jones, S. E. Field of proxemic behavior of young school children in three subcultural groups. *Journal of Personality and Social Psychology*, 1971, *19*, 351–356.

Albrecht, S. L., & Warner, L. G. The interactive effects of situational and personality factors on attitude-action consistency. Paper presented at the Southwest Sociological Convention, 1973.

Aldrich, C. A., & Hewitt, E. A self regulating feeding program for infants. *Journal of the American Medical Association*, 1947, *135*, 340–342.

Allen, D. E. *Analysis of Public Conversation*. Ann Arbor, Mich.: University of Michigan, 1961.

Allen, D. E. Family influence on academic performance. *International Journal of Sociology of the Family*, 1971, *1*, 106–115.

Allen, D. E., & Guy, R. F. *Conversation Analysis: The Sociology of Talk*. The Hague, the Netherlands: Mouton, 1974.

Allport, G. W. *The Nature of Prejudice*. Reading, Mass.: Addison-Wesley, 1954.

417

Allport, G. W. Attitudes. In *Attitude Theory and Measurement.* New York: Wiley, 1967.

Allport, G. W. The historical background of modern social psychology. In G. Lindzey and E. Aronson (Eds.), *The Handbook of Social Psychology.* Reading, Mass.: Addison-Wesley, 1968.

Almy, M., Chittenden, E., & Miller, P. *Young Children's Thinking.* New York: Teachers College Press, Columbia University, 1966.

Ambrose, J. A. Development of the smiling response in early infancy. In J. M. Foss (Ed.), *Determinants of Infant Behavior.* New York: Wiley, 1961.

Anderson, S. G. Abortion and the husband's consent. *Journal of Family Law,* 1973–1974, *13,* 311–331.

Angell, R. C. Charles Horton Cooley. In D. L. Sills (Ed.), *The International Encyclopedia of the Social Sciences* (Vol. 3). New York: Macmillan, 1947.

Angle, J. Mainland control of manufacturing and reward for bilingualism in Puerto Rico. *American Sociological Review,* 1976, *41,* 289–307.

Angrist, S. Mental illness and deviant behavior: Unsolved conceptual problems. *Sociological Quarterly,* 1966, *7,* 436–448.

Ankudinova, N. E. Ob-osobyennostyakh otsenki i samo-otsenki uchastikhsya I–IV klassov v uchebnoi dyeyatel 'nosti. [On appraisal and self-appraisal in student behavior in grades 1 to 4.] *Voprosy Psikhologii,* 1968, *3,* 131–138.

Arbuthnot, J. Relationships between maturity of moral judgment and measures of cognitive abilities. *Psychological Reports,* 1973, *33,* 945–946.

Argyle, M. *Psychology of Interpersonal Behavior.* Baltimore: Penguin, 1967.

Argyle, M. *Social Interaction.* Chicago: Aldine, 1969.

Argyle, M., & Little, B. R. Do personality traits apply to social behavior? *Journal for the Theory of Social Behavior,* 1972, *2,* 1–35.

Argyle, M., & Williams, M. Observer or observed? A reversible perspective on person perception. *Sociometry,* 1969, *32,* 396–412.

Armer, M., & Schnaiberg, A. Measuring individual modernity: a near myth. *American Sociological Review,* 1972, *37,* 301–316.

Aronfreed, J. *Conduct and Conscience: The Socialization of Internalized Control on Behavior.* New York: Academic Press, 1968.

Aronson, E., & Carlsmith, J. M. Experimentation in social psychology. In G. Lindzey and E. Aronson (Eds.), *Handbook of Social Psychology* (2nd ed.) (Vol. 2). Reading, Mass.: Addison-Wesley, 1968.

Aronson, E., & Mills, J. Effect of severity of initiation on liking for a group. *Journal of Abnormal and Social Psychology,* 1959, *59,* 177–181.

Aronson, E., Turner, J., & Carlsmith, J. Communicator credibility and communication discrepancy as determinants of social change. *Journal of Abnormal and Social Psychology,* 1963, *66,* 31–36.

Aronson, E., & Worchel, P. Similarity versus liking as determinants of interpersonal attractiveness. *Psychonomic Science,* 1966, *5,* 157–158.

Aronson, E., & Worchel, P. My enemy's enemy is my friend. *Journal of Personality and Social Psychology,* 1968, *8,* 8–12.

Aronson, V., Abrahams, D., & Rottman, L. Importance of physical attractiveness in dating behavior. *Journal of Personality and Social Psychology,* 1973, *25,* 151–176.

Asch, S. *Social Psychology.* Englewood Cliffs, N.J.: Prentice-Hall, 1952.

Atkin, C. K., & Bowen, L. Quality versus quantity in televised political ads. *Public Opinion Quarterly,* 1973, *37,* 209–224.

Austin, W., & Walster, E. Equity with the world: The transrelational effects of equity and inequity. *Sociometry*, 1975, *38*, 474–496.

Ausubel, D. P. *Readings in the Psychology of Cognition.* New York: Holt, Rinehart & Winston, 1965.

Back, K. W. Social research as a communications system. *Social Forces*, 1962, *41*, 61–68.

Back, K. W. Biological models of social change. *American Sociological Review*, 1971, *36*, 660–667.

Back, K. W., Bunker, S., & Dunnagan, C. Barriers to communication and measurement of semantic space. *Sociometry*, 1972, *35*, 347–357.

Bain, R. The self-and-other words of a child. *American Journal of Sociology*, 1936, *41*, 767–775.

Bakan, D. *David Bakan on Method: Toward a Reconstruction of Psychological Investigation.* San Francisco: Jossey-Bass, 1967.

Baker, R. Observer: VE day plus 7,305. *New York Times*, 1965.

Baker, W. Y. *Out on a Limb.* New York: McGraw-Hill (n.d.).

Bales, R. F. *Interaction Process Analysis: A Method for the Study of Small Groups.* Reading, Mass.: Addison-Wesley, 1950.

Bales, R. F. Equilibrium problem in small groups. In T. Parsons, R. Bales, and E. Shils, *Working Papers in the Theory of Action.* New York: Free Press, 1953.

Bales, R. F. *Personality and Interpersonal Behavior.* New York: Holt, Rinehart & Winston, 1970.

Bales, R. F., & Strodtbeck, F. L. Phases in group problem solving. *Journal of Abnormal and Social Psychology*, 1951, *46*, 485–489.

Ball-Rokeach, S. J. From pervasive ambiguity to a definition of the situation. *Sociometry*, 1973, *36*, 378–389.

Ballweg, J. A. Resolution of conjugal role adjustment. *Journal of Marriage and the Family*, 1967, *29*, 277–281.

Bandura, A. What TV violence can do to your child. In O. N. Larsen (Ed.), *Violence and the Mass Media.* New York: Harper & Row, 1968.

Bandura, A., & McDonald, F. J. The influence of social reinforcement and the behavior of models in shaping children's moral judgments. *Journal of Abnormal Social Psychology*, 1963, *67*, 274–281.

Bandura, A., Ross, D., & Ross, S. A. Imitation of film-mediated aggressive models. *Journal of Abnormal and Social Psychology*, 1963, *66*, 3–11.

Banton, M. *Roles: An Introduction to the Study of Social Relations.* London: Tavistock, 1965.

Bany, M. A., & Johnson, L. B. *Classroom Group Behavior.* New York: Macmillan, 1964.

Bardis, P. D. A technique for the measurement of attitudes toward abortion. *Journal of Sociology of the Family*, 1972, *2*, 98–104.

Barker, R. The social psychology of disability. *Journal of Social Issues*, 1948, *4*.

Barker, R. G., & Wright, H. F. *Midwest and Its Children: The Psychological Ecology of an American Town.* Evanston, Ill.: Row, Peterson, 1954.

Barker, R. M. *Ecological Psychology: Concepts and Methods for Studying the Environment of Human Behavior.* Stanford, Calif.: Stanford University Press, 1968.

Baron, R. A. Attraction toward the model and model's competence as determinants of adult imitative behavior. *Journal of Personality and Social Psychology*, 1970, *14*, 345–351.

Baron, R., Byrne, D., & Griffitt, W. *Social Psychology: Understanding Human Interaction*. Boston: Allyn & Bacon, 1974.

Barrett, C. J., Berg, P. I., Eaton, E. M., & Lisa, E. Implications of women's liberation and the future of psychotherapy. *Psychotherapy: Theory, Research, and Practice*, 1974, (Spring), 11–15.

Bartell, G. *Group Sex*. New York: Peter Wyden, 1971.

Bartlett, F. C. The aims of political propaganda. In D. Katz, D. Cartwright, S. Eldersveld, and A. M. Lee (Eds.), *Public Opinion and Propaganda*. New York: Dryden, 1954.

Basso, K. J. To give up on words: Silence in western Apache culture. In P. Giglioli (Ed.), *Language and Social Context*. Harmondsworth, England: Penguin, 1972.

Batchelor, J. P., & Goethals, G. Spatial arrangements in freely formed groups. *Sociometry*, 1972, *35*, 270–279.

Bates, A. P. Privacy: a useful concept? *Social Forces*, 1964, *42*, 429–434.

Bauer, W. Public opinion. In *Encyclopedia of the Social Sciences* (Vol. 12). New York: Macmillan, 1935.

Baxter, J. C., & Rozelle, R. M. Non-verbal expression as a function of crowding during a simulated police-citizen encounter. *Journal of Personality and Social Psychology*, 1975, *32*, 40–45.

BaYunus, I. *Shoplifting among college students: A study in the sociology of crime*. Unpublished doctoral dissertation, University of Michigan, 1970.

Beck, A. W. *Words and Waves*. New York: McGraw-Hill, 1967.

Beck, J. Sexist inequality triggers violence. Knight News Service, March 13, 1976.

Becker, E. Socialization, command of performance, and mental illness. *American Journal of Sociology*, 1962, *67*, 494–501.

Becker, E. *The Revolution in Psychiatry*. New York: Free Press, 1964.

Becker, E. *The Birth and Death of Meaning* (2nd ed.). New York: Free Press, 1968.

Becker, E. *The Denial of Death*. New York: Free Press, 1974.

Becker, H. S. *Outsiders: Studies in the Sociology of Deviance*. New York: Free Press, 1963.

Becker, H. S. What do they really learn at college? *Trans-Action*, 1964, *1*, 14–17.

Becker, H. S. The self and adult socialization. In *Sociological Work: Methods and Substance*. Chicago: Aldine, 1970.

Becker, H. S., Geer, B., Hughes, E. C., & Strauss, A. *Boys in White: Student Culture in Medical School*. Chicago: University of Chicago Press, 1961.

Becker, M. H. Sociometric location and innovativeness: Reformulation and extension of the diffusion model. *American Sociological Review*, 1970, *35*, 267–282.

Belknap, I. *Human Problems of a State Mental Hospital*. New York: McGraw-Hill, 1956.

Bell, G. D. Determinants of span control. *American Journal of Sociology*, 1967, *73*, 100–109.

Bell, R. R. *Marriage and Family Interaction* (Rev. ed.). Homewood, Ill.: Dorsey Press, 1967.

Bell, R. R. *Social Deviance: A Substantive Analysis*. Homewood, Ill.: Dorsey Press, 1971.

Bell, S. M., & Ainsworth, M. Infant crying and maternal responsiveness. *Child Development*, 1972, *43*, 1171–1190.

Bem, D. (Ed.). *Beliefs, Attitudes and Human Affairs*. Monterey, Calif.: Brooks/Cole, 1970.

Bengston, V. L. Generation and family effects in value socialization. *American Sociological Review*, 1975, *40*, 358–371.

Bennetts, L. Prostitution: A non-victim crime? *Issues in Criminology*, 1973, *8*, 137–162.

Bensman, J. American youth and the class structure. In H. Silverstein (Ed.), *The Sociology of Youth*. New York: Macmillan, 1973.

Benton, A. A. Productivity, distributive justice, and bargaining among children. *Journal of Personality and Social Psychology*, 1971, *18*, 68–78.

Berger, B. On the youthfulness of youth cultures. *Social Research*, 1963, (Autumn), 319–342.

Berger, P., & Kellner, H. Marriage and the construction of reality. *Diogenes*, 1964, *46*, 1–24.

Berger, P. L., & Luckman, T. *The Social Construction of Reality*. New York: Doubleday, 1967.

Berkowitz, L. *Social Psychology*. Glenview, Ill.: Scott, Foresman, 1972.

Berkowitz, L., & Daniels, L. Responsibility and dependency. *Journal of Abnormal and Social Psychology*, 1963, *66*, 429–436.

Berkowitz, W. R. The impact of antiVietnam demonstrations upon national public opinion and military indicators. *Social Science Research*, 1973, *2*, 1–14.

Berlo, D. K. *The Process of Communication*. New York: Holt, Rinehart & Winston, 1960.

Bernard, J. *Women, Wives and Mothers: Values and Options*. Chicago: Aldine, 1975.

Berne, E. *Games People Play*. New York: Grove Press, 1964.

Bernstein, B. A public language: Some sociological implications of a linguistic form. *British Journal of Sociology*, 1959, *10*, 311–326.

Bernstein, B. Social class, language, and socialization. In P. Giglioli (Ed.), *Language and Social Context*. Harmondsworth, England: Penguin, 1972.

Berrelson, B. *Graduate Education in the United States*. New York: McGraw-Hill, 1960.

Berscheid, E., Dion, K., Walster, E., & Walster, G. W. Physical attractiveness and dating choice: A test of the matching hypothesis. *Journal of Experimental Social Psychology*, 1971, *7*, 173–189.

Berscheid, E., & Walster, E. *Interpersonal Attraction*. New York: Addison-Wesley, 1969.

Bertalanffy, L. von. *General Systems Theory*. New York: Braziller, 1968.

Bettelheim, B. *The Empty Fortress: Infantile Autism and the Birth of Self*. New York: Free Press, 1967.

Bezdek, W., & Strodtbeck, F. L. Sex role identity and pragmatic action. *American Sociological Review*, 1970, *35*, 491–502.

Biddle, B. J., & Thomas, E. J. *Role Theory: Concepts and Research*. New York: Wiley, 1966.

Bierstedt, R. Sociology and humane learning. *American Sociological Review*, 1960, *25*, 3–9.

Bierstedt, R. *The Social Order* (3rd ed.). New York: McGraw-Hill, 1970.

Bird, C. *Born Female*. New York: McKay, 1974.

Birdwhistell, R. L. *Kinesics and Context: Essays on Body Motion Communication*. Philadelphia: University of Pennsylvania Press, 1970.

Birenbaum, A., & Sagarin, E. *People in Places: The Sociology of the Familiar*. New York: Praeger, 1973.

Black, C. R., Weinstein, E. A., & Tanur, J. M. Self-interest and expectations of altruism in exchange situations. *The Sociological Quarterly*, 1974, *15*, 242–252.

Blake, J. Abortion and public opinion. *Science*, 1971, *71*, 540–548.

Blake, R. R., & Mouton, J. S. Loyalty of ingroup representatives to ingroup positions during intergroup competition. *Sociometry*, 1961, *24*, 177–183.

Blalock, H. M. Estimating measurement error using multiple indicators and several points in time. *American Sociological Review*, 1970, *35*, 101–111.

Blatz, C. V. Accountability and answerability. *Journal for the Theory of Social Behavior*, 1972, *2*, 101–120.

Blau, P. M. *Exchange and Power in Social Life*. New York: Wiley, 1964.

Blau, P. M. Parameters of social structure. *American Sociological Review*, 1974, *39*, 615–636.

Blazer, J. A. Married virgins: A study of unconsummated marriages. *Journal of Marriage and the Family*, 1964, *26*, 213–214.

Blum, A. F., & McHugh, P. The social ascription of motives. *American Sociological Review*, 1971, *36*, 98–109.

Blumer, H. *An Appraisal of Thomas and Znaniecki's The Polish Peasant in Europe and America*. New York: Social Science Research Council, 1939.

Blumer, H. Collective behavior. In A. M. Lee (Ed.), *New Outline of the Principles of Sociology*. New York: Barnes & Noble, 1946.

Blumer, H. The mass, the public, and public opinion. In *Reader in Public Opinion and Communication*. Glencoe, Ill.: Free Press, 1953.

Blumer, H. *Symbolic Interactionism: Perspective and Method*. Englewood Cliffs, N.J.: Prentice-Hall, 1969.

Blumstein, P. W., & Weinstein, E. A. The redress of distributive injustice. *American Journal of Sociology*, 1969, *74*, 408–418.

Bogardus, E. S. *Fundamentals of Social Psychology*. New York: Appleton-Century-Crofts, 1931.

Bohrenstedt, G. W. A quick method for determining the reliability and validity of multiple item scales. *American Sociological Review*, 1969, *34*, 542–548.

Bolton, C. Is sociology a behavioral science? *Pacific Sociological Review*, 1963, *6*, 3–9.

Bond, J. R., & Vinacke, W. E. Coalitions in mixed-sex triads. *Sociometry*, 1961, *24*, 61–75.

Bonjean, C. M., Hill, R. J., & McLemore, S. D. Continuities in sociological measurement. In N. K. Denzin (Ed.), *Sociological Methods*. Chicago: Aldine, 1970.

Boocock, S. S. The life career game. In M. Inbar and C. Stoll (Eds.), *Simulation and Gaming in Social Science*. New York: Free Press, 1972.

Borgatta, E. F. On the work of Jacob L. Moreno. *Sociometry*, 1975, *38*, 148–152.

Borofsky, G. N., Stollock, G. E., & Messe, L. A. Sex differences in bystander reactions to physical assault. *Journal of Experimental Social Psychology*, 1971, 7, 313–318.

Bossard, J. Residential propinquity as a factor in mate selection. *American Journal of Sociology*, 1932, *38*, 219–224.

Bossard, J. *The Sociology of Child Development*. New York: Harper & Row, 1948.

Bott, E. Urban families: Conjugal roles and social networks. *Human Relations*, 1955, *8*, 345–486.

Boulanger, G. *Le Cris chez l'Enfant*. Paris: Vrin, 1968.

Bowen, D. D., & Seigel, J. P. A longitudinal study of reactions in small task groups to periodic performance feedback. *Human Relations*, 1973, *26*, 433–448.

Bowers, K. S. Situationism in psychology: An analysis and a critique. *Psychological Review*, 1973, *80*, 307–336.

Box, S. *Deviance, Reality, and Society*. London: Holt, Rinehart & Winston, 1971.

Boydell, C. L., & Grindstaff, C. F. Public opinion toward legal sanctions for crimes of violence. *Journal of Criminal Law and Criminology*, 1974, *65*, 113–116.

Brannon, R., Cyphers, G., Hesse, S., Hesselbart, S., Keane, R., Schuman, H., Viccaro, T., & Wright, D. Attitude and action: A field experiment joined to a general population survey. *American Sociological Review*, 1973, *38*, 625–636.

Braungart, R. G. Family status, socialization, and student politics: A multivariate analysis. *American Journal of Sociology*, 1971, 77, 108–130.

Breer, P. E., & Locke, E. A. *Task Experience as a Source of Attitudes*. Homewood, Ill.: Dorsey Press, 1965.

Brehm, J. W., & Cohen, A. R. *Explorations in Cognitive Dissonance*. New York: Wiley, 1962.

Brewer, J. Flow on communications, expert qualifications, and organizational structures. *American Sociological Review*, 1971, *36*, 475–484.

Breznitz, S., & Kugelmass, S. Intentionality in moral judgment: Developmental stages. *Child Development*, 1967, *38*, 469–479.

Brim, O. G., & Wheeler, S. *Socialization after Childhood*. New York: Wiley, 1967.

Brissett, D., & Edgley, C. *Life as Theater: A Dramaturgical Sourcebook*. Chicago: Aldine, 1975.

Brody, R. A., & Verba, S. Hawk and dove: The search for an explanation of Vietnam policy preferences. *Acta Politica*, 1972, *7*, 285–322.

Bronfenbrenner, U. *Two Worlds of Childhood: U.S. and U.S.S.R.* New York: Russell Sage Foundation, 1970.

Brown, R. *Words and Things*. Glencoe, Ill.: Free Press, 1958.

Brown, R., & Bellugi, U. Three processes in the child's acquisition of syntax. In J. Emig, J. Fleming, and H. Popp (Eds.), *Language and Learning*. New York: Harcourt Brace Jovanovich, 1964.

Brown, R., Cozden, C., & Bellugi, U. A child's grammar from I to III. In J. Hill (Ed.), *Minnesota Symposium on Child Psychology*. Minneapolis: University of Minnesota Press, 1969.

Bruwold, W. H. Consistency among attitudes, beliefs, and behavior. *Journal of Social Psychology*, 1972, *86*, 127–134.

Bryan, J. H., & Test, M. A. Models and helping: Naturalistic studies in aiding behavior. *Journal of Personality and Social Psychology*, 1967, *6*, 400–407.

Bugental, D., Love, L. R., & Gianetto, R. M. Perfidious feminine faces. *Journal of Personality and Social Psychology*, 1971, *17*, 314–318.

Burgess, E. W., & Locke, H. J. *The Family*. New York: American Book Co., 1953.

Burhans, D. T., Jr. Coalition game research: A reexamination. *American Journal of Sociology*, 1973, *79*, 389–408.

Burke, K. *A Grammar of Motives*. Englewood Cliffs, N.J.: Prentice-Hall, 1945.

Burke, K. *A Rhetoric of Motives*. Englewood Cliffs, N.J.: Prentice-Hall, 1950.

Burke, K. *Permanence and Change*. Indianapolis: Bobbs-Merrill, 1965.

Burr, W. R. An expansion and test of a role theory of marital satisfaction. *Journal of Marriage and the Family*, 1971, *33*, 368–372.

Byrne, D. Interpersonal attraction and attitude similarity. *Journal of Abnormal and Social Psychology*, 1961, *62*, 713–715.

Byrne, D. *The Attraction Paradigm*. New York: Academic Press, 1971.

Byrne, D., Baron, R., & Griffitt, W. *Social Psychology: Understanding Human Interaction*. Boston: Allyn & Bacon, 1974.

Byrne, D., & Griffitt, W. Similarity versus liking: A clarification. *Journal of*

Psychonomic Science, 1966, *6,* 295–296.

Byrne, D., London, O., & Reeves, K. The effects of physical attractiveness, sex, and attitude similarity on interpersonal attraction. *Journal of Personality,* 1968, *36,* 259–271.

Byrne, D., & McGraw, C. Interpersonal attraction toward Negroes. In H. C. Lindgren (Ed.), *Contemporary Research in Social Psychology.* New York: Wiley, 1969.

Cameron, B. *Informal Sociology: A Casual Introduction to Sociological Thinking.* New York: Random House, 1963.

Campbell, A., Converse, P. E., Miller, W. E., & Stokes, D. E. *The American Voter: An Abridgement.* New York: Wiley, 1964.

Campbell, O. T. Social attitudes and other acquired behavioral dispositions. In S. Kock (Ed.), *Psychology: A Study of a Science.* New York: McGraw-Hill, 1963.

Cancian, F. M. Interaction patterns in Zincanteco families. *American Sociological Review,* 1964, *29,* 540–550.

Carlsmith, J., Collins, B., & Helmreich, R. Studies in forced compliance. Effect of pressure for compliance on attitude change produced by face-to-face role playing and anonymous essay writing. *Journal of Personality and Social Psychology,* 1966, *4,* 1–33.

Carmichael, L., Roberts, S. O., & Wessell, N. Y. A study of judgment of manual expression as represented in still and motion pictures. *Journal of Social Psychology,* 1937, *8,* 115–142.

Carnap, R. *The Logical Syntax of Language.* Patterson, N.J.: Littlefield Adams, 1959.

Carr, L. G. The stole items and acquiescence. *American Sociological Review,* 1971, *36,* 287–293.

Cartwright, D. Risk taking by individuals and groups: An assessment of research employing choice dilemmas. *Journal of Personality and Social Psychology,* 1971, *20,* 178–361.

Cartwright, D., & Harary, F. Structure balance: A generalization of Heider's theory. *Psychological Review,* 1956, *63,* 277–293.

Cartwright, D., & Zander, A. (Eds.). *Group Dynamics: Research and Theory.* Evanston, Ill.: Row, Peterson, 1960.

Cassirer, E. *An Essay on Man.* New Haven, Conn.: Yale University Press, 1944.

Cater, D., & Adler, R. (Eds.). *Television as a Social Force: New Approaches to TV Criticism.* New York: Praeger, 1975.

Cater, D., & Strickland, S. *TV Violence and the Child: The Evolution and Fate of the Surgeon General's Report.* New York: Russell Sage Foundation, 1975.

Cavan, S. *Liquor License.* Chicago: Aldine, 1966.

Chaikin, A., Sigler, E., & Derlaga, V. Non-verbal mediators of teacher expectancy effects. *Journal of Personality and Social Psychology,* 1974, *30,* 144–149.

Chapanis, N., & Chapanis, A. Cognitive dissonance. *Psychological Bulletin,* 1964, *61,* 1–22.

Chapman, A. H. *The Games Children Play.* New York: Berkley, 1971.

Chave, E. J. A new type of scaling for measuring attitudes. *Religious Education,* 1928, *23,* 214–249.

Cherniss, C. Personality and ideology: A personological study of women's liberation. *Psychiatry,* 1972, (May), 109–125.

Cherry, C. *On Human Communication: A Review, a Survey, and a Criticism.* New York: Wiley, 1957.

Chesebro, J. W., Cragan, J. F., & McCullough, P. The small group technique of the radical revolutionary: A synthetic study of consciousness raising. *Speech Monographs*, 1973, *40*, 136–146.

Cheyne, J. A., & Efran, M. G. The effect of spatial and interpersonal variables on the invasion of group controlled territories. *Sociometry*, 1972, *35*, 477–489.

Chombart de Lauwe, M. J. Image de soi et images culturelles de l'enfant. *Psychologie Francaise*, 1971, *16*, 185–198.

Chombart de Lauwe, P. H. The interaction of person and society. *American Sociological Review*, 1966, *31*, 237–248.

Chomsky, C. *The Acquisition of Syntax in Children from 5 to 10*. Cambridge, Mass.: MIT Press, 1969.

Chomsky, N. *Aspects of the Theory of Syntax*. Cambridge, Mass.: MIT Press, 1965.

Chomsky, N. *Problems of Knowledge and Freedom*. London: Fontana, 1973.

Chomsky, N., & Halle, M. *The Sound Pattern of English*. New York: Harper & Row, 1968.

Chukovsky, K. *From Two to Five*. (M. Morton, Trans.). Los Angeles: University of California Press, 1963.

Cicourel, A. V. *Method and Measurement in Sociology*. Glencoe, Ill.: Free Press, 1964.

Cicourel, A. V. *The Social Organization of Juvenile Justice*. New York: Wiley, 1967.

Cicourel, A. V. *Cognitive Sociology: Language and Meaning in Social Interaction*. New York: Free Press, 1974.

Cicourel, A. V., Jennings, K., Jennings, S., Leiter, K., MacKay, R., Mehan, H., & Roth, D. *Language Use and School Performance*. New York: Academic Press, 1974.

Clark, C. D. Concept of the public. *Southwest Social Science Quarterly*, 1932–1933, *13*, 311–320.

Clark, R. D. III. Group-induced shift toward risk: A critical appraisal. *Psychological Bulletin*, 1971, *76*, 251–270.

Clausen, J. A. Perspectives of childhood socialization. In Clausen, Brim, Inkeles, Lippitt, Maccoby, and Smith, *Socialization and Society*. Boston: Little, Brown, 1968.

Clausen, J., & Yarrow, M. The impact of mental illness on the family. *Journal of Social Issues, 11*, 1955.

Clayton, R., & Tolone, W. Religiosity and attitudes toward induced abortion: An elaboration of the relationship. *Sociological Analysis*, 1973, *34*, 26–39.

Clift, E. The year of the woman. *Newsweek*, November 4, 1974, 20–25.

Clinard, M. *Sociology of Deviant Behavior*. New York: Holt, Rinehart & Winston, 1974.

Cloyd, J. S. Small group as a social institution. *American Sociological Review*, 1965, *30*, 394–402.

Cochran, W. G., Mosteller, F., & Tukey, J. W. Principles of sampling. *Journal of American Statistical Association*, 1954, *79*, 30–35.

Coe, W. C., & Sarbin, T. R. An alternative interpretation to the multiple composition of hypnotic scales: A single role-relevant skill. *Journal of Personality and Social Psychology*, 1971, *18*, 1–8.

Cohen, A. K. *Deviance and Control*. Englewood Cliffs, N.J.: Prentice-Hall, 1966.

Cohen, A. R. Some implications of self-esteem for social influence. In C. Hovland and I. Janis (Eds.), *Personality and Persuasibility* (Vol. 2). New Haven, Conn.: Yale University Press, 1959.

Cohen, A. R. Attitudinal consequences of induced discrepancies between cognitions and behavior. *Public Opinion Quarterly*, 1960, *24*, 297–318.

Cohen, E., & Sampson, E. E. Distributive justice: A preliminary study of children's equal and equitable allocations of rewards using the doll play technique. Paper presented at the meeting of the Eastern Psychological Association, New York, April, 1975.

Colburn, C. W. II. *Experimental Study of the Relationship in Persuasion.* Unpublished doctoral dissertation, Indiana University, 1967.

Cole, S., & LeJeune, R. Illness and legitimation of failure. *American Sociological Review*, 1972, *37*, 347–356.

Coleman, J. The adolescent subculture and academic achievement. *American Journal of Sociology*, 1960, *65*, 337–347.

Coleman, J. S. *The Adolescent Society.* New York: Free Press, 1963.

Collins, R., & Makowsky, M. *The Discovery of Society.* New York: Random House, 1972.

Colombotos, J. Physicians and Medicare: A before-after study of the effects of legislation on attitudes. *American Sociological Review*, 1969, *34*, 318–334.

Comer, R. J., & Piliavin, J. Effects of physical deviance upon face to face interaction: The other side. *Journal of Personality and Social Psychology*, 1972, *23*, 33–39.

Comte, A. *The Positive Philosophy.* New York: AMS Press, 1974. (Originally published, 1855.)

Comte, A. *System of Positive Polity.* New York: B. Franklin, 1968. (Originally published, 1875.)

Cooley, C. H. *Personal Competition.* New York: Macmillan, 1899.

Cooley, C. H. *Human Nature and the Social Order.* New York: Scribner's, 1902.

Cooley, C. H. *Social Organization.* New York: Scribner's, 1909.

Cooley, C. H. *Social Processes.* New York: Scribner's, 1918.

Cooley, C. H., Angell, R. C., & Carr, L. J. *Introductory Sociology.* New York: Scribner's, 1933.

Cooper, E., & Dinerman, H. Analysis of the film "Don't Be a Sucker": A study in communication. *Public Opinion Quarterly*, 1951, *15*, 243–264.

Cooper, G. L., & Mangham, I. L. *T-groups: A Survey of Research.* New York: Wiley Interscience, 1971.

Cooper, J., & Worchel, S. Role of undesired consequences in arousing cognitive dissonance. *Journal of Personality and Social Psychology*, 1970, *16*, 199–206.

Corsini, R. J., Shaw, M. E., & Blake, R. R. *Roleplaying in Business and Industry.* Glencoe, Ill.: Free Press, 1961.

Coser, L. A. Some functions of deviant behavior and normative flexibility. *American Journal of Sociology*, 1961, *68*, 172–181.

Coser, R. L. *Life in the Ward.* East Lansing, Mich.: Michigan State University Press, 1962.

Coser, R. L. Role distance, sociological ambivalence and transitional status systems. *American Journal of Sociology*, 1966, *72*, 173–187.

Costner, H. L. Utilizing causal models to discover flaws in experiments. *Sociometry*, 1971, *34*, 398–410.

Couch, C. Self-attitudes and degree of agreement with immediate others. *American Journal of Sociology*, 1958, *63*, 491–496.

Couto, W. Role playing vs. role taking: An appeal for clarification. *American Sociological Review*, 1951, *16*, 180–184.

Crano, W. D., & Cooper, R. E. Examination of Newcomb's extension of structural balance. *Journal of Personality and Social Psychology*, 1973, *27*, 344–353.

Crespi, I. What kinds of attitude measures are predictive of behavior? *Public Opinion Quarterly*, 1971, *35*, 327–334.

Crittenden, K., & Hill, R. J. Coding reliability and validity of interview data. *American Sociological Review*, 1971, *36*, 1073–1080.

Cromwell, J. Relative effect on audience attitude of first vs. second argumentative speech of a series. *Speech Monographs*, 1950, *17*, 105–122.

Cummings, E. E. *50 Poems*. New York: Grosset & Dunlap, 1940.

Curtis, R. F., & Jackson, E. F. Multiple indicators in survey research. *American Journal of Sociology*, 1962, *68*, 195–204.

Cuzzort, R. *Humanity and Modern Sociological Thought*. New York: Holt, Rinehart & Winston, 1969.

Cuzzort, R., King, E. W. *Humanity and Modern Social Thought* (2nd ed.). New York: Holt, Rinehart & Winston, 1976.

Daehler, M. W., Horowitz, A. B., Wynns, F. C., & Flavell, J. H. Verbal and nonverbal rehearsal in children's recall. *Child Development*, 1969, *40*, 443–453.

Dager, E. Z. Socialization and personality development in the child. In H. T. Christensen (Ed.), *Handbook of Marriage and the Family*. Chicago: Rand McNally, 1964.

Dank, B. M. Coming out in the gay world. In M. Truzzi (Ed.), *Sociology for Pleasure*. Englewood Cliffs, N.J.: Prentice-Hall, 1974.

Davis, F. Deviance disavowal. *Social Problems*, 1961, Fall, 120–132.

Davis, K. A. A final note on extreme isolation. *American Journal of Sociology*, 1940, *45*, 554–565.

Davis, K. The sociology of parent-youth conflict. *American Sociological Review*, 1940, *5*, 523–535.

Davis, K. Adolescence and the social structure. *The Annals of the American Academy of Political and Social Sciences*, 1944, *236*, 8–16.

Davis, M. S. *Intimate Relations*. New York: Free Press, 1973.

Dawson, C. A., & Gettys, W. E. *An Introduction to Sociology*. New York: Ronald Press, 1929.

Dean, L. M., Willis, F., & Hewitt, J. Initial interaction distance among individuals of equal and unequal military rank. *Journal of Personality and Social Psychology*, 1975, *32*, 294–299.

DeFleur, M. L., & Westie, F. R. Verbal attitudes and overt acts: An experiment on salience of attitudes. *American Sociological Review*, 1958, *23*, 667–673.

deHoyos, A., & deHoyos, G. The amigo system and alienation of the wife in the conjugal Mexican family. In B. Farber (Ed.), *Kinship and Family Organization*. New York: Wiley, 1966.

Delbecq, A. L., Van de Ven, A. H., & Gustafson, D. H. *Group Techniques for Program Planning: A Guide to Nominal Group and Delphi Processes*. Glenview, Ill.: Scott, Foresman, 1975.

DeLevita, D. H. *The Concept of Identity*. New York: Harper & Row, 1967.

Denes, P. B., & Pinson, E. *The Speech Chain: The Physics and Biology of Spoken Language*. New York: Anchor Doubleday, 1973.

Denney, N. W., & Duffy, D. M. Possible environmental causes of stages in moral reasoning. *Journal of Genetic Psychology*, 1974, *125*, 277–283.

Denzin, N. K. Symbolic interactionism and ethnomethodology, a proposed synthesis. *American Sociological Review*, 1969, *34*, 922–934.

Denzin, N. K. Symbolic interactionism and ethnomethodology. In J. Douglas (Ed.), *Understanding Everyday Life*. Chicago: Aldine, 1970.

DePalma, D. J. Effects of social class, moral orientation, and severity of punishment on boys' moral responses to transgression and generosity. *Developmental Psychology*, 1974, *10*, 890–900.

Desmonde, W. The position of George Herbert Mead. In G. Stone and H. Farberman (Eds.), *Social Psychology through Symbolic Interaction*. Boston: Ginn, 1970.

Deutsch, M., & Krauss, R. *Theories in Social Psychology*. New York: Basic Books, 1965.

Deutscher, I. *What We Say/What We Do: Sentiments and Acts*. Glenview, Ill.: Scott, Foresman, 1973.

Devereux, E. C., Bronfenbrenner, U., & Rodgers, R. Childrearing in England and the United States: A cross national comparison. *Journal of Marriage and the Family*, 1969, *31*, 257–270.

Devereux, E. C., Jr., Bronfenbrenner, U., & Suci, G. J. Patterns of parent behavior in America and West Germany: A cross-cultural comparison. *International Social Science Journal*, 1962, *3*, 488–506.

Dewey, J. *Human Nature and Conduct*. New York: Holt, Rinehart & Winston, 1922.

Dickson, S. Class attitudes on dental treatment. *British Journal of Sociology*, 1968, *19*, 206–211.

Diderot, D. Lettre sur les sourds et muets. In J. Assezat (Ed.), *Oeuvres completes de Diderot* (Vol. 1). Paris: Garnier Frères, 1875.

Dillman, D., & Christensen, J. Toward the assessment of public values. *Public Opinion Quarterly*, 1974, *38*, 206–221.

Dittman, A. T. The body-movement speech-rhythm relationship as a cue to speech encoding. In A. Seigman and B. Pope (Eds.), *Studies in Dyadic Communication*. New York: Pergamon Press, 1972.

Dittman, A. Uh-huhs of adults perfectly timed. *Oklahoma City Times*, 1973.

Dommermuth, W. P. How does the medium affect the message? *Journalism Quarterly*, 1974, *51*, 441–447.

Doob, L. W. The behavior of attitudes. *Psychological Review*, 1947, *54*, 135–156.

Douglas, J. *Deviance and Respectability: The Social Construction of Moral Meanings*. New York: Basic Books, 1970.

Douvan, E., & Adelson, J. The adolescent experience and identity. In M. Wertheimer (Ed.), *Confrontation*. Glenview, Ill.: Scott, Foresman, 1970.

Dressler, D. *Sociology: The Study of Human Interaction*. New York: Knopf, 1973.

Driscoll, R., Davis, K. E., & Lipetz, M. E. Parental interference and romantic love: The Romeo and Juliet effect. *Journal of Personality and Social Psychology*, 1972, *24*, 1–10.

Duncan, H. D. *Communication and Social Order*. New York: Bedminster Press, 1962.

Duncan, H. D. The search for a social theory of communication in American sociology. In F. E. X. Dance (Ed.), *Human Communication Theory: Original Essays*. New York: Holt, Rinehart & Winston, 1967.

Duncan, H. D. *Symbols in Society*. New York: Oxford, 1968.

Duncan, S., Rosenberg, M. J., & Finkelstein, J. The paralanguage of experimenter bias. *Sociometry*, 1969, *32*, 207–219.

Dunlap, K. Are there any instincts? *Journal of Abnormal Psychology*, 1919, *14*, 307–311.

Dunn, T., & Ziff, R. A new copytesting system. *Journal of Advertising Research*, 1974, *14*, 53–59.

Dunphy, D. C. Phases, roles and myths in self-analytic groups. *Journal of Applied Behavioral Science*, 1968, *4*, 195–225.

Dunphy, D. C. *The Primary Group: A Handbook for Analysis and Field Research*. New York: Appleton-Century-Crofts, 1972.

Durkheim, E. *On the Division of Labor in Society* (George Simpson, Trans.). New York: Macmillan, 1933. (Originally published, 1893.)

Dyer, E. F. Parenthood as crisis: A restudy. *Marriage and Family Living*, 1963, May, 196–201.

Eaton, C. Breaking a path for the liberation of women in the South. *The Georgia Review*, 1974, *28*, 187–199.

Eckhoff, E., Gauslaa, J., & Baldwin, A. L. Parental behavior toward boys and girls of preschool age. *Acta Psychologica*, 1961, *18*, 85–99.

Edgerly, J. W., & Gaither, G. Assessing attitude intensity among student factions: A behavioral model. *Journal of Human Relations*, 1971, *19*, 377–393.

Edgley, C. *Vocabularies of Motive and the Social Definition of Schizophrenia: An Exploratory Study.* Unpublished doctoral dissertation, State University of New York, Buffalo, 1970.

Edney, J. J., & Jordan-Edney, N. L. Territorial spacing on a beach. *Sociometry*, 1974, *37*, 92–194.

Edwards, D. W. Blacks vs. Whites: When is race a relevant variable? *Journal of Personality and Social Psychology*, 1974, *29*, 39–49.

Ehrlich, C. The male sociologist's burden: The place of women in marriage and family tests. *Journal of Marriage and the Family*, 1971, *33*, 421–430.

Eibl-Eibesfeldt, I. Zur Etnologie menschlichen Grussverhaltens: Das Grussverhalten und einige andere Muster freundlicher Kontaktaufnahme der Waika. *Tierpsychologie*, 1971, *29*, 196–213.

Eisenstadt, S. N. Archetypal patterns of youth. In E. Erikson (Ed.), *Youth: Change and Challenge.* New York: American Academy of Arts and Sciences, 1961.

Ekman, P., & Friesen, W. V. Nonverbal leakage and cues to deception. *Psychiatry*, 1969, *32*, 88–106. (a)

Ekman, P., & Friesen, W. V. The repertoire of nonverbal behavior: Categories, origins, usage, and coding. *Semiotica*, 1969, *1*, 49–98. (b)

Elder, G. H. Family structures and educational attainment: A cross national analysis. *American Sociological Review*, 1965, *30*, 81–96. (a)

Elder, G. H. Role relations, socio-cultural environments and autocratic family ideology. *Sociometry*, 1965, *28*, 173–196. (b)

Elder, G. H., & Bowerman, C. E. A family structure and childrearing patterns: The effect of family size and sex composition. *American Sociological Review*, 1963, *28*, 891–905.

Elkin, F., & Westley, W. The myth of the adolescent culture. *American Sociological Review*, 1955, *20*, 680–684.

Ellsworth, P., & Carlsmith, J. M. Eye contact and gaze aversion in an aggressive encounter. *Journal of Personality and Social Psychology*, 1973, *28*, 280–292.

Endler, N. S., & Hunt, J. McV. S-R inventories of hostility and comparisons of the proportions of variance from persons, responses, and situations for hostility and anxiousness. *Journal of Personality and Social Psychology*, 1968, *9*, 309–315.

Enroth, R. M. The homosexual church: An ecclesiastical extension of a subculture. *Social Compass*, 1974, *21*, 255–360.

Entwisle, D. Developmental sociolinguistics: Inner-city children. *American Journal of Sociology*, 1968, *74*, 37–49.

Epstein, A. L. Linguistic innovation and culture on the Copperbelt, Northern Rhodesia. In J. A. Fishman (Ed.), *Readings in the Sociology of Language.* The Hague, the Netherlands: Mouton, 1968.

Epstein, C. Encountering the male establishment limits on women's careers in the professions. *American Journal of Sociology*, 1970, *75*, 965–982.

Erikson, E. H. *Childhood and Society*. New York: Norton, 1950.

Erikson, E. H. *Young Man Luther*. New York: Norton, 1958.

Erikson, K. Notes on the sociology of deviance. *Social Problems*, 1962, *9*, 307–314.

Erikson, K. A comment on disguised observation in sociology. *Social Problems*, 1967, *14*, 366–373.

Etzioni, A. *A comparative analysis of complex organizations* (Rev. ed.). New York: Free Press, 1975.

Fairfield, D. *Communes, USA: The Modern Utopian*. San Francisco: Alternatives Foundation, 1972.

Fairweather, G. W. *Methods for Experimental Social Innovation*. New York: Wiley, 1968.

Fast, J. *Body Language*. New York: Pocket Books, 1970.

Feitelson, D., Weintraub, S., & Michaeli, O. Social interactions in heterogenous pre-schools in Israel. *Child Development*, 1972, *43*, 1149–1259.

Feldman, R. A. Interrelationships among three bases of group integration. *Sociometry*, 1968, *31*, 30–46.

Feldman, R. E. Response to compatriots and foreigners who seek assistance. *Journal of Personality and Social Psychology*, 1968, *10*, 202–214.

Feldstein, S. Temporal patterns of dialogues: Basic research and reconsiderations. In A. Siegman and B. Pope (Eds.), *Studies in Dyadic Communication*. New York: Pergamon Press, 1972.

Feree, M. A woman for president? Changing responses: 1958–1972. *Public Opinion Quarterly*, 1974, *38*, 390–399.

Fernandez, R. *The I, the Me and You: An Introduction to Social Psychology*. New York: Praeger, 1977.

Feshbach, N. D., & Roe, K. Empathy in six and seven year olds. *Child Development*, 1969, *39*, 133–149.

Festinger, L. *A Theory of Cognitive Dissonance*. Evanston, Ill.: Row, Peterson, 1957.

Festinger, L., & Carlsmith, J. Cognitive consequences of forced compliance. *Journal of Abnormal and Social Psychology*, 1959, *58*, 203–210.

Festinger, L., Riecken, H., & Schachter, S. *When prophecy fails*. Minneapolis: University of Minnesota Press, 1956.

Festinger, L., Schachter, S., & Back, K. *Social Pressures in Informal Groups*. New York: Harper & Row, 1950.

Filley, A. C. *Interpersonal Conflict Resolution*. Glenview, Ill.: Scott, Foresman, 1975.

Fink, D. G. Television. *Encyclopedia Britannica* (Vol. 21). Chicago: William Benton, 1972.

Fischer, E. Consistency among humanitarian and helping attitudes. *Social Forces*, 1973, *52*, 157–168.

Fisek, M. H., & Ofshe, R. The process of status evolution. *Sociometry*, 1970, *33*, 327–346.

Fishbein, M. Attitude and the prediction of behavior. In M. Fishbein (Ed.), *Attitude Theory and Measurement*. New York: Wiley, 1967.

Fishman, J. A. *Readings in the Sociology of Language*. The Hague, the Netherlands: Mouton, 1968.

Flacks, R. Social and cultural meanings of student revolt: Some informal comparative observations. *Social Problems*, 1970, *17*, 340–357.

Flavell, J. H., Beach, D. R., & Chinsky, J. M. Spontaneous verbal rehearsal in a memory task as a function of age. *Child Development*, 1966, *37*, 283–300.

Foote, Nelson. Identification as the basis for a theory of motivation. *American Sociological Review*, 1951, *16*, 14–21.

Frank, F., & Anderson, L. Effects of task and group size on group productivity and member satisfaction. *Sociometry*, 1971, *34*, 135–149.

Frazier, C. Between obedience and revolution. *Philosophy and Public Affairs*, 1972, *1*, 315–334.

Free, L., & Cantril, H. Political identification. In S. Welsh and J. Comer (Eds.), *Public Opinion*. Palo Alto, Calif.: Mayfield, 1975.

Freedman, J., Levy, A., Buchanan, R., & Price, J. Crowding and human aggressiveness. *Journal of Experimental and Social Psychology*, 1972, *8*, 528–548.

Freedman, N., Blass, T., Ripkin, A., & Quitkin, F. Body movements and the verbal encoding of aggressive affect. *Journal of Personality and Social Psychology*, 1973, *26*, 72–85.

Freeman, H., & Simmons, O. Feelings of stigma among relatives of former mental patients. *Social Problems*, 1961, *8*, 312–321.

Freeman, J. The origins of the women's liberation movement. *American Journal of Sociology*, 1973, *78*, 792–811.

Freidson, E. *Profession of Medicine*. New York: Dodd-Mead, 1970.

Freud, S. *Group Psychology and the Analysis of the Ego*. New York: Boni and Liveright, 1922. (Originally published, 1921.)

Freud, S. The passing of the oedipus complex. In S. Freud, *Collected Papers* (Vol. 2). London: Hogarth Press, 1924.

Freud, S. *Civilization and Its Discontents*. New York: Norton, 1929.

Freud, S. *The Basic Writings of Sigmund Freud*. New York: Modern Library, 1938.

Frideres, J., Warner, L. G., & Albrecht, S. L. The impact of social constraints on the relationship between attitudes and behavior. *Social Forces*, 1971, *50*, 101–112.

Friedan, B. *The Feminine Mystique*. New York: Dell, 1963.

Friedrichs, R. W. *A Sociology of Sociology*. New York: Free Press, 1970.

Friendenberg, E. Z. *Coming of Age in America*. New York: Vintage, 1961.

Friendenberg, E. Z. The image of the adolescent minority. *Dissent*, 1963, *10*, 149–158.

Fromm, E. *Escape from Freedom*. New York: Holt, Rinehart & Winston, 1941.

Fromme, D. K., & Schmidt, C. K. Affective role enactment and expressive behavior. *Journal of Personality and Social Psychology*, 1972, *24*, 413–419.

Gallagher, J., & Burke, P. J. Scapegoating and leader behavior. *Social Forces*, 1974, *52*, 481–488.

Gamson, W. A. A theory of coalition formation. *American Sociological Review*, 1961, *22*, 373–379.

Gamson, W. A. Violence and political power: The meek don't make it. *Psychology Today*, 1974, *8*, 35–41.

Gans, H. J. The positive functions of poverty. *American Journal of Sociology*, 1972, *78*, 278–283.

Garfinkel, H. Conditions of successful degradation ceremonies. *American Journal of Sociology*, 1956, *61*, 420–424.

Garfinkel, H. *Studies in Ethnomethodology*. Englewood Cliffs, N.J.: Prentice-Hall, 1967.

Gas looters grab fuel for free. *Associated Press* news release, December 13, 1975.

Gecas, V., Thomas, D., & Weigert, A. Social identities in Anglo and Latin adolescents. *Social Forces*, 1973, *51*, 477–484.

Gerard, H. B. Deviation, conformity and commitment. In I. D. Steiner and M.

Fishbein (Eds.), *Current Studies in Social Psychology*. New York: Holt, Rinehart & Winston, 1965.

Gerard, H. B. & Mathewson, G. C. Effect of severity of initiation on liking for a group. *Journal of Experimental Social Psychology*, 1966, *2*, 278–287.

Gergen, K. Personal consistency and the presentation of self. In C. Gordon and K. Gergen (Eds.), *The Self in Social Interaction*. New York: Wiley, 1968.

Gergen, K. *The Concept of Self*. New York: Holt, Rinehart & Winston, 1971.

Gergen, K. Social psychology as history. *Journal of Personality and Social Psychology*, 1973, *26*, 309–320.

Gerson, W. M. Violence as an American value theme. In O. N. Larson (Ed.), *Violence and the Mass Media*. New York: Harper & Row, 1968.

Geschwender, J. A. Continuities in the theories of status consistency and cognitive dissonance. *Social Forces*, 1967, *46*, 160–171.

Geschwender, J. A. Explorations in the theory of social movements and revolutions. *Social Forces*, 1968, *47*, 127–135.

Gibb, C. A. Leadership. In G. Lindzey and E. Aronson (Eds.), *The Handbook of Social Psychology* (Vol. 4). Reading, Mass.: Addison-Wesley, 1969.

Gibbs, J. P. Conceptions of deviant behavior: The old and the new. *Pacific Sociological Review*, 1966, *9*, 9–14.

Giesen, M., & McClaren, H. A. Discussion, distance, and sex: Changes in impressions and attraction during small group interaction. *Sociometry*, 1976, *39*, 60–70.

Gillespie, D. L. Who has the power? The marital struggle. *Journal of Marriage and the Family*, 1971, *33*, 445–458.

Gillig, P., & Greenwalk, A. Is it time to lay the sleeper effect to rest? *Journal of Personality and Social Psychology*, 1974, *29*, 132–139.

Glaser, B., & Strauss, A. *The Discovery of Grounded Theory*. Chicago: Aldine, 1967.

Glenn, N. D. Recent trends in intercategory differences in attitudes. *Social Forces*, 1974, *52*, 395–401.

Glock, C. Y., & Stark, R. Will ethics be the death of Christianity? *Trans-Action*, 1968, *7*, 7–14.

Glueck, S. Ten years of "Unraveling Juvenile Delinquency": An examination of criticisms. *Journal of Criminal Law, Criminology, and Police Science*, 1960, *51*, 196.

Glueck, S., & Glueck, E. *Unraveling Juvenile Delinquency*. New York: Commonwealth Fund, 1950.

Goffman, E. On face work. *Psychiatry*, 1955, *18*, 213–231.

Goffman, E. *Presentation of Self in Everyday Life*. New York: Doubleday, 1959.

Goffman, E. *Asylums*. New York: Doubleday, 1961. (a)

Goffman, E. *Encounters*. Indianapolis: Bobbs-Merrill, 1961. (b)

Goffman, E. *Behavior in Public Places*. London: Macmillan, 1963. (a)

Goffman, E. *Stigma: Notes on the Management of Spoiled Identity*. Englewood Cliffs, N.J.: Prentice-Hall, 1963. (b)

Goffman, E. *Interaction Ritual*. New York: Doubleday, 1967. (a)

Goffman, E. Characteristics of total institutions. In *Symposium on Preventive and Social Psychiatry*, at Walter Reed Army Institute of Research, Washington, D.C., 1967. (b)

Goffman, E. *Relations in Public*. New York: Basic Books, 1971.

Goldberg, G. N., & Kiesler, C. A. Visual behavior and face distance during interaction. *Sociometry*, 1969, *32*, 43–53.

Golden, M., Birns, B., Bridger, W., & Moss, A. Social class differentiation in cognitive development among Black preschool children. *Child Development*, 1971, *42*, 37–45.

Goldman-Eiser, F. *Psycholinguistics: Experiments in Spontaneous Speech*. New York: Academic Press, 1968.

Goldner, F. H., Ritti, R. R., & Ference, T. P. The production of cynical knowledge in organizations. *American Sociological Review*, 1977, *42*, 539–551.

Goldschmidt, J., Gergen, M., Quigley, K., & Gergen, K. The women's liberation movement: Attitudes and action. *Journal of Personality*, 1974, *42*, 601–617.

Goode, W. J. Encroachment, charlatanism and the emerging professions: Psychology, sociology, and medicine. *American Sociological Review*, 1960, *25*, 902–914.

Goode, W. J. *The Family*. Englewood Cliffs, N.J.: Prentice-Hall, 1964.

Goode, W. J. *Exploration in Social Theory*. New York: Oxford University Press, 1973.

Goodman, N. Adolescent norms. *Merrill Palmer Quarterly*, 1969, *15*, 199–211.

Goodman, P. *Growing Up Absurd*. New York: Vintage, 1964.

Goodman, P. Youth subculture and an unteachable generation. In M. Wertheimer (Ed.), *Confrontation*. Glenview, Ill.: Scott, Foresman, 1970.

Goranson, R. E. Media violence and aggressive behavior. In L. Berkowitz (Ed.), *Advances in Experimental Social Psychology* (Vol. 5). New York: Academic Press, 1970.

Gordon, C., & Gergen, K. *The Self in Social Interaction*. New York: Wiley, 1968.

Gordon, R. L. Interaction between attitude and the definition of the situation in the expression of opinion. *American Sociological Review*, 1952, *17*, 50–58.

Gould, R. *Transformations*. New York: Simon & Schuster, 1978.

Gouldner, A. The norm of reciprocity: A preliminary statement. *American Sociological Review*, 1960, *25*, 161–178.

Gouldner, A. *The Coming Crisis of Western Sociology*. New York: Basic Books, 1970.

Gove, W. R., & Geerken, M. R. Response bias in surveys of mental health: An empirical investigation. *American Journal of Sociology*, 1977, *82*, 1289–1318.

Grass, R. C., & Wallace, W. H. Advertising Communications: Print versus TV. *Journal of Advertising Research*, 1972, *14*, 19–23.

Green, A. W. *Sociology*. New York: McGraw-Hill, 1968.

Greenberg, B. S. British children and televised violence. *Public Opinion Quarterly*, 1974–1975, *38*, 531–547.

Greenberg, J. H. *Anthropological Linguistics: An Introduction*. New York: Random House, 1968.

Greenberg, M. S. Role playing: An alternative to deception. *Journal of Personality and Social Psychology*, 1967, *7*, 152–157.

Greer, G. *The Female Eunuch*. New York: McGraw-Hill, 1971.

Gross, E., & Stone, G. P. Embarrassment and the analysis of role requirements. *American Journal of Sociology*, 1964, *70*, 1–15.

Gross, L. The "real" world of television. *Today's Education*, 1974, *63*, 86–87.

Gross, N., Mason, W. S., & McEachern, A. W. *Exploration in Role Analysis: Studies of the School Superintendency Role*. New York: Wiley, 1957.

Guardo, C., & Bohan, J. Development of a sense of self identity in children. *Child Development*, 1971, *42*, 1909–1922.

Gubrium, J. *Living and Dying at Murray Manor*. New York: St. Martin's Press, 1975.

Guilford, J. P. An experiment in learning to read facial expressions. *Journal of Abnormal and Social Psychology*, 1929, *24*, 191.

Gullahorn, J., & Gullahorn, J. T. A non-random walk in the odyssey of a computer model. In M. Inbar and C. Stoll (Eds.), *Simulation and Gaming in Social Science.* New York: Free Press, 1972.

Gunther, M. Do commercials really sell you? *TV Guide,* 1974, November 9, 4–8.

Gusfield, J. R. *Protest, Reform and Revolt.* New York: Wiley, 1970.

Gustafson, D. P., & Gaumnitz, J. E. Consensus rankings in small groups: Self rankings included and excluded. *Sociometry,* 1972, *35,* 610–618.

Gutkin, D. C. An analysis of the concept of moral intentionality. *Human Development,* 1973, *16,* 371–381. (a)

Gutkin, D. C. *An Inquiry into the Development of Moral Intentionality.* Unpublished doctoral dissertation, Michigan State University, 1973. (b)

Guttman, L. A basis for scaling qualitative data. *American Sociological Review,* 1944, *9,* 139–150.

Guy, R. F. *A Study of Vocal Intensity in Dyadic Interaction.* Ann Arbor, Mich.: University Microfilms, 1971.

Haas, J. E. *Role Conception and Group Consensus: A Study of Disharmony in Hospital Work Groups.* Columbus: Ohio State University Press, 1964.

Haber, L. P., & Smith, R. T. Disability and deviance: Normative adaptations of role behavior. *American Sociological Review,* 1971, *36,* 87–97.

Haga, W. J., Graen, G., & Danserau, F. Professionalism in role making: A longitudinal investigation. *American Sociological Review,* 1974, *39,* 122–133.

Hagan, J., & Leon, J. Rediscovering delinquency: Social history, political ideology and the sociology of law. *American Sociological Review,* 1977, *42,* 587–598.

Hage, J., Aiken, M., & Marrett, C. Organization structure and communications. *American Sociological Review,* 1971, *36,* 860–871.

Hage, J., & Marwell, G. Toward the development of an empirically based theory of role relationships. *Sociometry,* 1968, *31,* 200–212.

Hall, E. T. *The Silent Language.* New York: Doubleday, 1959.

Hall, G. S. *Adolescence* (Vols. 1 and 2). New York: Appleton-Century-Crofts, 1916.

Hamblin, R. L. Mathematical experimentation and sociological theory: A critical analysis. *Sociometry,* 1971, *34,* 423–452.

Hamblin, R. L., Buckholt, D., Ferritor, D., Kosloff, M., & Blackwell, L. *The Humanization Processes: A Social Behavioral Analysis of Children's Problems.* New York: Wiley Interscience, 1971.

Hankin, J. *A Sociological Critique of Psychiatric Theories of Crime.* Madison: University of Wisconsin Press, 1972.

Hanson, R. C. The systematic linkage hypothesis and role consensus patterns in hospital community relations. *American Sociological Review,* 1962, *27,* 304–313.

Hanson, R. G., & Simmons, O. G. The role path: A concept and procedure for studying migration to urban communities. *Human Organization,* 1968, *27,* 152–167.

Harlow, H. F. The primate socialization motives. *Transactions of the Stud. Coll. Phys. Philadelphia,* 1966, *37,* 533–547.

Harlow, H. F. The heterosexual affection system in monkeys. In W. Bennis, E. S. Chein, F. Steele, and D. Berlew (Eds.), *Interpersonal Dynamics: Essays and Readings on Human Interaction.* Homewood, Ill.: Dorsey Press, 1968.

Harris, M., & Bauden, H. The language of altruism: Effects of language, dress, and ethnic group. *Journal of Social Psychology,* 1973, *91,* 37–41.

Harris, M., & Hassemer, W. G. Some factors affecting the complexity of children's sentences: The effects of modeling, age, sex, and bilingualism. *Journal of Experimental Child Psychology*, 1972, *13*, 445–447.

Harrison, R., & Lubin, B. Personality style, group composition and learning. *Journal of Applied Behavioral Science*, 1965, *1*, 286–301.

Hartley, E. *Problems in Prejudice*. New York: King's Crown Press, 1946.

Hastings, P. K., & Hoge, D. R. Religious change among college students over two decades. *Social Forces*, 1970, *49*, 16–28.

Hatfield, J. S., Ferguson, L. R., & Albert, R. Mother-child interaction and the socialization process. *Child Development*, 1967, *38*, 345–414.

Hawes, L. C. *Pragmatics of Analoguing: Theory and Model Construction in Communication*. Reading, Mass.: Addison-Wesley, 1975.

Hawkes, R. K. Norms, deviance, and social control: A mathematical exploration of concepts. *American Journal of Sociology*, 1975, *80*, 886–908.

Hayakawa, S. I. *Language in Action*. New York: Harcourt Brace Jovanovich, 1940.

Hayakawa, S. I. *The Use and Misuse of Language*. New York: Fawcett, 1962.

Hayakawa, S. I. Social change through TV. *Saturday Evening Post*, March 1974, 46.

Hayes, D., Meltzer, L., & Lundberg, S. Information distribution, interdependence, and activity levels. *Sociometry*, 1968, *31*, 162–179.

Hebb, D. O. *The Organization of Behavior*. New York: Wiley, 1949.

Heider, F. Attitudes and cognitive organization. *Journal of Psychology*, 1946, *21*, 107–112.

Heider, F. *The Psychology of Interpersonal Relations*. New York: Wiley, 1958.

Heine, P. J. *Personality in Social Theory*. Chicago: Aldine, 1971.

Heller, K. Interview structure and interviewer style in initial interviews. In A. Siegman and B. Pope (Eds.), *Studies in Dyadic Communication*. New York: Pergamon Press, 1972.

Helmreich, R., Aronson, E., & LeFan, J. To err is humanizing: Sometimes effects of self-esteem, competence and a pratfall on interpersonal attraction. *Journal of Personality and Social Psychology*, 1970, *16*, 259–264.

Henle, P. *Language, Thought, and Culture*. Ann Arbor: University of Michigan Press, 1965.

Henley, N. M. *Body Politics: Power, Sex, and Non-Verbal Communication*. Englewood Cliffs, N.J.: Prentice-Hall, 1977.

Hennessey, B. *Public Opinion*. Belmont, Calif.: Wadsworth, 1970.

Hennig, M. *Career Development for Women Executives*. Doctoral dissertation, Harvard University, 1970. (Book in press.)

Henry, J. *On Sham, Vulnerability, and Other Forms of Self Destruction*. New York: Vintage, 1973.

Henshel, A. M. Swinging: A study of decision making in marriage. *American Journal of Sociology*, 1973, *78*, 885–891.

Herman, S. N., & Schild, E. O. The stranger group in a cross-cultural situation. *Sociometry*, 1961, *24*, 165–176.

Hertzler, J. O. *A Sociology of Language*. New York: Random House, 1965.

Heshka, S., & Nelson, Y. Interpersonal speaking distance as a function of age, sex, and relationship. *Sociometry*, 1972, *35*, 491–498.

Hess, R. D., & Shipman, V. C. Early experience and the socialization of cognitive modes in children. *Child Development*, 1965, *36*, 869–886.

Hetherington, E. M. The effects of familial variables on sex typing, on parent-child similarity, and on imitation in children. In J. Hill (Ed.), *Minnesota Symposium on Child Psychology* (Vol. 1). Minneapolis: University of Minnesota Press, 1967.

Hewitt, J., & Stokes, R. Disclaimers. *American Sociological Review*, 1975, *40*, 1–11.

Higbee, K. L. Fifteen years of fear arousal: Research on threat appeals: 1953–1968. *Psychological Bulletin*, 1969, *72*, 426–444.

Hilton, I. Differences in the behavior of mothers toward first- and later-born children. *Journal of Personality and Social Psychology*, 1967, *3*, 282–290.

Himmelfarb, S. Studies in the perception of ethnic group members: Accuracy, response, bias, and anti-Semitism. *Journal of Personality and Social Psychology*, 1966, *4*, 347–355.

Hochschild, A. R. Disengagement theory: A critique and a proposal. *American Sociological Review*, 1975, *40*, 553–569.

Hodge, R. W., Siegel, P. M., & Rossi, P. H. Occupational prestige in the United States: 1925–1963. *American Journal of Sociology*, 1964, *70*, 286–302.

Hoffer, E. *The Ordeal of Change*. New York: Harper & Row, 1956.

Hofstadter, R. The pseudo-conservative revolt. In D. Bell (Ed.), *The Radical Right*. New York: Doubleday, 1963.

Hogan, R. Moral conduct and moral character: A psychological perspective. *Psychological Bulletin*, 1973, *79*, 217–232.

Hole, J., & Levine, E. *Rebirth of Feminism*. New York: Quadrangle, 1971.

Hollander, E. P. Conformity, status, and idiosyncracy credit. *Psychological Review*, 1958, *65*, 117–127.

Holloman, C. R. The perceived leadership role of military and civilian supervision in a military setting. *Personnel Psychology*, 1967, *20*, 199–211.

Holstein, O. M., Goldstein, J. W., & Bem, D. J. The importance of expressive behavior, involvement, sex, and need approval in inducing liking. *Journal of Experimental Social Psychology*, 1971, *7*, 534–544.

Homans, G. C. *The Human Group*. New York: Harcourt Brace Jovanovich, 1950.

Homans, G. C. Status among clerical workers. *Human Organizations*, 1953, *12*, 5–10.

Homans, G. C. *Social Behavior: Its Elementary Forms*. New York: Harcourt Brace Jovanovich, 1961.

Homans, G. C. Bringing men back in. *American Sociological Review*, 1964, *39*, 808–818.

Hooton, E. A. *Crime and the Man*. Cambridge: Harvard University Press, 1939.

Horn, M. J. *The Second Skin: An Interdisciplinary Study of Clothing*. Boston: Houghton-Mifflin, 1975.

Horowitz, I. A., & Rothschild, B. H. Conformity as a function of deception and role playing. *Journal of Personality and Social Psychology*, 1970, *14*, 224–226.

Horowitz, I. L., & Rainwater, L. On journalistic moralizers. *Trans-Action*, 1970, *7*.

Hovland, C. I., Janis, I. L., & Kelly, H. *Communication and Persuasion*. New Haven, Conn.: Yale University Press, 1953.

Hovland, C. I., Lumsdaine, A., & Sheffield, F. D. *Experiments on Mass Communication*. Princeton, N.J.: Princeton University Press, 1949.

Hovland, C. I., & Mandell, W. *Is There a Law of Primacy in Persuasion?* Paper presented to the Eastern Psychological Association, 1952.

Hovland, C. I., & Weiss, W. The influence of source credibility on communication effectiveness. *Public Opinion Quarterly*, 1951, *15*, 635–650.

Howard, J. *Please Touch*. New York: Dell, 1970.

Howard, J. R. *The Cutting Edge*. New York: Lippincott, 1974.

Hoyt, M., Henley, M., & Collins, B. Studies in forced compliance: Confluence of choice and consequences on attitude change. *Journal of Personality and Social Psychology*, 1972, *23*, 205–210.

Hudson, R. A., Wesley, H. H., Ages, J. W., & Shea, F. P. Health professionals' attitudes toward abortion. *Public Opinion Quarterly*, 1974, *38*, 159–173.

Huff, D. *How to Lie with Statistics*. New York: Harton, 1954.

Hughes, E. C. Dilemmas and contradictions of status. *American Journal of Sociology*, 1945, *50*, 353–359.

Hughes, E. Z. Angry in retirement. *Human Behavior*, 1974, September, 56–59.

Hughes, L. *The Langston Hughes Reader*. New York: George Braziller, 1958.

Humphreys, L. *Tearoom Trade: Impersonal Sex in Public Places*. Chicago: Aldine, 1970.

Hunt, W. H., Crane, W. W., & Wahlke, J. C. Interviewing political elites in cross cultural comparative research. *American Journal of Sociology*, 1964, *70*, 59–68.

Hurlock, E. B. *Child Development* (4th ed.). New York: McGraw-Hill, 1964.

Hurvitz, N. The marital roles inventory as a counseling instrument. *Journal of Marriage and the Family*, 1965, *27*, 492–501.

Husbands, C. T. Some social and psychological consequences of the American dating system. *Adolescence*, 1970, *5*, 451–462.

Huston, T. L. Ambiguity of acceptance, social desirability, and dating choice. *Journal of Experimental Social Psychology*, 1973, *9*, 32–42.

Hyman, H. The psychology of status. *Archives of Psychology*, 1942, *38*, 269–282.

Hyman, H. H., & Sheatsley, P. B. Attitudes on desegregation. *Scientific American*, 1964, *211*, 16–23.

Hymes, D. *The Ethnography of Speaking: Readings in the Sociology of Language*. The Hague, the Netherlands: Mouton, 1968.

Hymes, D. *Foundations in Sociolinguistics: An Ethnographic Approach*. Philadelphia: University of Pennsylvania Press, 1974.

Hymes, J. L. *Teaching the Child under Six*. Columbus, Ohio: Merrill, 1968.

Ichheiser, G. *Appearances and Realities*. San Francisco: Jossey-Bass, 1970.

Inkeles, A. Social structure and socialization. In D. A. Goslin (Ed.), *Handbook of Socialization Theory and Research*. Chicago: Rand McNally, 1969.

Ivey, R. D. Consultation with a male homosexual. *Personnel and Guidance Journal*, 1972, *50*, 749–754.

Iwawaki, S., Sumida, K., Okimo, S., & Cowen, E. L. Manifest anxiety in French, Japanese, and United States children. *Child Development*, 1967, *38*, 713–722.

Jacob, H. Problems of scale equivalency in measuring attitudes in American subcultures. *Social Science Quarterly*, 1971, *52*, 61–75.

Jacobson, R. Verbal communication. *Scientific American*, 1972, *227*, 73–80.

James, W. *The Principles of Psychology*. New York: Dover, 1890.

James, W. *Psychology, the Briefer Course*. New York: Holt, Rinehart & Winston, 1915.

Janis, I., & Feshback, S. Effects of fear-arousing communications. *Journal of Abnormal and Social Psychology*, 1969, *13*, 317–321.

Jansyn, L. R., Jr. Solidarity and delinquency in a street corner group. *American Sociological Review*, 1966, *31*, 600–614.

Jasso, G., & Rossi, P. H. Distributive justice and earned income. *American Sociological Review*, 1977, *42*, 639–652.

Jeffries, V., Turner, R., & Morris, R. The public perception of the Watts riot as social protest. *American Sociological Review*, 1971, *36*, 443–451.

Jenkins, J. Acquisition of language. In D. A. Goslin (Ed.), *Handbook of Socialization Theory and Research*. Chicago: Rand McNally, 1969.

Jennings, H. H. *Leadership and Isolation: A Study of Personality in Interpersonal Relations* (2nd ed.). New York: Longmans Green, 1950.

Jennings, K., & Jennings, S. Tests and experiments with children. In A. Cicounel (Ed.), *Language Use and School Performance*. New York: Academic Press, 1974.

Jett, M. The return of Rosie: Blue collar occupations attract more women, mainly for the money. *Wall Street Journal*, April 16, 1973.

Johnson, D. W. Use of role reversal in intergroup competition. *Journal of Personality and Social Psychology*, 1967, *7*, 135–141.

Johnson, H. H., & Issett, R. R. Relationship between authoritarianism and attitude change as a function of source credibility. *Journal of Personality and Social Psychology*, 1953, *48*, 79–92.

Johnson, L. A black perspective on social research: In response to Merton. *Issues in Criminology*, 1974, *9*, 55–70.

Johnson, S. Sociology of Christmas cards. *Trans-Action*, 1971, *8*(3), 40–45.

Jones, E. E. *Ingratiation*. New York: Appleton-Century-Crofts, 1964.

Jourard, S. Some factors in self-disclosure. *Journal of Abnormal and Social Psychology*, 1958, *56*, 91–98.

Juhasz, J. D., & Sarbin, T. R. On the false alarm metaphor in psychophysics. *Psychological Record*, 1966, *16*, 323–327.

Jung, J. Snoopology. *Human Behavior*, October 1975, 6–8.

Kahn, R. M., & Bowers, W. J. The social context of the rank-and-file student activist: A test of four hypotheses. *Sociology of Education*, 1970, *43*, 38–55.

Kantner, R. M. The organization child: Experience management in a nursery school. *Sociology of Education*, 1972, *45*, 186–212.

Katz, D. The functional approach to the study of attitude. *Public Opinion Quarterly*, 1960, *24*, 163–204.

Katz, D., & Brady, K. W. Verbal stereotypes and racial prejudice. In T. M. Newcomb (Ed.), *Readings in Social Psychology*. New York: Holt, Rinehart & Winston, 1947.

Katz, D., & Stotland, E. A preliminary statement to a theory of attitude structure and change. In S. Koch (Ed.), *Psychology: A Study of a Science* (Vol. 3). New York: McGraw-Hill, 1959.

Katz, E., & Lazarsfeld, P. *Personal Influence*. Glencoe, Ill.: Free Press, 1955.

Katzman, N. Television soap operas: What's been going on anyway? *Public Opinion Quarterly*, 1972, *36*, 200–212.

Keasey, C. B. The influence of opinion agreement and quality of supportive reasoning in the evaluation of moral judgments. *Journal of Personality and Social Psychology*, 1974, *30*, 477–482.

Keith, J. My own men's liberation. In J. H. Pleck and J. Sawyer (Eds.), *Men and Masculinity*. Englewood Cliffs, N.J.: Prentice-Hall, 1974.

Kelley, H. H., & Stahelski, A. J. Social interaction: Basis of cooperators' and competitors' beliefs about others. *Journal of Personality and Social Psychology*, 1970, *16*, 66–91.

Kelley, J. Causal chain models for the socioeconomic career. *American Sociological Review*, 1973, *38*, 481–493.

Kelly, K. D., & Chambliss, W. J. Status inconsistency and political attitudes. *American Sociological Review*, 1966, *31*, 375–382.

Kelman, H. C., & Hovland, C. I. Reinstatement of the communicator in delayed measurement of opinion change. *Journal of Abnormal and Social Psychology,* 1953, *48,* 327–335.

Keltner, J. W. *Interpersonal Speech Communication: Elements and Structures.* Belmont, Calif.: Wadsworth, 1970.

Kelvin, P. *The Bases of Social Behavior.* New York: Holt, Rinehart & Winston, 1970.

Kemper, T. D. Reference groups, socialization and achievement. *American Sociological Review,* 1968, *33,* 31–45.

Keniston, K. Stranded in the present. In M. Wertheimer (Ed.), *Confrontation.* Glenview, Ill.: Scott, Foresman, 1970.

Kenkel, W. F. The relationship between status consistency and political economic attitudes. *American Sociological Review,* 1956, *21,* 365–368.

Key, V. An introduction to public opinion and American democracy. In S. Welsh and J. Comer (Eds.), *Public Opinion.* Palo Alto, Calif.: Mayfield, 1975.

Kiesler, C. A., Collins, B. A., & Miller, N. *Attitude Change.* New York: Wiley, 1969.

Kikuchi, T. Studies on the development of self (I). *Tohuku Psychologica Folia,* 1968, *27,* 22–31.

Killinger, R. R. The counselor and gay liberation. *Personnel and Guidance Journal,* 1971, *49,* 715–719.

Kipnis, D. *The Powerholders.* Chicago: University of Chicago Press, 1976.

Kistyakovskaya, M. O stimulakh vizivayuschikh polozhitel'niye emotsi u rebyenka pervikhmesyatsev zhizni. [On visual stimulation of positive emotions in infants in the first months of life.] *Voprosy Psikhologii,* 1965, 129–140.

Kitsuse, J. Societal reaction to deviant behavior: Problems of theory and method. *Social Problems,* 1962, *9,* 247–256.

Klapp, O. E. *Symbolic Leaders: Public Dramas and Public Men.* Chicago: Aldine, 1964.

Klapp, O. E. *Collective Search for Identity.* New York: Holt, Rinehart & Winston, 1969.

Kleinfeld, J. S. Effects of nonverbal warmth on learning of Eskimo and White students. *Journal of Social Psychology,* 1974, *92,* 3–9.

Knapp, M. *Nonverbal Communication in Human Interaction.* New York: Holt, Rinehart & Winston, 1972.

Kohan, S., Demille, R., & Meyers, J. Two comparisons of attitude measures. *Journal of Advertising Research,* 1972, *12,* 29–34.

Kohlberg, L. *The Development of a Model of Moral Thinking in the Years Ten to Sixteen.* Unpublished doctoral dissertation, University of Chicago, 1958.

Kohlberg, L. *Stages in the Development of Moral Thought and Action.* New York: Holt, Rinehart & Winston, 1969.

Komarovsky, M. Some problems in role analysis. *American Sociological Review,* 1973, *38,* 649–662.

Komonova, I. M. Golosovia reaktsii dyetyei pervogo goda zhizni i ikh svyaz s raznoobraznimi formami povedenia. [Vocal reactions of children in the first year of life to various forms of behavior.] *Voprosy Psikhologii,* 1968, 119–126.

Kopkind, A. Mixed singles. *New Times,* 1976, *7*(7), 12–15.

Kornhauser, W. *The Politics of Mass Society.* New York: Free Press, 1959.

Korsch, B., & Negrete, V. F. Doctor-patient communication. *Scientific American,* 1972, *227,* 66–75.

Korzybski, A. *Science and Sanity.* Lancaster, Pa.: Science Press, 1933.

Koslin, B. L., Haarlow, R. N., Karlins, M. & Pargament, R. Predicting group status from members' cognitions. *Sociometry*, 1968, *31*, 64–75.

Krail, K. A., & Leventhal, G. The sex variable in the intrusion of personal space. *Sociometry*, 1976, *39*, 170–173.

Krauss, R. M., & Glucksberg, S. The development of communication: Competence as a function of age. *Child Development*, 1969, *40*, 255–266.

Kropotkin, P. *Mutual Aid: A Factor of Evolution*. Boston: Porter Sargent, 1960.

Kübler-Ross, E. *On Death and Dying*. New York: Macmillan, 1969.

Kübler-Ross, E. *Death: The Final Stage of Growth*. Englewood Cliffs, N.J.: Prentice-Hall, 1975.

Kuhn, M. Self-attitudes by age, sex, and professional training. *Sociological Quarterly*, 1960, *1*, 39–55.

Kuhn, M., & McPartland, T. An empirical investigation of self-attitude. *American Sociological Review*, 1954, *19*, 68–76.

Kuhn, T. *The Structure of Scientific Revolutions*. Chicago: University of Chicago Press, 1970.

Kulchitskaya, E. I. K probleme uravetennogo razvitaya rebenka. [Toward problems of the development of conscience in children.] *Voprosy Psikhologii*, 1966, *1*, 116–125.

Kurth, S. Friendships and friendly relations. In G. McCall, M. McCall, N. Denzin, G. Suttles, and S. Kurth (Eds.), *Social Relationships*. Chicago: Aldine, 1970.

Labov, W. Reflections of social processes in linguistic structures. In J. A. Fishman (Ed.), *Readings in the Sociology of Language*. The Hague, the Netherlands: Mouton, 1968.

Labov, W. *Language in the Inner City: Studies in the Black English Vernacular*. Philadelphia: University of Pennsylvania Press, 1972. (a)

Labov, W. *Sociolinguistic Patterns*. Philadelphia: University of Pennsylvania Press, 1972. (b)

Ladd, E. C. *Negro Political Leadership in the South*. Ithaca, N.Y.: Cornell University Press, 1966.

Laffal, J. *Pathological and Normal Language*. New York: Atherton, 1965.

Lambert, W., Gardner, R., Olton, R., & Tunstall, K. A study of the roles of attitudes and motivation in second-language learning. In J. A. Fishman (Ed.), *Readings in the Sociology of Language*. The Hague, the Netherlands: Mouton, 1968.

Lambley, P. Racial attitudes and segregation: Voting patterns of White English-speaking South Africans. *British Journal of Sociology*, 1974, *25*, 261–272.

Landers, A. Girls reveal sexual come-ons. *Tulsa Daily World*, October 23, 1976.

Landy, E. *An Investigation of the Relationships between Attitude and Two Causes of Overt Behavior*. Unpublished master's thesis, University of Illinois, 1966.

Lane, R. E., & Sears, D. O. The problem of intensity. In S. Welsh and J. Comer (Eds.), *Public Opinion*. Palo Alto, Calif.: Mayfield, 1975.

LaPiere, R. T. Attitudes versus actions. *Social Forces*, 1934, *13*, 230–237.

Largey, G. P., & Watson, D. R. The sociology of odors. *American Journal of Sociology*, 1972, *77*, 1021–1034.

Lason, R. F., & Leslie, G. R. Status hierarchy governing the serious dating relationships of university students. *Social Forces*, 1968, *47*, 195–202.

Lastrucci, C. *The Scientific Approach: Basic Principles of the Scientific Method*. Cambridge, Mass.: Schenkman, 1963.

Latane, B., & Dabbs, J. M., Jr. Sex, group size, and helping in three cities. *Sociometry*, 1975, *38*, 180–194.

Latane, B., & Darley, J. M. Bystander apathy. *American Scientist*, 1969, *57*, 244–268.

Latane, B., & Rodin, J. A lady in distress: Inhibiting effects of friends and strangers on bystanders' intervention. *Journal of Experimental and Social Psychology,* 1969, *5,* 189–202.

Laudicina, F. V. Toward new forms of liberation: A mildly utopian proposal. *Social Theory and Practice,* 1973, *2,* 275–288.

Lauer, H. L. The problems and values of attitude research. *Sociological Quarterly,* 1971, *12,* 247–252.

Lauer, R. H. Social movements: An interactionist analysis. *Sociological Quarterly,* 1972, *13,* 315–328.

Lazarsfeld, P. F. The controversy over detailed interviews—An offer for negotiation. *Public Opinion Quarterly,* 1944, *8,* 38–60.

Lazarsfeld, P., & Merton, R. Friendship as a social process. In M. Berger, T. Abel, and C. Page (Eds.), *Freedom and Control in Modern Society.* New York: Van Nostrand Reinhold, 1954.

LeBon, S. *The Crowd: A Study of the Popular Mind* (2nd ed.). London: Unwin, 1897.

Leggett, J. Economic insecurity and working class consciousness. *American Sociological Review,* 1964, *29,* 226–234.

Leinhardt, S. Developmental change in the sentiment structure of children's groups. *American Sociological Review,* 1972, *37,* 202–212.

Lemert, E. M. *Social Pathology: A Systematic Approach to the Theory of Sociopathic Behavior.* New York: McGraw-Hill, 1951.

Lemert, E. M. Paranoia and the dynamics of exclusion. *Sociometry,* 1962, *25,* 2–20.

Lemert, E. M. *Human Deviance, Social Problems, and Social Control.* Englewood Cliffs, N.J.: Prentice-Hall, 1967.

Lennard, H. L., & Bernstein, A. Interdependence of therapist and patient verbal behavior. In J. A. Fishman (Ed.), *Readings in the Sociology of Language.* The Hague, the Netherlands: Mouton, 1968.

Lennard, H. L., & Bernstein, A. *Patterns in Human Interaction.* San Francisco: Jossey-Bass, 1969.

Lenski, G. Status crystallization: A non-vertical dimension of social status. *American Sociological Review,* 1954, *19,* 405–413.

Lerman, P. Gangs, networks, and subcultural delinquency. *American Journal of Sociology,* 1967, *73,* 63–72.

Lerner, M. The justice motive: "Equity" and "parity" among children. *Journal of Personality and Social Psychology,* 1974, *29,* 539–550.

Lerner, R. M., & Gellert, E. Body build identification, preference, and aversion in children. *Developmental Psychology,* 1969, *1,* 456–462.

Leventhal, G. S. Influence of brothers and sisters on sex role behavior. *Journal of Personality and Social Psychology,* 1970, *16,* 452–465.

Leventhal, G. S., & Anderson, D. Self-interest and the maintenance of equity. *Journal of Personality and Social Psychology,* 1970, *15,* 57–62.

Leventhal, G. S., & Lane, D. W. Sex, age, and equity behavior. *Journal of Personality and Social Psychology,* 1970, *15,* 312–316.

Leventhal, H. Findings and theory in the study of fear communications. In L. Berkowitz (Ed.), *Advances in Experimental Social Psychology* (Vol. 5). New York: Academic Press, 1970.

Levine, D. N., Carter, E. B., & Gorman, E. M. Simmel's influence on American sociology. *American Journal of Sociology,* 1976, *81,* 1112–1132.

Levine, L. S. *Personal and Social Development.* New York: Holt, Rinehart & Winston, 1963.

Levinger, G., & Snoek, D. *Attraction in Relationships: A New Look at Interpersonal Attraction.* Morristown, N.J.: General Learning Press, 1972.

Levitan, S., & Johnston, W. B. *Work Is Here to Stay, Alas.* Salt Lake City, Utah: Olympus, 1973.

Levy, P., Lundgren, D., Ansel, M., Fell, D., Fink, B., & McGrath, J. Bystander effect in a demand without threat situation. *Journal of Personality and Social Psychology,* 1972, *24*, 166–171.

Levy-Bruhl, L. *The Philosophy of Auguste Comte.* London: Sonnenschein, 1903.

Lewin, K. *Field Theory in Social Science.* New York: Harper & Row, 1951.

Lewis, G. H. Bales' Monte Carlo model of small group discussions. *Sociometry,* 1970, *33*, 20–36.

Lewis, G. H. Role differentiation. *American Sociological Review,* 1972, *37*, 424–434.

Lichtenberg, G. *The Lichtenberg Reader.* Boston: Beacon, 1959.

Lichtenwaller, J. S., & Maxwell, J. W. The relationship of birth order and socioeconomic status to the creativity of pre-school children. *Child Development,* 1969, *40*, 1241–1250.

Lieberman, S. The effects of changes in roles on the attitudes of role occupants. *Human Relations,* 1956, *9*, 385–402.

Lieberson, S. Bilingualism in Montreal: A demographic analysis. *American Journal of Sociology,* 1965, *71*, 10–25.

Liebert, R. M. Modeling and the media. *School Psychology Digest,* 1975, *4*, 22–29.

Likert, R. A technique for the measurement of attitudes. *Archives of Psychology,* 1932, No. 140, 44–53.

Lindesmith, A., & Strauss, A. *Social Psychology.* New York: Holt, Rinehart & Winston, 1949.

Lindesmith, A., Strauss, A., & Denzin, N. *Social Psychology* (4th ed.). New York: Holt, Rinehart & Winston, 1975.

Lindskold, S., Albert, K., Baer, R., & Moore, W. Territorial boundaries of interacting groups and passive audiences. *Sociometry,* 1976, *39*, 71–76.

Lindzey, G., & Byrne, D. Measurement of social choice and interpersonal attractiveness. In G. Lindzey and E. Aronson (Eds.), *Handbook of Social Psychology* (Vol. 2). Reading, Mass.: Addison-Wesley, 1968.

Linn, E. L. Role behaviors in two dental clinics, a trial of Nadel's criteria. *Human Organization,* 1967, *26*, 141–148.

Linton, R. *The Study of Man.* New York: Appleton-Century-Crofts, 1936.

Linton, R. *The Cultural Background of Personality.* New York: Appleton-Century-Crofts, 1945.

Lippitt, R., & White, R. K. An experimental study of leadership and group life. In E. E. Maccoby, T. M. Newcomb, and E. L. Hartley (Eds.), *Readings in Social Psychology.* New York: Holt, Rinehart & Winston, 1958.

Lippman, W. *Public Opinion.* New York: Harcourt Brace Jovanovich, 1922.

Liska, A. E. Emergent issues in the attitude behavior consistency controversy. *American Sociological Review,* 1974, *39*, 261–272.

Litwak, E. Technological innovation and theoretical functions of primary groups and bureaucratic structures. *American Journal of Sociology,* 1968, *73*, 468–481.

Litwak, E., & Szelenyi, I. Primary group structures and their functions: Kin, neighbors and friends. *American Sociological Review,* 1969, *34*, 465–481.

Locke, J. *Selections* (S. P. Lamprecht, Ed.). New York: Scribner's, 1928.

Lofland, L. *A World of Strangers.* New York: Basic Books, 1973.

Lombroso, C. *Crime, Its Causes and Remedies*. (H. P. Horton, Trans.). Boston: Little, Brown, 1912.

Loomis, A. M. *A Technique for Observing Social Behavior of Nursery School Children*. New York: Teachers College Press, Columbia University, 1931.

Lott, A. J., & Lott, B. E. Group cohesiveness of interpersonal attraction. In T. Huston (Ed.), *Foundations of Interpersonal Attraction*. New York: Academic Press, 1965.

Lubman, S. A divorce trial, Peking style. *Wall Street Journal*, June 5, 1973.

Luft, J. *Group Processes: An Introduction to Group Dynamics* (2nd ed.). Palo Alto, Calif.: National Press, 1970.

Lundberg, C. C. Personality focused joking: Joking pattern and function. *Human Organization*, 1969, *28*, 22–28.

Lundberg, G. A. *Social Research*. New York: Longmans, Green, 1929.

Lundberg, G. A. *Foundations of Sociology*. New York: McKay, 1964.

Lundgren, D. C., & Bogart, D. H. Group size, member dissatisfaction, and radicalism. *Human Relations*, 1974, *27*, 339–355.

Luria, A. R., & Yudovich, F. Ia. *Speech and the Development of Mental Processes in the Child*. (J. Simon, Ed. and Trans.). Harmondsworth, England: Penguin, 1959.

Luttbeg, N. Patterns of leadership policy preference: A study of some assumptions in community research. In N. Luttbeg (Ed.), *Public Opinion and Public Policy*. Homewood, Ill.: Dorsey Press, 1968.

Lynd, H. *On Shame and the Search for Identity*. New York: Science Editions, 1958.

Lynn, D. B. *Parental and Sex Role Identification*. Berkeley, Calif.: McCutchan, 1969.

Lyons, J. E. Conversation with gay liberation: An interview. *Journal of College Student Personnel*, 1973, *14*, 165–170.

MacAndrew, C., & Edgerton, R. *Drunken Comportment*. Chicago: Aldine, 1969.

Maccoby, E. E. Woman's intellect. In S. Farber and R. Wilson (Eds.), *The Potential of Women*. New York: McGraw-Hill, 1963.

Maccoby, E. E., & Masters, J. Attachment and dependency. In *Carmichael's Manual of Child Psychology* (3rd ed.). New York: Wiley, 1970.

MacKinnon, D. W. Violations of prohibitions. In H. A. Murray (Ed.), *Explorations in Personality*. New York: Oxford University Press, 1938.

Mahoney, J. An analysis of the axiological structure of traditional and proliberation men and women. *Journal of Psychology*, 1975, *90*, 31–39.

Malinowski, B. *Crime and Custom in Savage Society*. Patterson, N.J.: Littlefield Adams, 1959.

Mann, L. Queue culture: The waiting line as a social system. *American Journal of Sociology*, 1969, *75*, 340–354.

Mannheim, K. *Ideology and Utopia*. New York: Harvest Books, 1936.

Manning, P. K., & Truzzi, M. (Eds.). *Youth and Sociology*. Englewood Cliffs, N.J.: Prentice-Hall, 1972.

Marsh, R. M. Lifetime commitment in Japan: Roles, norms, values. *American Journal of Sociology*, 1971, *76*, 795–812.

Marshall, V. W. Socialization for impending death in a retirement village. *American Journal of Sociology*, 1975, *80*, 1124–1144.

Martin, J. D. Suspicion and the experimental confederate: A study of role credibility. *Sociometry*, 1970, *33*, 178–192.

Martindale, D. *The Nature and Types of Sociological Theory*. Boston: Houghton Mifflin, 1960.

Martineau, H. *The Positive Philosophy of Auguste Comte*. London: J. Chapman, 1853.

Marwell, G., & Hage, J. The organization of role relationships: A systematic description. *American Sociological Review*, 1970, *35*, 884–910.

Marx, K., & Engels, F. *The Communist Manifesto*. New York: International Press, 1930.

Maslow, A. *Motivation and Personality*. New York: Harper & Row, 1954.

Masterman, M. The nature of a paradigm. In I. Lakatos and A. Musgrave (Eds.), *Criticism and the Growth of Knowledge*. Cambridge: Cambridge University Press, 1970.

Masters, W. The sexual response cycle of the human female. *Western Journal of Surgery*, 1960, *68*, 57–72.

Matarazzo, J. D., Weitman, M., Saslow, G., & Weins, A. Interviewer influence on durations of interviewee speech. *Journal of Verbal Learning and Verbal Behavior*, 1963, *1*, 451–458.

Matza, D. *Becoming Deviant*. Englewood Cliffs, N.J.: Prentice-Hall, 1969.

Mauss, M. *The Gift*. London: Cohen & West, 1954.

Maxwell, M. A. A quantity-frequency analysis of drinking behavior in the state of Washington. *Northwest Science*, 1958, *32*, 57–67.

Mayhew, B. H., & Levinger, R. L. On the emergence of oligarchy in human interaction. *American Journal of Sociology*, 1976, *81*, 1017–1049.

McBride, G. *Intrafamilial Interaction Analysis*. Unpublished doctoral dissertation, University of Michigan, 1973.

McCaghy, C. H., Skipper, J. K., & Lefton, M. *In Their Own Behalf: Voices from the Margin*. New York: Appleton-Century-Crofts, 1974.

McCall, G., & Simmons, J. L. *Identities and Interactions*. New York: Free Press, 1966.

McCandless, B. R. Childhood socialization. In D. A. Goslin (Ed.), *Handbook of Socialization Theory and Research*. Chicago: Rand McNally, 1969.

McCarthy, D. Language development of the preschool child. In R. Barker, J. Kounin, and H. Wright (Eds.), *Child Behavior and Development: A Course of Representative Studies*. New York: McGraw-Hill, 1943.

McCarthy, J. L., & Wolfe, D. Doctorates granted to women and minority groups. *Science*, 1975, *189*, 856–859.

McDonald, D. A caste. A culture. A market, I. A market, II. (Series of articles.) *The New Yorker*, November 22 and November 29, 1958.

McDougall, W. *Introduction to Social Psychology*. London: Methuen, 1908.

McGhee, P. E. Moral development and children's appreciation of humor. *Developmental Psychology*, 1974, *10*, 514–525.

McGovern, A. *Aeosop's Fables*. New York: Scholastic Book Services, 1963.

McGuire, W. J. Persistence of resistance to persuasion induced by various types of prior defenses. *Journal of Abnormal and Social Psychology*, 1961, *63*, 326–332. (a)

McGuire, W. J. Relative efficacy of active and passive prior defense in immunizing beliefs against persuasion. *Journal of Abnormal and Social Psychology*, 1961, *63*, 326–332. (b)

McGuire, W. J. Inducing resistance to persuasion. In L. Berkowitz (Ed.), *Advances in Experimental Social Psychology*, 1962, *64*, 241–248.

McGuire, W. J. The nature of attitudes and attitude change. In G. Lindzey and E. Aronson (Eds.), *Handbook of Social Psychology* (2nd ed.). Reading, Mass.: Addison-Wesley, 1969.

McGuire, W. J., & Papageorgis, D. Relative efficacy of various types of prior belief defense in producing immunity to persuasion. *Journal of Abnormal and Social Psychology*, 1961, *62*, 327–337.

McKee, J. *Introduction to Sociology*. New York: Holt, Rinehart & Winston, 1969.

McLuhan, M., & Fiore, Quentin. *The Medium is the Massage*. New York: Bantam, 1967.

McPartland, T. S., Cumming, J. H., & Garretson, W. Self-conception and ward behavior in two psychiatric hospitals. *Sociometry*, 1961, *24*, 111–124.

Mead, G. H. *Mind, Self, and Society*. Chicago: University of Chicago Press, 1934.

Mead, G. H. *The Philosophy of the Act*. Chicago: University of Chicago Press, 1938.

Mead, M. *Growing Up in New Guinea*. New York: New American Library, 1953.

Mechanic, D. Some factors in identifying and defining mental illness. *Mental Hygiene*, 1962, *46*, 66–74.

Mechanic, P., & Volkart, E. H. Stress, illness behavior and the sick role. *American Sociological Review*, 1961, *26*, 51–58.

Meddock, T. D., Parsons, J. A., & Hill, K. T. Effects of an adult's presence and praise on young child's performance. *Journal of Experimental Child Psychology*, 1971, *13*, 197–211.

Megargee, E. I. Influence of the sex roles on the manifestation of leadership. *Journal of Applied Psychology*, 1969, *53*, 377–382.

Mehrabian, A. *Silent Messages*. Belmont, Calif.: Wadsworth, 1971.

Mehrabian, A. *Nonverbal Communication*. New York: Aldine, Atherton, 1962.

Menninger, K. *What Ever Became of Sin?* New York: Hawthorne Press, 1973.

Merton, R. K. Social structure and anomie. *American Sociological Review*, 1938, *3*, 672–682.

Merton, R. K. Fact and factitiousness in ethnic opinionnaires. *American Sociological Review*, 1940, *5*, 13–27. (a)

Merton, R. K. Bureaucratic structure and personality. *Social Forces*, 1940, *18*. (b)

Merton, R. K. *Social Theory and Social Structure*. Glencoe, Ill.: Free Press, 1957.

Messenger, S., Sampson, H., & Towne, R. Life as theater: Some notes on the dramaturgic approach to social reality. *Sociometry*, 1962, *25*, 98–110.

Milgram, S. *Obedience to Authority*. New York: Harper & Row, 1975.

Milgram, S. *The Individual in a Social World*. Reading, Mass.: Addison-Wesley, 1977.

Miller, D. Adolescents and the high school system. *Community Mental Health*, 1970, *6*, 483–491.

Miller, G. A. Some preliminaries to psycholinguistics. *American Psychologist*, 1965, *20*, 15–20.

Miller, G. A. Psychology as a means of promoting human welfare. In Kouten et al., *Psychology and the Problems of Society*. Washington: American Psychological Association, 1970.

Miller, H., & Geller, D. Structural balance in dyads. *Journal of Personality and Social Psychology*, 1972, *21*, 135–178.

Mills, C. W. Situated actions and vocabularies of motive. *American Sociological Review*, 1940, *5*, 904–914.

Mintern, L., & Lambert, W. W. *Mothers of Six Cultures: Antecedents of Childrearing*. New York: Wiley, 1964.

Minton, C., Kagan, J., & Levine, J. A. Maternal control and obedience in the two year old child. *Child Development*, 1971, *42*, 1873–1894.

Mitchell, J. J. Moral dilemmas of early adolescence. *School Counselor*, 1974, *22*, 16–22.

Mitroff, I. I. Norms and counter-norms in a select group of the Apollo moon scientists. A case study of the ambivalence of scientists. *American Sociological Review*, 1974, *39*, 579–595.

Miyamoto, S., Dornbusch, F., & Dornbusch, S. M. A test of interactionist hypotheses of self-conception. *American Journal of Sociology*, 1956, *61*, 399–403.

Montessori, M. *The Absorbent Mind*. New York: Holt, Rinehart & Winston, 1967.

Moos, R. H. Sources of variance in response to questionnaires and in behavior. *Journal of Abnormal Psychology*, 1969, *74*, 405–412.

Morales, V. Children learn reading, writing, revolution: Marxism thriving in Mexico City shantytowns. *Associated Press*, March 10, 1976.

Moreno, J. L. *Who Shall Survive? A New Approach to the Problem of Human Interrelations*. Washington: Nervous and Mental Disease Publishing Co., 1934.

Morgan, E. A. Crib deaths. *Canadian Medical Association Journal*, 1969, *100*, 968–969.

Morris, C. *Signs, Language, and Behavior*. New York: Braziller, 1975.

Morris, J. *Conundrum*. New York: Harcourt Brace Jovanovich, 1974.

Mosteller, F., & Wallace, D. L. *Inference and Disputed Authorship: The Federalist*. Reading, Mass.: Addison-Wesley, 1964.

Mueller, C. *Politics of Communication: A Study of Political Sociology, Socialization, and Legitimation*. New York: Oxford University Press, 1973.

Mueller, E. The maintenance of verbal exchange between young children. *Child Development*, 1972, *43*, 930–978.

Murphy, G., Murphy, L. B., & Newcomb, T. M. *Experimental Social Psychology*. New York: Harper & Row, 1937.

Mussen, P. H. Early sex role development. In D. A. Goslin (Ed.), *Handbook of Socialization Theory and Research*. Chicago: Rand McNally, 1969.

Mussen, P. H., Conger, J. J., & Kagan, J. *Child Development and Personality*. New York: Harper & Row, 1969.

Myrdal, G. *An American Dilemma*. New York: Harper & Row, 1958.

Myrdal, G. *Asian Drama* (Vol. 3). New York: Pantheon, 1968.

Nader, L. Forums of justice: A cross-cultural perspective. *Journal of Social Issues*, 1975, *31*, 151–160.

Natanson, M. *The Journeying Self*. Reading, Mass.: Addison-Wesley, 1970.

Neisser, U. *Cognitive Psychology*. New York: Appleton-Century-Crofts, 1967.

Nelson, H. A. Leadership and change in an evolutionary movement: An analysis of change in the leadership structure of the southern civil rights movement. *Social Forces*, 1971, *49*, 353–371.

Nelson, H. A. Social movement transformation and pre-movement factor-effect: A preliminary inquiry. *Sociological Quarterly*, 1974, *15*, 127–142.

Nelson, J. I. Clique contacts and family orientations. *American Sociological Review*, 1966, *31*, 663–671.

Nelson, J. I., & Tallman, I. Local and cosmopolitan perception of conformity: A specification of parental influence. *American Journal of Sociology*, 1969, *75*, 193–207.

Nesbitt, P. D., & Steven, G. Personal space and stimulus intensity at a Southern California amusement park. *Sociometry*, 1974, *37*, 105–115.

Nettler, G. Shifting the load. *American Behavioral Scientist*, 1972, *15*, 361–379.

Newcomb, T. M. An approach to the study of communicative acts. *Psychological Review*, 1953, *60*, 404–593.

Newcomb, T. M. The prediction of interpersonal attraction. *American Psychologist*, 1956, *11*, 575–586.

Newcomb, T. M. *The Acquaintance Process*. New York: Holt, Rinehart & Winston, 1961.

Newcomb, T. M. Public attitudes toward welfare. *Social Work*, 1971, *16*, 83–90.

Newcomb, T. M., Rosenberg, J., & Tannenbaum, P. H. *Theories of Cognitive Consistency: A Sourcebook*. Chicago: Rand McNally, 1968.

Newson, J., & Newson, E. *Patterns of Infant Care in an Urban Setting*. Baltimore: Penguin, 1965.

Newton, E. *Mother Camp: Female Impersonators in America*. Englewood Cliffs, N.J.: Prentice-Hall, 1972.

Nisbet, R. A. *The Social Bond*. New York: Knopf, 1970.

Noble, G. Effect of filmed aggression on children's constructive and destructive play. *Journal of Personality and Social Psychology*, 1973, *26*, 54–59.

Nosanchuk, T. A., & Lightstone, J. Canned laughter and public and private conformity. *Journal of Personality and Social Psychology*, 1974, *29*, 153–156.

Ogburn, W. F. *Machines and Tomorrow's World* (Rev. ed.). Public Affairs Pamphlets, 1946, No. 26.

Ogden, C. K., & Richards, I. A. *The Meaning of Meaning*. New York: Harcourt Brace Jovanovich, 1923.

Olsen, N. J. Family structure and socialization patterns in Taiwan. *American Journal of Sociology*, 1974, *79*, 1395–1417.

Organ, D. W. Some variables affecting boundary role behavior. *Sociometry*, 1971, *34*, 524–537.

O'Riley, J. Review of current trends of business and finance: Does your wife work? *Wall Street Journal*, January 2, 1976.

Orne, M. T. On the social psychology of the psychological experiment, with particular reference to demand characteristics and their implications. *American Psychologist*, 1962, *17*, 776–783.

Orum, A. M. On participation in political protest movements. *Journal of Applied Behavioral Science*, 1974, *10*, 181–207.

Orum, A. M., & Cohen, R. S. Development of political orientation among black and white children. *American Sociological Review*, 1973, *38*, 62–74.

Orum, A. M., & Orum, A. W. The class and status bases of Negro student protest. *Social Science Quarterly*, 1968, *49*, 521–533.

Osborn, D. K., & Endsley, R. C. Emotional reactions of children to TV violence. *Child Development*, 1971, *42*, 321–331.

Osgood, C. E., & Tannenbaum, P. H. The principle of congruity in attitude change. *Psychological Review*, 1955, *62*, 42–55.

Ostorm, T. M. Item construction in attitude measurement. *Public Opinion Quarterly*, 1971–1972, *35*, 593–600.

O'Toole, R., & Dubin, R. An experiment in George Herbert Mead's taking the role of the other. *Journal of Personality and Social Psychology*, 1968, *10*, 59–65.

Papanek, M. Authority and sex roles in the family. *Journal of Marriage and the Family*, 1969, *31*, 88–114.

Park, R. *Race and Culture*. Glencoe, Ill.: Free Press, 1950.

Parker, F. B. Self-role strain and drinking disposition at a prealcoholic age level.

Journal of Social Psychology, 1969, *78*, 55–61.

Parker, J. S. The mutual interests of employees and management: Some problems and opportunities. *Vital Speeches*, 1960, *26*, 349–352.

Parsons, T. Age and sex in the social structure of the United States. *American Sociological Review*, 1942, *7*, 604–616.

Parsons, T. *Essays in Sociological Theory.* Glencoe, Ill.: Free Press, 1949.

Parsons, T. Deviant behavior and mechanisms of social control. In T. Parsons (Ed.), *The Social System.* New York: Free Press, 1951.

Parsons, T. The incest taboo in relation to social structure. *British Journal of Sociology*, 1954, *5*, 101–117.

Parsons, T. *Social Structure and Personality.* Glencoe, Ill.: Free Press, 1964.

Parsons, T. *Politics and Social Structure.* New York: Free Press, 1969.

Parsons, T., & Bales, R. F. *Family: Socialization and Interaction Process.* Glencoe, Ill.: Free Press, 1955.

Parsons, T., Bales, R. F., & Shils, E. *Working Papers in the Theory of Action.* Glencoe, Ill.: Free Press, 1953.

Patterson, G. H. A dyadic analysis of aggressive behavior. In J. Hill (Ed.), *Minnesota Symposia on Child Psychology.* Minneapolis: University of Minnesota Press, 1970.

Pavlov, I. *Conditioned Reflexes.* New York: Oxford University Press, 1927.

Payne, S., Summers, D., & Stewart, T. Value difference across three generations. *Sociometry*, 1973, *36*, 20–30.

Perinbanayagam, R. S. Towards a theory of social change: A delineation of an approach. *Trans-Actions, Missouri Academy of Science*, 1967, *1*, 66–74.

Perinbanayagam, R. S. The definition of the situation: An analysis of the ethnomethodological and dramaturgic view. *Sociological Quarterly*, 1974, *15*, 521–541.

Peters, R. S. *The Concept of Motivation.* London: Routledge & Kegan Paul, 1958.

Peterson, D. R., & Migliorino, G. Pancultural factors of parental behavior in Sicily and the U.S. *Child Development*, 1967, *38*, 967–991.

Peterson, R., & Thurstone, L. L. *Motion Pictures and the Social Attitudes of Children.* New York: Macmillan, 1933.

Petroni, F. A. Social class, family size and the sick role. *Journal of Marriage and the Family*, 1969, *31*, 728–735.

Pettigrew, T. *Profile of the Negro American.* New York: Van Nostrand Reinhold, 1964.

Pfeil, E. Role expectations when entering into marriage. *Journal of Marriage and the Family*, 1968, *30*, 161–165.

Pfuetze, P. *The Social Self.* New York: Bookman, 1954.

Phifer, M. K. Influence of the process of discrimination on the selection of statements for an attitude scale. *Public Opinion Quarterly*, 1971–1972, *35*, 601–605.

Phillips, D. *Knowledge from What?* Chicago: Rand McNally, 1971.

Phillips, D. *Abandoning Method.* San Francisco: Jossey-Bass, 1973.

Phillips, D., & Clancy, K. J. Response biases in field studies of mental illness. *American Sociological Review*, 1970, *35*, 503–514.

Phillips, D. P., & Converse, R. H. Measuring the structure and boundary properties of groups: Some uses of information theory. *Sociometry*, 1972, *35*, 235–254.

Piaget, J. *Judgment and Reasoning in the Child.* Patterson, N.J.: Littlefield Adams, 1959. (a)

Piaget, J. *The Thought and Language of the Child* (3rd ed.). London: Routledge & Kegan Paul, 1959. (b)

Piaget, J. *The Child's Concept of Physical Causality*. Patterson, N.J.: Littlefield Adams, 1960. (Originally published, 1930.)

Piaget, J. *Moral Judgment of the Child*. New York: Free Press, 1965.

Piaget, J. *The Child's Conception of Movement and Speed*. New York: Ballantine, 1971.

Pittneger, R. C., Hockett, C., & Danehy, J. *The First Five Minutes*. New York: Martineau, 1960.

Platt, W. Personal communication, 1976.

Plowman, E. E. *The Jesus Movement in America*. Elgin, Ill.: David C. Cook, 1971.

Pollock, D. F. *Sociology and Philosophy*. New York: Free Press, 1953.

Polsky, N. *Hustlers, Beats, and Others*. New York: Anchor, 1967.

Popova, M. N. Osobennosti rechevikh proyavlenii dyetyei pervogo polgoda vtorogo goda zhizni. [Certain speech phenomena in children in the first half year of the second year of life.] *Voprosy Psikhologii*, 1968, 116–122.

Porterfield, A. *Youth in Trouble*. Fort Worth, Texas: Leo Potishman Foundation, 1946.

Portes, A. Political primitivism, differential socialization, and lower-class leftist radicalism. *American Sociological Review*, 1971, *36*, 820–835.

Price, K. O., Harburg, E., & Newcomb, T. M. Psychological balance in situations of negative interpersonal attitudes. *Journal of Personality and Social Psychology*, 1966, *3*, 265–271.

Price, W. H., & Whatmore, P. B. Behavior disorders and patterns of crime among XYY males identified at a maximum security hospital. *British Medical Journal*, 1967, *1*, 533–537.

Pugh, D. Role activation conflict: A study of industrial inspection. *American Sociological Review*, 1966, *31*, 835–842.

Punyodyana, B. Later life socialization and differential social assimilation of Chinese in urban Thailand (Bangkok). *Social Forces*, 1974, *50*, 232–238.

Quint, J. The impact of mastectomy. *American Journal of Nursing*, 1963, *63*, 88–92.

Raab, E., & Lipset, S. The prejudiced society. In E. Raab (Ed.), *American Race Relations Today*. New York: Anchor, 1962.

Ralston, N. C., & Patience, T. G. America's artificial adolescents. *Adolescence*, 1972, *7*, 137–142.

Rardin, D. R., & Moan, C. E. Peer interaction and cognition development. *Child Development*, 1971, *42*, 1658–1699.

Reckless, W., Dinitz, S., & Murray, E. Self-concept as an insulator against delinquency. *American Sociological Review*, 1958, *21*, 744–748.

Reeder, L. G., & Donohue, G. A. Conceptions of self and others. *American Journal of Sociology*, 1960, *66*, 153–159.

Reese, H. W., & Lipsitt, L. P. *Experimental Child Psychology*. New York: Academic Press, 1970.

Reich, C. *The Greening of America*. New York: Bantam, 1970.

Rest, J., Cooper, D., Coder, R., Masanz, J., & Anderson, D. Judging the important issues in moral dilemmas—An objective measure of development. *Developmental Psychology*, 1974, *10*, 491–501.

Rheingold, H. L. The social and socializing infant. In D. A. Goslin (Ed.), *Handbook of Socialization Theory and Research*. Chicago: Rand McNally, 1969.

Richardson, S. A. The effect of physical disability on the socialization of the child. In D. A. Goslin (Ed.), *Handbook of Socialization Theory and Research*. Chicago: Rand McNally, 1969.

Riesman, D. *The Lonely Crowd*. New Haven, Conn.: Yale University Press, 1950.

Riley, M. W., Foner, A., Hess, B., & Toby, M. L. Socialization for the middle and later years. In D. A. Goslin (Ed.), *Handbook of Socialization Theory and Research*. Chicago: Rand McNally, 1969.

Ritchie, O. W., & Koller, M. R. *Sociology of Childhood*. New York: Appleton-Century-Crofts, 1964.

Ritzer, G. *Sociology: A Multiple Paradigm Science*. Englewood Cliffs, N.J.: Prentice-Hall, 1975.

Robinson, H. F., & Spodek, B. *New Directions in the Kindergarten*. New York: Teachers College Press, Columbia University, 1965.

Rock, P. The sociology of deviancy and conceptions of moral order. *British Journal of Criminology*, 1974, *14*, 139–149.

Rodgers, D. A., & Ziegler, F. J. Social role theory, the marital relations of girls and the use of ovulation suppressors. *Journal of Marriage and the Family*, 1968, *30*, 584–591.

Roethlisberger, F. J. Barriers to communication between men. In S. I. Hayakawa (Ed.), *Use and Misuse of Language*. New York: Fawcett, 1962.

Roethlisberger, F. J., & Dickson, W. J. *Management and the Worker*. Cambridge, Mass.: Harvard University Press, 1939.

Rogers, C. *Carl Rogers on Encounter Groups*. New York: Harper & Row, 1970.

Rogler, L. H., & Hollingshead, A. B. *Trapped: Families and Schizophrenia*. New York: Wiley, 1965.

Rokeach, M. Change and stability in American value systems. *Public Opinion Quarterly*, 1974, *38*, 222–238.

Romano-V, O. I. Institutions in modern society: Caretakers and subjects. *Science*, 1974, *183*, 722–725.

Rommetveit, R. Words, contexts and verbal message transmission. In E. Carswell and R. Rommetveit (Eds.), *Social Context of Messages*. New York: Academic Press, 1971.

Rootman, I. Voluntary withdrawal from a total adult socializing organization: A model. *Sociology of Education*, 1972, *45*, 258–270.

Rosen, G. Social change and psychopathology in the emotional climate of millennial movements. *American Behavioral Scientist*, 1972, *16*, 153–167.

Rosenbaum, J. E. The stratification of socialization processes. *American Sociological Review*, 1975, *40*, 48–54.

Rosenberg, M. *Society and the Adolescent Self Image*. Princeton, N.J.: Princeton University Press, 1965. (a)

Rosenberg, M. When dissonance fails: On eliminating evaluation apprehension from attitude measurement. *Journal of Personality and Social Psychology*, 1965, *1*, 28–42. (b)

Rosenblatt, P. C. Communication in the practice of love magic. *Social Forces*, 1971, *49*, 482–487.

Rosenhan, D. L. On being sane in insane places. *Science*, 1973, *179*, 250–258.

Rosenthal, A. M. *Thirty-Eight Witnesses*. New York: McGraw-Hill, 1964.

Rosenthal, R., & Jacobson, L. *Pygmalion in the Classroom: Teacher Expectation and Pupil's Intellectual Development*. New York: Holt, Rinehart & Winston, 1968.

Ross, E. A. *Social Psychology*. New York: Macmillan, 1908.

Ross, M., & DiTecco, D. An attributional analysis of moral judgment. *Journal of Social Issues*, 1975, *31*, 91–109.

Rossi, A. Naming children in middle class families. *American Sociological Review*, 1965, *30*, 499–513.

Roszak, T. *The Making of a Counterculture.* New York: Anchor, 1969.

Rotenberg, M., & Sarbin, T. Impact of differentially significant others on role involvement: An experiment with prison social types. *Journal of Abnormal Psychology,* 1971, *77,* 97–107.

Rothbart, M. K., & Maccoby, E. Parents' differential reaction to sons and daughters. *Journal of Personality and Social Psychology,* 1966, *4,* 237–243.

Rothchild, E. Emotional aspects of sexual development. *Pediatric Clinics of North America,* 1969, *16.*

Rotter, G. S. Attitudinal points of agreement and disagreement. *Journal of Social Psychology,* 1972, *86,* 211–218.

Rousseau, J. J. *Discourse on the Origin and Foundation of Inequality among Mankind.* New York: P. F. Collier, 1910.

Rozhina, L. N. Nekotoriye uslovia vozniknovenia interesa k perekhivanism i mislam literaturnikh geroyev u detyei mladshego shkolnogo vozrasta. [Some conditions for the origin of an interest in experiences and thoughts on literary heroes in children of early school age.] *Voprosy Psikhologii,* 1966, *2,* 139–146.

Rubin, Z. Measurement of romantic love. *Journal of Personality and Social Psychology,* 1970, *16,* 265–273.

Rubin, Z. *Liking and Loving.* New York: Holt, Rinehart & Winston, 1973.

Rubin, Z. Who believes in a just world? *Journal of Social Issues,* 1975, *31,* 65–89.

Ruddock, R. *Roles and Relationships.* London: Routledge & Kegan Paul, 1969.

Ruesch, J. *Therapeutic Communication.* New York: Norton, 1961.

Rush, G. B. Status consistency and right wing extremism. *American Sociological Review,* 1967, *32,* 86–92.

Ryckman, R. M., Martern, J. L., Rhodda, W. C., & Sherman, M. F. Locus of control and attitudes toward women's liberation in a college population. *Journal of Social Psychology,* 1972, *87,* 157–158.

Sachs, H. An initial investigation of the usability of conversational data for doing sociology. In D. Sudnow (Ed.), *Studies in Social Interaction.* New York: Free Press, 1972.

Sagarin, E. *Deviants and Deviance: An Introduction to the Study of Disvalued People and Behavior.* New York: Praeger, 1975.

Sample, J., & Warland, R. Attitude and prediction of behavior. *Social Forces,* 1973, *51,* 292–304.

Sampson, E. E. Studies of status congruence. In L. Berkowitz (Ed.), *Advances in Experimental Social Psychology* (Vol. 4). New York: Academic Press, 1969.

Sampson, E. E. On justice as equality. *Journal of Social Issues,* 1975, *31,* 45–64.

Sampson, H., Messinger, S., & Towne, R. Family processes and becoming a mental patient. *American Journal of Sociology,* 1962, *68,* 88–96.

Sandels, S. Young children in traffic. *British Journal of Educational Psychology,* 1970, *40,* 111–116.

Sanders, W. B. *The Sociologist as Detective.* New York: Praeger, 1976.

Sandhu, H. S. *A Study on Prison Impact.* Chandigarh, India: Punjab University Publication Bureau, 1968.

Sandhu, H. S. *Modern Corrections.* Springfield, Ill.: Thomas, 1974.

Sapir, E. *Culture, Language, and Personality.* Berkeley: University of California Press, 1964.

Sarbin, T. R. A preface to a psychological analysis of the self. *Psychological Review,* 1962, *59,* 11–22.

Sarbin, T. R., & Allen, V. L. Role theory. In G. Lindzey and E. Aronson (Eds.), *Hand-*

book of Social Psychology (Vol. 1). Reading, Mass.: Addison-Wesley, 1968.

Sartorius, R. Individual conduct and social norms: A utilitarian account. *Ethics*, 1972, *82*, 200–218.

Sashkin, M., & Maier, R. F. Sex effects in delegation. *Personnel Psychology*, 1971, *24*, 471–476.

Satir, V. *Peoplemaking*. Palo Alto, Calif.: Science and Behavior Books, 1972.

Savitz, L. Delinquency and migration. In M. Wolfgang, L. Savitz, and N. Johnston (Eds.), *The Sociology of Crime and Delinquency*. New York: Wiley, 1962.

Sawyer, J. The altruism scale: A measure of cooperative, individualistic, and competitive interpersonal orientation. *American Journal of Sociology*, 1966, *71*, 407–416.

Scanzoni, J. Socialization, achievement, and achievement values. *American Sociological Review*, 1967, *32*, 449–456.

Scarlett, H. H., Press, A. H., & Crockett, W. H. Children's descriptions of peers: A Wernerian developmental analysis. *Child Development*, 1971, *42*, 439–452.

Schafer, R., & Kloglan, G. Application of the rule of distributive justice in a normative organization. *Pacific Sociological Review*, 1974, *17*, 199–213.

Schatzman, L., & Strauss, A. *Field Research Strategies for a Natural Sociology*. Englewood Cliffs, N.J.: Prentice-Hall, 1973.

Scheff, T. *Being Mentally Ill: A Sociological Theory*. Chicago: Aldine, 1966.

Scheff, T. (Ed.). *Mental Illness and Social Processes*. New York: Harper & Row, 1967.

Scheff, T. Negotiating reality: Notes on power in the assessment of responsibility. *Social Problems*, 1968, *16*, 3–17.

Schellenberg, J. A. *Masters of Social Psychology*. New York: Oxford University Press, 1978.

Schettler, C. *Public Opinion in American Society*. New York: Harper & Row, 1960.

Schilder, P. *The Image and Appearance of the Human Body*. New York: International Universities Press, 1935.

Schmitt, R. L. Major role change and self change. *Sociological Quarterly*, 1966, *7*, 311–322.

Schneider, D. J. *Social Psychology*. Reading, Mass.: Addison-Wesley, 1976.

Schoenherr, R. A., & Greeley, A. M. Role commitment processes and the American Catholic priesthood. *American Sociological Review*, 1974, *39*, 407–426.

Schooler, C. Childhood family structure and adult characteristics. *Sociometry*, 1972, *35*, 255–269.

Schulman, G. I. Asch conformity studies: Conformity to the experimenter and/or to the group. *Sociometry*, 1967, *30*, 26–40.

Schuman, H., & Gruenberg, B. Impact of city on racial attitudes. *American Journal of Sociology*, 1970, *76*, 213–261.

Schur, E. *Labeling Deviant Behavior: Its Sociological Implications*. New York: Harper & Row, 1971.

Schutz, A. On multiple realities. *Philosophy and Phenomenological Research*, 1945, *5*, 523–531.

Schutz, A. *Collected Papers II: Studies in Social Theory*. The Hague, the Netherlands: Martinus Nijhoff, 1964.

Schwartz, B. The social psychology of the gift. *American Journal of Sociology*, 1967, *73*, 1–11.

Schwartz, B. The social psychology of privacy. *American Journal of Sociology*, 1968, *73*, 740–752.

Schwartz, C. G. The psychological meaning of mental illness in the family. *Journal of Social Issues*, 1955, *11*, 12–24.

Schwartz, C. G. Perspectives on deviance: Wives' definitions of their husband's mental illness. *Psychiatry*, 1957, *20*, 275–291.

Scodel, A., & Austrin, H. The perception of Jewish photographs by non-Jews and Jews. *Journal of Abnormal and Social Psychology*, 1957, *54*, 278–280.

Scott, J. F. *Internalization of Norms: A Sociological Theory of Normative Commitment.* Englewood Cliffs, N.J.: Prentice-Hall, 1971.

Scott, J., & Franklin, J. The changing nature of sex references in mass circulation magazines. *Public Opinion Quarterly*, 1972, *36*, 80–86.

Scott, M. B. Functional analysis: A statement of problems. In G. Stone and H. Farberman (Eds.), *Social Psychology through Symbolic Interaction.* Boston: Ginn, 1970.

Scott, M. B., & Lyman, S. M. Accounts. *American Sociological Review*, 1968, *33*, 46–62.

Scott, R. A. The socialization of blind children. In D. A. Goslin (Ed.), *Handbook of Socialization Theory and Research.* Chicago: Rand McNally, 1969.

Scott, W. A. Attitude measurement. In C. Lindzey and E. Aronson (Eds.), *Handbook of Social Psychology* (Vol. 2). Reading, Mass.: Addison-Wesley, 1968.

Scully, D., & Bart, P. A funny thing happened on the way to the office: Women in gynecology textbooks. *American Journal of Sociology*, 1973, *78*, 1045–1049.

Searles, R., & Williams, J. A. Negro college students' participation in sit-ins. *Social Forces*, 1962, *40*, 215–219.

Sears, R. R. Relation of early socialization experiences to self concepts and gender role in middle childhood. *Child Development*, 1970, *41*, 267–290.

Sebald, H. *Adolescence: A Sociological Analysis.* New York: Appleton-Century-Crofts, 1968.

Secord, P. F., & Backman, C. W. *Social Psychology.* New York: McGraw-Hill, 1964.

Second, P. F., & Backman, C. W. *Social Psychology* (2nd ed.). New York: McGraw-Hill, 1974.

Seeley, J. *The Americanization of the Unconscious.* New York: Science House, 1967.

Seeman, M. The signals of '68: Alienation in pre-crisis France. *American Sociological Review*, August 1972, 385–402.

Selman, R. L. Taking another's perspective in role taking. *Child Development*, 1971, *42*, 1721–1734.

Semenova, A. P. *Psikhologicheski Analiz Ponemania Alegorii, Metafor, i Sravnenia.* [*Psychological Analysis of the Comprehension of Allegory, Metaphor, and Equivalences.*] Leningrad: Leningradskogo Instituta Imeni A. I. Gerzena, 1941.

Shaw, M. E. Communication networks. In L. Berkowitz (Ed.), *Advances in Experimental Social Psychology* (Vol. 1). New York: Academic Press, 1964.

Shaw, M. E. *Group Dynamics: The Psychology of Small Groups.* New York: McGraw-Hill, 1971.

Shaw, M. E., & Costanzo, P. R. *Theories of Social Psychology.* New York: McGraw-Hill, 1970.

Sheehy, G. *Passages.* New York: Bantam, 1976.

Sheldon, W. *The Varieties of Temperament.* New York: Harper & Row, 1942.

Sheldon, W. H., Stevens, S. S., & Tucker, W. P. *The Varieties of Human Physique.* New York: Harper & Row, 1940.

Sherif, M. *Groups in Harmony and Tension.* New York: Harper & Row, 1953.

Sherif, M., & Sherif, C. *Reference Groups*. New York: Harper & Row, 1964.

Sherif, M., White, B. J., & Harvey, O. J. Status in experimentally produced groups. *American Journal of Sociology*, 1955, *60*, 370–379.

Sherman, S. Effects of choice and incentive on attitude change in a discrepant behavior situation. *Journal of Personality and Social Psychology*, 1970, *15*, 245–252.

Sherwood, J. J., Barron, J. W., & Fitch, H. G. Cognitive dissonance: Theory and research. In R. V. Wagner and J. J. Sherwood (Eds.), *The Study of Attitude Change*. Monterey, Calif.: Brooks/Cole, 1969.

Shibutani, T. *Society and Personality*. Englewood Cliffs, N.J.: Prentice-Hall, 1961.

Shirley, M. M. Common content in the speech of preschool children. *Child Development*, 1938, *9*, 333–346.

Short, J. F., Jr., & Strodtbeck, F. L. Response of gang leaders to status threat: Observation of group process and delinquent behavior. *American Journal of Sociology*, 1963, *68*, 571–579.

Shuman, H. Attitudes versus action versus attitudes versus attitudes. *Public Opinion Quarterly*, 1972, *36*, 347–354.

Shurakova, T. N. O mekhanizmakh dyetskogo slovotorchestba. [On mechanisms of work creation in children.] *Voprosy Psikhologii*, 1969, *1*, 62–67.

Sieber, S. D. The integration of fieldwork and survey methods. *American Journal of Sociology*, 1973, *78*, 1335–1359.

Sieber, S. D. Toward a theory of role accumulation. *American Sociological Review*, 1974, *39*, 567–578.

Sigall, H., Aronson, E., & VanHoose, T. The cooperative subject: Myth or reality? *Journal of Experimental Social Psychology*, 1970, *6*, 1–10.

Silverstein, C., & Stang, D. J. Seating position and interaction in triads: A field study. *Sociometry*, 1976, *39*, 166–170.

Simmel, G. *The Sociology of Georg Simmel* (K. Wolff, Ed.). New York: Free Press, 1950.

Simmel, G. *Bruecke und Tuer*. Stuttgart, Germany: Koehler Verlag, 1957.

Simmel, G. *Soziologie*. Berlin: Dunker & Humbolt, 1958.

Simmons, J. L. *Deviants*. San Francisco: Glendessary Press, 1969.

Simmons, R. G. Role conflict and the first line supervision: An experimental study. *American Journal of Sociology*, 1968, *74*, 482–495.

Simmons, R. G., & Rosenberg, M. Functions of children's perceptions of the stratification system. *American Sociological Review*, 1971, *36*, 235–249.

Simon, H. A. How big is a chunk? *Science*, 1974, *183*, 482–488.

Simon, S. B., Howe, L. W., & Kirschenbaum, H. *Values Clarification*. New York: Hart, 1972.

Simon, W., & Gagnon, J. Psychosexual development. *Trans-Action*, 1969, *6*, 9–17.

Simpson, E. L. Moral development research. *Human Development*, 1974, *17*, 81–106.

Skinner, B. F. *Walden Two*. New York: Macmillan, 1948.

Skinner, B. F. *Beyond Freedom and Dignity*. New York: Knopf, 1971.

Skolnick, J. H. *The Politics of Protest: Report to the National Commission on the Causes and Prevention of Violence*. New York: Ballantine, 1969.

Slaby, A. E., & Sealy, J. R. Black liberation, women's liberation. *American Journal of Psychiatry*, 1973, *130*, 196–200.

Smith, B. L., Laswell, H. D., & Casey, R. D. *Propaganda, Communication and Public Opinion*. Princeton, N.J.: Princeton University Press, 1946.

Smith, D. M. Adolescence: A study of stereotyping. *The Sociological Review*, 1970, *18*, 197–211.

Smith, T. S. Aestheticism and social structure: Style and social network in the dandy life. *American Sociological Review*, 1974, *39*, 725–743.

Snoek, J. D. Role strain in diversified role sets. *American Journal of Sociology*, 1966, *71*, 363–372.

Snow, C. E. Mother's speech to children learning language. *Child Development*, 1972, *43*, 549–565.

Sommer, R. Sociofugal space. *American Journal of Sociology*, 1967, *72*, 656–660.

Sommer, R. *Personal Space: The Behavioral Basis of Design.* Englewood Cliffs, N.J.: Prentice-Hall, 1969.

Speer, A. *Inside the Third Reich.* New York: Avon, 1970.

Speier, M. *How to Observe Face to Face Communication: A Sociological Introduction.* Palisades, Calif.: Goodyear, 1973.

Spencer, H. *First Principles.* New York: Burt, 1962.

Spiegel, J. P., & Machotka, P. *Messages of the Body Mime.* New York: Free Press, 1974.

Spinetta, J. J., & Rigler, D. The child-abusing parent: A psychological review. *Psychological Bulletin*, 1972, *77*, 296–304.

Spitz, R. A. Hospitalism. An inquiry into the genesis of psychiatric conditions in early childhood. *Psychoanalytic Study of the Child*, 1945, *1*, 53–74.

Spitzer, S., & Denzin, N. *The Mental Patient: Studies in the Sociology of Deviance.* New York: McGraw-Hill, 1968.

Spock, B. *Baby and Child Care.* New York: Pocket Books, 1957.

Sponberg, H. A study of the relative effectiveness of climax and anti-climax order in argumentative speech. *Speech Monographs*, 1946, *13*, 35–44.

Sprey, J. The family as a system in conflict. *Journal of Marriage and the Family*, 1969, *31*, 699–706

Stallings, R. A. Patterns of belief in social movements: Clarifications from an analysis of environmental groups. *Sociological Quarterly*, 1973, *14*, 465–480.

Stayton, D. J., Hohan, R., & Ainsworth, M. Infant obedience and maternal behavior: The origins of socialization reconsidered. *Child Development*, 1972, *42*, 1057–1069.

Stebbins, R. A. *Commitment to Deviance: The Nonprofessional Criminal in the Community.* Westport, Conn.: Greenwood, 1971.

Stein, T. R. Identifying emergent leaders from verbal and nonverbal communications. *Journal of Personality and Social Psychology*, 1975, *32*, 125–135.

Steiner, I. D. *Group Processes and Productivity.* New York: Academic Press, 1972.

Stogdill, R. *Handbook of Leadership.* New York: Macmillan, 1974.

Stoloff, C. Who joins women's liberation? *Psychiatry*, 1973, *36*, 325–340.

Stone, G. Appearance and the self. In A. Rose (Ed.), *Human Behavior and Social Processes.* Boston: Houghton Mifflin, 1962.

Stone, G., & Farberman, H. On the edge of rapprochement: Was Durkheim moving toward the perspective of symbolic interaction? *Sociological Quarterly*, 1967, *8*, 149–164.

Stone, G., & Farberman, H. (Eds.). *Social Psychology through Symbolic Interaction.* Boston: Ginn, 1970.

Stone, G., & Gross, E. Embarrassment and the analysis of role requirements. *American Journal of Sociology*, 1964, *70*, 1–15.

Stouffer, S. Sociological factors favoring innovations. In L. H. Clark (Ed.), *Consumer Behavior*. New York: Harper & Row, 1958.

Stouwie, R. J. Inconsistent verbal instructions and children's resistance to temptation behavior. *Child Development*, 1972, *42*, 1517–1531.

Strauss, A. *Mirrors and Masks: The Search for Identity*. Glencoe, Ill.: Free Press, 1959.

Strauss, A. (Ed.). *George Herbert Mead on Social Psychology*. Chicago: University of Chicago Press, 1964.

Strauss, A., & Schatzman, L. *Field Research: Strategies for a Natural Sociology*. Englewood Cliffs, N.J.: Prentice-Hall, 1973.

Strauss, J. H., & Strauss, M. A. Family roles and sex differences in creativity of children in Bombay and Minneapolis. *Journal of Marriage and the Family*, 1968, *30*, 46–53.

Strauss, M. A. Communication, creativity, and problem solving ability of middle and working class families in three societies. *American Journal of Sociology*, 1968, *73*, 417–430.

Stream, H. S. Role theory: Its implications for social casework treatment. In M. C. Nelson (Ed.), *Roles and Paradigms in Psychotherapy*. New York: Grune & Stratton, 1968.

Strodtbeck, F. L. The family as a three-person group. In G. Handel (Ed.), *The Psychosocial Interior of the Family*. Chicago: Aldine, 1967.

Strodtbeck, F. L., James, R. M., & Hawkins, C. Social status in jury deliberations. *American Sociological Review*, 1957, *22*, 713–719.

Stryker, S. Identity salience and role performance: The relevance of symbolic interaction theory for family research. *Journal of Marriage and the Family*, 1968, *30*, 558–570.

Suchman, E. A. The "hang-loose" ethic and the spirit of drug use. *Journal of Health and Social Behavior*, 1968, *9*, 140–155.

Sullivan, H. S. The psychiatric interview. In H. S. Sullivan, *Collected Works* (Vol. 1). New York: Norton, 1953.

Sullivan, H. S. The illusion of personal individuality. In H. S. Sullivan, *The Fusion of Psychiatry and Social Science*. New York: Norton, 1964.

Summerhayes, D. L., & Suchner, R. W. Power implications of touch in male-female relationships. *Sex Roles*, 1978, *4*(1), 103–110.

Sutherland, E. H. *White Collar Crime*. New York: Holt, Rinehart & Winston, 1949.

Suttles, G. Friendship as a social institution. In M. McCall, N. Denzin, G. Suttles, and S. Kurth, *Social Relationships*. Chicago: Aldine, 1970.

Swanson, G. Mead and Freud: Their relevance for social psychology. In J. Manis and B. Meltzer (Eds.), *Symbolic Interaction*. Boston: Allyn & Bacon, 1967.

Sykes, G. M., & Matza, D. Techniques of neutralization. *American Sociological Review*, 1957, *22*, 667–669.

Szasz, T. S. *The Myth of Mental Illness*. New York: Dell, 1961.

Szasz, T. S. *Law, Liberty, and Psychiatry*. New York: Collier, 1963.

Szasz, T. S. *Ideology and Insanity*. New York: Doubleday, 1970.

Szasz, T. S. *The Second Sin*. New York: Doubleday, 1973.

Szasz, T. S. *Ceremonial Chemistry*. New York: Anchor, 1974.

Tallman, I. Spousal role differentiation and the socialization of severely retarded children. *Journal of Marriage and the Family*, 1965, *27*, 37–42.

Tarde, G. *The Laws of Imitation*. New York: Holt, Rinehart & Winston, 1903.

Taylor, H. F. *Balance in Small Groups*. New York: Van Nostrand Reinhold, 1970.

Taylor, K. W., & Frideres, J. Issues versus controversies: Substantive and statistical significance. *American Sociological Review*, 1972, 37, 464–472.

Tec, N. Family and differential involvement with marijuana: A study of suburban teenagers. *Journal of Marriage and the Family*, 1970, 32, 656–664.

Tedeschi, J. T., Schdenkes, B. R., & Bonoma, T. V. *Conflict, Power, and Games*. Chicago: Aldine, 1973.

Tedesco, J. F., & Fromme, D. K. Cooperation, competition, and personal space. *Sociometry*, 1974, 37, 116–121.

Tennis, G. H., & Dabbs, J. M., Jr. Sex, setting, and personal space: First grade through college. *Sociometry*, 1975, 38, 385–384.

Thayer, S., & Schiff, W. Eye contact, facial expression, and experience of time. *Journal of Social Psychology*, 1975, 95, 117–124.

Thibaut, J. W., & Kelley, H. H. *Social Psychology of Groups*. New York: Wiley, 1959.

Thomas, W. I. *The Unadjusted Girl*. Boston: Little, Brown, 1923.

Thomas, W. I. *Primitive Behavior: An Introduction to the Social Sciences*. New York: McGraw-Hill, 1937.

Thomas, W. I., & Znaniecki, F. *The Polish Peasant in Europe and America*. Chicago: University of Chicago Press, 1918.

Thornberg, H. D. Peers: Three distinct groups. *Adolescence*, 1971, 6, 59–76.

Thornton, R., & Nardi, P. M. Dynamics of role acquisition. *American Journal of Sociology*, 1975, 80, 870–885.

Thurstone, L. Attitudes can be measured. *American Journal of Sociology*, 1928, 33, 529–554.

Thurstone, L., & Chave, E. J. *The Measurement of Attitudes*. Chicago: University of Chicago Press, 1929.

Tizard, J. *Community Services for the Mentally Handicapped*. London: Oxford University Press, 1964.

Todd, V. E., & Hefferman, H. *The Years before School: Guiding Preschool Children*. London: Macmillan, 1970.

Tonkova-Yampolskaya, A. Razvitie rechevoi intonatsii u dyetyei pervikh dvukh lyet zhizni. [Development of speech intonation for children in the first two years of life.] *Voprosy Psikhologii*, 1968, 94–101.

Treiman, D. J. Status discrepancy and prejudice. *American Journal of Sociology*, 1966, 71, 651–664.

Triandis, H. C. Cultural influences upon cognitive processes. In L. Berkowitz (Ed.), *Advances in Experimental Social Psychology* (Vol. 1). New York: Academic Press, 1964.

Tsarapkina, E. S. K voprosu ob uchenii dyetyei inostannomu yaziky v dyetskom sadu. [On questions of teaching children foreign language in kindergarten.] *Voprosy Psikhologii*, 1965, 2, 141–147.

Tucker, J., & Friedman, S. T. Population density and group size. *American Journal of Sociology*, 1972, 77, 742–749.

Tulkin, S. R., & Kagan, J. Mother-child interaction in the first year of life. *Child Development*, 1972, 43, 31–41.

Turk, A. Prospects for theories of criminal behavior. *Journal of Criminal Law, Criminology, and Police Science*, 1964, 55, 454–461.

Turk, H. Instrumental values and popularity of instrumental leaders. *Social Forces*, 1961, 39, 252–259.

Turner, C. Conjugal roles and social networks. *Human Relations*, 1967, 20, 121–130.

Turner, R. Role taking: Process vs. conformity. In A. Rose (Ed.), *Human Behavior and Social Processes*. Boston: Houghton Mifflin, 1962.

Turner, R., & Edgley, C. Death as theater: A dramaturgical analysis of the American funeral. *Sociology and Social Research*, 1976, *60*, 377–392.

TV sex and violence. *U.S. News and World Report*, January 13, 1975, 31–33.

Twain, M. *The Adventures of Huckleberry Finn*. New York: Harper & Row, 1884.

Twain, M. The turning point of my life. In M. Twain, *What Is Man? And Other Essays*. New York: Harper & Row, 1935.

Udry, J. R. The importance of being beautiful: A reexamination and racial comparison. *American Journal of Sociology*, 1977, *83*, 154–161.

Uesugi, T. K., & Vinacke, W. E. Strategy in a feminine game. *Sociometry*, 1963, *26*, 75–88.

Van Gennep, A. *The Rites of Passage*. Chicago: University of Chicago Press, 1960.

Veevers, J. E. Drinking attitudes and drinking behavior: An exploratory study. *Journal of Social Psychology*, 1971, *85*, 103–109.

Veltfort, H., & Lee, G. The Cocoanut Grove fire: A study in scapegoating. *Journal of Abnormal and Social Psychology*, 1943, 138–154.

Verba, S. *Small Groups and Political Behavior*. Princeton, N.J.: Princeton University Press, 1961.

Verlarde, A. J., & Warlick, M. Massage parlors: The sensuality business. *Society*, November/December 1973, 101–110.

Vinacke, W. Sex roles in a three person game. *Sociometry*, 1959, *22*, 342–360.

Vinacke, W., & Gulickson, G. Age and sex differences in the formation of coalitions. *Child Development*, 1964, *33*, 1217–1231.

Vogel, E. F., & Bell, N. W. The emotionally disturbed child as the family scapegoat. In E. Vogel and N. Ball (Eds.), *A Modern Introduction to the Family*. Glencoe, Ill.: Free Press, 1960.

von Hoffman, N. The sociological snoopers. *Washington Post*, January 30, 1970.

Vygotsky, L. Thought and speech. *Psychiatry*, 1939, *2*, 29–52.

Vygotsky, L. S. *Thought and Language* (E. Hanfmann and G. Vacar, Trans.). Cambridge, Mass.: MIT Press, 1962.

Vygotsky, L. S. Igra u eye rol' y psikhicheskom razvitii rebyenka. [Play and its role in the psychic development of children.] *Voprosy Psikhologii*, 1966, 62–75.

Wagner, W. The increasing importance of the peer group during adolescence. *Adolescence*, 1971, *6*, 53–58.

Wahba, M. Preferences among alternative forms of equity: The apportionment of coalition reward in males and females. *Journal of Social Psychology*, 1972, *87*, 107–115.

Waller, W. The rating and dating complex. *American Sociological Review*, 1937, *2*, 727–734.

Walster, E., Aronson, V., Abrahams, D., & Rottman, V. Assignment of responsibility for an accident. *Journal of Personality and Social Psychology*, 1966, *3*, 73–79.

Walster, E., Berscheid, E., & Walster, G. W. New directions in equity research. *Journal of Personality and Social Psychology*, 1973, *25*, 151–176.

Walster, E., & Walster, G. W. Equity and social justice. *Journal of Social Issues*, 1975, *31*, 21–43.

Walter, G. A. Effects of video tape feedback and modeling on behavior of task group members. *Human Relations*, 1975, *28*, 121–138.

Wamsley, G. L. Contrasting institutions of Air Force socialization: Happenstance or bellwether? *American Journal of Sociology*, 1972, *78*, 399–417.

Warner, L. G., & DeFleur, M. L. Attitudes as an interactional concept: Social constraints and social distance as intervening variables between attitudes and action. *American Sociological Review*, 1969, *34*, 153–169.

Warren, V. L., & Cairns, R. B. Social reinforcement satiation: An outcome of frequency or ambiguity? *Journal of Experimental Child Psychology*, 1972, *13*, 249–260.

Warwick, D. Social scientists ought to stop lying. *Psychiatry Today*, February 1975, 10–13.

Watson, G. L. Social structure and social movements: The Black Muslims in the U.S.A. and the Ras-Tofarians in Jamaica. *British Journal of Sociology*, 1973, *24*, 188–204.

Watzlawick, P., Beavin, J. H., & Jackson, D. *Pragmatics of human communication: A study of interactional patterns, pathologies, and paradoxes.* New York: Norton, 1967.

Wax, M. L. Tenting with Malinowski. *American Sociological Review*, 1972, *37*, 1–13.

Way, H. F. *Liberty in the Balance: Current Issues in Civil Liberties.* New York: McGraw-Hill, 1964.

Webb, E. J., Campbell, D. T., Schwartz, R. D., & L. Seechrest. *Unobtrusive Measures: Non-Reactive Research in the Social Sciences.* Chicago: Rand McNally, 1966.

Weber, M. *The Sociology of Max Weber* (E. Fischoff, Trans.). Boston: Beacon Press, 1963. (Originally published, 1922.)

Weber, M. *The Protestant Ethic and the Spirit of Capitalism* (T. Parsons, Trans.). London: George Allen & Unwin, 1930.

Weber, R., & Schaffer, W. Public opinion and American state policy-making. *Midwest Journal of Political Science*, 1972, *16*, 683–699.

Weigert, A. J., & Hastings, R. Identity loss, family, and social change. *American Journal of Sociology*, 1977, *82*, 1171–1186.

Weilbacker, W. What happens to advertisements when they grow up? *Public Opinion Quarterly*, 1970, *34*, 216–223.

Weinberg, M., & Williams, C. *Male Homosexuals.* New York: Penguin, 1974.

Weinstein, M. A. The sociology of public morality: Talcott Parsons and phenomenology. *Sociological Focus*, 1973, *6*, 10–31.

Weitzman, L. J. Sex-role socialization in picture books for pre-school children. *American Journal of Sociology*, 1972, *77*, 1125–1150.

Weitzman, L. J. Sex-role socialization. In J. Freeman (Ed.), *Women, a Feminist Perspective.* Palo Alto, Calif.: Mayfield, 1975.

Weitzman, L. J., Eifler, D., Hokada, E., & Ross, C. Sex role socialization in picture books for pre-school children. *American Journal of Sociology*, 1972, *77*, 1125–1150.

Welsh, S., & Comer, J. *Public Opinion.* Palo Alto, Calif.: Mayfield, 1975.

Wesley, C. The women's movement and psychotherapy. *Social Work*, 1975, *20*, 120–124.

Wheeler, S. Role conflict in correctional communities. In D. R. Cressey (Ed.), *The Prison: Studies in Institutional Organization and Change.* New York: Holt, Rinehart & Winston, 1961.

Wheeler, S. Socialization in correctional institutions. In D. A. Goslin (Ed.), *Handbook of Socialization Theory and Research.* Chicago: Rand McNally, 1969.

White, L. *The Science of Culture.* New York: Harper & Row, 1940.

Whitehead, A. N. *The Principle of Relativity.* Cambridge, England: Cambridge University Press, 1922.

Whiteman, P. A., & Kosier, K. P. Development of children's moralistic judgments: Age, sex, IQ, and certain personal experiential variables. *Child Development,* 1964, *35,* 843–850.

Whorf, B. L. *Language, Thought, and Reality.* Cambridge, Mass.: MIT Press, 1956.

Whyte, W. F. *Street Corner Society.* Chicago: University of Chicago Press, 1955.

Wiener, M., & Mehrabian, A. *Language within a Language.* New York: Appleton-Century-Crofts, 1968.

Wiessburg, N. C. On DeFleur and Westie's "Attitudes as a Scientific Concept." *Social Forces,* 1965, *43,* 422–425.

Wilensky, H. L., & Ladinsky, J. From religious community to occupational group: Structural assimilation among professors, lawyers, and engineers. *American Sociological Review,* 1967, *32,* 541–561.

Wilkenson, G. Mental disorder as dramaturgical incompetence. *Sociological Quarterly,* 1974, *15,* 143–158.

Willard, D., & Strodtbeck, F. L. Latency of verbal response and participation in small groups. *Sociometry,* 1972, *35,* 161–175.

Williams, G. H. *The Radical Reformation.* Philadelphia: Westminster, 1962.

Williams, W., & Warner, W. Reliable recency effects. *Psychological Reports,* 1969, *25,* 311–317.

Wilmot, W. W. *Dyadic Communication: A Transactional Perspective.* Reading, Mass.: Addison-Wesley, 1975.

Winch, R. F. Family and kinship. In N. J. Smelser (Ed.), *Sociology: An Introduction.* New York: Wiley, 1967.

Winick, C. Some reasons for the increase in drug dependence among middle-class youths. In H. Silverstein (Ed.), *The Sociology of Youth.* New York: Macmillan, 1973.

Winthrop, H. *Ventures in Social Interpretation.* New York: Appleton-Century-Crofts, 1968.

Wispe, L. G., & Freshley, H. B. Race, sex, and sympathetic helping behavior: The broken bag caper. *Journal of Personality and Social Psychology,* 1971, *17,* 59–65.

Wittgenstein, L. *Tractatus Logico-Philosophicus.* London: Routledge & Kegan Paul, 1922.

Wittgenstein, L. *Philosophical Investigations.* London: Blackwell, 1958.

Woelfel, J., & Haller, A. O. Significant others: The self-reflexive act and the attitude formation process. *American Sociological Review,* 1971, *36,* 74–87.

Wolf, C. P. The Durkheim thesis: Occupational groups and moral integration. *Journal for the Scientific Study of Religion,* 1970, *9,* 17–32.

Wolff, K. (Ed.). *The Sociology of Georg Simmel.* Glencoe, Ill.: Free Press, 1950.

Wolkon, G. H., & Haldeman, R. B. Role position salience and social functioning of psychiatric patients. *Journal of Social Psychology,* 1969, *78,* 113–119.

Worchel, S., Andreoli, V., & Eason, J. Is the medium the message? A study of the effects of media, communicator, and message characteristics on attitude change. *Journal of Applied Social Psychology,* 1975, *5,* 157–172.

Wright, P. L. Analyzing media effects on advertising responses. *Public Opinion Quarterly,* 1974, *38,* 192–205.

Wrightsman, L. *Assumptions about Human Nature: A Social Psychological Approach.* Monterey: Brooks/Cole, 1974.

Wrong, D. H. The oversocialized conception of man in modern sociology. *American Sociological Review*, 1961, *26*, 183–193.

Wyer, R., & Weatherley, D. A. Social role, aggression, and academic achievement. *Journal of Personality and Social Psychology*, 1965, *1*, 645–649.

Wylie, R. C. *The Self-Concept: A Critical Survey of Pertinent Research Literature.* Lincoln: University of Nebraska Press, 1961.

Yakovlyev, N. M. Rebyenok i ego obshchestvo. [The child and his society.] *Voprosy Psikhologii*, 1966, *4*, 142–151.

Yankelovich, D. CBS reports: Generations apart. In A. Daigon and R. T. LaConte (Eds.), *Dig USA*. New York: Bantam, 1970.

Young, C. Community application of social psychology. In L. Wrightsman, *Social Psychology in the Seventies*. Monterey, Calif.: Brooks/Cole, 1972.

Zajonc, R. B. The concepts of balance, congruity, and dissonance. *Public Opinion Quarterly*, 1960, *24*, 280–296.

Zajonc, R. B. Social facilitation. *Science*, 1965, *149*, 269–274.

Zaleska, M., & Kogan, N. Level of risk selected by individuals in groups when deciding for self or others. *Sociometry*, 1971, *34*, 198–213.

Zeitlin, M. Economic insecurity and the political attitudes of Cuban workers. *American Sociological Review*, 1966, *31*, 31–51.

Zicklin, G., A conversation concerning face-to-face interaction. *Psychiatry*, 1968, *31*, 236–249.

Zigler, E., & Child, E. L. Socialization. In G. Lindzey and E. Aronson (Eds.), *Handbook of Social Psychology*. Reading, Mass.: Addison-Wesley, 1969.

Zimmerman, D., & Wieder, D. L. Ethnomethodology and the problem of order. In J. Douglas (Ed.), *Understanding Everyday Life*. Chicago: Aldine, 1970.

Zipf, G. K. *The Psychobiology of Language: An Introduction to Dynamic Philology.* Cambridge, Mass.: MIT Press, 1965.

Znaniecki, F. *Social Relations and Social Rules.* San Francisco: Jossey-Bass, 1965.

Zygmunt, J. F. Movements and motives: Some unresolved issues in the psychology of social movements. *Human Relations*, 1972, *25*, 449–467.

Name Index

Subject Index